SETTLE ANY ARGUMENT
WITH THE DEFINITIVE
REFE...
TO OUR W...
P9-BEE-415
...NT

HOW LOW CAN YOU GO?: Dennis Walston, limbo dancer extraordinaire, passed under a flaming bar placed six inches off the floor on March 2, 1991! [p. 290]

HOLD THE HEADSTONE, PLEASE: Michel Lotito of France, who has been eating metal and glass since 1959, once ate an airplane! [p. 28]

NOW YOU SEE IT, NOW YOU DON'T: Eldon D. Wigton, known as Dr. Eldoonie, performed 225 different tricks in two minutes on April 21, 1991! [p. 297]

PLUS!!!!
THE SIZE-26 FEET! [p. 18]
THE SEVENTEEN-MILE TAPDANCE! [p. 640]
TWENTY-SIX YEARS OF SOAKING! [p. 305]
THE 1,973-BLADE PENKNIFE! [p. 390]

AND
THE MOST HAM RADIO CONTACTS [p. 278],
THE TINIEST WRITING [p. 406],
THE LONGEST OPERA [p. 265], AND THE
LARGEST PEARL [p. 120].

Bantam Books in the Guinness Series

THE GUINNESS BOOK OF RECORDS 1997

CONTENTS

FEATURES

TIPS

from the
RECORD BREAKERS

LARGEST WURLITZER ORGAN

Eddie Layton, page 269

MOST SUCCESSFUL SOUL SINGER

Aretha Franklin, page 283

EGG DROPPING

David Donoghue, page 326

LARGEST FLAG

Ski Demski, page 389

GRAPE CATCHING

Paul Tavilla, page 397

HITTING

Wade Boggs, page 441

 *• Oldest senator, page 11 • Organ transplants, page 33 • California condor, page 49 •Most distant object from Earth, page 86 • Longest underwater cave, page 94 • Highest prime number, page 140• Longest time in space, page 148 • Largest search for extraterrestrial intelligence, page 151 • Largest amusement park, page 165 • Land-speed record, page 191 • Highest traffic density, page 200 • Best-selling book, page 255• Largest bequest, page 316 • Largest religion, page 351 • Stilt-walking, page 403 • Tiddlywinks, page 405 • Largest blue marlin, page 487 • Lowest golf score, page 508 • Fastest speed on skis, page 566 •*

INTRODUCTION

WELCOME TO THE 40TH ANNIVERSARY EDITION OF *THE GUINNESS BOOK OF RECORDS.*

The Guinness Book of Records was the brainchild of Sir Hugh Beaver, the managing director of Guinness Brewing. In 1951, after a day of game shooting in Ireland, Beaver and his shooting party were involved in an argument as to whether the golden plover was Europe's fastest game bird. Beaver could not find the answer in any of the reference books in his host's house, Castlebridge House. Three years later, the dispute flared again.

UNABLE TO FIND the answer a second time, Beaver thought that there must be numerous such arguments going on nightly in pubs and inns throughout the British Isles, while patrons partook of his employer's brew. He decided to produce a book that would settle these disagreements. Beaver commissioned Norris and Ross McWhirter, editors and statisticians in London, to compile a book of records. The first copy was bound by the printers in 1955. The book shot to the top of the British best-seller list, and each successive annual edition has done the same.

OVER THE LAST 40 years the book has become a worldwide success. The first United States edition was published in 1956. Editions in France (1962) and Germany (1963) followed. The 1997 edition will be published in 77 different countries in 38 different languages. Total sales of all editions passed 50 million in 1984, 75 million in 1994 and will pass the 100 million mark early in the next millenium.

THE GUINNESS BOOK
OF RECORDS

EDITOR
Mark C. Young

MANAGING EDITOR
Christine Heilman

RESEARCH MANAGER
John W. Hansen

RESEARCH ASSISTANT
C. Meghan Smith

CONTRIBUTING WRITERS
Janet Buell, Tobey Grumet,
Karen Romano Young,
Glenn M. Speer, David Winkler

ACKNOWLEDGMENTS

The creation of a new edition of *The Guinness Book of Records* is very much a team effort. Space prevents me from mentioning all of the talented and dedicated people who put together the 1997 edition. There are, however, certain individuals whose contributions have been especially valuable. They are as follows:

Judy Dunbar, Michael Cipriano and Pat Collins of Penguin USA, Richard Cerrone of the New York Yankees, Liz Berry and Phil de Picciatto of Advantage International, Edgar Vincent and Joe Reese of Vincent and Farrell Associates, Virginia Ensesa, Dennis Brown, Susan Hale, Geoff Baker, Louise Willi of the Liechtenstein Prime Minister's Office, James Edward Cross, Stephen E. Ambrose, Rick Thompson and Nathan Benn of Picture Network International, Peter Orlowsky and Jackie Jeske of Allsport Photography, Bill Syrett of the Department of Meteorology at Penn State University, Don Bowden of Associated Press/World Wide Photos, Pat McLaughlin of Animals Animals, Phillip Littlemore, Amanda Mitchell, Nicholas Heath-Brown, Stewart Newport, Amanda Brooks, Teri Grenert, Muriel Ling, Roselle Le Sauteur, Matt Harper, Angela Turner.

I would also like to thank the individuals and organizations who took time to help us with our research, and the record-breakers, whose enthusiasm and hard work inspire us to make the book better every year.

Mark C. Young
Editor

10 TIPS

from the
RECORD BREAKERS

Choose to beat a record that is in the current edition.

◆

Remember that if the record you want to try to beat is not in the book, your chances of its being introduced are slim. You might improve those chances by ensuring that your record activity is a measurable one with plenty of popular appeal.

◆

If you wish to attempt a published record, please write to the following address, requesting the guidelines for that event:

◆

The Guinness Book of World Records
Guinness Media, Inc.
Six Landmark Square
Stamford, CT 06901-2704

Check with us about two months before you proceed. The record you have in mind could easily have changed since publication.

◆

If you would like to attempt a potential new record category, you should submit a written proposal outlining your idea to the address above.

◆

The criteria used to establish a record are as follows: the record must be measurable, must be independently corroborated, must be completely objective, and should preferably be the subject of worldwide interest and participation. Unique skills, unusual happenings, one-of-a-kind occurrences or "firsts" do not normally qualify for entry into the book.

◆

Follow the guidelines on rules and authentication that we can provide for your record attempt.

◆

Produce documentation at all stages. We cannot send out witnesses, so we need all the proof you can gather.

◆

We are a very small editorial team, and we receive hundreds of letters every week. Please submit your request at least two months in advance of your attempt so that we can give your inquiry the attention it deserves.

◆

Please be patient. Regrettably, it can take four to six weeks for us to get back to you, longer if your claim requires further research on our part.

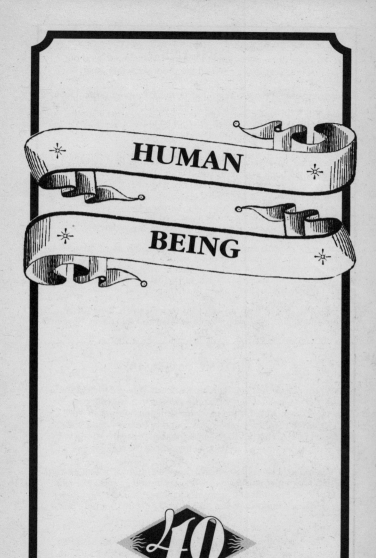

HUMAN

BEING

40

ORIGINS

Earliest primates   Primates appeared in the Paleocene epoch, about 65 million years ago. The earliest members of the suborder Anthropoidea are known from both Africa and South America in the early Oligocene, 30–34 million years ago. Finds from the Fayum, Egypt may represent primates from the Eocene period, 37 million years ago.

Earliest hominoid   A jawbone with three molars, found in the Otavi Hills, Namibia on June 4, 1991, was dated at 12–13 million years and named *Otavi pithecus namibiensis.*

Earliest hominid   An Australopithecine jawbone with two molars, each two inches long, was found near Lake Baringo, Kenya in February 1984 and dated to 4 million years ago by associated fossils and to 5.4–5.6 million years ago through rock correlation by potassium–argon dating.

Earliest of the genus **Homo**   *Homo habilis*, or "handy man," from Olduvai Gorge, Tanzania was identified and named by Louis Leakey, Philip Tobias and John Napier in 1964 after a suggestion from Prof. Raymond Arthur Dart (1893–1988). The greatest age attributed to fossils of this genus is about 2.4 million years for a piece of cranium found in western Kenya in 1965.

   The earliest stone tools are abraded core-choppers dating from *c.* 2.7 million years ago. They were found in Hadar, Ethiopia in November–

OLDEST MUMMY

A mummy at the Nevada State Museum, thought to be about 2,000 years old when it was discovered in a Nevada cave in 1940, was tested using modern dating techniques in April 1996. The Spirit Caveman was found to be more than 9,400 years old. Anthropologists hope the well-preserved body will give insights into life at the end of the ice age.

Egyptian   The oldest known Egyptian mummy is that of a high-ranking young woman who was buried *c.* 2600 B.C. near the Great Pyramid of Cheops at Giza, or Al-Gizeh, Egypt. Her remains were discovered on March 17, 1989, but only her skull was intact.

The oldest complete Egyptian mummy is of Wati, a court musician of *c.* 2400 B.C., from the tomb of Nefer in Saqqara, Egypt, found in 1944.

December 1976 by Hélène Roche (France). Finger-held (as opposed to fist-held) quartz slicers found by Roche and Dr. John Wall (New Zealand) near the Hadar site by the Gona River can also be dated to *c*. 2.7 million years ago.

Earliest Homo erectus The oldest example of *Homo erectus* ("upright man"), the direct ancestor of *Homo sapiens*, was discovered by Eugène Dubois (Netherlands) in Trinil, Java in 1891. Javan *H. erectus* was redated to 1.8 million years in 1994.

Earliest Homo sapiens *Homo sapiens* ("wise man") appeared about 300,000 years ago as the successor to *Homo erectus*.

United States In 1968, a burial site containing bones of two individuals believed to be an infant and an adolescent was uncovered by construction workers at Flathead Creek, just south of Wilsall, MT. Various bone fragments were dated to at least 10,940 years ago. The remains are believed to be from the Paleo-Indian culture, with artifacts in the style of the Clovis Age.

Over 500 artifacts 11,000 to 16,000 years old were found in Washington Co., PA in April 1973 after being brought to the attention of the University of Pittsburgh by Albert Miller, whose family owned the land. The site dates to the Pre-Clovis Paleo-Indian culture and it is believed that *Homo sapiens* Paleo-Indians were the initial inhabitants of the site. The dig, led by Dr. James Adovasio, started in June 1973 and lasted until June 1983.

BIRTH AND FAMILIES

MOTHERHOOD

Most children born to one mother In a total of 27 confinements, the wife of Feodor Vassilyev, a peasant from Shuya (near Moscow), Russia, gave birth to a total of 69 children, comprising 16 pairs of twins, seven sets of triplets and four sets of quadruplets. The case was reported to Moscow by the Monastery of Nikolskiy on February 27, 1782. Only two of the children born to Mme. Vassilyev in the period *c*. 1725–65 died in infancy.

Leontina Albina (née Espinosa) of San Antonio, Chile produced her 55th and last child in 1981. Her husband, Gerardo Secunda Albina (Alvina), states that they were married in Argentina in 1943 and had five sets of triplets (all boys) before coming to Chile. Only 40 children (24 boys and 16 girls) survive.

Oldest mother Rossanna Della Corte of Canino, Italy gave birth at age 63 on July 18, 1994.

BABIES

Heaviest single birth Anna Bates (née Swan; 1846–88), a 7-ft.-5½-in. Canadian woman, gave birth to a boy weighing 23 lb. 12 oz. (length 30

REMAINS TO THIS DAY

Mummies are synonymous with Egypt, pyramids, pharaohs, golden artifacts and the preservation of human remains. But a spate of recent discoveries demonstrate that the human body can be preserved accidentally as well as deliberately in many environments: in ice, peat bogs, deserts and caves. In fact, Egyptian mummies are not even the oldest bodies. Highlighted here are a selection of the oldest bodies found around the world: from China to Chile, Greenland to Peru, and, most recently, in Nevada. Will even older bodies be discovered someday? That, of course, remains to be seen.

Spirit Caveman

- 9,400 years old
- found by S.M. and G. Wheeler at Spirit Caves, Nevada in 1940
- originally thought to be 2,000 years old; kept in a sealed box until 1996, when it was redated with modern techniques

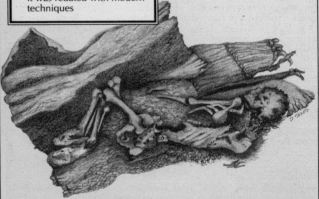

Chinchorro mummies

- 7,000 years old
- found in the Atacama Desert in Chile in 1983
- prehistoric fishing culture had developed elaborate mummification procedures 2,000 years before the practice arose in Egypt

Otzi

- 5,300 years old
- found by two German hikers in a melting glacier in the Otztal Alps in 1991
- probably a shepherd, hunter or trader who died in a snowstorm

Oldest Egyptian mummy

- 4,400 years old
- body of a court musician, found in the tomb of Nefer in Saqqara, Egypt
- a slightly older but incomplete mummy—only the head was intact—was found in Giza, Egypt in 1989

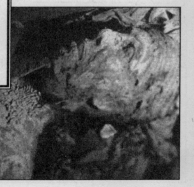

Xinjiang mummies

- 4,000 years old
- found in Urumqui, China in 1987 by Prof. Victor Mair
- Caucasian features raise questions about involvement of Europeans in China's history

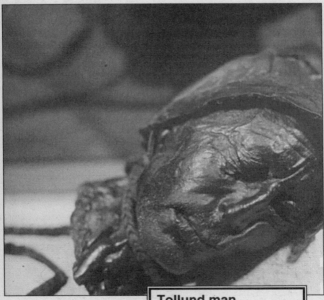

Tollund man

- 2,000 years old
- found in 1950 by archeologist Peter Glob in Tollund Fen, a peat bog in Denmark
- lived during times when Germanic people sacrificed kinfolk to the bog and was found with a noose around his neck

Inca maiden

- 500 years old
- found in 1995 by archeologist Johan Reinhard at the top of Mount Ampato in the Peruvian Andes
- sacrificed by her people, probably to appease their mountain god

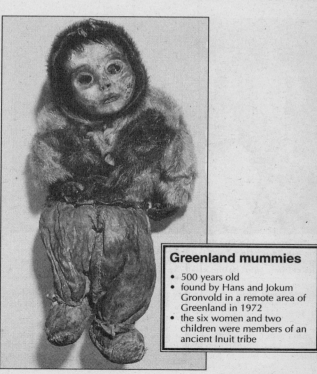

Greenland mummies

- 500 years old
- found by Hans and Jokum Gronvold in a remote area of Greenland in 1972
- the six women and two children were members of an ancient Inuit tribe

inches) in Seville, OH on January 19, 1879, but the baby died 11 hours later.

The heaviest baby born to a normal-size mother was a boy weighing 22 lb. 8 oz. who was born to Carmelina Fedele of Aversa, Italy in September 1955.

Heaviest twins The world's heaviest twins, collectively weighing 27 lb. 12 oz., were born to Mrs. J.P. Haskin of Fort Smith, AR on February 20, 1924.

Heaviest quadruplets Two girls and two boys weighing a total of 22 lb. 15¾ oz., were born to Tina Saunders at St. Peter's Hospital, Chertsey, England on February 7, 1989.

Heaviest quintuplets Two sets of quintuplets have been born with a combined weight of 25 pounds, the first on June 7, 1953 to Mrs. Lui Saulian of Zhejiang, China, and the second to Mrs. Kamalammal of Pondicherry, India on December 30, 1956.

Seven-generation family
Augusta Bunge (née Pagel) of Wisconsin became a great-great-great-great-grandmother at age 109. Her great-great-great-great-grandson, Christopher John Bollig, was born on January 21, 1989.

Lightest single birth A 9.9-ounce premature baby girl named Madeline was born at the Loyola University Medical Center, Maywood, IL on June 27, 1989.

Lightest twins Two sets of twins have been born with a total weight of 30.33 ounces. Roshan Maralyn (17.28 ounces) and Melanie Louise (13.05 ounces) were born to Katrina Gray in Brisbane, Australia on November 19, 1993. Anne Faith Sarah (14.81 ounces) and John Alexander (15.52

ounces) were born to Wendy Kay Morrison in Ontario, Canada, January 14, 1994.

Most-premature baby   James Elgin was born to Brenda and James Gill on May 20, 1987 in Ottawa, Ontario, Canada 128 days premature and weighing 1 lb. 6 oz.

United States   Ernestine Hudgins was born on February 8, 1983 in San Diego, CA about 18 weeks premature and weighing 17 ounces.

Most-premature twins   Joanna and Alexander Bagwell were born 114 days premature on June 2, 1993 in Oxford, England.

United States   Joshua and Evan Ernsteen were born 112 days premature on August 18, 1992 at Evanston Hospital, Evanston, IL. Sarah and Riley Winstead were also born 112 days premature, on May 3, 1994, at Trinity Hospital, Minot, ND.

Most-premature triplets   The most-premature triplets in the United States were Brandi, Christian and Kelli Karasiewicz, born to Rick and Gwen Karasiewicz on December 9, 1980 in Columbia, SC, 88 days premature and weighing 1 lb. 11 oz., 1 lb. 15 oz. and 1 lb. 10 oz.

Most-premature quadruplets   Tina Piper of St. Leonards-on-Sea, England had quadruplets on April 10, 1988, after exactly 26 weeks of pregnancy. Oliver, 2 lb. 9 oz. (d. February 1989), Francesca, 2 lb. 2 oz., Charlotte, 2 lb. 4½ oz., and Georgina, 2 lb. 5 oz., were all born at The Royal Sussex County Hospital, Brighton, England.

MULTIPLE BIRTHS

Longest-parted twins   With the help of New Zealand's television program *Missing* on April 27, 1989, Iris Johns (born Iris Haughie) and Aro Campbell (born Aro Haughie), who were born on January 13, 1914, were reunited after 75 years' separation.

United States   Lloyd Earl and Floyd Ellsworth Clark were born on February 15, 1917 in Nebraska. They were parted when they were four months old and lived under their adopted names, Dewayne Gramly (Lloyd) and Paul Forbes (Floyd). Both men knew that they had been born twins, but they were not reunited until June 16, 1986, after 69 years of separation.

Longest interval between births   Mrs. Danny Petrungaro (née Berg) of Rome, Italy gave birth to a girl, Diana, on December 22, 1987, but the other twin, Monica, was delivered by cesarean on January 27, 1988, 36 days later.

Highest number at a single birth   The highest number reported at a single birth were two boys and eight girls in Bacacay, Brazil on April 22, 1946. Reports of 10 at a single birth were also received from Spain in 1924 and from China on May 12, 1936.

The highest number medically recorded is nine (nonuplets), born to Geraldine Broderick at Royal Hospital for Women, Sydney, Australia on

June 13, 1971. None of the five boys (two stillborn) and four girls lived for more than six days. The birth of nine children has also been reported on at least two other occasions: in Philadelphia, PA on May 29, 1971; and in Bagerhat, Bangladesh c. May 11, 1977; in both cases none of the babies survived.

Most-identical twins
The International Twins Association was founded in 1934 and has staged its national "Most Identical Twins" contest annually since 1937. John and William Reiff of Phoenixville, PA have won a record 21 titles, including their current 12-year winning streak, between 1957 and 1995.

Most multiple births in a family Quadruplets Four sets, to Mme. Feodor Vassilyev, Shuya, Russia (b. 1707) (see MOTHERHOOD).

Triplets 15 sets, to Maddalena Granata, Italy (1839–*fl*. 1886).

Twins 16 sets, to Mme. Vassilyev (see above). Barbara Zulu of Barbeton, South Africa had three sets of girls and three mixed sets in seven years (1967–73). Anna Steynvaait of Johannesburg, South Africa produced two sets within 10 months in 1960.

DESCENDANTS

Most descendants   At his death on October 15, 1992, Samuel S. Must, age 96, of Fryburg, PA had 824 living descendants: 11 children, 97 grandchildren, 634 great-grandchildren and 82 great-great-grandchildren.

Mrs. Peter L. Schwartz (1902–88) of Missouri had 14 children, 175 grandchildren, 477 great-grand-children, and 20 great-great-grandchildren.

Longest lineage   The lineage of K'ung Ch'iu or Confucius (551–479 B.C.) can be traced further than that of any other family. His great-great-great-great-grandfather K'ung Chia is known from the eighth century B.C. Seven of K'ung Chia's 86th lineal descendants are still alive today.

LONGEVITY

Oldest person   The oldest person in the world whose date of birth can be authenticated is Jeanne Louise Calment, who was born in France on February 21, 1875. Now 121 years old, she lives in a nursing home in Arles, France.

United States   The oldest person in the United States was Carrie White (née Joyner), who was born on November 18, 1874 and died on February 14, 1991 at the age of 116 yr. 88 days.

40 years ago *Strom Thurmond was a first-term Democratic senator.* **Today** *he is the senior Republican member of the Senate and the oldest person ever elected to that body.*

"The secrets of your health are your exercise, your diet and your attitude to life . . . the greatest accomplishment in history is helping people. My motto is helping people."—Sen. Strom Thurmond (oldest senator), April 11, 1996

Oldest twins   Eli Shadrack and John Meshak Phipps were born on February 14, 1803 in Affington, VA. Eli died first, on February 23, 1911 at age 108 yr. 9 days.

On June 17, 1984, identical twin sisters Mildred Widman Philippi and

Mary Widman Franzini of St. Louis, MO celebrated their 104th birthday. Mildred died on May 4, 1985, 44 days short of their 105th birthday.

Oldest triplets   Faith, Hope and Charity Cardwell were born on May 18, 1899 in Elm Mott, TX. Faith died first, on October 2, 1994, at the age of 95 yr. 137 days. Charity died on January 6, 1995. Hope now lives in California.

Oldest quadruplets   The Ottman quads of Munich, Germany—Adolf, Anne-Marie, Emma and Elisabeth—were born on May 5, 1912. Adolf was the first to die, on March 17, 1992, at the age of 79 yr. 316 days.

United States   The Morlok quads of Lansing, MI—Edna, Wilma, Sarah and Helen—celebrated their 66th birthday on May 19, 1996.

Most living ascendants   Megan Sue Austin of Bar Harbor, ME had a full set of grandparents and great-grandparents and five great-great-grandparents, making 19 direct ascendants, when she was born on May 16, 1982.

THE BODY

HEIGHT

Tallest man   The tallest man in medical history of whom there is ir-refutable evidence was Robert Pershing Wadlow, born on February 22, 1918 in Alton, IL. Weighing 8½ pounds at birth, he began his abnormal growth at the age of two, following a double hernia operation. At age 10 he was 6 ft. 5 in. tall.

On June 27, 1940, Dr. C.M. Charles of Washington University's School of Medicine in St. Louis, MO, and Dr. Cyril MacBryde measured Robert Wadlow at 8 ft. 11.1 in. (arm span 9 ft. 5¾ in.) in St. Louis.

TALLEST LIVING WOMAN

Sandy Allen, born June 18, 1955 in Chicago, IL, weighed 6½ pounds at birth, but started growing abnormally soon afterwards. At 10 years of age she stood 6 ft. 3 in.

Allen measured 7 ft. 1 in. when she was 16. On July 14, 1977, at 7 ft. 7¼ in., Allen underwent a pituitary gland operation that inhibited further growth. She now weighs 462 pounds and takes a size 16EEE shoe.

See feature (right)

Sandy Allen

Along with being the tallest woman in the world, there's a good chance that Sandy Allen might also have the largest heart. From her home in Indiana, Allen told Guinness what it's like to be a record-holder, and how growing up with her extra height affected her life.

"It wasn't all that much fun because the kids—especially the boys—teased me a lot, and the girls basically ignored me. When I got into junior high and high school, it got steadily worse. So I just plugged on on my own," she explains.

But life changed for Allen as she got older, and becoming a part of *The Guinness Book of World Records* holds a special spot in her heart. "I know it sounds silly, but getting into your book really made things happen for me. I remember back in the 70s, I was on the Tom Snyder show with a band called Split Enz, and they ended up writing a song called 'Hello Sandy Allen.' I was really flattered by that. But Guinness gave me the opportunity to travel and to turn what seemed to be a problem into something good."

Right now, Sandy's life is just fine. She's very proud of her size and the other things that make her different from the crowd, and she spends a lot of time helping kids understand that being different isn't as bad as it seems. "What I try to do is encourage people who might be down on their lives, and down on life itself, and show them that if you don't give up easily, you'll get your problems solved. I don't give up easily—I'll tell you that right now."

But Sandy's dream in life is one of big construction. "What I want more than anything is to get a house custom-built to my size. And it'll have a big old bathtub! The last time I did a promotion for Guinness was back a few years ago in London, and I got stuck in the bathtub in my hotel room. Literally stuck! I couldn't get out of the thing. After I sat in the water for about half an hour, I guess I shriveled up like a prune and finally managed to get out. It would be nice to get a house made with taller, wider doorways, higher countertops in the kitchen, and just lots of space everywhere!"

Wadlow died 18 days later on July 15, 1940, as a result of a septic blister on his right ankle caused by a poorly fitting brace. He was buried in Oakwood Cemetery, Alton, IL in a coffin measuring 10 ft. 9 in.

Wadlow's greatest recorded weight was 491 pounds on his 21st birthday. His shoes were size 37AA (18½ inches) and his hands measured 12¾ inches from the wrist to the tip of the middle finger.

Tallest woman   The tallest woman in medical history was Zeng Jinlian of Yujiang village in the Bright Moon Commune, Hunan Province, central China, who measured 8 ft. 1¾ in. when she died on February 13, 1982. This figure represented her height with assumed normal spinal curvature, because she suffered from severe scoliosis (curvature of the spine) and could not stand up straight.

Zeng began to grow abnormally at the age of four months and stood 5 ft. 1½ in. before her fourth birthday. Her hands measured 10 inches and her feet were 14 inches long.

Tallest living person   There are two claimants to the title of tallest person in the world: Haji Mohammad Alam Channa of Bachal Channa, Sehwan Sharif, Pakistan, and the world's tallest living woman, Sandy Allen, both of whom are 7 ft. 7¼ in. tall.

Most variable stature   Adam Rainer, born in Graz, Austria (1899–1950), measured 3 ft. 10½ in. at age 21. He then suddenly started growing at a rapid rate, and by 1931 he had reached 7 ft. 1¾ in. He became so weak as a result that he was bedridden for the rest of his life.

At the time of Rainer's death on March 4, 1950, age 51, he measured 7 ft. 8 in. and was the only person in medical history to have been both a dwarf and a giant.

Tallest married couple   Anna Hanen Swan (1846–88) of Nova Scotia, Canada was said to be 8 ft. 1 in. but actually measured 7 ft. 5½ in. In London, England on June 17, 1871 she married Martin van Buren Bates (1845–1919) of Whitesburg, KY, who stood 7 ft. 2½ in., making them the tallest married couple on record.

Most dissimilar couple   Fabien Pretou, 6 ft. 2 in. tall, married Natalie Lucius, 3 ft. 1 in. tall, in Seyssinet-Pariset, France on April 14, 1990.

Tallest identical twins   Michael and James Lanier (1969–   ) of Troy, MI measured 7 ft. 1 in. at age 14 and later reached 7 ft. 4 in.

Heather and Heidi Burge (1971–   ) of Palos Verdes, CA are 6 ft. 4¾ in. tall. Both sisters play professional basketball, Heidi in Italy and Heather in Australia.

Shortest man   The shortest mature person of whom there is independent evidence is Gul Mohammad of Delhi, India. On July 19, 1990, when he was examined at Ram Manohar Hospital, New Delhi, he was 22½ inches tall and weighed 37½ pounds.

Shortest woman   Pauline Musters was born in Ossendrecht, Netherlands, on February 26, 1876 and measured 12 inches at birth. At nine years of age she was 21.65 inches tall and weighed only 3 lb. 5 oz. She died on March 1, 1895 in New York City at age 19.

Although Musters was billed at 19 inches, a postmortem examination showed her to be exactly 24 inches tall (there was some elongation after death). Her mature weight varied from 7½ to 9 pounds.

Shortest living woman Madge Bester of Johannesburg, South Africa, is 25½ inches tall. She suffers from osteogenesis imperfecta, a disease characterized by brittle bones and skeletal deformities, and she is confined to a wheelchair. Bester's mother, Winnie, is not much taller, measuring 27½ inches.

Shortest twins Matjus and Bela Matina (1903–*c*. 1935) of Budapest, Hungary, who later became United States citizens, were both 30 inches tall.

Shortest living twins The shortest living twins are John Rice of West Palm Beach, FL and Greg Rice of Manalapan, FL (1951–), who stand 34 inches tall.

Oldest dwarf Hungarian-born Susanna Bokoyni ("Princess Susanna") of Newton, NJ died at age 105 on August 24, 1984. She was 3 ft. 4 in. tall.

WEIGHT

Heaviest man The heaviest person in medical history was Jon Brower Minnoch of Bainbridge Island, WA, who had been obese since childhood. The 6-ft.-1-in. former taxi driver weighed 392 pounds in 1963, 700 pounds in 1966, and 975 pounds in September 1976.

In March 1978, Minnoch was rushed to University Hospital, Seattle, saturated with fluid and suffering from heart and respiratory failure. It took a dozen firemen and an improvised stretcher to move him from his home to a ferryboat. When he arrived at the hospital he was put in two beds lashed together. It took 13 people just to roll him over. Consultant endocrinologist Dr. Robert Schwartz calculated that Minnoch must have weighed more than 1,400 pounds when he was admitted. A great deal of this was water accumulation due to his congestive heart failure. After nearly 16 months on a 1,200-calorie-a-day diet, Minnoch was discharged at 476 pounds. In October 1981, he had to be readmitted, having put on 197 pounds. When he died on September 10, 1983 he weighed more than 798 pounds.

Heaviest woman The heaviest woman ever recorded is Rosalie Bradford (U.S.; b. 1944), who registered a peak weight of 1,200 pounds in January 1987. In August of that year she developed congestive heart failure and was rushed to a hospital. She was put on a carefully controlled diet and by February 1994 weighed 283 pounds.

Heaviest twins Billy Leon and Benny Loyd McCrary, alias McGuire, of Hendersonville, NC weighed 743 pounds (Billy) and 723 pounds (Benny) and had 84-inch waists in November 1978. As professional tag-team wrestling performers they were billed at weights up to 770 pounds. Billy died in Niagara Falls, Ontario, Canada on July 13, 1979.

Greatest weight loss Dieting The greatest recorded slimming feat by a man was that of Jon Brower Minnoch (see HEAVIEST MAN), who had reduced to 476 pounds by July 1979, a weight loss of at least 920 pounds in 16 months.

TIPS

from the
RECORD BREAKERS

GREATEST WEIGHT LOSS

In January 1987, Rosalie Bradford weighed 1,200 pounds. Eight months later, her heart failed and she was rushed to the hospital. Placed on a controlled diet, Bradford began her remarkable transformation. Her commitment to recovery helped her shed 917 pounds over seven years. Today Bradford's weight remains under 300 pounds, and she is determined to lose a further 100 pounds. Here she outlines her tips for success.

◆

Commit to a healthy food plan that will serve you for life.

Bradford initially looked for "a magic wand to dump all that fat on the floor." That approach won't work. "It happens in small steps," she says.

◆

Understand that slips are not failures.

Afraid of failure, Bradford resisted help from family and friends. A telephone call from TV diet guru Richard Simmons sparked her total commitment. "I had to lose 500 pounds before I could even stand up," she recalls.

◆

Send your large-size clothing to Goodwill.

"It's going to be a lifelong effort," Bradford proclaims. "You won't be needing those large clothes again."

Rosalie Bradford (see HEAVIEST WOMAN) went from a weight of 1,200 pounds in January 1987 to 283 pounds in February 1994, a loss of a record 917 pounds.

Sweating   Ron Allen sweated off 21½ pounds of his weight of 239 pounds in Nashville, TN in 24 hours in August 1984.

Greatest weight gain   The reported record for weight gain is held by Jon Brower Minnoch (see HEAVIEST MAN) at 196 pounds in seven days in October 1981 before his readmission to University Hospital, Seattle, WA. Arthur Knorr (U.S.; 1916–60) gained 294 pounds in the last six months of his life.

Most dissimilar couple   The greatest weight difference for a married couple is approximately 1,300 pounds, for Jon Brower Minnoch (see HEAVIEST MAN) and his 110-pound wife Jeannette in March 1978.

Lightest person   The lightest adult was Lucia Zarate (Mexico, 1863–89). At age 17, she measured 26½ inches and weighed 4.7 pounds. She "fattened up" to 13 pounds by her 20th birthday. At birth she had weighed 2½ pounds.

HANDS AND FEET

Longest fingernails   Fingernails grow at a rate of about 0.02 inches a week—four times faster than toenails. As of March 12, 1996, the aggregate measurement of the fingernails of Shridhar Chillal of Pune, Maharashtra, India was 231 inches for the five nails on his left hand (thumb 53 inches, index finger 41 inches, middle finger 44 inches, ring finger 47 inches, and pinkie 46 inches). He last cut his nails in 1952.

Shridhar Chillal's thumbnail accounts for 53 inches of his record 231 inches of fingernails.

Matthew McGrory steps out in his size 26 shoes.

Largest feet If cases of elephantiasis are excluded, then the biggest feet currently known are those of Matthew McGrory (1973–   ) of Pennsylvania, who wears size 26 shoes.

Balancing on one foot The longest recorded duration for balancing on one foot is 55 hr. 35 min., by Girish Sharma in Deori, India, October 2–4, 1992. In this contest the disengaged foot may not be rested on the standing foot, nor may any object be used for support or balance.

Motionlessness Radhey Shyam Prajapati (India) stood motionless for 18 hr. 5 min. 50 sec. at Ghandi Bhawan, Bhopal, India on January 25–26, 1996.

HAIR AND SKIN

Longest beard The beard of Hans N. Langseth (Norway) measured 17½ feet at the time of his burial in Kensett, IA in 1927. The beard was presented to the Smithsonian Institution in 1967.

The beard of Janice Deveree, "the bearded lady," of Bracken Co., KY was measured at 14 inches in 1884.

Fastest shaving   Denny Rowe shaved 1,994 men in 60 minutes with a retractor safety razor in Herne Bay, England on June 19, 1988, taking an average of 1.8 seconds per volunteer and drawing blood four times.

Tom Rodden of Chatham, England shaved 278 volunteers in 60 minutes with a straight razor on November 10, 1993, averaging 12.9 seconds per face. He drew blood only once.

Longest mustache   The mustache of Kalyan Ramji Sain of Sundargarth, India, grown since 1976, reached a span of 133$^{1}/_{2}$ inches (right side 67$^{3}/_{4}$ inches, left side 65$^{3}/_{4}$ inches) in July 1993.

United States   Paul Miller of Alta Loma, CA had grown a mustache measuring nine feet long as of February 3, 1995.

Longest hair   The longest documented hair belongs to Mata Jagdamba of Ujjain, India. Her hair measured 13 ft. 10$^{1}/_{2}$ in. on February 21, 1994.

United States   The hair of Diane Witt of Worcester, MA measured over 12 ft. 8 in. in March 1993. Witt has not measured (or cut) her hair since then.

Most tattoos   The ultimate in being tattooed is represented by Tom Leppard of the Isle of Skye, Scotland. He has a leopard-skin design, with the skin between the spots tattooed saffron yellow. Approximately 99.2 percent of his body is covered.

The world's most decorated woman is strip artiste "Krystyne Kolorful" (Canada). Her 95 percent bodysuit took 10 years to complete.

Bernard Moeller of Pennsylvania has the most separate designs, with 14,002 individual tattoos as of April 1, 1996.

TEETH

Hardest substance   Tooth enamel, the hardest substance in the body, is the only part of the human body that remains basically unchanged throughout life.

Earliest teeth   The first deciduous or milk teeth, the upper and lower jaw first incisors, normally appear in infants at 5–8 months. Molars usually appear at 24 months, but in a case published in Denmark in 1970, a 6-week-premature baby was documented with eight teeth at birth.

Most dedicated dentist   Brother Giovanni Battista Orsenigo of the Ospedale Fatebenefratelli, Rome, Italy, a dentist, saved all the teeth he extracted during the time he practiced his profession from 1868 to 1904. In 1903, the number was found to be 2,000,744 teeth, indicating an average of 185 teeth, or nearly six total extractions, each day.

Oldest false teeth   From discoveries made in Etruscan tombs, partial dentures of bridgework type were being worn in what is now the Tuscany region of Italy as early as 700 B.C. Some were permanently attached to existing teeth and others were removable.

Lifting and pulling with teeth   Walter Arfeuille (Belgium) lifted weights totaling 621 pounds a distance of 6³/₄ inches off the ground with his teeth in Paris, France on March 31, 1990.

Robert Galstyan of Masis, Armenia pulled two railroad cars coupled together, weighing a total of 483,197 pounds, a distance of 23 feet along a railroad track with his teeth at Shcherbinka, Greater Moscow, Russia on July 21, 1992.

BONES

Longest bone   The thigh bone or femur is the longest bone in the body. It usually constitutes 27.5 percent of a person's stature, and may be expected to be 19³/₄ inches long in a 6-foot-tall man. The longest bone was the 29.9-inch femur of the German giant Constantine, who died in Mons, Belgium on March 30, 1902, at age 30.

Smallest bone   The stapes or stirrup bone, one of the three auditory ossicles in the middle ear, measures 0.10–0.13 inches long and weighs 0.03–0.066 grains.

VISION

Highest acuity   The human eye is capable of judging relative position with remarkable accuracy, reaching limits of between three and five seconds of arc.

In April 1984, Dr. Dennis M. Levi of the College of Optometry, University of Houston, Houston, TX repeatedly identified the relative position of a thin bright green line within 0.85 seconds of arc, equivalent to a displacement of one fourth of an inch at a distance of one mile.

Light sensitivity   Working in Chicago, IL in 1942, Maurice H. Pirenne detected a flash of blue light of 500 nm in total darkness, when as few as five quanta or photons of light were available to be absorbed by the rod photoreceptors of the retina.

BRAINS

Heaviest brain   In December 1992, Dr. T. Mandybur and Karen Carney of the Department of Pathology and Laboratory Medicine at the University of Cincinnati, Cincinnati, OH reported a brain from a 30-year-old man that weighed 5 lb. 1.1 oz.

Lightest brain   The lightest "normal" or non-atrophied brain on record was one weighing 1 lb. 8 oz. It belonged to Daniel Lyon (Ireland), who died in 1907 at age 46 in New York. He measured just over five feet tall and weighed 145 pounds.

Mathematical computation   Shakuntala Devi multiplied two randomly selected 13-digit numbers (7,686,369,774,870 × 2,465,099,745,779) at Imperial College, London, England on June 18, 1980, in 28 seconds. Her answer, which was correct, was 18,947,668,177,995,426,462,773,730.

Memorization Bhandanta Vicittabi Vumsa (1911–93) recited 16,000 pages of Buddhist canonical texts in Yangon, Myanmar in May 1974. Gon Yangling, 26, memorized more than 15,000 telephone numbers in Harbin, China, according to the Xinhua News Agency.

Memorizing cards Dominic O'Brien (Great Britain) memorized on a single sighting a random sequence of 40 separate decks of cards (2,080 cards in all) that had been shuffled together, with only one mistake, at the BBC studios, Elstree, England on November 26, 1993. The fastest time to memorize a single deck of shuffled cards is 42.01 seconds, by Tom Groves at Jesus College, Cambridge, England on November 3, 1994.

Memorizing pi Hiroyuki Goto of Tokyo, Japan recited pi to 42,195 places at the NHK Broadcasting Center, Tokyo on February 18, 1995.

Longest and shortest dreams Dreaming sleep is characterized by rapid eye movements known as REM. The longest recorded period of REM is one of 3 hr. 8 min. by David Powell at the Puget Sound Sleep Disorder Center, Seattle, WA on April 29, 1994. At the other extreme, in July 1984, the Sleep Research Center, Haifa, Israel recorded no REM in a 33-year-old male with a shrapnel brain injury.

MUSCLES

Largest muscle The bulkiest of the 639 named muscles in the human body is usually the gluteus maximus or buttock muscle, which extends the thigh. The uterus, which normally weighs about one ounce, can increase its weight during pregnancy to more than 2.2 pounds.

Smallest muscle The stapedius, which controls the stapes (see SMALLEST BONE), is less than 0.05 inches long.

Longest muscle The sartorius, a narrow, ribbonlike muscle, runs from the pelvis across the front of the thigh to the top of the tibia below the knee.

Strongest muscle The two masseters, one on each side of the mouth, are responsible for the action of biting. In August 1986, Richard Hofmann of Lake City, FL achieved a bite strength of 975 pounds for about two seconds in a gnatho-dynamometer test at the College of Dentistry, University of Florida. This is more than six times the normal biting strength of these muscles.

Most active muscle It is estimated that the eye muscles move 100,000 times a day or more. Many of these movements take place during the dreaming phase of sleep.

Longest muscle name The *levator labii superioris alaeque nasi* has one branch running to the upper lip and the other to the nostril. It is the muscle that curls the upper lip.

Largest biceps   Denis Sester of Bloomington, MN has a right bicep measuring 30¾ inches cold.

CHESTS, WAISTS AND NECKS

Largest chest measurement   Robert Earl Hughes (U.S.) had a chest measurement of 124 inches.

Isaac Nesser of Greensburg, PA has the largest muscular chest measurement, at 74 ¹/₁₆ inches.

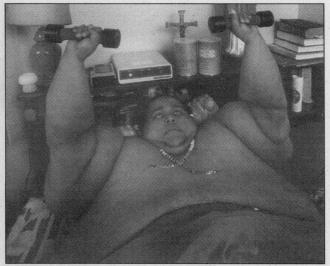

Walter Hudson's waist, the largest ever recorded, measured 119 inches.

Largest waist   The waist of Walter Hudson (1944–91) of New York measured 119 inches at his peak weight of 1,197 pounds.

Smallest waist   The smallest waist in someone of normal stature was that of Ethel Granger (1905–82) of Peterborough, England, reduced from a natural 22 inches to 13 inches over the period 1929–39. The same measurement was also claimed for the French actress Mlle. Polaire (Emile Marie Bouchand; 1881–1939).

Longest neck   The longest measured extension of the neck by the successive fitting of copper coils, as practiced by the women of the Padaung or Kareni tribe of Myanmar, is 15¾ inches.

TIPS

from the
RECORD BREAKERS

LARGEST CHEST

After 20 years of daily workouts, Isaac Nesser's chest expanded to a mind-bulging 74 $1/16$ inches by May 20, 1993. The Guinness Book of World Records asked our peak pecs personality to give aspiring record breakers some tips.

◆

Develop your own personalized lifting program.
Nesser lifts twice a day in 2-hour shifts. His program includes bench-pressing 560 pounds in a series of three to five repetitions and curling 300-pound barbells in a similar series.

◆

Build up slowly.
Nesser started lifting weights at eight years old. The key to his success is dedication and consistency, not attempting outrageous weights to impress friends. That can only lead to injury.

◆

Don't get the flu.
Nesser's longest break from the weights was caused by a bout of influenza. He lost 20 pounds in one week and his chest "slimmed" by two inches.

VOICE AND BREATHING

Lung power   The inflation of a standard 35-ounce meteorological balloon to a diameter of eight feet in a timed contest was achieved by Nicholas Mason (England) in 45 min. 2.5 sec. for the BBC *Record Breakers* television program on September 26, 1994.

Greatest range   The normal intelligible outdoor range of a man's voice in still air is 600 feet. The silbo, the whistled language of the island of La Gomera in the Canaries, is intelligible across the valleys at five miles under ideal conditions. There is a recorded case of the human voice being detectable at a distance of $10^1/2$ miles across still water at night.

Fastest talker   Few people are able to speak articulately at a sustained speed greater than 300 words per minute.

Steve Woodmore of Orpington, England spoke 595 words in a time of 56.01 seconds, or 637.4 words per minute, on the British TV program *Motor Mouth* on September 22, 1990.

Sean Shannon, a Canadian residing in Oxford, England, recited Hamlet's soliloquy "To be or not to be" (260 words) in a time of 24 seconds (equivalent to 650 words per minute) on BBC Radio Oxford on October 26, 1990.

Talking backwards   Steve Briers of Kilgetty, Wales recited the entire lyrics of Queen's album *A Night at the Opera* backwards at BBC North-West Radio 4's *Cat's Whiskers* on February 6, 1990 in a time of 9 min. 58.44 sec.

Loudest scream   Simon Robinson of McLaren Vale, South Australia produced a scream of 128 decibels at a distance of 8 ft. 2 in. at The Guinness Challenge in Adelaide, Australia in 1988.

Loudest shout   Annalisa Wray of Comber, Northern Ireland achieved 121.7 decibels when shouting the word "quiet" at the Citybus Challenge, Belfast, Northern Ireland on April 16, 1994.

Loudest whistle   Roy Lomas produced a whistle of 122.5 decibels at a distance of 8 ft. 2 in. in the Deadroom at the BBC studios in Manchester, England on December 19, 1983.

Sneezing   The longest sneezing fit ever recorded is that of Donna Griffiths of Pershore, England. She started sneezing on January 13, 1981 and sneezed an estimated 1 million times in the first 365 days. Griffiths achieved her first sneeze-free day on September 16, 1983—the 978th day.

The fastest speed at which particles expelled by sneezing have ever been measured to travel is 103.6 MPH.

Loudest snoring   Kåre Walkert of Kumla, Sweden, who suffers from the breathing disorder apnea, recorded peak levels of 93 dBA while sleeping at the Örebro Regional Hospital, Sweden on May 24, 1993.

Fastest yodeling   The most rapid recorded yodel is 22 tones (15 falsetto) in one second, by Thomas Scholl of Munich, Germany on February 9, 1992.

TIPS

from the
RECORD BREAKERS

FASTEST TALKER
*Sean Shannon blazed through Hamlet's soliloquy in 24
seconds on October 26, 1990. Potential record-breakers
shouldn't get tongue-tied if they follow his suggestions.*

◆

Speak clearly.
"The judges are not tolerant of any errors," says Shannon.
"Record attempts are taped and digitized—each word has to
correspond to its digital computer pattern."

◆

Memorize the speech.
Shannon doesn't think anyone could read it aloud quickly
enough to break the record.

◆

Don't be surprised if you start to make mistakes.
"If you repeat the speech more than once or twice in a single
session," Shannon says, "you make more errors. It's difficult to
continue talking at this rate for more than a few seconds."

BLOOD

Most common blood group   On a world basis, Group O is the most common (46 percent), but in some areas, for example Norway, Group A predominates.

United States   The subgroup O+ is found in 38 percent of the United States population.

Rarest blood type   The rarest type in the world is a type of Bombay blood (subtype h-h) found so far only in a Czechoslovak nurse in 1961, and in a brother (Rh positive) and sister (Rh negative) surnamed Jalbert in Massachusetts, reported in February 1968.

United States   The rarest generic blood group is AB–, which occurs in only 0.7 percent of persons in the United States.

Largest blood transfusion   A 50-year-old hemophiliac, Warren C. Jyrich, required 2,400 donor units of blood, equivalent to 1,900 pints of blood, when undergoing open heart surgery at the Michael Reese Hospital, Chicago, IL in December 1970.

Largest vein   The largest is the inferior vena cava, which returns the blood from the lower half of the body to the heart.

Largest artery   The largest is the aorta, which is 1.18 inches in diameter where it leaves the heart. By the time it ends at the level of the fourth lumbar vertebra it is about 0.68 inches in diameter.

Highest blood sugar level   Blair Zickmund of Massapequa, NY was admitted to Winthrop-University Hospital, Long Island, NY on November 1, 1995 with a blood sugar reading of 1,696 mg/dl while conscious. Zickmund, who has juvenile diabetes, recovered and is now in good health.

Highest blood alcohol level   The University of California Medical School, Los Angeles reported in December 1982 the case of a confused but conscious 24-year-old female, who was shown to have a blood alcohol level of 1,510 mg per 100 ml. After two days, the woman discharged herself.

CELLS

Largest cell   The megakaryocyte, a blood cell, measures 200 microns. It is found in the bone marrow, where it produces the platelets that play an important role in blood clotting.

Smallest cells   The smallest cells are the brain cells in the cerebellum, which measure about 0.005 mm.

Longest cells   Motor neurons can be $4\frac{1}{4}$ feet long. They have cell bodies in the lower spinal cord with axons that carry nerve impulses down to the big toe.

Fastest turnover of body cells   The body cells with the shortest life are in the lining of the alimentary tract (gut), where the cells are shed every three days.

Longest-living cells   Brain cells last for life. They may be three times as old as bone cells, which live 25–30 years.

Most abundant cell   The body contains approximately 30 billion red blood cells. The function of these cells is to carry oxygen around the body.

MEDICAL EXTREMES

Highest body temperature   Willie Jones, 52, was admitted to Grady Memorial Hospital, Atlanta, GA with heatstroke on July 10, 1980. His temperature was 115.7°F. Jones was discharged 24 days later.

Lowest body temperature   The lowest body temperature was 57.5°F, for Karlee Kosolofski, age two, of Regina, Saskatchewan, Canada on February 23, 1994. She had been accidentally locked out of her house for six hours in a temperature of –8°F. Despite severe frostbite, which required the amputation of her left leg above the knee, she made a full recovery.

Cardiac arrest   Norwegian fisherman Jan Egil Refsdahl fell overboard off Bergen on December 7, 1987. His heart stopped for four hours and his body temperature dropped to 77°F , but he recovered after he was connected to a heart–lung machine at Haukeland Hospital.

Longest coma   Elaine Esposito of Tarpon Springs, FL never regained consciousness after an appendectomy on August 6, 1941, when she was age six. She died on November 25, 1978, having been in a coma for 37 yr. 111 days.

The largest gallbladder weighed three times as much as the average newborn baby.

Eating   Michel Lotito of Grenoble, France, known as Monsieur Mangetout ("Mr. Eat-Everything"), has been eating metal and glass since 1959. His diet since 1966 has included 10 bicycles, a supermarket cart, seven TV sets, six chandeliers, a Cessna light aircraft and a computer.

Longest without food and water   The longest recorded case of survival without food *and* water is 18 days, by Andreas Mihavecz of Bregenz, Austria, a passenger in a car crash who was put in a holding cell in Höscht on April 1, 1979 and forgotten by the police until April 18, when he was close to death.

Largest gallbladder   On March 15, 1989 at the National Naval Medical Center in Bethesda, MD, Prof. Bimal C. Ghosh removed a 23-pound gallbladder from a 69-year-old woman. The woman recovered and left the hospital 10 days later.

Largest gallstone   A gallstone weighing 13 lb. 14 oz. was removed from an 80-year-old woman by Dr. Humphrey Arthure at Charing Cross Hospital, London, England on December 29, 1952.

Most gallstones   In August 1987, it was reported that 23,530 gallstones had been removed from an 85-year-old woman by Dr. K. Whittle Martin at Worthing Hospital, Sussex, England.

Highest g force endured   Race car driver David Purley (1945–85) survived a deceleration from 108 MPH to zero in a crash at Silverstone, near Towcester, England on July 13, 1977 that involved a force of 179.8 *g*. He suffered 29 fractures, three dislocations and six heart stoppages.

Hemodialysis   Brian Wilson of Edinburgh, Scotland has suffered from kidney failure since 1964, and has been on hemodialysis since May 30, 1964.

United States   Carl Toscano of Haverhill, MA has been on hemodialysis since May 31, 1967.

Hiccupping   Charles Osborne (1894–1991) of Anthon, IA hiccupped every 1½ seconds for 69 yr. 5 mo., until February 1990. Osborne began hiccupping in 1922 when he was slaughtering a hog.

Longest hospital stay   Martha Nelson was admitted to the Columbus State Institute for the Feeble-Minded in Ohio in 1875 and died in January 1975 at age 103 yr. 6 mo. in the Orient State Institution, OH after spending more than 99 years in hospitals.

Munchausen's syndrome   The most extreme recorded case of Munchausen's syndrome was William McIloy (1906–83), who cost Britain's National Health Service an estimated £2.5 million ($4 million). Over 50 years, he had 400 operations and stayed at 100 hospitals using 22 aliases.

Most injections   Samuel L. Davidson of Glasgow, Scotland has had 77,200 insulin injections since 1923.

Longest in "iron lung"   Dorothy Stone of Liss, England has been in a negative pressure respirator since 1947.

Pill-taking   The highest recorded total of pills swallowed by a patient is 565,939 between June 9, 1967 and June 19, 1988 by C.H.A. Kilner (1926–88) of Bindura, Zimbabwe.

Swallowing   The worst reported case of compulsive swallowing of objects involved a 42-year-old woman who complained of a "slight abdominal pain." She proved to have 2,533 objects, including 947 bent pins, in her stomach. These were removed in June 1927 at the Ontario Hospital, Canada.

The heaviest object extracted from a human stomach was a 5-lb.-3-oz. ball of hair from a 20-year-old female compulsive swallower at the South Devon and East Cornwall Hospital, England in March 1895.

Largest tumor   An ovarian cyst weighing an estimated 328 pounds was drained and then successfully removed from a patient by Dr. Arthur Spohn in Texas in 1905.

The largest tumor ever removed *intact* was a multicystic mass of the ovary weighing 303 pounds. The 3-foot-diameter growth was removed in October 1991 from the abdomen of an unnamed 35-year-old woman by Prof. Katherine O'Hanlan of Stanford University Medical Center, California. The patient weighed 210 pounds after the 6-hour operation and made a full recovery.

Underwater submergence   In 1986, 2-year-old Michelle Funk of Salt Lake City, UT made a full recovery after spending 66 minutes under water.

ILLNESS AND DISEASE

Commonest diseases   The commonest noncontagious diseases are periodontal diseases such as gingivitis. Few people completely escape the effects of tooth decay during their lives.

The commonest contagious disease in the world is coryza or acute nasopharyngitis (the common cold).

Highest mortality   There are a number of diseases that are considered to be universally fatal. AIDS and rabies encephalitis are well-known examples.

Pneumonic plague, which caused the Black Death of 1347–51, killed everyone who caught it—some 75 million people worldwide.

Leading cause of death   In industrialized countries, roughly half of all deaths are caused by diseases of the heart and blood vessels, including heart attacks, strokes, and gangrene of the lower limbs due to atheroma obstructing the flow of blood.

United States   Heart disease claimed 725,710 lives during the year ending October 31, 1995.

BALAMURALI K. AMBATI

Balamurali K. Ambati was 10 years old when he paged through *The Guinness Book of World Records* and spied the record for the world's youngest doctor. "I'd always wanted to be a doctor," he says now. "I must have filed it away in the back of my mind, and then when I was in medical school it came back to me. I thought, 'Hey! I can do that!'"

Indeed he could. Ambati graduated from medical school—Mount Sinai School of Medicine in New York—at 17 years, 10 months of age. Now doing his residency (for Harvard) at North Shore Hospital in Long Island, Ambati plans a career in ophthalmology.

Most people finish medical school at about age 26, but Ambati has never done what "most people" do. He started kindergarten at five, but graduated from high school at age 12 (that's about two grades per school year) and finished his bachelor's degree in biology at New York University at 13 years 10 months.

"I was always tall for my age," Ambati recalls. "I was 5'10" at 10 years old. Most people didn't know how old I was for a couple of weeks, and by then they were used to me and didn't care."

What about his patients? "It doesn't make a difference to a 75-year-old patient if I'm 18 or 26. They figure the person treating them is going to be younger than they are anyway, and as long as that person is fully competent and caring, they're open-minded." The soft-spoken doctor has never had a patient object to being treated by him.

Outside the hospital, Ambati sees himself as a normal teen. "I go to movies, play sports, and watch TV like other people my age," he says. "In the hospital, most of my friends are older because that's who's there." But being among older people is comfortable for him, and even seems to run in the family. Ambati's older brother, an ophthalmologist, earned his M.D. and his Ph.D. at age 23. His father and grandfather graduated from high school early, his father at 14 and his grandfather at 11.

Ambati immigrated to the United States at age three with his family, all of whom are now U.S. citizens. His father, an engineer for the City of New York, and his mother, a math professor at Queens College, encouraged their sons to do well in school. "When I was quite young, my mother was a graduate student and took me along to her classes and to the college library."

He explains the family attitude further: "When children are young, there's enthusiasm and excitement about everything, but somehow most kids seem to lose interest in things. I think it's wrong that everyone takes their kids to Little League, but they don't get as involved in school."

"My parents encouraged me to have high ideals, to work hard, and to keep my enthusiasm. Without them, I wouldn't be where I am today."

Ambati hopes his next big accomplishment will be one that is of lasting value to medical science: "I want to research retinal regeneration and work on the development of a silicon retina that would cure irreversible blindness."

Ambati's advice to other high-reaching teens? "I think most people don't reach their full potential. It's important for kids to know that there's a whole big world out there, and they can do anything."

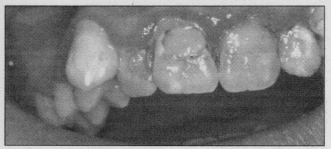

Periodontal diseases like gingivitis are the world's most common noncontagious diseases.

Most dispensed drug The estrogen replacement drug Premarin was dispensed 44,301,000 times in the United States in 1995, a nine percent increase over the previous year.

Greatest drug sales The anti-ulcer drug Zantac was the drug with the highest dollar sales in 1995, at $2,145,062,000. Zantac accounted for 20 percent of the total dollar sales for the top 10 drugs combined.

DOCTORS

Most dedicated doctor Between 1943 and 1993, Dr. M.C. Modi, a pioneer of mass eye surgery in India, performed as many as 833 cataract operations in one day. He visited 46,120 villages and 12,118,630 patients, and performed 610,564 operations.

Dr. Robert B. McClure of Toronto, Ontario, Canada performed 20,423 major operations, 1924–78.

YOUNGEST DOCTOR

Balamurali Ambati (b. July 29, 1977) of Hollis Hills, NY graduated from the Mount Sinai School of Medicine in New York on May 19, 1995, when he was 17 years old.

See feature (previous page)

OPERATIONS

Longest operation An operation of 96 hours was performed on Mrs. Gertrude Levandowski from February 4 to February 8, 1951 in Chicago, IL to remove an ovarian cyst. During the operation, her weight fell from 616 pounds to 308 pounds.

Most operations endured   From July 22, 1954, to the end of 1994, Charles Jensen of Chester, SD had 970 operations to remove the tumors associated with basal cell nevus syndrome.

Most common inpatient procedure   The most frequently performed inpatient procedure is diagnostic ultrasound, which was carried out 1,420,000 times in 1994.

Oldest patient   The greatest recorded age at which anyone has undergone an operation is 111 yr. 105 days in the case of James Henry Brett, Jr. (1849–1961) of Houston, TX. He had a hip operation on November 7, 1960.

Longest surviving heart transplant patient   Dirk van Zyl of Cape Town, South Africa (1926–94) survived for 23 yr. 57 days, having received an unnamed person's heart in 1971.

Youngest heart transplant patient   Olivia Maize of Murphy, NC received a heart transplant at Loma Linda Hospital, Loma Linda, CA on July 1, 1994 at the age of 1 hr. 40 min. She died a month later as a result of rejection complications.

Most kidney transplants   From 1954 through 1995, there were 169,880 kidney transplants in the United States. The greatest number performed in one year is 11,788, in 1995.

Longest surviving kidney transplant patients   Johanna Leanora Rempel (née Nightingale; b. 1948) of Red Deer, Alberta, Canada was given a kidney from her identical twin sister Lana Blatz on December 28, 1960 at the Peter Bent Brigham Hospital, Boston, MA.

40 years ago organ transplant procedures were still in the experimental stage, with only a handful of kidney transplants performed prior to 1956. **Today** thousands of transplants are performed each year in the United States, including heart, kidney, lung, pancreas and liver transplants.

"More than 19,000 people received organ transplants in 1995, but the number of individuals needing lifesaving transplants has also reached record highs, now greater than 45,000. With more donors, more lives can be saved." —Bruce Lucas, M.D., President, United Network for Organ Sharing, May 15, 1996

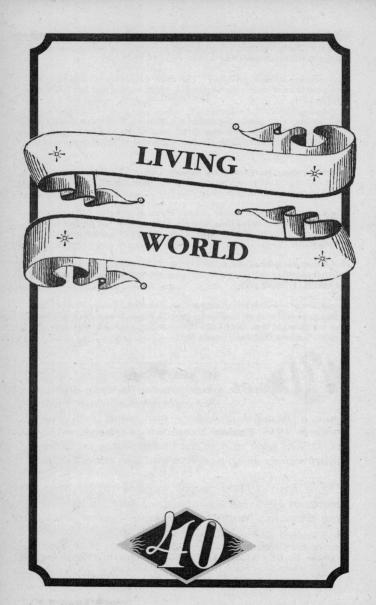

LIVING
WORLD

40

ANIMAL KINGDOM

MAMMALS

Tallest mammal The tallest giraffe ever recorded was a male Masai giraffe (*Giraffa camelopardalis tippelskirchi*) named George, received at Chester Zoo, Chester, England on January 8, 1959 from Kenya. His horns almost grazed the roof of the 20-foot-high Giraffe House when he was nine years old. George died in 1969.

Smallest mammal Savi's white-toothed pygmy shrew (*Suncus etruscus*) has a head and body length of 1.32–2 inches and a tail length of 0.94–1.14 inches, and weighs 0.05–0.09 ounces. It is found along the Mediterranean coast and southwards to Cape Province, South Africa.

Fastest land mammals Over a short distance (i.e., up to 600 yards) the cheetah (*Acinonyx jubatus*) of the open plains of East Africa, Iran, Turkmenistan and Afghanistan has a probable maximum speed of about 60 MPH on level ground.

The pronghorn antelope (*Antilocapra americana*) of the western United States, southwestern Canada, and northern Mexico has been observed to travel at 35 MPH for four miles, at 42 MPH for one mile, and at 55 MPH for half a mile.

Slowest mammal The three-toed sloth of tropical South America (*Bradypus tridactylus*) has an average ground speed of 6–8 feet per minute (0.07–0.1 MPH), but in the trees it can accelerate to 15 feet per minute (0.17 MPH).

Oldest mammal No other mammal can match the age of 120 years attained by humans, but it is probable that the closest approach is made by the Asiatic elephant (*Elephas maximus*). The greatest age that has been verified with certainty is 78 years in the case of a female named Modoc, which died in Santa Clara, CA on July 17, 1975. Certain whale species are believed to live even longer, although little is known about this. The fin whale (*Balaenoptera physalis*) is probably the longest-lived, with a maximum attainable lifespan estimated at 90–100 years.

WHALES

Largest mammal The largest mammal, and the largest animal ever recorded, is the blue whale (*Balaenoptera musculus*). Newborn calves are 20–26 feet long and weigh up to 6,600 pounds.

Heaviest A female blue whale weighing 190 tons and measuring 90 ft. 6 in. was caught in the Southern Ocean on March 20, 1947.

Longest In 1909, a female blue whale measuring 110 ft. 2½ in. long was landed at Grytviken, South Georgia, Falkland Islands.

Largest toothed mammal A male sperm whale (*Physeter macrocephalus*) 67 ft. 11 in. long was captured in the summer of 1950 off the Kurile Islands, in the northwest Pacific.

Fastest marine mammal In October 1958, a male killer whale (*Orcinus orca*) was timed at 34.5 MPH in the North Pacific. Similar speeds have been reported for Dall's porpoise (*Phocoenoides dalli*) in short bursts.

Deepest dive In August 1969, a male sperm whale (*Physeter macrocephalus*) was killed 100 miles south of Durban, South Africa after it surfaced from a dive lasting 1 hr. 52 min. Inside its stomach were two *Scymnodon*, small sharks found only on the sea floor, which suggested that the whale had descended over 9,840 feet. The deepest measured dive was made in 1991 by a sperm whale off the coast of Dominica. Scientists from the Woods Hole Oceanographic Institute recorded a dive of 6,560 feet, lasting a total of 1 hr. 13 min.

Loudest animal sound The low-frequency pulses made by blue whales have been measured at up to 188 decibels, making them the loudest sounds emitted by any living source. They have been detected 530 miles away.

Greatest animal weight loss During a 7-month lactation period, a 132-ton female blue whale can lose up to 25 percent of her body weight nursing her calf.

ELEPHANTS

Largest modern land mammal The largest African bush elephant (Loxodonta africana africana) ever recorded was a male shot on November 7, 1974, in Mucusso, Angola. It measured 13 ft. 8 in. in a projected line from the highest point of the shoulder to the base of the forefoot, indicating that its standing height must have been about 13 feet. Its weight was computed to be 13.5 tons.

Tallest The tallest recorded elephant was a male shot in Damaraland, Namibia on April 4, 1978, after it allegedly killed 11 people and caused widespread crop damage. Lying on its side, it measured 14½ feet in a projected line from the shoulder to the base of the forefoot, indicating a standing height of about 13 ft. 10 in. It weighed an estimated 8.8 tons.

Sleepiest mammals Some armadillos (Dasypodidae), opossums (Didelphidae) and sloths (Bradypodidae and Megalonychidae) spend up to 80 percent of their lives sleeping or dozing. The least active are the three species of 3-toed sloths in the genus *Bradypus*.

Highest-living mammal By a small margin, the highest-living mammal is the large-eared pika (*Ochtona macrotis*), which has been recorded at a height of 20,106 feet in mountain ranges in Asia. The yak (*Bos mutus*), of Tibet and the Sichuanese Alps, China, climbs to an altitude of 20,000 feet when foraging.

Largest herds The largest herds on record were those of the springbok (*Antidorcas marsupialis*) during migration across the plains of the western parts of southern Africa in the 19th century. One herd estimated to be 15 miles wide and more than 100 miles long was reported from Karree Kloof, Orange River, South Africa in July 1896.

Largest litter   The greatest number of young born to a *wild* mammal at a single birth is 31 (30 of which survived) in the case of the tailless tenrec (*Tenrec ecaudatus*), found in Madagascar and the Comoro Islands.

Longest gestation period   The Asiatic elephant (*Elephas maximus*) has an average gestation period of 609 days (over 20 months) and a maximum of 760 days.

Shortest gestation period   The shortest mammalian gestation period is 12–13 days, which is common in a number of species. These include the Virginia opossum (*Didelphis marsupialis*) of North America, and the water opossum or yapok (*Chironectes minimus*) of central and northern South America. On rare occasions, gestation periods of as little as eight days have been recorded for some of these species.

Youngest breeder   The female true lemming (*Lemmus lemmus*) of Scandinavia can become pregnant at the age of 14 days. The gestation period is 16–23 days. Lemmings are also prolific animals; one pair reportedly produced eight litters in 167 days.

Largest tusks   The longest tusks (excluding prehistoric examples) are a pair from an African elephant (*Loxodonta africana*) preserved in the New York Zoological Society (Bronx Zoo), New York City. The right tusk measures 11 ft. 5½ in. along the outside curve and the left tusk measures 11 feet. The combined weight of the tusks is 293 pounds.

Heaviest   A pair of African elephant (*Loxodonta africana*) tusks from a male shot in Kenya in 1897, weighed 240 pounds (length 10 ft. 2½ in.) and 225 pounds (length 10 ft. 5½ in.) respectively, giving a total weight of 465 pounds.

Longest horns   The longest horns of any living animal are those of the water buffalo (*Bubalus arnee = B. bubalis*). One male shot in 1955 had horns measuring 13 ft. 11 in. from tip to tip along the outside curve across the forehead.

Domestic animal   The largest spread on record is 10 ft. 6 in. for a Texas longhorn steer. The horns are currently on exhibition at the Heritage Museum, Big Springs, TX.

Largest antlers   The record antler spread or rack of any living species is 6 ft. 6½ in. from a moose (*Alces alces*) killed near the Stewart River in the Yukon Territory, Canada in October 1897. The antlers are now on display in the Field Museum, Chicago, IL.

CARNIVORES

Largest carnivore The largest of all carnivores is the polar bear (*Ursus maritimus*). Adult males typically weigh 880–1,300 pounds and have a nose-to-tail length of 95–102 inches.

Smallest carnivore The least or dwarf weasel (*Mustela nivalis*) has a head–body length of 4.3–10.2 inches, a tail length of 0.5–3.4 inches, and a weight of 1–7 ounces. This species varies in size more than any other mammal; the smallest individuals are females from Siberia and the Alps.

Largest feline Male Siberian tigers (*Panthera tigris altaica*) average 10 ft. 4 in. long from the nose to the tip of the tail, stand 39–42 inches at the shoulder and weigh about 585 pounds.

An Indian tiger (*Panthera tigris tigris*) shot in Uttar Pradesh in November 1967 measured 10 ft. 7 in. between pegs (11 ft. 1 in. over the curves) and weighed 857 pounds (compared with 9 ft. 3 in. and 420 pounds for an average adult male).

Smallest feline The rusty-spotted cat (*Priongilurus rubiginosus*) of southern India and Sri Lanka has a head–body length of 13.8–18.9 inches and an average weight of 2 lb. 7 oz. (female) and 3 lb. 5 oz.–3 lb. 8 oz. (male).

Polar bears are the largest carnivores.

SEALS AND SEA LIONS

Largest pinniped The largest of the 34 known species of pinniped is the southern elephant seal (*Mirounga leonina*) of the sub-Antarctic islands. Males average 16½ feet long from the tip of the inflated snout to the tips of the outstretched tail flippers, have a maximum girth of 12 feet, and weigh 4,400–7,720 pounds. The largest accurately measured specimen was a male weighing at least 4 tons and measuring 21 ft. 4 in. after flensing (stripping of the blubber or skin). Its original length was estimated to be about 22½ feet. The seal was killed in the South Atlantic at Possession Bay, South Georgia on February 28, 1913.

Live The largest reported live specimen is a male from South Georgia, nicknamed Stalin. It was tranquilized by members of the British Antarctic Survey on October 14, 1989, when it weighed 5,869 pounds and measured 16 ft. 8 in. long.

Smallest pinniped The smallest pinniped, by a small margin, is the Galápagos fur seal (*Arctocephalus galapagoensis*). Adult females average 47 inches long and weigh about 60 pounds. Males are usually larger, averaging 59 inches long and weighing around 140 pounds.

Oldest pinniped The greatest authenticated age for a pinniped has been estimated by scientists at the Limnological Institute, Irkutsk, Russia to be 56 years for the female Baikal seal (*Phoca sibirica*) and 52 years for the male.

Fastest swimmer The maximum swimming speed recorded for a pinniped is a short spurt of 25 MPH by a California sea lion (*Zalophus californianus*).

Deepest dive In May 1989, scientists testing the diving abilities of northern elephant seals (*Mirounga angustirostris*) off the coast of San Miguel Island, CA documented an adult male that reached a maximum depth of 5,017 feet.

BATS

Most acute hearing Because of their ultrasonic echo-location abilities, bats have the most acute hearing of any terrestrial animal. Most bats use frequencies in the 20–80 kHz range, although some can hear frequencies as high as 120–250 kHz. This compares with a limit of almost 20 kHz for humans, and 280 kHz for common dolphins (*Delphinus delphis*).

Largest bat The largest bat in terms of wingspan is the Bismarck flying fox (*Pteropus neohibernicus*) of the Bismarck Archipelago and New Guinea. One specimen preserved in the American Museum of Natural History in New York City had a wingspan of 5 ft. 5 in.

United States Mature specimens of the large mastiff bat (*Eumops perotis*), found in southern Texas, California, Arizona and New Mexico, have a wingspan of 22 inches.

Smallest bat The smallest bat in the United States is the Western pipistrelle (*Pipistrellus hesperus*), found in the western United States. Mature specimens have a wingspan of 7.9 inches.

Oldest bat The greatest age reliably reported for a bat is 32 years for a banded female little brown bat (*Myotis lucifugus*) in the United States in 1987.

Largest colony The largest concentration of bats is in Bracken Cave, San Antonio, TX, where up to 20 million Mexican free-tailed bats (*Tadarida brasiliensis*) assemble.

Deepest descent The little brown bat (*Myotis lucifugus*) has been recorded at a depth of 3,805 feet in a zinc mine in New York State.

RODENTS

Largest colony of animals The black-tailed prairie dog (*Cynomys ludovicianus*), a rodent of the family Sciuridae found in the western United States and northern Mexico, builds huge colonies. One single "town" discovered in 1901 contained about 400 million individuals and was estimated to cover 24,000 square miles.

Largest rodent The capybara (*Hydrochoerus hydrochaeris*), of northern South America, has a head and body length of 3¼–4½ feet and can weigh up to 145 pounds, although one exceptional cage-fat specimen attained 250 pounds.

Smallest rodent The northern pygmy mouse (*Baiomys taylori*), found in Mexico, Arizona and Texas, and the Baluchistan pygmy jerboa (*Salpingotus michaelis*) of Pakistan both have head–body lengths of as little as 1.42 inches and a tail length of 2.84 inches.

Oldest rodent The greatest reliable age reported for a rodent is 27 yr. 3 mo. for a Sumatran crested porcupine (*Hystrix brachyura*) that died in the National Zoological Park, Washington, D.C. on January 12, 1965.

Highest density A population of house mice (*Mus musculus*) numbering 83,000/acre was found in the dry bed of Buena Vista Lake, Kern County, CA in 1926–27.

Longest hibernation Arctic ground squirrels (*Spermophilus parryi*), found in Canada and Alaska, hibernate for nine months of the year.

DEER

Largest deer An Alaskan moose (*Alces alces gigas*) standing 7 ft. 8 in. between pegs and weighing an estimated 1,800 pounds was shot on the Yukon River in the Yukon Territory, Canada in September 1897.

Smallest deer The smallest true deer (family Cervidae) is the southern pudu (*Pudu puda*), which is 13–15 inches tall at the shoulder and weighs 14–18 pounds. It is found in Chile and Argentina.

Oldest deer A red deer (*Cervus elaphus scoticus*) named Bambi (b. June 8, 1963) died on January 20, 1995, at the advanced age of 31 yr. 8 mo. The deer was owned by the Fraser family of Kiltarlity, Scotland.

KANGAROOS

Largest kangaroo The male red kangaroo (*Macropus rufus*) of central, southern and eastern Australia measures up to 5 ft. 11 in. tall when standing in its normal position, and up to 9 ft. 4 in. in total length (including the tail). It can weigh up to 198 pounds.

Fastest kangaroo The fastest speed recorded for a marsupial is 40 MPH for a mature female eastern gray kangaroo (*Macropus giganteus*).

Longest kangaroo jump During a chase in New South Wales, Australia in January 1951, a female red kangaroo made a series of bounds that included one of 42 feet. There is also an unconfirmed report of an eastern gray kangaroo jumping nearly 44½ feet on level ground.

PRIMATES

Noisiest land animal The male howler monkey (*Alouatta*) of Central and South America makes a sound that has been described as a cross between the bark of a dog and the bray of a donkey, and can be heard clearly for distances of up to 3.1 miles.

The tallest primate was a mountain gorilla like this one from Zaire.

Largest primate The male eastern lowland gorilla (*Gorilla g. graueri*) of eastern Zaire has a bipedal standing height of up to 5 ft. 11 in. and weighs up to 386 pounds.

Tallest The greatest height (top of crest to heel) recorded for a gorilla in the wild is 6 ft. 5 in. for a male mountain gorilla shot in the eastern Congo (Zaire) on May 16, 1938.

TIPS

from the

RECORD BREAKERS

LARGEST DOMESTIC ANIMAL HORNS

The largest set of domestic animal horns is displayed at the Heritage Museum in Big Springs, TX. The 10-ft.-6-in.-long record-breaker is one of 53 sets of horns found in the Longhorn Room. Curator Angie Way offers some tips on showcasing a record-breaker.

◆

Clean and protect.

The horns are waxed every six months with a treatment recommended by the British Museum, and the Longhorn Room is kept at a constant temperature of 70 degrees, with a relative humidity of 55 percent, to preserve the leather holder that joins the set.

◆

Watch for natural pests.

Carpet beetles are common in western Texas and the museum maintains a constant watch for dust trails left by these hungry pests. "The museum is sprayed every quarter," Way says, "because carpet beetles would literally eat the horns."

◆

Be prepared for skepticism.

Visiting school groups are frequently a skeptical audience. "Children often ask if the horns are made of plastic," Way comments, "but real horns have a layered structure that the staff can easily demonstrate." Relating the length of the horns is another challenge readily met by the museum. "The horns are roughly the same size as three children lying head-to-toe," Way chuckles, "and we always have plenty of volunteers."

Heaviest   The heaviest gorilla ever kept in captivity was a male of uncertain subspecies named N'gagi, who died in the San Diego Zoo in California on January 12, 1944 at age 18. He weighed 683 pounds at his heaviest in 1943 and was 5 ft. 7¾ in. tall.

Smallest primate   The smallest true primate (excluding tree shrews, which are normally classified separately) is the rufous mouse lemur (*Microcebus rufus*) of Madagascar. It has a head–body length of 4–4.9 inches, a tail length of 5–5.9 inches, and a weight of 1.6–3.2 ounces.

Oldest primate   The greatest irrefutable age recorded for a nonhuman primate is 59 yr. 5 mo. for a chimpanzee (*Pan troglodytes*) named Gamma, who died at the Yerkes Primate Research Center in Atlanta, GA on February 19, 1992. Gamma was born at the Florida branch of the Yerkes Center in September 1932.

Monkey   The world's oldest monkey, a male white-throated capuchin (*Cebus capucinus*) named Bobo, died on July 10, 1988 at age 53.

HORSES

Largest horse   The tallest documented horse was the shire gelding Sampson, bred by Thomas Cleaver of Toddington Mills, England. Foaled in 1846, this horse measured 21.2½ hands (7 ft. 2½ in.) in 1850 and was said to have weighed 3,360 pounds.

Largest mules   Apollo (foaled 1977) and Anak (foaled 1976), owned by Herbert L. Mueller of Columbia, IL, are the largest mules on record. Apollo measures 19.1 hands (6 ft. 5 in.) and weighs 2,200 pounds, with Anak at 18.3 hands (6 ft. 3 in.) and 2,100 pounds. Both are the hybrid offspring of Belgian mares and mammoth jacks.

Smallest horse   The stallion Little Pumpkin (foaled April 15, 1973), owned by J.C. Williams Jr. of Della Terra Mini Horse Farm, Inman, SC, stood 14 inches tall and weighed 20 pounds on November 30, 1975.

Breed   The Falabela was developed by Julio Falabela (Argentina). The smallest example was a 15-inch-tall mare that weighed 26¼ pounds.

Oldest horse   The greatest age reliably recorded for a horse is 62 years in the case of Old Billy (foaled 1760), bred by Edward Robinson of Woolston, England. Old Billy died on November 27, 1822.

Oldest pony   The greatest age reliably recorded for a pony is 54 years, shared by two ponies. Teddy E. Bear, owned by Kathy Pennington of Virginia Beach, VA, can still gallop but no longer takes riders, and his teeth are somewhat worn. The other stallion (foaled 1919) was owned by a farmer in central France.

DOGS

Largest dog   The heaviest and longest dog ever recorded is Aicama Zorba of La-Susa (whelped September 26, 1981), an Old English mastiff owned by Chris Eraclides (Great Britain). In November 1989, Zorba weighed 343 pounds, stood 37 inches at the shoulder, and measured 8 ft. 3 in. from nose to tail.

Tallest Shamgret Danzas (whelped 1975), owned by Wendy and Keith Comley of Milton Keynes, England, was 41½ inches tall, or 42 inches when his hackles were raised, and weighed up to 238 pounds. He died on October 16, 1984.

Smallest dog The smallest dog on record was a Yorkshire terrier owned by Arthur Marples of Blackburn, England. This dog, which died in 1945 at the age of nearly two years, stood 2½ inches at the shoulder and measured 3¾ inches from its nose to the root of its tail. It weighed four ounces.

United States The smallest dog in the United States is Chelsi Dijon, a 28-ounce toy poodle belonging to Dollie Childs of Dothan, AL.

Oldest dog An Australian cattle-dog named Bluey, owned by Les Hall of Rochester, Victoria, Australia, was obtained as a puppy in 1910 and worked for nearly 20 years. He was put to sleep on November 14, 1939 at the age of 29 yr. 5 mo.

Longest-serving guide dog The longest period of active service reported for a guide dog is 14 yr. 8 mo. (August 1972–March 1987) in the case of a Labrador retriever bitch named Cindy-Cleo (whelped January 20, 1971), owned by Aaron Barr of Tel Aviv, Israel. The dog died on April 10, 1987.

Hearing Donna, a hearing guide dog owned by John Hogan of Pyrmont Point, Australia, completed 18 years of active service in New Zealand and Australia before her death in 1995 at age 20 yr. 20 mo.

Most guide dogs placed The United States record for the most guide dogs placed with people in a single year is held by Guide Dogs for the Blind, Inc. of San Rafael, CA, with 287 placements in 1995.

The overall record for the most guide dogs placed with people is held by the Seeing Eye of Morristown, NJ, with a total of 11,226 placements as of April 30, 1996.

Most prolific sire The greatest sire ever was the champion greyhound Low Pressure, nicknamed Timmy (whelped September 1957), owned by Bruna Amhurst of London, England. From December 1961 until his death on November 27, 1969, he fathered over 3,000 puppies.

Highest jump The canine "high jump" record for a leap and a scramble over a smooth wooden wall (without ribs or other aids) is 12 ft. 2½ in., achieved by an 18-month-old lurcher dog named Stag at the annual Cotswold Country Fair in Cirencester, England on September 27, 1993. The dog is owned by Mr. and Mrs. P.R. Matthews of Redruth, England.

Longest jump A greyhound named Bang jumped 30 feet while chasing a hare at Brecon Lodge, Gloucestershire, England in 1849. He cleared a 4-ft.-6-in. gate and landed on a hard road, damaging his pastern bone.

TIPS

from the
RECORD BREAKERS

SMALLEST DOG

Weighing in at 28 ounces and measuring 8¹/₂ inches from the tip of his nose to the base of his tail, Chelsi Dijon is the smallest fully-grown dog in the United States. His owner, Dollie Childs, shares her tips for caring for one of The Guinness Book of Records' *tiniest record-breakers.*

♦

Take care of those tiny teeth.

Chelsi visits the veterinarian every three months to get his teeth cleaned. "It takes the vet two hours," says Childs, "but it's very important. Tooth decay can lead to a number of problems for small dogs." Childs also gets Chelsi's hair clipped regularly to prevent ear infections.

♦

Be prepared for around-the-clock feeding.

The smallest puppy in a litter of three, Chelsi was rejected by his mother. Childs fed him a mixture of infant milk formula and iron supplements from a dropper every two hours for several months. Today, he has a sweet tooth. "He loves Cheerios and graham crackers," and, his owner admits, "I often give him slices of cheese."

♦

Beware of squirrels.

Chelsi loves to play within the confines of his back yard. He's good friends with Childs' other dog, Alexandria, a Maltese. Squirrels, however, are not so friendly. "The squirrels are bigger than Chelsi and they chase him in the yard . . . I'm always watching for those squirrels. I don't like them scaring my Chelsi."

MOST PETTED DOG

Josh the Wonder Dog has been petted by 408,127
people since October 1989. Josh, a 15-year-old terrier
mix, lives and travels with author Richard Stack of Glen
Burnie, MD.

See feature (right)

Best tracker In 1925, a Doberman pinscher named Sauer, trained by Detective-Sergeant Herbert Kruger, tracked a stock thief 100 miles across the Great Karroo, South Africa by scent alone.

Top show dog The greatest number of Best-in-Show awards won by any dog in all-breed shows is 275, by the German shepherd bitch Altana's Mystique (b. May 1987). The dog was formerly owned by Jane Firestone and is now owned and trained by James A. Moses of Alpharetta, GA.

Largest dog show The centennial of the annual Crufts show, held at the National Exhibition Center, Birmingham, England on January 9–12, 1991, attracted a record 22,993 entries.

Most registrations There were 132,051 Labrador retrievers registered in the United States in 1995, according to the American Kennel Club.

Drug sniffing Iowa, a black Labrador retriever used by the Port of Miami, made 155 drug seizures worth a record $2.4 billion. Iowa was trained by Armando Johnson and handled by Chuck Meaders, Chief of Canine Operations for the Port of Miami.

The greatest number of seizures by dogs is 969 (worth $182 million) in 1988 alone by Rocky and Barco, a pair of Malinoises patrolling the Rio Grande Valley ("Cocaine Valley") along the Texas border, where the pair were so proficient that Mexican drug smugglers put a $30,000 price on their heads. The dogs hold the rank of honorary Sergeant Major and always wear their stripes when they are on duty.

Dog walking The Great North Dog Walk took place on July 9, 1995 in South Shields, England and involved 327 dogs (of 72 different breeds) and their owners. Each dog was kept on a leash throughout the 3-mile walk.

CATS

Largest cat The heaviest domestic cat was a neutered male tabby named Himmy, owned by Thomas Vyse of Redlynch, Queensland, Australia. Himmy weighed 46 lb. 15$\frac{1}{4}$ oz. (waist 33 inches, length 38 inches).

Smallest cat A male blue point Himalayan-Persian cat named Tinker Toy, owned by Katrina and Scott Forbes of Taylorville, IL, is just 2$\frac{3}{4}$ inches tall and 7$\frac{1}{2}$ inches long.

JOSH, THE WONDER DOG

When Josh the Wonder Dog first adopted owner Richard Stack, who could have known he would eventually become a Guinness record-holder? Not Stack, and certainly not Josh. But Josh is now the world's most petted dog.

Back in 1984, Stack was watching a cartoon with naughty raccoons trying to save their lake from a developer. "It just had all the wrong values," says Stack. "The raccoons stole, and when one of them was being punished, the others helped him escape from their parents' clutches. So I said to a friend, 'Hey, I could do better!' And she said, 'Go ahead!'"

Stack started writing a children's book called The Doggonest Christmas starring Josh the Wonder Dog, and asked his uncle to illustrate it. "I told my uncle what I wanted Josh to look like, but he drew him completely different than I had asked."

"About a week later, a dog wandered onto my lawn. He looked just like the dog my uncle had drawn! So I took him in, and four and a half years later, I finally had my book completed."

When it hit the schools, they promptly asked Stack if he could bring his dog in for visits. "Of course, all the children wanted to pet him, and we set up petting lines. One day, I heard someone comment that this dog must be the most petted in the world, so we started keeping affidavits."

"Josh has a lot of problems," says Stack. "He was shot in 1987 by some crazy person in my neighborhood. He had neurosurgery to get the bullet out and now he can't wag his tail or eat a regular diet. And in addition to that, he isn't a pedigree, and he's really nothing special—at least to look at. But we think that if Josh can overcome his problems and do the amazing things he does, then so can any kid."

Oldest cat The oldest reliably recorded cat was the female tabby Ma, owned by Alice St. George Moore of Drewsteignton, England. This cat was put to sleep on November 5, 1957 at age 34.

Largest cat show The largest cat show in the United States was the International Cat Show held at McCormick Place, Chicago, IL, November 17–18, 1995. It attracted a record 1,200 entries.

Most registrations The Cat Fanciers' Association reported that the most popular breed of cat in the United States in 1995 was the Persian, with 44,735 registrations.

Most prolific cat A tabby named Dusty (b. 1935) of Bonham, TX produced 420 kittens during her life.

RABBITS

Largest rabbit In April 1980, a French lop doe weighing 26.45 pounds was exhibited at the Reus Fair in Spain.

Smallest rabbit The Netherland dwarf and the Polish dwarf have a weight range of 2–2½ pounds when fully grown.

Most prolific rabbits The most prolific domestic breeds are the New Zealand white and the Californian. Does produce 5–6 litters a year, each comprising 8–12 kittens, during their breeding life (compare with five litters and 3–7 young for the wild rabbit).

Longest ears "Sweet Majestic Star," a champion black English lop rabbit owned by Therese and Cheryl Seward of Exeter, England, had ears measuring 28½ inches long and 7¼ inches wide. He died on October 6, 1992.

BIRDS

Largest bird Male ostriches (*Struthio c. camelus*) have been recorded up to nine feet tall and 345 pounds in weight.

Heaviest flying bird The heaviest flying birds are the Kori bustard (*Ardeotis kori*) of northeast and southern Africa and the great bustard (*Otis tarda*) of Europe and Asia. Weights of 42 pounds have been reported for the Kori bustard, and the heaviest recorded great bustard weighed 39 lb. 11 oz.

Tallest flying bird Cranes (Gruidae) can stand almost 6 ft. 6 in. high.

Heaviest bird of prey An adult male Andean condor (*Vultur gryphus*) has an average weight of 20–27 pounds. An oversized male California condor (*Gymnogyps californianus*) now preserved in the California Academy of Sciences in San Francisco weighed 31 pounds. This species rarely exceeds 23 pounds.

Largest wingspan   The wandering albatross (*Diomedea exulans*) has the largest wingspan of any living bird. A male with a wingspan of 11 ft. 11 in. was caught in the Tasman Sea in September 1965.

Smallest bird   Adult male bee hummingbirds (*Mellisuga helenae*) of Cuba and the Isle of Pines are 2.24 inches long and weigh 0.056 ounces (females are slightly larger).

Smallest bird of prey   The black-legged falconet (*Microhierax fringillarius*) and the white-fronted or Bornean falconet (*Microhierax latifrons*) each have an average length of 5½–6 inches (excluding a 2-inch tail) and weigh about 1¼ ounces.

Most talkative bird   A female gray parrot (*Psittacus erythacus*) named Prudle, cared for by Iris Frost of Seaford, England, won the "Best Talking Parrot-like Bird" title at the National Cage and Aviary Bird Show in London for 12 consecutive years (1965–76). Prudle, who had a vocabulary of nearly 800 words, was taken from a nest at Jinja, Uganda in 1958. She retired undefeated.

40 years ago the California condor population had been reduced to an estimated 60 individuals by hunters and museum exhibitors. *Today* the population stands at 120 (17 living in the wild and 103 in captivity), due to the efforts of the California Condor Recovery Program, which trapped the nine condors remaining in the wild in 1985 to save the species from extinction.

"The California condor was saved from extinction by a combination of factors: zoo facilities found a new mission to breed wild domestic species so that they could be preserved as well as displayed; increased public awareness led to the support of environmental legislation and the field program executed the breeding program."—Robert Mista, Condor Program Coordinator, U.S. Fish & Wildlife Service, June 10, 1996

Largest vocabulary   Puck, a budgerigar owned by Camille Jordan of Petaluma, CA, had a vocabulary estimated at 1,728 words.

Fastest-flying bird   In one series of German experiments, a velocity of 168 MPH was recorded for a peregrine falcon (*Falco peregrinus*) at a 30-degree angle of descent, rising to a maximum of 217 MPH at an angle of 45 degrees.

Fastest wing-beat   The wing-beat of the horned sungem (*Heliactin cornuta*), a hummingbird living in tropical South America, is 90 beats per second.

Fastest bird on land   The ostrich can run at a speed of up to 40 MPH when necessary.

Fastest swimmer   The gentoo penguin (*Pygoscelis papua*) has a maximum burst of speed of c. 17 MPH.

Slowest-flying bird   American woodcocks (*Scolopax minor*) and Eurasian woodcocks (*S. rusticola*) can fly at 5 MPH.

Oldest bird   An 80-year-old male sulfur-crested cockatoo (*Cacatua galerita*) named Cocky died at London Zoo, London, England in 1982.

Domestic   The longest-lived domesticated bird is the domestic goose (*Anseranser domesticus*), which can live for 25 years. In December 1976, a gander named George, owned by Florence Hull of Thornton, England, died at the age of 49 yr. 8 mo. He was hatched in April 1927.

Longest flight   The greatest distance covered by a banded bird is 14,000 miles, by an Arctic tern (*Sterna paradisaea*). The tern was banded as a nestling on July 5, 1955 in the Kandalaksha Sanctuary on the White Sea coast, Russia, and was captured alive by a fisherman eight miles south of Fremantle, Western Australia on May 16, 1956. The bird had probably flown south via the Atlantic Ocean and then circled Africa before crossing the Indian Ocean.

Highest-flying bird   The highest irrefutable altitude recorded for a bird is 37,000 feet for a Ruppell's vulture (*Gyps rueppellii*) that collided with a commercial aircraft over Abidjan, Ivory Coast on November 29, 1973. The impact damaged one of the aircraft's engines, but the plane landed safely. Feather remains allowed the National Museum of Natural History in Washington, D.C. to identify the bird.

Most airborne bird   The sooty tern (*Sterna fuscata*) remains continuously aloft from 3–10 years as a sub-adult before returning to land to breed.

Longest feathers   The longest feathers are those of the Phoenix fowl or Yokohama chicken (a strain of red junglefowl *Gallus gallus*), which has been bred in southwestern Japan since the mid-17th century. In 1972, a tail covert 34 ft. 9½ in. long was reported for a rooster owned by Masasha Kubota of Kochi, Shikoku, Japan.

Deepest dive   In 1990, a depth of 1,584 feet was recorded for an emperor penguin (*Aptenodytes forsteri*) in the Ross Sea, Antarctica.

Sharpest vision   It has been calculated that a large bird of prey can detect a target object at a distance three or more times greater than that achieved by humans; thus a peregrine falcon (*Falco peregrinus*) can spot a pigeon at a range of over five miles under ideal conditions.

Greatest field of vision   The woodcock (*Scolopax rusticola*) has eyes set so far back on its head that it has a 360-degree field of vision, enabling it to see all around and over the top of its head.

Highest g force   Experiments have revealed that the beak of the red-headed woodpecker (*Melanerpes erythrocephalus*) hits the bark of a tree with an impact velocity of 13 MPH. When the head snaps back the brain is subject to a deceleration of about 10 *g*.

Longest bill   The bill of the Australian pelican (*Pelicanus conspicillatus*) is 13–18½ inches long. The longest bill in relation to overall body length belongs to the sword-billed hummingbird (*Ensifera ensifera*) of the Andes from Venezuela to Bolivia. The bill measures four inches long and is longer than the bird's body.

Largest egg   On June 28, 1988, a 2-year-old cross between a northern and a southern ostrich (*Struthio c. camelus* and *Struthio c. australis*) laid an egg weighing a record 5.1 pounds at the Kibbutz Ha'on collective farm, Israel.

Smallest egg   The vervain hummingbird (*Mellisuga minima*), of Jamaica and nearby islets, lays the smallest eggs. Two specimens measuring less than 0.39 inches long weighed 0.0128 ounces and 0.0132 ounces.

An ostrich egg dwarfs a chicken egg.

Mounds built by the mallee fowl are the largest bird's nests.

Longest incubation   The longest incubation period is that of the wandering albatross (*Diomedea exulans*), with a range of 75–82 days.

Shortest incubation   The shortest incubation period is 10 days for the shore lark (*Eremophila alpestris*), lesser whitethroat (*Sylvia curruca*) and a number of other small passerine species.

Largest nest   The incubation mounds built by the mallee fowl (*Leipoa ocellata*) of Australia measure up to 15 feet high and 35 feet across, and it has been calculated that their construction may involve the mounding of 8,830 cubic feet of material weighing 330 tons.

Smallest nest   The nest of the vervain hummingbird (*Mellisuga minima*) is about half the size of a walnut, while the deeper one of the bee hummingbird (*M. helenea*) is thimble-sized.

Bird-watching   Since 1965, Phoebe Snetsinger of Webster Groves, MO has seen 8,040 of the 9,700 known bird species, all of the families on the official list and over 90 percent of the genera.

24 hours   The greatest number of species spotted in a 24-hour period is 342, by Kenyans Terry Stevenson, John Fanshawe and Andy Roberts on day two of the Birdwatch Kenya '86 event held November 29–30.

REPTILES AND AMPHIBIANS

CROCODILIANS

Largest crocodile   There are four protected estuarine crocodiles at the Bhitarkanika Wildlife Sanctuary, Orissa State, India that measure more than 19 ft. 8 in. long. The largest individual is over 23 feet long.

Smallest crocodilian The dwarf caiman (*Paleosuchus palpebrosus*) of northern South America is the smallest living crocodilian. Females rarely exceed a length of four feet, and males rarely grow to more than 4 ft. 11 in.

Oldest crocodilian The greatest age authenticated for a crocodilian is 66 years for a female American alligator (*Alligator mississippiensis*) that arrived at Adelaide Zoo, South Australia on June 5, 1914 as a 2-year-old, and died there on September 26, 1978.

LIZARDS

Largest lizard Adult male komodo dragons or oras (*Varanus komodoensis*), found on the Indonesian islands of Komodo, Rintja, Padar and Flores, average 7 ft. 5 in. long and weigh about 130 pounds. The largest specimen to be accurately measured was a male presented to an American zoologist in 1928 by the Sultan of Bima. In 1937, this animal was put on display at St. Louis Zoological Gardens, St. Louis, MO for a short period. It then measured 10 ft. 2 in. long and weighed 365 pounds.

Longest lizard The Salvadori or Papuan monitor (*Varanus salvadori*) of Papua New Guinea has been measured at up to 15 ft. 7 in. long, but nearly 70 percent of the total length is taken up by the tail.

Smallest lizard *Sphaerodactylus parthenopion*, a tiny gecko indigenous to the island of Virgin Gorda, one of the British Virgin Islands, is the world's smallest lizard. It is known from only 15 specimens, including some pregnant females found August 10–16, 1964. The three largest females measured 0.70 inches from snout to vent, with a tail of approximately the same length.

Komodo dragons, the world's largest lizards, sometimes attack humans.

Oldest lizard   The greatest age recorded for a lizard is over 54 years for a male slow worm (*Anguis fragilis*) kept in the Zoological Museum in Copenhagen, Denmark from 1892 until 1946.

Fastest lizard   The highest speed measured for any reptile on land is 21.7 MPH for a spiny-tailed iguana (*Ctenosaura*) from Costa Rica, in a series of experiments by Professor Raymond Huey from the University of Washington, Seattle, WA, and colleagues at the University of California, Berkeley, CA.

TURTLES

Largest turtle   A male leatherback found dead on the beach at Harlech, Wales on September 23, 1988 measured 9 ft. 5½ in. long from nose to tail, and nine feet across the front flippers. The turtle weighed an astonishing 2,120 pounds.

United States   The greatest weight reliably recorded in the United States is 1,908 pounds for a male leatherback captured off Monterey, CA on August 29, 1961, which measured 8 ft. 4 in.

Smallest turtle   The stinkpot or common musk turtle (*Sternotherus odoratus*) has an average shell length of three inches when fully grown, and a weight of only eight ounces.
   The smallest marine turtle is the Atlantic ridley (*Lepidochelys kempii*), which has a shell length of 19.7–27.6 inches and a maximum weight of 175 pounds.

Fastest turtle   The fastest speed claimed for any reptile in water is 22 MPH by a Pacific leatherback turtle.

Deepest dive   In May 1987, it was reported by Dr. Scott Eckert that a leatherback turtle (*Dermochelys coriacea*) fitted with a pressure-sensitive recording device had dived to a depth of 3,973 feet off the Virgin Islands in the West Indies.

Largest tortoise   A Galápagos tortoise (*Geochelone elephantopus*) named Goliath, who has lived at the Life Fellowship Bird Sanctuary in Seffner, FL since 1960, measures 54 inches long, 40½ inches wide, and 27½ inches high, and weighs 911 pounds.

Oldest tortoise   The greatest age recorded for a tortoise is over 152 years for a male Marion's tortoise (*Testudo sumeirii*), brought from the Seychelles to Mauritius in 1766 by the Chevalier de Fresne, who presented it to the Port Louis army garrison. This specimen was accidentally killed in 1918.

SNAKES

Longest snake   A reticulated python (*Python reticulatus*) measuring 32 ft. 9½ in. was shot in Celebes, Indonesia in 1912. This species is also found in southeast Asia and the Philippines.

United States   There are three species of snake in the United States with average measurements of 8 ft. 6 in. These include the indigo snake (*Drymarchon corais*), the eastern coachwhip (*Masticophis flagellum*) and the black ratsnake (*Elaphe obsoleta*), all found in the southeastern United States.

Longest venomous snake   The king cobra (*Ophiophagus hannah*), also called the hamadryad, averages 12–15 feet long and is found in southeast Asia and India. An 18-ft.-2-in. specimen, captured alive near Fort Dickson in the state of Negri Sembilan, Malaysia in April 1937, later grew to 18 ft. 9 in. in London Zoo, England.

Shortest snake   The very rare thread snake (*Leptotyphlops bilineata*) is known only from Martinique, Barbados and St. Lucia. The longest known specimen measured 4¼ inches, and had such a thin body that it could have entered the hole left in a standard pencil after the lead has been removed.

Shortest venomous snake   The namaqua dwarf adder (*Bitis schneider*) of Namibia has an average length of eight inches.

Heaviest snake   The anaconda (*Eunectes murinus*) of tropical South America and Trinidad is nearly twice as heavy as a reticulated python (*Python reticulatus*) of the same length. A female shot in Brazil *c.* 1960 was not weighed, but as it measured 27 ft. 9 in. long with a girth of 44 inches, it must have weighed about 500 pounds. The average adult length is 18–20 feet.

Heaviest venomous snake   The eastern diamondback rattlesnake (*Crotalus adamanteus*) of the southeastern United States is probably the heaviest venomous snake. One specimen, measuring 7 ft. 9 in. long, weighed 34 pounds.

Oldest snake   The greatest reliable age recorded for a snake is 40 yr. 3 mo. 14 days for a male common boa (*Boa constrictor constrictor*) named Popeye, who died at the Philadelphia Zoo, Phildelphia, PA on April 15, 1977.

Most venomous snake   All sea snakes are venomous. *Hydrophis belcheri*, which lives around the Ashmore Reef in the Timor Sea, has a myotoxic venom 100 times as toxic as that of any land snake.

Most venomous land snake   The 5-ft.-7-in. small-scaled or fierce snake (*Oxyuranus microlepidotus*) is found mainly in the Diamantina River and Cooper's Creek drainage basins in Channel County, Queensland, and western New South Wales, Australia. Its venom is several times more toxic than that of the tiger snake (*Notechis scutatus*) of South Australia and Tasmania. One specimen of tiger snake yielded 0.00385 ounces of venom after milking, enough to kill 250,000 mice.

United States   The most venomous snake in the United States is the coral snake (*Micrurus fulvius*). In a standard LD99–100 test, which kills 99–100 percent of all mice injected with the venom, it takes 0.55 grain of venom per 2.2 pounds of mouse weight injected intravenously. In this test, the smaller the dosage, the more toxic the venom.

Most snakebites   More people die of snakebites in Sri Lanka than in any comparable area in the world. An average of 800 people are killed annually on the island by snakes, and more than 95 percent of the fatalities are caused by the common krait (*Bungarus caeruleus*), the Sri Lankan cobra (*Naja n. naja*), and Russell's viper (*Vipera russelli pulchella*).

The saw-scaled or carpet viper (*Echis carinatus*) bites and kills more people in the world than any other species. Its geographical range extends from West Africa to India.

Longest fangs   The highly venomous gaboon viper (*Bitis gabonica*) of tropical Africa has the longest fangs of any snake. In one 6-foot-long specimen, they measured almost two inches long.

Fastest snake   The fastest-moving land snake is probably the aggressive black mamba (*Dendroaspis polylepis*) of the eastern part of tropical Africa. This snake can achieve speeds of 10–12 MPH in short bursts over level ground.

Most snakes milked   Over a 10-year period ending in December 1970, Bernard Keyter, a supervisor at the South African Institute for Medical Research in Johannesburg, South Africa, milked 780,000 venomous snakes, obtaining 1,046 gallons of venom. He was never bitten.

Bernard Keyter milked more snakes than anyone else.

FROGS

Largest frog   The rare African giant frog or goliath frog (*Conraua goliath*) is found in Cameroon and Equatorial Guinea. A specimen captured in April 1989 on the Sanaga River, Cameroon by Andy Koffman of Seattle, WA had a snout-to-vent length of 14½ inches (34½ inches overall with legs extended) and weighed 8 lb. 1 oz. on October 30, 1989.

Smallest frog   *Sminthillus limbatus* of Cuba measures 0.34–0.5 inches long (snout-to-vent) when fully grown. It is the smallest frog and the smallest amphibian.

Longest jump by a frog   Distances in frog-jumping competitions represent the aggregate of three consecutive leaps. The greatest distance covered by a frog in a triple jump is 33 ft. 5½ in. by a South African sharp-nosed frog (*Ptychadena oxyrhynchus*) named Santjie at a frog derby held at Lurula Natal Spa, Paulpietersburg, Natal, South Africa on May 21, 1977.

United States   At the annual Calaveras Jumping Jubilee held at Angels Camp, CA, an American bullfrog (*Rana catesbeiana*) called Rosie the Ribeter, owned and trained by Lee Guidici of Santa Clara, CA, leaped 21 ft. 5¾ in. on May 18, 1986.

Most poisonous animal   The brightly colored poison-arrow frogs (*Dendrobates* and *Phyllobates*) of South and Central America secrete some of the most deadly biological toxins ever discovered. The skin secretion of the golden poison-arrow frog (*Phyllobates terribilis*) of western Colombia is the most poisonous; this frog is so dangerous that scientists have to wear thick gloves to pick it up in case they have cuts or scratches on their hands.

FISH

Strongest animal bite   Experiments carried out with a Snodgrass gnathodynamometer (shark-bite meter) at the Lerner Marine Laboratory, Bimini, Bahamas showed that a 6-ft.-6¾-in.-long dusky shark (*Carcharhinus obscurus*) could exert a force of 132 pounds between its jaws. This is equivalent to a pressure of 22 tons per square inch at the tips of the teeth. The bites of larger sharks, such as the great white (*Carcharodon carcharias*), must be considerably stronger but have never been measured.

Largest fish   The rare plankton-feeding whale shark (*Rhincodon typus*) is found in the warmer areas of the Atlantic, Pacific, and Indian Oceans. The longest specimen to have been scientifically measured was captured off Baba Island near Karachi, Pakistan on November 11, 1949. It measured 41½ feet long, 23 feet around the thickest part of the body and weighed an estimated 16½–23 tons.

Largest predatory fish   The largest predatory fish is the great white shark (*Carcharodon carcharias*). Adult specimens average 14–15 feet long and weigh 1,150–1,700 pounds. There are many claims of huge specimens up to 33 feet long and, although few have been properly authenticated, there is plenty of circumstantial evidence to suggest that some great whites grow to more than 20 feet long.

Largest freshwater fish   The largest fish that spends its whole life in fresh or brackish water is the rare pla buk or pa beuk (*Pangasianodon gigas*) found only in the Mekong River and its major tributaries in China, Laos, Cambodia and Thailand. The largest specimen, captured in the River Ban Mee Noi, Thailand, was reportedly 9 ft. 10¼ in. long and weighed 533½ pounds.

The largest fish is the whale shark, which eats plankton.

Smallest fish   The shortest marine fish—and the shortest vertebrate—is the dwarf goby (*Trimmatom nanus*) of the Chagos Archipelago, central Indian Ocean. In one series of 92 specimens collected by the 1978–79 Joint Services Chagos Research Expedition of the British Armed Forces, the adult males averaged 0.34 inches long and the adult females 0.35 inches.

Smallest freshwater fish   The shortest and lightest freshwater fish is the dwarf pygmy goby (*Pandaka pygmaea*), a colorless and nearly transparent species found in the streams and lakes of Luzon in the Philippines. Adult males measure only 0.28–0.38 inches long and weigh 0.00014–0.00018 ounces.

Fastest fish   The cosmopolitan sailfish (*Istiophorus platypterus*) is considered to be the fastest species of fish over short distances, although the practical difficulties of measuring make data extremely difficult to secure. In a series of speed trials carried out at the Long Key Fishing Camp, FL, one sailfish took out 300 feet of line in three seconds, which is equivalent to a velocity of 68 MPH (compare with 60 MPH for the cheetah).

Deepest-living fish   Brotulids of the genus *Bassogigas* are generally regarded as the deepest-living vertebrates. The greatest depth from which a fish has been recovered is 27,230 feet in the Puerto Rico Trench in the Atlantic by Dr. Gilbert L. Voss of the U.S. research vessel *John Elliott*, who caught a 6½-inch-long *Bassogigas profundissimus* in April 1970. It was only the fifth such brotulid ever caught.

Oldest fish   In 1948, the death of an 88-year-old female European eel (*Anguilla anguilla*) named Putte was reported by the aquarium at Hälsingborg Museum, Sweden. She was allegedly born in 1860 in the Sargasso Sea, in the North Atlantic, and was caught in a river as a 3-year-old elver.

Oldest goldfish   Goldfish (*Carassius auratus*) have been reported to live for over 50 years in China, although there are few authenticated records. A goldfish named Fred, owned by A.R. Wilson of Worthing, England, died on August 1, 1980 at 41 years of age.

Shortest-lived fish   Certain species of the family Cyprinodontidae (killifish), found in Africa, the Americas, Asia and the warmer parts of Europe, normally live for about eight months.

Most eggs   The ocean sunfish (*Mola mola*) produces up to 300 million eggs at a single spawning, each of them measuring about 0.05 inches in diameter.

Fewest eggs   The mouth-brooding cichlid *Tropheus moorii* of Lake Tanganyika, East Africa, produces seven eggs or fewer during normal reproduction.

Most valuable fish   The Russian sturgeon (*Huso huso*) is the most valuable fish. In 1924, a 2,706-pound female was caught in the Tikhaya Sosna River; it yielded 541 pounds of best-quality caviar, which would be worth $300,000 on today's market.

The 30-inch-long Ginrin Showa koi, which won the supreme championship in nationwide Japanese koi shows in 1976, 1977, 1979 and 1980, was sold two years later for 17 million yen (about $165,000). In March 1986, this 15-year-old ornamental carp was acquired by Derry Evans, owner of the Kent Koi Centre near Sevenoaks, England, for an undisclosed sum, but the fish died five months later.

Most ferocious fish   The razor-toothed piranhas of the genera *Serrasalmus* and *Pygocentrus* are generally considered to be the most ferocious freshwater fish in the world. They live in large rivers in South America, and will attack any creature, regardless of size, if it is injured or making a commotion in the water. On September 19, 1981, more than 300 people were reportedly killed and eaten when an overloaded passenger-cargo boat capsized and sank as it was docking at the Brazilian port of Obidos.

Most venomous fish   The most venomous fish are the stonefish (Synanceidae) that live in the tropical waters of the Indo-Pacific, and in particular *Synanceia horrida*, which also has the largest venom glands. Direct contact with the spines of its fins, which contain a strong neurotoxic poison, can prove fatal.

Most electric fish   The electric eel (*Electrophorus electricus*) is found in the rivers of Brazil, Colombia, Venezuela and Peru. An average-sized specimen can discharge one amp at 400 volts, but measurements up to 650 volts have been recorded.

LOTS OF GOOD FISH

THE MONTEREY BAY AQUARIUM

*M*onterey Bay is a big dip of coastal waters gouged from the coast of California. Deep, pristine, and rich with an astonishing abundance of wildlife from blue whales to tiny krill, the bay is the largest national marine sanctuary in the United States.

The Monterey Bay Aquarium sits on the site of Cannery Row, the fish-packing plants made famous in John Steinbeck's book of the same name. No more fish are packed here; instead, they are protected in this habitat that is a nursery to crabs and sea turtles, a kindergarten to kelp and sea otters, and home to schools of all kinds of fish from sunfish (mola mola) to moonfish (opah). Monterey's diversity of species stems from its diversity of depths, from shallow coves to the underwater Monterey Canyon, two miles deep. The bay is a perfect laboratory for learning about the workings of the ocean and the life that is found here in abundance.

A Building With Gills

If a building could wish, this aquarium would choose to be a fish. It's situated right in the water rather than on the shore. Unique filters—like big gills—pump in bay water, feeding, flushing, and seeding the exhibits in a way that mirrors what goes on in the waters outside. Spores of tiny microorganisms stream in, stay, and grow. They colonize the display tanks and help create an environment where larger species—reptiles, fish, mammals, invertebrates, birds, and plants—can thrive.

The Monterey Bay Aquarium opened in October, 1984. Before the staff took a wildlife census, they estimated that the exhibits held 124,000 animals and plants—10 times more than any other aquarium in the United States. The census surprised them: aquarists counted 571 species and 364,593 individuals, from a lone long-billed curlew to the strawberry anemones that number over 100,000. Then, in March 1996, the Outer Bay exhibit opened. This million-gallon tank and its inhabitants—pelagic (open-ocean) creatures like leopard sharks and yellow-fin tuna—will send the population sky-high. The 35-foot tank is fronted by the world's largest aquarium window, a 36-ton acrylic panel that covers 958.8 square feet, and is 13 inches thick.

Have Tuna, Will Travel

It's one thing to build a giant fish tank, but quite another to fill it. Like the other Monterey displays, the Outer Bay exhibit's smaller species come in through the "gills." But big pelagic fish must be studied, found, caught, and carefully brought back to the aquarium. Large species are captured in several ways—through netting, rod-and-reel fishing, and anesthetics. Spotter planes fly over areas that fishermen have named as likely. And the great sunfish—mola mola—come to the surface to let seagulls remove parasites from their bodies.

Senior Collector of Fishes John O'Sullivan explains the process of starting a collection of big yellow-fin tuna. "First we checked the literature—our records and anything we could find about the fish. Then we went to the pros: Our sister aquarium [Tokyo Sea Life Park] in Japan taught us about tuna, and local commercial fishermen helped us find them."

Other aquariums had used tanks to bring in large fish—but none this large. O'Sullivan gathered advice and used it to build a 3,000-gallon transport tank that goes on a 48-foot semi and holds 18 yellow fin tuna. "We call it the Finnebago," he grins. It took several trips to move the whole catch of nearly 80 tuna 450 miles from San Diego to Monterey.

Run Silent, Run Deep

"Monterey Bay is a habitat like the woodlands or a bog or the Serengeti," says O'Sullivan. "You can track elephants from one place to another and see what they eat, how they stay in one place for a few days and move on. It's the same concept in open water: you can have tons of tuna move through an area and the next day be gone. They used food, produced waste, and the whole ecosystem changed in 12 hours. And now they're gone—where? There is so much in the ocean that just passes through, from whales to the tiniest thing. You can't sit back and watch [as on a safari]. If wildebeests are running, you can hear them. But so much in the ocean is silent."

When it comes to exploring the ocean, O'Sullivan says, Monterey is just getting its feet wet. Moon fish (opahs) top his fish wish list. These red fish with blue spots and giant forked tails show up in the fish market some times, but he has never caught one alive.

The Deep Ocean exhibit, slated to open in 2000, will hold species found at 300 feet or deeper. With the Outer Bay exhibit, this display will allow the Monterey Bay Aquarium to open doors on the world's two largest habitats.

STARFISH

Largest starfish   The largest of the 1,600 known species of starfish is the very fragile brisingid *Midgardia xandaras*. One specimen, collected by the Texas A & M University research vessel *Alaminos* in the southern part of the Gulf of Mexico in 1968, measured 4½ feet tip to tip, but the diameter of its disc was only 1.02 inches.

Smallest starfish   The asterinid sea star *Patiriella parvivipara* was discovered by Wolfgang Zeidler on the west coast of the Eyre Peninsula, South Australia in 1975. It has a maximum radius of only 0.18 inches and a diameter of less than 0.35 inches.

Most destructive starfish   The crown of thorns (*Acanthaster planci*) of the Indo-Pacific region and the Red Sea has 12–19 arms and can measure up to 24 inches in diameter. It feeds on coral polyps and can destroy 46–62 square inches of coral in one day. It has been responsible for the destruction of large parts of the Great Barrier Reef off Australia.

CRUSTACEANS

Largest crustacean   The takashigani or giant spider crab (*Macrocheira kaempferi*) is the largest, although not the heaviest, of all Crustacea (a category that includes crabs, lobsters, shrimp, prawns, crawfish, etc.). It is found in deep waters off the southeastern coast of Japan. One specimen had a claw-span of 12 ft. 1½ in. and weighed 41 pounds.

Freshwater   A species of crayfish or crawfish (*Astacopis gouldi*) found in the streams of Tasmania, Australia has been measured up to two feet long and weighing as much as nine pounds. In 1934, an unconfirmed weight of 14 pounds (total length 29 inches) was reported for one specimen caught at Bridport, Tasmania, Australia.

Heaviest crustacean   The heaviest crustacean, and the largest species of lobster, is the American or North Atlantic lobster (*Homarus americanus*). On February 11, 1977, a specimen weighing 44 lb. 6 oz. and measuring 3 ft. 6 in. from the end of the tail fan to the tip of the largest claw was caught off Nova Scotia, Canada. This lobster was later sold to a New York restaurant owner.

Greatest concentration   U.S. scientists tracked a swarm of krill (*Euphasia superba*) estimated to weigh 11 million tons off Antarctica in March 1981.

SPIDERS

Largest spider The largest spider is the goliath bird-eating spider (*Theraphosa leblondi*) of the coastal rain forests of Surinam, Guyana, and French Guiana, but specimens have also been reported from Venezuela and Brazil. A male specimen collected by members of the Pablo San Martin Expedition at Rio Cavro, Venezuela in April 1965 had a leg span of 11.02 inches.

Heaviest spider Female bird-eating spiders are more heavily built than males, and in February 1985 Charles J. Seiderman of New York City captured a female example near Paramaribo, Surinam that weighed a record peak 4.3 ounces before its death from molting problems in January 1986. Other measurements included a maximum leg span of 10½ inches, a total body length of four inches, and 1-inch-long fangs.

Smallest spider *Patu marplesi* (family Symphytognathidae) of Western Samoa in the Pacific is the smallest spider. The type specimen (male), found in moss at *c.* 2,000 feet in Madolelei, Western Samoa in January 1965, measured 0.017 inches overall, which means that it was about the size of a period on this page.

Oldest spider The longest-lived of all spiders are the tropical bird-eaters (family Theraphosidae). One female specimen collected in Mexico in 1935 lived for an estimated 26–28 years. It is believed that a 25-year lifespan is not unusual for bird-eating spiders, putting them among the longest-lived of all terrestrial invertebrates.

A bird-eating spider lives up to its name.

United States   The longest-lived species of American spider is *Rhecosticta californica* of the family Theraphosidae, which has an average life span of 25 years.

Most venomous spider   The most venomous spiders are the Brazilian wandering spiders of the genus *Phoneutria*, and particularly the Brazilian huntsman *P. fera*, which has the most active neurotoxic venom of any living spider. These large and highly aggressive creatures frequently enter human dwellings and hide in clothing or shoes. When disturbed they bite furiously several times, and hundreds of accidents involving these species are reported annually. When deaths do occur, they are usually in children under the age of seven. Fortunately, an effective antivenin is available.

Fastest spider   The long-legged sun spiders of the order Solifugae live in the arid semidesert regions of Africa and the Middle East. They feed on geckos and other lizards and can reach speeds of over 10 MPH.

SCORPIONS

Largest scorpion   The largest of the 800 or so species of scorpion is a species called *Heterometrus swannerderdami* from southern India. Males frequently attain a length of more than seven inches from the tips of the pincers to the end of the sting. One specimen found during World War II measured 11.5 inches in overall length. The tropical emperor or imperial scorpion (*Pandinus imperator*) of West Africa also grows to seven inches; the largest on record is a male from Sierra Leone that measured 9.01 inches.

Smallest scorpion   *Microbothus pusillus*, found on the Red Sea coast, measures about half an inch long.

Most venomous scorpion   The Palestine yellow scorpion (*Leiurus quinquestriatus*) ranges from the eastern part of North Africa through the Middle East to the shores of the Red Sea. Fortunately, the amount of venom it delivers is very small (0.000009 ounces) and adult lives are seldom endangered; however, it has been responsible for a number of fatalities among children under the age of five.

INSECTS

Greatest concentration of animals   A swarm of Rocky Mountain locusts (*Melanoplus spretus*) that flew over Nebraska on July 20–30, 1874 covered an area estimated at 198,600 square miles. The swarm must have contained at least 12.5 trillion insects with a total weight of about 27.5 million tons.

Fastest animal reproduction A single cabbage aphid (*Brevicoryne brassicae*) could theoretically (with unlimited food and no predators) give rise in a year to a mass of descendants weighing 906 million tons.

Most acute sense of smell The male emperor moth (*Eudia pavonia*) has the most acute sense of smell in the animal kingdom. It can detect the sex attractant of the female at a range of 6.8 miles upwind. The chemoreceptors on the male moth's antennae are so sensitive that they can detect a single molecule of scent.

Strongest animal In proportion to their size, the strongest animals are beetles of the family Scarabaeidae. In one test, a rhinoceros beetle (Dynastinae) supported 850 times its own weight on its back (compared with 25 percent of its body weight for an adult elephant). Humans can support 17 times their own body weight in a trestle lift.

Most prodigious eater The larva of the Polyphemus moth (*Antheraea polyphemus*) of North America consumes an amount equal to 86,000 times its own birth weight in the first 56 days of its life. In human terms, this would be equivalent to a 7-pound baby taking in 300 tons of nourishment.

Oldest insect The longest-lived insects are the splendor beetles (Buprestidae). On May 27, 1983, a specimen of *Buprestis aurulenta* appeared from the staircase timber in the the home of Mr. W. Euston of Prittlewell, England, after 47 years as a larva.

Heaviest insect The heaviest insects are the Goliath beetles (family Scarabaeidae) of Equatorial Africa. The largest are *Goliathus regius*, *G. meleagris*, *G. goliathus* (= *G. giganteus*) and *G. druryi*, and in one series of fully grown males (females are smaller) the lengths from the tips of the

The male emperor moth's antennae can detect a single molecule of scent.

small frontal horns to the end of the abdomen measured up to 4.33 inches and the weights ranged from 2½ to 3½ ounces.

Longest insect *Pharnacia kirbyi* is a stick insect from the rain forests of Borneo. A specimen in the British Museum (Natural History), London, England has a body length of 12.9 inches and a total length, including legs, of 20 inches.

Smallest insect The feather-winged beetles of the family Ptiliidae (= Trichopterygidae) and the battledore-wing fairy flies of the family Mymaridae are smaller than some species of protozoa (single-celled animals).

Lightest insect The male bloodsucking banded louse (*Enderleinellus zonatus*) and the parasitic wasp (*Caraphractus cinctus*) may each weigh as little as 5,670,000 to an ounce. Eggs of the latter each weigh 141,750,000 to an ounce.

Loudest insect At 7,400 pulses per minute, the tymbal organs of the male cicada (family Cicadidae) produce a noise (described by the U.S. Department of Agriculture as "tsh-ee-EEEE-e-ou") detectable more than a quarter of a mile distant.

Fastest-flying insect A maximum speed of 36 MPH has been recorded for the Australian dragonfly *Austrophlebia costalis*.

Fastest wing-beat The fastest wing-beat of any insect is 62,760 beats per minute by a midge of the genus *Forcipomyia*. The contraction–expansion cycle of 0.00045 seconds is the fastest muscle movement ever measured.

Slowest wing-beat The slowest wing-beat of any insect is 300 beats per minute by the swallowtail butterfly (*Papilio machaon*).

Fastest-moving insect The fastest-moving insects are large tropical cockroaches; the record is 3.36 MPH, or 50 body lengths per second, registered by *Periplaneta americana* at the University of California at Berkeley in 1991.

Most legs The centipede *Himantarum gabrielis*, found in southern Europe, has 171–177 pairs of legs. (By definition, all insects have six legs; centipedes are officially classed as myriapodous arthropods.)

Largest egg The 6-inch-long Malaysian stick insect *Heteropteryx dilitata* lays ½-inch-long eggs. Mantids and cockroaches lay larger egg cases, but these contain up to 200 individual eggs.

Highest g force The click beetle (*Athous haemorrhoidalis*) endures 400 *g* when "jack-knifing" into the air to escape predators. One specimen measuring half an inch long and weighing 0.00014 ounces that jumped to a height of 11¾ inches was calculated to have endured a peak brain deceleration of 2,300 *g*.

Largest cockroach A preserved female cockroach (*Megaloblatta longipennis*) in the collection of Akira Yokokura of Yamagata, Japan is 3.81 inches long and 1.77 inches across.

Largest termite mound   In 1968, W. Page photographed a mound south of Horgesia, Somalia estimated to be 28½ feet tall.

Largest grasshopper   An unidentified species of grasshopper from the Malaysia–Thailand border measures 10 inches long and can leap 15 feet.

Largest flea   The largest of the 1,830 recognized flea varieties is *Hystrichopsylla schefferi*, which was described from a specimen taken from the nest of a mountain beaver (*Aplodontia rufa*) in 1913. Females are up to 0.3 inches long.

Longest flea jump   The cat flea (*Ctenocephalides felis*) has been known to reach a height of 34 inches in a single jump. The common flea (*Pulex irritans*) is capable of similar feats. In one American experiment carried out in 1910, a specimen performed a long jump of 13 inches and a high jump of 7¾ inches. In jumping 130 times its own height, a flea subjects itself to a force of 200 *g*.

Largest dragonfly   *Megaloprepus caruleata* of Central and South America has been measured at 4.72 inches long with a wingspan of 7.52 inches.

United States   The giant green darner (*Anax walsinghami*) has a body length of up to 4½ inches.

Smallest dragonfly   The smallest dragonfly is *Agriocnemis naia* of Myanmar. One specimen had a wing spread of 0.69 inches and a body length of 0.71 inches.

United States   The elfin skimmer (*Nannothaemis bella*) has a body length of ⅘ of an inch.

Largest butterfly   Females of the Queen Alexandra's birdwing butterfly (*Ornithoptera alexandrae*) of Papua New Guinea may have a wingspan of 11 inches and weigh 0.9 ounces.

United States   The largest native butterfly in the United States is the giant swallowtail (*Papilio cresphontes*), with a wingspan of up to six inches.

Smallest butterfly   The micro-moth *Stigmella ridiculosa,* found in the Canary Islands, has a wingspan of 0.079 inches.

Longest butterfly migration   A tagged monarch butterfly (*Danaus plexippus*) released by Donald Davis near Brighton, Ontario, Canada in September 1986 was recaptured 2,133 miles away near Angangueo, Mexico in January 1987. This distance was obtained by measuring a line from the release site to the recapture site, but the actual distance traveled could be double this figure.

MOLLUSKS

Largest mollusk   The giant squid, *Architeuthis dux*, is the largest invertebrate and the largest mollusk. The heaviest ever recorded was a 2.2-ton specimen that ran aground in Thimble Tickle Bay, Newfoundland, Canada on November 2, 1878. Its body was 20 feet long, and one tentacle measured 35 feet long.

Gastropod   The largest known gastropod is the trumpet or baler conch (*Syrinx aruanus*) of Australia. One specimen collected off Western Australia in 1979 and now owned by Don Pisor of San Diego, CA had a shell 30.4 inches long with a maximum girth of 39.75 inches. It weighed nearly 40 pounds when alive.

Largest animal eye   The giant squid has the largest eye of any animal, living or extinct. The squid found in Thimble Tickle Bay (see LARGEST MOLLUSK) had eyes 15^3/$_4$ inches wide—almost as wide as this open book.

Longest mollusk   A 57-foot giant *Architeuthis longimanus* was washed up on Lyall Bay, Cook Strait, New Zealand in October 1887. Its two long, slender tentacles each measured 49 ft. 3 in.

Most venomous mollusk   The two closely related species of blue-ringed octopus, *Hapalochlaena masculosa* and *H. lunulata*, found around the coasts of Australia and parts of southeast Asia, carry a neurotoxic venom so potent that their bite can kill in a matter of minutes. It has been estimated that each individual carries sufficient venom to cause the paralysis (or even death) of 10 adult people. Fortunately, blue-ringed octopuses are not considered aggressive and normally bite only when they are taken out of the water and provoked. These mollusks have a radial spread of just 4–8 inches.

Gastropods   The most venomous gastropods are cone shells (genus Conus), all of which can deliver a fast-acting neurotoxic venom. Several species are capable of killing people, but the geographer cone (*Conus geographus*) of the Indo-Pacific is considered to be one of the most dangerous.

Longest suspended animation   In 1846, two specimens of the desert snail (*Eremina desertorum*) were presented to the British Museum (Natural History) in London as dead exhibits. They were placed on display, but four years later, in March 1850, it was found that one of the snails was still alive. This snail lived for another two years before it fell into a torpor and then died.

Slowest animal growth   The deep-sea clam (*Tindaria callistiformis*) of the North Atlantic takes roughly 100 years to reach a length of ^{1}/$_3$ of an inch.

Snail racing   A garden snail named Archie, owned by Carl Bramham of Pott Row, England, covered a 13-inch course in 2 minutes in July 1995.

WORMS

Longest earthworm   The species *Microhaetus rappi* (= *M. microhaetus*) is found in South Africa. Around 1937, a giant earthworm measuring 22 feet long when naturally extended and 0.8 inches in diameter was collected in the Transvaal.

The longest earthworm is found in South Africa.

Shortest earthworm   *Chaetogaster annandalei* measures less than 0.02 inches long.

Worm-charming   At the first World Worm Charming Championship held in Willaston, Cheshire, England on July 5, 1980, Tom Shufflebotham charmed a record 511 worms out of the ground (a 9.84-square-foot plot) in 30 minutes. In this contest, garden forks or other implements are vibrated in the soil by competitors to coax up the worms, but water is banned.

JELLYFISH AND CORALS

Largest jellyfish   An Arctic giant jellyfish (*Cyanea capillata arctica*) that washed up in Massachusetts Bay had a bell diameter of 7 ft. 6 in. and tentacles stretching 120 feet.

Most venomous jellyfish   The Australian sea wasp or box jellyfish (*Chironex fleckeri*) is the most venomous cnidarian in the world. Its cardiotoxic venom has caused the deaths of at least 70 people off the coast of Australia alone in the past century, with some victims dying within four minutes if medical aid is not available.

Largest animal-made structure   The largest structure ever built by living creatures is the 1,260-mile-long Great Barrier Reef, off Queensland, Australia, covering 80,000 square miles. It consists of millions of dead and living stony corals (order Madreporaria or Scleractinia). Over 350 species of coral are currently found on this reef, and its accretion is estimated to have taken some 600 million years.

SPONGES

Greatest powers of regeneration   The sponges (Porifera) can regrow from tiny fragments of themselves. If a sponge is pushed through a fine-meshed silk gauze, each piece of separated tissue will live as an individual and grow into a full-sized sponge.

Largest sponge   The barrel-shaped loggerhead sponge (*Spheciospongia vesparium*) of the West Indies and the waters off Florida can measure up to 3 ft. 6 in. high and three feet in diameter.

Heaviest sponge   In 1909, a wool sponge (*Hippospongia canaliculatta*) measuring six feet in circumference was collected off the Bahamas. When taken from the water it weighed 80–90 pounds, but after it had been cleaned and dried it weighed 12 pounds. This sponge is now kept in the National Museum of Natural History, Washington, D.C.

Smallest sponge   The widely distributed *Leucosolenia blanca* measures 0.11 inches in height when fully grown.

Deepest-living sponges   Sponges have been recovered from depths of up to 18,500 feet.

MICROBES

Most dangerous animal   Malarial parasites of the genus *Plasmodium*, carried by mosquitos of the genus *Anopheles*, have probably been responsible for half of all human deaths, excluding deaths caused by wars and accidents, since the Stone Age.

Smallest free-living entity   *Mycoplasma laidlawii* has a diameter during its early existence of only 0.0000001m. Examples of the strain known as H.39 have a diameter of 0.0000003m and weigh 0.0000000000000001g.

Largest modern protozoan   The largest existing protozoan, a species of *Stannophyllum* (Xenophyophorida), can reach $9^{3/4}$ inches in length but does not exceed the volume of the extinct calcareous foraminifera of the genus *Nummulites* (see LARGEST PROTOZOAN).

Fastest protozoan   *Monas stigmatica* has been found to move a distance equivalent to 40 times its length in a second. Humans cannot cover even seven times their own length in a second.

Largest bacterium   *Epulopiscium fishelsoni* inhabits the intestinal tract of the brown surgeonfish (*Acanthurus nigrofuscus*) from the Red Sea and the Great Barrier Reef. Measuring 80 by 600mm or more and therefore visible to the naked eye, it is a million times larger than the human food poisoner *Escherichia coli*.

Fastest bacterium   The rod-shaped bacillus *Bdellovibrio bacteriovorus*, which is two micrometers long, can move 50 times its own length in one second, using a polar flagellum rotating 100 times per second. This is equivalent to a human sprinter reaching 200 MPH.

Highest-living bacterium   In April 1967, the National Aeronautics and Space Administration (NASA) reported that bacteria had been discovered at an altitude of $25^{1/2}$ miles.

Toughest bacterium   The bacterium *Micrococcus radiodurans* can withstand atomic radiation of 6.5 million röntgens, or 10,000 times the dose that would be fatal to the average person. In March 1983, John Barras (University of Oregon) reported bacteria from sulfurous seabed vents thriving at 583°F in the East Pacific Rise at Lat. 21° N.

Oldest bacterium   Viable bacteria were reported in 1991 to have been recovered from sediments 3–4 million years old from the Sea of Japan.

Living   In 1991, live bacteria were found in the flesh of a mastodon from Ohio that died 12,000 years earlier. The bacteria gave the flesh a bad smell even after such a long time.

FUNGI

Largest fungus   A single living clonal growth of the underground fungus *Armillaria ostoyae* was reported in May 1992 as covering some 1,500 acres in the forests of Washington State. Estimates based on its size suggest that the fungus is 500–1,000 years old, but no attempts have been made to estimate its weight. Also known as the honey or shoestring fungus, it fruits above ground as edible gilled mushrooms.

Largest edible fungus   A giant puffball (*Calvatia gigantea*) measuring 8 ft. 8 in. in circumference and weighing 48$\frac{1}{2}$ pounds was found by Jean-Guy Richard of Montreal, Canada in 1987.

Largest tree fungus   In 1995, the bracket fungus (*Rigidoporus ulmarius*) growing on the grounds of the International Mycological Institute in Kew, England measured 64 by 55 inches, with a circumference of 189 inches.

United States   In April 1992, Freda Kaplan of San Ramon, CA found a puffball (*Langermannia gigantea*) measuring 7 ft. 3 in. in circumference on the Wiedemann ranch in San Ramon.

Heaviest fungus   A clonal growth of *Armillaria bulbosa* was reported on April 2, 1992 to be covering about 37 acres of forest in Michigan. It was

The death cap kills more people than any other poisonous fungus.

calculated to weigh over 110 tons, which is comparable with the weight of a blue whale. The organism is thought to have originated from a single fertilized spore at least 1,500 years ago.

Heaviest edible fungus A chicken of the woods mushroom (*Laetiporus sulphureus*) weighing 100 pounds was found in the New Forest, England by Giovanni Paba of Broadstone, Dorset, England on October 15, 1990.

Most poisonous fungus The yellowish-olive death cap (*Amanita phalloides*) is responsible for 90 percent of fatal poisonings caused by fungi. The estimated lethal amount for humans, depending on body weight, is about $1^3/4$ ounces of fresh fungus. Six to 15 hours after eating the fungus, the victim experiences vomiting and delirium, followed by collapse and death.

PREHISTORIC LIFE

Heaviest dinosaur A titanosaurid from Argentina, *Argentinosaurus*, was estimated in 1994 to have weighed up to 110 tons based on its vast vertebrae.

Largest dinosaurs The sauropod dinosaurs, a group of long-necked, long-tailed, 4-legged plant-eaters, lumbered around the world during the Jurassic and Cretaceous periods, 208-65 million years ago. They ranged in length from 80 feet to over 150 feet. Weight estimates range from 15 tons to 100 tons.

Tallest dinosaurs *Brachiosaurus brancai* ("arm lizard") from the Tendaguru site in Tanzania is dated as Late Jurassic (150–144 million years ago). The site was excavated by German expeditions during the period 1909–11, and a complete skeleton was constructed from the remains of several individuals and put on display at the Humboldt Museum in Berlin in 1937. This is the largest mounted dinosaur skeleton, measuring 72 ft. 9½ in. long and 46 feet tall.

LARGEST PREDATORY DINOSAUR

In 1995, the largest dinosaur skull was found in southwest Morocco. The 5-ft.-4-in.-long skull belonged to a flesh-eater called *Carcharodontosaurus saharicus,* which is estimated to have been over 40 feet long, larger than *Tyrannosaurus rex* and *Giganotosaurus carolinii,* although the size ranges of these three creatures may have overlapped.

See feature (at right)

PAUL C. SERENO

Carcharodontosaurus saharicus lived and died 90 million years ago, at the end of the Jurassic period. It roamed the land that is now Morocco after the great split of the supercontinent into two land masses, at the time when dinosaur diversity was at its peak. It was huge: even bigger than its relative, *Tyrannosaurus rex*, with immense triangular teeth.

Now, in the late 20th century A.D., it was hiding, embedded in a rocky cliff in the Kem Kem region of the Moroccan desert, waiting for someone to see it for what it was. In the 1920s, clues had been found that indicated *Carcharodontosaurus saharicus* ("shark-toothed reptile of the Sahara") once existed. Dr. Paul Sereno, a University of Chicago paleontologist, had studied the clues for years, then targeted the Kem Kem as a likely spot—with well-exposed rock of just the right age—to search.

Very little of Africa has been sifted for dinosaur remains. Sereno, age 38, says, "It was a great quest, like being in North America in the 19th century." Sereno spotted the cliff from across a valley one summer day. He and his team of searchers were just four days from going home. "We had been finding bones since the first day out—lots of broken pieces and toe bones—and kept searching from dawn until the light fell so precariously that we were afraid we wouldn't be able to get down." Toe bones alone didn't prove the existence of the world's largest dinosaur, but Sereno had a hunch about that cliff.

"At first I didn't realize how high I was climbing. I was tiptoeing along, and there it was, across my path—a big piece of bone the size of a grapefruit. I've studied dinosaurs long enough—I knew: it was the back end of a predatory dinosaur's skull." What's more, it was a clean, fresh break. "It had dropped from the piece of cliff above me, which must have been weathering right through the skull." Sereno gazed up. "Twenty feet up, I spied the other piece. The jaws were headed straight into the cliff. It was an exact fit." Sereno went back to the group. "I felt very emotional, because we had all worked so hard, but I said just, 'We've got four days left in the field. I want you to find a skull!' They looked at me funny, and one got suspicious: 'Have you found something?'"

Sereno took the crew to the site of his find, and they worked together to extricate the skull—50 pieces of it—from the cliff. "It could be none other than *Carcharodontosaurus saharicus*," Sereno reported. "To be the one to find it was really spectacular. I came home with a euphoric sense of having made a mark on this discipline."

Longest dinosaur   In 1991, a sauropod discovered in New Mexico, *Seismosaurus halli*, was estimated to be 128–170 feet long based on comparisons of individual bones.

Longest neck   The sauropod *Mamenchisaurus* ("mamenchi lizard") of the Late Jurassic had the longest neck of any animal that has ever lived. The neck measured 36 feet—half the total length of the dinosaur.

Largest footprints   In 1932, the gigantic footprints of a large bipedal hadrosaurid measuring 53½ inches long and 32 inches wide were discovered in Salt Lake City, UT, and other reports from Colorado and Utah refer to footprints 37–40 inches wide. Footprints attributed to the largest brachiosaurids also range up to 40 inches wide for the hind feet.

Largest dinosaur eggs   *Hypselosaurus priscus* ("high ridge lizard"), a 40-foot-long titanosaurid that lived about 80 million years ago, laid the largest eggs. Examples found in the Durance valley near Aix-en-Provence, France in October 1961 would have had, uncrushed, a length of 12 inches and a diameter of 10 inches (capacity 5.8 pints).

Smallest dinosaur   The chicken-sized *Compsognathus* ("pretty jaw") of southern Germany and southeast France, and an undescribed plant-eating fabrosaurid from Colorado, both measured 29½ inches from the snout to the tip of the tail and weighed about 15 pounds.

Most brainless dinosaur   *Stegosaurus* ("plated lizard"), which roamed across Colorado, Oklahoma, Utah and Wyoming about 150 million years ago, was up to 30 feet long but had a 2½-ounce brain. This represented 0.004 of 1 percent of its body weight of 1.9 tons (compare with 0.074 of 1 percent for an elephant and 1.88 percent for a human).

Largest flying creature   A 65 million-year-old bone found in Jordan in 1943 is thought to be a neck vertebra from a pterosaur called *Arambourgiania philadelphiae*, estimated to have a wingspan of over 39 feet.

Oldest reptile fossil   *Westlothiana lizziae* is estimated to be 340 million years old, 40 million years older than previously discovered reptiles.

Largest land mammal   *Indricotherium* was a long-necked, hornless rhinocerotid that roamed across western Asia and Europe about 35 million years ago. A restoration in the American Museum of Natural History, New York City measures 17 ft. 9 in. to the top of the shoulder hump and 37 feet in total length. The most likely maximum weight of this gigantic browser is 12–22 tons.

Oldest bird fossil   Two partial bird skeletons were found in Texas in rocks dating from 220 million years ago. Named *Protoavis texensis* in 1991, the pheasant-sized creature has caused much controversy by pushing the age of birds back many millions of years from the previous record, that of the more familiar *Archeopteryx lithographica* from Germany.

Oldest insect fossil   A shrimplike creature found in 1991 in rocks 420 million years old may be the oldest insect. Found in Western Australia, this 5-inch-long euthycarcinoid was a freshwater predator.

Oldest land animals   Animals moved from the sea to the land at least 414 million years ago. The first known land animals include two kinds of centipede and a tiny spider found among plant debris. However, all three species were fairly advanced predators—and must therefore have been preying on animals that lived on land even before they did.

Oldest DNA   The oldest fossil DNA was found in a 120–135 million-year-old weevil encased in amber from Lebanon.

Largest protozoan   The largest known protozoans in terms of volume are the extinct calcareous foraminifera (*Foraminiferida*) of the genus *Nummulites*. Individuals up to six inches wide have been found in the Middle Eocene rocks of Turkey.

Oldest flower fossil   A flower believed to be 120 million years old was identified in 1989 by Dr. Leo Hickey and Dr. David Taylor of Yale University from a fossil discovered near Melbourne, Victoria, Australia. The flowering angiosperm, which resembles a modern black pepper plant, had two leaves and one flower and is known as the Koonwarra plant.

PLANT KINGDOM

Oldest plant   "King Clone," a creosote plant (*Larrea tridentata*) found in southwest California, was estimated in February 1980 by Prof. Frank C. Vasek to be 11,700 years old.

Northernmost plant   The yellow poppy (*Papaver radicatum*) and the Arctic willow (*Salix arctica*) grow at Lat. 83° N.

Southernmost plant   The southernmost flowering plant is the Antarctic hair grass (*Deschampsia antarctica*), which was located at Lat. 68° 21′ S on Refuge Island, Antarctica on March 11, 1981.

Highest-living plant   The greatest certain altitude at which any flowering plants have been found is 21,000 feet on Mt. Kamet (25,447 feet) in the Himalayas by N.D. Jayal in 1955. They were *Ermania himalayensis* and *Ranunculus lobatus*.

Deepest-living plant   Plant life was found underwater at a depth of 884 feet by Mark and Diane Littler off San Salvador Island, Bahamas in October 1984.

Deepest roots   The greatest reported depth to which roots have penetrated is a calculated 400 feet for a wild fig tree at Echo Caves, near Ohrigstad, Transvaal, South Africa.

Longest roots   A single winter rye plant (*Secale cereale*) has been shown to produce 387 miles of roots in 1.8 cubic feet of earth.

Fastest-growing plant Some species of the 45 genera of bamboo have been found to grow up to three feet per day.

Largest cactus The saguaro (*Cereus giganteus* or *Carnegiea gigantea*) is found in Arizona, southeastern California and Sonora, Mexico. A specimen found in the Maricopa Mountains, near Gila Bend, AZ on January 17, 1988, had candelabra-like branches rising to 57 ft. 11¾ in.

An armless cactus 78 feet high was measured in April 1978 by Hube Yates in Cave Creek, AZ. It was toppled in a windstorm in July 1986 at an estimated age of 150 years.

The largest cactus is the saguaro, found in southwestern North America.

FLOWERS

Largest bloom   *Rafflesia arnoldi* of southeast Asia has blooms three feet across and weighing as much as 36 pounds.

Inflorescence   The largest inflorescence is that of *Puya raimondii*. Its panicle (diameter eight feet) emerges to a height of 35 feet, and each panicle bears up to 8,000 white blooms.

Smallest flowering and fruiting plant   The floating, flowering aquatic duckweed (*Wolffia angusta*) of Australia is only 0.024 inches long and 0.013 inches wide. It weighs about .00001 ounces and its fruit, which resembles a minuscule fig, weighs .000025 ounces.

United States   The smallest plant regularly flowering in the United States is *Wolffia globosa*, which is found in the San Joaquin Valley, California, and in rivers draining the Sierra Nevada Mountains. The plant is 0.015–0.027 inches long and 0.011 inches wide.

Fastest-growing flowering plant   It was reported from Tresco Abbey, Isles of Scilly, Great Britain in July 1978 that a *Hesperoyucca whipplei* grew 12 feet in 14 days, a rate of about 10 inches per day.

Slowest-flowering plant   The panicle of *Puya raimondii* (see LARGEST BLOOM) emerges after 80–150 years of the plant's life and then dies.

Tallest orchid   Specimens of *Grammatophyllum speciosum*, a native of Malaysia, have been recorded up to 25 feet high. There are five species of vanilla orchid that are vines and can spread to almost any length depending on the environment.

Rafflesia arnoldi **has the largest of all blooms.**

Largest orchid flower The petals of *Pathiopedilum sanderianum* are reported to grow up to three feet long in the wild. A specimen grown in Somerset, England in 1991 had three flowers averaging two feet from the top of the dorsal sepal to the bottom of the ribbon petals, giving a record stretched length of four feet.

United States The largest flowering orchid in the United States is the yellow ladyslipper (*Cypripedium calceolus*). Its petals grow up to seven inches long.

Largest rose tree A Lady Banks rose tree at Tombstone, AZ has a trunk 163 inches in circumference, stands nine feet high and covers an area of 8,660 square feet. It is supported by 77 posts and several thousand feet of piping, which allows 150 people to be seated under the arbor.

Largest leaves The largest leaves of any plant belong to the raffia palm (*Raphia farinifera* = *R. raffia*) of the Mascarene Islands in the Indian Ocean, and the Amazonian bamboo palm (*R. taedigera*) of South America, both of which have leaf blades that measure up to 65½ feet long, with petioles up to 13 feet.

United States The leaves of the climbing fern (*Lygodium japonicum*) of the Gulf coast can grow to 23 feet.

Most-leafed clovers A 14-leafed white clover (*Trifolium repens*) was found by Randy Farland near Sioux Falls, SD on June 16, 1975. A 14-leafed red clover (*T. pratense*) was reported by Paul Haizlip in Bellevue, WA on June 22, 1987.

SEEDS

Largest seed The single-seeded fruit of the giant fan palm *Lodoicea maldivica* (= *L. callipyge, L. seychellarum*) can weigh 44 pounds. Commonly known as the double coconut or coco de mer, it is found wild only in the Seychelles in the Indian Ocean.

Smallest seed The smallest are those of epiphytic orchids, at 28,129.81 million seeds per ounce (compare with grass pollens at up to 6 billion grains per ounce).

Most durable seed A plausible but inconclusive claim for the longevity of seeds has been made for the Arctic lupine (*Lupinus arcticus*) found in frozen silt at Miller Creek, Yukon, Canada in July 1954 by Harold Schmidt. The seeds were germinated in 1966 and were radiocarbon dated to at least 8000 B.C. and more probably to 13,000 B.C.

GRASSES

Commonest grass Bermuda grass (*Cynodon dactylon*) is native to tropical Africa and the Indo-Malaysian region, but it extends from Lat. 45° N to 45° S. It is possibly the most troublesome weed of the grass family, affecting 40 crops in over 80 countries.

Tallest grass A thorny bamboo culm (*Bambusa arundiancea*) felled at Pattazhi, Travancore, India in November 1904 was 121½ feet tall.

WEEDS

Largest weed The giant hogweed (*Heracleum mantegazzianum*), originally from the Caucasus, reaches 12 feet tall and has leaves three feet long.

Most damaging weed The purple nutsedge, nutgrass or nutsedge (*Cyperus rotundus*) is a land weed native to India. It attacks 52 crops in 92 countries, including the United States, where it is found primarily in the southern states.

Aquatic The most widespread aquatic weed is the water hyacinth (*Eichhornia crassipes*), which is a native of the Amazon basin but extends from Lat. 40° N to 45° S.

Tallest weed The tallest weed in the United States is the Melaleuca tree (*Melaleuca quinquenervia*). Growing to an average of 39 feet, it has infested 3.7 million of the 4.7 million acres of Florida wetlands.

TREES

Oldest tree species The maidenhair tree (*Ginkgo biloba*), which first appeared about 160 million years ago during the Jurassic era, survives today as a living species. It has been grown since c. 1100 in Japan.

Oldest tree The potential life span of a bristlecone pine (*Pinus longaeva*) is estimated at nearly 5,500 years, and that of a giant sequoia (*Sequoiadendron giganteum*) at 6,000 years. The oldest recorded tree was the "Eon Tree," a coast redwood (*Sequioa sempervirens*) in Humboldt County, CA. This tree, which fell in December 1977, stood about 250 feet tall and was believed to be at least 6,200 years old.

Living A bristlecone pine named Methuselah, growing at 10,000 feet on the California side of the White Mountains, has been confirmed as 4,700 years old. In March 1974, it was reported that this tree had produced 48 live seedlings.

Most massive tree General Sherman, a giant sequoia (*Sequoiadendron giganteum*) standing in Sequoia National Park, CA, is 275 feet tall. In 1991, it had a girth of 102.6 feet, measured 4½ feet above the ground. In terms of total volume, General Sherman is considered the largest living thing in the world.

Greatest spread The great banyan (*Ficus benghalensis*) in the Indian Botanical Garden, Calcutta, India has 1,775 prop or supporting roots and a circumference of 1,350 feet. It covers some three acres and dates from before 1787.

Greatest girth A circumference of 190 feet was recorded for the European chestnut (*Castanea sativa*) known as the "Tree of the Hundred Horses"

(Castagno di Cento Cavalli) on Mount Etna, Sicily, Italy in 1770 and 1780. It is now in three parts, widely separated.

United States   The giant sequoia named General Sherman in Sequoia National Park, CA has a girth of 102.6 feet, measured 4½ feet above the ground.

Tallest tree   An Australian eucalyptus (*Eucalyptus regnans*) at Watts River, Victoria, Australia, was reported in 1872 to measure 435 feet tall. It almost certainly measured over 500 feet originally.

Living   The tallest tree currently standing is the "National Geographic Society" coast redwood (*S. sempervirens*) in Redwood National Park, Orick, CA. It was measured at 365 ft. 6 in. by researchers with the National Geographic Society and Oregon State University in March 1995.

Fastest-growing tree   Discounting bamboo, which is not classified as a tree but as a woody grass, the fastest rate of growth recorded is 35 ft. 3 in. in 13 months by an *Albizzia falcata* planted on June 17, 1974 in Sabah, Malaysia.

Slowest-growing tree   Excluding *bonsai*, the extreme in slow growth is represented by *Dioon edule* (Cycadaceae) in Mexico, whose average annual growth rate is 0.03 inches; a specimen 120 years old measured four inches high.

Most isolated tree   It is believed that the nearest companion to a solitary Norwegian spruce on Campbell Island in the Pacific Ocean is over 120 nautical miles away in the Auckland Islands.

Largest forest   The largest forested areas in the world are the coniferous forests of northern Russia, lying between Lat. 55° N and the Arctic Circle. The total wooded area amounts to 2.7 billion acres (25 percent of the

Wrangell-St. Elias National Park and Preserve covers 13.2 million acres in Alaska.

world's forests), of which 38 percent is Siberian larch. In comparison, the largest area of forest in the tropics is the Amazon basin, with some 815 million acres.

United States   The largest forest in the United States is the Tongass National Forest (16.7 million acres) in Alaska. The United States is 32.25 percent forested.

ZOOS, AQUARIUMS AND PARKS

Oldest zoo   The Zoological Society of London, England was founded in 1826. In June 1996, the collection comprised 14,494 specimens, housed in Regent's Park, London, England and at Whipsnade Park, England.

United States   The Philadelphia Zoo received its charter from the state of Pennsylvania in 1859, but did not open to the public until 1874.

Lincoln Park Zoo, a 60-acre public park owned by the city of Chicago, received a gift of two swans from Central Park, New York City in 1868 to start its collection. The current facility covers 35 acres. According to the American Association of Zoological Parks and Aquariums, Lincoln Park Zoo is also the top zoo for attendance, with 4 million visitors each year.

Largest aquarium   In terms of volume, the Living Seas Aquarium, opened in 1986 at the Epcot Center near Orlando, FL, is the largest, with a capacity of almost 6.7 million gallons. It contains over 3,000 fish, representing 65 species.

The Monterey Bay Aquarium in California contains over 364,593 specimens (571 species) of fauna and flora. The average annual attendance is 1.7 million visitors; however, in 1985, there were 2.3 million visitors, the highest for any aquarium in the United States.

Largest park   The National Park of North-Eastern Greenland covers 375,289 square miles and stretches from Liverpool Land in the south to Odaaq Ø, off Pearyland. Established in 1974, the park is largely covered by ice and is home to a variety of protected flora and fauna, including polar bears, musk-ox and birds of prey.

United States   The largest public park in the United States is Wrangell-St. Elias National Park and Preserve in Alaska. The National Park section covers 8.33 million acres and the Preserve comprises 4.88 million acres.

Most national parks visited   Alan K. Hogenauer of Oakdale, NY has visited 1,002 different parts of the U.S. National Park System, including the 369 official units, since 1953.

Largest game reserve   Etosha National Park, Namibia was established in 1907, and now covers an area of 38,427 square miles.

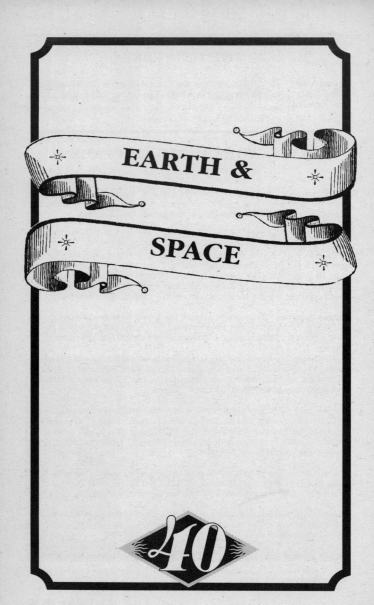

EARTH & SPACE

40

THE UNIVERSE

Largest structure in the Universe In June 1994, the discovery of a cocoon-shaped shell of galaxies about 650 million light-years across was announced by Georges Paturel (France) and his colleagues.

Remotest object The record red shift is 4.897 for the quasar PC 1247 + 3406. This quasar appears to be 13.2 billion light-years away.

Remotest galaxy The remotest galaxy is the radio galaxy 8C 1435 + 635. It has a red shift of 4.25, equivalent to a distance of 13 billion light-years. Tentative evidence was obtained during 1994 by a European Southern Observatory (ESO) team for a galaxy of red shift 4.38, equivalent to a distance of 13.1 billion light-years.

Largest galaxy The central galaxy of Abell 2029 is 1.07 billion light-years away in the Virgo cluster. The galaxy has a major diameter of 5.6 million light-years, which is 80 times the diameter of the Milky Way galaxy, and a light output 2 trillion times that of the Sun.

Brightest object The most luminous object in the sky is the quasar HS 1946 + 7658, which is 1.5×10^{15} times more luminous than the Sun. This quasar is 12.4 billion light-years away.

Most luminous galaxy The highest luminosity reported for a galaxy is 4.7×10^{14} times that of the Sun for the hyperluminous IRAS (Infra Red Astron-

The Great Galaxy in Andromeda is the most distant object visible to the naked eye.

omy Satellite) galaxy FSC 10214 + 4724, which has a red shift of 2.282, equivalent to a distance of 11.6 billion light-years. However, this value is 10 to 100 times too large due to the lensing effect of intervening galaxies. If that is so, the brightest galaxy would then be the hyperluminous IRAS F15307 + 3252, with a luminosity 1.0×10^{13} times that of the Sun. Although it has a red shift of only 0.926, equivalent to a distance of 8.1 billion light-years, the luminosity of this galaxy may also be enhanced by lensing.

Farthest visible object   The remotest object visible to the naked eye is the Great Galaxy in Andromeda (magnitude 3.47). Known as Messier 31, it is a rotating spiral nebula at a distance of about 2.31 million light-years from Earth.

Under ideal conditions, Messier 33, the Spiral in Triangulum (magnitude 5.79), can be glimpsed by the naked eye at a distance of 2.53 million light-years.

STARS

Nearest star   The closest star other than the Sun is the very faint Proxima Centauri, which is 4.225 light-years away.

The nearest star visible to the naked eye is the Southern Hemisphere binary Alpha Centauri (4.35 light-years away), which has an apparent magnitude of –0.27.

Largest star   Betelgeuse (Alpha Orionis) is 310 light-years away. It has a diameter of 400 million miles, about 500 times greater than the diameter of the Sun, and it is surrounded by a gas halo up to 530 billion miles in diameter.

Most massive star   The variable Eta Carinae, 9,100 light-years away in the Carina Nebula, is estimated to have a mass 150–200 times greater than the mass of the Sun. The most massive stars whose masses have actually been determined are the two stars of the binary known as Plaskett's Star (discovered by K. Plaskett in 1992), which both have masses 60–100 times greater than the Sun.

Smallest star   Neutron stars, which may weigh up to three times as much as the Sun, have diameters of only 6–19 miles. Although black holes are pointlike sources, their distortion of local space–time means that they appear as black stars, with a diameter of 37 miles for one weighing 10 times the mass of the Sun.

Lightest star   The white dwarf companion to the millisecond pulsar PSR B1957 + 20 has a mass of only 0.02 that of the Sun (20 Jupiter masses) and is being evaporated away by the fast-spinning neutron star. The brown dwarf star Gliese 229B has a mass estimated to be between 20 and 50 Jupiter masses. Normal stars (those undergoing continuous fusion of hydrogen) cannot have a mass less than 80 times that of Jupiter.

Brightest star   If all the stars could be viewed at the same distance, Eta Carinae would be the brightest, with a total luminosity 6.5 million times that of the Sun. However, the visually brightest star viewed through a telescope is the hypergiant Cygnus OB2 No. 12, which is 5,900 light-years away. It has an absolute visual magnitude of –9.9 and is therefore visually 810,000 times brighter than the Sun.

Brightest star seen from Earth   Sirius A (Alpha Canis Majoris), 8.64 light-years away, is the brightest star in the sky, with an apparent magnitude of –1.46. It has a mass 2.14 times the mass of the Sun and is visually 24 times brighter.

Faintest star   The faintest star is the brown dwarf Gliese 229B, orbiting 4.1 billion miles from the main star Gliese 229A, which is 18.6 light-years away

Alpha Canis Majoris is the brightest star as seen from Earth.

from Earth. The B star has a luminosity 500,000 times less than the Sun and a visual brightness 500 million times less. Its surface temperature of less than 1,300°F is the lowest observed stellar temperature.

Youngest stars   The youngest stars appear to be two protostars known collectively as IRAS–4 buried deep in dust clouds in the nebula NGC 1333, which is 1,100 light-years away. These protostars will not blaze forth as full-fledged stars for at least another 100,000 years.

Slowest pulsar   The pulsar with the slowest spin-down rate, and therefore the most accurate stellar clock, is PSR J0034 - 0534, at only 6.7×10^{-21} seconds per second.

Fastest pulsar   For pulsars whose spin rates have been accurately measured, the fastest-spinning is PSR B1937 + 214. It is in the constellation Vulpecula, 11,700 light-years away, and has a pulse period of 1.5578064949 milliseconds, which is equivalent to a spin rate of 641.9285218 revolutions per second.

Brightest supernova   The brightest supernova ever seen is believed to be SN 1006, seen near Beta Lupi in April 1006. It flared for two years and attained an estimated magnitude of –9 to –10.

Largest constellation   Hydra (the Sea Serpent) covers 1302.844 square degrees, or 3.16 percent of the whole sky, and contains at least 68 stars visible to the naked eye. The constellation Centaurus (Centaur), which ranks ninth in area, contains at least 94 such stars.

Zodiacal   Virgo is the largest, with an area of 1,294.428 square degrees. Taurus has the most bright stars, with 125 down to magnitude 6.

Smallest constellation   Crux Australis (Southern Cross) has an area of only 0.16 percent of the sky, or 68.477 square degrees, compared with the 41,252.96 square degrees of the whole sky.

Zodiacal   The smallest is Capricornus (Capricorn), with an area of 413.947 square degrees.

THE SOLAR SYSTEM

Largest model of the solar system   The biggest scale model of the solar system was developed by the Lakeview Museum of Arts and Sciences in Peoria, IL and inaugurated in April 1992. The planetary orbit of the model measures 60 miles across.

THE SUN

Largest object in the solar system   The Sun is classified as a yellow dwarf type G2, but its mass of 2 octillion tons is 332,946.04 times the mass of

Earth and represents over 99 percent of the total mass of the solar system. The Sun's diameter is 865,040 miles.

Greatest Earth–Sun distance   Earth's orbit is elliptical, so its distance from the Sun varies. At aphelion, the outermost point, Earth is 94,509,200 miles from the Sun, compared with 91,402,600 miles at perihelion, the closest point.

Largest sunspot   A sunspot recorded on April 8, 1947 had an area of about 7 billion square miles, with an extreme longitude of 187,000 miles and an extreme latitude of 90,000 miles.

Most sunspots   In October 1957, a smoothed sunspot count showed 263, the highest recorded index since records started in 1755.

Longest-lasting sunspot   In 1943, one sunspot persisted for 200 days, from June to December.

PLANETS

Largest planet   Jupiter, with an equatorial diameter of 88,846 miles, has a mass 317.828 times, and a volume 1,323.3 times, that of Earth. It also has the shortest period of rotation; Jupiter's day is 9 hr. 50 min. 30.003 sec. long at the equator.

Smallest planet   Pluto has a diameter of 1,442 miles.

Coldest planet   Although the surface temperature of Pluto is only approximately known, its surface composition suggests that the temperature must be similar to the value of –391°F measured for Neptune's moon Triton, the lowest observed surface temperature of any natural body in the solar system.

Hottest planet   Venus has an estimated surface temperature of 864°F, based on measurements taken by the Russian *Venera* and U.S. *Pioneer* surface probes.

Outermost planet   The Pluto–Charon system orbits at a mean distance from the Sun of 3.674 billion miles.
   The remotest solar system object is the Kuiper Belt object 1995 WY2, which orbits at a mean distance of 4.420 billion miles.

Nearest planet to Earth   Venus can come to within 24 million miles of the Earth, but its average distance is 25.7 million miles inside Earth's orbit.

Fastest planet   Mercury, which orbits the Sun at an average distance of 35,983,100 miles, has an orbital period of 87.9686 days, thus giving it the highest average speed in orbit of 107,030 MPH.

Highest surface feature   The highest surface feature of any planet is Olympus Mons in the Tharsis region of Mars. It has a diameter of 310–370 miles and an estimated height of 16 miles above the surrounding plain.

Brightest planet   Viewed from Earth, the brightest of the five planets normally visible to the naked eye (Jupiter, Mars, Mercury, Saturn, and Venus) is Venus, with a maximum magnitude of –4.4.

Faintest planet   Uranus, with a magnitude of 5.5, can be seen with the naked eye under certain conditions. The faintest of the nine planets as seen from Earth is Pluto (magnitude 15.0), which can only be viewed through a telescope.

Densest planet   Earth has an average density 5.515 times that of water.

Least dense planet   Saturn has an average density only about an eighth of Earth's density or 0.685 times the density of water.

Greatest conjunction   The most dramatic recorded conjunction of the seven principal members of the solar system besides Earth (Sun, Moon, Mercury, Venus, Mars, Jupiter and Saturn) occurred on February 5, 1962, when 16° covered all seven during an eclipse in the Pacific area.

SATELLITES

Largest satellite   The largest and heaviest satellite is Ganymede (Jupiter III), which is 2.017 times as heavy as Earth's moon and has a diameter of 3,273 miles, compared with 2,159.3 miles for Earth's moon.

Smallest satellite   Of satellites whose diameters have been measured, the smallest is Deimos, the irregularly shaped outermost moon of Mars, which has an average diameter of 7.8 miles.

Most satellites   Of the 61 satellites in the solar system, 18 belong to Saturn.

Shortest planet–satellite distance   Phobos orbits Mars at a distance of 5,287 miles from the planet's center.

Longest planet–satellite distance   Jupiter's outer satellite Sinope orbits the planet at 14.7 million miles from its center.

ASTEROIDS

Largest asteroid   The largest asteroid is 1 Ceres, with an equatorial diameter of 596 miles.

Smallest asteroid   The smallest asteroid is 1993KA2, with a diameter of about 16 feet.

Brightest asteroid   The brightest asteroid is 4 Vesta (discovered on March 29, 1807) with an absolute magnitude of 3.16.

Faintest asteroid   The faintest asteroid is 1993KB2, whose absolute magnitude of 29 makes it the faintest object ever detected.

Nearest to the Sun   Most of the estimated 45,000 asteroids orbit between Mars and Jupiter, but the orbits of only about 7,200 have been computed.

The Aten asteroid 1995 CR (discovered on February 3, 1995) is only 11,130,000 miles from the Sun at perihelion.

Farthest from the Sun   The Kuiper belt object 1994 JS is 4.933 billion miles away from the Sun at aphelion.

Closest approach to Earth   The asteroid 1994XM₁, which is 33 feet in diameter, was discovered by James Scotti (U.S.) on December 9, 1994, 14 hours before it passed within 62,000 miles of Earth.

THE MOON

Shortest Earth–Moon distance   In this century, the closest approach to Earth by the Moon (the smallest perigee) was 221,441 miles center-to-center on January 4, 1912.

Longest Earth–Moon distance   On March 2, 1984, the Moon was 252,718 miles from Earth, the farthest distance this century.

Largest craters   The largest impact basin on the Moon, and the largest and deepest crater in the solar system, is the far-side South-Pole-Aitken, which is 1,550 miles in diameter and an average 39,000 feet deep.
   The largest wholly visible crater is the walled plain Bailly, which is 183 miles across, with walls rising to 14,000 feet.

Highest mountains   In the absence of a sea level, lunar altitudes are measured relative to an adopted reference sphere with a radius of 1,080 miles. On this basis, the highest elevation is 26,000 feet for the highlands north of the Korolev Basin, on the far side of the Moon.

Highest temperature   When the Sun is overhead, the temperature on the lunar equator reaches 243°F.

Lowest temperature   Around sunset, the temperature at the lunar equator is 58°F, and after nightfall it sinks to –261°F.

ECLIPSES

Longest eclipse   The maximum possible duration of a solar eclipse is 7 min. 31 sec. The longest recent eclipse was on June 20, 1955 (7 min. 8 sec.), west of the Philippines, although it was clouded out along most of its track.

Most eclipses in one place   The only recent example of three total solar eclipses occurring in one location was at a point 44° N, 67° E in Kazakhstan, in September 1941, July 1945, and February 1952.

COMETS

Brightest periodical comet   Appearances of Halley's Comet, which has a period of 76 years, have been traced back to 467 B.C. It was first depicted in the Nuremburg Chronicle of A.D. 684.

Largest comet   The object 2060 Chiron has a diameter of 113 miles. The largest coma was that of the comet of 1811, at 1.2 million miles in diameter. The tail of the Great Comet of 1843 trailed for 205 million miles.

Longest period   The longest period computed for a comet is 1,550 years, for Comet McNaught-Russell, equivalent to a mean distance from the Sun of 12 billion miles.

Shortest period   The periodic comet that returns most frequently is the increasingly faint Encke's Comet, first identified in 1786. It has an orbital period of 1,198 days (3.28 years) and has the closest approach to the Sun (30.8 million miles at perihelion, when its speed is 158,000 MPH).

Closest approach to Earth   On July 1, 1770, Lexell's Comet, traveling at 86,100 MPH relative to the Sun, came within 745,000 miles of Earth. Earth is believed to have passed through the tail of Halley's Comet on May 19, 1910.

METEORITES

Oldest meteorite   The Krähenberg meteorite has been dated at 4.6 billion ± 20 million years, which is just within the initial period of solar system formation.

Largest meteorite   The largest known meteorite was found in 1920 at Hoba West, near Grootfontein in Namibia. It is a block nine feet long by eight feet wide, estimated to weigh 65 tons.

The largest meteorite exhibited in a museum is the "Cape York" meteorite, weighing 68,000 pounds, now on display in the Hayden Planetarium in New York City.

Greatest explosion   There was an explosion of 10–15 megatons in the basin of the Podkamennaya Tunguska River, in Siberia, Russia, on June 30, 1908. The blast devastated an area of 1,500 square miles and the shock was felt 620 miles away. This explosion was probably caused by the disintegration at an altitude of 33,000 feet of a 100-foot-diameter stony asteroid traveling at hypersonic velocity.

Largest crater   In 1962, a crater 150 miles in diameter and half a mile deep in Wilkes Land, Antarctica was attributed to a meteorite. The crater could have been created by a 14.33 billion-ton meteorite striking at 44,000 MPH.

There is a craterlike formation or astrobleme 275 miles in diameter on the eastern shore of Hudson Bay, Canada.

The largest and best-preserved crater that was definitely formed by an asteroid is the Coon Butte or Barringer Crater, near Canyon Diablo, Winslow, AZ. It is 4,150 feet in diameter and now about 575 feet deep, with a parapet rising 130–155 feet above the surrounding plain. It has been estimated that an iron–nickel mass of some 2.2 million tons and with a diameter of 200–260 feet gouged out this crater *c.* 25,000 B.C.

Largest meteor shower   On the night of November 16–17, 1966, the Leonid meteors were visible between western North America and eastern Russia. Meteors passed over Arizona at a rate of 2,300 per minute for a period of 20 minutes starting at 5 A.M. on November 17, 1966.

THE EARTH

CONTINENTS

Largest continent Of the earth's surface, only about 57,151,000 square miles (29.02 percent) is land above water, with a mean height of 2,480 feet above sea level. The Eurasian landmass is the largest, with an area (including islands) of 20,700,000 square miles.

The Afro-Eurasian landmass, separated artificially by the Suez Canal, covers an area of 32,700,000 square miles.

There is strong evidence that about 300 million years ago, the earth's land surface comprised a single primeval continent of 60 million square miles, now termed Pangaea.

Smallest continent The Australian mainland has an area of 2,941,526 square miles.

Land farthest from the sea The point of land remotest from the sea is at Lat. 46° 16.8′ N, Long. 86° 40.2′ E in the Dzungarian Basin, which is in the Xinjiang Uygur autonomous region of China. It is at a straight-line distance of 1,645 miles from the nearest open sea—Baydaratskaya Guba to the north (Arctic Ocean), Feni Point to the south (Indian Ocean) and Bohai Wan to the east (Yellow Sea).

Largest peninsula The world's largest peninsula is Arabia, with an area of about 1.25 million square miles.

United States The Alaskan peninsula is the longest in the United States, with a length of 471 miles. The longest in the conterminous 48 states is the Florida peninsula, at 383 miles.

ROCKS

Oldest rock The greatest reported age for any scientifically dated rock is 3.962 billion years in the case of the Acasta Gneisses, found about 200 miles north of Yellowknife, Northwest Territories, Canada.

Older minerals that are not rocks have also been identified. Zircon crystals discovered in the Jack Hills, 430 miles north of Perth, Western Australia, were found to be 4.276 billion years old. These are the oldest fragments of the earth's crust discovered so far.

United States The oldest rocks in the United States are the 3.6 billion-year-old Morton Gneisses, scattered over an area of 50 miles from New Ulm to Renville Co., MN.

Largest rock The largest exposed monolith in the world is Ayers Rock, known to Aborigines as Uluru, which rises 1,143 feet above the surrounding desert plain in Northern Territory, Australia. It is 1.5 miles long and a mile wide.

Longest natural arch   Kolob Arch in Zion National Park, Utah, has a span of 290–310 feet, a width of 41 feet and its height to the top surface is 330 feet. While Kolob Arch is set 50 feet from the wall of a cliff, Landscape Arch, in Arches National Park, Utah is a stand-alone arch with a span of 291–306 feet and the height to the top surface is 106 feet. In one place erosion has narrowed it to six feet wide.

CAVES

Longest cave   The most extensive cave system in the world is in Mammoth Cave National Park, KY. Explorations by many groups of cavers have revealed that interconnected cave passages beneath the Flint, Mammoth Cave, Toohey and Joppa ridges make up a system with a total mapped length that is now 350 miles.

Largest cave   The world's largest cave chamber is the Sarawak Chamber, Lubang Nasib Bagus, in the Gunung Mulu National Park, Sarawak, Malaysia. Its length is 2,300 feet, its average width is 980 feet, and it is not less than 230 feet high at any point.

Longest underwater cave   The Nohoch Nah Chich cave system in Quintana Roo, Mexico has 31.88 miles of mapped passages. Exploration of the system, which began in November 1987, has been carried out by the CEDAM Cave Diving Team under the leadership of Mike Madden (U.S.)

Longest dive into a cave   The longest dive into a single flooded cave passage is 13,300 feet into the Doux de Coly, Dordogne, France by Olivier Issler (Switzerland) on April 4, 1991.

The longest underwater traverse in a cave is 10,000 feet from King Pot to Keld Head, North Yorkshire, England by Geoff Yeadon and Geoff Crossley on August 3, 1991.

The deepest cave dive was to 925 feet in Zacaton, Mexico by Jim Bowden (U.S.) in April 1994.

40 years ago no underwater caves had been mapped. **Today** the longest measured underwater cave is Nohoch Nah Chich, located in the Yucatan Peninsula. Exploration began in 1987, and to date 31.88 miles have been mapped.

"This cave system could be one of the 10 largest in the world. Divers will be exploring here throughout my children's lifetimes. I believe that in five years, over 100 miles will have been mapped."—Mike Madden, leader CEDAM team, June 19, 1996

A diver explores the Nohoch Nah Chich cave system.

Deepest descent into a cave The world depth record was set by the Groupe Vulcain in the Gouffre Jean Bernard, France at 5,256 feet in 1989. However, this cave has never been entirely descended, so the "sporting" record for the greatest descent into a cave is recognized as 4,947 feet in the Shakta Pantjukhina in the Caucasus Mountains of Georgia by a team of Ukrainian cavers in 1988.

Longest stalactite The longest freehanging stalactite in the world is believed to be one measuring over 40 feet long in Gruta do Janelão, Minas Gerais, Brazil.

Tallest stalagmite The tallest known stalagmite in the world is one measuring 200 feet high in the cave of Tham Nam Klong Ngu, at Kanchanaburi, Thailand. It is difficult to see whether or not it is joined to the cave roof; if it is, it should correctly be termed a cave column. The tallest stalagmite may in that case be one measuring 105 feet tall in the Krásnohorská cave, near Rožňava in Slovakia.

The tallest known cave column is considered to be the Flying Dragon Pillar, 128 feet high, in Daji Dong, Guizhou, China.

Deepest cave The deepest cave in the United States is Lechuguilla Cave in Carlsbad Caverns National Park, Carlsbad, NM, which currently measures 1,567 feet deep and has a mapped length of 89.35 miles.

Highest rock pinnacle The highest rock pinnacle is Ball's Pyramid, near Lord Howe Island in the Pacific, which is 1,843 feet high but has a base axis of only 660 feet.

MOUNTAINS

Highest mountain Recent satellites indicate that Mt. Everest, a peak in the eastern Himalayas on the Tibet–Nepal border, is 29,029 feet high.

The mountain whose summit is farthest from the earth's center is the Andean peak of Chimborazo (20,561 feet), 98 miles south of the equator in Ecuador. Its summit is 7,054 feet further from the earth's center than the summit of Mt. Everest.

The highest island mountain in the world is Puncak Jaya in Irian Jaya, Indonesia, at 16,023 feet.

United States The highest mountain in the United States is Mt. McKinley in Alaska, at 20,320 feet.

The highest mountain in the 48 conterminous states is Mt. Whitney in California, with a highest point of 14,494 feet.

Tallest mountain Measured from its submarine base in the Hawaiian Trough to its peak, Mauna Kea (White Mountain), on the island of Hawaii, has a total height of 33,480 feet, of which 13,796 feet are above sea level.

Longest mountain range The submarine Mid-Ocean Ridge extends 40,000 miles from the Arctic Ocean, around Africa, Asia and Australia, to North America. Its highest point is 13,800 feet above the base ocean depth.

Land The longest land mountain range is the Andes of South America, which is 4,700 miles long.

Highest mountain range The Himalaya-Karakoram range contains 96 of the world's 109 peaks of over 24,000 feet.

Longest line of sight Vatnajökull (6,952 feet), Iceland has been seen by refracted light from the Faeroe Islands 340 miles away.

United States In Alaska, Mt. McKinley (20,320 feet) has been sighted from Mt. Sanford (16,237 feet), a distance of 230 miles.

Greatest plateau The most extensive high plateau in the world is the Tibetan Plateau in Central Asia. Its average altitude is 16,000 feet and its area is 715,000 square miles.

Highest sea cliffs The cliffs on the north coast of Moloka'i, HI near Umilehi Point descend 3,300 feet to the sea at an average inclination of more than 55°.

VALLEYS

Deepest valley The Yarlung Zangbo valley in the Himalayas is 16,650 feet deep. The peaks of Namche Barwa (25,436 feet) and Jala Peri (23,891 feet) are 13 miles apart, with the Yarlung Zangbo River in between.

Largest gorge The Grand Canyon on the Colorado River in north-central Arizona extends from Marble Gorge to the Grand Wash Cliffs, a distance of 277 miles. It averages 10 miles in width and is one mile deep.

The submarine Labrador Basin, between Greenland and Labrador, Canada, is 2,150 miles long.

Deepest canyon A canyon or gorge is generally defined as a valley with steep rock walls and a considerable depth in relation to its width. The Grand Canyon (see *Largest Gorge*) has the characteristic vertical sections of wall, but is much wider than its depth. The Vicos Gorge in the Pindus mountains of northwest Greece is 2,950 feet deep and 3,600 feet between its rims.

United States The deepest canyon in the United States is Kings Canyon, Clovis, CA, which runs through Sierra and Sequoia National Forests. The deepest point, which measures 8,200 feet, is in the Sierra National Forest section of the canyon.

Deepest submarine canyon The submarine canyon 25 miles south of Esperance, Western Australia is 6,000 feet deep and 20 miles wide.

DESERTS

Largest desert The Sahara in North Africa stretches 3,200 miles from east to west at its widest point. From north to south it is 800–1,400 miles long, and it covers 3,579,000 square miles.

United States The Mojave Desert is the largest in the United States. It covers 15,000 square miles.

Largest sand dunes The world's highest measured sand dunes are those in the Saharan sand sea of Isaouane-N-Tifernine of east-central Algeria. They have a wavelength of three miles and are as high as 1,526 feet.

OCEANS

Largest ocean The Pacific Ocean represents 45.9 percent of the world's oceans and covers 64,186,300 square miles. Its average depth is 12,925 feet.

Deepest ocean The deepest point of the world's oceans is in the Marianas Trench in the Pacific Ocean. It was pinpointed in 1951 by the British Survey Ship Challenger, and on January 23, 1960, the manned U.S.N. bathyscaphe *Trieste* descended to the bottom. On March 24, 1995, the unmanned Japanese probe Kaiko also reached the bottom and recorded a depth of 35,797 feet.

Smallest ocean The Arctic Ocean covers 5,105,700 square miles. Its average depth is 3,407 feet.

Largest sea The South China Sea has an area of 1,148,500 square miles.

Remotest spot from land The world's most distant point from land is a spot in the South Pacific, 47° 30′ S, 120° W, which is 1,600 miles from Pitcairn Island, Ducie Island and Cape Dart, Antarctica. Surrounding this spot is a circle of water with an area of 8,041,200 square miles—about a million square miles larger than Russia, the world's largest country.

Largest bay The largest bay measured by shoreline length is Hudson Bay, Canada, which has a shoreline of 7,623 miles and an area of 476,000 square miles. Measured by area, the Bay of Bengal, in the Indian Ocean, is larger, at 839,000 square miles.

Largest gulf　The Gulf of Mexico covers 596,000 square miles and has a shoreline extending 3,100 miles, from Cape Sable, FL to Cabo Catoche, Mexico.

Longest fjord　The Nordvest Fjord arm of the Scoresby Sound in eastern Greenland extends 195 miles inland from the sea.

Highest seamount　The highest submarine mountain, or seamount is near the Tonga Trench, between Samoa and New Zealand. It rises 28,500 feet from the seabed, with its summit 1,200 feet below the surface.

Most southerly ocean　The most southerly part of the oceans is located at 87° S, 151° W, at the snout of the Scott Glacier, 200 miles from the South Pole.

Lowest sea temperature　The temperature of water at the surface of the White Sea can be as low as 28°F.

Highest sea temperature　In the shallow areas of the Persian Gulf, the surface temperature can reach 96°F in summer.

The highest temperature recorded in the ocean is 759°F in a hot spring 300 miles off the west coast of the United States, measured in 1985 by an American research submarine.

Clearest sea　The Weddell Sea, 71° S, 15° W off Antarctica, has the clearest water of any sea. A Secchi Disk one foot in diameter was visible to a depth of 262 feet on October 13, 1986, as measured by Dutch researchers at the German Alfred Wegener Institute. Such clarity is comparable to the clarity of distilled water.

The Pacific Ocean is the largest and deepest ocean.

The surface temperature of the White Sea can drop to 28°F.

STRAITS

Longest straits The Tatarskiy Proliv or Tartar Straits, between Sakhalin Island and Russia, run 500 miles from the Sea of Japan to Sakhalinsky Zaliv.

Broadest straits The broadest named straits in the world are the Davis Straits between Greenland and Baffin Island, Canada, with a minimum width of 210 miles. The Drake Passage, a deep waterway between the Diego Ramirez Islands, Chile and the South Shetland Islands, is 710 miles across.

Narrowest strait The narrowest navigable strait is the Strait of Dofuchi, between Shodoshima Island and Mae Island, Japan. At the bridge linking the two islands, the strait is 32 ft. 7 in. wide.

WAVES

Highest waves The highest officially recorded sea wave was calculated at 112 feet from trough to crest; it was measured during a 68-knot hurricane by Lt. Frederic Margraff (U.S.N.) from the U.S.S. Ramapo, traveling from Manila, Philippines to San Diego, CA on the night of February 6–7, 1933. The highest instrumentally measured wave was 86 feet high, and was recorded by the British ship Weather Reporter in the North Atlantic on December 30, 1972 at Lat. 59° N, Long. 19° W.

Highest tsunamis On July 9, 1958, a landslip on land caused a 100-MPH wave to wash 1,720 feet high along the fjord-like Lituya Bay in Alaska.

The highest tsunami triggered by an underwater landslide struck the island of Lanai in Hawaii *c.* 105,000 years ago. It deposited sediment up to an altitude of 1,230 feet.

The highest tsunami caused by an offshore earthquake appeared off Ishigaki Island, Ryukyu island chain, Japan on April 24, 1771. It was possibly 279 feet high, and it tossed an 830-ton block of coral more than 1½ miles inland.

Most deadly tsunami   The worst tsunami in the United States occurred on September 8, 1900 in Galveston, TX, killing more than 5,000 people.

CURRENTS

Greatest ocean current   On the basis of measurements taken in 1982 in the Drake Passage, between Chile and Antarctica, the Antarctic Circumpolar Current or West Wind Drift was found to be flowing at a rate of 4.3 billion cubic feet per second. Results from computer modeling in 1990 estimate a higher figure of 6.9 billion cubic feet per second.

Strongest currents   In Nakwakto Rapids, Slingsby Channel, British Columbia, Canada (Lat. 51° 06′ N, Long. 127° 30′ W), the flow rate may reach 16 knots.

TIDES

Greatest tide   The greatest tides occur in the Bay of Fundy, which divides the peninsula of Nova Scotia, Canada from Maine and the Canadian province of New Brunswick. Burntcoat Head in the Minas Basin, Nova Scotia has the greatest mean spring range, at 52 ft. 6 in. Comparable tides have been reported in Leaf Basin, in Ungava Bay, Quebec.

Least tide   Tahiti, in the mid-Pacific Ocean, experiences virtually no tide.

Highest and lowest tide   The highest and lowest tide in the United States is at Sunrise, AK. Its range is 33.3 feet.

ISLANDS

Largest island   Discounting Australia, which is usually regarded as a continental landmass, the largest island in the world is Greenland, with an area of about 840,000 square miles.

Sand   The largest sand island in the world is Fraser Island, Queensland, Australia, with a sand dune 75 miles long.

Freshwater   The largest island surrounded mostly by fresh water (18,500 square miles) is the Ilha de Marajó in the mouth of the Amazon River, Brazil.

Remotest island   Bouvet Island (Bouvetøya), an uninhabited Norwegian dependency in the South Atlantic, is 1,050 miles north of the nearest land, Queen Maud Land in Antarctica.
   The remotest inhabited island is Tristan da Cunha in the South Atlantic. The nearest inhabited land is the island of St. Helena, 1,315 nautical miles away.

Northernmost land   The islet of Odaaq Ø, 100 feet across and 0.8 miles north of Kaffeklubben Ø off Pearyland, Greenland, is 438.9 miles from the North Pole.

Southernmost land The South Pole, unlike the North Pole, is on land. At the South Pole the ice sheet is drifting at a rate of 33 feet per year away from the geographic pole along the 40th meridian west of Greenwich.

Greatest archipelago The world's greatest archipelago is the crescent of more than 17,000 islands, 3,500 miles long, that forms Indonesia.

Largest atoll The largest atoll in the world is Kwajalein in the Marshall Islands, in the central Pacific Ocean. Its slender coral reef 176 miles long encloses a lagoon of 1,100 square miles.

The atoll with the largest land area is Christmas Atoll, in the Line Islands in the central Pacific Ocean. It has an area of 251 square miles, of which 124 square miles is land.

Longest reef The Great Barrier Reef off Queensland, northeastern Australia is 1,260 miles long. It actually consists of thousands of separate reefs. Large areas of the central section have been devastated by the crown-of-thorns starfish (*Acanthaster planci*).

RIVERS

Longest rivers The longest rivers in the world are the Nile, flowing into the Mediterranean, and the Amazon, flowing into the South Atlantic. Which one is longer is more a matter of definition than of measurement.

The Amazon has several mouths that widen toward the sea, so the exact point where the river ends is uncertain. If the Pará estuary is counted, its length is 4,195 miles. The length of the Nile before the loss of a few miles of meanders due to the construction of the Aswan High Dam was 4,145 miles.

United States The Mississippi is 2,348 miles long. It flows from its source at Lake Itasca, MN through 10 states to the Gulf of Mexico. The entire Mississippi River system, including the eastern and western tributaries, flows through 25 states.

Shortest rivers As with the longest river, two rivers could be considered to be the shortest named rivers. The Roe River, which flows into the Missouri River near Great Falls, MT, is fed by a large freshwater spring. It has two forks, measuring 201 feet (East Fork Roe River) and 58 feet (North Fork Roe River). The D River, in Lincoln City, OR, connects Devil's Lake to the Pacific Ocean. Its length is officially quoted as 120 ± 5 feet.

Largest river basin The Amazon basin covers about 2,720,000 square miles. It has countless tributaries and subtributaries, including the Madeira, which at 2,100 miles is the longest tributary in the world.

Longest estuary The Ob, in northern Russia, is 550 miles long. It is up to 50 miles wide, and is also the widest river that freezes solid.

Largest delta The delta created by the Ganges and Brahmaputra in Bangladesh and West Bengal, India covers 30,000 square miles.

LARGEST MARSH

The Everglades is a vast plateau of subtropical saw-grass marsh in southern Florida, covering 2,185 square miles. Fed by water from Lake Okeechobee, the Everglades is the largest subtropical wilderness in the continental United States.

See feature (right)

United States   The Mississippi River delta has an area of about 10,100 square miles.

Greatest flow   The Amazon discharges an average of 7.1 million cusec into the Atlantic Ocean, increasing to more than 12 million cusec in full flood. The flow of the Amazon is 60 times greater than the flow of the Nile.

Largest submarine river   In 1952, a 190-mile-wide submarine river, known as the Cromwell Current, was discovered flowing eastward below the surface of the Pacific for 4,000 miles along the equator. It flows at depths of up to 1,300 feet, and its volume is 1,000 times the volume of the Mississippi.

Longest waterway   The longest transcontinental waterway is 6,637 miles long and links the Beaufort Sea in northern Canada with the Gulf of Mexico in the United States. It starts at Tuktoyaktuk on the Mackenzie River and ends at Port Eads on the Mississippi delta.

Largest swamp   The world's largest tract of swamp is the Pantanal, in the states of Mato Grosso and Mato Grosso do Sul, Brazil. It is about 42,000 square miles in area.

Largest river bore   At spring tides, the bore (wave of tidal water) on the Qiantong Jiang in eastern China reaches a height of up to 25 feet and a speed of 13–15 knots. It can be heard advancing at a range of 14 miles.

The annual downstream flood wave on the Mekong, in southeast Asia, can reach a height of 46 feet.

WATERFALLS

Highest waterfall   The highest waterfall (as opposed to vaporized "bridal-veil fall") in the world is the Salto Angel (Angel Falls) in Venezuela, on a branch of the Carrao River, an upper tributary of the Caroni, with a total drop of 3,212 feet; the longest single drop is 2,648 feet.

United States   The tallest continuous waterfall in the United States is Ribbon Falls in Yosemite National Park, CA, with a drop of 1,612 feet. This is a seasonal waterfall and is generally dry from late July to early September.

Yosemite Falls, also in Yosemite National Park, has the greatest total

WORKING TO SAVE THE

EVERGLADES

At 2,185 square miles, Everglades National Park is the largest subtropical wilderness in the continental United States. Conservationist Marjory Stoneman Douglas dubbed it "River of Grass" because of its level landscape of saw-grass marsh. This "river" runs continuously and slowly toward the sea and the Gulf of Mexico, fed only by rain.

South Florida has only been above ground since the Ice Age, and the rock that lies under the Everglades is practically brand-new—just 6,000 to 8,000 years old. The highest elevation in the Everglades is only eight feet above sea level. Despite its recent arrival on the scene, this area is of paramount importance because of the wildlife that flourishes here.

Palm trees, swamp lilies, and red mangroves grow in abundance. Migrating birds winter here on their routes from North America to South America. Manatees, American alligators, crabs, osprey, loggerhead turtles and more form a gorgeous diversity of native animals that thrived here until the rapid population growth of Florida began to change things.

The Everglades' watershed area begins on the Kissimmee River basin in central Florida and extends from Lake Okeechobee south. In the past, shallow Lake Okeechobee filled and overflowed to form the 50-mile-wide River of Grass. Never deeper than three feet, the River flowed about 100 miles a day to the Gulf of Mexico. Now, increased use of water by people has threatened the Everglades' water supply.

The Everglades was made a national park in 1947 to help protect the marsh. A system of canals and levees controls the water levels and shunts rain to areas that need it. Still, the level of water is often much less than it needs to be in order for the area to stay flooded. Sometimes canal flow coincides with rainfall, and water floods high, dry areas such as those where alligators make their nests. Many native Everglades animals are endangered, from the Florida panther to the tiniest frog egg. Everglades wading birds have experienced a shocking 93 percent decline.

Recently, Congress extended the park boundary to protect nesting areas and shellfish nurseries, making the Everglades one of the world's largest ecosystem restoration projects.

drop at 2,425 feet, but actually consists of three distinct waterfalls. These are the Upper (1,430 feet), Middle (675 feet) and Lower falls (320 feet).

Largest waterfall   On the basis of average annual flow, the greatest waterfall in the world is the Boyoma Falls in Zaire, with 600,000 cusec.

The waterfall with the greatest peak flow was the Guaíra (Salto das Sete Quedas) on the Alto Paraná River between Brazil and Paraguay, which on occasions reached 1.75 million cusec, until the completion of the Itaipú Dam gates in 1982.

Widest waterfall   The Khône Falls in Laos are 6.7 miles wide and 50–70 feet high, with a flood flow of 1.5 million cusec.

LAKES

Largest lake   The Caspian Sea (in Azerbaijan, Russia, Kazakhstan, Turkmenistan and Iran) is the largest inland sea or lake. It is 760 miles long and covers 143,550 square miles. Its maximum depth is 3,360 feet and its surface is 93 feet below sea level.

United States   The largest lake entirely within the United States is Lake Michigan, with a water surface area of 22,300 square miles, a length of 307 miles, a breadth of 118 miles and a maximum depth of 923 feet. Both Lake Superior and Lake Huron have larger areas, but they straddle the border between Canada and the United States.

Deepest lake   Lake Baikal in Siberia, Russia is 385 miles long and 20–46 miles wide. The deepest part of the lake is 5,371 feet deep.

United States   Crater Lake, a 6-mile-long lake in the Cascade Mountains of Oregon, is 1,932 feet deep at its deepest point, and has an average depth of 1,500 feet. Crater Lake has no inlets or outlets; it is filled by precipitation.

Highest lake   The highest lake in the world is an unnamed lake in Tibet at an altitude of about 19,000 feet above sea level (Lat. 34°16′ N, Long. 85°43′ E). The lake has a maximum length of five miles and a maximum width of three miles. The highest *named* lake in the world, Burog Co, lies just to the north of it at an altitude of around 18,400 feet above sea level. Burog Co has a maximum length of 11 miles and a maximum width of five miles.

Largest freshwater lake   Measured by surface area, Lake Superior is the largest freshwater lake. It covers 31,800 square miles, of which 20,700 square miles are in Minnesota, Wisconsin and Michigan and 11,100 square miles are in Ontario, Canada.

The freshwater lake with the greatest volume is Lake Baikal in Siberia, Russia, with an estimated volume of 5,500 cubic miles. (See DEEPEST LAKE.)

Largest lagoon   Lagoa dos Patos, located near the seashore in Rio Grande do Sul, Brazil, is 174 miles long and extends over 3,803 square miles, separated from the Atlantic Ocean by long sand strips. It has a maximum width of 44 miles.

Largest underground lake   The surface of the lake in the Drachenhauchloch cave, near Grootfontein, Namibia, is 217 feet underground, and its depth is 276 feet.

United States   The Lost Sea in the Craighead Caverns, Sweetwater, TN is 300 feet underground and covers 4½ acres.

Largest lake in a lake   The largest lake inside another lake is Manitou Lake (41.09 square miles) on the world's largest lake island, Manitoulin Island (1,068 square miles), in Lake Huron.

ICE

Longest glacier   The Lambert Glacier, which drains about a fifth of the East Antarctic ice sheet, is up to 40 miles wide and, with its seaward extension, the Amery Ice Shelf, it measures at least 440 miles long.

Fastest glacier   The fastest-moving major glacier is the Columbia Glacier, between Valdez and Anchorage, AK, which travels an average of 82 feet per day.

Thickest ice   The greatest recorded thickness of ice is 2.97 miles, measured by radio echo soundings from a U.S. Antarctic research aircraft at 69° 56′ 17″ S, 135° 12′ 9″ E, 270 miles from the coast of Wilkes Land, Antartica on January 4, 1975.

Deepest permafrost   A permafrost of more than 4,500 feet was reported from the upper reaches of the Viluy River, Siberia, Russia in February 1982.

Largest iceberg   A tabular iceberg 208 miles long and 60 miles wide was sighted 150 miles west of Scott Island, in the South Pacific Ocean, by the U.S.S. *Glacier* on November 12, 1956.

Tallest iceberg   In 1958, the U.S. icebreaker *East Wind* reported a 550-foot-high iceberg off western Greenland.

Most southerly arctic iceberg   An arctic iceberg was sighted in the Atlantic by a U.S.N. weather patrol at Lat. 28° 44′ N (approximately the same latitude as Miami, FL), Long. 48° 42′ W, in April 1935.

Most northerly antarctic iceberg   A remnant of an antarctic iceberg was seen in the Atlantic by the ship *Dochra* at Lat. 26° 30′ S (roughly the same latitude as Rio de Janeiro, Brazil), Long. 25° 40′ W, on April 30, 1894.

WEATHER

Lowest ozone levels   Ozone levels reached a record low between October 9 and 14, 1993 over the South Pole, when an average figure of 91 Dobson units was recorded. The minimum level needed to shield the earth from solar ultraviolet radiation is 300 DU.

TIPS

from the
RECORD BREAKERS

COLDEST PLACE

International Falls, MN nestles next to the Canadian border. Officially recognized as having the lowest annual mean temperature in the United States, the town beats the cold with its warm community spirit. "The cold doesn't stop us . . . life goes on," declares Mayor Jack Murray. Here's how residents stay toasty and cozy in the cold.

◆

Wear lots of layers.

Sub-zero temperatures are common during the winter, so people wear plenty of layers. "I walk three to four miles each morning," says Murray, who usually wears "a T-shirt, pajama bottoms, long johns, a long-sleeved sweatshirt, a wool shirt, heavy wool stag pants, a down-filled jacket, wool socks, insulated boots, heavy mittens and a fur cap."

◆

Go outside and have fun.

In January, International Falls holds its "Icebox Days Festival." The town participates in bowling frozen turkeys, frozen lake baseball, and the "Freeze Your Gizzard Blizzard Race."

◆

Beware low flying crystals.

Visitors who doubt the severity of the cold are quickly convinced by a simple experiment. "Bring a pan of water to boiling point," instructs Murray, "then step outside and fling the water in the air. As soon as the hot water hits the air, it crystallizes."

TIPS

from the
RECORD BREAKERS

HOTTEST PLACE
Death Valley, California is the hottest place in the United States. Temperatures hover at the 120-degree mark during the summer. Martha Watkins of the Death Valley Chamber of Commerce offers some hints for living with heat.

◆

Don't get dehydrated.
Watkins advises people to stop to drink at least once an hour. Local residents tend to stay indoors during the peak heat hours and wear hats when they do venture out. "I wear a damp dish towel under my hat that drapes down my neck and over my shoulders," Watkins says.

◆

Forget about river rafting.
Death Valley's grand landscapes attract thousands of visitors each year. "The most surprising request for information that I have ever received was, 'Where can I go river rafting?'" laughs Watkins. "The Amargosa River runs through parts of the valley, but it's largely subterranean."

◆

Make sure your sneakers have extra-strength glue.
Each summer runners participate in a road race through the valley, from Badwater to Mount Whitney, 83 miles away. "The ground temperature can reach 300 degrees, and quite often the glue in the shoes melts."

Most equable temperature   Between 1911 and 1990, the Brazilian offshore island of Fernando de Noronha had a minimum temperature of 63.9°F on February 27, 1980 and a maximum of 90.0°F on March 3, 1968, December 25, 1972 and April 17, 1973, giving an extreme range of 26.1°F.

Greatest temperature range   The greatest recorded temperature ranges are around the Siberian "cold pole" in Russia. Temperatures in Verkhoyansk (67° 33′ N, 133° 23′ E) have ranged 188 degrees, from –90°F to 98°F.

The greatest variation recorded in a day is 100 degrees (a fall from 44°F to –56°F) in Browning, MT on January 23–24, 1916.

The most freakish rise was 49 degrees in two minutes in Spearfish, SD, from –4°F at 7:30 A.M. to 45°F at 7:32 A.M. on January 22, 1943.

Highest shade temperature   The highest shade temperature ever recorded is 136°F at Al'Aziziyah, Libya on September 13, 1922.

Hottest place   At Marble Bar, Western Australia (maximum temperature 120.5°F), 160 consecutive days with maximum temperatures of 100°F or higher were recorded between October 31, 1923 and April 7, 1924.

United States   The highest temperature recorded in the United States was 134°F at Greenland Ranch, Death Valley, CA on July 10, 1913. In Death Valley, maximum temperatures of over 120°F were recorded on 43 consecutive days, between July 6 and August 17, 1917.

Driest place   The annual rainfall on the coast of Chile between Arica and Antofagasta is less than 0.004 inches.

United States   In 1929, no precipitation was recorded for Death Valley, CA. Currently, the driest state is Nevada, with an annual rainfall of only nine inches.

Longest drought   The Atacama Desert, in northern Chile, experiences virtually no rain, although several times a century a squall may strike a small area of it.

United States   The most intense drought in the United States lasted 57 months, from May 1952 to March 1957, in western Kansas. The Drought Severity Index reached a lowest point ever of –6.2, in September 1956. Below –4.0 on this index indicates extreme drought conditions.

Most sunshine   The annual average at Yuma, AZ is 91 percent of the possible hours of sunshine (4,055 hours out of 4,456 possible hours in a year).

St. Petersburg, FL recorded 768 consecutive sunny days from February 9, 1967 to March 17, 1969.

Lowest screen temperature   A record low of –128.6°F was registered at Vostok, Antarctica (alt. 11,220 feet) on July 21, 1983.

The coldest permanently inhabited place is the village of Oymyakon, Siberia, Russia, where the temperature reached –90°F in 1933, and an unofficial –98°F has been published more recently.

United States   The lowest temperature ever recorded in the United States was –79.8°F on January 23, 1971 in Prospect Creek, AK. The lowest temperature in the conterminous states was –69.7°F in Rogers Pass, MT on January 20, 1954.

Coldest place Polyus Nedostupnosti, Antarctica, at 78° S, 96° E, is the coldest location in the world, with an extrapolated annual mean of –72°F.

United States Langdon, ND had 41 days below 0°F, from November 11, 1935 to February 20, 1936. Langdon also holds the record for most consecutive days below 32°F, with 92 days from November 30, 1935 to February 29, 1936.

International Falls, MN has an annual mean temperature of 36.5°F, the lowest in the United States.

Wettest place By average annual rainfall, the wettest place in the world is Mawsynram, in Meghalaya State, India, with 467½ inches per year.

United States The wettest state is Louisiana, with an annual rainfall of 56 inches.

Most rainy days Mt. Wai-‘ale-‘ale (5,148 feet), Kauai, HI has up to 350 rainy days per year.

Most intense rainfall The rainfall of 1.5 inches in one minute in Basse Terre, Guadeloupe on November 26, 1970 is the most intense recorded with modern methods.

Greatest rainfall A record 73.62 inches of rain fell in 24 hours in Cilaos (alt. 3,940 feet), Réunion, Indian Ocean on March 15 and 16, 1952. This is equal to 8,327 tons of rain per acre. For a calendar month, the record is 366 inches, at Cherrapunji, Meghalaya, India in July 1861.

The 12-month record was also set at Cherrapunji, with 1,041.8 inches between August 1, 1860 and July 31, 1861.

United States In the United States, the 24-hour record is 43 inches in Alvin, TX, on July 25–26, 1979. Over a 12-month period, 739 inches fell in Kukui, Maui, HI from December 1981 to December 1982. The annual record for the conterminous states is 184.56 inches, in Wynoochee Oxbow, WA in 1931.

Longest-lasting rainbow A rainbow was continuously visible for six hours over Sheffield, England on March 14, 1994.

Deadliest flood The most deaths from a flood in the United States was more than 2,000 people, in Johnstown, PA on May 31, 1889. The water formed a wall 20–30 feet high, rushing through the valley on the way to Johnstown at a rate of 15 MPH.

Greatest flood In 1993, scientists reported the discovery of the largest freshwater flood in history. It occurred *c.* 18,000 years ago when an ancient ice dam lake in the Altay Mountains in Siberia, Russia broke and allowed the water to pour out. The lake was estimated to be 75 miles long and 2,500 feet deep, and the main flow of water was probably about 1,600 feet deep and traveling at 100 MPH.

Worst flood damage   As of August 10, 1993 it was reported that $12 billion in property and agricultural damage had been caused by the great Midwest flood of 1993. The flood affected parts of nine states and covered an area estimated at twice the size of New Jersey.

Windiest place   Commonwealth Bay, George V Coast, Antarctica, where gales reach 200 MPH, is the world's windiest place.

Highest surface wind speed   A surface wind speed of 231 MPH was recorded on Mt. Washington (6,288 feet), NH on April 12, 1934.

The fastest speed at a low altitude was registered on March 8, 1972 at the U.S.A.F. base in Thule, Greenland, when a peak speed of 207 MPH was recorded. The fastest speed measured to date in a tornado is 280 MPH in Wichita Falls, TX on April 2, 1958.

Deadliest hurricane   The greatest number of fatalities from an American hurricane is an estimated 6,000 deaths on September 8, 1900 in Galveston Island, TX.

Fastest hurricane winds   The fastest sustained winds in a hurricane in the United States measured 200 MPH, with 210-MPH gusts, on August 17–18, 1969, when Hurricane Camille hit the Mississippi–Alabama coast at Pass Christian, MS.

Fastest-moving hurricane   The greatest forward speed by a hurricane in the United States was in excess of 60 MPH, with an average speed of 58 MPH, for the Great New England Hurricane on September 21, 1938, when it struck central Long Island at Babylon, NY. The hurricane continued on to landfall at Milford, CT.

Costliest hurricane   Hurricane Andrew hit southern Florida on August 24, 1992, crossed the Gulf of Mexico and caused further destruction in Louisiana. The hurricane killed 76 people, left approximately 258,000 people homeless and caused an estimated $46.5 billion in damages, making it the most costly hurricane ever in the United States.

Deadliest tornado   The most deaths from one tornado in the United States is 695, on March 18, 1925 in Missouri, Illinois and Indiana. This tornado also ranks first as the tornado with the longest continuous track on the ground, 219 miles; first with a 3.5-hour continuous duration on he ground;

MOST LIGHTNING STRIKE SURVIVORS

On July 4, 1995, 38 people were struck by a single bolt of lightning while waiting to watch the fireworks in Castalia, NC. Although they suffered considerable pain and trauma, all 38 survived the incident.

See feature (next page)

The Earth   ●   111

KATHERINE STRANGE

*A*lmost everyone has seen a massive bolt of lightning at one time or another, but how would it feel to be the target of this force of nature? Just ask Katherine Strange of Castalia, NC. She can tell you exactly what it's like. She and 37 other people know all too well—they were struck by the same bolt of lightning.

*O*n the Fourth of July, 1995, Strange threw her annual party for friends and family. Little did they know when they left their gathering to go to the Castalia fireworks that they'd see more than the rockets' red glare.

"*W*e were just getting ready to watch the fireworks," says Strange, "which were supposed to start at 9:15, so we were all sitting on the ground. Then my son moved to a tarp with a crane under it. Well, it looked like a good spot to see everything, so we all moved on over there with him. I remember asking what time it was, and my brother-in-law told me it was 14 minutes after nine—and all of a sudden, BOOM! We were hit by a giant bolt of lightning!"

*S*trange goes on to say that her nephew lost his heartbeat on the spot, and had to be revived twice by paramedics, once right after the strike and once in the ambulance on the way to the hospital. "My son Corey also lost his heartbeat, but he was revived by CPR at the scene. I was paralyzed from the waist down for a few hours, and truthfully, we all thought we were going to die. The pain was just unreal—there's nothing to describe it. All I could think was, 'I'm 33 years old, and this is how I'm going to die, and I have no control over it!' And I realized then and there that you just don't have any choice in the matter."

*S*trange also realizes how bizarre the experience was, and she explains that life might never be the same for her or for the others involved. "We're really lucky that we all have each other. I think that's what's really kept us sane. People don't understand what a trauma it was for us because we don't have any real physical injuries that they can see. We're trying to just get on with things, and we're doing pretty well, but sometimes when there's a storm or any really loud noise, we all get pretty petrified. The funniest part of the whole thing is that some of our friends and relatives were right next to us when the lightning struck, but because they had shoes on and weren't sitting down, they didn't feel a thing!"

first in total area of destruction, covering 164 square miles; first in dimensions, with the funnel sometimes exceeding one mile wide; and third in forward speed, reaching a maximum of 73 MPH, while averaging 62 MPH over its duration.

Most tornadoes The state with the most tornadoes recorded in a year is Texas, with 232 in 1967.

Most tornadoes in 24 hours The southern and midwestern United States experienced 148 tornadoes on April 3–4, 1974.

Heaviest hailstones The heaviest hailstones on record, weighing up to 2¼ pounds, are reported to have killed 92 people in Bangladesh on April 14, 1986.

United States The heaviest hailstone in the United States weighed 1.671 pounds and had a diameter of 5.62 inches. It fell in Coffeyville, KS on September 3, 1970.

Greatest snowfall A total of 1,224½ inches of snow fell over a 12-month period from February 19, 1971 to February 18, 1972 at Paradise, Mt. Rainier, WA.
   The record for a single snowstorm is 189 inches at Mt. Shasta Ski Bowl, CA, February 13–19, 1959, and for a 24-hour period, the record snowfall is 78 inches, at Mile 47 Camp, Cooper River Division, AK on February 7, 1963.
   The greatest depth of snow on the ground was 37 ft. 7 in. at Tamarac, CA in March 1911.

Most times struck by lightning Ex-park ranger Roy C. Sullivan was struck by lightning seven times. His attraction for lightning began in 1942, when he lost his big toenail. He was hit again in July 1969 (lost eyebrows), in July 1970 (left shoulder seared), on April 16, 1972 (hair set on fire), on August 7, 1973 (hair set on fire again and legs seared), and on June 5, 1976 (ankle injured), and he was sent to Waynesboro Hospital, Waynesboro, VA with chest and stomach burns on June 25, 1977 after being struck while fishing.

Highest pressure The highest barometric pressure ever recorded was 32 inches at Agata, Siberia, Russia (alt. 862 feet) on December 31, 1968.

Lowest pressure The lowest sea-level barometric pressure was 25.69 inches in Typhoon Tip, 300 miles west of Guam, Pacific Ocean, at Lat. 16° 44′ N, Long. 137° 46′ E, on October 12, 1979.

Foggiest place Sea-level fogs—with visibility less than 0.56 miles—persist for weeks on the Grand Banks, Newfoundland, Canada, with the average being more than 120 days of fog per year.

EARTHQUAKES

Strongest earthquake The most commonly used measure of the size of an earthquake is its surface magnitude (Ms), based on amplitudes of surface waves, usually at a period of 20 seconds. The largest reported magnitudes on this scale, known as the Richter scale, are about 8.9, but the scale does not properly represent the size of the very largest earthquakes, above Ms about 8, for which it is better to use the concept of seismic moment, Mo.

Moment can be used to derive a "moment magnitude," Mw. The largest recorded earthquake on the Mw scale was the Chilean shock of May 22, 1960, which had Mw = 9.5, but measured only 8.3 on the Ms scale.

United States   The strongest earthquake in American history, measuring 8.4 on the Richter scale and 9.2 on the Mw scale, was near Prince William Sound, AK (80 miles east of Anchorage) on March 27, 1964. It killed 131 people and caused an estimated $750 million in damage; it also caused a 50-foot tsunami that traveled 8,445 miles at 450 MPH. The town of Kodiak was destroyed, and tremors were felt in California, Hawaii and Japan.

Deadliest earthquake   The greatest estimate of the death toll in an earthquake is the 830,000 fatalities in a quake in the Shaanxi, Shanxi and Henan provinces of China on February 2, 1556.

Most destructive earthquake   The greatest physical devastation was in the earthquake on the Kanto plain, Japan, on September 1, 1923 (Mag. Ms = 8.2). In Tokyo and Yokohama, 575,000 dwellings were destroyed. The number of people killed and missing in this quake and the resultant fires was 142,807.

DEADLIEST NATURAL DISASTERS

Circular Storm
1,000,000 killed; Ganges Delta Islands, Bangladesh; November 12–13, 1970.

Flood
900,000 killed; Hwang-ho River, China; October 1887.

Earthquake
830,000 killed; Shaanxi, Shanxi and Henan Provinces, China; February 1556.

Landslides
180,000 killed; Kansu Province, China; December 16, 1920.

Volcanic Eruption
92,000 killed; Tambora, Sumbawa, Indonesia; April 5–10, 1815.

Avalanches
c. 18,000 killed; Yungay, Huascarán, Peru; May 31, 1970.

Tornado
c. 1,300 killed; Shaturia, Bangladesh; April 26, 1989.

Hail
246 killed; Moradabad, Uttar Pradesh, India; April 20, 1888.

Lightning
81 killed; airliner struck by lightning near Elkton, MD; December 8, 1963.

United States   The insured property loss of the Los Angeles earthquake of January 17, 1994 amounts to $2.5 billion. It is estimated that the overall loss could reach $20 billion, making it the third most expensive disaster ever for insurers. The earthquake measured 7.5 on the Richter scale.

VOLCANOES

Greatest explosion   The greatest explosion in historic times occurred on August 27, 1883, with an eruption of Krakatoa, an island (then 18 square miles) in the Sunda Strait, between Sumatra and Java, in Indonesia. The explosion, which was about 26 times as powerful as the largest hydrogen bomb ever tested, wiped out 163 villages, and 36,380 people were killed by the wave it caused. Pumice was thrown 34 miles high and dust fell 3,313 miles away 10 days later. The explosion was recorded four hours later on the island of Rodrigues, 2,968 miles away, as "the roar of heavy guns," and was heard over one-thirteenth of the surface of the globe.

Deadliest volcano   Volcanic activity in Tambora, Sumbawa, Indonesia in April 1815 killed about 92,000 people.

United States   The most deaths from a volcanic eruption in the United States was 60 people, on May 18, 1980 from the eruption of Mt. St. Helens, WA.

Greatest volume of discharge   The total volume of matter discharged in the eruption of Tambora, a volcano on the Indonesian island of Sumbawa, April 5–10 1815, was 36–43 cubic miles. A crater five miles in diameter was formed and the height of the island was lowered from 13,450 feet to 9,350 feet. More than 92,000 people were killed in the eruption, or died in the subsequent famine.

Most violent eruption   The ejecta in the Taupo eruption in New Zealand *c.* A.D. 130 has been estimated at 33 billion tons of pumice moving at one time at 400 MPH. It flattened 6,200 square miles. Less than 20 percent of the 15.4 billion tons of pumice carried up into the air in this most violent of all documented volcanic events fell within 125 miles of the vent.

Longest lava flow   The longest lava flow in historic times was a mixture of ropey lava (twisted cordlike solidifications) and blocky lava resulting from the eruption of Laki in 1783 in southeast Iceland, which flowed 40½–43½ miles. The largest known prehistoric flow is the Roza basalt flow in North America *c.* 15 million years ago, which had an unsurpassed length (190 miles), area (15,400 square miles) and volume (300 cubic miles).

Most active volcano   Kilauea in Hawaii has erupted continuously since 1983. Lava is being discharged at a rate of seven cubic yards per second.

Largest active volcano   Of the 1,343 active volcanoes in the world (many of which are submarine), Mauna Loa in Hawaii is the largest. It has the shape of a broad, gentle dome 75 miles long and 31 miles wide (above sea level), with lava flows that occupy more than 1,980 square miles of the island. It has a total volume of 10,200 cubic miles, of which 84.2 percent is below sea level. Its caldera or volcano crater, Mokuaweoweo, measures four square miles and is 500–600 feet deep. Mauna Loa rises 13,680 feet and erupts approximately every ten years. Its last eruption, however, occurred in 1984.

Highest active volcano   The highest volcano regarded as active is Ojos del Salado, at a height of 22,595 feet, on the frontier between Chile and Argentina.

Northernmost volcano   Mt. Beerenberg (7,470 feet), on the island of Jan Mayen in the Greenland Sea, erupted on September 20, 1970.

Southernmost volcano   The most southerly active volcano is Mt. Erebus (12,447 feet), on Ross Island in the Antarctic Ocean.

Largest volcano crater   The world's largest volcano crater is that of Toba, Sumatra, Indonesia, covering 685 square miles.

AVALANCHES

Greatest avalanche   The greatest natural avalanches occur in the Himalayas, but no estimates of their volume have been published. It was estimated that 120 million cubic feet of snow fell in an avalanche in the Italian Alps in 1885.

United States   The 250-MPH avalanche triggered by the Mt. St. Helens eruption in Washington State on May 18, 1980 was estimated to measure 96 billion cubic feet.

GEYSERS

Tallest geyser   The Waimangu geyser in New Zealand erupted to a height of more than 1,500 feet in 1903. Although the ground in the area is still hot, Waimangu itself has not been active since late 1904.
 The tallest active geyser is the Steamboat Geyser in Yellowstone National Park, WY. During the 1980s, it erupted at intervals ranging from 19 days to over four years, although there were occasions in the 1960s when it erupted every 4–10 days. Its maximum height is 195–380 feet.

GEMS AND PRECIOUS METALS

DIAMONDS

Largest diamond   The Cullinan, weighing 3,106 carats, was found on January 26, 1905 in the Premier Mine, Pretoria, South Africa. It was later cut into 106 polished diamonds and produced the largest cut fine quality colorless diamond, weighing 530.2 carats.

Largest cut diamond   The 545.67-carat gem known as the Golden Jubilee Diamond was made from a 775.5-carat rough into a fire rose cushion cut.

The Golden Jubilee Diamond acted as the forerunner to the Centenary Diamond, the world's largest flawless top color modern fancy cut diamond at 273.85 carats.

Smallest brilliant-cut diamond A 0.0000743-carat diamond fashioned by hand by Pauline Willemse at Coster Diamonds B.V., Amsterdam, Netherlands, 1991–94, is 0.0063–0.0067 inches in diameter and 0.0043 inches high.

Highest-priced diamond On May 17, 1995, a 100.1-carat pear-shaped "D" flawless diamond was sold at Sotheby's, Geneva, Switzerland to Sheikh Ahmed Fitaihi (Saudi Arabia).

The highest price paid for a rough diamond was $10 million for a 255.1-carat stone from Guinea, by the William Goldberg Diamond Corporation in partnership with the Chow Tai Fook Jewellery Co. Ltd. of Hong Kong, in March 1989.

The record per carat is $926,315 for a 0.95-carat fancy purplish-red stone sold at Christie's, New York on April 28, 1987.

EMERALDS

Largest cut emerald An 86,136-carat natural beryl was found in Carnaiba, Brazil in August 1974. It was carved by Richard Chan in Hong Kong and valued at $1,120,080 in 1982.

Largest emerald crystal The largest single emerald crystal of gem quality was 7,025 carats. It was found in 1969 at the Cruces Mine, near Gachala, Colombia.

Highest-priced emerald The highest price for a single emerald is $2,126,646, for a 19.77-carat emerald and diamond ring made by Cartier in 1958, which was sold at Sotheby's, Geneva, Switzerland on April 2, 1987.

RUBIES

Largest star ruby The Eminent Star ruby, believed to be of Indian origin, is the largest ruby, at 6,465 carats.

Highest-priced ruby A ruby ring with a stone weighing 15.97 carats was sold at Sotheby's, New York on October 18, 1988 for $227,300.

SAPPHIRES

Largest star sapphire The 9,719.5-carat gem The Lone Star was cut in London, England in November 1989.

Highest-priced sapphire A step-cut stone of 62.02 carats was sold as part of a sapphire and diamond ring at Sotheby's, St. Moritz, Switzerland on February 20, 1988 for $2,791,723.

TOPAZ

Largest topaz The 22,892.5-carat American Golden Topaz has been on display at the Smithsonian Institution, Washington, D.C. since May 4, 1988.

TIPS

from the
RECORD BREAKERS

SMALLEST CUT DIAMOND

Pauline Willemse decided to display her skill as a diamond cutter and polisher by cutting the world's smallest diamond. It took three years, but in 1994 she finished her task. Her diamond was 50 times smaller than the head of a ballpoint pen. Here she describes how to polish off this record.

♦

Concentrate.

"Diamond cutting is sensitive work," explains Willemse. "The feel of the diamond must flow right through to the cutter." Willemse believes the successful cutter is born with certain vital abilities: "Techniques can be learned, but precision, patience and concentration are part of your personality."

♦

Be a perfectionist.

To gain certification as a diamond cutter in the Netherlands, students must meet high standards. "If you make two big mistakes, you're removed from the group," says Willemse. The diamond must also be perfect. "Never cut a diamond that has inclusions (black spots)," warns Willemse, "or it will crack."

♦

Don't lose the diamond.

Two attempts at the record failed when the cutting disk dislodged the diamond from the holder. "Big diamonds can be knocked out, too, but you can find them," laughs Willemse. "Mine were so small that I lost them among the cut slivers. It was tough," she says, "but I wanted the record so badly that I started again . . . and third time was lucky."

OPALS

Largest opal   The largest gem-quality white opal was 26,350 carats, found in July 1989 at the Jupiter Field at Coober Pedy in South Australia.

Largest black opal   A stone found on February 4, 1972 at Lightning Ridge, New South Wales, Australia produced a finished gem of 1,520 carats, called the Empress of Glengarry.

Largest rough black opal   The largest gem-quality uncut black opal was also found at Lightning Ridge, on November 3, 1986. It weighs 1,982.5 carats and measures 4 by 2⅝ by 2½ inches.

PEARLS

Largest pearl   The 14-lb.-1-oz. Pearl of Lao-tze was found at Palawan, Philippines in May 1934 in the shell of a giant clam.

Largest abalone pearl   A baroque abalone pearl measuring 2¾ by 2 by 1⅛ inches and weighing 469.13 carats was found at Salt Point State Park, CA in May 1990.

Largest cultured pearl   A 1½-inch round, 138.25-carat cultured pearl weighing 1 ounce was found near Samui Island, off Thailand, in January 1988.

Highest-priced pearl   La Régente, a pearl weighing 302.68 grains and formerly part of the French crown jewels, was sold at Christie's, Geneva, Switzerland on May 12, 1988 for $864,280.

AMBER

Largest piece of amber   Burma Amber weighs 33 lb. 10 oz. and is located in the Natural History Museum, London, England.

JADE

Largest piece of jade   A single lens of nephrite jade weighing 636 tons was found in the Yukon Territory of Canada in 1992.

GOLD

Largest mass of gold   The Holtermann Nugget, found in 1872 in the Beyers & Holtermann Star of Hope mine in New South Wales, Australia, contained 2,640 troy ounces of gold in a 7,560-troy-ounce slab of slate.

Largest pure gold nugget   The Welcome Stranger, found at Moliagul, Victoria, Australia in 1869, yielded 2,248 troy ounces of pure gold from 2,280¼ troy ounces.

PLATINUM

Largest platinum nugget   A 340-ounce nugget of platinum was found in the Ural Mountains in Russia in 1843.

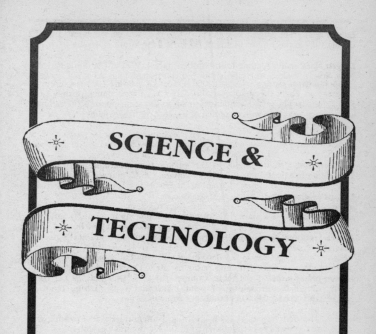

SCIENCE & TECHNOLOGY

40

ELEMENTS

Rarest natural element   Only 0.0056 ounces of astatine (At) is present in the earth's crust; the isotope astatine 215 (At 215) accounts for only 1.6×10^{-10} ounces. The least abundant element in the atmosphere is the radioactive gas radon (Rn), with a volume of 6×10^{-18} parts by volume.

Most common element   Hydrogen (H) accounts for over 90 percent of all known matter in the universe and 70.68 percent by mass in the solar system.
   The commonest element in the earth's atmosphere is nitrogen (N), which is present at 78.08 percent by volume (75.52 percent by mass). Iron (Fe) is the most common element in the earth itself, making up 36 percent of the planet's mass.

Newest element   Element 111, provisional name unununium (Uuu), was discovered in 1994 at the Gesellschaft für Schwerionenforschung, Darmstadt, Germany by a joint German, Russian, Slovakian, and Finnish team.

Highest and lowest density Solid   The densest solid at room temperature is osmium (Os) at 0.8161 pounds per cubic inch. The least dense element at room temperature is the metal lithium (Li) at 0.01927 pounds per cubic inch, although the density of solid hydrogen at its melting point of –434.546°F is only 0.00315 pounds per cubic inch.

Gas   The densest gas at NTP (Normal Temperature and Pressure, 0°C and one atmosphere) is radon (Rn) at 0.6274 pounds per cubic foot. The lightest gas is hydrogen (H) at 0.005612 pounds per cubic foot.

Highest melting and boiling points   Metallic tungsten or wolfram (W) melts at 6,177°F. The graphite form of carbon (C) sublimes directly to vapor at 6,699°F and can only be obtained as a liquid above a temperature of 8,546°F and a pressure of 100 atmospheres.

Lowest melting and boiling points   Helium (He) cannot be obtained as a solid at atmospheric pressure; the minimum pressure is 24.985 atmospheres at –458.275°F. Helium also has the lowest boiling point, at –458.275°F. Mercury (Hg) has the lowest melting and boiling points of any metallic element, at –37.892°F and 673.92°F respectively.

Hardest element   The diamond allotrope of carbon (C) has a Knoop value of 8,400.

Highest and lowest thermal expansion   The element with the highest expansion is cesium (Cs), at 94×10^{-5} per degree C, while the diamond allotrope of carbon (C) has the lowest expansion at 1.0×10^{-6} per degree C.

Most ductile element   One ounce of gold (Au) can be drawn to a length of 43 miles.

One use for helium, the element with the lowest melting and boiling points.

Highest tensile strength   Boron (B) has a tensile strength of 5.7 GPa 8.3 × 10^5 lbf/in².

Strongest pure metal   The strongest pure metal appears to be iridium (Ir) with a typical tensile strength of 550MPa (8.0 × 10^4 lbf/in²).

Shortest and longest liquid ranges   Based on the differences between melting and boiling points, the element with the shortest liquid range (on the Celsius scale) is neon (Ne), at only 2.542 degrees (from −248.594°C to −246.052°C [−415.469°F to −410.894°F]). The radioactive element neptunium (Np) has the longest liquid range, at 3,453 degrees (from 637°C to 4,090°C [1,179°F to 7,394°F]).

Most toxic element   The severest restriction placed on any element in the form of a radioactive isotope is 2.4 × 10^{-16} g/m³ in air for thorium 228 (Th-228) or radiothorium. The most severely restricted nonradioactive element is beryllium, with a threshold limit value in air of 2 g/m³.

Most and fewest isotopes   There are at least 2,570 isotopes, and cesium (Cs) has the most, with 37. The greatest number of stable isotopes is 10, for the metallic element tin (Sn). Hydrogen (H) has the fewest isotopes, with just three.

CHEMICAL EXTREMES

Strongest acid   The strongest super acid is an 80 percent solution of antimony pentafluoride in hydrofluoric acid (fluoroantimonic acid HF: SbF_5).

This solution has not been measured directly, but a 50 percent solution is 10^{18} times stronger than concentrated sulfuric acid.

Bitterest substance   The bitterest-tasting substances are based on the denatonium cation and have been produced commercially as benzoate and saccharide. Taste detection levels are as low as one part in 500 million, and a dilution of one part in 100 million will leave a lingering taste.

Sweetest substance   Talin from katemfe (*Thaumatococcus daniellii*), discovered in West Africa, is 6,150 times as sweet as a 1 percent sucrose solution.

Most powerful nerve gas   Ethyl S-2-diisopropylaminoethylmethylphosphonothiolate or VX, developed at the Chemical Defense Experimental Establishment, Porton Down, England in 1952, is 300 times more powerful than the phosgene ($COCl_2$) used in World War I. The lethal dosage is 10 mg-minute per cubic meter airborne or 0.3 mg orally.

Most lethal man-made chemical   TCDD (2, 3, 7, 8-tetrachloro-dibenzo-p-dioxin), the most dangerous dioxin, is 150,000 times more deadly than cyanide.

Most absorbent substance   "H-span" or Super Slurper, composed of one-half starch derivative and one-fourth each of acrylamide and acrylic acid, can, when treated with iron, retain water 1,300 times its own weight.

Most refractory substance   The most refractory substance is tantalum carbide ($TaC_{0.88}$), which melts at 7,214°F.

Most heat-resistant substance   The existence of a complex material known as NFAARr or Ultra Hightech Starlite was announced in April 1993. Invented by Maurice Ward (Great Britain), it can temporarily resist plasma temperature (18,032°F).

Highest superconducting temperature   In 1993, bulk superconductivity with a transition to zero resistance at −221.3°F was achieved at the Laboratorium für Festkörperphysik, Zurich, Switzerland, in a mixture of oxides of mercury, barium, calcium and copper, $HgBa_2Ca_2Cu_3O_{1+x}$ and $HgBa_2CaCu_2O_{6+x}$.

Least dense solids   In February 1990, a silica aerogel with a density of only five ounces per cubic foot was produced at Lawrence Livermore National Laboratory in Livermore, CA.

PHYSICAL EXTREMES

Highest temperature   The highest temperature produced in a laboratory is 918,000,000°F on February 17, 1995, in the Tokamak Fusion Test Reactor at the Princeton University Plasma Physics Laboratory, Princeton, NJ using a deuterium-tritium plasma mix (See GREATEST FUSION POWER).

Hottest flame   The hottest-burning substance is carbon subnitride (C_4N_2), which, at one atmosphere pressure, can produce a flame calculated to reach 9,010°F.

Lowest temperature   Absolute zero, 0 K on the Kelvin scale, corresponds to −459.67°F. The lowest temperature ever reached is 2.8×10^{-10}K in a nuclear demagnetization device at the Low Temperature Laboratory, Helsinki University of Technology, Finland, announced in 1993.

Highest pressure   A sustained laboratory pressure of 170 GPa (11,000 tons per square inch) was achieved in the giant hydraulic diamond-faced press at the Carnegie Institution's Geophysical Laboratory, Washington, D.C. and reported in June 1978.

Using dynamic methods and impact speeds of up to 18,000 MPH, momentary pressures of 7,000 GPa (540,000 tons per square inch) were reported in the United States in 1958.

Highest vacuum   In January 1991, K. Odaka and S. Ueda of Japan obtained a vacuum of 7×10^{-16} atmospheres in a stainless steel chamber.

Lowest friction   The lowest coefficient of static and dynamic friction of any solid is 0.03, for Hi-T-Lube with an MOS2 burnished (B) exterior. The 0.03 result was achieved by sliding Hi-T-Lube (B) against Hi-T-Lube (B). This material was developed for NASA in 1965 by General Magnaplate Corp., Linden, NJ.

MOST EFFICIENT LUBRICANT

Tufoil, manufactured by Fluoramics Inc. of Mahwah, NJ, has a coefficient of friction of .029.

See feature (next page)

Highest velocity   The highest velocity at which any solid visible object has been projected is 334,800 MPH in the case of a plastic disc at the Naval Research Laboratory, Washington, D.C., in August 1980.

Most magnetic substance   The most magnetic substance is neodymium iron boride ($Nd_2Fe_{14}B$) with a maximum energy product of up to 280 kJ per cubic meter.

Strongest magnetic field   The strongest continuous field strength achieved was a total of 35.3 ± 0.3 teslas at the Francis Bitter National Magnet Laboratory, Massachusetts Institute of Technology, Cambridge, MA, on May 26, 1988.

Most powerful electric current   If fired simultaneously, the 4,032 capacitors comprising the Zeus capacitor at the Los Alamos Scientific Laboratory,

Whoever would have known that years ago, as Frank Reick flew his plane above the Hudson River and contemplated the city beneath him, a Guinness record was being hatched?

"In the early 1970s, I was flying my airplane down the Hudson River, and as I looked down into the canyons of New York, I could see this brown ooze coming out of them which I knew was car exhaust. So in the great modesty which is characteristic of all inventors, I said, 'I'm going to have to do something about that,'" explains Reick, president, founder, and chief inventor of Fluoramics Inc., Mahwah, NJ. And so began the invention of Tufoil, the world's slipperiest substance. "I wanted to make a lubricant that was very slippery so we could idle machines down for a tighter carburetor and less exhaust."

"I went back to the lab and made up a couple of dispersions that I thought were great, put it in two cars, and seized every single valve lifter—and you've never heard such a racket in your life! So I had to pull the engines apart, and fish out the valve lifters. Out of them, I got these big chewing gum-like curds, and it was pretty obvious that I was going to have to do some development work on it. But when I put the machines back together, I noticed that they were very smooth and quiet. I had obviously done something to improve the performance of the engines even though I had made a bloody mess out of the things. So I worked steadily from the early 1970s up to the 80s on this, doing a lot of work on engines, laboratory work, engine testing—and finally, in the 1980s, we started marketing in the New Jersey area."

But the road to success was not as smooth as Reick would have liked. "Around the time Tufoil was first being marketed, many other companies decided to use Teflon in oil and make claims on it," says Reick. "We didn't like to be put in the same bucket as these operations. I was getting patents in, and we sort of scooped the field in terms of the technology. I also started publishing scientific articles. This helped make Tufoil a well-respected product." But Fluoramics did make one mistake. "We didn't go in for fancy packaging early on," Reick notes. "I was more concerned with the technology."

Tufoil is now sold all over the world. It can be used to tame a roaring engine or a noisy washing machine. But Reick hasn't hung up his inventing gloves just yet. "The funny thing about inventing is that once you've done it, you stand around and wonder what you're going to do next. Setting records never entered my mind when I started this, but you get a nice warm feeling after you've done something that you know is worthwhile."

NM would produce, for a few microseconds, twice as much current as that generated anywhere else on earth.

Highest voltage The highest potential difference obtained in a laboratory was 32 ± 1.5 million volts by the National Electrostatistics Corporation, Oak Ridge, TN on May 17, 1979.

Brightest light The brightest artificial sources are laser pulses generated at the Los Alamos National Laboratory, Los Alamos, NM. A 1-picosecond ultraviolet flash (1×10^{-12} seconds) is intensified to 5×10^{15} watts.

Longest echo There is a 15-second echo following the closing of the door of the Chapel of the Mausoleum, Hamilton, Scotland, built 1840–55.

SCIENTIFIC INSTRUMENTS

Largest scientific instrument The Large Electron–Positron (LEP) storage ring at CERN, Geneva, Switzerland is 12½ feet in diameter and 17 miles in circumference.

Finest balance The Sartorius Model 4108, manufactured in Göttingen, Germany, can weigh objects of up to 0.018 ounces to an accuracy of 3.5×10^{-10} ounces, equivalent to little more than ⅟₆₀th of the weight of the ink on this period.

Oldest measures The oldest known measure of weight is the beqa of the Amratian period of Egyptian civilization *c.* 3800 B.C., found at Naqada, Egypt. The cylindrical weights weigh 6.65–7.45 ounces.

Smallest thermometer Dr. Frederich Sachs, a biophysicist at the State University of New York at Buffalo, developed an ultra-microthermometer for measuring the temperature of single living cells. The tip is one micron in diameter, about ⅟₅₀th the diameter of a human hair.

Largest barometer An oil-filled barometer, of overall height 42 feet, was constructed by Allan Mills and John Pritchard of the Department of Physics and Astronomy, University of Leicester, Leicester, England in 1991. It attained a standard height of 40 feet (at which pressure mercury would stand at 2½ feet).

Smallest microphone Prof. Ibrahim Kavrak of Bogazici University, Istanbul, Turkey developed a microphone for fluid flow pressure measurement in 1967. It has a frequency response of 10 Hz–10 kHz and measures 0.06 × 0.03 inches.

Finest cut The large optics diamond turning machine at the Lawrence Livermore National Laboratory, Livermore, CA was reported in June 1983 to be able to sever a human hair 3,000 times lengthwise.

Sharpest objects The sharpest manufactured objects are glass micropipette tubes whose beveled tips have an outer diameter of 0.02 μm and a 0.01-μm inner diameter. The latter is 6,500 times thinner than a human hair. The tubes are used in intracellular work on living cells.

Most powerful microscope The scanning tunneling microscope (STM) invented at the IBM Zürich research laboratory, Switzerland, in 1981 has a magnification of 100 million times and a resolution of $\frac{1}{100}$th the diameter of an atom (3×10^{-10} m), making it the world's most powerful microscope.

Most powerful laser The "Nova" laser at the Lawrence Livermore National Laboratory, Livermore, CA produces laser pulses capable of generating 100×10^{12} W of power, much of which is delivered to a target the size of a grain of sand in 1×10^{-9} seconds. For this instant, that power is 200 times greater than the combined output of all the electrical generating plants in the United States. The laser itself is 300 feet long and about three stories high.

Most powerful particle accelerator The world's highest-energy "atom-smasher" is the 1.25-mile-diameter proton synchroton "Tevatron" at the Fermi National Accelerator Laboratory (Fermilab) near Batavia, IL. On November 30, 1986 a center of mass energy of 1.8 TeV (1.8×10^{12} eV) was achieved by colliding protons and antiprotons.

Fastest centrifuge The highest rotary speed ever achieved is 4,500 MPH by a tapered 6-inch carbon fiber rod in a vacuum at Birmingham University, Birmingham, England, reported on January 24, 1975.

Heaviest magnet The heaviest magnet is in the Joint Institute for Nuclear Research at Dubna, near Moscow, Russia, for the 10 GeV synchrophasotron measuring 196 feet in diameter and weighing 42,000 tons.

The 300-foot-long Nova laser is the world's most powerful laser.

Largest electromagnet   The octagonal electromagnet in the L3 detector, an experiment on LEP (Large Electron–Positron collider), consists of 7,055 tons of low carbon steel yoke and 1,213 tons of aluminum coil. Thirty thousand amperes of current flow through the aluminum coil to create a uniform magnetic field of five kilogauss. The total weight of the magnet, including the frame, coil and inner support tube, is 7,810 tons, and it is composed of more metal than is contained in the Eiffel Tower.

POWER

Oldest water mill   The water mill with the oldest continuous commercial use is at Priston Mill near Bath, England, first mentioned in A.D. 931 in a charter to King Athelstan (924/5–939). It is driven by the Conygre Brook.

Oldest steam engine   The oldest steam engine in working order is the Smethwick Engine, dating from 1779. Designed by James Watt (1736–1819) and built by the Birmingham Canal Company, the pump originally had a 24-inch bore and a stroke of eight feet. It worked on the canal locks at Smethwick, England until 1891. The engine was presented to the Birmingham Museum of Science and Industry in 1960 and is regularly steamed for the public.

Largest steam engine   The largest ever single-cylinder steam engine was designed by Matthew Loam of Cornwall, England and built by the Hayle Foundry Co. in 1849 for land draining at Haarlem, Netherlands. The cylinder was 12 feet in diameter and each stroke lifted 16,140 gallons of water.

Most efficient steam engine   The most efficient steam engine recorded was Taylor's engine, built by Michael Loam for United Mines of Gwennap, England in 1840. It registered only 1.7 pounds of coal per horsepower per hour.

Greatest fusion power   The highest level of controlled fusion power attained is 10.7 MW, in the Tokamak Fusion Test Reactor at the Princeton University Plasma Physics Laboratory, Princeton, NJ in November 1994.

Largest generator   A turbo generator of 1,450 MW (net) is being installed at the Ignalina atomic power station in southern Lithuania.

Largest power plant   The most powerful power station is the Itaipu power station on the Paraná River near the Brazil–Paraguay border. Opened in 1984, the station has now attained its ultimate rated capacity of 13,320 MW.

Largest transformers   The world's largest single-phase transformers are rated at 1,500,000 kVA. Eight of these are in service with the American Electric Power Service Corporation. Of these, five step down from 765 to 345 kV.

The Itaipu power station has a rated capacity of 13,320 MW.

Longest transmission lines The longest span between pylons of any power line is 17,638 feet, across the Ameralik Fjord near Nuuk, Greenland. Erected by A.S. Betonmast of Oslo, Norway in 1991–92 as part of the 132 kV line serving the 45 MW Buksefjorden Hydro Power Station, the line weighs 42 tons.

Highest transmission lines The transmission lines across the Straits of Messina, Italy have towers of 675 feet (Sicily side) and 735 feet (Calabria side), 11,900 feet apart.

Highest-voltage transmission lines The highest voltages carried on a DC are 1,330 kV over a distance of 1,224 miles on the DC Pacific Inter-Tie in the United States, which stretches from approximately 100 miles east of Portland, OR to a location east of Los Angeles, CA.

The highest voltages carried on a 3-phase AC are 1,200 kV in Russia over a distance greater than 1,000 miles. The first section carries the current from Siberia to the province of North Kazakhstan, while the second takes the current from Siberia to Ural.

Biggest blackout The greatest power failure in history struck seven northeastern U.S. states and Ontario, Canada on November 9–10, 1965. About 30 million people in 80,000 square miles were plunged into darkness. Two people died as a result of the blackout. In New York City the power failed at 5:27 P.M. and was not fully restored for 13½ hours.

Largest nuclear reactor The largest single nuclear reactor in the world is the Ignalina station, Lithuania, which came fully on line in January 1984 and has a net capacity of 1,380 MW.

Largest nuclear power station The 6-reactor Zaporozhe power station in the Ukraine gives a gross output of 6,000 MW.

The largest nuclear power complex in the United States is in Wintersburg, AZ. The three Palo Verde units (1,221 MW each) have a net summer capability of 3,663 MW.

The largest unit in the country is found in Bay City, TX. The South Texas 1 unit has a capability of 1,251 MW; the South Texas 2 unit's capability is 1,250 MW.

Largest solar power plant   In terms of nominal capacity, the largest solar electric power plant is the Harper Lake Site in the Mojave Desert, California, run by UC Operating Services. The two solar electric generating stations have a nominal capacity of 160 MW. The site covers 1,280 acres.

Largest wind generators   The GEC MOD-5A installation on the north shore of Oahu, HI produces 7,300 kW with its 400-foot rotors when the wind reaches 32 MPH.

Largest turbines   The largest hydraulic turbines are 32 feet in diameter with a 449-ton runner and a 350-ton shaft. Rated at 815 MW, they were installed by Allis-Chalmers (now Voith Hydro) at the Grand Coulee Third Powerplant in Washington State.

Smallest turbine   A gas turbine with compressor and turbine wheels measuring 1.6 inches and an operating speed of 100,000 RPM, was developed at the University of New South Wales, Sydney, Australia.

Largest battery   The 10 MW lead-acid battery in Chino, CA has a design capacity of 40 MW/h. It is currently used at an electrical substation for leveling peak demand loads. This project is a cooperative effort by Southern California Edison Company Electric Power Research Institute and International Lead Zinc Research Organization, Inc.

MINES AND DRILLING

Deepest penetration into the earth   A geological exploratory drilling near Zapolarny in the Kola Peninsula of Arctic Russia, begun on May 24, 1970, was reported in April 1992 to have surpassed a depth of 40,230 feet.
   The deepest penetration made into the ground by human beings is in the Western Deep Levels Mine at Carletonville, Transvaal, South Africa, where a record depth of 11,749 feet was attained on July 12, 1977. The virgin rock temperature at this depth is 131°F.

Shaft sinking   The one-month (31-day) world record is 1,251 feet for a standard shaft 26 feet in diameter at Buffelsfontein Mine, Transvaal, South Africa, in March 1962.

Deepest ocean drilling   In 1993, the Ocean Drilling Program's vessel *JOIDES Resolution* drilled 6,926 feet into the seabed in the eastern equatorial Pacific. The deepest site at which drilling has been conducted is 23,077 feet below the surface on the western wall of the Mariana Trench, Pacific Ocean, by the Deep Sea Drilling Project's vessel *Glomar Challenger*.

The world's longest crude oil pipeline is 2,353 miles long.

Deepest ice-core drilling   The deepest borehole in ice was reported in July 1993 to have reached the bottom of the Greenland ice sheet at a depth of 10,018 feet after five years' drilling by American researchers.

Fastest drilling   The most footage drilled in one month is 34,574 feet, in June 1988 by Harkins & Company Rig Number 13 during the drilling of four wells in McMullen County, TX.

Deepest water bore   The Stensvad Water Well 11-W1 is 7,320 feet deep, and was drilled by the Great Northern Drilling Co. Inc. in Rosebud County, MT in October–November 1961.

Deepest steam well   The Thermal Power Co. geothermal steam well, begun in Sonoma County, CA in 1955, is down to 9,029 feet.

OIL

Largest oil producer   Saudi Arabia produced 8,231,000 barrels per day in 1995.

Largest oil importer   In 1995, the United States imported 8,835,000 barrels per day of crude oil and its by-products. Venezuela was the leading supplier, providing 1,480,000 barrels per day, which represented 16.8 percent of U.S. imports.

Largest oil consumer   The United States used 17.7 barrels per day in 1994, 26 percent of the world's total.

Largest refinery   Amoco Oil Company's Texas City, TX refinery has a capacity of 433,000 barrels per day.

Largest catalytic cracker   The Tosco Refining Company plant in Linden, NJ had a peak fresh feed rate of 159,500 barrels (6,699,700 gallons) per day in 1995. Tosco Refining Company is a division of Tosco Corporation of Stamford, CT.

Largest oil field   The largest oil field is the Ghawar Field in Saudi Arabia, developed by Aramco and measuring 150 by 22 miles, with an estimated ultimate recovery of 82 billion barrels.

Largest oil tanks   The five ARAMCO 1½-million-barrel storage tanks at Ju'aymah, Saudi Arabia are 72 feet tall with a diameter of 386 feet and were completed in March 1980.

Heaviest platform   The Pampo platform in the Campos Basin off Rio de Janeiro, Brazil was built and is operated by Petrobrás. It weighs 26,455 tons and processes 33,000 barrels per day. The platform operates 377 feet above the seabed.

Tallest platform   In April 1996, Shell Oil Company's "Mars" tension leg platform was installed in the Gulf of Mexico. It set a new water-depth record for a production platform, extending 2,940 feet from seabed to surface.

The Tosco Refining Company's catalytic cracker processes 6.8 million gallons of oil per day.

Greatest oil gusher The greatest wildcat ever recorded blew at Alborz No. 5 well, near Qum, Iran on August 26, 1956. The oil gushed to a height of 170 feet at 120,000 barrels per day. It was closed after 90 days' work by B. Mostofi and Myron Kinley of Texas.

Worst oil spill A marine blow-out beneath the drilling rig *Ixtoc I* in the Gulf of Campeche, Gulf of Mexico on June 3, 1979 produced a slick that reached 400 miles by August 5, 1979. It was capped on March 24, 1980 after a loss of 505,600 tons.

On January 19, 1991, Iraqi president Saddam Hussein ordered the pumping of Kuwaiti crude oil into the Persian Gulf. Estimates put the loss at 6–8 million barrels.

The *Exxon Valdez* struck a reef in Prince William Sound, AK on March 24, 1989, spilling 10 million gallons of crude. The slick spread over 2,600 square miles.

NATURAL GAS

Largest gas producer The Commonwealth of Independent States (CIS) produced 24.9 trillion cubic feet of natural gas in 1995.

Largest gas deposit The gas deposit at Urengoi, Russia has an EUR (estimated ultimate recovery) of 285 trillion cubic feet.

Greatest gas fire A gas fire burned at Gassi Touil in the Algerian Sahara from November 13, 1961 to April 28, 1962. The pillar of flame rose 450 feet. It was eventually extinguished by Paul Neal ("Red") Adair of Houston, TX, using 550 pounds of dynamite.

ENGINEERING

Strongest alloy Carbon-manganese steel music wire measuring 0.004 inches wide has a required tensile strength in the range of 3.40–3.78 GPa (4.93×105 to 5.48×10^5 lbf/in.²).

Largest blast furnace The no. 5 furnace at the Cherepovets works in Russia has a volume of 5,500 cubic meters.

Longest conveyor belt The longest single-flight conveyor belt is 18 miles long. It is in Western Australia and was installed by Cable Belt Ltd. of Camberley, England.

Most powerful gantry crane The 92.3-foot-wide Rahco gantry crane at the Grand Coulee Dam Third Powerplant in Washington State was tested to lift a load of 2,460 tons in 1975. It lowered a 1,972-ton generator rotor with an accuracy of 1.32 inches.

Tallest mobile crane The 890-ton Rosenkranz K10001, with a lifting capacity of 1,100 tons, and a combined boom and jib height of 663 feet, is carried on 10 trucks, each limited to a length of 75 ft. 8 in. and an axle weight of 130 tons. It can lift 33 tons to a height of 525 feet.

Greatest load raised The heaviest lifting operation in engineering history was the raising of the entire 1-mile-long offshore Ekofisk complex in the North Sea, Great Britain, after subsidence of the seabed. The complex consists of eight platforms weighing 44,090 tons. During August 17–18, 1987 it was raised 21 ft. 4 in. by 122 hydraulic jacks and a computer-controlled hydraulic system.

Most powerful diesel engines Five 12RTA84 type diesel engines have been constructed by Sulzer Brothers of Winterthur, Switzerland, for containerships built for the American President Lines. Each 12-cylinder power unit gives a maximum continuous output of 57,000 bhp at 95 revolutions per minute.

Largest earthmover The giant wheeled loader developed for open-air coal mining in Australia by SMEC, a consortium of 11 manufacturers in Tokyo, Japan, is 55 feet long, weighs 198 tons, and has rubber tires 11½ feet in diameter. The bucket has a capacity of 671 cubic feet.

SMALLEST MACHINE

The microscopic machine developed by Sandia National Laboratories in New Mexico is etched from a silicon wafer. Its smallest part is a gear 50 microns in diameter (approximately the same diameter as a human hair).
See feature (right)

Fastest elevators   The fastest domestic passenger elevators in the world are in the 70-story, 971-foot-tall Yokohama Landmark Tower in Yokohama, Japan, opened to the public on July 16, 1993. Designed and built by Mitsubishi Electric Corporation of Tokyo, the elevators operate at 28 MPH, taking passengers from the second floor to the 69th floor observatory in 40 seconds.

Much higher speeds are achieved in the winding cages of mine shafts. A hoisting shaft 6,800 feet deep, owned by Western Deep Levels Ltd. in South Africa, winds at speeds of up to 41 MPH. Otitis media (popping of the ears) presents problems above even 10 MPH.

Longest escalator   The 4-section outdoor escalator at Ocean Park, Hong Kong has an overall length of 745 feet and a total vertical rise of 377 feet.

Shortest escalator   The escalator at Okadaya More's shopping mall, Kawasaki-shi, Japan has a vertical height of 32.83 inches. It was installed by Hitachi Ltd.

Longest moving sidewalks   The moving sidewalks installed in 1970 in the Neue Messe Center, Düsseldorf, Germany measure 738 feet between comb plates.

Longest ropeway   The COMILOG installation, built in 1959–62 for the Moanda manganese mine in Gabon, extends for 47 miles. It has 858 towers and 2,800 buckets, with 96 miles of wire rope running over 6,000 idler pulleys.

Highest cable car   The highest and longest passenger-carrying aerial ropeway in the world is the *Teleférico Mérida* in Venezuela, from Mérida City (5,379 feet) to the summit of Pico Espejo (15,629 feet), a rise of 10,250 feet. The ropeway is in four sections, involving three car changes in the 8-mile ascent in one hour. The fourth span is 10,070 feet long.

Largest forging   The largest forging on record is one of a 225-ton, 55-foot-long generator shaft, forged by the Bethlehem Steel Corporation of Pennsylvania in October 1973.

Most powerful forklifts   Kalmar LMV of Sweden in 1991 manufactured three counterbalanced forklift trucks capable of lifting loads of up to 99 tons at a load center of 90.5 inches.

ERNEST GARCIA

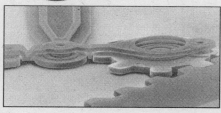

Nowadays, everything seems to come in smaller sizes, from compact computers to compact cars. As often as not, if it's smaller, it's better! Ernest Garcia, senior member of the technical staff of the Electromechanical Engineering Department at Sandia National Laboratories, would have to agree with this philosophy after creating the world's smallest machine.

"It's called a microengine, and it's a microscopic machine, originally created for defense purposes. The process that's used to fabricate this is borrowed from the process that's used to make integrated circuits—in other words, tiny transistors and things like that. It's a technique known as photolithography—which is one of the processes used to define the shapes of this very small part," says Garcia. "Because it's so small, we're able to drive the thing faster than any other electrically driven device—about 300,000 RPM. The gear is 50 microns in diameter [roughly the same diameter as a human hair], but some of the other parts are bigger than that. The entire machine is fabricated on the same kind of silicon wafer that you might put integrated circuits on."

Applications Garcia foresees for his microscopic machine include medical tools and material manipulation tools. For defense, he's looking toward safety mechanisms in weapons. "It'll have a lot of applications for inspection—you could drive machinery to inspect the insides of things you can't usually get to. Like the insides of a bigger machine or even the human body," he says. "As of now, this particular device has been used to drive a gear train of some other gears—so it's the first electrically driven machine that's able to drive a mechanical load." Garcia explains that the machine is really converting linear motion to rotary motion, and is equivalent to a full-size motor. "The implications are great because up until now, there hasn't been a good way to drive a mechanical load at these dimensions—about two and a half microns by two microns. That's the size of those thin films of polycrystal and silicon that make up the output gear of the machine. But to that is then connected some linkages which are operated by electrostatic linear actuators."

So what will this tiny leap for mankind mean in the future? "It will probably be the equivalent of the revolution that occurred when we went to integrated circuits from discrete electrical devices—which enabled you to make very powerful computers on a chip which was very small and could be mass-produced."

Thinnest glass   The thinnest glass, type D263, has a minimum thickness of 0.00098 inches and a maximum thickness of 0.00137 inches. It is made by Deutsche Spezialglas AG, Grünenplan, Germany for use in electronic and medical equipment.

Largest sheet of glass   The biggest sheets of glass ever manufactured were 71 feet long and 9 ft. 6 in. wide. They were made by the Saint Gobain Co. in France and installed in the Chantereine-Thourotte factory near Compiègne in August 1966.

Largest blown glass vessel   A bottle standing 7 ft. 8 in. tall with a capacity of about 188 gallons was blown at Wheaton Village, Millville, NJ on September 26–27, 1992 by a team led by glass artist Steve Tobin. The attempt was made during the "South Jersey Glass Blast," part of a celebration of the local glassmaking heritage.

Largest lathe   A 126-foot-long, 460-ton giant lathe was built by Waldrich Siegen of Germany in 1973 for the South African Electricity Supply Commission at Rosherville.

Largest nuts   The largest nuts ever made weigh five tons each with an outside diameter of 52 inches and a 25-inch thread. Known as "Pilgrim Nuts," they were manufactured by Pilgrim International Ltd. of Oldham, England for use on the columns of a large forging press.

Longest pipeline *Natural gas*   The longest natural gas pipeline in the world is the TransCanada pipeline, which transported a record 2,351.5 billion cubic feet of gas over 8,671 miles of pipe in 1995.

Oil   The longest crude oil pipeline in the world is the Interprovincial Pipe Line Inc. installation, which spans the North American continent from Edmonton, Alberta, Canada through Chicago, IL to Montreal, Quebec, a distance of 2,353 miles. Eighty-two pumping stations maintain a flow of 1.6 million barrels of oil per day.

Most expensive pipeline   The total cost of the Alaska oil pipeline, running 800 miles from Prudhoe Bay to Valdez, was $9 billion. The pipe's capacity is 2.1 million barrels per day.

Most powerful presses   The world's two most powerful production machines are forging presses in the United States. The Loewy closed-die forging press, owned and operated by the Wyman-Gordon Company at North Grafton, MA, weighs 10,438 tons and stands 108 ft. 2½ in. high. It has a rated capacity of 50,000 tons and became operational in October 1955. A press of similar weight, height and rated capacity is in operation at the plant of the Aluminum Company of America in Cleveland, OH.

The greatest press force of any sheet metal forming press is 116,840 tons for a QUINTUS fluid cell press delivered by ASEA to BMG AG in Munich, Germany in January 1986.

Largest radar installation   The largest of the three installations in the U.S. Ballistic Missile Early Warning System (BMEWS) is near Thule, in Greenland, 931 miles from the North Pole. It was completed in 1960 at a cost of $500 million.

Largest ropes The longest wire ropes are the four made at British Ropes Ltd., Wallsend, England, each measuring 15 miles long. The ropes are 1.3 inches in diameter, weigh 120 tons each, and were ordered by the CEGB for use in the construction of the 2,000 MW cross-Channel power cable.

Largest steel producer The Nippon Steel Corporation of Japan produced 30.52 million tons of crude steel in the year ending March 1992, compared with 31.959 million tons in 1991. It now has 37,388 employees.

United States The largest producer of steel in the United States is USX Corporation, of Pittsburgh, PA, which produced 12.2 million tons of raw steel in 1995. The annual sales figure for the U.S. Steel Group of USX was $6.5 billion and the number of employees for the year was 20,845.

Largest wind tunnel The largest test section of the NASA Ames Research Center wind tunnel in Mountain View, Palo Alto, CA measures 79 by 118 feet and is powered by six 22,500 horsepower motors, giving a top speed of 115 MPH.

MATHEMATICS

Largest numbers The largest lexicographically accepted named number in the system of successive powers of 10 is the centillion, first recorded in 1852. It is the hundredth power of a million, or 1 followed by 600 zeros.

Highest prime number The highest known prime number was discovered by David Slowinski and Paul Gage at Cray Research Inc. in Eagan, MN in January 1994, while they were conducting tests on a CRAY C90 Series supercomputer. This prime number has 258,716 digits, enough to fill over 21 pages of *The Guinness Book of World Records*. In mathematical notation it is expressed as $2^{859,433} - 1$, which denotes two multiplied by itself 859,433 times, minus one. Numbers expressed in this form are known as Mersenne prime numbers, named after Father Marin Mersenne, a 17th-century French monk who spent years searching for prime numbers of this type.

The largest known twin primes are $1,706,595 \times 2^{11,235} - 1$ and $1,706,595 \times 2^{11,235} + 1$, found on August 6, 1989 by a team in Santa Clara, CA.

Lowest composite number The lowest nonprime or composite number (excluding 1) is 4.

Lowest and highest perfect numbers A number is said to be perfect if it is equal to the sum of its divisors other than itself, e.g., $1 + 2 + 4 + 7 + 14 = 28$. The lowest perfect number is 6 $(= 1 + 2 + 3)$.

The highest known perfect number is $(2^{859,433} - 1) \times 2^{859,433}$. It has a total of 517,430 digits (enough to fill over 41 pages of *The Guinness Book of World Records*), and it is derived from the largest known Mersenne prime.

Most difficult math problem Fermat's last theorem has precipitated more incorrect proofs than have been published for any other theorem. Pierre de

Fermat inspired centuries of hopeless searching when he wrote the theorem in a notebook, adding, "I have found an admirable proof of this theorem, but the margin is too narrow to contain it." In June 1993, Andrew J. Wiles of Princeton University announced his discovery of the proof of the theorem. Subsequent study revealed flaws, but in early 1995, Prof. Wiles corrected them. He is now writing up the proof.

Most-proved theorem   A book published in 1940 entitled *The Pythagorean Proposition* contained 370 different proofs of Pythagoras' theorem.

---

40 years ago the highest known prime number was $2^{2281} -1$, a 687-digit number discovered by Professor D. H. Lehmer using a S.W.A.C. computer in October 1952. **Today** the highest known prime number is a 258,716-digit Mersenne prime discovered by David Slowinski and Paul Gage, who used a CRAY C90 Series supercomputer.

"Mersenne numbers go on and on. You just never know when another Mersenne prime will be among them." —Paul Gage, June 28, 1996

"It's a fun programming challenge. Computers are a thousand times faster than they were 15 years ago. The future is impossible to predict."—David Slowinski, July 8, 1996

Longest proof   The proof of the classification of all finite simple groups is spread over more than 14,000 pages in nearly 500 papers in mathematical journals, contributed by more than 100 mathematicians over a period of more than 35 years.

Most prolific mathematician   Leonard Euler (Switzerland; 1707–83) was so prolific that his papers were still being published for the first time more than 50 years after his death. His collected works have been printed bit by bit since 1910 and will eventually occupy more than 75 large volumes.

Oldest mathematical puzzle   *"As I was going to St. Ives, I met a man with seven wives. Every wife had seven sacks, every sack had seven cats, every cat had seven kits. Kits, cats, sacks and wives, how many were going to St. Ives?"*

Apart from slight differences in wording, this is identical to a puzzle found in an Egyptian scroll copied by the scribe Ahmes *c.* 1650 B.C.

***Most accurate version of* pi**   The most decimal places to which pi (π) has been calculated is 6,442,450,000. Professor Yasumasa Kanada (Japan) made two independent calculations by different methods and compared the results using computer programs written by Daisuke Takahasi. The main program was run for 116 hr. 38 min., September 24–29, 1995 and the verification program was run October 6–11, 1995 on a HITAC S-3800/480 supercomputer.

***Most inaccurate version of* pi**   In 1897, the General Assembly of Indiana enacted Bill No. 246, stating that *pi* was *de jure* 4.

COMPUTING

Fastest computer   The fastest general-purpose vector-parallel computer is the CRAY Y-MP C90 supercomputer, with two gigabytes (gigabyte = one billion bytes) of central memory and with 16 CPUs (central processing units), giving a combined peak performance of 16 gigaflops (gigaflop = one billion floating point operations per second).

Several suppliers now market "massively parallel" computers which, with enough processors, have a theoretical aggregate performance exceeding that of a C90, though the performance on real-life applications can be less. This is because it may be harder to harness effectively the power of a large number of small processors than a small number of large ones.

Fastest chip   The world's fastest microprocessor is the Alpha 21164, developed by Digital Equipment Corporation of Maynard, MA. It can run at 300 MHz.

Largest computer network   The Internet is accessed by 60 million users on 3,864,000 computers in 81 countries. It is estimated that by 2003, 5 billion people worldwide will be on the Internet.

Fastest transistor   A transistor capable of switching 230 billion times per second was announced by the University of Illinois at Urbana–Champaign in October 1986. The devices were made of indium gallium arsenide and aluminum gallium arsenide and were developed in collaboration with General Electric Company.

Smallest modem   The smallest modem is the SRM-3A, which is 2.4 inches long, 1.2 inches wide, and 0.8 inches high, and weighs 1.1 ounces. It is currently manufactured by RAD Data Communications Ltd. of Tel Aviv, Israel.

Smallest robot   The world's smallest robot is the "Monsieur" microbot, developed by the Seiko Epson Corporation of Japan in 1992. The light-sensitive robot measures less than 0.06 cubic inches, weighs 0.05 ounces and is made of 97 separate watch parts (equivalent to two ordinary watches). Capable of speeds of 0.4 inches per second for about five minutes when charged, the "Monsieur" has earned a design award at the International Contest for Hill-Climbing Micromechanisms.

CLOCKS AND WATCHES

Most accurate clock   A commercially available atomic clock manufactured by Hewlett-Packard of Palo Alto, CA was unveiled in December 1991. Designated the HP 5071A primary frequency standard with cesium II technology, the device, costing $54,000 and about the size of a desktop computer, is accurate to one second in 1.6 million years.

Oldest clock   The faceless clock, dating from 1386, or possibly earlier, at Salisbury Cathedral in England was restored in 1956, having struck the hours for 498 years and ticked more than 500 million times.

Largest clock   The astronomical clock in the Cathedral of St.-Pierre, Beauvais, France was constructed between 1865 and 1868. It contains 90,000 parts and is 40 feet high, 20 feet wide and nine feet deep.

Largest clock face   The clock face on the floral clock constructed at Matsubara Park, Toi, Japan on June 18, 1991 is 101 feet in diameter.

Highest clock   The highest clock is at the top of the Morton International Building, Chicago, IL. It is 580 feet above street level.

Largest sundial   Designed by Arata Isozaki of Tokyo, Japan as the centerpiece of the Walt Disney World Co. headquarters in Orlando, FL, the largest sundial has a base diameter of 122 feet and is 120 feet high, with a gnomon (projecting arm) of the same length.

Most expensive clock   The highest price paid for a clock is $1,652,500 for the Alexander III 25th Wedding Anniversary Clock made by Fabergé, sold on April 18, 1996 at Christie's, New York City.

Longest pendulum   The longest pendulum measures 73 ft. 9¾ in. and is part of the water-mill clock installed by the Hattori Tokeiten Co. in the Shinjuku NS building in Tokyo, Japan in 1983.

Largest watch   A Swatch 531 ft. 6 in. long and 65 ft. 7½ in. in diameter was made by D. Tomas Feliu and set up on the site of the Bank of Bilbao building, Madrid, Spain, December 7–12, 1985.

Smallest watches   Jaeger le Coultre of Switzerland produces the smallest watches. Equipped with a 15-jeweled movement, they measure just over half an inch long and ³⁄₁₆ inches wide. Movement and case weigh under a quarter of an ounce.

Most expensive watch The record price paid for a watch is SFr4.95 million ($3,315,000) at Habsburg Feldman, Geneva, Switzerland on April 9, 1989 for a Patek Philippe Calibre '89.

TELEPHONES AND FAXES

Most telephones The country with the most phones is the United States, with 165 million as of March 1994. Monaco has the most per capita, with 96 per 100.

Most mobile phones The country with the greatest number of cellular telephone subscribers is the United States, with 34.9 million at the end of 1995. The country with the greatest penetration is Sweden, with 229 subscribers per 1,000 people.

Largest telephone The world's largest operational telephone was exhibited at a festival on September 16, 1988 to celebrate the 80th birthday of Centraal Beheer, an insurance company based in Apeldoorn, Netherlands. It was 8 ft. 1 in. high and 19 ft. 11 in. long, and weighed 3.8 tons. The handset, which was 23 ft. 5 in. long, had to be lifted by crane.

Smallest telephone An operational telephone measuring 1 $^9/_{16}$ by $^5/_8$ by 1 $^5/_{16}$ inches was created by Zbigniew Rózanek (Poland) in August 1995.

Busiest telephone route The busiest international phone route is between the United States and Canada. In 1994, there were 4.3 billion minutes of telephone traffic between the two countries.

Busiest telephone exchange GPT (GEC Plessey Telecommunications Ltd.) demonstrated the ability of the "System X" telephone exchange to handle 1,558,000 calls in an hour through an exchange in Nottingham, England on June 27, 1989.

Largest switchboard The switchboard in the Pentagon, Arlington, VA has 34,500 lines and handles over 1 million calls per day. Its busiest day was June 6, 1994—the 50th anniversary of D-Day—when there were 1,502,415 calls.

Longest telephone cable The longest submarine telephone cable is FLAG (Fiber-optic Link Around the Globe), which runs for 16,800 miles from Japan to the United Kingdom and can carry 600,000 phone calls at a time.

Longest fiber optics transmission The longest distance over which signals have been transmitted without repeaters is 156.3 miles, by British Telecom, Martlesham Heath, England in 1985.

Largest fax machine Manufactured by WideCom Group Inc. of Mississauga, Ontario, Canada, the "WIDEFax 36" can process documents up to 36 inches.

TIPS

from the
RECORD BREAKERS

LONGEST SPACE WALK

Kathryn Thornton has flown on four shuttle missions. During her second flight, she completed the longest space walk by a woman astronaut. She offers some pointers on reaching for the stars.

♦

Get good grades.

"Good grades are critical to gaining acceptance to the astronaut training program," says Thornton. She recommends studying math, science and technical studies. "Keep trying," she adds. "Very few people are accepted on their first try."

♦

Be healthy.

There are no specific requirements for astronaut selection. "I underwent a week of medical tests," says Thornton, "but that was only to establish that I was healthy." Not even flying experience is needed. "I had never flown on anything larger than a commercial airliner," she says, "and I've never tried to gain a pilot's license."

♦

Wear boxing gloves to do home repairs.

The cosmic environment, 300-pound space suits and heavy padded gloves reduce mobility and dexterity. "The walk is always choreographed during training," says Thornton. Water tanks and air-bearing floors simulate conditions in space. "Stopping in space is difficult," says Thornton. Undoing screws is an even bigger challenge. "It once took hours to unscrew nine small screws that didn't match our power tools. A couple of them floated away and they're still up there."

Smallest fax machine   The Real Time Strategies, Inc. hand-held device Pagentry combines various functions including the transmission of fax messages. It measures 3 by 5 by ³/₄ inches.

SPACE FLIGHT

Highest rocket velocity   The fastest escape velocity from Earth was 34,134 MPH, achieved by the ESA *Ulysses* spacecraft, powered by an IUS–PAM upper stage after deployment from the space shuttle *Discovery* on October 7, 1990, en route to an orbit around the Sun via a flyby of Jupiter.

Most powerful rocket   The NI booster of the former USSR, first launched from the Baikonur Cosmodrome at Tyuratam, Kazakhstan on February 21, 1969, had a thrust of 5,200 tons but exploded at takeoff + 70 seconds. Its current booster, *Energya*, first launched on May 15, 1987 from the Baikonur Cosmodrome, has a thrust of 3,900 tons. It is capable of placing 116 tons into low Earth orbit. Four strap-on boosters powered by single RD-170 engines were used.

Most powerful rocket engine   The most powerful rocket engine was built in the former USSR by Scientific Industrial Corporation of Energetic Engineering in 1980. The engine has a thrust of 900 tons in open space and 830 tons at Earth's surface. The RD-170 burns liquid oxygen and kerosene.

Largest objects orbited   The 440-pound U.S. RAE (Radio Astronomy Explorer) B, or *Explorer 49*, launched on June 10, 1973, was the largest object orbited, with antennae 1,500 feet from tip to tip. The heaviest object orbited was the combined Russian *Mir 1* space station and U.S. space shuttle *Atlantis*, which docked on June 29, 1995 and together weighed 245.8 tons. The longest object ever placed in space was the Italian Tethered Satellite, deployed from *Columbia STS 75*, which extended 12.3 miles before the tether snapped on February 26, 1996. The satellite and the length of tether continued to orbit until March 19, 1996.

Closest approach to the Sun by a spacecraft   The research spacecraft *Helios B* approached within 27 million miles of the Sun, carrying both U.S. and German instrumentation, on April 16, 1976.

Fastest spacecraft   The fastest solar system speed of approximately 158,000 MPH is reached by the NASA–German *Helios B* solar probe when it reaches the perihelion of its solar orbit.

Remotest man-made object   *Pioneer 10*, launched from Cape Canaveral, FL, crossed the mean orbit of Pluto on September 29, 1995 at a distance of approximately 6 billion miles from Earth.

Longest manned spaceflight   Dr. Valeriy Polyakov (Russia) was launched to *Mir* aboard *Soyuz TM-18* on January 8, 1994. He landed in *Soyuz TM-20* on March 22, 1995, after a spaceflight lasting 438 days 18 hr. The longest space flight by a woman was 169 days 5 hr. 21 min. 20 sec. by Yelena Kondakova (Russia), who was launched to *Mir* on *Soyuz TM-20* on October 3, 1994 and landed in the same spacecraft on March 22, 1995. She is also the woman with the most space experience.

Under the FAI Category P for aerospacecraft, the longest spaceflight is by mission *STS-78* aboard *Columbia,* which lasted 16 days 21 hr. 48 min., June 20–July 7, 1996.

Shortest manned spaceflight Cdr. Alan B. Shepard, Jr. (U.S.N.) made a spaceflight aboard *Mercury 3* on May 5, 1961. His suborbital mission lasted 15 min. 28 sec.

Fastest spaceflight The fastest speed at which humans have traveled is 24,791 MPH, when the command module of *Apollo 10,* carrying Col. (now Brig. Gen.) Thomas Patten Stafford (U.S.A.F.), Cdr. Eugene Andrew Cernan (U.S.N.) and Cdr. (now Capt.) John Watts Young (U.S.N.), reached this maximum value at the 75.7-mile altitude interface on its trans-Earth round-trip flight on May 26, 1969.

Most journeys Capt. John Watts Young (U.S.N. ret.) completed his sixth spaceflight on December 8, 1983, when he relinquished command of *Columbia STS 9/Spacelab* after a space career of 34 days 19 hr. 41 min. 53 sec. Young flew *Gemini 3, Gemini 10, Apollo 10, Apollo 16 STS 1* and *STS 9.* The women's record is five, by Shannon Lucid (*STS 419, 31, 45, 58* and *76*).

Most time in space Valeriy Polyakov, a physician and research cosmonaut, has the most accumulated time in space, with 16,312 hr. 36 min. (nearly 680 days) in two missions (August 29, 1988–April 27, 1989 and January 8, 1994–March 22, 1995). The most experienced female space traveler is Yelena Kondakova (Russia), who has spent 169 days 5 hr. 21 min. 20 sec. in space (See LONGEST MANNED SPACEFLIGHT).

United States Norm Thagard has spent more time in space than any other American. He left Earth with the Russian team *Mir 18* on a *Soyuz* spacecraft on March 14, 1995 and returned July 7, 1995 on the U.S. shuttle *Atlantis,* after 115 days 8 hr. 44 min. in space. Shannon Lucid is the American woman with the most space experience, with 34 days 22 hr. 52 min.

Oldest astronaut The oldest astronaut was Vance DeVoe Brand (U.S.; b. May 9, 1931), age 59 yr. 7 mo. 1 day, while aboard *Columbia STS 35,* December 2–10, 1990. The oldest woman was Shannon Lucid (U.S.), age 53 yr. 6 mo. 4 days as of July 18, 1996, on *Atlantis STS 76.*

Youngest astronaut Major (later Lt.-Gen.) Gherman Stepanovich Titov (b. September 11, 1935) was 25 yr. 329 days old when launched in *Vostok 2* on August 6, 1961. The youngest woman in space was Valentina Tereshkova, age 26.

United States The youngest American astronaut was Sally Ride (b. May 26, 1951), who on June 18, 1983, aged 32 yr. 23 days, was launched aboard *Challenger STS 7.*

Largest crew The largest crew on a single space mission was eight, launched on October 30, 1985 on *Challenger STS 61A*, the 22nd shuttle

Space shuttle *Endeavour* lifts off from Kennedy Space Center in Florida.

mission, which carried the German *Spacelab D1* laboratory. The mission, commanded by Hank Hartsfield, lasted 7 days 44 min. 51 sec.

The largest crew on a single spacecraft was 10, when the crew of the *Soyuz TM 21* mission (two Russians and one American) joined the crew of the *Atlantis STS 71* mission (five Americans and two Russians) aboard the Russian *Mir 1* space station on June 29, 1995.

Most people in space   The greatest number of people in space at one time was 13, by the crews of the 7-person American mission *STS-67* aboard *Endeavour*, and the combined Russian teams *Soyuz TM-20* and *Soyuz TM-21*, each of which consisted of three crew members (one American). From March 14 to March 18, 1995, all parties were in space conducting joint scientific experiments.

40 years ago humankind had not ventured into space. The first manned spaceflight took place on April 12, 1961, with Soviet cosmonaut Yuri Gagarin at the controls of Vostok I. Gagarin ejected and parachuted to earth after 118 minutes. **Today** the longest continuous duration in space is 437 days 17 hours 58 minutes 16 seconds by Russian Cosmonaut Valeriy Poliyakov, who was launched to the Mir space station aboard Soyuz TM18 on January 8, 1994 and returned to earth aboard Soyuz TM20 on March 22, 1995.

"Duration records will continue to evolve.... Humans will go to Mars, no question. We have the guidance, propulsion, hardware and navigational capabilities. We just need the political will. An expedition to Mars would be a 2-year round trip journey, with a 2-week stopover on the planet."—Brian Welch, NASA Chief of News and Information, June 21, 1996

Farthest person from Earth   The greatest distance from Earth attained by humans was when the crew of *Apollo 13* were at apocynthion (i.e., their furthest point), 158 miles above the Moon and 248,655 miles from Earth, at 1:21 A.M. EST on April 14, 1970. The crew consisted of Capt. James Arthur Lovell, Jr. (U.S.N.), Fred Wallace Haise, Jr. and John L. Swigert.

Most isolated human being   The farthest a human has been removed from the nearest living fellow human is 2,235 miles, by the command module pilot Alfred M. Worden on the U.S. *Apollo 15* lunar mission of July 30–August 1, 1971, while David Scott and James Irwin explored the moon's surface.

Longest spacewalk   The longest spacewalk ever made was 8 hr. 29 min., by Pierre Thuot, Rick Hieb and Tom Akers on *Endeavour STS 49* on May 13, 1992. The longest spacewalk by a woman was 7 hr. 49 min., by Kathryn Thornton (U.S.) on *Endeavour STS 49* on May 14, 1992.

Untethered   Capt. Bruce McCandless II (U.S.N.), from the space shuttle *Challenger*, was the first to engage in untethered EVA (extravehicular activity), at an altitude of 164 miles above Hawaii, on February 7, 1984.

Most spacewalks   Russian cosmonaut Aleksandr Serebrov completed a record ninth spacewalk on October 22, 1993.

United States   During the 11-day *Endeavour* shuttle mission to repair the Hubble Telescope, Lt. Col. Thomas Akers made his fifth spacewalk, the most by any U.S. astronaut. Akers had logged 29 hr. 40 min. walking in space by December 7, 1993. Dave Scott also made five spacewalks, during *Apollo* missions *9* and *15* in 1969 and 1971.

Most flights by a shuttle   As of July 22, 1995, *Discovery* had flown 21 missions.

Greatest spaceflight disaster   The greatest published number to perish in a spaceflight is seven, aboard *Challenger 51L* on January 28, 1986, when an explosion occurred 73 seconds after liftoff, at a height of 47,000 feet.

TELESCOPES

Largest telescope   The world's largest telescopes are Keck I and Keck II on Mauna Kea, HI. Each one has a 10-meter primary mirror made up of 36 segments. Keck I and Keck II work together as an interferometer. Theoretically, they would be able to see a car's headlights separately from a distance of 15,500 miles.

Largest reflector   The largest single-mirror telescope now in use is the 19-ft.-8-in. reflector on Mount Semirodriki, near Zelenchukskaya, Russia.

United States   The largest single-mirror telescope in the United States is the 200-inch Hale reflector at Mount Palomar.

Largest infrared reflector   The UKIRT (United Kingdom Infrared Telescope) on Mauna Kea, HI has a 147-inch mirror. It is so good that it can be used for visual work as well as infrared.

Largest metal-mirror reflector   A 72-inch reflector was set up at Birr Castle, County Offaly, Ireland in 1845 by the third Earl of Rosse. The reflector was last used in 1909, but it is being restored and should be operational again by 1997.

Largest multiple-mirror telescope   The MMT (Multiple-Mirror Telescope) at the Whipple Observatory at Mount Hopkins, AZ uses six 72-inch mirrors together, giving a light-grasp equal to a single 176-inch mirror.

Largest solar telescope   The McMath solar telescope at Kitt Peak, AZ has a 6-ft.-11-in. primary mirror; the light is sent to it via a 32° inclined tunnel from a coelostat (rotatable mirror) at the top end.

Largest submillimeter telescope   The James Clerk Maxwell telescope on Mauna Kea, HI has a 49-ft.-3-in. paraboloid primary, and is used for studies of the submillimeter part of the electromagnetic spectrum (0.01–0.03 inches).

Largest refractor   A 62-foot-long refractor completed in 1897 is situated at the Yerkes Observatory, Williams Bay, WI and belongs to the University of Chicago, IL. The 40-inch refractor is still in full use on clear nights.

Largest radio dish   The world's largest radio telescope is the partially-steerable ionospheric assembly built over the natural bowl at Arecibo, Puerto Rico. The dish is 1,000 feet in diameter and covers 18½ acres suspended under a 600-ton platform.

Largest radio installation   The Australia Telescope includes dishes at Parkes, Siding Spring and Culgoora. There are also links with tracking stations at Usuada and Kashima, Japan, and with the TDRS (Tracking and Data Relay Satellite). This is equivalent to a radio telescope with an effective diameter of 17,102 miles.

United States   The VLA (Very Large Array) of the U.S. National Science Foundation is Y-shaped, with each arm 13 miles long and with 27 mobile antennae (each 82 feet in diameter) on rails. It is 50 miles west of Socorro, NM.

Largest Schmidt telescope   The largest Schmidt telescope is the 6-ft.-6¾-in. instrument at the Karl Schwarzschild Observatory in Tautenberg, Germany. It has a clear aperture of 52¾ inches with a 78¾-inch mirror, focal length 13 feet.

Largest space telescope   The Edwin P. Hubble Space Telescope weighs 12 tons and is 43 feet in overall length, with a 94½-inch reflector. It was placed in orbit at 381 miles altitude by a U.S. space shuttle on April 24, 1990.

Oldest observatory   The oldest observatory building is the "Tower of the Winds" used by Andronichus of Cyrrhus in Athens, Greece *c.* 100 B.C.

Highest observatory   The observatory on Chacaltaya, Bolivia is at 17,060 feet. It is equipped with gamma ray sensors rather than telescopes.

Lowest observatory   The lowest "observatory" is at Homestake Mine, SD, where the "telescope" is a tank of cleaning fluid (perchloroethylene), which contains chlorine, and can trap neutrinos from the sun. The installation is 1.1 miles below ground level so that experiments are not confused by cosmic rays.

Oldest planetarium   The Adler Planetarium in Chicago, IL, which opened on May 12, 1930, is the oldest planetarium in the United States. Its dome is 68 feet in diameter, and it seats 450 people.

---

40 years ago the systematic search for extraterrestrial life had not yet begun. When the first program was launched in 1960 at the National Radio Astronomy Observatory in Green Bank, WV, astronomers eavesdropping on the universe were limited to two star systems and one channel in the radio spectrum. **Today** the largest SETI (search for extraterrestrial intelligence) effort is Project Phoenix, based in Mountain View, CA. Project Phoenix will scrutinize 1,000 nearby star systems and 2 billion channels in the radio spectrum.

"Our goal is to find a signal broadcast by a transmitter. We would then have an answer to the question: Do we have cosmic company? I don't know if that would be a record, but it would be the greatest discovery in history."—Seth Shostack, astronomer, SETI Institute, Project Phoenix, June 14, 1996

Largest planetarium   The planetarium at the Ehime Prefectural Science Museum, Niihama City, Japan has a dome with a diameter of 98 ft. 5 in. Up to 25,000 stars can be displayed, and viewers can observe space as it would look from other planets.

United States   The Kelly Space Voyager Planetarium in Charlotte, NC has a dome 78½ feet in diameter and seats 307 people.

The American Museum of Natural History–Hayden Planetarium, New York City has a dome diameter of 75 ft. 2 in., but has the largest seating capacity of any planetarium in the United States, with 650 seats.

Longest extraterrestrial search   The longest-running SETI (search for extraterrestrial intelligence) project is the Ohio SETI Program at Ohio State University, Columbus, OH, which has searched the universe for extraterrestrial radio signals for 23 years, beginning in 1973.

Largest extraterrestrial search   The most comprehensive search for extraterrestrial life is Project Phoenix (originally NASA SETI), which is conducted by the SETI Institute of Mountain View, CA. The project will be stationed in Green Bank, WV from the fall of 1996, using a 140-foot-diameter telescope to listen for extraterrestrial radio signals from the neighborhoods of approximately 1,000 nearby sunlike stars by the year 2000.

BUILDINGS &

STRUCTURES

40

ORIGINS

Oldest human structure In January 1960, Dr. Mary Leakey discovered what may be the footings of a windbreak built 1.75 million years ago in the Olduvai Gorge, Tanzania. The site consists of a rough circle of loosely piled lava blocks associated with artifacts and bones on a work-floor.

United States Samples taken from the remains of a circular structure near Akron, OH in 1992 confirmed that it was a Native American hunting camp 11,000 years ago.

Oldest freestanding structure The megalithic temples of Mgarr, Skorba and Ggantija in Malta date from *c*. 3250 B.C., three and a half centuries before the first Egyptian pyramid.

Oldest wooden structure The oldest extant wooden buildings in the world are the Pagoda, Chumanar Gate and Temple of Horyu (Horyu-ji) in Nara, Japan, dating from *c*. A.D. 670.

BUILDINGS FOR LIVING

Oldest habitation The remains of 21 huts containing hearths or pebble-lined pits and delimited by stake-holes, found in October 1965 at the Terra Amata site in Nice, France, are thought to belong to the Acheulian culture of approximately 400,000 years ago.

Northernmost habitation The Danish scientific station set up in 1952 in Pearyland, Greenland is more than 900 miles north of the Arctic Circle and is manned every summer.

Southernmost habitation The United States' Amundsen-Scott South Polar Station was completed in 1957 and replaced in 1975. It is permanently manned.

CASTLES

Oldest castle The castle at Gomdan, Yemen originally had 20 stories and dates from before A.D. 100.

Largest ancient castle Hradcany Castle, Prague, Czech Republic dates from the ninth century and covers 18 acres.

Tallest sand castle A sand castle measuring 21 ft. 6 in. high, constructed only with hands, buckets and shovels, was made by a team led by Joe

The Amundsen-Scott South Polar Station is the world's most southerly habitation.

Maize, George Pennock and Ted Siebert in Harrison Hot Springs, British Columbia, Canada on September 26, 1993.

Longest sand castle A sand castle 5.2 miles long was made by staff and pupils of Ellon Academy, near Aberdeen, Scotland, on March 24, 1988.

PALACES

Largest palace The Imperial Palace (Gugong) in the center of Beijing, China covers a rectangle 3,150 by 2,460 feet (an area of 178 acres). The

The Imperial Palace in Beijing, China covers 178 acres.

outline survives from the construction of the third Ming emperor, Yongle (1402–24), but most of the five halls and 17 palaces date from the 18th century.

The Palace of Versailles, 14 miles southwest of Paris, France, has a facade 1,903 feet long, with 375 windows. The building, completed in 1682 for Louis XIV (1643–1715), occupied over 30,000 workmen under the supervision of Jules Hardouin-Mansart (1646–1708).

Residential Istana Nurul Iman, the palace of the Sultan of Brunei in the capital Bandar Seri Begawan, completed in January 1984 at a reported cost of $350 million, is the largest residence in the world, with 1,788 rooms and 257 bathrooms. The underground garage holds the sultan's 153 cars.

Largest ice palace The ice palace built by TMK Construction Specialties for the St. Paul, MN Winter Carnival in January 1992 used 18,000 blocks of ice weighing 10.8 million pounds, stood 166 ft. 8 in. tall, and covered an area the size of a football field, making it the largest-ever ice construction.

Largest snow palace The largest snow construction was a snow palace with a volume of 3,658,310.2 cubic feet and a height of 99 ft. 5 in. unveiled on February 8, 1994 at Asahikawa, Hokkaido, Japan.

Largest moat From plans drawn by French sources, it appears that the moats surrounding the Imperial Palace in Beijing measure 161 feet wide and have a total length of 10,794 feet.

HOUSING

According to the National Association of Realtors, as of December 31, 1995, the median price of existing homes sold in the 135 largest metropolitan areas in the United States is $112,900, and for new homes the median price is $132,000. The metropolitan area with the highest median price is Honolulu, HI, at $331,800.

Largest house The 250-room Biltmore House in Asheville, NC is owned by George and William Cecil, grandsons of George Washington Vanderbilt II (1862–1914). The house was built between 1890 and 1895 on an estate of 119,000 acres, at a cost of $4.4 million; it is now valued at $5.5 million, with 12,000 acres.

Largest gingerbread house A gingerbread house 52 feet high and 32 feet square was built by David Sunken and Roger A. Pelcher of the Bohemian Club of Des Moines, IA and 100 volunteers on December 2, 1988. The house was made of 2,000 sheets of gingerbread and 1,650 pounds of icing.

Most expensive house The most expensive private house ever built is the Hearst Ranch at San Simeon, CA. It was built 1922–39 for William Randolph Hearst (1863–1951), at a cost of over $30 million. It has more than 100 rooms, a 104-foot-long heated swimming pool, an 83-foot-long assembly hall and a garage for 25 limousines. The house was originally maintained by 60 servants.

Largest nonpalatial residence St. Emmeram Castle, Regensburg, Germany, valued at more than $177 million, contains 517 rooms with a floor space of 231,000 square feet. Only 95 rooms are used by the family of the late Prince Johannes von Thurn und Taxis.

Longest continuous house construction Winchester House in San Jose, CA was under construction for 38 years. The original house was an 8-room farmhouse with separate barn on the 161-acre estate of Oliver Winchester. Sarah Winchester, widowed in 1886, consulted a psychic in Boston, who told her that she alone could balance the ledger for those killed by Winchester firearms by never stopping construction on the estate. Mrs. Winchester moved to California, where she transformed the farmhouse into a mansion, which now has 13 bathrooms, 52 skylights, 47 fireplaces, 10,000 windows, 40 staircases, 2,000 doorways and closets opening into blank walls, secret passageways, trapdoors, three $10,000 elevators and more. The constant remodeling of the house was intended to confuse the resident ghosts.

Camping out The silent Indian *fakir* Mastram Bapu ("contented father") remained on the same spot by the roadside in the village of Chitra for 22 years, from 1960 to 1982.

Pole sitting Modern records do not come close to that of St. Simeon the Younger (*c.* A.D. 521–97), called Stylites, a monk who spent his last 45 years on top of a stone pillar on the Hill of Wonders, near Antioch, Syria. His achievement is the longest-standing record in *The Guinness Book of World Records*.

Mellissa Sanders lived in a shack measuring six feet by seven feet at the top of a pole in Indianapolis, IN, from October 26, 1986 to March 24, 1988, a total of 516 days.

Rob Colley stayed in a 180-gallon barrel at the top of a 43-foot pole in Dartmoor Wildlife Park, near Plymouth, England, for 42 days 35 min. from August 13 to September 24, 1992.

Tallest apartment building The 1,127-foot John Hancock Center in Chicago, IL is 100 stories high; floors 44–92 are residential.

The tallest purely residential apartment house is Lake Point Tower, Chicago, IL, which has 879 units consisting of 70 stories, standing 639 feet high.

HOTELS

Oldest hotel The Hoshi Ryokan in Awazu, Japan dates from A.D. 717, when Garyo Hoshi built an inn near a spring that was said to have miraculous healing powers. The waters are still celebrated for their recuperative effects, and the Ryokan now has 100 bedrooms.

Largest hotel The MGM Grand Hotel/Casino in Las Vegas, NV consists of four 30-story towers on a 112-acre site. The hotel has 5,005 rooms with suites of up to 6,000 square feet, and the complex also includes a 15,200-seat arena and a 33-acre theme park. The complex was started in 1991 and opened officially in December 1993. Its total cost was $1 billion.

Largest lobby The lobby at the Hyatt Regency, San Francisco, CA is 350 feet long and 160 feet wide, and with its 170-foot ceiling is as tall as a 17-story building.

Tallest hotel Measured from the main entrance to the top, the 73-story Westin Stamford in Raffles City, Singapore "topped out" in March 1985 at 742 feet tall. However, the Westin Stamford Detroit Plaza in Detroit, MI is 748 feet tall when measured from the rear entrance.

Most expensive room The Galactic Fantasy Suite in the Nassau Marriot Resort and Crystal Palace Casino in the Bahamas can be rented for $25,000 per night. The price includes high-tech toys such as a Lucite piano that produces images as well as music, a rotating sofa and bed, and a thunder and lightning sound and light show.

Most mobile hotel The 3-story brick Hotel Fairmount in San Antonio, TX, which weighs 1,600 tons, was moved on 36 dollies with pneumatic tires approximately five blocks and over a bridge, which had to be reinforced. The move, by Emmert International of Portland, OR, took six days, March 30–April 4, 1985, and cost $650,000.

Largest fumigation During the restoration of the Mission Inn complex in Riverside, CA, June 28–July 1, 1987, Fume Masters Inc. of Riverside carried out the largest fumigation ever conducted to rid the buildings of termites. More than 350 tarpaulins were used to completely cover the 70,000-square-foot site and buildings—domes, minarets, chimneys and balconies, some of which were more than 100 feet high.

BUILDINGS FOR WORKING

Largest construction project The Madinat Al-Jubail Al-Sinaiyah project in Saudi Arabia is the largest public works project in modern times. Construction started in 1976 on an industrial city covering 250,705 acres. At the peak of construction, nearly 52,000 workers were employed.

Tallest scaffolding Regional Scaffolding and Hoisting Co. Inc. of Bronx, NY erected scaffolding with a total height of 650 feet and a volume of 4.8 million cubic feet around the New York City Municipal Building in 1988. The work required 12,000 scaffold frames and 20,000 aluminum planks, and was in place until 1992.

Largest scaffolding The largest scaffolding was erected by Thyssen Hünnebeck GmbH of Ratingen, Germany around the City Palace in Berlin. The scaffolding, which had a total volume of 6,360,000 feet and stood 102 feet high, was in place from May 1993 until October 1994.

Largest demolition project The biggest building demolished by explosives was the 21-story Traymore Hotel, Atlantic City, NJ on May 26, 1972 by Controlled Demolition Inc. of Towson, MD. This 600-room hotel had a

The Petronas Towers are 1,483 feet tall.

Controlled Demolition Inc. of Towson, MD. This 600-room hotel had a volume of 6.5 million cubic feet.

The tallest structure ever demolished by explosives was the Matla Power Station chimney, Kriel, South Africa, on July 19, 1981. It stood 902 feet tall and was brought down by the Santon (Steeplejack) Co. Ltd. of Manchester, England. Fifteen members of the Aurora Karate Do demolished a 7-room house in Prince Albert, Saskatchewan, Canada in 3 hr. 9 min. 59 sec., using only feet and bare hands, on April 16, 1994.

Largest industrial building   The largest multilevel industrial building that is one discrete structure is the container freight station of Asia Terminals Ltd. at Hong Kong's Kwai Chung containerport. The 15-level building was completed in 1994 and has a total area of 9,320,867 square feet. The building measures 906 by 958 feet, with a height of 359 ft. 3 in. The entire area in each floor is directly accessible by 46-foot container trucks, and the building includes 16.67 miles of roadway and 2,609 container truck parking bays.

Bricklaying   Sammy Joe Wingfield of Arlington, TN laid 1,048 bricks in 60 minutes on May 20, 1994. The record was set under the normal working conditions of an average bricklayer.

Largest brickworks   The Midland Brick Company Pty. Ltd. at Middle Swan Headquarters, WA covers an area of 119 ha and has a weekly production capacity of 7.7 million brick equivalents.

Tallest fountain   The fountain in Fountain Hills, AZ, built for McCulloch Properties Inc., can reach 625 feet when all three pumps are on and weather conditions are favorable.

Largest commercial building   In terms of floor area, the largest commercial building in the world under one roof is the flower auction building Bloemenveiling Aalsmeer (VBA) in Aalsmeer, Netherlands. The floor surface of the building measures 7.6 million square feet.

The world's largest building in terms of volume is the Boeing Company's main assembly plant in Everett, WA. The building had a volume of 196,476,000 cubic feet in 1968, but subsequent expansion programs increased the volume to 472 million cubic feet. The site covers 1,025 acres.

Largest wooden building   In 1942–43, 16 wooden blimp hangars for Navy airships were built at various locations throughout the United States. They measure 1,040 feet long, 150 ft. 4 in. high at the crown and 296 ft. 6 in. wide at the base. There are only nine remaining—two each in Tillamook, OR, Moffett Field and Santa Ana, CA and Lakehurst, NJ, and one in Elizabeth City, NC.

Largest kitchen   An Indian government field kitchen set up during a famine in April 1973 in Ahmadnagar, Maharashtra provided 1.2 million subsistence meals daily.

Longest stairway   The service staircase for the Niesenbahn funicular near Spiez, Switzerland rises 5,476 feet. It has 11,674 steps and a banister.

Tallest spiral staircase   The staircase on the outside of the Bòbila Almirall chimney in Tarrasa, Spain, built by Mariano Masana i Ribas in 1956, is 207 feet high and has 217 steps.

Longest spiral staircase   The staircase in the Mapco–White County Coal Mine, Carmi, IL is 1,103 feet deep and has 1,520 steps. It was installed by Systems Control in May 1981.

Stair climbing   The 100-story record for stair climbing was set by Dennis W. Martz in the Detroit Plaza Hotel, Detroit, MI on June 26, 1978, at 11 min. 23.8 sec.

Brian McCauliff ran a vertical mile (ascending and descending eight times) on the stairs of the Westin Hotel, Detroit, MI in 1 hr. 38 min. 5 sec. on February 2, 1992.

The record for the 1,760 steps (vertical height 1,122 feet) in the world's tallest freestanding structure, the CN Tower, Toronto, Canada, is 7 min. 52 sec. by Brendan Keenoy on October 29, 1989.

Geoff Case raced up the 1,575 steps of the Empire State Building, New York City in 10 min. 18 sec. on February 16, 1993.

Largest garbage dump   Reclamation Plant No. 1, Fresh Kills, Staten Island, NY, opened in March 1948, is the world's largest sanitary landfill. The facility covers 3,000 acres and processes 4,368,000 tons of garbage per year, or 14,000 tons a day, six days a week.

Largest gas tanks   In Fontaine-l'Evêque, Belgium, disused mines have been adapted to store up to 17.6 billion cubic feet of gas at normal pressure.

The largest conventional gas tank is in Simmering, Vienna, Austria. It has a height of 275 feet and a capacity of 10.6 million cubic feet.

Largest refuse electrical generation plants   The South Meadow, Hartford County, CT plant and the Refuse and Coal Plant, Franklin County, OH, both with a capacity of 90 MW, are the biggest refuse electrical generation plants in the United States.

Largest sewage works   The Stickney Water Reclamation Plant (formerly the West–Southwest Sewage Treatment Works) in Stickney, IL began operation in 1939 on a 570-acre site and serves an area containing 2,193,000 people. Its 622 employees treated an average of 802 million gallons of waste per day in 1995.

OFFICES

Largest administrative building   The largest ground area covered by any office building is that of the Pentagon, in Arlington, VA. Built to house the U.S. Defense Department's offices, it was completed on January 15, 1943 and cost an estimated $83 million. Each of the outermost sides is 921 feet long, and the perimeter of the building is about 4,610 feet. Its five stories enclose a floor area of 149.2 acres. The corridors total 17.5 miles in length, and there are 7,754 windows to be cleaned. There are 23,000 people working in the building.

Largest office building   The complex with the largest rentable space is the World Trade Center in New York City, with a total of 12 million square feet of rentable space available in seven buildings, including 4.37 million square feet in each of the twin towers. Each tower has 99 elevators and 43,600 windows containing 600,000 square feet of glass. There are 50,000 people working in the complex and 70,000 visitors daily.

Tallest office building   In March 1996, the Petronas Towers in Malaysia overtook the Sears Tower's 22-year-old record as the world's tallest building. The 241-foot stainless steel pinnacles placed on top of the 88-story towers brought their height to 1,483 feet.

Tallest indoor waterfall   The waterfall in the lobby of the International Center Building, Detroit, MI measures 114 feet tall.

WALLS, WINDOWS AND DOORS

Longest wall   The Great Wall of China has a main-line length of 2,150 miles. Completed during the reign of Qin Shi Huangdi (221–210 B.C.), it has a further 2,195 miles of branches and spurs. It is 15–39 feet high and up to 32 feet thick.

The Great Wall of China is 2,150 miles long.

Thickest walls   Ur-nammu's city walls at Ur (now Muqayyar, Iraq), destroyed by the Elamites in 2006 B.C., were 88 feet thick and made of mud brick.

Longest fence   The dingo-proof wire fence enclosing the main sheep areas of Australia is six feet high, one foot underground and stretches for 3,437 miles. The Queensland state government discontinued full maintenance in 1982.

Tallest fences   The world's tallest fences are security screens 65 feet high erected by Harrop-Allin of Pretoria, South Africa in November 1981 to protect fuel depots and refineries at Sasolburg from rocket attack.

Largest windows   The windows in the Palace of Industry and Technology at Rondpoint de la Défense, Paris, France have an extreme width of 715 feet and a maximum height of 164 feet.

Oldest stained glass window   The oldest complete stained glass window is in the Cathedral of Augsburg, Germany. It dates from the second half of the 11th century.

United States   The stained glass window in Christ Church, Pelham Manor, NY was designed by William Jay Bolton and John Bolton in 1843.

Largest stained glass window   The window of the Resurrection Mausoleum in Justice, IL measures 22,381 square feet in 2,448 panels.
    The Basilica of Our Lady of Peace (Notre Dame de la Paix) at Yamoussoukro, Ivory Coast contains stained glass windows covering a total area of 80,000 square feet.

Tallest stained glass window   The back-lit glass mural installed in 1979 in the atrium of the Ramada Hotel, Dubai is 135 feet high.

Largest doors   The four doors in the Vehicle Assembly Building near Cape Canaveral, FL are 460 feet high.

Heaviest door   The radiation shield door in the Natural Institute for Fusion Science in Toki, Gifu, Japan weighs 793 tons and is 38 ft. 6 in. high, 37 ft. 5 in. wide and 6 ft. 7 in. thick.

BUILDINGS FOR ENTERTAINMENT

STADIUMS

Largest stadium   The Strahov Stadium in Prague, Czech Republic was completed in 1934 and could accommodate 240,000 spectators.

Largest in use   The Maracanã Municipal Stadium in Rio de Janeiro, Brazil has a normal capacity of 205,000, of whom 155,000 can be seated. A crowd of 199,854 was accommodated for the World Cup soccer final between Brazil and Uruguay on July 16, 1950.

United States   The largest stadium in the United States is Michigan Football Stadium, Ann Arbor, MI, which has a seating capacity of 102,501. The largest crowd ever to attend an event there was 106,851 for the Michigan vs. Ohio State game on September 11, 1993. Ohio State won 27–23.

Largest covered stadium   The Aztec Stadium, Mexico City, opened in 1968, has a capacity of 107,000 for soccer, although a record attendance of 132,274 was achieved for boxing on February 20, 1993. Nearly all seats are under cover.

Largest indoor stadium   The 273-foot-tall Louisiana Superdome in New Orleans, LA, covering 13 acres, has a maximum seating capacity of 97,365 for conventions or 76,791 for football.

Largest roof   The transparent acrylic "marquee" roof over the Munich Olympic Stadium, Germany measures 914,940 square feet in area, resting on a steel net supported by masts.

The largest roofspan in the world is 787 ft. 4 in. for the major axis of the elliptical Texas Stadium, completed in 1971 in Irving, TX.

Largest retractable roof   The roof covering the SkyDome, Toronto, Ontario, Canada, completed in June 1989, covers eight acres, spans 674 feet at its widest point and rises to 282 feet.

Largest air-supported building   The 80,311-capacity octagonal Pontiac Silverdome Stadium, Pontiac, MI is 600 feet wide and 770 feet long. The 10-acre translucent Fiberglas roof is 202 feet high and is supported by compressed air. Geiger-Berger Associates of New York City were the structural engineers.

Largest dome   The Louisiana Superdome, New Orleans, LA has a diameter of 680 feet.

SHOPPING CENTERS

Largest shopping center   The West Edmonton Mall in Alberta, Canada covers 5.2 million square feet on a 121-acre site and contains over 800 stores and services as well as 11 major department stores. Parking is provided for 20,000 cars, and more than 20 million shoppers visited in 1995.

United States   The Mall of America in Bloomington, MN covers 4.2 million square feet. It contains 350 stores, eight night clubs, and a 7-acre amusement park. There are parking spaces for 12,750 cars, and approximately 750,000 people shop there every week.

Largest wholesale center   The Dallas Market Center on Stemmons Freeway, Dallas, TX covers nearly 6.9 million square feet in five buildings. The whole complex covers 175 acres and houses some 2,580 permanent showrooms displaying merchandise of more than 30,000 manufacturers. The center attracts 800,000 buyers each year to its 50 annual markets and trade shows.

Longest mall   The £40-million ($68-million) shopping center in Milton Keynes, England is 2,360 feet long.

BARS AND RESTAURANTS

Largest bar   The largest beer-selling establishment in the world is the Mathäser, Bayerstrasse 5, Munich, Germany, where daily sales reach

84,470 pints. It was established in 1829, demolished in World War II and rebuilt by 1955. It seats 5,500 people.

Tallest bar   The bar at Humperdink's Seafood and Steakhouse in Irving, TX is 25 ft. 3 in. high with two levels of shelving containing over 1,000 bottles. The lower level has four rows of shelves approximately 40 feet across and can be reached from floor level. The upper level, with five rows of shelves, is reached by ladder.

Longest bar   The world's longest permanent continuous bar is the 405-ft.-10-in.-long counter in the Beer Barrel Saloon at Put-in-Bay, South Bass Island, OH, opened in 1989. The bar is fitted with 56 beer taps and surrounded by 160 bar stools. Longer temporary bars have been erected, notably for beer festivals.

Largest restaurant   The Royal Dragon (Mang Gorn Luang) restaurant in Bangkok, Thailand, opened in October 1991, can seat 5,000 customers. In order to cover the 4-acre service area more quickly, the 541 service staff wear roller skates. Up to 3,000 dishes are served every hour.

Highest restaurant   The restaurant in the Chacaltaya ski resort, Bolivia is at an altitude of 17,519 feet.

RESORTS

Largest amusement resort   Disney World is set in 30,000 acres of Orange and Osceola counties, 20 miles southwest of Orlando, FL. It was opened on October 1, 1971 after a $400 million investment and has attracted more than 350 million visitors.

40 years ago *"the largest holiday camp in the world" was Butlin's Filey Holiday Camp in England. It covered 498 acres and 150,000 people vacationed there each year.* **Today** *the largest and most popular amusement resort is Disney World in Orlando, FL, which covers 30,000 acres and has attracted more than 350 million visitors.*

"Staying on vacation the longest. I would like to take the longest vacation."—George C. Wolfe, Tony award winning director of "Bring in Da Noise, Bring in Da Funk," June 24, 1996

Largest recreational beach   Virginia Beach, VA has 28 miles of beachfront on the Atlantic and 10 miles of estuary frontage on Chesapeake Bay. The area covers 310 square miles, with 147 hotel properties and 2,323 campsites.

Largest casino   Foxwoods Resort Casino in Ledyard, CT includes a total gaming area of 193,000 square feet. There are 3,854 slot machines, 234 table games and 3,500 bingo seats.

Largest slot machine jackpot   The biggest beating handed to a "one-armed bandit" was $6,814,823.48, by Cammie Brewer, 61, at the Club Cal-Neva, Reno, NV on February 14, 1988.

Largest naturist resort   Domaine de Lambeyran, near Lodève in southern France, covers 840 acres. The Helio-Marin Center at Cap d'Agde, also in southern France, is visited by around 250,000 people per year.

United States   The largest naturist club in the United States in terms of total acreage is Oaklake Trails, Tulsa, OK, which covers 418 acres. Club Paradise, Land O'Lakes, FL, had 75,000 visitors in 1995.

FAIRS

Largest fair   The Louisiana Purchase Exposition in St. Louis, MO in 1904 covered 1,271.76 acres and was attended by 19,694,855 people. Events of the 1904 Olympic Games were staged in conjunction with the fair.

Largest exhibition center   The International Exposition Center in Cleveland, OH is situated on a 188-acre site adjacent to Hopkins International Airport in a building that measures 2.5 million square feet. An indoor terminal provides direct rail access and parking for 10,000 cars, and the Center accommodates 200 different events each year.

Largest Ferris wheel   The Cosmoclock 21 in Yokohama City, Japan is 344$\frac{1}{2}$ feet high and 328 feet in diameter, with 60 8-seat gondolas. It features illumination by laser beams and acoustic effects by synthesizers. The 60 arms holding the gondolas serve as second hands for the 42$\frac{1}{2}$-foot-long clock mounted at the hub.

Largest swing   A glider swing 30 feet high was constructed by Kenneth R. Mack, Langenburg, Saskatchewan, Canada for Uncle Herb's Amusements in 1986. The swing is capable of taking its four riders 25 feet off the ground.

Tallest scarecrow   "Stretch II," constructed by the Speers family of Paris, Ontario, Canada and a crew of 15 at the Paris, Ontario Fall Fair on September 2, 1989, measured 103 ft. 6$\frac{3}{4}$ in. tall.

Largest bonfire   Residents and off-duty firefighters from Workington, England lit a bonfire 122 ft. 6 in. high, with an overall volume of 250,700 cubic feet, on November 5, 1993.

Largest Ferris Wheel
The tallest Ferris wheel in the United States is the Texas Star at Fair Park in Dallas, TX, built in 1985. It is 212 ft. 6 in. high with 41 gondolas and a seating capacity of 244 riders.

ROLLER COASTERS

Oldest operating roller coaster *Rutschebahnen* (Scenic Railway) Mk.2 was constructed at the Tivoli Gardens, Copenhagen, Denmark, in 1913. This coaster opened to the public in 1914.

United States The oldest operating roller coaster in the United States is the *Zippin Pippin*, constructed at Libertyland Amusement Park, Memphis, TN in 1915.

Longest roller coaster *The Ultimate* at Lightwater Valley Theme Park in Ripon, England has a run of 1.42 miles.

Superman The Escape is the tallest and fastest roller coaster.

United States *The Beast* at Kings Island, Cincinnati, OH has a run of 1.40 miles, including 800 feet of tunnels and a 540-degree banked helix.

Tallest roller coaster The tallest and fastest roller coaster in the world is *Superman The Escape* at Six Flags Magic Mountain, Valencia, CA. This linear-powered reverse-free-fall coaster was designed by Intamin AG of Switzerland and features a 415-foot steel support structure and a design speed of 100 mph.

The tallest traditional complete-circuit roller coaster is *Fujiyama* at the Fujikyu Highland Amusement Park, Japan. It is 259 feet tall and has a lift height of 235 feet, a vertical drop of 230 feet and a design speed of 81 mph.

Greatest number of loops/inversions The most for any complete circuit multi-element coaster is the Dragon Khan at Port Aventura, Salou, Spain. It was designed by Bolliger and Mabillard of Mothey, Switzerland. Riders are turned upside-down eight times over the steel track, which extends for 4,166 ft. 2 in.

Most roller coasters Cedar Point Amusement Park in Sandusky, OH offers a choice of two wood and nine steel track coasters.

Largest maze The largest maze ever constructed was made in a cornfield in Shippensburg, PA. It had a total path length of 2.03 miles and covered an area of 172,225 square feet, and was in existence for two months in August–September 1995.

Permanent The largest permanent maze is the hedge maze in Ruurlo, Netherlands, which has an area of 94,080 square feet. It was created from beech hedges in 1891.

The maze with the greatest path length is at Longleat, Warminster, England. It was opened on June 6, 1978 and has 1.69 miles of paths flanked by 16,180 yew trees.

BUILDINGS FOR WORSHIP

Oldest church The oldest standing church in the United States is the Newport Parish Church, commonly known as St. Luke's, in Isle of Wight County, VA, four miles south of Smithfield, VA. The church was built *c.* 1632 and was originally called Warrisquioke Parish Church. Its present name was instituted in 1957.

Oldest synagogue The oldest synagogue in the United States is Touro Synagogue, Newport, RI. Construction was started in 1759 and completed in 1763.

Largest temple The largest religious structure ever built is Angkor Wat ("City Temple"), enclosing 402 acres in Cambodia. It was built to the Hindu god Vishnu by the Khmer King Suryavarman II in the period A.D. 1113–50. Its curtain wall measures $5/8$ square mile and its population, before it was abandoned in 1432, was 80,000. The whole complex of 72 monuments, begun *c.* A.D. 900, extends over 15 by 5 miles.

LARGEST SYNAGOGUE

Temple Emanu-El, on Fifth Avenue at 65th Street, New York City, was completed in September 1929. It has a frontage of 150 feet on Fifth Avenue and 253 feet on 65th Street. The sanctuary proper can accommodate 2,500 people, and the adjoining Beth-El Chapel seats 350. When all the temple's facilities are in use, 5,800 people can be accommodated.

See feature (next page)

Worship, Web Site and Freedom

$\mathscr{T}$he entire gamut of architecture: skyscrapers, hotels, apartment buildings, department stores, museums, libraries and places of worship line the length of Fifth Avenue in New York City. Many of them are large, many are grand, many are inspirational and some are sacred. One building that embodies all these qualities is Congregation Emanu-El of the City of New York, the world's largest synagogue.

"The origin of the Congregation is traced back to 1845. It began very humbly with 33 recently arrived immigrants from Western Europe," says Dr. Ronald B. Sobel, the Senior Rabbi of Temple Emanu-El. The Congregation expanded steadily during the 19th century and relocated several times. At the turn of the 20th century, New York City experienced a new wave of immigration from Europe, which included a large influx of Eastern European Jews. Temple Emanu-El was active in helping new immigrants, and many joined the Congregation. In the late 1920s the Congregation consolidated with Temple Beth-El and a decision was made to build the synagogue at 65th Street.

Rabbi Sobel points out that at that time it was the intention of the Congregation to build the largest Jewish house of worship in the world: "It was very much in their mind. That was a conscious, deliberate and well-thought-through design." He adds, "They wanted a grandeur that would be expressed with simplicity. They wanted an inner space wherein the worshipper could feel as if he or she was reaching upward towards the vastness of the universe where there would be an overwhelming sense of sanctity."

Statistics don't match the grandeur of architecture, but they do highlight the size of Temple Emanu-El. Rabbi Sobel recites them from memory: "There are 2,500 seats in the main sanctuary. There are 350 seats in the adjoining Beth-El Chapel, over 1,000 seats in the Lowenstein Sanctuary, 450 seats in the Greenwald Hall and approximately 1,500 seats in the Isaac Mayer Wise Hall. That's a total of about 5,800 seats. The Congregation today is approximately 3,000 families, and if you translate that into individuals, it's about 10,000." The intimacy of worship, however, is not compromised. "The brilliance of the architectural design allows the rabbinate in the pulpit to relate to the congregation in the pew with an intimacy that one would not expect in so large a space."

Temple Emanu-El is not bound by its capacious walls. The Friday evening service was first aired on radio in 1931 and has been broadcast every week since 1944. Last year Temple Emanu-El launched its own web site. "This past Passover, we made the Seder available on the Internet for the first 39 hours of Passover. There were in excess of 122,000 hits from 32 nations around the world, and by the end of the entire week of Passover there were more than 224,000 visitors on our web site," says Rabbi Sobel.

The structure is more than a building to Rabbi Sobel; it is "a symbol of the unique freedom that the United States has accorded the Jewish people." He explains: "Unlike historic Europe, where synagogues had to be erected on side streets, here the Congregation was able to erect on one of the most important thoroughfares of this country, Fifth Avenue, a sanctuary to take its place alongside the sanctuaries of other great religious traditions. The temple's very presence on Fifth Avenue speaks eloquently to the great freedoms accorded by America's glorious experiment in democracy."

Highest temple The Rongbu temple, between Tingri and Shigatse in Tibet, is at an altitude of *c*. 16,750 feet, just 25 miles from Mt. Everest. It contains nine chapels, and is inhabited by lamas and nuns.

Largest cathedrals The Gothic cathedral church of the Episcopal Diocese of New York, St. John the Divine, in New York City, has a floor area of

St. John the Divine in New York City is the largest cathedral.

121,000 square feet and a volume of 16,822,000 cubic feet. The cornerstone was laid on December 27, 1892, and work on the building was stopped in 1941. Work was restarted in July 1979, but is still not finished. The nave is the world's longest at 601 feet, with a vaulting 124 feet in height.

The cathedral with the largest area is that of Santa María de la Sede in Seville, Spain. It was built between 1402 and 1519, and is 414 feet long, 271 feet wide and 100 feet high to the vault of the nave.

Smallest cathedral   The Christ Catholic Church, Highlandville, MO, consecrated in July 1983, measures 14 by 17 feet and seats 18 people.

Largest church   The church of the Basilica of Our Lady of Peace (Notre Dame de la Paix) in Yamoussoukro, Ivory Coast was completed in 1989 at a cost of $180 million. It has a total area of 323,000 square feet, with seating for 7,000 people. Including its golden cross, it is 518 feet high.

The elliptical Basilica of St. Pius X (Sant-Pie X) in Lourdes, France was completed in 1957 at a cost of $5.6 million. It is 660 feet long and has a capacity of 20,000.

Angkor Wat, the largest religious structure in the world, covers 402 acres.

Longest   The crypt of the underground Civil War Memorial Church in the Guadarrama Mountains, 28 miles from Madrid, Spain, is 853 feet long. It took 21 years (1937–58) to build, at a reported cost of $392 million, and is surmounted by a cross 492 feet tall.

Smallest church   The chapel of Santa Isabel de Hungría is irregular in shape and has a floor area of just 21⅛ square feet. It is inside the Colomares, a monument to Christopher Columbus, in Benalmádena, Málaga, Spain.

Tallest spire   The tallest cathedral spire in the world is that of the Protestant Cathedral of Ulm in Germany. The building is early Gothic and was begun in 1377. The tower was not finally completed until 1890 and is 528 feet high.

The Chicago Temple/First United Methodist Church, Chicago, IL consists of a 22-story skyscraper surmounted by a steeple cross at 568 feet above street level.

Largest mosque   The total area of the Shah Faisal Mosque, near Islamabad, Pakistan, is 46.87 acres, with the covered area of the prayer hall being 1.19 acres. It can accommodate 100,000 worshippers in the prayer hall and the courtyard, and a further 200,000 people in the adjacent grounds.

Tallest minaret   The minaret of the Great Hassan II Mosque, Casablanca, Morocco measures 656 feet high. The cost of construction of the mosque was $540 million.

MONUMENTS

Tallest monument   The stainless-steel Gateway to the West arch in St. Louis, MO, completed on October 28, 1965, is a sweeping arch spanning 630 feet and rising to 630 feet. It cost $29 million and was designed in 1947 by the Finnish-American architect Eero Saarinen (1910–61).

Tallest menhir   The 330-ton Grand Menhir Brisé in Locmariaquer, Brittany, France originally stood 59 feet high, but it is now in four pieces.

Largest trilithons   The largest trilithons are at Stonehenge, Salisbury Plain, England, with single sarsen blocks weighing over 50 tons. The blocks would have required at least 550 men to drag them up a 9-degree gradient. The earliest stage of construction is dated to 2950 B.C.

PYRAMIDS

...id   The largest pyramid, and the largest monument ever ... the Quetzalcóatl Pyramid at Cholula de Rivadabia, 63 miles ... exico City. It is 177 feet tall and its base covers an area of ... Its total volume has been estimated at 4.3 million cubic

The largest single block in a pyramid is from the Third Pyramid (Pyramid of Mycerinus) at El Gizeh, Egypt and weighs 320 tons.

Oldest pyramid   The Djoser step pyramid in Saqqara, Egypt dates from *c.* 2630 B.C. It was constructed by Imhotep to a height of 204 feet.

Largest ziggurat   The Ziggurat of Choga Zambil, 18.6 miles from Haft Tepe, Iran, had an outer base 344 by 344 feet, and the fifth "box," nearly 164 feet above, measured 92 by 92 feet.

STATUES AND COLUMNS

Tallest monumental column   Constructed 1936–39, the tapering column that commemorates the Battle of San Jacinto (April 21, 1836), on the bank of the San Jacinto River near Houston, TX, is 570 feet tall, 47 feet square at the base, and 30 feet square at the observation tower, which is topped by a star weighing 220 tons.

Tallest columns   The 36 fluted marble pillars in the colonnade of the Education Building, Albany, NY are 90 feet tall, with a base diameter of 6 ft. 6 in.

The Temple of Amun has the world's tallest load-bearing columns.

Load-bearing   The tallest load-bearing stone columns are in the Hall of Columns of the Temple of Amun at Karnak, Egypt. They are 69 feet tall and were built in the 19th dynasty during the reign of Rameses II *c.* 1270 B.C.

Tallest floodlights   The tallest lighting columns are the six towers of the Melbourne Cricket Ground, Melbourne, Victoria, Australia. They are 246 feet high and weigh 132 tons each.

Largest obelisk   The obelisk of Tuthmosis III, brought from Aswan, Egypt by Emperor Constantius in the spring of A.D. 357, was repositioned in the

Piazza San Giovanni in Laterano, Rome on August 3, 1588. Once 118 ft. 1 in. tall, it now stands 107 ft. 7 in. and weighs 502 tons.

An unfinished obelisk, probably commissioned by Queen Hatshepsut *c.* 1490 B.C., *in situ* at Aswan, Egypt is 136 ft. 10 in. long and weighs 1,287 tons.

Tallest statue   A bronze statue of Buddha 394 feet high was completed in Tokyo, Japan in January 1993. It is 115 feet wide and weighs 1,100 tons. The statue took seven years to make, and was a joint Japanese–Taiwanese project.

United States   The Statue of Liberty was designed and built in France to commemorate the friendship of France and the United States. The 152-foot statue was then shipped to New York City, where its copper sheets were assembled. President Cleveland accepted the statue for the United States on October 28, 1886.

CEMETERIES AND TOMBS

Largest cemetery   Ohlsdorf Cemetery in Hamburg, Germany covers 990 acres, with 972,020 burials and 408,471 cremations as of December 31, 1995. It has been in use since 1877.

United States   The largest cemetery in the United States is Arlington National Cemetery, situated on the Potomac River in Virginia. It covers 612 acres, and more than 200,000 members of the armed forces are buried there.

Tallest cemetery   The Memorial Necrópole Ecumênica, located in Santos, near São Paulo, Brazil, is 10 stories high, occupying an area of 4.4 acres.

Largest crematorium   The Nikolo-Arkhangelskiy Crematorium, east Moscow, Russia has seven twin cremators. It was completed in March 1972 and covers an area of 519 acres.

Largest artificial mound   The gravel mound on the summit of Nemrud Dagi, Malatya, Turkey measures 197 feet tall and covers 7.5 acres. It was built as a memorial to the Seleucid King Antiochus I (r. 69–34 B.C.).

Largest tomb   The Mount Li tomb, the burial place of Qin Shi Huangdi, the First Emperor of Qin, was built during his reign, 221–210 B.C. and is situated 25 miles east of Xianyang, China. The two walls surrounding the grave measure 7,129 by 3,195 feet and 2,247 by 1,896 feet respectively. The tomb contained an estimated 8,000 terracotta soldiers and horses that are life-size and larger.

Largest mass tomb   A tomb housing 180,000 World War II dead in Okinawa, Japan was enlarged in 1985 to accommodate another 9,000 bodies.

Grave digging   Johann Heinrich Karl Thieme, sexton of Aldenburg, Germany, dug 23,311 graves during a 50-year career. In 1826, his apprentice dug *his* grave.

BRIDGES

Oldest bridge   The oldest datable bridge still in use is the slab stone single-arch bridge over the River Meles in Izmir, Turkey, which dates from *c.* 850 B.C.

Busiest bridge   The Howrah Bridge across the River Hooghly in Calcutta, India carries 57,000 vehicles per day and an incalculable number of pedestrians across its 1,500-foot-long, 72-foot-wide span.

Fastest bridge building   A team of British soldiers from 21 Engineer Regiment, based in Nienburg, Germany, constructed a bridge across a 26-ft.-3-in. gap using a 5-bay single-story MGB (medium-girder bridge) in 8 min. 44 sec. in Hameln, Germany on November 3, 1995.

Bridge sale   The largest antique ever sold was London Bridge, in England in March 1968. Ivan F. Luckin of the Court of Common Council of the Corporation of London sold it to the McCulloch Oil Corporation of Los Angeles, CA for £1,029,000 ($2,469,600). The 11,800 tons of stonework were reassembled in Lake Havasu City, AZ and rededicated in October 1971.

Longest bridge   The Second Lake Pontchartrain Causeway, which joins Mandeville and Metairie, LA, is 126,055 feet (23.87 miles) long.

Longest cable suspension bridge   The main span of the Humber Estuary Bridge, Humberside, England is 4,626 feet long. The towers are 533 ft. 1⅝ in. tall. Including its two side spans, the bridge stretches 1.37 miles.

Cable-stayed   The Pont de Normandie in Le Havre, France has a cable-stayed main span of 2,808 feet.
   The Mackinac Straits Bridge between Mackinac City and St. Ignace, MI is the longest suspension bridge between anchorages (1.58 miles), and has an overall length, including approaches, of five miles.

United States   The Verrazano–Narrows Bridge measures 4,260 feet. The bridge spans Lower New York Bay and connects Staten Island to Brooklyn.

Suspension bridge walking   Donald H. Betty of Lancaster, PA has walked over the 13 longest suspension bridges in the world.

Longest cantilever bridge   The Quebec Bridge over the St. Lawrence River in Canada is 1,800 feet between the piers and 3,239 feet overall.

Longest covered bridge   The covered bridge in Hartland, New Brunswick, Canada measures 1,282 feet overall.

Longest floating bridge The Second Lake Washington Bridge, Seattle, WA has a total length of 12,596 feet and a floating section that measures 7,518 feet.

Longest railroad bridge The 40,374-foot-long Seto-Ohashi double-deck road and rail bridge links Kojima, Honshu with Sakaide, Shikoku, Japan.

United States The Huey P. Long Bridge, Metairie, LA has a railroad section 23,235 feet long, including approach roads.

The Golden Gate Bridge has the world's tallest bridge towers.

Longest concrete arch bridge   The Jesse H. Jones Memorial Bridge, which spans the Houston Ship Canal in Texas, measures 1,500 feet.

Longest steel arch bridge   The New River Gorge Bridge, near Fayetteville, WV, has a span of 1,700 feet.

Longest stone arch bridge   The 3,810-foot-long Rockville Bridge, north of Harrisburg, PA, has 48 spans containing 216,050 tons of stone.

Widest long-span bridge   The 1,650-foot Sydney Harbor Bridge, Sydney, Australia is 160 feet wide. It carries two railroad tracks, eight road lanes, and bicycle and pedestrian lanes.

Highest bridge   The suspension bridge in the Royal Gorge in Colorado is 1,053 feet above the Arkansas River and has a main span of 880 feet.

Highest railroad bridge   The Mala Reka viaduct of Yugoslav Railways at Kolašin on the Belgrade–Bar line is 650 feet high.

Highest road bridge   The road bridge at the highest altitude in the world, 18,380 feet, is the 98.4-foot-long Bailey Bridge, near Khardung-La, in Ladakh, India.

Tallest bridge towers   The towers of the Golden Gate Bridge, which connects San Francisco and Marin Co., CA, stand 745 feet above the water. The bridge has an overall length of 8,966 feet.

Longest railway viaduct   The rock-filled Great Salt Lake Railroad Trestle, carrying the Southern Pacific Railroad 11.85 miles across the Great Salt Lake, UT, was opened as a pile and trestle bridge on March 8, 1904, but converted to rock fill in 1955–60.

Longest ancient aqueduct   The aqueduct of Carthage in Tunisia ran 87.6 miles from the springs of Zaghouan to Djebel Djougar. It was built by the Romans during the reign of Publius Aelius Hadrianus (A.D. 117–138), also known as Hadrian. In 1895, 344 arches still survived. Its original capacity was 7 million gallons per day.

Longest modern aqueduct   The California State Water Project aqueduct, completed in 1974, has a total length of 826 miles, of which 385 miles is canalized.

TUNNELS

Longest tunnel   The longest tunnel of any kind is the New York City West Delaware water-supply tunnel, begun in 1937 and completed in 1944. It has a diameter of 13½ feet and runs for 105 miles from the Rondout Reservoir into the Hillview Reservoir in Yonkers, NY.

Longest rail tunnel　The 33.46-mile-long Seikan Rail Tunnel was bored to 787 feet beneath sea level and 328 feet below the seabed of the Tsugaru Strait between Tappi Saki, Honshu, and Fukushima, Hokkaido, Japan.

Undersea　The Channel Tunnel runs under the English Channel between Folkestone, England and Calais, France. The length of each twin rail tunnel is 31.03 miles and the diameter 24 ft. 11 in. The undersea section is 9.1 miles longer than the undersea section of the Seikan rail tunnel (see above), although the overall length of the Channel Tunnel is less.

United States　The longest railroad main-line tunnel in the United States is the Cascade Tunnel, which runs between Spokane and Seattle, WA on the Burlington Northern railway. The tunnel is 7 mi. 1,397 yd. long.

Longest subway tunnel　The Moscow Metro Kaluzhskaya underground railroad line from Medvedkovo to Bittsevsky Park is 23½ miles long.

Longest road tunnel　The 10.14-mile-long 2-lane St. Gotthard road tunnel from Göschenen to Airolo, Switzerland opened to traffic on September 5, 1980.

United States　The longest road tunnel in the United States is the 1.69-mile-long twin Eisenhower Memorial Tunnel on Interstate 70 under the Continental Divide in Colorado.

Largest road tunnel　The largest-diameter road tunnel in the world is the one blasted through Yerba Buena Island, San Francisco, CA. It is 77 ft. 10 in. wide, 56 feet high and 540 feet long. More than 250,000 vehicles pass through on its two decks every day.

Deepest road tunnel　The Hitra Tunnel in Norway, which links the mainland to the island of Hitra, reaches a depth of 866 feet below sea level. It is 3½ miles long and has three lanes.

Longest hydroelectric irrigation tunnel　The 51½-mile-long Orange–Fish Rivers tunnel, South Africa, was bored between 1967 and 1973. The lining to a minimum thickness of nine inches gave a completed diameter of 17 ft. 6 in.

Largest sewerage tunnel　The Chicago Water Reclamation District Tunnel and Reservoir Project (TARP) in Illinois, also known as the "Deep Tunnel," will have 131 miles of sewerage tunneling when it is complete. As of January 1996, 75.4 miles were in operation and 18 miles were under construction. The estimated cost of the total project, including the three 41-billion-gallon total capacity reservoirs, is $3.7 billion.

Longest bridge-tunnel　The Chesapeake Bay bridge-tunnel extends 17.65 miles from the Eastern Shore region of the Virginia Peninsula to Virginia Beach, VA. It was opened to traffic on April 15, 1964. The longest bridged section is Trestle C (4.56 miles long) and the longest tunnel section is the Thimble Shoal Channel Tunnel (1.09 miles).

Longest and largest canal-tunnel　The Rove Tunnel on the Canal de Marseille au Rhône in the south of France was completed in 1927 and is 23,359 feet long, 72 feet wide and 37 feet high. Built to be navigated by seagoing ships, it was closed in 1963 following a collapse and has not been reopened.

Oldest navigable tunnel   The Malpas tunnel on the Canal du Midi in southwest France was completed in 1681 and is 528 feet long. Its completion enabled vessels to navigate from the Atlantic Ocean to the Mediterranean Sea via the river Garonne to Toulouse and via the Canal du Midi to Sète.

Longest unsupported tunnel   The longest unsupported machine-bored tunnel is the Three Rivers water tunnel, 5.82 miles long with a 10-ft.-6-in. diameter, constructed for the city of Atlanta, GA from April 1980 to February 1982.

DAMS AND RESERVOIRS

Most massive dam   Measured by volume, the largest dam is New Cornelia Tailings, an earth-fill dam on Ten Mile Wash in Arizona, which has a volume of 274.5 million cubic yards.

Largest concrete dam   The Grand Coulee Dam on the Columbia River, WA has a crest length of 4,173 feet, is 550 feet high, and contains 285 million cubic feet (21.5 million tons) of concrete.

Highest dam   The 984-foot high Nurek dam, on the River Vakhsh, Tajikistan, is the world's highest dam.

United States   The embankment–earthfill Oroville Dam, spanning the Feather River in California, is the United States' highest dam, rising to 754 feet.

The Grand Coulee Dam is the world's largest concrete dam.

Strongest dam The 804-foot-high Sayano-Shushenskaya Dam on the River Yenisey, Russia is designed to bear a load of 20 million tons from a fully filled reservoir of 41 billion cubic yards capacity.

Longest dam The Kiev Dam across the Dnieper, Ukraine, completed in 1964, has a crest length of 25.6 miles.

Largest tidal river barrier The Oosterscheldedam, a storm-surge barrier in the southwestern corner of the Netherlands, has 65 concrete piers and 62 steel gates, and covers a total length of 5½ miles.

Largest levees The most massive levees ever built were the Mississippi River levees, begun in 1717 but vastly augmented by the federal government after the disastrous floods of 1927. They extended for 1,732 miles along the main river from Cape Girardeau, MO to the Gulf of Mexico and comprised more than a billion cubic yards of earthworks. Levees on the tributaries comprised an additional 2,000 miles.

Longest breakwater The granite South Breakwater protecting the Port of Galveston, TX is 6.74 miles long.

Largest reservoir The largest man-made reservoir in terms of volume is the Bratskoye reservoir, on the Angara River in Siberia, Russia, with a volume of 40.6 cubic miles and an area of 2,111 square miles. It extends for 372 miles with a width of 21 miles.

The world's largest artificial lake measured by surface area is Lake Volta, Ghana, formed by the Akosombo Dam. The lake has an area of 3,275 square miles, with a shoreline 4,505 miles long.

United States The largest wholly artificial reservoir in the United States is Lake Mead in Nevada, formed by the Hoover Dam. It has a capacity of 1,241,445 million cubic feet and a surface area of 28,255,000 acre-feet.

Largest waterwheel The Mohammadieh Noria wheel at Hamah, Syria is 131 feet in diameter and dates from Roman times.

CANALS AND LOCKS

Longest ancient canal The Grand Canal of China was begun in 540 B.C. and not completed until A.D. 1327, by which time it extended (including canalized river sections) for 1,107 miles. The estimated work force *c.* A.D. 600 reached 5 million on the Bian section.

Longest modern canal The Belomorsko-Baltiyskiy Canal from Belomorsk to Povenets, Russia is 141 miles long and has 19 locks. The canal cannot accommodate ships of more than 16 feet in draft.

The world's longest big-ship canal is the Suez Canal linking the Red Sea with the Mediterranean, opened on November 17, 1869. It is 100.8 miles long from the Port Said lighthouse to Suez Roads, and ranges from 984 feet to 1,198 feet wide. It took 10 years and a work force of 1.5 million people to build the canal; 120,000 workers died during construction.

United States The longest canal in the United States is the Erie Barge Canal, connecting the Hudson River at Troy, NY with Lake Erie at Buffalo, NY. It is 365 miles long, 150 feet wide and 12 feet deep.

Busiest ship canal Germany's Kiel Canal, linking the North Sea with the Baltic Sea, had more than 43,287 transits in 1995. The busiest in terms of tonnage of shipping is the Suez Canal, with 417,852,000 gross registered tons in the fiscal year 1995.

The Corinth Canal is 3.93 miles long and 26 feet deep.

Longest irrigation canal The Karakumsky Canal stretches 745 miles from Haun-Khan to Ashkhabad, Turkmenistan. The course length is 500 miles.

Largest canal system The seawater cooling system associated with the Madinat Al-Jubail Al-Sinaiyah construction project in Saudi Arabia brings 388 million cubic feet of seawater per day to cool the industrial establishments.

Longest artificial seaway The St. Lawrence Seaway is 189 miles long along the New York State–Canada border from Montreal to Lake Ontario. It enables ships up to 728 feet long and weighing up to 29,100 tons to sail 2,342 miles from the North Atlantic up the St. Lawrence estuary and across the Great Lakes to Duluth, MN.

Largest lock The Berendrecht lock, which links the River Scheldt with docks in Antwerp, Belgium, is the largest sea lock in the world. It has a length of 1,640 feet, a width of 223 feet and a sill level of 44 feet.

Deepest lock   The Zhaporozhe lock on the River Dniepr, Ukraine can raise or lower barges 123 feet.

United States   The deepest lock in the United States is the John Day dam lock on the River Columbia, in Oregon and Washington. It can raise or lower barges 113 feet.

Highest lock elevator   The lock elevator at Ronquières on the Charléroi–Brussels Canal, Belgium rises to 225 feet.

Largest cut   The Corinth Canal, Greece, opened in 1893, is 3.93 miles long, 26 feet deep, 81 feet wide at the surface and has an extreme depth of cutting of 259 feet.

MASTS AND TOWERS

Tallest mast   The tallest-ever structure in the world was the guyed Warszawa Radio mast in Konstantynow, Poland. Prior to its fall during renovation work on August 10, 1991, it was 2,120⅔ feet tall. The mast was put into operation on July 22, 1974. It was designed by Jan Polak and weighed 606 tons.

The world's tallest structure is now a stayed television transmitting tower 2,063 feet tall, between Fargo and Blanchard, ND. It was built at a cost of about $500,000 for Channel 11 of KTHI-TV in 30 days (October 2–November 1, 1963) by 11 men from Hamilton Erection, Inc. of York, SC.

Tallest tower   The tallest building and freestanding tower (as opposed to a guyed mast) in the world is the $63 million CN Tower in Toronto, Ontario, Canada, which rises to 1,815 ft. 5 in. Excavation began on February 12, 1973 for the erection of the 143,300-ton reinforced, post-tensioned concrete structure, which was completed on April 2, 1975. The 416-seat restaurant revolves in the Sky Pod at 1,150 feet, from which diners can see hills 75 miles away.

Tallest LEGO tower   A LEGO tower measuring 74 ft. 4 in. tall was built by 4,660 children in Tåstrup, Denmark on July 29, 1995.

Largest cooling tower   The cooling tower adjacent to the nuclear power plant in Uentrop, Germany is 590 feet tall and was completed in 1976.

Tallest water tower   The Waterspheroid in Edmond, OK rises to a height of 218 feet, and has a capacity of 500,000 gallons. The tower was manufactured by Chicago Bridge and Iron Na-Con Inc.

Tallest house of cards   The greatest number of stories achieved in building a free-standing house of standard playing cards is 100, to a height of 19 ft. 2 in., built by Bryan Berg of Spirit Lake, IA in Copenhagen, Denmark and completed on May 10, 1996. No adhesives were used.

TIPS

from the
RECORD BREAKERS

TALLEST HOUSE OF CARDS

Architecture student Bryan Berg's card house record has been broken several times, but he keeps coming back to top it. Here, Berg offers his tips on getting the cards stacked in your favor.

♦

Build from the ground up.

"The limiting factor is not just the ceiling, but how large you make the base." Berg has built card towers on the air for television networks, and jitters over the size of his audience have dictated changes in his houses. "I usually make 4-card links on the bottom, but when I went on CBS I used 5-card links. I didn't want it to fall over in front of all those people."

♦

Stock up on cards.

Berg's card houses use up 500–1,000 decks of playing cards. "I get funny looks in the check-out line at the store," he says. Although he'd gladly recycle cards, he doesn't often get the chance. At one building session, audience members waited patiently for Berg to topple his tower, then rushed the platform and carried off 27,000 cards.

♦

Deal with skeptics.

"What kind of fruitcake would do something like this?" Berg gets that kind of question a lot, as well as queries about the brand of glue he uses (none) and what happens if someone blows on the tower (he directs a huge fan at it to prove its strength). His favorite question of all: "Do you start building from the top or the bottom?"

The tallest cooling tower, rising to 590 feet, is in Uentrop, Germany.

Tallest chimney   The Ekibastuz, Kazakhstan coal power plant No. 2 stack, completed in 1987, is 1,377 feet tall. The chimney tapers from 144 feet in diameter at the base to 46 ft. 7 in. at the top, and it weighs 53,600 tons.

Most massive chimney   The 1,148-foot chimney at Puentes de Garcia Rodriguez, northwest Spain, built by M.W. Kellogg Co. for Empresa Nacional de Electricidad S.A., has an internal volume of 6.7 million cubic feet.

Tallest flagpole   The flagpole at Panmunjon, North Korea, near the border with South Korea, is 525 feet high and flies a flag 98 ft. 6 in. long.

The tallest unsupported flagpole is the 282-foot-tall steel pole erected on August 22, 1985 at the Canadian Expo 86 exhibition in Vancouver, British Columbia. The flagpole supports a gigantic hockey stick 205 feet long.

Tallest totem pole   A 180-ft.-3-in.-tall pole known as the *Spirit of Lekwammen* was raised on August 4, 1994 in Victoria, British Columbia, Canada prior to the Commonwealth Games taking place there. It was a Spirit of Nations project developed by Richard Krentz of Campbell River, also in British Columbia, and took nine months to carve.

Tallest maypole   The tallest maypole ever erected was 127 ft. 6 in. tall and was put up in New Westminster, British Columbia, Canada on May 20, 1995.

Tallest lighthouse   The 348-foot steel tower near Yamashita Park in Yokohama, Japan has a power of 600,000 candelas and a visibility range of 20 miles.

The lights with the greatest range are 1,089 feet above the ground on the Empire State Building, New York City. Each 4-arc mercury bulb is visible 80 miles away on the ground and 300 miles away from aircraft.

TRANSPORT

AUTOMOBILES

PRODUCTION

Largest annual production The number of vehicles constructed worldwide in 1995 was a record 52,273,000, of which a record 37,291,000 were automobiles.

Largest manufacturer The world's largest manufacturer of motor vehicles and parts (and the largest manufacturing company) is General Motors Corporation of Detroit, MI. The company has on average 709,000 employees. In 1994, General Motors produced 5,543,012 cars.

Largest plant The largest single automobile plant in the world is the Volkswagenwerk in Wolfsburg, Germany, with 60,000 employees and a capacity for producing 4,000 vehicles per week (208,000 per year). The factory buildings cover an area of 371 acres and the whole plant covers 1,878 acres, with 46 miles of rail sidings.

United States The largest automobile plant in the United States is the Nissan Motor Manufacturing Corp.'s Smyrna, TN plant. The plant had a capacity of 450,000 cars and compact pickup trucks at the end of 1993. The plant covers an area of 5.1 million square feet.

Longest in production A total of 21,240,657 Volkswagen "Beetles" have been produced since 1937. Two production lines continue to produce the car—Puebla, Mexico and São Paulo, Brazil.

The Morgan 4/4, built by the Morgan Motor Car Co. of Malvern, England, celebrated its 60th birthday in December 1995. There is still a waiting list of 6–8 years to buy this model.

United States The oldest mass-production model still being made is the Chrysler Imperial, which was in production from 1926 to 1984 and 1990–present. The luxury model Cadillac Fleetwood has been in continuous production since 1936.

Largest car Of cars produced for private use, the largest was the Bugatti "Royale" type 41. First built in 1927, this machine has an 8-cylinder engine of 12.7-liter capacity, and measures over 22 feet long. The hood is over seven feet long.

Longest car A 26-wheeled limo measuring 100 feet long was designed by Jay Ohrberg of Burbank, CA. It has many special features, including a swimming pool and a king-sized water bed. It was designed so that it can be driven as one piece, or changed to bend in the middle.

Largest engine The largest engine capacity of a production car is 13.5 liters, for the U.S. Pierce-Arrow 6–66 Raceabout of 1912–18, the U.S. Peerless 6–60 of 1912–14, and the Fageol of 1918.

Most powerful car The most powerful current production car is the McLaren F1 6.1; it develops in excess of 627 BHP.

Heaviest car The heaviest car recently in production (up to 25 were made annually) appears to be the Soviet-built Zil–41047 limousine with a 12.72-foot wheelbase. It weighs 7,352 pounds (3.7 tons).

A "stretched" Zil was used by former USSR president Mikhail Gorbachev until December 1991. It weighed 6.6 tons and was made of 3-inch armor-plated steel. The 8-cylinder, 7-liter engine guzzled fuel at a rate of six miles per gallon.

Lightest car Louis Borsi of London, England has built and driven a 21-pound car with a 2.5-cc engine. It is capable of 15 MPH.

Smallest street-legal car The smallest registered street-legal car in the United States has an overall length of 88³/₄ inches and a width of 40¹/₂ inches. It was built by Arlis Sluder and is now owned by Jeff Gibson.

Jeff Gibson owns the smallest street-legal car in the United States.

Most expensive car The most expensive car ever built was the U.S. Presidential 1969 Lincoln Continental Executive delivered to the U.S. Secret Service on October 14, 1968. It has an overall length of 21 ft. 6¹/₄ in. with a 13-ft.-4-in. wheelbase, and with the addition of 2.2 tons of armor plate, weighs six tons (12,000 pounds). The estimated cost of research, development and manufacture was $500,000, but it is rented at $5,000 per year. Even if all four tires were shot out it could travel at 50 MPH on inner rubber-edged steel discs.

Used The greatest confirmed price paid is $15 million, including commission, for the 1931 Bugatti Type 41 Royale Sports Coupé by Kellner, sold to Meitec Corporation of Japan on April 12, 1990.

Most inexpensive car The cheapest car of all time was the 1922 Red Bug Buckboard, built by the Briggs & Stratton Co. of Milwaukee, WI, listed at $125–$150. It had a 62-inch wheelbase and weighed 245 pounds. Early models of the King Midget cars were sold in kit form for self-assembly for as little as $100 in 1948.

Largest antique car collection   Harold LeMay of Tacoma, WA has an automobile collection consisting of 1,900 antique and vintage vehicles.

Longest parade of cars   A parade of 2,223 Corvettes traveled from the Bloomington Gold Corvette Show in Springfield, IL to Athens, IL and back again on June 25, 1994.

Most expensive license plate   License plate No. 9 was sold at a Hong Kong government auction for HK$13 million (approximately $1.7 million) on March 19, 1994 to Albert Yeung Sau-Shing. "Nine" sounds like the word "dog" in Chinese, and the purchase was considered lucky because 1994 was the Year of the Dog.

Car wrecking   In a career lasting 40 years until his retirement in 1993, stuntman Dick Sheppard of Gloucester, England wrecked 2,003 cars.

Some of Harold LeMay's 1,900 antique and vintage cars.

Tire supporting   The greatest number of tires supported in a freestanding lift is 96, by Gary Windebank of Romsey, England in February 1984. The total weight was 1,440 pounds. The tires used were Michelin XZX 155 × 13.

SPEED

Fastest land vehicle   The *official* 1-mile land-speed record is 633.468 MPH, set by Richard Noble on October 4, 1983 over the Black Rock Desert, NV in his 17,000-pound-thrust Rolls-Royce Avon 302 jet-powered *Thrust 2*, designed by John Ackroyd.

Fastest rocket-engined vehicle   The fastest speed attained by any wheeled land vehicle is 631.367 MPH by *The Blue Flame*, a rocket-powered 4-wheeled vehicle driven by Gary Gabelich (U.S.) on the Bonneville Salt Flats, UT on October 23, 1970. Gabelich momentarily exceeded 650 MPH. The car was powered by a liquid natural gas/hydrogen peroxide rocket engine developing a thrust of up to a maximum 22,000 pounds.

The fastest reputed land speed figure in one direction is 739.666 MPH, or Mach 1.0106, by Stan Barrett (U.S.) in the *Budweiser Rocket*, a rocket-engined 3-wheeled car, at Edwards Air Force Base, CA on December 17, 1979. This published speed of Mach 1.0106 is not officially sanctioned by the U.S.A.F., as the Digital Instrument Radar was not calibrated or certified. The radar information was not generated by the vehicle directly but by an operator aiming a dish using a TV screen.

Fastest piston-engined car   The fastest speed measured for a wheel-driven car is 432.692 MPH by Al Teague in *Speed-O-Motive/Spirit of '76* at Bonneville Salt Flats, UT on August 21, 1991 over the final 132 feet of a mile run (av. 425.230 MPH for the whole mile).

 **40 years ago** *the official world land speed record stood at 394.196 mph. The car was powered by two 12-cyclinder Napier-Lion engines developing 2,860 horsepower.* **Today** *the official record is 633.468 mph, set by Richard Noble on October 4, 1983 in a vehicle powered by a 17,000-pound-thrust Rolls-Royce Avon 302 jet-engine.*

"The idea of breaking a record is absurd. I don't even drive."—Barbara Walters, TV broadcaster, June 4, 1996

Fastest diesel-engined car   The prototype 3-liter Mercedes C 111/3 attained 203.3 MPH in tests on the Nardo Circuit, southern Italy, October 5–15, 1978, and in April 1978 averaged 195.4 MPH for 12 hours, thus covering a world record 2,344.7 miles.

Fastest steam car   On August 19, 1985 Robert E. Barber broke the 79-year-old record for a steam car driving No. 744, *Steamin' Demon*, built by the Barber-Nichols Engineering Co., which reached 145.607 MPH at Bonneville Salt Flats, UT.

Fastest electric car   The highest speed achieved by an electric vehicle is 183.822 MPH over a 2-way flying kilometer by General Motors' *Impact*, driven by Clive Roberts (Great Britain) at Fort Stockton Test Center in Texas on March 11, 1994.

Fastest road car Various revved-up track cars have been licensed for road use but are not normal production models.

The fastest speed ever attained by a standard production car is 217.1 MPH for a Jaguar XJ220, driven by Martin Brundle at the Nardo Circuit, Italy on June 21, 1992.

The highest road-tested acceleration reported for a street-legal car is 0–60 MPH in 3.07 seconds for a Ford RS200 Evolution, driven by Graham Hathaway at the Boreham Proving Ground, Essex, England on May 25, 1994.

DRIVING

Amphibious circumnavigation The only circumnavigation by an amphibious vehicle was by Ben Carlin (Australia) in the amphibious jeep _Half-Safe_. He completed the last leg of the Atlantic crossing (the English Channel) on August 24, 1951. He arrived back in Montreal, Canada on May 8, 1958, having completed a circumnavigation of 39,000 miles over land and 9,600 miles by sea and river. He was accompanied on the transatlantic stage by his ex-wife Elinore (U.S.) and on the long transpacific stage (Tokyo, Japan to Anchorage, AK) by Broye Lafayette De-Mente (U.S.).

One-year drive The greatest distance ever covered in one year is 354,257 miles, by two Opel Rekord 2-liter passenger sedans, both of which covered this distance between May 18, 1988 and the same date in 1989 without any major mechanical breakdowns. The vehicles were manufactured by the Delta Motor Corporation, Port Elizabeth, South Africa, and were driven on tar and gravel roads in the Northern Cape by a team of company drivers from Delta.

Don Champion with his 1979 Cadillac DeVille.

Trans-Americas drive   Garry Sowerby (Canada), with Tim Cahill (U.S.) as co-driver and navigator, drove a 1988 GMC Sierra K3500 4-wheel-drive pickup truck powered by a 6.2-liter V8 Detroit diesel engine from Ushuaia, Tierra del Fuego, Argentina to Prudhoe Bay, AK, a distance of 14,739 miles, in a total elapsed time of 23 days 22 hr. 43 min. from September 29 to October 22, 1987. The vehicle and team were surface-freighted from Cartagena, Colombia to Balboa, Panama so as to bypass the Darién Gap.

Oldest car to cross the United States   Raymond H. Carr drove across the United States in a 1902 Northern, the oldest car ever to make the trip. Traveling at 15–20 MPH, Carr left San Diego, CA on May 8, 1994 and arrived at Jekyll Island, GA on May 31, 1994.

Carr also crossed the United States in a 1912 Baker Electric Runabout, the oldest electric car to make the crossing, starting in Astoria, OR on May 28, 1995 and finishing in Atlantic City, NJ on July 3, 1995.

Longest skid marks   The skid marks made by the jet-powered *Spirit of America*, driven by Craig Breedlove, after the car went out of control at Bonneville Salt Flats, UT, on October 15, 1964, were nearly six miles long.

Highest mileage   The highest recorded mileage for a car is 1,592,503 miles as of January 10, 1996, for a 1963 Volkswagen Beetle owned by Albert Klein of Pasadena, CA.

The highest recorded mileage for a car with the original gasoline motor without an overhaul is 661,183 miles to June 1, 1996 for a 1979 Cadillac DeVille owned by Don Champion of Louisville, KY.

Lowest gas consumption   A team of students from Lycée St. Joseph La Joliverie, Nantes, France achieved 7,591 MPG in the Shell Mileage Marathon at Silverstone, England on July 17, 1992.

This 1902 Northern is the oldest car to cross the United States.

Longest fuel range The greatest distance driven without refueling on a single fill-up in a standard vehicle (38.2 gallons carried in factory-optional twin fuel tanks) is 1,691.6 miles, by a 1991 Toyota LandCruiser diesel station wagon. Driven by Ewan Kennedy with Ian Lee (observer) from Nyngan, New South Wales, Australia to Winton, Queensland, Australia and back from May 18 to May 21, 1992, the car averaged 37.3 MPH, giving 44.2 MPG.

The greatest distance traveled by an unmodified production car on the contents of a standard fuel tank is 1,338.1 miles, giving 75.94 MPG. Stuart Bladon and Robert Procter drove the length of Great Britain, July 26–28, 1992, from John o' Groat's to Land's End, and returned to Scotland driving an Audi 100 TD1 diesel car. The fuel in the 17.62-gallon fuel tank ran out after 35 hr. 18 min.

Driving in reverse Charles Creighton and James Hargis of Maplewood, MO drove their Model A Ford 1929 roadster in reverse for 3,340 miles from New York to Los Angeles, CA, from July 26 to August 13, 1930 without once stopping the engine. They arrived back in New York in reverse on September 5, having completed 7,180 miles in 42 days.

Brian "Cub" Keene and James "Wilbur" Wright drove their Chevrolet Blazer 9,031 miles in reverse in 37 days (August 1–September 6, 1984) through 15 states and Canada.

The highest average speed attained in any nonstop reverse drive exceeding 500 miles was achieved by Gerald Hoagland, who drove a 1969 Chevrolet Impala 501 miles in 17 hr. 38 min. at Chemung Speed Drome, NY, July 9–10, 1976, to average 28.41 MPH.

Longest battery-powered car journey David Turner and Tim Pickhard of Turners of Boscastle Ltd., Cornwall, England traveled 875 miles from Land's End to John o' Groat's, Great Britain in a Freight Rover Leyland Sherpa, powered by a Lucas electric motor, December 21–25, 1985.

Two-side-wheel driving Car On May 24, 1989 Bengt Norberg of Äppelbo, Sweden drove a Mitsubishi Colt GTi-16V on two side wheels nonstop for a distance of 192.873 miles in a time of 7 hr. 15 min. 50 sec. He also achieved a distance of 27.842 miles in one hour at Rattvik Horse Track, Sweden on the same day.

Sven-Erik Söderman (Sweden) achieved a speed of 102.14 MPH over a 100-meter (328.1-foot) flying start on two wheels of an Opel Kadett at Mora Siljan Airport, Mora, Sweden on August 2, 1990. Söderman achieved a record speed for the flying kilometer of 152.96 km/h (95.04 MPH) at the same venue on August 24, 1990.

Truck Sven-Erik Söderman drove a Daf 2800 7.5-ton truck on two wheels for a distance of 6.73 miles at Mora Siljan Airport, Mora, Sweden on May 19, 1991.

Bus Bobby Ore (Great Britain) drove a double-decker bus a distance of 810 feet on two wheels at North Weald Airfield, England on May 21, 1988.

Most durable driver Goodyear Tire and Rubber Co. test driver Weldon C. Kocich drove 3,141,946 miles from February 5, 1953 to February 28, 1986, thus averaging 95,210 miles per year.

Oldest drivers   Layne Hall (b. December 24 or 25, 1884 or March 15, 1880) of Silver Creek, NY was issued a driver's license valid until his birthday in 1993, when, based on the birthdate on the license, he would have been 113 years old. However, he died on November 20, 1990 at age 105, according to the death certificate.

Mrs. Maude Tull of Inglewood, CA, who took up driving at age 91 after her husband died, was issued a license renewal on February 5, 1976 when she was 104.

Driving tests   The easiest tests are those in Egypt, in which the ability to drive 19.64 feet forward and the same in reverse has been deemed sufficient. In 1979, it was reported that an accurate reversing test had been added.

Mrs. Fannie Turner of Little Rock, AR passed the *written* test for drivers on her 104th attempt in October 1978.

Worst driver   It was reported that a 75-year-old male driver received 10 traffic tickets, drove on the wrong side of the road 4 times, committed 4 hit-and-run offenses and caused 6 accidents, all within 20 minutes, in McKinney, TX on October 15, 1966.

Most parking tickets   Mrs. Silvia Matos of New York City set a record for unpaid parking tickets, totaling $150,000. She collected the 2,800 tickets between 1985 and 1988, but authorities were unable to collect any money; she registered her car under 19 addresses and 36 license plates and could not be found.

SPECIALIZED VEHICLES

Largest automotive land vehicle   "Big Muskie," a 13,200 ton walking dragline (a machine that removes dirt from coal), was built by Bucyrus Erie for the Central Ohio Coal Co.'s Muskingum, OH site. It is no longer in use.

Longest land vehicle   The Arctic Snow Train, owned by Steve McPeak (U.S.), has 54 wheels and is 572 feet long. It was built by R.G. Le Tourneau, Inc. of Longview, TX for the U.S. Army. Its gross train weight is 441 tons, with a top speed of 20 MPH, and it was driven by a crew of six when used as an "overland train" for the military. It generates 4,680 shp and has a fuel capacity of 7,832 gallons.

Heaviest load   On July 14–15, 1984, John Brown Engineers & Contractors BV moved the Conoco Kotter Field production deck with a roll-out weight of 325 tons for the Continental Netherlands Oil Co. of Leidsenhage, Netherlands.

BUSES

Longest buses   The articulated DAF Super CityTrain buses of Zaire have room for a total of 350 passengers each. The buses are 105.64 feet long and weigh 32 tons empty.

Rigid   The longest rigid single bus, built by Van Hool of Belgium, is 49 feet long and carries 69 passengers.

Largest bus fleet   The 11,282 single-deck buses in São Paulo, Brazil make up the world's largest bus fleet.

Longest bus route   Operated by Expreso Internacional Ormeño S.A., the regular scheduled 6,003-mile-long service between Caracas, Venezuela and Buenos Aires, Argentina takes 214 hours, with a 12-hour stopover in Santiago, Chile and a 24-hour stopover in Lima, Peru.

United States   The longest scheduled bus route currently in use in the United States is operated by Greyhound from Chicago to San Francisco. It is 2,294 miles long and takes 51 hr. 49 min. to complete, employing seven drivers, with no change of bus.

Greatest passenger volume   The city with the greatest passenger volume in the United States as of December 1994 was New York City, with unlinked passenger trips of 605.7 million for buses and 1.31 billion for trains. In 1994, the city with the highest aggregate for passenger miles traveled was also New York City, where riders logged approximately 7 billion miles.

CAMPERS

Largest camper   In 1990, Sheik Hamad Bin Hamdan Al Nahyan of Abu Dhabi, United Arab Emirates built a 2-wheeled, 5-story vehicle measuring 66 feet long, 39 feet wide and 39 feet high. Weighing 120 tons, it has 8 bedrooms, 8 bathrooms, 4 garages and water storage for 6,340 gallons.

Longest camper journey   Harry B. Coleman and Peggy Larson covered 143,716 miles in 133 countries in a Volkswagen Camper, August 20, 1976–April 20, 1978.

Fastest camper   A Roadster camper towed by a 1990 Ford EA Falcon, driven by Charlie Kovacs, achieved 126.76 MPH at Mangalore Airfield, Seymour, Victoria, Australia on April 18, 1991.

CRAWLERS

Largest crawler   The two Marion 8-caterpillar crawlers, used for conveying spacecraft to their launch pads at Cape Canaveral, FL, each measure 131 ft. 4 in. by 114 feet. The loaded train weight is 9,000 tons.

FIRE ENGINES

Greatest pumping capacity   The fire appliance with the greatest pumping capacity is the 860-hp 8-wheel Oshkosh firetruck, which weighs 66 tons and

One of the largest crawlers moves a space shuttle.

is used for aircraft and runway fires. It can discharge 50,200 gallons of foam through two turrets in 2 min. 30 sec.

Fire pumping   The greatest gallonage stirrup-pumped by a team of eight in an 80-hour charity pump is 37,898 gallons, by firefighters at the Knaresborough Fire Station, Knaresborough, England, June 25–28, 1992.

Fire pump handling   The longest unaided tow of a fire appliance in excess of 1,120 pounds in 24 hours on a closed circuit is 223 miles, by a 32-man team from the Dublin Fire Brigade with a 1,144-pound fire pump, Dublin, Ireland, June 20–21, 1987.

GO-KARTS

Highest go-kart mileage   The highest mileage recorded in 24 hours on an outdoor circuit by a 4-man team is 1,034²/₅ miles, on a ⁴/₅-mile track in Weybridge, England on February 24–25, 1995, by Stefan Dennis, David Brabham, and Russ and Steve Malkin.

The highest mileage recorded in 24 hours on an indoor track by a 4-man team driving 160-cc karts is 883.9 miles, at the Welsh Karting Centre, Cardiff, Wales on November 26, 1993. The drivers were Ian O'Sullivan, Paul Marram, Richard Jenkins and Michael Watts.

LAWN MOWERS

Widest lawn mower The widest gang mower in the world is the 5-ton 60-foot-wide 27-unit "Big Green Machine" used by turf farmer Jay Edgar Frick of Monroe, OH. It mows an acre in 60 seconds.

Longest lawn mower drive Ian Ireland of Harlow, England drove an Iseki SG15 power lawn mower 3,034 miles between Harlow and Southend Pier, England, August 13–September 7, 1989.

ROCKET-POWERED SLEDS

Fastest speed on ice *Oxygen*, driven by Sammy Miller on Lake George, NY on February 15, 1981, reached 247.93 MPH.

SNOW PLOWS

Largest snow-plow blade A blade measuring 50¼ feet long and four feet high, with a clearing capacity of 1,095 cubic feet in one pass, was made by Aero Snow Removal Corporation of New York, NY in 1992 for operation at JFK International Airport.

SNOWMOBILES

Longest snowmobile ride John W. Outzen (U.S.) and Andre, Carl and Dennis Boucher traveled 10,252.3 miles from Anchorage, AK to Dartmouth, Nova Scotia, Canada, in 56 riding days, January 2–March 3, 1992, on four Arctic Cat Panther Deluxe Snowmobiles.

Tony Lenzini of Duluth, MN drove his 1986 Arctic Cat Cougar snowmobile a total of 7,211 miles in 60 riding days, December 28, 1985–March 20, 1986.

SOLAR-POWERED VEHICLES

Fastest solar-powered land vehicle The fastest speed attained by a solely solar-powered land vehicle is 48.71 MPH, by Molly Brennan, driving the General Motors *Sunraycer* at Mesa, AZ on June 24, 1988.

The fastest speed of 83.88 MPH using solar/battery power was achieved by Star Micronics' solar car *Solar Star*, driven by Manfred Hermann on January 5, 1991 at Richmond R.A.A.F. Base, Richmond, Australia.

TANKS

Heaviest tank The heaviest tank ever constructed was the German Panzer Kampfwagen Maus II, which weighed over 210 tons. By 1945, it had reached only the experimental stage and was not developed further.

The heaviest operational tank used by any army was the 83-ton 13-man French Char de Rupture 2C bis of 1922. It carried a 155-mm howitzer and had two 250-hp engines giving a maximum speed of 7.5 MPH.

United States The heaviest tank in the United States Army is the M1A1 Abrams, which weighs 67 tons when combat loaded, is 32 ft. 3 in. long, and can reach 41.5 MPH.

Most heavily armed tank   The most heavily armed tank is the Soviet T-72, which has a $4^7/_8$-inch high-velocity gun and is the only rocket-gun tank with explosive reactive armor.

Fastest tank   The fastest tracked armored reconnaissance vehicle is the British Scorpion, which can reach 50 MPH with a 75 percent payload.

The American experimental tank M1936, built by J. Walter Christie, was clocked at 64.3 MPH during official trials in Great Britain in 1938.

Most tanks produced   More than 50,000 of the Soviet T-54/55 series tanks were built between 1954 and 1980 in the USSR alone, with further production in the one-time Warsaw Pact countries and China.

TAXIS

Largest taxi fleet   Mexico City has a taxi fleet of 60,000 taxis, including regular taxis, communal fixed-route taxis and airport taxis.

United States   On January 1, 1994, New York City had 11,787 registered yellow medallion cabs and 40,000 licensed drivers serving an estimated 226 million passengers yearly. In addition, there are approximately 30,000 For Hire Vehicle (FHV) cabs serving out of 600 bases stationed throughout the city's five boroughs.

Most durable taxi driver   Carmen Fasanella was continuously licensed as a taxicab owner and driver in the Borough of Princeton, NJ for 68 yr. 243 days, February 1, 1921–November 2, 1989.

Longest taxicab ride   The longest taxicab ride on record is one of 21,691 miles at a cost of £40,000 (approximately $68,000). Jeremy Levine, Mark Aylett and Carlos Aresse traveled from London, England to Cape Town, South Africa and back, June 3–October 17, 1994.

TRACTORS

Largest tractor   The $459,000 U.S. Department of Agriculture Wide Tractive Frame Vehicle, completed by Ag West of Sacramento, CA in June 1982, measures 33 feet between its wheels, which are designed to run on permanent paths, and weighs 24.5 tons.

Longest tractor journey   The Young Farmers Group of Devon, England left their native country on October 18, 1990 in one tractor and supporting trailer, and drove overland to Zimbabwe, a total of 14,500 miles, arriving on March 4, 1991.

TROLLEYS

Oldest trolley   Motor cars 1 and 2 of the Manx Electric Railway date from 1893. They run regularly on the $17^3/_4$-mile railroad between Douglas and Ramsey, Isle of Man, Great Britain.

Most extensive trolley system   St. Petersburg, Russia has the most extensive trolley system, with 2,402 cars on 64 routes and 429.13 miles of track.

40 years ago the country with the greatest number of vehicles per mile of road was the United Kingdom, with 29 vehicles per mile of road, or one every 60 yards. **Today** Gibraltar has the world's highest traffic density. At the last count, in 1993, there were 767 vehicles per mile, or one every 6 ft. 10½ in.

"Whoever wrecked the most cars is a record-holder I admire. I'll probably get close to that soon."—Steffi Graf, tennis champion, July 17, 1996

Longest trolley journey The longest trolley journey now possible is from Krefeld St. Tönis to Witten Annen Nord, Germany. With luck at the eight interconnections, the 65½-mile trip can be completed in five and a half hours.

TRUCKS

Largest truck The Terex Titan 33-19 manufactured by General Motors Corporation and now in operation at Westar Mine, British Columbia, Canada has a loaded weight of 604.7 tons and a capacity of 350 tons. When tipped, its height is 56 feet. The 16-cylinder engine delivers 3,300 hp.

Most powerful truck Les Shockley of Galena, KS drove his Jet Truck *ShockWave*, powered by three Pratt & Whitney jet engines developing 36,000 hp, to a record speed of 256 MPH in 6.36 seconds over a quarter-mile from a standing start on June 4, 1989 at Autodrome de Monterrey, Mexico. He set a further record for the standing mile at 376 MPH at Paine Field, Everett, WA on August 18, 1991.

Largest tires Bridgestone Corporation of Tokyo, Japan manufactures tires measuring 12 ft. 6¼ in. in diameter for giant dump trucks.

Longest wheelie Steve Murty, driving a Pirelli High Performer, established the record for the longest wheelie in a truck, covering 1,794.9 feet in Blackpool, England on June 28, 1991.

WRECKERS

Most powerful wrecker The Twin City Garage and Body Shop's 22.7-ton, 36-foot-long International M6-23 "Hulk" 1969 is stationed at Scott City, MO. It can lift in excess of 325 tons on its short boom.

SERVICES

Largest filling station   There are 204 pumps—96 Tokheim Unistar and 108 Tokheim Explorer—in Jeddah, Saudi Arabia.

Highest filling station   The highest filling station in the world is at Leh, Ladakh, India, at 12,001 feet, operated by the Indian Oil Corporation.

Largest garage   The largest private garage is one of two stories built outside Bombay, India for the private collection of 176 cars owned by Pranlal Bhogilal.

The KMB Overhaul Center, operated by the Kowloon Motor Bus Co. (1933) Ltd., Hong Kong, is the world's largest multistory service center. Built expressly for double-decker buses, it has four floors occupying more than 11.6 acres.

Largest parking lot   The lot in the West Edmonton Mall, Edmonton, Alberta, Canada can hold 20,000 vehicles, and there are overflow facilities for 10,000 more cars.

Longest tow   Great Britain's Automobile Association used a Land Rover to tow a replica Model T Ford van 4,995 miles, starting in Ascot, England on May 4, 1993 and ending up in Widmerpool, England on May 12, 1993.

ROADS

Greatest length of road   The United States has more miles of road than any other country, with 3,906,544 miles of graded road. The state with the most miles of road is Texas, with 294,491 miles, while Hawaii has the fewest, with 4,106 miles.

Longest driveable road   The Pan-American Highway, from northwest Alaska to Santiago, Chile, then eastward to Buenos Aires, Argentina and terminating in Brasilia, Brazil, is over 15,000 miles long. There is, however, a small incomplete section in Panama and Colombia known as the Darién Gap.

United States   The longest highway solely in the United States is US-20, which runs 3,370 miles from Boston, MA to Newport, OR. The longest highway in the interstate system is I-90, 3,107 miles from Boston, MA to Seattle, WA.

Worst exit to miss   The longest distance between controlled access exits in the United States is 51.1 miles from Florida Turnpike exit 193 (Yeehaw Junction, FL) to exit 242 (Kissimmee, FL). The longest distance on any interstate highway is 37.7 miles from I-80 exit 41 (Knolls, UT) to exit 4 (Bonneville Speedway, UT).

Highest trail   The highest trail in the world is an 8-mile stretch of the Gangdise between Khaleb and Xinji-fu, Tibet, which in two places exceeds 20,000 feet.

Highest road   The highest road in the world is Khardungla Pass in India, at an altitude of 18,640 feet. It links the town of Leh, Ladakh, with a military outpost on the Siachen Glacier in the Karakoram mountains in Kashmir.

Lowest road   The lowest road is along the Israeli shores of the Dead Sea at 1,290 feet below sea level.

Widest road   The Monumental Axis runs for 1½ miles from the Municipal Plaza to the Plaza of the Three Powers in Brasilia, the capital of Brazil. The dual 6-lane boulevard, opened in April 1960, is 820.2 feet wide.

Highest traffic volume   The most heavily traveled stretch of road is Interstate 405 (San Diego Freeway), in Orange County, CA, which has a rush-hour volume of 25,500 vehicles. This volume occurs on a 0.9-mile stretch between Garden Grove Freeway and Seal Beach Boulevard.

Highest traffic density   In 1993, Gibraltar had 767 vehicles per mile of serviceable road, giving a density of 6 ft. 10½ in. per vehicle.

Longest traffic jam   On February 16, 1980, a traffic jam stretching 109.3 miles from Lyons to Paris, France was reported. A record traffic jam was reported for 1.5 million cars crawling bumper-to-bumper over the East–West German border on April 12, 1990.

Longest street   The longest designated street in the world is Yonge Street, running north and west from Toronto, Ontario, Canada. The first stretch, completed on February 16, 1796, ran 34 miles. Its official length, now extended to Rainy River on the Ontario–Minnesota border, is 1,178.3 miles.

Narrowest street   The world's narrowest street is in the village of Ripatransone in the Marche region of Italy. It is called *Vicolo della Virilita* ("Virility Alley") and is 1 ft. 5 in. wide.

Shortest street   Elgin Street, in Bacup, England, measures just 17 feet long.

Steepest street   Baldwin Street, Dunedin, New Zealand has a maximum gradient of 1 in 1.266.

United States   The crookedest and steepest street in the United States is Lombard Street, San Francisco, CA. It has eight consecutive 90-degree turns of 20-foot radius.

BICYCLES

Longest bicycle   The longest true bicycle (i.e., without a third stabilizing wheel) was designed and built by Terry Thessman of Pahiatua, New Zealand. It measures 72 ft. 11½ long and weighs 750 pounds. It was ridden by four riders a distance of 807 feet on February 27, 1988. Turning corners proved to be a problem.

Smallest bicycle   The smallest-wheeled ridable bicycle has 0.76-inch-diameter wheels. It was ridden by its constructor, Neville Patten of Gladstone, Queensland, Australia for a distance of 13 ft. 5½ in. on March 25, 1988.

   The smallest ridable bicycle in terms of length was built by Jacques Puyoou of Pau, Pyrénées-Atlantiques, France, whose tandem is 14.1 inches long. The bicycle has been ridden by him and Madame Puyoou.

Largest bicycle   The largest bicycle as measured by the front-wheel diameter is "Frankencycle," built by Dave Moore of Rosemead, CA and first ridden by Steve Gordon of Moorpark, CA, on June 4, 1989. The wheel diameter is 10 feet and the bicycle itself is 11 ft. 2 in. high.

Largest tricycle   The Dillon Colossal Tricycle was designed by Arthur Dillon. It has rear wheels 11 feet in diameter, constructed by David Moore, and a front wheel 5 ft. 10 in. high.

Longest wheelie   Leandro Henrique Basseto set a record of 10 hr. 40 min. 8 sec. in Madaguari, Paraná, Brazil on December 2, 1990.

Underwater tricycling   A team of 32 divers pedaled a distance of 116.66 miles in 75 hr. 20 min. on a standard tricycle at Diver's Den, Santa Barbara, CA on June 16–19, 1988.

HUMAN-POWERED VEHICLES

Fastest human-powered vehicle   The world speed records for human-powered vehicles (HPVs) over a 200-meter (656.2-foot) flying start (single rider) are 65.484 MPH by Fred Markham at Mono Lake, CA on May 11, 1986 and 62.92 MPH (multiple riders) by Dave Grylls and Leigh Barczewski at the Ontario Speedway, CA, on May 4, 1980.

   The 1-hour standing start (single rider) record is held by Pat Kinch, riding *Kingcycle Bean*, averaging a speed of 46.96 MPH on September 8, 1990 at Millbrook Proving Ground, Bedford, England.

Fastest water cycle   The men's 6,562-foot (single rider) record is 12.84 MPH, by Steve Hegg in *Flying Fish* off Long Beach, CA on July 20, 1987.

UNICYCLES

Tallest unicycle   The tallest unicycle ever mastered is 101 ft. 9 in. tall. It was ridden by Steve McPeak (with a safety wire suspended by an overhead crane) for a distance of 376 feet in Las Vegas, NV in October 1980.

Smallest unicycle   Peter Rosendahl (Sweden) rode an 8-inch-high unicycle with a wheel diameter of 0.78 inches, with no attachments or extensions fitted, a distance of 7 ft. 2 in. in Hamburg, Germany on December 14, 1995.

One hundred miles   Takayuki Koike of Kanagawa, Japan set a unicycle record for 100 miles of 6 hr. 44 min. 21.84 sec. on August 9, 1987 (average speed 14.83 MPH).

Akira Matsushima on his record-breaking unicycle ride.

Longest unicycle journey   Akira Matsushima (Japan) unicycled 3,261 miles from Newport, OR to Washington, D.C. from July 10 to August 22, 1992.

Unicycling backwards   Ashrita Furman (U.S.) rode backwards for a distance of 53 miles 300 yards at Forest Park, Queens, NY on September 16, 1994.

Fastest unicycle sprint   Peter Rosendahl set a sprint record for 100 meters (328.1 feet) of 12.11 seconds (18.47 MPH) in Las Vegas, NV on March 25, 1994.

MOTORCYCLES

In January 1993, it was estimated that there were 4,001,000 registered motorcycles in the United States.

Longest motorcycle Gregg Reid of Atlanta, GA designed and built a Yamaha 250-cc motorcycle that measures 15 ft. 6 in. long and weighs 520 pounds. It is street legal and has been insured.

Smallest motorcycle Simon Timperley and Clive Williams of Progressive Engineering Ltd., Ashton-under-Lyne, England designed and constructed a motorcycle with a 4.25-inch wheelbase, a seat height of 3.75 inches and a wheel diameter of 0.75 inches for the front and 0.95 inches for the back. It was ridden 3.2 feet.

SPEED

Fastest speeds Dave Campos (U.S.), riding a 23-foot-long streamliner named *Easyriders*, powered by two 91-cubic-inch Ruxton Harley-Davidson engines, set AMA and FIM absolute records with an overall average of 322.150 MPH and completed the faster run at an average of 322.870 MPH on Bonneville Salt Flats, UT on July 14, 1990.

The fastest time for a single run over 440 yards from a standing start is 6.19 seconds by Tony Lang (U.S.) riding a supercharged Suzuki at Gainesville, FL in 1994.

The highest terminal velocity at the end of a 440-yard run from a standing start is 231.24 MPH, by Elmer Trett (U.S.) at Virginia Motorsports Park, Petersburg, VA, in 1994.

Fastest production road machine The 151-hp 1-liter Tu Atara Yamaha Bimota 6th edition EI has a road-tested top speed of 186.4 MPH.

RIDING

Longest scooter ride A Kinetic Honda DX 100 cc, ridden by Har Parkash Rishi, Amarjeet Singh and Navjot Chadha, covered a distance of 19,241 miles nonstop in 1,001 at Traffic Park, Pune, Maharashtra, India between April 22 and June 3, 1990.

Largest pyramid The "Schwet Ashwas" team from the Indian Military Police Corps established a record with a pyramid of 133 men on 11 motorcycles. The pyramid was held together by muscle and determination only, with no straps, harnesses or other aids. It traveled a distance of 382 yards at Bangalore, India on August 22, 1995.

Longest wheelie Yasuyuki Kudo covered 205.7 miles nonstop on the rear wheel of his Honda TLM 220 R 216-cc motorcycle at the Japan Automobile Research Institute, Tsukuba, Japan on May 5, 1991.

LONGEST MOTORCYCLE RIDE

Emilio Sciotto of Buenos Aires, Argentina rode over 456,729 miles across 214 countries from January 17, 1985 to April 2, 1995. He set off on his Honda Gold Wing, which he nicknamed "The Black Princess," with $300 and no previous travel experience. Along the way, Sciotto learned five languages, became a Muslim, and married his girlfriend in India.

Fastest wheelie The highest speed attained on a rear wheel of a motorcycle is 157.87 MPH, by Jacky Vranken (Belgium) on a Suzuki GSXR 1100 at St. Truiden Military Airfield, Belgium on November 8, 1992.

Wall of death The greatest endurance feat on a "wall of death" was 7 hr. 0 min. 13 sec., by Martin Blume, Berlin, Germany on April 16, 1983. He rode over 12,000 laps on the 33-foot-diameter wall on a Yamaha XS400, averaging 30 MPH for the 181½ miles.

Most on one machine The record for the most people on a single machine is 47, established by the Army Corps of Brasília, Brazil on a 1,200-cc Harley Davidson on December 15, 1995.

Ramp jumping The longest distance ever achieved by a motorcycle long-jumping is 251 feet, by Doug Danger on a 1991 Honda CR500 at Loudon, NH on June 22, 1991.

RAILROADING

TRAINS

Fastest train The fastest speed attained by a railed vehicle is Mach 8, by an unmanned rocket sled over the 9½-mile-long rail track at White Sands Missile Range, NM on October 5, 1982.

The fastest speed recorded on any national rail system is 320.2 MPH by the French SNCF high-speed train TGV Atlantique between Courtalain and Tours on May 18, 1990. The TGV Sud-Est was brought into service on September 27, 1981. TGV Atlantique and Nord services now run at up to 186 MPH. The fastest point-to-point schedule is between Paris and St. Pierre des Corps, near Tours. The 144 miles are covered in 55 minutes—an average of 157 MPH. The Eurostar service from London to Paris also runs at 186 MPH on the French side of the Channel. New Series 500 trains for Japan's JR West rail system are also designed to run at 186 MPH in regular service.

Fastest steam locomotive The highest speed ever ratified for a steam locomotive was 125 MPH over 1,320 feet, by the LNER 4–6–2 No. 4468 *Mallard* (later numbered 60022), which hauled seven coaches weighing 267.9 tons down Stoke Bank, near Essendine, England on July 3, 1938. Driver Joseph Duddington was at the controls with Fireman Thomas Bray. The engine suffered some damage to the middle big-end bearing.

Largest steam locomotive The largest operating steam locomotive is the 207-ton South African Railways GMA Garratt type 4-8-2+2-8-4, built between 1952 and 1954.

Most powerful steam locomotive In terms of tractive effort, the most powerful steam locomotive was No. 700, a triple-articulated or triplex 6-cylinder 2–8–8–8–4 engine built by the Baldwin Locomotive Works in 1916 for the Virginian Railway. It had a tractive force of 166,300 pounds when working compound and 199,560 pounds when working simple.

Strongest rail carrier The 36-axle "Schnabel" has a capacity of 890 tons, measures 301 ft. 10 in. long, and was built for a U.S. railroad by Krupp, Germany in March 1981.

The heaviest load ever moved on rails is the 11,971-ton Church of the Virgin Mary (built in 1548 in the village of Most, Czech Republic), which was obstructing coal operations. In October–November 1975, it was moved 2,400 feet at 0.0013 MPH over four weeks, at a cost of $17 million.

Longest and heaviest train On August 26–27, 1989, a 4½-mile-long train weighing 77,720 tons (excluding locomotives) made a run on the 3-ft.-6-in.-gauge Sishen–Saldanha railroad in South Africa. Carrying the largest number of cars ever recorded, the train consisted of 660 cars each loaded to 105 tons gross, a tank car, and a caboose. It was moved by nine 50 kV electric and seven diesel-electric locomotives distributed along the train. It traveled 535 miles in 22 hr. 40 min.

United States The longest and heaviest freight train was about four miles long. It comprised 500 coal motor cars with three 3,600-hp diesels pulling and three more in the middle; the total weight was nearly 47,040 tons. The train traveled 157 miles from Iaeger, WV to Portsmouth, OH on the Norfolk and Western Railway on November 15, 1967.

Longest passenger train A train belonging to the National Belgium Railway Company measured 1,895 yards long, consisted of 70 coaches, and had a total weight of over 3,071 tons. The train was powered by one electric locomotive and took 1 hr. 11 min. 5 sec. to complete the 38-mile journey from Ghent to Ostend on April 27, 1991.

TRACKS

Longest track The world's longest run without change of train is one of 5,777 miles on the Trans-Siberian line from Moscow to Vladivostok, Russia. There are 70 stops on the fastest regular journey, which is scheduled to take 6 days 12 hr. 45 min.

Longest straight track The Commonwealth Railways Trans-Australian line over the Nullarbor Plain, from Mile 496 between Nurina and Loongana, Western Australia to Mile 793 between Ooldea and Watson, South Australia, is 297 miles dead straight, although it is not level.

United States The longest straight track in the United States is 78.86 miles on CSX Railroad, between Wilmington and Hamlet, NC.

Widest and narrowest gauge The widest in standard use is 5 ft. 6 in. This width is used in Spain, Portugal, India, Pakistan, Bangladesh, Sri Lanka, Argentina and Chile. The narrowest gauge on which public services are operated is 10¼ inches on the Wells Harbor (0.7 miles) and Wells–Walsingham Railways (four miles) in Norfolk, England.

Highest line At 15,806 feet above sea level, the standard gauge (4 ft. 8½ in.) track on the Morococha branch of the Peruvian State Railways at La Cima is the highest in the world.

Lowest line The Seikan Tunnel, which crosses the Tsugaro Strait between Honshu and Hokkaido, Japan, reaches a depth of 786 feet below sea level. The tunnel was opened on March 13, 1988 and is 33.46 miles long.

Steepest railway The Katoomba Scenic Railway in the Blue Mountains of New South Wales, Australia is 1,020 feet long, with a gradient of 1 in 0.82. A 220-hp electric winding machine hauls the car by twin steel cables of ⅞-inch diameter. The ride takes 1 min. 40 sec., and the railway carries about 420,000 passengers a year.

Greatest length of railroad As of 1994, the United States had 168,776 miles of road (route miles) operated for all classes of track. There were 123,335 miles of class I track (freight only) and 45,441 miles of non-class I track operated. There was a total of 183,685 miles of track owned by class I railroads, including sidings and yards.

Steepest gradient The world's steepest gradient worked by adhesion is 1 in 11, between Chedde and Servoz on the meter-gauge SNCF Chamonix line, France.

Busiest system The railroad carrying the largest number of passengers is the East Japan Railway Co., which in 1994 carried 16,600,000 passengers daily, providing it with a revenue of $19.5 billion.

Spike driving In the World Championship Professional Spike Driving Competition, held at the Golden Spike National Historic Site in Utah, Dale C. Jones, 49, of Lehi, UT, drove six 7-inch railroad spikes in a time of 26.4 seconds on August 11, 1984. He incurred no penalty points under the official rules.

TRAIN TRAVEL

Most countries in 24 hours The greatest number of countries traveled through entirely by train in 24 hours is 11, by Alison Bailey, Ian Bailey, John English and David Kellie, May 1–2, 1993. Their journey started in Hungary and continued through Slovakia, the Czech Republic, Austria, Germany, back into Austria, Liechtenstein, Switzerland, France, Luxembourg, Belgium and the Netherlands, where they arrived 22 hr. 10 min. after setting off.

Most miles traveled John E. Ballenger of Dunedin, FL logged 76,485 miles of unduplicated rail routes in North and South America.

United States H. Frank Martin of Muscatine, IA traveled 22,857 unduplicated miles on Amtrak, May 13–June 13, 1994.

Most miles in one week Andrew Kingsmell and Sean Andrews of Bromley, England and Graham Bardouleau of Crawley, England traveled 13,105 miles on the French National Railway System in 6 days 22 hr. 38 min., November 28–December 5, 1992.

Fastest handpumped railcars A speed of 20.58 MPH for a 984-foot course was achieved by a 5-man team (one pusher, four pumpers) at Rolvenden, England, August 21, 1989, recording a time of 32.61 seconds.

STATIONS

Highest station Condor Station in Bolivia is situated at 15,705 feet on the meter-gauge Rio Mulato-to-Potosi line.

Largest waiting rooms The four waiting rooms in Beijing Station, Chang'an Boulevard, Beijing, China, which were opened in September 1959, have a total standing capacity of 14,000.

Longest railroad platform The Kharagpur platform in West Bengal, India measures 2,733 feet long.

Largest freight yard Bailey Yard in North Platte, NE covers 2,850 acres and has 260 miles of track. It handles an average of 108 trains and some 8,500 freight cars every day.

SUBWAY SYSTEMS

Most extensive subway system   The most extensive underground or rapid transit railway system in the world is the London Underground, England, with 244 miles of route, of which 86 miles is bored tunnel and 20 miles is "cut and cover." The whole system is operated by a staff of 14,000; there are 267 stations, and 3,985 cars form a fleet of 547 trains. Passengers made 764 million journeys in 1994–95.

Most stations   The subway with the most stations is the Metropolitan Transportation Authority/New York City Transportation Authority subway. There are 468 stations in a network that covers 238 route miles. It serves an estimated 7.1 million passengers per day.

Traveling the New York subway   The record time for traveling the whole system is 26 hr. 21 min. 08 sec., set by Kevin Foster (U.S.), October 25–26, 1989.

Busiest subway system   Greater Moscow Metro (opened 1935) in Russia had as many as 3.3 billion passenger journeys per year at its peak, but the figure has now declined to 3.2 billion. It has 4,143 railcars, 158 stations and 158.9 miles of track.

Longest subway platform   The State Street Center subway platform on "The Loop" in Chicago, IL measures 3,500 feet long.

Worst subway disaster   The worst subway accident in the United States occurred on November 1, 1918, in Brooklyn, NY, when a BRT Line train derailed on a curve on Malbone St. in the Brighton Beach section. There were 97 fatalities on the scene, and five more people died later from injuries sustained in the crash. The BRT line went bankrupt on December 31, 1918 as a result of the tragedy.

E. VIRGIL CONWAY

Each year hundreds of thousands tour New York City. They spend their visits zipping around from one record-breaking site or event to another. What makes this zipping possible? The Metropolitan Transit Authority (MTA). The MTA operates two of the city's record holders: Grand Central Station, the world's largest train station, and the New York City Subway, the system with the most stations. One person oversees this mass of mass transit: E. Virgil Conway, the chairman of the MTA.

"I believe in using the system myself. I live in Bronxville and take the train into Grand Central," he says. "When I go downtown to City Hall, I take the subway." Metro-North Railroad runs Grand Central Station and the New York Transit Authority operates the subway. "There's a unity to the general operation, but the individual operations require different ex-

pertise," explains Conway. Grand Central Station is undergoing an extensive restoration project that Conway follows closely. "Grand Central Station is a symbol of the vigor and vitality of our city. This project will restore the grandeur it had when originally built."

The subway is not known for its grandeur, but Conway staunchly defends the maligned system: "The subway system is much changed. The trains are air-conditioned, they're graffiti-free and the crime rate has dropped." He adds, "It's the fastest way to get from one part of the city to another."

Conway is also a firm believer in public service. He accepts no salary for his job, an appointed position. "I was a banker for a lot of my career but have always had a public service job of one sort or another," he says. And does the chairman want to try for the Guinness subway riding record? "No," he says. "My overriding goal is to provide safe and secure transportation to five million New Yorkers each day."

AIRCRAFT AND FLIGHT

AIRCRAFT

Largest wingspan The Hughes H4 Hercules flying boat (*Spruce Goose*) had a wingspan of 319 ft. 11 in. and measured 218 ft. 8 in. long. The 8-engined 213-ton aircraft was raised 70 feet into the air in a test run of 3,000 feet, piloted by Howard Hughes, off Long Beach Harbor, CA, on November 2, 1947, but after this it never flew again.

Among current aircraft, the Ukrainian Antonov An-124 has a span of 240 ft. 5³⁄₄ in. The U.S.A.F. C-5B cargo plane has a wingspan of 222 ft. 8¹⁄₂ in., which is the greatest for any United States military aircraft.

Heaviest aircraft The Ukrainian Antonov An-225 *Mriya* has the highest standard maximum takeoff weight, at 661 tons (1,322,750 pounds). This aircraft lifted a payload of 344,582 pounds to a height of 40,715 feet on March 22, 1989. The flight was achieved by Capt. Aleksandr Galunenko and his crew of seven pilots.

Most capacious aircraft The Aero Spacelines Super Guppy, a converted Boeing C-97, has a cargo hold with a usable volume of 49,790 cubic feet and a maximum takeoff weight of 87.5 tons. Its wingspan is 156 ft. 3 in. and its length 141 ft. 3 in. Its cargo compartment is 108 ft. 10 in. long with a cylindrical section 25 feet in diameter.

Heaviest commercial cargo Ukrainian aircraft designer Antonov and British charter company Air Foyle carried out the heaviest commercial air cargo movement, by taking three transformers weighing 47.4 tons each and other equipment from Barcelona, Spain to Nouméa, New Caledonia (Pacific), January 10–14, 1991. The total weight carried in the An-124 *Ruslan* was 154.3 tons.

Air Foyle and Antonov also set the record for carrying the heaviest single piece of cargo, by flying a 136.7-ton power plant generator from Düsseldorf, Germany to New Delhi, India on September 22, 1993. Again, the aircraft used was the Ukrainian An-124 *Ruslan*. Because of the huge weight, the plane had to make six refueling stops during the 5,600-mile flight.

Smallest aircraft The smallest biplane ever flown was the *Bumble Bee Two*, designed and built by Robert H. Starr of Arizona. It was 8 ft. 10 in. long, with a wingspan of 5 ft. 6 in., and weighed 396 pounds empty. The fastest speed it attained was 190 MPH. On May 8, 1988, after flying to a height of approximately 400 feet, it crashed, and was totally destroyed.

Bombers Heaviest The former Soviet 4-jet Tupolev Tu-160 has a maximum takeoff weight of over 600,270 pounds.

Longest The Boeing B-52G is the longest bomber in the U.S.A.F. at 160 ft. 11 in. The B-52H has the greatest thrust of a bomber in the U.S. fleet, at 136,000 pounds, and the greatest unrefueled range of over 8,800 miles.

The B-52 is the longest bomber in the U.S.A.F.

Fastest The world's fastest operational bombers include the French Dassault Mirage IV, which can fly at Mach 2.2 at 36,000 feet.

The American variable-geometry or "swing-wing" General Dynamics FB-111A has a maximum speed of Mach 2.5, and the Soviet swing-wing Tupolev Tu-22M has an estimated over-target speed of Mach 2.0 but could be as fast as Mach 2.5.

Fastest time to refuel The Sky Harbor Air Service line crew refueled a 1975 Cessna 310 (N29HH) with 102.7 gallons of 100 octane avgas in 3 min. 42 sec. on July 5, 1992. The plane had landed at Cheyenne Airport in Wyoming during an around-the-world air race.

Largest aircraft manufacturer The world's largest aerospace company is Boeing of Seattle, WA, with 1994 sales of $21.9 billion and a workforce of 115,000 people worldwide. Cessna Aircraft Company of Wichita, KS has manufactured the most aircraft, with 178,000 since 1911.

AIRLINERS

Oldest jet airliner According to the British-based aviation information and consultancy service company Airclaims, the oldest jet airliner still flying is a Boeing 707-138 currently in operation with the Royal Saudi Arabian Air Force. It was completed on February 11, 1959 and delivered to Qantas; Saudi Arabia acquired the airliner in 1987.

Largest jet airliner The highest capacity jet airliner is the Boeing 747-400, which entered service with Northwest Airlines on January 31, 1989. It has a wingspan of 213 feet, a range of 8,290 miles and can carry up to 566 passengers. The original Boeing 747-100 "Jumbo Jet" has a capacity of 385–560 and cruises at a speed of 640 MPH. Its wingspan is 195 ft. 8 in. and its length 231 ft. 10 in. The plane entered service in January 1970.

Greatest passenger load The greatest passenger load carried by any single commercial airliner was 1,088 during *Operation Solomon*, which began on May 24, 1991 when Ethiopian Jews were evacuated from Addis Ababa to Israel on a Boeing 747 belonging to El Al airline. This figure includes two babies born during the flight.

Most flights by a propeller-driven airliner General Dynamics (formerly Convair) reported in March 1994 that some of its CV-580 turboprop airliners had logged over 150,000 flights, typically averaging no more than 20 minutes, in short-haul operations.

Most flights by a jet airliner A McDonnell Douglas DC-9 Series 14 had made 100,746 flights by February 1, 1996. It was originally delivered to Delta Airlines in September 1966 and is currently in service with Northwest Airlines.

The most hours recorded by a jet airliner still in service is 99,825 hours reported for a Boeing 747-200F on March 1, 1996. The aircraft was delivered to Lufthansa in March 1972 and is now in service with Korean Air.

The Boeing 747 is the largest jet airliner.

HELICOPTERS

Fastest helicopter Under FAI rules, the world's speed record for helicopters was set by John Trevor Eggington with co-pilot Derek J. Clews, who averaged 249.09 MPH over Somerset, England on August 11, 1986 in a Westland Lynx company demonstrator helicopter.

Largest helicopter The former Soviet Mil Mi-12 was powered by four 6,500-hp turboshaft engines and had a span of 219 ft. 10 in. over its rotor tips, with a length of 121 ft. 4½ in. It weighed 114 tons. The aircraft was demonstrated at the Paris Air Show but never entered formal service.

The largest rotorcraft was the Piasecki Heli-Stat, which used four Sikorsky S-58 airframes attached to a Goodyear ZPG-2 airship. Powered by four

1,525-hp piston engines, it was 343 feet long, 111 feet high and 149 feet wide.

Smallest helicopter   The single-seat Seremet WS-8 ultralight helicopter was built in Denmark in 1976. It had a a rotor diameter of 14 ft. 9 in. and an empty weight of 117 pounds.

Highest helicopter altitude   Jean Boulet flew an Aérospatiale SA315B Lama at 40,820 feet over Istres, France on June 21, 1972.

Longest hover   Doug Daigle, Brian Watts and Dave Meyer of Tridair Helicopters, together with Rod Anderson of Helistream, Inc. of California, maintained a continuous hovering flight in a 1947 Bell 47B model for 50 hr. 50 sec. from December 13 to December 15, 1989.

Greatest load lifted   On February 3, 1982 at Podmoscovnoe in the USSR, a Mil Mi-26 heavy-lift helicopter, crewed by G.V. Alfeurov and L.A. Indeyev, lifted a mass of 62.58 tons to a height of 6,560 feet.

Longest helicopter flight   Under FAI rules, the record for the longest unrefueled nonstop flight was set by Robert Ferry, flying a Hughes YOH-6A, over a distance of 2,213.1 miles from Culver City, CA to Ormond Beach, FL in April 1966.

Fastest helicopter circumnavigation   Ron Bower (U.S.) flew around the world in his Bell 206B-3 JetRanger III helicopter in 24 days 4 hr. 36 min. 24 sec. Bower left from Fort Worth, TX on June 28, 1994, flying eastward, and arrived back in Fort Worth on July 22 after a journey involving 85 stops.

AIRLINES

Oldest airline   Koninklijke-Luchtvaart-Maatschappij NV (KLM), the national airline of the Netherlands, was established on October 7, 1919. It opened its first scheduled service (Amsterdam–London, England) on May 17, 1920.

KLM, established in 1919, is the oldest airline.

TIPS

from the
RECORD BREAKERS

FASTEST HELICOPTER CIRCUMNAVIGATION

Helicopter industry executive and veteran pilot Ron Bower set the circumnavigation speed mark in 1994. The trip took eight months of planning and 24 days of flying. He offers these tips to aspiring record-breaking pilots.

◆

Make a commitment.

Travel requires planning; circumnavigation requires commitment to the plan. "Plan your work and work your plan," says Bower. Hundreds of tasks are involved. Visas, supplies, fuel, maintenance backup and maps have to be obtained for each leg of the trip.

◆

Utilize new resources.

"Political and technological changes enabled me to break the '82 record," says Bower. He was able to fly across Russia and use Global Positioning Satellite navigation systems. "There's always opportunity in change. I looked for change and took advantage of it."

◆

Minimize risk.

Bad weather, barren landscapes and ocean crossings are just a sampling of the hazards. "Team building is important to minimizing risks." Bower adds, "I had a dedicated group of sponsors and co-participants providing support along the route." He carried quipment for every emergency: rafts, clothing, tools, spare parts—and, over Russia, an interpreter. The Bell 206 JetRanger itself had only one modification: a larger fuel tank.

Chalk's International Airline has been flying amphibious planes from Miami, FL to the Bahamas since July 1919. The founder, Albert "Pappy" Chalk, flew from 1911 to 1975.

Largest airline   The Russian state airline Aeroflot was instituted on February 9, 1923. In its last complete year of formal existence (1990) it employed 600,000 people (more than the top 18 U.S. airlines put together) and flew 139 million passengers, with 20,000 pilots, along 620,000 miles of domestic routes.

Since the breakup of the Soviet Union, the company that carries the greatest number of passengers is Delta Air Lines, with 89,992,109 in 1995. The German airline Lufthansa has the longest route network, covering 546,399 miles.

Busiest airline system   The country with the busiest airline system is the United States, where the total number of passengers for air carriers in scheduled domestic operations exceeded 498.6 million in 1995.

Busiest international route   The city-pair with the highest international scheduled passenger traffic is London/Paris. More than 3.3 million passengers fly between the two cities annually. The busiest intercontinental route is London/New York, with more than 2.3 million passengers flying between the two cities annually.

AIRPORTS

Largest airport   The King Khalid International Airport, Riyadh, Saudi Arabia covers 87 square miles (55,040 acres).
Terminal   The terminal at Hartsfield International Airport, Atlanta, GA has floor space covering 5.7 million square feet (approximately 131 acres) and is still expanding.

In 1995, the terminal serviced 57,734,755 passengers, although it has a capacity for 70 million.

The Hajj Terminal at the King Abdul-Aziz Airport near Jeddah, Saudi Arabia is the world's largest roofed structure, covering 370 acres.

Busiest airport   O'Hare International Airport, Chicago, IL had a total of 67,253,358 passengers and 892,330 operations in 1995. This represents, on average, a takeoff or landing every 35 seconds.

BAA Heathrow, London, England handles more international traffic than any other airport, with 46,810,000 international passengers in 1995, but, including domestic flights, it is only the fourth busiest airport overall (see LARGEST AIRPORT).

Bien Hoa Air Base, South Vietnam, handled 1,019,437 takeoffs and landings in 1970.

Largest heliport   The heliport at Morgan City, LA, owned and operated by Petroleum Helicopter Inc., is one of a string used by helicopters flying energy-related offshore operations into the Gulf of Mexico. The heliport is spread over 52 acres and has pads for 48 helicopters.

The world's largest helipad was at An Khe, South Vietnam, during the Vietnam war. It covered an area of $1\frac{1}{4}$ by $1\frac{3}{4}$ miles and could accommodate 434 helicopters.

TIPS

from the
RECORD BREAKERS

AIRSICKNESS BAG COLLECTION

*Marketing and investment consultant Niek Vermeulen has
2,112 airline airsickness bags from 470 different airlines and
heads a list of over 50 serious collectors. Vermeulen guards
his sources, but did agree to throw up a few tips for Guinness.*

◆

Network.

Collecting airline memorabilia, such as wing pins, is a
popular hobby. "I can't fly every airline, so I attend aviation
shows and trade with other collectors," says Vermeulen.
Having well-traveled friends also helps. "I have friends who
fly all over the world. They always get bags for me."

◆

Remember that it's only a hobby.

"My bags are not stamps. Do not expect to gain monetary
value," says Vermeulen. What about unusual designs?
"Tellair's bag has a connect-the-dots drawing of William Tell.
Air Afrique's has a lovely sketch of a native hut." He even has
a bag from Mount Everest Air. "A friend sent me that one,"
he says.

◆

Aim high.

"There are a lot of airlines out there. Russia currently has 400
registered airlines," he says. There is plenty of competition. "A
Czech collector closed to within 40 bags of my total. I had to
work hard to pull away again." There is one bag out of reach,
though. "I really want a space shuttle bag." He adds, "NASA
said no, it's government property."

Highest landing field   The highest is La Sa (Lhasa) Airport, Tibet, People's Republic of China, at 14,315 feet.

Highest heliport   The heliport at Sonam, on the Siachen Glacier in Kashmir, is at an altitude of 19,500 feet.

Lowest landing field   The lowest landing field is El Lisan on the east shore of the Dead Sea, 1,180 feet below sea level, but during World War II BOAC Short C-class flying boats operated from the surface of the Dead Sea at 1,292 feet below sea level.

The lowest international airport is Schiphol, Amsterdam, Netherlands, at 15 feet below sea level.

Longest runway   The runway at Edwards Air Force Base, Muroc, CA measures 37,676 feet (7.13 miles) long.

Civil   The runway at Pierre van Ryneveld Airport, Upington, South Africa is 3.04 miles long. It was constructed in five months from August 1975 to January 1976.

Largest hangar   Hangar 375 ("Big Texas") at Kelly Air Force Base, San Antonio, TX has four doors each 250 feet wide, 60 feet high, and weighing 681 tons. The high bay is 2,000 by 300 by 90 feet in area and is surrounded by a 44-acre concrete apron. It is the largest freestanding hangar in the world.

Tallest control tower   The tower at Denver International Airport, Denver, CO is 327 feet tall, giving air traffic controllers a 3-mile view.

SCHEDULED FLIGHTS

Longest scheduled flight   The longest nonstop scheduled flight currently operating is the 7,968-mile flight from New York to Johannesburg on South African Airways.

In terms of time taken, the longest is 15 hr. 10 min. for the flight from Osaka to Istanbul on Turkish Airlines.

Shortest scheduled flight   Using Britten-Norman Islander twin-engined 10-seat transports, Loganair has been flying between the Orkney Islands of Westray and Papa Westray, Great Britain since September 1967. The check-in time for the 2-minute flight is 20 minutes.

Fastest circumnavigation   The fastest time for a circumnavigation on scheduled flights is 44 hr. 6 min., by David J. Springbett of Taplow, England, January 8–10, 1980. His route took him from Los Angeles, CA eastwards via London, Bahrain, Singapore, Bangkok, Manila, Tokyo and Honolulu, over a 23,069-mile course. A minimum distance of 22,858.8 miles (the length of the Tropic of Cancer or Capricorn) must be flown.

Antipodal points   David Sole of Edinburgh, Scotland traveled around the world on scheduled flights, taking in exact antipodal points, in 64 hr. 2 min., May 2–5, 1995. Leaving from London Heathrow, he flew to Madrid,

Spain, back to Heathrow, and then to Napier, New Zealand via Singapore and Auckland. From Napier he went by helicopter to Ti Tree Point, the point exactly opposite Madrid Airport on the other side of the world. Returning to London via Los Angeles, Sole traveled a total distance of 25,917 miles.

Brother Michael Bartlett of Sandy, England achieved a record time for flying around the world on scheduled flights, but just taking in the airports closest to antipodal points, when he flew via Shanghai, China and Buenos Aires, Argentina in a time of 58 hr. 44 min. He started and finished at Zürich, Switzerland and traveled a distance of 25,816 miles, February 13–16, 1995.

Most flights in 24 hours Brother Michael Bartlett made 42 scheduled passenger flights with Heli Transport of Nice, France between Nice, Sophia Antipolis, Monaco and Cannes in 13 hr. 33 min. on June 13, 1990.

SPEED

Official airspeed record Capt. Eldon W. Joersz and Major George T. Morgan, Jr. flew at 2,193.2 MPH in a Lockheed SR-71A "Blackbird" near Beale Air Force Base, CA over a 15½-mile course on July 28, 1976.

Fastest fixed-wing aircraft The U.S. North American Aviation X-15A-2, powered by a liquid oxygen and ammonia rocket-propulsion system, flew for the first time (after modification from the X-15A) on June 25, 1964. The landing speed was 242 MPH. The fastest speed attained was Mach 6.7, by Major William J. Knight (U.S.A.F.) on October 3, 1967.

The space shuttle *Columbia*, commanded by Capt. John W. Young (U.S.N.) and piloted by Capt. Robert L. Crippen (U.S.N.), was launched from the Kennedy Space Center, Cape Canaveral, FL on April 12, 1981. *Columbia* broke all records in space by a fixed-wing craft, with 16,600 MPH at main engine cutoff. After reentry from 75.8 miles, experiencing temperatures of 3,920°F, it glided home weighing 107 tons, and with a landing speed of 216 MPH, on Rogers Dry Lake, CA on April 14, 1981.

Fastest jet The U.S.A.F. Lockheed SR-71, a reconnaissance aircraft, was first flown in its definitive form on December 22, 1964. It has an altitude ceiling of 85,000 feet, and its reported range at Mach 3 is 2,982 miles at 78,750 feet.

Fastest airliner The Tupolev Tu-144, first flown on December 31, 1968, was reported to have reached Mach 2.4, but normal cruising speed was Mach 2.2. Scheduled services began on December 26, 1975, flying freight and mail.

The supersonic BAC/Aérospatiale Concorde, first flown on March 2, 1969, cruises at up to Mach 2.2 and became the first supersonic airliner used in passenger service on January 21, 1976. The New York–London, England record is 2 hr. 54 min. 30 sec., set on April 14, 1990.

Fastest biplane The fastest is the Italian Fiat CR42B, with a 1,010-hp Daimler-Benz DB601A engine, which attained 323 MPH in 1941. Only one was built.

Fastest piston-engined aircraft On August 21, 1989, in Las Vegas, NV, the *Rare Bear*, a modified Grumman Bearcat F8F piloted by Lyle Shelton, set the FAI-approved world record for a 3-km run of 528.3 MPH.

Fastest propeller-driven aircraft The fastest propeller-driven aircraft in use is the former Soviet Tu-95/142 "Bear" with four 14,795-hp engines driving 8-blade counter-rotating propellers with a maximum level speed of Mach 0.82.

Fastest coast-to-coast flight The record aircraft time from coast to coast is 67 min. 54 sec. by Lt. Col. Ed Yeilding, pilot, and Lt. Col. J. T. Vida, reconnaissance systems officer, aboard the SR-71 Blackbird spy plane on March 6, 1990. The Blackbird refueled over the Pacific Ocean at 27,000 feet before starting a climb to 83,000 feet, heading east from the west coast near Los Angeles and crossing the east coast near Washington. D.C.

Fastest transatlantic flight Major James V. Sullivan (U.S.) and Major Noel F. Widdifield (U.S.) flew eastwards across the Atlantic in 1 hr. 54 min. 56.4 sec. in a Lockheed SR-71A Blackbird on September 1, 1974. The average speed, slowed by refueling from a KC-135 tanker aircraft, for the New York–London stage of 3,461.53 miles was 1,806.96 MPH.

Solo On March 12, 1978, Capt. John J.A. Smith flew from Gander, Newfoundland, Canada to Gatwick, London, England in 8 hr. 47 min. 32 sec., in a Rockwell Commander 685 twin-turboprop. He achieved an average speed of 265.1 MPH.

Fastest London–New York flight The record time from central London, England to downtown New York City by helicopter and Concorde is 3 hr. 59 min. 44 sec., and for the return, 3 hr. 40 min. 40 sec., both by David J. Springbett and David Boyce, February 8–9, 1982.

Evelyn Bryan Johnson has logged more flying hours than any other woman pilot.

Fastest circumnavigational flight   The fastest flight under the FAI rules, which permit flights that exceed the length of the Tropic of Cancer or Capricorn (22,858.8 miles), was one of 31 hr. 27 min. 49 sec. by an Air France Concorde (Capt. Michel Dupont and Capt. Claude Hetru) flying east from JFK airport in New York via Toulouse, Dubai, Bangkok, Guam, Honolulu and Acapulco on August 15–16, 1995. There were 80 passengers and 18 crew on board flight AF1995.

Fastest climb   Heinz Frick of British Aerospace took a Harrier GR5 powered by a Rolls-Royce Pegasus 11-61 engine from a standing start to 39,370 feet in 2 min. 6.63 sec. above the Rolls-Royce flight test center, Filton, England on August 15, 1989.

Aleksandr Fedotov (USSR) flew a Mikoyan E 266M (MiG-25) aircraft to establish the fastest time-to-height record on May 17, 1975. He reached 114,830 feet in 4 min. 11.7 sec. after takeoff from Podmoscovnoe, Russia.

United States   The fastest time-to-height record for a United States aircraft is to 62,000 feet in 2 min. 2.94 sec., by Major Roger J. Smith (U.S.A.F.), in an F-15 Eagle on January 19, 1975.

DURATION RECORDS

Longest nonservice flight   The longest flight on record is 64 days 22 hr. 19 min. 5 sec., by Robert Timm and John Cook in the Cessna 172 *Hacienda*. They took off from McCarran Airfield, Las Vegas, NV just before 3:53 P.M. local time on December 4, 1958 and landed at the same airfield just before 2:12 P.M. on February 7, 1959. They covered a distance equivalent to six times around the world, being refueled without any landings.

The longest nonstop flight by a commercial airliner was one of 10,008 nautical miles (11,523 miles) from Auckland, New Zealand to Le Bourget, Paris, France in 21 hr. 46 min., June 17–18, 1993 by the Airbus Industrie A340–200. It was the return leg of a flight that had started at Le Bourget the previous day.

PERSONAL AVIATION RECORDS

Oldest and youngest passengers   Airborne births are reported every year. The oldest person to fly was Mrs. Jessica S. Swift (b. Anna Stewart), who was 110 yr. 3 mo. old when she flew from Vermont to Florida in December 1981.

Oldest pilot   Col. Clarence Cornish (b. November 10, 1898) of Indianapolis, IN flew a Cessna 172 on August 16, 1995, when he was 96 years old. His first flight was on May 6, 1918 and his first solo flight 21 days later.

Circumnavigation   Strict circumnavigation of the globe requires the aircraft to pass through two antipodal points, covering a minimum distance of 24,859.73 miles. Fred Lasby completed a solo around-the-world flight at age 82 in his single-engined Piper Comanche. He left Fort Meyers, FL on June 30, 1994, flew 23,218 miles with 21 stops, and arrived back in Fort Meyers on August 20, 1994.

Most flying hours Pilot John Edward Long (U.S.) logged 61,510 hours of flight time as a pilot between May 1933 and April, 1996. This adds up to more than seven years.

Evelyn Bryan Johnson, manager of Moore Murrell Airport, Morristown, TN, logged the women's record of 54,600 hours in flight as a pilot and flight instructor, 1945–95.

David Huxley pulls a 747-400.

Passenger   The record for a supersonic passenger is held by Fred Finn, who has made 707 Atlantic crossings on Concorde. He commutes regularly from New Jersey to London, England, and had flown a total distance of 11,023,000 miles by the end of March 1995.

Most planes flown   Capt. Eric Brown (January 21, 1919–   ) has flown 487 different basic types of aircraft as a command pilot. A World War II fighter pilot, he became chief naval test pilot at the Royal Aircraft Establishment in Farnborough, England and is Britain's leading test pilot of carrier-based aircraft.

United States   James B. Taylor, Jr. (1897–1942) flew 461 different types of aircraft during his 25 years as a test and demonstration pilot for the U.S. Navy and a number of aircraft manufacturers.

Most transatlantic flights   Between March 1948 and his retirement on September 1, 1984, Flight Service Manager Charles M. Schimpf logged a total of 2,880 Atlantic crossings.

Longest-serving flight attendant   Juanita Carmichael has been a flight attendant on American Airlines since July 10, 1944.

Most experienced passenger   Edwin A. Shackleton of Bristol, England has been a passenger in 572 different types of aircraft. His first flight was in March 1943 in D.H. Dominie R9548; other aircraft have included helicopters, gliders, microlights, and balloons.

Plane pulling   David Huxley single-handedly pulled a Qantas Boeing 747-400 weighing 206 tons a distance of 179 ft. 6 in. across the tarmac at Sydney Airport, Australia on April 2, 1996.

Sixty people pulled a 226-ton British Airways Boeing 747 328 feet in 61.0 seconds at Heathrow Airport, London, England, May 25, 1995.

Wing walking   Roy Castle flew on the wing of a Boeing Stearman airplane for 3 hr. 23 min. on August 2, 1990, from Gatwick, England to Le Bourget, near Paris, France.

AIRSHIPS

Largest airship   The 235-ton German *Hindenburg* (LZ 129) and its sister ship *Graf Zeppelin II* (LZ 130) each had a length of 803 ft. 10 in. and a capacity of 7,062,100 cubic feet. The *Hindenburg* first flew in 1936 and the *Graf Zeppelin II* in 1938.

Nonrigid   The largest nonrigid airship ever constructed was the U.S. Navy ZPG 3-W, which had a capacity of 1.5 million cubic feet, a length of 403 feet, a diameter of 85.1 feet and a crew of 21. It first flew in 1958 but crashed into the sea in 1960.

Longest flight   The longest recorded flight by an airship (without refueling) is 264 hr. 12 min. by a U.S. Navy Goodyear-built ZPG-2 class ship (Cdr. J.R. Hunt, U.S.N.) that flew 9,448 miles, leaving from South Weymouth Naval Air Station, MA on March 4, 1957 and landing in Key West, FL, on March 15.

The FAI-accredited straight-line distance record for airships is 3,967.1 miles, set by the German *Graf Zeppelin* LZ 127, captained by Dr. Hugo Eckener, October 29–November 1, 1928.

From November 21 to November 25, 1917, the German *Zeppelin* (L 59) flew from Yambol, Bulgaria to a point south of Khartoum, Sudan and returned, covering a minimum of 4,500 miles.

Greatest passenger load   The most people ever carried in an airship was 207, in the U.S. Navy *Akron* in 1931. The transatlantic record is 117, carried by the German *Hindenburg* in 1937. This airship exploded into a fireball at Lakehurst, NJ on May 6, 1937.

HELIUM BALLOONING

Longest balloon flight   The record distance traveled by a balloon is 5,435.82 miles, by Steve Fossett in a Cameron R-150 helium balloon, February 17–21, 1995. The journey started in Seoul, Korea and ended in Mendham, Saskatchewan, Canada.

Richard Abruzzo and Troy Bradley set the FAI endurance record for a gas and hot-air balloon in *Team USA*. They crossed the Atlantic Ocean from Bangor, ME to Ben Slimane, Morocco, a distance of 3,318.2 miles, in 144 hr. 16 min., September 16–22, 1992.

Highest balloon altitude Unmanned   The highest altitude attained by an unmanned balloon was 170,000 feet, by a Winzen balloon with a 47.8 million-cubic-foot capacity, launched at Chico, CA in October 27, 1972.

Manned   The highest altitude reached in a manned balloon is an unofficial 123,800 feet, by Nicholas Piantanida (1933–66) of Bricktown, NJ, from Sioux Falls, SD on February 1, 1966. He landed in a cornfield in Iowa but did not survive.

The official record (closed gondola) is 113,740 feet by Cdr. Malcolm D. Ross (U.S.N.R.) and Lt. Cdr. Victor A. Prother (U.S.N.), in an ascent from the deck of the U.S.S. *Antietam* over the Gulf of Mexico on May 4, 1961 in a balloon of 12 million-cubic-foot capacity.

Scientists Harold Froelich and Keith Lang of Minneapolis, MN made an unplanned ascent in an open gondola, without pressure suits or goggles, to an altitude of 42,126 feet on September 26, 1956.

Largest balloon   The largest balloon ever built had an inflatable volume of 70 million cubic feet and stood 1,000 feet tall. It was unmanned, and was manufactured by Winzen Research Inc. (now Winzen Engineering Inc.) of South St. Paul, Minnesota. The balloon did not get off the ground and was destroyed at launch on July 8, 1975.

HOT-AIR BALLOONING

Largest mass ascent   On August 15, 1987, 128 participants at the Ninth Bristol International Balloon Festival in Bristol, England made the greatest mass ascent of hot-air balloons from a single site within one hour.

Highest hot-air balloon ascent   Per Lindstrand (Great Britain) reached 64,997 feet in a Colt 600 hot-air balloon over Laredo, TX on June 6, 1988.

Most passengers in a balloon   The balloon *Super Maine*, with a capacity of 2.6 million cubic feet, was built by Tom Handcock of Portland, ME. Tethered, it rose to a height of 50 feet with 61 passengers on board on February 19, 1988.

Henk Brink (Netherlands) made an untethered flight, with 50 passengers and crew, in the 850,000-cubic-foot capacity *Nashua Number One* on August 17, 1988. The flight began at Lelystad Airport, Netherlands and lasted 25 minutes; the balloon reached an altitude of 328 feet.

LONGEST HOT-AIR BALLOON JOURNEY

Richard Branson (Great Britain) and his pilot, Per Lindstrand (Great Britain), crossed the Pacific in the *Virgin Otsuka Pacific Flyer* from the southern tip of Japan to Lac la Matre, Yukon, Canada, January 15–17, 1991 in a 2.6 million-cubic foot capacity hot-air balloon (the largest ever flown) to set FAI records for duration (46 hr. 15 min.) and distance (great circle 4,768 miles).

See feature (next page)

SHIPS

Oldest vessel   A pinewood dugout found in Pesse, Netherlands was dated to *c.* 6315 B.C. ± 275 years.

Oldest boat   A 27-foot-long, 2½-foot-wide wooden canoe dated to *c.* 4490 B.C. was discovered at Tybrind Vig on the Baltic island of Fünen.

Oldest paddle wheeler   The D/S *Skibladner*, built in Minnesund, Norway by the Swedish shipyard Motala Mek. Werkstad, has continuously plied Lake Mjøsa, Norway since 1856.

Oldest active sailing ship   The oldest square rigged vessel that is still seaworthy is the iron barque *Star of India*. It was built in 1863 in Ramsey, Isle of Man as a full-rigged, 1,197-ton ship, then named *Euterpe*. The vessel is

Richard Branson

Adventurer, businessman, co-pilot . . . Richard Branson is his own alphabet travel game. Roadside billboards, however, do not line the Atlantic Ocean or the jet stream—the venues for Branson's daring record-setting journeys. In 1986 his boat broke the trans-Atlantic speed mark, and a year later he set another Atlantic crossing record, piloting a hot-air balloon with Per Lindstrand. The ballooning standards set in 1987 were surpassed in 1991, when Branson teamed with Lindstrand again—this time to cross the Pacific Ocean.

"The idea of going in a balloon and just being blown about by the wind" has been a dream of Branson's since childhood. "I let a helium balloon go and watched it go beyond the horizon from my garden," he says. A distant cousin of the South Pole explorer Captain Robert Scott, Branson caught the adventure bug early in life. "My father used to take me to see Scott's boat in London. The sad thing is that most exploits have already been achieved . . . I was very fortunate to have a chance to push myself on my boating and ballooning adventures."

The first trans-Atlantic boat attempt ended when Branson and four others were rescued by helicopter; the trans-Atlantic balloon flight ditched in the Irish Sea and the Pacific flight landed 1,700 miles off-course on a frozen lake in Canada. How does Branson prepare for the risks? For the balloon flights special precautions are taken. "We had to practice skydiving in case something went wrong," he says, "and we carried equipment that would be suitable for an arctic landing or a sea landing."

The balloons themselves are record-breakers. The balloon that crossed the Atlantic was the largest ever flown at 2.3 million cubic feet capacity, but that mark was topped by the balloon used in the Pacific crossing, 2.6 million cubic feet. Branson and Lindstrand travel in specially designed pressurized capsules, rather than traditional baskets. But comfort is not a consideration on these flights: "We didn't sleep on either the Atlantic or Pacific flights."

How do you steer such an enormous balloon? "You just go the way the winds go," says Branson. "We have instruments to see where we are going and where we are." He adds, "In the Pacific the winds got stronger

and stronger. We found we were going at 270–280 MPH. That meant we crossed the Pacific twice as quickly as expected."

Branson's exploits extend beyond ballooning and boating. He is the founder and chairman of the Virgin Group, which includes Virgin Atlantic Airways. "The challenge of trying to start and build companies and motivate staff is a similar sort of challenge to ballooning. I love to push myself to the limits and see what I'm capable of. If somebody says it's impossible I like to prove them wrong. I love the pure adventure of it."

Next is a trans-global flight. "We'll be ready to launch between November and January. It's the worst time of the year, but the strongest time for the wind to take us around the world." Branson's advice to adventurers: "Don't take no for an answer. Go for it," he says. "But go for it with a smile."

now preserved as a museum ship in San Diego, CA, but makes occasional daytrips under sail.

Longest canoe   The "Snake Boat" *Nadubhagóm*, 135 feet long, from Kerala, southern India, has a crew of 109 rowers and nine "encouragers."

Heaviest wooden ship   The *Richelieu*, 333 ft. 8 in. long and weighing 9,548 tons, was launched in Toulon, France on December 3, 1873.

Longest wooden ship   The New York-built *Rochambeau* (1867–72), formerly the *Dunderberg*, measured 377 ft. 4 in. overall.

Largest human-powered ship   *Tessarakonteres*, a 3-banked catamaran galley with 4,000 rowers, built for Ptolemy IV *c.* 210 B.C. in Alexandria, Egypt, measured 420 feet, with eight men to a 57-foot oar.

Largest and most powerful tug   The *Nikolay Chiker* (SB-135) and *Fotiy Krylov* (SB-134) were commissioned in 1989 and built by Hollming Ltd. of Finland for V/O Sudoimport, in the former USSR. They have 25,000 bhp, are capable of 291 tons bollard pull at full power, and measure 325 feet long and 64 feet wide. *Fotiy Krylov* is reported to be under charter to the Tsavliris Group of Companies of Piraeus, Greece, and may for a time have been named *Tsavliris Giant*.

Most powerful icebreakers   The *Rossiya* and its sister ships *Sovetskiy Soyuz* and *Oktyabryskaya Revolutsiya* are the most powerful icebreakers in the world. The *Rossiya* weighs 28,000 tons, is 460 feet long, and is powered by 75,000 hp nuclear engines. It was built in Leningrad (now St. Petersburg), Russia and completed in 1985.

Most powerful dredger   The 468.2-foot-long *Prins der Nederlanden*, weighing 10,586 gross tons, can dredge up 22,400 tons of sand from a depth of 115 feet via two suction tubes in less than an hour.

Largest propeller   The largest propeller is a triple-bladed screw of 36 ft. 1 in. diameter made by Kawasaki Heavy Industries, Japan, and delivered on March 17, 1982 for the 233,787-ton bulk carrier *Hoei Maru* (now renamed *New Harvest*).

Largest hydrofoil   The 212-foot-long *Plainview* (346 tons full-load) naval hydrofoil was launched by the Lockheed Shipbuilding and Construction Co. at Seattle, WA on June 28, 1965. It has a service speed of 57.2 MPH.

Message in a bottle   A message in a bottle was released on the seabed 24 miles southwest of the island of Foula on June 12, 1914 by Capt. C.H. Brown of the Scottish Office Agriculture and Fisheries Department as part of a survey of currents. The bottle was found 81 years later, floating on the surface 20 miles south of Foula on August 6, 1995 by John Derudder, a Belgian fisherman.

PORTS

Largest port The Port of New York and New Jersey has a navigable waterfront of 755 miles (295 miles in New Jersey), stretching over 92 square miles, with a total berthing capacity of 391 ships at a time. The total warehouse floor space covers 422.4 acres.

Busiest port The busiest port harbor is Rotterdam, Netherlands, which covers 38 square miles, with 76 miles of quays. It handled 325 million tons of seagoing cargo in 1995.

Although the port of Hong Kong handles less tonnage than Rotterdam in total seaborne cargo, it is the world's leading containerport, and handled 12,528,692 TEUs in 1995.

United States The busiest port in the United States is South Louisiana, LA, which handled 184,855,712 short tons of cargo in 1994.

Largest dry dock With a maximum shipbuilding capacity of 1.2 million deadweight tons, the Daewoo Okpo No. 1 Dry Dock, Koje Island in South Korea measures 1,740 feet long by 430 feet wide and was completed in 1979. The dock gates, 46 feet high and 33 feet thick at the base, are the world's most massive.

The Port of New York and New Jersey is the world's largest port.

OCEAN CROSSINGS

Fastest Atlantic crossing Under the rules of the Hales Trophy, which recognizes the highest average speed rather than the shortest duration, the record is held by the 222-foot Italian powerboat *Destriero*, with an average speed of 53.09 knots between the Nantucket Light Buoy and Bishop Rock Lighthouse, Isles of Scilly, Great Britain, August 6–9, 1992, in a time of 58 hr. 34 min. 4 sec.

Fastest Pacific crossing The fastest crossing from Yokohama, Japan to Long Beach, CA—4,840 nautical miles (5,567.64 miles)—took 6 days 1 hr. 27 min. (June 30 to July 6, 1973) by the containership *Sea-Land Commerce* (56,353 tons), at an average speed of 33.27 knots (38.31 MPH).

San Francisco to Boston Richard B. Wilson and Bill Biewenga sailed from San Francisco to Boston via Cape Horn in 69 days 19 hr. 44 min. They left San Francisco in the 53-foot trimaran *Great American II* on January 27 and arrived in Boston on April 7, 1993.

Longest solo ocean row Peter Bird spent 304 days 14 hr. nonstop rowing at sea during a trans-Pacific voyage, which began on May 12, 1993 and was ended prematurely on March 12, 1994.

Fastest circumnavigation Peter Blake (New Zealand) and Robin Knox-Johnson (Great Britain) won the Jules Verne Trophy when they arrived back in France on April 1, 1994, after circling the globe nonstop in 74 days 22 hr. 17 min. in the catamaran *Enza*.

MERCHANT SHIPPING

Shipbuilding Worldwide production completed in 1995, excluding naval auxiliaries, nonpropelled vessels, the U.S. Reserve Fleet, vessels restricted to harbor or river/canal service, and vessels of less than 100 gross registered tonnage, was 22.5 million gross registered tonnage. The figures for Russia, Ukraine, the People's Republic of China and Denmark are incomplete. Japan completed 9.3 million gross registered tonnage (41 percent of the world total) in 1995.

The world's leading shipbuilder in 1995 was Hyundai Heavy Industries Co. Ltd. of South Korea, which completed 43 ships of 2.27 million gross tons.

Largest ship owner The Japanese NYK Group's fleet of owned vessels totaled 11,921,701 gross tonnage on February 1, 1995.

United States Exxon Corporation's fleets of owned/managed and chartered tankers in 1987 totaled a daily average of 10.42 million deadweight tons.

Largest fleet Panama's merchant fleet had a gross registered tonnage of 71.9 million tons at the end of 1995.

Fastest shipbuilding The fastest times in which complete ships of more than 10,000 tons were ever built were achieved at Kaiser's Yard, Portland, OR during the World War II program for building 2,742 Liberty ships. In 1942, No. 440, named *Robert E. Peary*, had its keel laid on November 8, was launched on November 12, and was operational on November 15 after 4 days 15½ hr. It was broken up in 1963.

Fastest riveting The world record for riveting is 11,209 rivets in nine hours, by John Moir at the Workman Clark Ltd. shipyard, Belfast, Northern Ireland in June 1918. His peak hour was his seventh, with 1,409 rivets, an average of nearly 23½ per minute.

CARGO VESSELS

Largest cargo vessel The largest ship carrying dry cargo is the Norwegian ore carrier *Berge Stahl*, 402,082.6 tons deadweight, built in South Korea for the Norwegian owner Sig Bergesen. It has a length of 1,125 feet, a beam measuring 208 feet and was launched on November 5, 1986.

Largest containership The *Regina Maersk* was built at Odense, Denmark and completed in January 1996. The vessel has a gross tonnage of 81,488 and a capacity of 6,000 TEU.

Largest barges The largest RoRo (roll-on, roll-off) vessels are five 730-foot-long barges operated by Crowley American Transport of Jacksonville, FL.

Largest ferry The largest car and passenger ferry is the 59,914 gross registered tonnage *Silja Europa*, which entered service in 1993 between Stockholm, Sweden and Helsinki, Finland. Operated by the Silja Line, the ferry is 662 feet long and can carry 3,000 passengers, 350 cars and 60 trucks.

Fastest ferry Built in Finland, Stena Line's HSS *Explorer* has a cruising speed of 40 knots and a top speed of 44 knots. The ferry can carry 1,500 passengers and 375 cars. The catamaran hulls are 415 feet long and 131 feet abeam.

The largest containership is the *Regina Maersk*.

PASSENGER VESSELS

Largest passenger liner The longest passenger liner ever built is the *Norway*, completed in 1960, measuring 1,035 ft. 7½ in. long, of 76,049 gross registered tonnage, and with a capacity of 2,022 passengers and 900 crew. It cruises in the Caribbean for the Royal Viking Line and is based at Miami, FL.

The largest cruise liner in service is the P&O Group's *Sun Princess*. It has a gross registered tonnage of 76,500 and a passenger capacity of 1,950. The liner was commissioned in December 1995 and built by the Fincantieri yard in Italy.

Largest riverboat The world's largest inland boat is the 382-foot *Mississippi Queen*, designed by James Gardner of London, England. The vessel was commissioned on July 25, 1976 in Cincinnati, OH and is now in service on the Mississippi River.

Largest yacht Royal The Saudi Arabian royal yacht *Abdul Aziz*, built in Denmark and completed in 1984 at Vospers Yard, Southampton, England, is 482 feet long.

Nonroyal The largest private yacht is the *Alexander*, a former ferry converted to a private yacht in 1986, at 400 feet overall.

Largest passenger hydrofoil Three 185-ton Supramar PTS 150 Mk III hydrofoils can carry 250 passengers at 40 knots across the Öre Sound between Malmö, Sweden and Copenhagen, Denmark. They were built by Westermoen Hydrofoil Ltd. of Mandal, Norway.

SAILING SHIPS

Oldest active sailing ship The oldest active sailing vessel is the *Star of India* (formerly *Euterpe*), built on the Isle of Man in 1863. It is 205 feet long, with a gross tonnage of 1318. It originally carried passengers between Great Britain and New Zealand. Today it is operated by the Maritime Museum Association of San Diego, CA.

Largest sailing ship The *France II*, weighing 5,806 gross registered tons, was launched at Bordeaux, France in 1911. The ship was a steel-hulled, 5-masted barque with a hull measuring 418 feet overall. It was wrecked off New Caledonia on July 12, 1922.

Largest in service The 357-foot-long *Sedov* was built in 1921 in Kiel, Germany. It is 48 feet wide, with a displacement of 6,944 tons, a gross registered tonnage of 3,556 and a sail area of 45,123 square feet.

Largest sails The largest spars ever carried were those in HM Battleship *Temeraire*, completed at Chatham, England on August 31, 1877 and broken up in 1921. The fore and main yards measured 115 feet long. The foresail contained 5,100 feet of canvas weighing 2.24 tons, and the total sail area was 25,000 square feet.

Tallest mast *Zeus*, an American-built sloop completed in 1994, is said to be the tallest single-masted yacht in the world. The yacht is 150 feet long and the mast is 173 feet high.

HOVERCRAFT

Fastest hovercraft The 78-foot-long 110-ton U.S. Navy test hovercraft SES-100B attained a speed of 91.9 knots (105.8 MPH) on January 25, 1980 on the Chesapeake Bay Test Range, MD.

Largest hovercraft The SRN4 Mk III, a British-built civil hovercraft, weighs 341 tons and can carry 418 passengers and 60 cars. It is 185 feet long and can travel at over 65 knots.

Longest hovercraft journey   Under the leadership of David Smithers, the British Trans-African Hovercraft Expedition traveled 5,000 miles through eight West African countries in a Winchester class SRN6, between October 15, 1969 and January 3, 1970.

Highest hovercraft   The highest altitude reached by a hovercraft was on June 11, 1990 when *Neste Enterprise* and her crew of 10 reached the navigable source of the Yangzi River, China at 16,050 feet.

SUBMARINES

Largest submarines   The Russian Typhoon class submarine is believed to have a dive displacement of 29,211 tons, to measure 562.7 feet overall and to be armed with 20 multiple warhead SS-NX-20 missiles with a range of 4,500 nautical miles. Six of these submarines are now in service.

United States   The largest submarines in the U.S. Navy are of the Ohio class. Each of the 16 ships in active service has a displacement of 18,700 tons and a length of 560 feet.

Smallest submarine   William G. Smith of Bognor Regis, England constructed a fully functional submarine 9 ft. 8 in. long, 3 ft. 9 in. wide and 4 ft. 8 in. high. It can reach depths of around 100 feet and remain underwater for four hours.

Fastest submarine   The Russian Alpha class nuclear-powered submarines had a reported maximum speed of over 40 knots, and were believed to be able to dive to 2,500 feet. It is thought that only one now remains in service, used for testing purposes.

Deepest submarine dive   The U.S. Navy deep submergence vessel *Sea Cliff* (DSV 4), 30 tons, commissioned in 1973, reached a depth of 20,000 feet in March 1985.

Longest submarine patrol   The longest submerged and unsupported patrol made public is 111 days, by HM Submarine *Warspite* in the South Atlantic, November 25, 1982–March 15, 1983.

Fastest human-powered submarine   On March 30, 1996, *SubStandard*, designed, built and crewed by William Nicoloff (U.S.), set a record for the fastest speed attained by a human-powered propeller submarine of 6.696 ± 0.06 knots (11.3 feet per second).

Nonpropeller   The fastest speed attained by a human-powered nonpropeller submarine is 2.9 ± 0.1 knots (4.88 feet per second), by *SubDUDE* on August 21, 1992. The submarine was designed by the Scripps Institution of Oceanography, University of California, San Diego.

TANKERS

Largest tanker   The largest ship of any kind is *Jahre Viking*, which weighs 622,534 tons deadweight. The tanker measures 1,504 feet long overall, with a beam of 225 ft. 11 in., and a draft of 80 ft. 9 in.

Largest wreck   The 354,041-ton deadweight very large crude carrier (VLCC) *Energy Determination* blew up and broke in two in the Strait of Hormuz, Persian Gulf on December 12, 1979.

Largest wreck removal   In 1979, Smit Tak International removed the remains of the 120,000-ton French tanker *Betelgeuse* from Bantry Bay, Republic of Ireland. The exercise took 20 months.

Most massive collision   On December 16, 1977, 22 miles off the coast of southern Africa, the tanker *Venoil* (330,954 deadweight tons) struck its sister ship *Venpet* (330,869 deadweight tons).

WARSHIPS

Largest aircraft carriers   The warships with the largest full-load displacement are the Nimitz class U.S. Navy aircraft carriers U.S.S. *Nimitz, Dwight D. Eisenhower, Carl Vinson, Theodore Roosevelt, Abraham Lincoln, George Washington*, and *John C. Stennis*, the last three of which displace 114,240 tons. The ships are 1,092 feet in length overall, with 4½ acres of flight deck, and can reach speeds in excess of 30 knots. Their full complement of personnel is 5,986.

Most aircraft landings   The greatest number of landings on an aircraft carrier in one day was 602, achieved by Marine Air Group 6 of the United States Pacific Fleet Air Force aboard the U.S.S. *Matanikau* on May 25, 1945 between 8 A.M. and 5 P.M.

Largest battleships   The Japanese battleships *Yamato* (sunk southwest of Kyushu, Japan by U.S. planes on April 7, 1945) and *Musashi* (sunk in the Philippine Sea on October 24, 1944) were the largest battleships ever commissioned, each with a full-load displacement of 78,387 tons. With an overall length of 863 feet, a beam of 127 feet and a full-load draft of 35 ft. 5 in., they were armed with nine 18.1-inch guns that fired 3,200-pound projectiles.

United States   The largest battleships were the U.S.S. *Missouri*, an Iowa class battleship, and the U.S.S. *Wisconsin*, 887 feet long with a full load displacement of 64,400 tons. Both were first commissioned in 1944 and then recommissioned in 1986 and 1988 respectively. Both ships have now been withdrawn from service.

Fastest armed vessel   A U.S. Navy hovercraft, the 78-foot-long 110-ton test vehicle SES-100B, achieved a speed of 91.9 knots (105.8 MPH), on January 25, 1980. (See FASTEST HOVERCRAFT.)

Fastest destroyers   The fastest speed attained by a destroyer was 45.25 knots (51.83 MPH) by the 3,120-ton French destroyer *Le Terrible* in 1935. It was built in France and was powered by four Yarrow small-tube boilers and two Rateau geared turbines, giving 100,000 shp.

United States   The fastest destroyers in the U.S. Navy arsenal are the Spruance class and Kidd class ships, which can reach 33 knots (38 MPH).

MODEL AIRCRAFT

Highest model aircraft flight Maynard L. Hill (U.S.), flying a radio-controlled model, established the world record for altitude of 26,919 feet on September 6, 1970.

Fastest model aircraft The speed record is 245.84 MPH by a model flown on control lines by Leonid Lipinski (USSR) in 1971. The record for a radio-controlled model is 242.91 MPH, set by Walter Sitar (Austria) in 1977.

Longest model aircraft flight Maynard Hill and Robert Rosenthal (U.S.) hold the closed-circuit distance record, with 776.7 miles, achieved on June 26, 1995.

Hill and Rosenthal also hold the record for the longest flight in a straight line to a nominated landing point, with 458.5 miles, from Bealeton, VA to Ridgeland, SC in 8 hr. 43 min on August 29, 1995.

The record duration is 33 hr. 39 min. 15 sec. by Maynard Hill, with a powered model, October 1–2, 1992.

Maynard Hill and Robert Rosenthal hold several records.

An indoor model with a wound rubber motor, designed by Robert Randolph (U.S.), set a duration record of 55 min. 6 sec. on December 5, 1993.

Jean-Pierre Schiltknecht flew a solar-driven model aircraft for 10 hr. 43 min. 51 sec. in Wetzlar, Germany on July 10, 1991.

Largest model aircraft The largest radio-controlled model aircraft was a glider weighing 45 pounds, with a wingspan of 18 ft. 6 in. and a length of 16 ft. 6 in. It was made by Simon Cocker of Congleton, England.

Largest paper aircraft The largest flying paper airplane, with a wingspan of 45 ft. 10 in., was constructed by a team of students from the Faculty of Aerospace Engineering at Delft University of Technology, Netherlands and flown on May 16, 1995. It was launched indoors and flew 114 ft. 2 in.

Longest paper aircraft flight The level flight duration record for a hand-launched paper aircraft is 18.80 seconds, by Ken Blackburn in a hangar at John F. Kennedy International Airport, New York City on February 17, 1994.

An indoor distance of 193 feet was recorded by Tony Felch at the La Crosse Center, La Crosse, WI on May 21, 1985.

MODEL BOATS

Longest model boat run Members of the Lowestoft Model Boat Club crewed a radio-controlled model boat on August 17–18, 1991 in Doncaster, England and set a 24-hour record of 111.18 miles.

24-hour run David and Peter Holland of Doncaster, England, of the Conisbrough and District Modelling Association, crewed a 28-inch-long scale model boat of the trawler *Margaret H* continuously on one battery for 24 hours, and recorded a distance of 33.45 miles, at The Dome, Doncaster Leisure Park, Doncaster, England, August 15–16, 1992.

MODEL CARS

Smallest car Nippondenso of Kariya, Japan created a motorized scale model car of Toyota's 1936 Model AA Sedan. The model measures 0.189 inches long, 0.068 inches wide, and 0.068 inches high, and has a top speed of 0.011 MPH.

Longest drive A Scalextric Jaguar XJ8 ran nonstop for 866 hr. 44 min. 54 sec. and covered 1,771.2 miles from May 2 to June 7, 1989. The event was organized by the Rev. Bryan G. Apps and church members of Southbourne, Bournemouth, England.

24-hour slot car race On September 4–5, 1994, H.O. Racing and Hobbies of San Diego, CA achieved a distance of 375.079 miles for a 1:64 scale car.

Under the rules of the B.S.C.R.A. (British Slot Car Racing Association), the 24-hour distance record by a 1:64 scale car is 198.987 miles, set by a team of four in Derby, England on November 11–12, 1995.

On July 5–6, 1986, the North London Society of Model Engineers team achieved a 24-hour distance record of 305.949 miles for a 1:32 scale car in Southport, England.

Longest slot car track   The longest slot car track measures 958 feet and was built at Mallory Park Circuit, Leicester, England on November 22, 1991. One car successfully completed a full lap.

MODEL TRAINS

Longest run   A standard Life-Like BL2 HO scale electric train pulled six 8-wheel coaches for 1,207.5 hours without stopping, from August 4 to September 23, 1990, and covered a distance of 909.5 miles. The event was organized by Ike Cottingham and Mark Hamrick of Mainline Modelers of Akron, OH.

24-hour run   The 7¼-inch-gauge model steam locomotive "Peggy" covered 167.7 miles in 24 hours at Weston Park Railway, Weston Park, England, June 17–18, 1994.

Smallest model railroad   A miniature model railroad with a scale of 1:1,400 was made by Bob Henderson of Gravenhurst, Ontario, Canada. The engine runs on a 4½-volt battery and measures ³/₁₆ of an inch overall.

"Peggy" sets a 24-hour distance record.

ARTS &

ENTERTAINMENT

40

ART

PAINTINGS

Largest painting   A painting of Elvis Presley measuring 76,726 square feet was completed by students of Savannah College of Art and Design and members of the local community in Tybee Island, GA on April 8, 1995.

Most valuable painting   The "Mona Lisa" (*La Gioconda*), by Leonardo da Vinci (1452–1519), in the Louvre, Paris, France was assessed for insurance purposes at $100 million for its move to Washington, D.C. and New York City for exhibition from December 14, 1962 to March 12, 1963. However, insurance was not purchased because the cost of the closest security precautions was less than that of the premiums.

Most prolific painter   Pablo Picasso (1881–1973) was the most prolific of all painters in a career that lasted 78 years. It has been estimated that Picasso produced about 13,500 paintings or designs, 100,000 prints or engravings, 34,000 book illustrations and 300 sculptures or ceramics. The complete body of his work has been valued at over $800 million.

Finest standard paintbrush   The finest standard brush sold is the 000 in Series 7 by Winsor and Newton, known as a "triple goose." It is made of 150–200 Kolinsky sable hairs weighing 0.000529 ounces.

GALLERIES

Largest art gallery   Visitors would have to walk 15 miles to see the 322 galleries of the Winter Palace and the neighboring Hermitage in St. Petersburg, Russia. The galleries house nearly 3 million works of art and objects of archaeological interest.

Most heavily endowed gallery   The J. Paul Getty Museum in Malibu, CA was established with an initial $1.4 billion budget in January 1974 and now has an annual budget of $180 million for acquisitions to stock its 38 galleries.

MOSAICS

Largest mosaic   The mosaic on the walls of the central library of the Universidad Nacional Autónoma de México in Mexico City is the largest in the world. The two largest of the four walls measure 12,949 square feet, and the scenes on each represent the pre-Hispanic past.

MURALS

Oldest mural   In 1961, clay relief leopards were discovered by James Malaart on manmade walls at level VII at Catal Hüyük in southern Anatolia, Turkey. They date from *c.* 6200 B.C.

Largest mural The Pueblo Levee Project in Colorado produced the world's largest mural, at 178,200 square feet.

POSTERS

Largest poster A poster measuring 236,119 square feet was made by the Community Youth Club of Hong Kong on October 26, 1993. The poster commemorated the International Year of the Family, and was displayed in Victoria Park, Hong Kong.

SCULPTURE

Oldest sculpture An animal head carved on a woolly rhinoceros vertebra from Tolbaga, Siberia is thought to be 34,860 years old. The oldest stone figurine is a 31,790-year-old serpentine female statuette from Galgenberg, Austria. About 32,000 years ago, several ivory figurines of humans and animals were deposited in Hohler Stein, Geissenklösterle and Vogelherd caves in southern Germany. Remarkably, these are generally more sophisticated and more animated than the sculpture of subsequent periods.

Largest sculpture The mounted figures of Jefferson Davis (1808–89), Gen. Robert E. Lee (1807–70) and Gen. Thomas "Stonewall" Jackson (1824–63) cover 1.33 acres on the face of Stone Mountain, near Atlanta, GA. They are 90 feet high. Roy Faulkner was on the mountain face for 8 yr. 174 days with a thermo-jet torch, working with sculptor Walker Kirtland Hancock and other helpers, from September 12, 1963 through March 3, 1972.

Sand sculptures The longest sand sculpture ever made was the 86,535-ft.-6-in.-long sculpture named "The GTE Directories Ultimate Sand Castle" built by over 10,000 volunteers at Myrtle Beach, SC on May 31, 1991.
   The tallest was the "Invitation to Fairyland," which was 56 ft. 2 in. high, and was built by 2,000 local volunteers at Kaseda, Japan on July 26, 1989 under the supervision of Gerry Kirk (U.S.) and Shogo Tashiro (Japan).

Largest ground figures In the Nazca Desert, 185 miles south of Lima, Peru, there are straight lines (one more than seven miles long), geometric shapes, and outlines of plants and animals that were drawn on the ground some time between 100 B.C. and A.D. 600. They were first detected from the air around 1928 and have been described as the world's longest works of art.

Modern The painted straw representation of Will the Great Buffalo in northeast Wyoming, completed by Robert Berks in September 1993, is half a mile long.

Largest hill figures A 330-foot-tall figure was found on a hill above Tarapacá, Chile in August 1968.

HIGHEST PRICES

Most expensive painting On May 15, 1990, *Portrait of Dr. Gachet* by Vincent Van Gogh was sold for $82.5 million at Christie's, New York City.

The largest sculpture is carved into the face of Stone Mountain.

The painting depicts Van Gogh's physician and was completed only weeks before the artist's suicide in 1890. The buyer was subsequently identified as Ryoei Saito, Japan's second-largest paper manufacturer.

20th-century   The record bid at auction for a 20th-century painting is $51.65 million for a painting by Pablo Picasso, at Druout, Binoche and Godeau, Paris, France in November, 1989.

Living artist   The highest price paid at auction for a work by a living artist is $20.68 million for *Interchange*, an abstract by the American painter Willem de Kooning, at Sotheby's, New York City on November 8, 1989. Painted in 1955, it was bought by Japanese dealer-collector "Mountain Tortoise."

Most expensive miniature   The record price is £352,000 ($621,600), paid by the Alexander Gallery of New York at Christie's, London, England on November 7, 1988 for a 2⅛-inch-high miniature of George Washington. It was painted by the Irish-American miniaturist John Ramage in 1789.

Most expensive print   The record price for a print at auction was £561,600 ($786,000) for a 1655 etching of *Christ Presented to the People* by Rembrandt (1606–69) at Christie's, London on December 5, 1985.

Most expensive drawing   On November 14, 1990, at Christie's, New York City, an anonymous buyer paid $8.36 million for the pen-and-ink scene *Jardin de Fleurs*, drawn by Vincent Van Gogh in Arles, France in 1888.

Most expensive poster   The record price for a poster is £68,200 (*c.* $93,000) for an advertisement for the 1895 Glasgow exhibition by Charles Rennie Macintosh, sold at Christie's, London on February 4, 1993.

Most expensive sculpture   The record price for a sculpture at auction is £6.82 million ($12 million) at Sotheby's, London on December 7, 1989 for a bronze garden ornament, *The Dancing Faun*, made by the Dutch-born sculptor Adrien de Vries (1545/6–1626). London dealer Cyril Humpris bought the figure from a couple who had paid £100 ($240) for it in the 1950s and in whose garden it had stood undiscovered for 40 years.

The highest price paid for the work of a sculptor during his lifetime is $1,265,000 at Sotheby's, New York City on May 21, 1982 for the 75-inch-long elmwood *Reclining Figure* by Henry Moore (Great Britain; 1898–1986).

United States   The highest price paid at auction for a sculpture by an American sculptor is $4.4 million for *Coming Through the Rye*, by Frederic Remington (1861–1909), at Christie's, New York City on May 25, 1989.

ANTIQUES

HIGHEST PRICES

All prices quoted are inclusive of the buyer's premium, and all records were set at public auction unless otherwise stated.

Art nouveau   The highest auction price for any piece of art nouveau is $1.78 million for a standard lamp in the form of three lotus blossoms by the Daum Brothers and Louis Majorelle of France, sold at Sotheby's, New York City on December 2, 1989.

Armor   The highest auction price paid for a suit of armor was £1,925,000 ($3,657,000), by B. H. Trupin (U.S.) on May 5, 1983 at Sotheby's, London, England, for a suit made in Milan by Giovanni Negroli in 1545 for Henri II of France. It came from the Hever Castle Collection in Kent, England.

Blanket   A Navajo Churro hand-spun serape dated *c.* 1852 sold for $115,500 at Sotheby's, New York City on October 22, 1983.

Bottle   A rare Korean Punch'ong bottle was sold at Christie's, New York City on November 17, 1993 for $376,500.

Box   A Cartier jeweled vanity case, set with a fragment of an ancient Egyptian stela, was sold at Christie's, New York City for $189,500 on November 17, 1993.

Carpet   On June 9, 1994, a Louis XV Savonnerie carpet was sold at Christie's, London to Djanhanguir Riahi for £1,321,000 ($2,113,600).
  The most expensive carpet ever made was the Spring carpet of Khusraw, made for the Sassanian palace at Ctesiphon, Iraq. It comprised about 7,000 square feet of silk and gold thread, and was encrusted with emeralds. The carpet was cut up as booty by looters in A.D. 635, but from the realization value of the pieces must have had an original value of some $170 million.

Ceramics   The highest auction price for any ceramic is £3.74 million ($6.4 million) for a Chinese Tang dynasty (A.D. 618–906) horse sold by the British Rail Pension Fund and bought by a Japanese dealer at Sotheby's, London, on December 12, 1989.

Furniture   The highest price ever paid for a single piece of furniture is £8.58 million ($15 million) at Christie's, London, on July 5, 1990 for the 18th-century Italian "Badminton Cabinet" owned by the Duke of Beaufort. It was bought by Barbara Piasecka Johnson (U.S.).

United States   The highest price ever paid for a single piece of American furniture is $12.1 million at Christie's, New York City on June 3, 1989 for a mahogany desk-cum-bookcase, made in the 1760s. It was bought by dealer Israel Sack.

Glass   The auction record is £520,000 ($1,175,200) for a Roman glass cage-cup of *c*. A.D. 300, measuring seven inches in diameter and four inches in height, sold at Sotheby's, London, on June 4, 1979 to Robin Symes.

Gun   An 1873 .45 caliber Colt single-action army revolver, Serial No. 1, was sold for $242,000 at Christie's New York City on May 14, 1987.

Helmet   The highest price ever paid for an item of headwear is $66,000 by the Alaska State Museum at an auction in New York City in November 1981 for a native North American Tlingit Kiksadi ceremonial frog helmet dating from *c*. 1600.

Jewelry   The world's largest jewelry auction, which included a Van Cleef and Arpels 1939 ruby and diamond necklace, realized over $50 million when the collection belonging to the Duchess of Windsor (1896–1986) was sold at Sotheby's, Geneva, Switzerland on April 3, 1987.

The highest auction price for individual items of jewelry is $6.2 million for two pear-shaped diamond drop earrings of 58.6 and 61 carats bought and sold anonymously at Sotheby's, Geneva, Switzerland, on November 14, 1980.

A Harry Winston diamond necklace was bought for $4.40 million at Sotheby's, New York City on April 14, 1994 by Saudi Arabian businessman Ahmed Fitahi.

Music box   The highest price paid for a music box is £20,900 ($22,990) for a Swiss example made for a Persian prince in 1901 and sold at Sotheby's, London, on January 23, 1985.

Playing cards   The highest price for a deck of playing cards is $143,352, paid by the Metropolitan Museum of Art, New York City at Sotheby's, London, on December 6, 1983. The cards, dating from c. 1470–85, constituted the oldest known *complete* hand-painted set.

The highest price paid for a single card was $7,450 for a card dated 1717, which was used as currency in Canada. It was sold by the dealer Yasha Beresiner to Lars Karlson (Sweden) in October 1990.

Silver   The record for silver is $3,386,440 for a Hanover chandelier from the collection of M. Hubert de Givenchy, sold at Christie's, Monaco on December 4, 1993.

Surgical instrument   The record price paid a surgical instrument was $34,848 for a 19th-century German mechanical chain saw sold at Christie's, London, on August 19, 1993.

Tapestry   The highest auction price for a tapestry is £638,000 ($1,124,794), paid by Swiss dealer Peter Kleiner at Christie's, London, on July 3, 1990 for a fragment of a Swiss example woven near Basle in the 1430s.

Teddy bear   A Steiff bear named Teddy Girl was sold for £110,000 ($171,578) by Christie's, London on December 5, 1994 to Japanese businessman Yoshihiro Sekiguchi. The bear was made in 1904, only a year after Steiff made the first jointed plush teddy bear, and had a particularly well documented history.

Toy The most expensive antique toy was sold for $231,000 to an anonymous telephone bidder at Christie's, New York City on December 14, 1991. The work is a hand-painted tinplate replica of the "Charles" hose reel, a piece of fire-fighting equipment pulled by two firemen, measuring 15 by 23 inches and built around 1870 by George Brown & Co. of Forestville, CT.

Most expensive atlas The highest price paid for an atlas is $1,925,000 for a version of Ptolemy's *Cosmographia* dating from 1492, which was sold at Sotheby's, New York City on January 31, 1990.

Most expensive book The highest price paid for any book is £8.14 million ($11.9 million) for the 226-leaf manuscript *The Gospel Book of Henry the Lion, Duke of Saxony* at Sotheby's, London on December 6, 1983. The book, which measures 13½ by 10 inches, was illuminated *c.* 1170 by the monk Herimann at Helmershansen Abbey, Germany with 41 full-page illustrations.

Printed Tokyo booksellers Maruzen Co. Ltd. paid $5.39 million for an Old Testament (Genesis to the Psalms) Gutenberg Bible printed in 1455 in Mainz, Germany at Christie's, New York City on October 22, 1987.

Most expensive broadsheet On June 13, 1991, Donald J. Scheer of Atlanta, GA paid $2,420,000 for one of the 24 known copies of the Declaration of Independence, printed by John Dunlap in Philadelphia, PA in 1776.

Most expensive manuscript An illustrated manuscript by Leonardo da Vinci known as the "Codex Hammer," in which da Vinci predicted the invention of the submarine and the steam engine, was sold for a record $30.8 million at Christie's, New York City on November 11, 1994. The buyer was Bill Gates (see RICHEST MEN). It is the only da Vinci manuscript in private hands.

United States On December 16, 1992, a manuscript written by Abraham Lincoln was sold for $1.54 million. The one-page script was written in preparation for a speech, and is the first surviving formulation of his "house divided" doctrine, written in the winter of 1857 or 1858. The manuscript was bought by Seth Kaller of Kaller Historical Documents.

Musical The auction record for a musical manuscript is $4,394,500 at Sotheby's, London, on May 22, 1987 for a 508-page bound volume measuring 8½ by 6½ inches and containing nine complete symphonies in Mozart's hand. The manuscript is owned by Robert Owen Lehman and is on deposit at the Pierpont Morgan Library in New York City.

The record price paid for a single musical manuscript is £1.1 million (*c.* $2 million), paid at Sotheby's, London, on December 6, 1991 for the autograph copy of the Piano Sonata in E minor, opus 90, by Ludwig van Beethoven (1770–1827).

Most expensive autograph letter The highest price ever paid on the open market for a single signed autograph letter was $748,000 on December 5, 1991 at Christie's, New York City for a letter written by Abraham Lincoln on January 8, 1863 defending the Emancipation Proclamation. It was sold to Profiles in History of Beverly Hills, CA.

MUSEUMS

Oldest museum   The world's oldest museum is the Ashmolean in Oxford, England, built between 1679 and 1683 and named after the collector Elias Ashmole (1617–92).

Largest museum   The Smithsonian Institution comprises 16 museums containing over 140 million items and has over 6,000 employees.

The American Museum of Natural History in New York City was founded in 1869 and comprises 23 interconnected buildings in an 18-acre park. The buildings of the museum and the planetarium cover 1.2 million square feet of floor space, accommodating more than 30 million artifacts and specimens. Its exhibits are viewed by more than 3 million visitors each year.

Most popular museum   The highest attendance on a single day for any museum is over 118,437 on April 14, 1984 at the Smithsonian's National Air and Space Museum, Washington, D.C., opened in July 1976. The record-setting day required the doors to be temporarily closed.

Airplanes hang from the ceiling of the Smithsonian National Air and Space Museum.

LANGUAGE

Commonest language   Chinese is spoken by an estimated 1 billion people.

Most widespread language   English is spoken by an estimated 800 million people; more generous estimates put the figure at 1.5 billion. Of these, 350 million are native speakers, 220 million of whom are in the United States.

Greatest concentration of languages   Papua New Guinea has the greatest concentration of separate languages in the world. Each of the estimated 869 languages has about 4,000 speakers.

Most complex language   The Ample language of Papua New Guinea has over 69,000 finite forms and 860 infinitive forms of the verb. Haida, a North American Indian language, has the most prefixes, with 70. Tabassaran, a language of Daghestan, Azerbaijan, uses the most noun cases, 48. Inuit uses 63 forms of the present tense, with simple nouns having as many as 252 inflections.

Most irregular verbs   According to *The Morphology and Syntax of Present-day English* by Prof. Olu Tomori, English has 283 irregular verbs, 30 of which are formed merely by adding prefixes.

Rarest sounds   The rarest speech sound is probably that written "ř" in Czech and termed a "rolled post-alveolar fricative." In the southern Bushman language !xo, there is a click articulated with both lips, which is written ☉. This sound, essentially a kiss, is termed a "velaric ingressive bilabial stop."

Commonest sound   No language is known to be without the vowel "a" (as in the English "father").

Largest vocabulary   The English language contains about 616,500 words plus another 400,000 technical terms, the most in any language, but it is doubtful if any individual speaker uses more than 60,000. William Shakespeare, for instance, employed a vocabulary of only about 33,000 words.

Most languages spoken   Dr. Harold Williams (1876–1928), a journalist from New Zealand, was reputed to speak 58 languages and many dialects fluently.

Ziad Fazah (Brazil) speaks and writes 58 languages. He was tested in a live interview in Athens, Greece in July 1991, when he surprised audience members by talking to them in their various native tongues.

Alexander Schwartz of New York City *worked* with 31 languages as a translator for the United Nations between 1962 and 1986.

Longest debate   Students of University College Galway, Galway, Ireland, with staff and guest speakers, debated the motion that "This house has all the time in the world" for exactly 28 days, February 2–March 2, 1995.

ALPHABET

Earliest alphabetic writing A clay tablet of 32 cuneiform letters was found at Ugarit (now Ras Sharma), Syria, and dated to *c*. 1450 B.C.

Oldest letter The letter "O" has not changed in shape since its adoption in the Phoenician alphabet *c*. 1,300 B.C.

Longest alphabet The language with the most letters in its alphabet is Cambodian, with 74.

Shortest alphabet Rotokas of central Bougainville Island, Papua New Guinea, has the fewest letters, with 11 (a, b, e, g, i, k, o, p, ř, t and u).

Most and fewest consonants The language with the greatest number of distinct consonantal sounds was Ubykh, with 80–85. Ubykh speakers migrated from the Caucasus to Turkey in the 19th century and the language is now extinct. The language with the fewest consonants is Rotokas, with six.

Most and fewest vowels The language with the most vowels is Sedang, a central Vietnamese language with 55 distinguishable vowel sounds. The Caucasian language Abkhazian has the fewest, with two.

WORDS

Longest word A compound "word" of 195 Sanskrit characters (which transliterates into 428 letters in the Roman alphabet) describes the region near Kanci, Tamil Nadu, India. The word appears in a 16th-century work by Tirumalāmbā, Queen of Vijayanagara.

English The longest word in the Oxford English Dictionary is *pneumonoultramicroscopicsilicovolcanoconiosis*, which has 45 letters and means "a lung disease caused by the inhalation of very fine silica dust." It is, however, described as "factitious" by the editors of the dictionary.

Longest palindromes The longest palindromic word (a word that reads the same backward or forward) is saippuakivikauppias (19 letters), which is Finnish for "a dealer in lye." The longest in English is tattarrattat, with 12 letters, which appears in the Oxford English Dictionary.

Longest anagrams The longest nonscientific English words that can form anagrams are the 17-letter transpositions *representationism* and *misrepresentation*. The longest scientific transposals are *hydroxydesoxycorticosterone* and *hydroxydeoxycorticosterones*, with 27 letters.

Longest abbreviation The initials S.K.O.M.K.H.P.K.J.C.D.P.W.B. stand for the Syarikat Kerjasama Orang-orang Melayu Kerajaan Hilir Perak Kerana Jimat Cermat Dan Pinjam-meminjam Wang Berhad. This is the Malay name for The Cooperative Company of the Lower State of Perak Government's Malay People for Money Savings and Loans Ltd., in Teluk Anson, Perak, West Malaysia (formerly Malaya). The abbreviation for the abbreviation is Skomk.

LONGEST WORDS

Spanish
Superextraordinarisimo (22)
extraordinary

Portuguese
Inconstitucionalissimamente (27)
with the highest degree of unconstitutionality

French
Anticonstitutionnellement (25)
anticonstitutionally

Swedish
Nordöstersjökustartilleriflygspaningssimulatoranläggningsmaterielunderhåsuppföljningssystemdiskussionsinläggsförberedel-searbeten (130)
Preparatory work on the contribution to the discussion on the maintaining system of support of the material of the aviation survey simulator device within the northeast part of the coastartillery of the Baltic

Japanese
Chi-n-chi-ku-ri-n (12 letters)
a very short person (slang)

Italian
Precipitevolissimevolmente (26)
as fast as possible

Russian
Ryentgyenoelyektrokardiografichyeskogo (33 Cyrillic letters)
of the X-ray electrocardiographic

Dutch
Kindercarnavalsoptochtvoorbereidingswerkzaamheden (49)
preparation activities for a children's carnival procession

German
Donaudampfschiffahrtselektrizitaetnhauptbetriebswerkbauunter-beamtengesellschaft (80)
The club for subordinate officials of the head office management of the Danube steamboat electrical services

---

Shortest abbreviation   The 55-letter full name of Los Angeles (El Pueblo de Nuestra Señora la Reina de los Angeles de Porciuncula) is abbreviated to L.A., or 3.63 percent of its length.

Longest acronym   The longest acronym is NIIOMTPLABOPARMBET-ZHELBETRABSBOMONIMONKONOTDTEKHSTROMONT with 56 letters (54 in Cyrillic) in the *Concise Dictionary of Soviet Terminology, Institutions and Abbreviations (1969)*, meaning: the Laboratory for Shuttering,

Reinforcement, Concrete and Ferroconcrete Operations for Composite-monolithic and Monolithic Constructions of the Department of the Technology of Building-Assembly Operations of the Scientific Research Institute of the Organization for Building Mechanization and Technical Aid of the Academy of Building and Architecture of the USSR.

Commonest words and letters The most frequently used words in written English are, in descending order of frequency: *the, of, and, to, a, in, that, is, I, it, for* and *as.* The most commonly used in conversation is "*I.*" The commonest letter is "e." More words begin with the letter "s" than with any other, but the most commonly *used* initial letter is "t" as in "the," "to," "that" or "there."

Most synonyms There are more synonyms for being intoxicated than for any other condition or object in the English language. *Dickson's Word Treasury,* compiled by Paul Dickson of Garrett Park, MD, lists 2,660 synonyms for this condition.

PERSONAL NAMES

Oldest name The oldest surviving personal name belongs to a predynastic king of Upper Egypt *ante* 3,050 B.C., who is represented by the hieroglyphic sign for a scorpion. It has been suggested that the name should be read as Sekhen.

Longest personal name The longest name to appear on a birth certificate is Rhoshandiatellyneshiaunneveshenk Koyaanisquatsiuth Williams, born to Mr. and Mrs. James Williams in Beaumont, TX on September 12, 1984. On October 5, 1984, Mr. Williams filed an amendment that expanded his daughter's first name to 1,019 letters and her middle name to 36 letters.

Most first names A. Lindup-Badarou of Truro, England, formerly known as A. Hicks, had a total of 3,530 first names as of March 1995.

Commonest family name The commonest surname in the English-speaking world is Smith. There are an estimated 2,382,509 Smiths in the United States.

PLACE-NAMES

Longest place-name The official name for Bangkok, the capital Thailand, is Krungthep Mahanakhon. However, the full name is Krungthep Mahanakhon Bovorn Ratanakosin Mahintharayutthaya Mahadilokpop Noparatratchathani Burirom Udomratchanivet Mahasathan Amornpiman Avatarnsathit Sakkathattiyavisnukarmprasit, which in its scholarly transliteration emerges with 175 letters.

   The longest place-name now in use is Taumatawhakatangihangakoauauotamateaturipukakapikimaungahoronukupokaiwhenuakitanatahu, the unofficial 85-letter version of the name of a hill (1,002 feet above sea level) in the Southern Hawke's Bay district of North Island, New Zealand. The Maori translation means "The place where Tamatea, the man with the big knees, who slid, climbed and swallowed mountains, known as landeater, played his flute to his loved one."

The official name for Bangkok is the longest-ever place-name.

United States   The longest place-name recognized by the United States Board on Geographic Names belongs to Nunathloogagamiutbingoi Dunes in the Bethel borough of Alaska. The dunes are three miles long and are located on the southeast coast near the Nunivak Islands, one mile north of Cape Mendon Hall.

Most spellings   The spelling of the Dutch town of Leeuwarden has been recorded in 225 versions since A.D. 1046.

LITERATURE

Oldest book   The oldest handwritten book still intact is a Coptic Psalter dated to about 1,600 years ago, found in 1984 at Beni Suef, Egypt.

Oldest mechanically printed work   The oldest surviving printed work is the Dharani scroll or *sutra* from wooden printing blocks found in the foundations of the Pulguk Sa pagoda, Kyongju, South Korea on October 14, 1966. It has been dated to no later than A.D. 704.

Smallest book   The smallest marketed bound printed book is printed on 22-gsm paper and measures $1/25$ by $1/25$ inches. It contains the children's story *Old King Cole!* and was published in 85 copies in March 1985 by The Gleniffer Press of Paisley, Scotland. The pages can be turned only by using a needle.

Largest publication The *Yongle Dadian* (the great thesaurus of the Yongle reign) comprises 22,937 manuscript chapters (370 of which still survive) in 11,095 volumes. It was written by 2,000 Chinese scholars between 1403 and 1408.

Largest dictionary *Deutsches Wörterbuch*, started by Jacob and Wilhelm Grimm in 1854, was completed in 1971 and consists of 34,519 pages and 33 volumes.

English language The second edition of the 20-volume *Oxford English Dictionary*, published in March 1989, comprises 21,543 pages and over 231,000 main entries. The longest entry is for the verb *set*, with over 60,000 words of text.

United States The largest English-language dictionary published in the United States is *Webster's Third New International Dictionary Unabridged*, published in 1986 by Merriam-Webster, Inc. It defines approximately 472,000 word-forms, with 99,370 illustrative quotations.

Largest encyclopedia The Chinese *Yongle Dadian* (see LARGEST PUBLICATION) was the largest encyclopedia ever compiled.

Currently, the largest encyclopedia is *La Enciclopedia Universal Ilustrada Europeo-Americana* (J. Espasa & Sons, Madrid and Barcelona), totaling 105,000 pages, with an annual supplement of 165.2 million words.

Largest work of fiction The novel *Tokugawa Ieyasu* by Sohachi Yamaoka has been serialized in Japanese daily newspapers since 1951. Now completed, it would require nearly 40 volumes if published.

BEST-SELLING BOOKS

Most copies sold The world's best-selling and most widely distributed book is the Bible, with an estimated 2.5 billion copies sold, 1815–1975. By the end of 1993, the whole Bible had been translated into 337 languages; 2,062 languages have translations of at least one book of the Bible.

Excluding noncopyright books, such as the Bible and the Koran, the all-time best-selling book is *The Guinness Book of Records*, first published in October 1955 by the Guinness Brewery. Global sales in 37 languages had reached more than 79 million in April 1996.

Most weeks on the best-seller list The longest duration on the *New York Times* best-seller list was *The Road Less Traveled* by M. Scott Peck, which had its 598th week on the list as of April 14, 1995. Over 5 million copies of the book, which is published by Touchstone, are currently in print.

PUBLISHERS AND PRINTERS

Largest printer The largest printer in 1994 was Bertelsmann in Germany. In 1993, the company had sales of $10,956 million with profits of $289 million. It employed 14,696 people.

United States The largest printer in the United States is R.R. Donnelley & Sons Co. of Chicago, IL. The company, founded in 1864, has 200 manufacturing facilities, offices, service centers and subsidiaries in 26 countries. In 1995, Donnelley had 41,000 employees worldwide, and turned out $6.5 billion worth of work.

The largest printer under one roof is the United States Government Printing Office (founded 1861) in Washington, D.C. Encompassing 34.4 acres of floor space, the central office processes an average of 1,464 print orders daily, and uses 93.2 million pounds of paper annually.

Highest printings It is believed that in the United States, Van Antwerp Bragg and Co. printed some 60 million copies of the 1879 edition of *The McGuffey Reader*, compiled by Henry Vail in the pre-copyright era for distribution to public schools.

The highest order for an initial print-run of a work of fiction is 2.8 million, ordered by Doubleday for John Grisham's sixth novel, *The Rainmaker*.

40 years ago the first edition of The Guinness Book of Records *did not list a category for the best-selling book.* **Today** *it is calculated that more than 2.5 billion copies of the Bible had been sold worldwide by 1977. By 1993, complete versions of the Bible had been translated into 3,378 languages.*

"I think that the greatest record achieved is that the Bible is the world's best-selling and most widely distributed book."—Elizabeth Dole, June 29, 1996

Oldest publisher Cambridge University Press has a continuous history of printing and publishing since 1584. The University received a Royal Letters Patent to print and sell all manner of books on July 20, 1534.

United States The firm of Williams and Wilkins (formerly Lea and Febiger) of Baltimore, MD has a continuous history of publishing since 1785.

Most prolific publisher At its peak in 1989, Progress Publishers (founded in 1931 as the Publishing Association of Foreign Workers in the former USSR) of Moscow, Russia printed over 750 titles in 50 languages annually.

Fastest publishing Two thousand bound copies of *The Book Fair Book*, published by the Zimbabwe International Book Fair Trust and printed by Print Holdings (Pvt) Ltd., were produced from raw disk in 5 hr. 23 min. at the Zimbabwe International Book Fair in Harare on August 5, 1993. The time for 1,000 copies was 4 hr. 50 min., and Braille, large print, CD-ROM, and audiotape formats were produced simultaneously.

BOOKSTORES AND LIBRARIES

Largest bookstore   The bookstore with the most titles and the longest shelving (30 miles) in the world is W. & G. Foyle Ltd. of London, England. First established in 1904 in a small store, the company now has a site of 75,825 square feet.

The most capacious individual bookstore in the world measured by square footage is the Barnes & Noble Bookstore at 105 Fifth Avenue at 18th Street, New York City. It covers 154,250 square feet and has 12.87 miles of shelving.

Oldest library   The first library in America was established at Harvard University in 1638. The first subscription library in the country was the Philadelphia Library Company in 1731. The first library in America that meets the definition of a modern public library was established in Peterboro, NH, on April 9, 1833.

The first library in the United States was established at Harvard University in 1698.

Largest library   The United States Library of Congress (founded on April 24, 1800) in Washington, D.C. contains 108,433,370 items—including 16,764,805 books in the classified collections, 25,934,708 other print materials, and 82,498,662 audio and visual materials. The library has 532 miles of shelving and employs 4,600 people.

Nonstatutory   The largest nonstatutory library—not funded or operated by the state—is the New York Public Library (founded 1895) on Fifth Avenue, New York City with a floor space of 525,276 square feet and 172 miles of shelving, plus an underground extension with the capacity for an additional 84 miles. Its collection, including 82 branch libraries, contains 4.6 million volumes and 38 million items of research material.

Public The largest public library in the United States is the Harold Washington Library Center, Chicago, IL, which opened on October 7, 1991. The 10-story, 756,640-square-foot building contains 70.85 miles of bookshelves and cost $144 million. The collection includes 1.7 million books, 13,300 periodical titles, and more than 8 million microforms, recordings and other items.

University The largest university library in the United States is believed to be Harvard University Library, in Cambridge, MA, which consists of more than 90 separate libraries and a total of 13,143,330 volumes.

Largest CD-ROM library MicroPatent of East Haven, CT, the commercial publisher of patent information, has a collection of 1,730 discs containing almost 20 million pages listing every US utility patent from 1976 to the present day.

Most overdue book A book in German on the Archbishop of Bremen, published in 1609, was borrowed from Sidney Sussex College, Cambridge, England by Colonel Robert Walpole, 1667–68. It was found by Prof. Sir John Plumb in the library at Houghton Hall, Norfolk, England and returned 288 years later. No fine was charged.

United States A book on febrile diseases (London, 1805, by Dr. J. Currie) was checked out in 1823 from the University of Cincinnati Medical Library and returned December 7, 1968 by the borrower's great-grandson. The fine of $2,264 was waived.

AUTHORS

Top-selling fiction author The world's top-selling writer of fiction is Agatha Christie (1890–1976), whose 78 crime novels have sold an estimated 2 billion copies in 44 languages. Royalty earnings from her works are estimated to be worth $4.25 million per year.

Brazilian author Jorge Amado has had his 32 novels published in 48 different languages in 60 countries. His first book, *O País do Carnaval*, appeared in 1931; his most recent book, *A Descoberta da América pelos Turcos*, was published in 1994.

Oldest author Sarah Louise Delaney's second book, *The Delaney Sisters' Book of Everyday Wisdom*, was published by Kodansha America in October 1994, when she was 105 years old. Her sister and co-author, A. Elizabeth Delaney (who died in September 1995), was 103.

Longest poem The longest poem ever published was the Kirghiz folk epic *Manas*, which appeared in printed form in 1958 but has never been translated into English. According to the *Dictionary of Oriental Literatures*, this 3-part epic runs to about 500,000 lines.

English language   A poem on the life of King Alfred by John Fitchett (1766–1838) of Liverpool, England ran to 129,807 lines and took 40 years to write. His editor, Robert Riscoe, added the concluding 2,585 lines.

DIARIES AND LETTERS

Longest-kept diary   Col. Ernest Loftus of Harare, Zimbabwe began his daily diary on May 4, 1896 at age 12 and continued it until his death on July 7, 1987 at the age of 103 yr. 178 days. George C. Edler of Bethesda, MD kept a handwritten diary continuously from September 20, 1909 until his death in 1987, a total of 78 years.

Longest and most letters   From July 1961 until the death of his bedridden wife, Mitsu, in March 1985, Uichi Noda wrote her 1,307 letters, amounting to 5 million characters, during his overseas trips. The letters were published in 25 volumes totaling 12,404 pages.

Rev. Canon Bill Cook and his fiancée/wife Helen of Diss, England exchanged 6,000 love letters during their 4¼-year separation from March 1942 to May 1946.

Most presidential signatures   The only known document that bears eleven U.S. presidential signatures is a letter sent by President Franklin Delano Roosevelt to Richard C. Corbyn, then of Dallas (now of Amarillo), TX, dated October 26, 1932. It was later signed by Herbert Hoover, Harry S Truman, Dwight D. Eisenhower, Gerald Ford, Lyndon Johnson, Jimmy Carter, Ronald Reagan, George Bush and Bill Clinton. Richard Nixon's first signature was signed with an auto-pen but he later re-signed it.

Most Christmas cards   The most personal Christmas cards sent by an individual is believed to be 62,824, by Werner Erhard of San Francisco, CA in December 1975.

NEWSPAPERS

Most newspaper readers   The country with the most newspaper readers is Sweden, where 580 newspapers are sold for every 1,000 people.

Highest circulation   The highest circulation for any newspaper was for *Komsomolskaya Pravda* (founded 1925), the youth paper of the former Soviet Communist Party, which reached a peak daily circulation of 21,975,000 copies in May 1990.

The 8-page weekly newspaper *Argumenty i Fakty* (founded 1978) of Moscow, Russia attained a figure of 33,431,100 copies in May 1990, when it had an estimated readership of over 100 million.

The highest circulation for any *currently* published newspaper is that of *Yomiuri Shimbun*, founded 1874, which publishes morning and evening editions, and had a combined daily circulation of 14,565,474 in January 1996.

United States   The highest-circulation daily newspaper in the United States is the *Wall Street Journal* (founded 1889), published by Dow Jones & Co. In March 1996, its circulation was 1,841,188 copies.

Oldest newspaper   A copy has survived of a news pamphlet published in Cologne, Germany in 1470.

The oldest existing newspaper in the world is the Swedish official journal *Post och Inrikes Tidningar*, founded in 1645 and published by the Royal Swedish Academy of Letters.

The oldest existing commercial newspaper is the *Haarlems Dagblad/ Oprechte Haarlemsche Courant*, published in Haarlem, Netherlands, first issued as the *Weeckelycke Courante van Europa* on January 8, 1656. A copy of issue No. 1 survives.

United States   The oldest continuously published newspaper in the United States is the *Hartford Courant*, established by Thomas Greene on October 29, 1764. Its current circulation figures are 227,792 daily and 316,058 Sunday papers, as of July 1996.

Largest newspaper   The most massive single issue of a newspaper was the September 14, 1987 edition of the Sunday *New York Times*, which weighed 12 pounds and had 1,612 pages.

The largest page size ever used was 55.9 by 39.2 inches for the June 14, 1993 edition of *Het Volk*, which was published in Gent, Belgium.

Smallest newspaper   A newspaper called "Tit Bits from all the Most Interesting Books, Periodicals and Newspapers in the World," dated September 5, 1885 and owned by Mark Sundquist of Shoreline, WA, has an original page size of $2^{1}/_{8}$ by $2^{3}/_{4}$ inches.

Longest editorship   Sir Etienne Dupuch of Nassau, Bahamas was editor-in-chief of *The Tribune* from April 1, 1919 to 1972, and a contributing editor until his death on August 23, 1991— a total of 72 years.

Most belated apology   The *Hartford Courant* issued an apology to Thomas Jefferson, 193 years late. In 1800, the newspaper ran a vehement editorial opposing his election, and expounding on the ways in which the country would be irrevocably damaged as a result. At the 250th anniversary of his birth, in 1993, the *Courant* finally admitted the error of its judgment with a formal apology, and the words: "It's never too late to admit a mistake."

Most Pulitzer prizes   The *New York Times* has won 73 Pulitzer prizes, more than any other news organization.

Most durable feature   Mary MacArthur of Port Appin, Scotland has contributed a regular feature to *The Oban Times and West Highland Times* since 1926.

Most durable advertiser   The Jos Neel Co., a clothing store in Macon, GA, ran an ad in the *Macon Telegraph* in the upper-left-hand corner of page two every day from February 22, 1889 to August 16, 1987. This constituted 35,291 consecutive advertisements.

Most widely syndicated columnist   Ann Landers appears in over 1,200 newspapers with an estimated readership of 90 million.

CIRCULATION CHAMPION

No sports section, no weather maps, no gossip and hardly any photographs. "The Wall Street Journal is a serious newspaper for serious people," says publisher Peter R. Kann. It's also the most widely purchased newspaper in the United States, with an average daily circulation of 1,841,188 copies. "It's a paradox. Our goal isn't the numbers," says Kann. "It's more important to have an audience that's fairly cohesive, highly loyal and responds to the publication." *The Wall Street Journal* has that audience: business people.

The first issue hit the newsstands on July 8, 1889. A 4-page afternoon paper, it was edited by Charles H. Dow, co-founder of the Dow Jones Company, which still owns the newspaper. "The editorial philosophy has remained constant. Free people, free markets, free enterprise and free flows of capital, information and people," summarizes Kann. Content and emphasis, however, has changed with the times. "Twenty years ago *The Wall Street Journal* concentrated on Fortune 500 companies," says Kann. "Today the pages are full of technology companies and the service component of the American economy, marketing, personal finance and international business coverage reflecting the interdependence of and the competition of the global economy."

The other significant change is electronic delivery. Kann relishes the opportunity provided by the technology revolution: "It's exciting. The paper is now fully available on the World Wide Web and has 400,000 registered users. It's neat: it gives you the full content of the *Journal* and the full content of our overseas editions. It's constantly updated during the

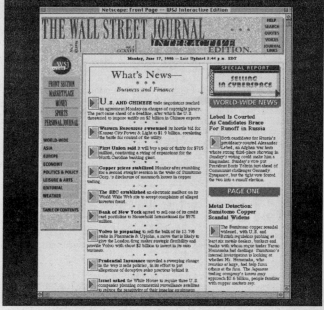

day, minute-by-minute in some cases." He adds, "The next step is to start charging for it. In August 1996 we will be the first publisher to start charging a real price."

Looking further ahead, Kann does not forecast the demise of the printed newspaper. "I think there will still be printed newspapers. They're a handy way to absorb information. They're portable, they're convenient, you can stick them in your briefcase, take them to the bathroom, scribble on them." There will be changes, though. "In 15 years, we won't devote 20 pages to stock quotes. Information of that sort will be easy to access electronically from your armchair." The publisher does not see these advances as a threat. "There are better uses to which you can put those pages and *The Wall Street Journal* would be better off devoting that space to thoughtful analytic coverage of issues. The two [print and electronic] are not in conflict; they complement each other."

Kann sees himself "as ultimately responsible for the content, quality and success of the publication." He emphasizes: "You stay successful by sticking to basic standards which I think do not and should not change, even if subject areas do. It's important to have independent, unbiased coverage not influenced by trends in pack-journalism, political correctness and social or business orthodoxy. We do have to keep the publication contemporary, but it has to stick with certain values, editorially, and those really matter."

PERIODICALS

Oldest periodical   The oldest continuing periodical in the world is *Philosophical Transactions of the Royal Society*, published in London, England, which first appeared on March 6, 1665.

United States   The oldest continuously published periodical in the United States is *The Old Farmer's Almanac*, started in Massachusetts by Robert Thomas, a teacher and amateur astronomer, in 1792.

Largest circulations   The total dispersal through noncommercial channels by Jehovah's Witnesses of *The Truth that Leads to Eternal Life*, published by the Watchtower Bible and Tract Society of New York City on May 8, 1968, reached 107,686,489 in 117 languages by June 1996.

The world's highest-circulation periodical is *TV Guide*, with a circulation of 13,175,000 as of December 31, 1995.

In its 47 basic international editions, *Reader's Digest* (established February 22, 1922) circulates more than 27 million copies monthly in 18 languages. In the United States, the magazine sells 15,126,664 copies per month.

Parade, the syndicated color magazine, is distributed with 334 U.S. newspapers every Sunday, and as of July 21, 1996, had a peak circulation of 36.156 million.

Largest consumer magazine   The January 1992 issue of *Hong Kong Toys*, published by the Hong Kong Trade Development Council, ran to 1,356 pages.

Most advertising pages   The greatest number of pages of advertisements sold in a single issue of a periodical is 829.54 in the October 1989 issue of *Business Week*.

COMIC STRIPS

Most durable comic strip   The longest-lived newspaper comic strip is "The Katzenjammer Kids" (Hans and Fritz), created by Rudolph Dirks and first published in the *New York Journal* on December 12, 1897. The strip, currently drawn by cartoonist Hy Eisman, has been taken over by King Features Syndicate and is now syndicated in approximately 50 Sunday newspaper publications.

Most widely syndicated cartoon strip   Charles Schulz's comic strip *Peanuts*, which first appeared in October 1950, currently appears in 2,620 newspapers in 75 countries and 26 languages.

Political cartoons   Ranan R. Lurie (U.S.) is the most widely syndicated political cartoonist in the world. As of June 1996, his work was published in 103 countries in 1,105 newspapers with a total circulation of 104 million copies.

MAPS

Oldest map   A clay tablet depicting the river Euphrates flowing through northern Mesopotamia (Iraq) dates to *c.* 2250 B.C. The earliest printed map in the world is one of western China dated to 1115.

Largest map The largest 2-dimensional map measures 49,000 square feet and was painted by students of O'Hara Park School, Oakley, CA in the summer of 1992.

Relief The Challenger relief map of British Columbia, Canada, measuring 6,080 square feet, was designed and built in the period 1945–52 by the late George Challenger and his son Robert. It is now on display at the Pacific National Exhibition in Vancouver, British Columbia.

Smallest map In 1992, Dr. Jonathon Mamin of IBM's Zurich laboratory used sudden electrical impulses to create a map of the Western Hemisphere from atoms. The map has a scale of one trillion to one, and a diameter of about one micron or $\frac{1}{100}$th the diameter of a human hair.

MUSIC

SONGS

Oldest song The *shaduf* chant has been sung since time immemorial by irrigation workers on the Nile in Egypt.

The oldest known harmonized music performed today is the English song "Sumer Is Icumen In," which dates from *c.* 1240.

Oldest national anthem The words of the "Kimigayo" of Japan date from the ninth century, although the music was written in 1881. The oldest music belongs to the anthem of the Netherlands, "Vilhelmus," which was written *c.* 1570.

Shortest national anthems The anthems of Japan, Jordan and San Marino each have four lines.

Longest rendering of a national anthem "God Save the King" was played nonstop 16 or 17 times by a German military band on the platform of Rathenau railroad station, Brandenburg, Germany on the morning of February 9, 1909. The reason was that King Edward VII was struggling to put on a German field-marshal's uniform inside the train before he could emerge.

Most renditions of the national anthem Susan R. Jeske sang "The Star-Spangled Banner" live at 17 official events in California, attended by approximately 60,000 people, within a 24-hour period, July 3–4, 1992. She traveled to the functions by automobile, helicopter and boat.

Most frequently sung songs The most frequently sung songs in English are "Happy Birthday to You" by Mildred Hill and Patty Smith Hill (written in 1893 and under copyright from 1935 to 2010); "For He's a Jolly Good Fellow" (originally the French "Malbrouk"), known at least as early as 1781; and "Auld Lang Syne" (originally the Strathspey "I Fee'd a Lad at Michaelmass"), some words of which were written by Scottish poet Robert Burns (1759–96).

Most successful songwriters   In terms of number-one singles, the most successful songwriters are John Lennon and Paul McCartney. McCartney is credited as writer on 32 number-one hits in the United States to Lennon's 26 (with 23 co-written), whereas Lennon authored 29 British number-ones to McCartney's 28 (25 co-written).

Oldest hymns   The music and parts of the text of a hymn in the *Oxyrhynchus Papyri* from the second century are the oldest known hymnody. The oldest exactly datable hymn is the "Heyr Himna Smióur (Hear, the Maker of Heaven)" from 1208 by the Icelandic bard and chieftain Kolbeinn Tumason (1173–1208).

Longest published hymn   "Sing God's Song," a hymn by Carolyn Ann Aish of Inglewood, New Zealand, is 754 verses or 3,016 lines long, with an additional 4-line refrain to each verse.

Most prolific hymnist   Frances (Fanny) Jane van Alstyne (née Crosby, 1820–1915) of the United States wrote 8,500 hymns.

Highest and lowest voices   Madeleine Marie Robin (1918–60), the French operatic coloratura, could produce and sustain the B above high C in the Lucia mad scene in Donizetti's *Lucia di Lammermoor*.

Ivan Rebroff, the Russian singer, has a voice that extends easily over four octaves, from low F to high F, one and a quarter octaves above C.

Dan Britton of Branson, MO can produce the note E-flat$_3$ (18.84 Hz).

The highest note put into song is g^4, occurring in Mozart's *Popoli di Tessaglia*. The lowest vocal note in the classical repertoire is in Mozart's *Die Entführung aus dem Serail* in Osmin's aria, which calls for a low D (73.4 Hz).

Oldest choral society   The oldest active choral society in the United States is the Old Stoughton Musical Society of Stoughton, MA, founded in 1786.

Largest choir   Excluding sing-alongs in stadiums, the greatest choir was one of 60,000 that sang in unison as a finale to a choral contest held in Breslau, Germany on August 2, 1937.

Fastest rapper   Rebel X.D. of Chicago, IL rapped 674 syllables in 54.9 seconds at the Hair Bear Recording Studio, Alsip, IL on August 27, 1992.

COMPOSERS

Most prolific composer   Georg Philipp Telemann (1681–1767) of Germany composed 12 complete sets of services for a year, 78 services for special occasions, 40 operas, 600 to 700 orchestral suites, 44 passions, plus concertos, sonatas and other chamber music.

Longest symphony   The symphony *Victory at Sea*, written by Richard Rodgers (1902–79) and arranged by Robert Russell Bennett in 1952 for the NBC television series of the same name, lasted 13 hours.

Longest solo piano composition   The longest continuous nonrepetitious piano piece ever published is *The Well-Tuned Piano* by La Monte Young, first presented by the Dia Art Foundation at the Concert Hall, Harrison St., New York City on February 28, 1980. The piece lasted 4 hr. 12 min. 10 sec.

Longest silence   The longest interval between the known composition of a piece by a major composer and its performance in the manner intended is from March 3, 1791 until October 9, 1982, in the case of Mozart's *Organ Piece for a Clock*, a fugue fantasy in F minor (K 608), arranged by the organ builders Wm. Hill & Son and Norman & Beard Ltd. at Glyndebourne, England.

OPERA

Longest opera   *The Heretics* by Gabriel von Wayditch (1888–1969) is orchestrated for 110 pieces and lasts 8½ hours. The longest commonly performed opera is *Die Meistersinger von Nürnberg* by Richard Wagner (1813–83) of Germany. A normal performance entails 5 hr. 15 min. of music.

Shortest opera   *The Sands of Time* by Simon Rees and Peter Reynolds was first performed by Rhian Owen and Dominic Burns on March 27, 1993 at The Hayes, Cardiff, Wales; it lasted 4 min. 9 sec. An even shorter performance, lasting only 3 min. 34 sec., was directed by Peter Reynolds at BBC Television Centre, London, England on September 14, 1993.

Largest opera house   The Metropolitan Opera House, Lincoln Center, New York City completed in September 1966 at a cost of $45.7 million, has a standing and seating capacity of 4,065 with 3,800 seats in an auditorium 451 feet deep.

Longest aria   The longest single aria, in the sense of an operatic solo, is Brünnhilde's immolation scene in Wagner's *Götterdämmerung*. It has been timed at 14 min. 46 sec.

Oldest opera singers   Ukrainian bass Mark Reizen (b. July 3, 1895) sang the substantial role of Prince Gremin in Tchaikovsky's *Eugene Onegin* at the Bolshoi Theatre in Moscow on his 90th birthday. Danshi Toyotake (b. Yoshie Yokota, 1891–1989) of Hyogo, Japan sang traditional Japanese narrative for 91 years from age seven. Her career spanned 81 years.

Most curtain calls   On February 24, 1988, Luciano Pavarotti received 165 curtain calls and was applauded for 1 hr. 7 min. after singing the part of Nemorino in Gaetano Donizetti's *L'Elisir d'amore* at the Deutsche Oper in Berlin, Germany.

Oldest opera company   The oldest opera company in the United States is the Metropolitan Opera Company of New York City; its first season was in 1883.

Longest operatic encore   The Austro-Hungarian emperor Leopold II (r. 1790–92) ordered an encore of the entire opera *Il Matrimonio Segreto* by Cimarosa at its premiere in 1792.

PLACIDO DOMINGO

$\mathcal{M}$ost roles performed, most recordings made and the biggest-selling CD in classical music history; good things do come in threes for Placido Domingo. His collaboration with Luciano Pavarotti and José Carreras as the Three Tenors has made music history, but the Spanish tenor's prolific output as a performer, recording artist and conductor sets him apart in the opera world. "Three things are important: the style of the role, the language and the vocal weight of the role," Domingo says of his approach to a role. He has performed 109 different roles during his career, the most of any tenor. "You have one voice with which you must try to find the right color for each part. From the light, beautiful and romantic color you use in Rodolfo's 'O Mimi tu piu non torni' (from *La Boheme*) to the commanding ferocity of Otello's 'Abasso le spade.'"

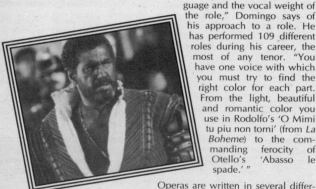

Operas are written in several different languages, and it is a must to have a grasp of the language being sung. "It's much better if you speak the language fluently that you're singing, but if you don't you really have to know all the meaning of the words to make sense dramatically," says Domingo. He speaks four languages fluently (Spanish, English, Italian and French) but reveals: "I will sing *Pique Dame* in Russian."

Domingo attributes his success with his wide-ranging repertoire to his excellent technique. "In the beginning I sang as a baritone. I had to work hard to become a tenor, laying the foundation for every higher note almost like a stone mason, brick by brick. I applied a great deal of thinking and actual work to achieve the proper technique." The maestro adds, "I like challenges and constantly set myself new ones. For me, only thus is life truly interesting."

All the world's major opera houses have been graced by Domingo. More recently, his work with the Three Tenors has led him to arena and stadium tours. His approach in either setting is unchanged. "I don't use a different vocal technique for singing at the Metropolitan Opera in New York or in an arena-type surrounding. It is the same voice, the same vocal production, the same aim for perfection and the same attention to style," declares the maestro. Discovering new opera talent is his passion: "Finding an exciting young singer is like a re-affirmation that my first love, which is opera, will live on and on."

The Three Tenors

First drawn together to celebrate the 1990 World Cup soccer tournament in Italy, the performances of the Three Tenors—Placido Domingo, Luciano Pavarotti and José Carreras—have set music industry records for CD and video sales. Despite their outstanding success, the Three Tenors have drawn criticism from opera purists who do not like to hear their champions singing Broadway show tunes and other popular music songs.

Domingo reacts strongly to this criticism. "I have little use for people who criticize us for singing popular music. Whatever we have programmed is beautiful music in its own right and we are certainly not the first to have sung songs from the musical theater and the movies." His colleague José Carreras agrees: "Singing some of the light repertory sometimes is nothing else but following the legacy of artists such as Enrico Caruso, Beniamino Gigli, McCormack, Schippa and Di Stefano." Adds Domingo: "Basically, what is being criticized is the fact that a song like 'Granada' is recognized by millions and therefore is popular. Have people forgotten how happy Mozart and Verdi were when people would whistle their music on the street? Why should music be sacrosanct?"

INSTRUMENTS

Largest organ   The largest and loudest musical instrument ever constructed is the now only partially functional Auditorium Organ in Atlantic City, NJ. Completed in 1930, this instrument had two consoles, 1,477 stop controls and 33,112 pipes.

The largest fully functional organ is the 6-manual 30,067-pipe Grand Court Organ in the Wanamaker Department Store, Philadelphia, PA. The organ has a 64-foot tone gravissima pipe.

Loudest organ stop   The Ophicleide stop of the Grand Great in the Solo Organ in the Atlantic City Auditorium has a pure trumpet note of more than six times the volume a locomotive whistle.

Grandest piano   The grandest weighed 1.4 tons and was 11 ft. 8 in. long. It was made by Chas H. Challen & Son Ltd. of London, England in 1935. Its longest string measured 9 ft. 11 in.

Most expensive piano   On March 26, 1980, a non-pianist paid $390,000 for a c. 1888 Steinway grand piano sold by the Martin Beck Theater at Sotheby Parke Bernet, New York City.

Largest brass instrument   A contrabass tuba standing 7½ feet tall, with 39 feet of tubing and a bell 3 ft. 4 in. across, was constructed for a world tour by the band of American composer John Philip Sousa, c. 1896–98.

Largest movable stringed instrument   A pantaleon with 270 strings stretched over 50 square feet was used by George Noel in 1767.

Largest double bass   A double bass measuring 14 feet tall was built in 1924 in Ironia, NJ by Arthur K. Ferris. It weighed 1,301 pounds, and its low notes could be felt rather than heard.

Largest playable guitar   Students of Shakamak High School in Jasonville, IN made a guitar measuring 38 ft. 2 in. tall, 16 feet wide and weighing 1,865 pounds. It was unveiled on May 17, 1991.

Acoustic   A guitar 28 ft. 5 in. long and 3 ft. 2 in. deep is on display at the Stradivarium exhibition in The Exploratory, Bristol, England. Its dimensions were enlarged from the proportions of a Stradivarius classical guitar.

Most expensive guitar   A Fender Stratocaster belonging to legendary rock guitarist Jimi Hendrix (1942–70) was sold by his former drummer Mitch Mitchell to an anonymous buyer for £198,000 ($338,580) at Sotheby's, London on April 25, 1990.

Most valuable violin   The highest price paid at auction for a violin is £902,000 ($1.7 million) for the 1720 "Mendelssohn" Stradivarius. It was sold to a mystery buyer at Christie's, London on November 21, 1990.

Largest cello   Master violin-maker Christian Urbista of Cordes, France built the world's largest playable cello. The instrument is 24.4 feet tall.

TIPS

from the
RECORD BREAKERS

LARGEST WURLITZER ORGAN

Eddie Layton plays the organ at Radio City Music Hall, which houses the Mighty Wurlitzer Organ. He divides his time between Radio City and Yankee Stadium, where, he reckons, he's played the "Charge" song nearly 50,000 times in his lifetime. Should you have the opportunity to play a big organ, follow Layton's tips.

◆

Learn not to fear large audiences.

"One day the regular organist at Radio City was ill. The stage manager asked me to fill in and play the Mighty Wurlitzer. I froze. That first day there were 6,000 people in the Music Hall, but everyone in the orchestra gave me the thumbs-up sign and I knew I had it."

◆

Get a rise out of your audience.

One day in Yankee Stadium the bases were loaded and I played 'Hava Nagila.' Everyone stood up to clap." Music Hall crowds were just as responsive: "At the end of the overture they brought the Mighty Wurlitzer on for the last eight measures. At the very end I'd reach over with my foot and touch the thunder button. It gave a boom that shook, rattled, and rolled the Music Hall and really excited the audience."

◆

Study, study, study.

Want to play a musical instrument? "Please study the three things that make the sound of music, which are harmony, arranging, and music theory. Then go on and develop your own unique style."

A guitar that belonged to Jimi Hendrix was the most expensive guitar sold at auction.

Most valuable cello The highest auction price for a cello is £682,000 ($1.2 million) at Sotheby's, London on June 22, 1988 for a Stradivarius known as "The Cholmondeley," which was made in Cremona, Italy *c.* 1698.

Largest drum A drum with a 13-foot diameter was built by the Supreme Drum Co., London, England and played at the Royal Festival Hall, London on May 31, 1987.

Largest drum kit A drum kit consisting of 308 pieces—153 drums, 77 cymbals, 33 cowbells, 12 hi-hats, 8 tambourines, 6 wood blocks, 3 gongs, 3 bell trees, 2 maracas, 2 triangles, 2 rain sticks, 2 bells, 1 ratchet, 1 set of chimes, 1 xylophone, 1 afuche, and 1 doorbell—was built by Dan McCourt of Pontiac, MI in 1994.

Most drums played Rory Blackwell played 400 separate drums in 16.2 seconds at Finlake Leisure Park, Chudleigh, England on May 29, 1995.

Longest alphorn An alphorn 154 ft. 8 in. long (excluding mouthpiece) and weighing 227 pounds was made by Swiss-born Peter Wutherich, of Boise, ID in December 1989.

Highest and lowest notes The extremes of orchestral instruments (excluding the organ) range from a handbell tuned to g^5 (6,272 cycles per second, or 6,272 Hz) to the sub-contrabass clarinet, which can reach C_4 (16.4 Hz). In 1873, a sub-double bassoon able to reach B_4 (14.6 Hz) was made, but no surviving specimen is known. The extremes for the organ are g^6 (12,544 cycles per second, or 12,544 Hz) and C_5 (8.12 Hz), obtainable from $^3/_4$-inch and 64-foot pipes respectively.

ORCHESTRAS

Oldest orchestra The oldest existing symphony orchestra, the Gewandhaus Orchestra of Leipzig, Germany, was established in 1743.

United States The oldest orchestra in the United States is the Philharmonic-Symphony Society of New York, founded in 1842.

Largest orchestra On June 17, 1872, Johann Strauss the younger (1825–99) conducted a 987-piece orchestra supported by a choir of 20,000, at the World Peace Jubilee in Boston, MA. The number of first violinists was 400.

On December 14, 1991, the 2,000-piece "Young People's Orchestra and Chorus of Mexico," consisting of 53 youth orchestras from Mexico plus musicians from Venezuela and the former USSR, gave a full classical concert conducted by Fernando Lozano and others in Mexico City, Mexico.

Bottle orchestra The Brighton Bottle Orchestra—consisting of Terry Garoghan and Peter Miller—performed a musical medley on 444 Gordon's Gin bottles at the Brighton International Festival, England on May 21, 1991.

Most prolific conductor Herbert von Karajan (Austria; 1908–89), principal conductor of the Berlin Philharmonic Orchestra for 35, made over 800 recordings of all the major works.

Longest-serving conductor Dr. Aloys Fleischmann (1910–92) conducted the Cork Symphony Orchestra (Cork, Republic of Ireland) for 58 seasons, ending in 1991–92.

United States The Chicago Symphony Orchestra was directed by Frederic Stock from 1905 until his death in 1942, a total of 37 seasons.

Longest-serving society orchestra leader   Lester Lanin has directed and played over 12,480 engagements around the world over six decades.

Largest band   The most massive band was one of 20,100 players at the Ullevaal Stadium, Oslo, Norway from Norges Musikkorps Forbund bands on June 28, 1964.

Largest one-man band   Rory Blackwell (Great Britain), aided by his double left-footed perpendicular percussion-pounder, plus his 3-tier right-footed horizontal 22-pronged differential beater, and his 12-outlet bellow-powered horn-blower, played 108 different instruments simultaneously in Dawlish, England on May 29, 1989.

Largest marching band   On June 27, 1993, a marching band of 6,017 people, including 927 majorettes and standard-bearers, marched 3,084 feet at Stafsberg Airport, Hamar, Norway.

Musical chairs   The largest game on record started with 8,238 participants. It was held at the Anglo-Chinese School, Singapore on August 5, 1989.

Baton twirling   The greatest number of complete spins done between tossing a baton into the air and catching it is 10, by Donald Garcia, on December 9, 1986. The women's record is eight spins, by Danielle Novakowski, in South Bend, IN on July 24, 1993.

CONCERTS

Classical concert   An estimated record 800,000 attended a free open-air concert by the New York Philharmonic conducted by Zubin Mehta, on the Great Lawn of Central Park, New York City on July 5, 1986.

Rock/pop festival   Steve Wozniak's 1983 U.S. Festival in San Bernardino, CA attracted an audience of 725,000.

Solo performer   The largest *paying* audience ever attracted by a solo performer was an estimated 180,000–184,000 in the Maracanã Stadium, Rio de Janeiro, Brazil to hear Paul McCartney on April 21, 1990.

Rod Stewart's *free* concert at Copacabana Beach, Rio de Janeiro, Brazil on New Year's Eve, 1994 attracted an audience of 3.5 million.

Most successful concert tour   The Rolling Stones' 1989 "Steel Wheels" North American tour earned an estimated $310 million and was attended by 3.2 million people in 30 cities.

Most rock concerts performed   The Grateful Dead performed 2,317 documented rock concerts, 1965–95. They played live in front of an estimated 25 million Deadheads and played 454 different songs and jams.

Three continents in a day   Def Leppard played concerts on three continents on October 23, 1995. Each concert lasted at least one hour and was attended by 200 or more people. The first concert began at 12:23 A.M. in

Morocco. The band flew to London for the second concert and finished their tour in Vancouver at 11:33 P.M.

Most durable musicians The Romanian pianist Cual Delavrancea (1887–1991) gave her last public recital, receiving six encores, at the age of 103.

The longest international career in the history of Western music is held by Polish pianist Mieczyslaw Horszowski (1892–1993), who played for Emperor Franz-Joseph in Vienna, Austria in 1899 and was still playing in 1989.

The world's oldest active musician is Jennie Newhouse (b. July 12, 1889) of High Bentham, England, who has been the regular organist at the Church of St. Boniface in Bentham since 1920.

Most successful concert series Michael Jackson sold out for seven nights at Wembley Stadium, London, England in the summer of 1988. A total of 504,000 people saw Jackson perform July 14–16, 22–23, and August 26–27, 1988.

Largest concert On July 21, 1990, Potsdamer Platz, straddling East and West Berlin, was the site of the largest rock concert in terms of participants. Roger Waters' production of Pink Floyd's "The Wall" had 600 people performing on stage. An estimated 200,000 people gathered for the symbolic building and demolition of a wall made of 2,500 styrofoam blocks.

TELEVISION

Most durable shows The most durable TV show is NBC's *Meet the Press*, first transmitted on November 6, 1947 and broadcast weekly since September 12, 1948. As of July 28, 1996, 2,515 shows had been broadcast.

The last televised broadcast of the *Joe Franklin Show* aired in August 1993. Starting in 1951, Franklin hosted 31,015 episodes of the show and conducted 309,136 interviews.

Stock Market Observer is the longest-running television show in terms of total hours of air time. Since August 1967, it has broadcast more than 39,779 hours of New York Stock Exchange floor trading.

Most episodes Since 1949, over 150,000 individual episodes of the TV show *Bozo the Clown*, by Larry Harmon Pictures, have been aired daily on 150 stations in the United States and abroad.

Most hours on camera The most hours on camera on U.S. national television is 10,448 hours by TV personality Hugh Downs in 49 years up to July 4, 1996.

Most spinoffs The U.S. television series with the most spinoffs is *Star Trek*, which has evolved into five syndicated programs: *Star Trek* (1966–69), *Star Trek* cartoon (1973–75), *Star Trek: The Next Generation* (1987–94), *Star*

BARBARA WALTERS

*T*he President, the First Lady and Barbra Streisand: a trio expected to be seen at Inaugural Balls and Hollywood fundraisers, but not as the guests on a brand-new television show.

*R*ewind to 1976: President-elect Jimmy Carter, his wife Rosalyn, and Streisand were the first guests on a new show called *The Barbara Walters Special*. A new type of show—the prime-time special—was born. Marking its 20th anniversary this year, *The Barbara Walters Special* is the longest-running prime-time interview special. "I had imagined it would be like a magazine show, with celebrities, political people, and other people in the news," recalls Walters. "Audiences didn't like the political interview and the ratings went down, so the show became more celebrity oriented." At first Walters didn't realize she was creating a new type of television show. "The specials were a great success, but I didn't consider them a breakthrough." Reruns now air in syndication on cable stations. Laughs Walters: "I never thought they would go on for 20 years. Now I think they're going to outlive me."

*T*he Barbara Walters Special was an offshoot of Walters' move to ABC to become co-anchor on the evening news. She was the first woman correspondent to gain the prestigious post, but the experience was a painful one. "It was as if I was some chorus girl. There would never have been the same type of antipathy had Harry Reasoner had Mike Wallace as a partner," says Walters. But Walters believes this harsh experience helped her: "It may have been the best thing for me to have to work my way back. It not only helped me to grow, I proved to myself that it wasn't all luck."

*A*fter the Reasoner partnership dissolved, the specials continued, as did Walters' work as a news correspondent. In 1984 she joined *20/20*, and she is now one of television's most renowned journalists. The specials, in fact, have always been secondary to her other work at ABC. "The specials were never first and foremost in my mind—they were never the only thing I did," she says. Keeping the show fresh is a challenge. "There have been times when I think I cannot do any more stars," admits Walters. "And then there is someone new again." The format of the specials will change in the future. "We came up with 'Fascinating People' which has show business stars but also has Nelson Mandela and Barry Diller. It's a more varied program. After 20 years you need to make some changes and keep it fresh." And her favorite interview? "I'd probably pick Anwar Sadat. It was a time when I was covering the Middle East and I think he changed the course of history."

Trek: Deep Space Nine (1993–present) and *Star Trek: Voyager* (1995–present). It has also spawned seven feature films.

Greatest audience   On January 28, 1996, 138.48 million viewers watched Super Bowl XXX.

The program that attracted the highest-ever rating share was the final episode of *M*A*S*H*, transmitted by CBS on February 28, 1983 to 60.2 percent of households in the United States. An estimated 125 million people tuned in, taking a 77 percent share of all viewing.

Most watched show   *Baywatch*, with an estimated weekly audience of 2,396,839,980 people throughout 103 countries and every continent, claims to be the most widely watched television show in the world.

Highest rated talk show   *The Oprah Winfrey Show* has led all talk shows in ratings for a record nine consecutive seasons spanning 1986–95.

Most expensive television rights   In November 1991, a group of U.S. and European investors, led by CBS, paid $8 million for the television rights to *Scarlett*, the sequel to Margaret Mitchell's *Gone With the Wind*, written by Alexandra Ripley.

Most Emmy Awards   The most Emmys won by any individual is 17, by television producer Dwight Arlington Hemion. He also holds the record for most nominations, with 44.

Sesame Street (PBS) has won the most awards for a series, with 64 between 1970 and 1996. *Cheers* has received the most nominations, with 117 (winning 27) between 1983 and 1993. The most Emmys awarded to a miniseries was 9, to *Roots* (ABC) in 1977. In 1977, *Eleanor and Franklin: The White House Years* (ABC) received the most Emmys, 11, for a television movie.

Most expensive TV production   *War and Remembrance* was the most expensive TV production, costing $110 million. The 14-episode ABC miniseries won the 1989 Emmy for best miniseries.

Most prolific TV scriptwriter   The most prolific television writer in the world was the Rt. Hon. Lord Willis (1918–92). He created 41 series, 37 stage plays and 39 feature films, and had 29 plays produced.

Most prolific TV producer   The most prolific producer was game show producer Mark Goodson. Goodson produced over 39,000 episodes totaling more than 21,240 hours of airtime.

Aaron Spelling has produced more than 2,993 TV episodes totaling 2,576.5 hours of airtime.

Largest TV set   The Sony Jumbo Tron color TV screen at the Tsukuba International Exposition '85 near Tokyo, Japan measured 80 by 150 feet.

Smallest TV set   The Seiko TV-Wrist Watch has a 1.2-inch screen and weighs 2.8 ounces. Including the receiver unit and headphones, the black and white system, costing 108,000 yen ($1,038), weighs 1.3 ounces.

The smallest single-piece set is the Casio-Keisanki TV-10, weighing 11.9 ounces with a 2.7-inch screen.

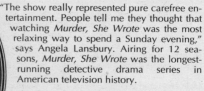

Angela Lansbury

"The show really represented pure carefree entertainment. People tell me they thought that watching *Murder, She Wrote* was the most relaxing way to spend a Sunday evening," says Angela Lansbury. Airing for 12 seasons, *Murder, She Wrote* was the longest-running detective drama series in American television history.

The first episode, entitled "The Murder of Sherlock Holmes," premiered on September 30, 1984. The main character, Jessica Fletcher, was played by Lansbury. Each week Fletcher, a mystery writer, solved a baffling murder case, usually one that occurred in Cabot Cove, ME, where she lived.

Most mysteriously, it would seem now, Lansbury was not the original choice for the Fletcher role. "CBS first offered it to Jean Stapleton, who declined," explains Lansbury. She, however, quickly accepted the part. "It was a great stroke of luck . . . it was an extraordinary career move." Although an immediate hit, Lansbury didn't expect the show to last as long as it did. "I never for a moment thought of myself in the show for more than two years at the maximum." She attributes the show's success to the appeal of the Fletcher character: "Jessica was a marvelous role model for women of a certain age. She had an innate youthfulness . . . she never thought as an older person." Adds Lansbury, "I tried to keep her consistent. You could depend on her to react to certain situations in a certain way."

Lansbury readily acknowledges that ratings success is the key to a long-running series. "You never stop worrying about ratings," she says. The right spot on the TV schedule is also critical. "We were placed on Sunday at 8 P.M., following *60 Minutes* . . . it was the perfect time slot." Once the show was established, hard work followed. "We made a complete movie every eight days and on the ninth day started the next one," recalls Lansbury. "The writers were challenged constantly. It was always a hard row to hoe."

The last episode of *Murder, She Wrote* aired on May 19, 1996. But Jessica Fletcher hasn't put her typewriter into mothballs just yet. "We're developing scripts for the Movie of the Week. We'll probably have one by 1997." Lansbury is excited by the prospect: "We'd like to involve Jessica in some really interesting plot lines and take her out of Cabot Cove . . . we've bumped off enough people there already."

The smallest and lightest color set is the Casio CV-1, with dimensions of 2.4 by 0.9 by 3.6 inches, weighing, with batteries, only six ounces. It has a screen size of 1.4 inches and retails in Japan for 40,000 yen (about $350).

Best-selling video The world's best-selling video is Walt Disney's animated feature *Aladdin*, which was released in North America in October 1993 and had sold over 41 million copies worldwide through May 1, 1995.

PHOTOGRAPHY

Oldest photograph In 1827, Joseph Niépce used a camera obscura to photograph the view from his window. The photo is now in the Gernsheim Collection at the University of Texas, Austin, TX.

Most expensive photograph A photograph by Alfred Stieglitz called *Georgia O'Keeffe: A Portrait—Hands with Thimble*, was sold at Christie's, New York City on October 8, 1993 for a record $398,500.

Largest camera The largest industrial camera ever built is the 30-ton Rolls-Royce camera now owned by BDC Holdings Ltd. of Derby, England. It was commissioned in 1956, and measures 8 ft. 10 in. high, 8¼ feet wide and 46 feet long. The lens is a 63-inch f16 Cooke Apochromatic.

A pinhole camera was created from a Portakabin unit measuring 34 by 9½ by 9 feet by photographers John Kippen and Chris Wainwright at the National Museum of Photography, Film and Television in Bradford, England on March 25, 1990. The unit produced a direct positive measuring 33 feet by 4 ft. 2 in.

Largest lens The National Museum of Photography, Film and Television, Bradford, England displays the largest lens, made by Pilkington Special Glass Ltd., St. Asaph, Wales. Its dimensions are: focal length 333 inches, diameter 54 inches, weight 474 pounds. Its focal length allows writing on the museum's walls to be read from 40 feet away.

Smallest camera Apart from cameras built for espionage and intracardiac surgery, the smallest is the Japanese "Petal" camera, with a diameter of 1.14 inches. Its focal length is 0.47 inches.

Fastest camera A camera built by The Blackett Laboratory of Imperial College of Science and Technology, London, England registers images at a rate of 33 billion per second.

The fastest production camera is currently the Imacon 675, made by Hadland Photonics Ltd. of Bovington, England, at up to 600 million frames per second.

Camera auction The record total for any camera auction is £296,043 ($503,000) for a collection of "spy," subminiature and detective cameras sold at Christie's, London, England on December 9, 1991.

The highest auction price for a camera is £55,750 ($86,415) for a rare

Enjalbert gun camera, a revolver-shaped spy camera made in France and patented in 1882, sold at Christie's, London, England on August 31, 1995.

Longest negative   On May 6, 1992, Thomas Bleich of Austin, TX produced a negative measuring 23 ft. 4½ in. by 10½ inches using a 10½-inch focal length Turner-Reich lens and Kodak No. 10 Cirkut Camera. The photograph was a portrait of 3,500 attendants at a concert in Austin.

RADIO

Most durable programs   *Rambling with Gambling*, the early morning program on WOR, New York City, was first broadcast in March 1925 and celebrated its 22,271st show on July 29, 1996. The show has been hosted by three generations of the Gambling family: John B. Gambling (1925–59), John A. Gambling (1959–89) and John R. Gambling (1985–present). The show currently airs six days a week, year-round.

The Grand Ole Opry has broadcast continuously since November 1925.

The weekly sports report "The Tenpin Tattler" was first broadcast on WCFL, Chicago, IL on August 24, 1935. More than 2,900 broadcasts later, it continues on WGN, Chicago with the original host, Sam Weinstein, who is the longest continuing host of a program.

Most hours broadcast per week   Larry King's radio and television programs were broadcast a combined 36 hours per week from 1985 through May 27, 1994. Since May 30, 1994, King's television show has aired simultaneously on radio and television six hours per week in 210 countries.

Most radio stations   The United States had 12,074 authorized broadcast stations as of June 30, 1996, more than any other country.

Largest audience   Surveys carried out in over 100 countries showed that the global estimated audience for the British Broadcasting Corporation World Service was 140 million regular listeners in 1995—greater than any other international broadcaster. The World Service is now broadcast in 41 languages.

Largest response   The largest recorded response to a radio show occurred June 21–27, 1993, when FM Osaka 85.1 in Osaka, Japan received a total of 8,091,309 calls in response to a phone-in lottery. The prize was 100,000 yen (around $1,500), and a chance to win it was offered for a 20-minute period every hour, for 10 hours each day. The maximum call count in one day of phone-ins (3 hr. 20 min.) was 1,540,793 on June 23, 1993.

Biggest radio prize   Mary Buchanan, 15, won a prize of $25,000 for 40 years (or $1 million) on WKRQ Cincinnati on November 21, 1980.

Most assiduous radio ham   The late Richard C. Spenceley of KV4AA in St. Thomas, VI built his contacts (QSOs) to a record level of 48,100 in 365 days in 1978.

RECORDED SOUND

Oldest recordings   The oldest existing recording was made in 1878 by Augustus Stroh, but it remains on the mandrel of his machine and has never been played.

The oldest playable record is believed to be an engraved metal cylinder made by Frank Lambert in 1878 or 1879 and voicing the hours on the clock. The recording is owned by Aaron Cramer of New York City.

Smallest recorder   In April 1983, Olympic Optical Industry Co. of Japan marketed a micro-cassette recorder measuring $4^1/_5$ by 2 by $^1/_2$ inches and weighing 4.4 ounces.

Smallest cassette   The NT digital cassette made by the Sony Corporation of Japan for use in dictating machines measures just $^1/_5$ by $^4/_5$ by $^1/_5$ inches.

Smallest functional record   Six titles of $1^5/_{16}$-inch diameter were recorded by HMV's studio at Hayes, England on January 26, 1923 for Queen Mary's Doll House. Some 92,000 of these miniature records were pressed, including 35,000 of God Save the King.

Largest record store   HMV opened the world's largest record store at 150 Oxford Street, London, England on October 24, 1986. Its selling area measures 36,684 square feet.

TOP RECORDING ARTISTS

Most successful solo recording artist   Although no independently audited figures have ever been published for Elvis Presley (1935–77), he had over 170 hit singles and over 80 top-selling albums starting in 1956. Aretha Franklin is the female solo artist with the most million-selling singles, with 14, 1967–73.

FASTEST SELLING DEBUT ALBUM

Cracked Rear View by Hootie and the Blowfish, released on July 5, 1994, is the fastest-selling debut album. It was certified at 14 million copies in the United States as of June 13, 1996.

See feature (next page)

Most successful group   The singers with the greatest sales of any group were the Beatles. The group, from Liverpool, England, comprised George

HOOTIE AND THE BLOWFISH

Jim Sonefeld, drummer for Hootie and the Blowfish, remembers his start back in the early years of his life known as college. And the more he remembers, the more he has to pinch himself now that his band holds the record for the fastest-selling debut album in the world.

"**B**ack in those days, we were definitely a college band back at the University of South Carolina," he reminisces. "We played weekend gigs and fraternity parties for beer. It wasn't until we were about to graduate in 1989 that we really got serious about things."

Serious is the right word to use for Hootie's first album, *Cracked Rear View*, which has sold more than 14 million copies. "When we decided to go all the way and start thinking of our band as a career more than a hobby, we realized that we had degrees that we worked for, but we were going to have to put them down if we wanted to be really intent on our music," Sonefeld says. "Being a musician, you're this big dreamer type where it doesn't matter how far away you are, you still think you're close to the top. That's what kept us going."

The band members held their jobs for a while, struggling to make ends meet, and stayed in South Carolina. "We just worked and tried to get off as early as we could for the weekend—and then just bolt," Sonefeld recalls. "We played a few gigs at a time, and as they started to increase, our bosses said, 'You've got to make a choice here: be in a band or have a job.'" Sonefeld admits now that this was exactly the kick in the pants that Hootie needed to break away. "We needed to just get on the road seriously—even if it meant starving a little bit."

The real surprise for Hootie and the Blowfish was the success that hit them when their record was finally released. "I think the reason we did so well was that we really touched people who weren't out buying records in force," Sonefeld muses. "We did a lot of televised events including Letterman, the opening ceremony at the Special Olympics and Frank Sinatra's 80th birthday party. People started to recognize us, and they just decided that we had a certain sound or something that they liked. I think our music is simple enough and nonaggressive enough to not scare anyone away," he adds. "We're pop music. We're not breaking any musical barriers—but maybe that's the catch. Maybe we're just simple enough that people can understand it and accept it."

Sonefeld does admit that breaking records is not what the band set out to do. "We're artists and musicians; we were thinking about how we were going to pay the rent next month. We knew that it was a really good thing that we got a chance to record a full-length album. That's all we wanted at that time. If you think past that, if you dream farther than that, or if you set your goal so high—you're in for a big fall. We just never wanted for that to happen."

Harrison, John Lennon, Paul McCartney and Ringo Starr. The all-time Beatles sales have been estimated by EMI at over a billion discs and tapes.

Most gold, platinum, and multiplatinum discs   The only *audited* measure of gold, platinum and multiplatinum singles and albums within the United States is certification by the Recording Industry Association of America (RIAA), introduced on March 14, 1958.

The Rolling Stones have the most certified gold discs for any group, with 41 (36 albums, 5 singles). The group with the most multiplatinum albums is the Beatles, with 13.

The recording artist with the most certified titles ever is Elvis Presley. Of his 61 gold albums, 29 went platinum, and 25 of his 50 gold singles went platinum. The female solo artist to receive the most gold discs is Barbra Streisand, with 43 (36 albums, 7 singles).

Elvis Presley holds the record for most platinum albums, with 29. Chicago, the Beatles and the Rolling Stones jointly hold the record for most platinum albums by a group, with 18. Billy Joel holds the record for the most multiplatinum albums for an individual, with 12. Barbra Streisand holds the platinum record for a female solo artist, with 23, and the record for most multiplatinum by a female recording artist, with 10.

Most recordings   A set of 180 compact discs containing the complete authenticated works of Mozart was produced by Philips Classics for release in 1990/91 to commemorate the bicentennial of the composer's death. The complete set comprises over 200 hours of music and would occupy 6½ feet of shelving.

Most Grammy Awards   An all-time record 32 awards to an individual (including a special Trustees' award presented in 1967 and a lifetime achievement award presented in 1996) have been won by the Hungarian-born British conductor Sir Georg Solti.

The most won by a solo pop performer is 18 (including a lifetime achievement award), by Stevie Wonder. The most won by a group is eight, by Manhattan Transfer. The greatest number won in one year is eight, by Michael Jackson, in 1984.

BIGGEST SELLERS

Singles   The greatest seller of any phonograph record to date is *White Christmas* by Irving Berlin, recorded by Bing Crosby on May 29, 1942. North American sales alone reached 170,884,207 copies by June 30, 1987.

The highest claim for any rock record is an unaudited 25 million for *Rock Around the Clock*, copyrighted in 1953 by James E. Myers under the name Jimmy De Knight and Max C. Freedmann and recorded on April 12, 1954 by Bill Haley and the Comets.

The highest certified singles, at 4 million copies, are "I Will Always Love You" by Whitney Houston; "Whoomp! (There It Is)" by Tag Team; "We Are The World" by USA for Africa; and "Bambi" by Disney.

Albums   The best-selling album of all time is *Thriller* by Michael Jackson, with United States sales of 24 million copies to date. The best-selling album by a group is the Eagles' *Greatest Hits, 1971–75* with over 22 million sales by July 1996.

TIPS

from the
RECORD BREAKERS

MOST SUCCESSFUL SOUL SINGER

Aretha Franklin has set the standards by which other singers are judged. Known worldwide as "the Queen of Soul," Franklin has set a stack of music records during her legendary career. Here she offers her advice on making records— including the Guinness kind.

◆

Love the music.

"I just started with just the love of singing," comments Franklin. And that's still the case. "Music crosses barriers," she notes. "That's a tremendous gratification. Music is moving and significant . . . and in some way special. That is just super terrific!"

◆

Dare to tour.

Touring is fun at first, but Franklin warns that it is a great challenge. "When you're younger and new to the industry you're excited and don't realize what 20 or 30 one-nighters mean," says Franklin. "It becomes very grueling living out of your suitcase," she adds. "Touring is rough on inexperienced and experienced performers."

◆

Seek out support.

Franklin tells aspiring singers, "If you must be in music, then try to have the best people manage you . . . in terms of a manager, road manager, booking agent and lawyer." And the secret to longevity? "Well, fabulous fans, that's for sure!" Franklin continues. "Good fans and my love for music . . . I think that's about it."

"WE WERE A GREAT LITTLE ROCK 'N' ROLL BAND"

—Paul McCartney

Beatles records? Are you kidding? They've got 'em in spades—but we couldn't possibly fit them all on these four pages. Here are some highlights of these all-time favorite record-makers (and record-breakers) extraordinaires!

Yesterday

"Such an easy game to play . . ."
—Yesterday

"Yesterday" has been played on the radio over 6 million times in the United States alone.

More than 3,000 covers have been made of "Yesterday," more than any other song. Artists range from Elvis Presley to Boyz II Men, Frank Sinatra to James Brown, Gladys Knight to Nat King Cole.

The song reportedly came to Paul McCartney in a dream. He woke up, went to the piano, turned on the tape recorder, and played the song, then spent the next few weeks trying to figure out whether he'd heard the song before or just made it up in his sleep. Some dream . . . some record!

Top-Selling Singles

"What I've got I'll give to you . . ."
—Can't Buy Me Love

The records came so hard and fast in the early years that even the record-keepers (producer EMI) got confused as to which Beatles song sold best in the United States.

The biggest advance orders for a song were for "Can't Buy Me Love," which sold 2,100,000 copies.

"I Want to Hold Your Hand" shares top billing because of the speed of its sales. Within three days of its release, 250,000 copies had been sold; after two weeks, one million copies were sold; and at 20 days, "I Want to Hold Your Hand" was selling 10,000 copies an hour in New York City alone.

But the hands-down winner is "Hey, Jude," (Apple) with more than 8 million copies sold in the United Kingdom and the United States.

Today

"The long and winding road that leads to your door . . ."
—The Long and Winding Road

With the *Beatles Anthology*, a vast compendium of first takes, out-takes, studio sessions, and unheard versions of beloved Beatles songs, the Beatles have done what every band since the Sixties has been trying to do: beat the Beatles.

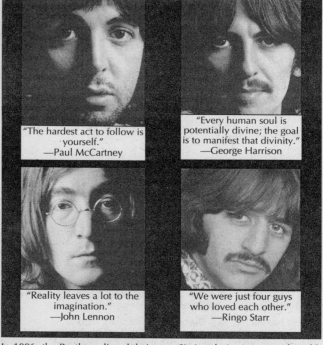

"The hardest act to follow is yourself."
—Paul McCartney

"Every human soul is potentially divine; the goal is to manifest that divinity."
—George Harrison

"Reality leaves a lot to the imagination."
—John Lennon

"We were just four guys who loved each other."
—Ringo Starr

In 1996, the Beatles eclipsed their own Sixties glories in terms of worldwide sales and audience. The *Beatles Anthology* television documentary was seen in 94 countries. Of great interest to the Beatles is the number of young people flocking to their recordings; 41% of buyers of *Beatles Anthology Volume 1* were teenagers.

Tomorrow

"You'll be older too . . ."
—When I'm Sixty-Four

• Volume 3 of the *Beatles Anthology* is expected to bring the year's total of sales for the Beatles to 33 million albums.

• In June 1996, Her Majesty Queen Elizabeth II opened the Liverpool Institute for Performing Arts. Founded by Paul McCartney, the school is housed in McCartney's old grammar school. A long-time dream of the Beatles legend, the project received backing from George Harrison, Ringo Starr, Yoko Ono and 2,000 other supporters. The aim is to help reinvigorate Liverpool by bringing in students from around the world to study dance, music and art with native Liverpudlians.

Interview: Paul McCartney

Paul McCartney drew the largest-ever stadium crowd to Maracanã Stadium, Rio de Janeiro, where 184,000 Brazilians turned out for his show. He talked to The Guinness Book of Records about what it's like to be on top of the world.

GBR: Did the Beatles expect to set so many records?

PM: We certainly didn't realize we were going to get into the record book, though we wanted to like everyone else. It's an honor for a kid who sat in the pub and hoped to be the tiddlywinks champion of the world to get to our level of success.

GBR: What's in the future for the Beatles?

PM: Most of the sales are to young people, which is funny because we all assumed it would be a lot of older people like ourselves on a nostalgia trip. I've got young kids myself. My son, for instance, will listen to one of our records and say, "Hey, it's funny!" Without being too immodest, I think that the writing was very good and it still holds up.

Top-Selling Double CD Album

Beatles Anthology Volume 1 and *Volume 2* sold 13 million double-CD albums in the first six months of release. *Volume 1*, released in November 1995, smashed the world record set by Michael Jackson's *HIStory* (391,000) by selling an incredible 855,473 copies for the first week of United States sales. *Volume 2* came in at number 3, with 441,788 copies. *Volume 2*, which covered the time period from February 1965, to February 1968—"the years of dash and daring"—was the Beatles' 17th number one album in the United States, more than any other band.

"Let's pretend that John's gone on holiday, he's rung up and said we've nearly finished the album, but there's this song that I kind of liked but I haven't finished yet. Will you finish it up for me? I trust you."

—Paul McCartney, recalling the Beatles' decision to record "Free As a Bird" based on the John Lennon tape that Yoko Ono agreed to release. "It was pretty emotional," recalls McCartney. "I warned Ringo to have his hanky ready when he listened to it."

Boston by Boston, released in 1976, is the best-selling debut album of all time. It has sold over 15 million copies in the United States.

Soundtrack   The best-selling movie soundtrack is *Saturday Night Fever*, with sales of over 26.5 million by May 1987.

Classical album   The best-selling classical album is *In Concert*, with sales of 2 million to date. It was recorded by José Carreras, Placido Domingo and Luciano Pavarotti at the 1990 Soccer World Cup Finals in Rome, Italy.

THE CHARTS

U.S. singles   "One Sweet Day" by Mariah Carey and Boyz II Men spent 16 weeks at Number 1 in 1995–96.

The Beatles have had the most No. 1 singles (20), Conway Twitty the most Country No. 1's (40) and Aretha Franklin and Stevie Wonder the most Rhythm and Blues No. 1's (20 each). Elvis Presley has had the most hit singles on *Billboard*'s Hot 100—149 from 1956 to 1983.

Bing Crosby's *White Christmas* spent a total of 86 weeks on the charts between 1942 and 1962. *Tainted Love* by Soft Cell stayed on the charts for 43 *consecutive* weeks from January 1982.

Albums   *South Pacific* was No. 1 for 69 weeks (nonconsecutive) from May 1949. *Dark Side of the Moon* by Pink Floyd was on the *Billboard* charts for 741 weeks to October 1988.

The Beatles had the most No. 1 albums (17). Elvis Presley was the most successful male soloist (9). Presley has had the most hit albums (93 from 1956 to January 1995).

DANCING

Largest dance   An estimated 48,000 people took part in a Chicken Dance held during the 1994 Oktoberfest-Zinzinnati in Cincinnati, OH in September 1994.

Longest dance   The most taxing marathon dance staged as a public spectacle was by Mike Ritof and Edith Boudreaux, who logged 214 days 12 hr. 28½ min. to win $2,000 at Chicago's Merry Garden Ballroom, Belmont and Sheffield, IL, August 29, 1930–April 1, 1931. Rest periods were progressively cut from 20 to 10 to 5 to zero minutes per hour, with 10-inch steps and a maximum of 15 seconds for closure of eyes.

The longest distance danced by one person was 13.1 miles, by Elizabeth Ursic, who tap-danced the Arizona Half Marathon in Tempe, AZ on January 10, 1993.

Rosie Radiator led 12 tap dancers through the streets of San Francisco, CA in a routine covering 9.61 miles on July 11, 1994.

Ballet *Fastest entrechat douze*   In the *entrechat*, the starting and finishing position each count as one, so that in an *entrechat douze* there are five crossings and uncrossings. This feat was performed by Wayne Sleep for the British Broadcasting Corporation *Record Breakers* TV program on January 7, 1973. He was in the air for 0.71 seconds.

Grands jetés   On November 28, 1988, Wayne Sleep completed 158 *grands jetés* along the length of Dunston Staiths, Gateshead, England in two minutes.

Most turns   The greatest number of spins called for in classical ballet choreography is 32 *fouettés rond de jambe en tournant* in *Swan Lake* by Piotr Ilyich Tchaikovsky (1840–93). Delia Gray (Great Britain) achieved 166 such turns at The Playhouse, Harlow, England on June 2, 1991.

Most curtain calls   Dame Margot Fonteyn and Rudolf Nureyev received 89 curtain calls after a performance of *Swan Lake* at the Vienna Staatsoper, Austria in October 1964.

Most successful ballroom dancers   The professional ballroom dancing champions Bill and Bobbie Irvine won 13 world titles between 1960 and 1968.

Oldest ballroom dancer   The oldest competitive ballroom dancer was Albert J. Sylvester (1889–1989) of Corsham, England, who retired at age 94.

United States   The oldest competitive ballroom dancer in the United States is Lorna S. Lengfeld, who was still competing at age 90.

Longest conga line   The Miami Super Conga, held in conjunction with Calle Ocho—a party to which Cuban-Americans invite the rest of Miami for a celebration of life—consisted of 119,986 people. The event was held on March 13, 1988.

The largest country line dance took place in Redwood City, CA.

Largest country line dance A total of 3,770 people danced for five minutes to "T-R-O-U-B-L-E" by Travis Tritt in Redwood City, CA on July 6, 1996.

Longest dancing dragon On May 19, 1995, 610 people brought to life a dancing dragon measuring 5,550 feet from nose to tail. The dragon danced for five minutes at Tiantan, Beijing, China.

Fastest flamenco dancer Solero de Jerez attained 16 heel taps per second in Brisbane, Australia in September 1967.

Lowest limbo dancer Dennis Walston, alias King Limbo, passed under a flaming bar that was just six inches off the floor in Kent, WA on March 2, 1991.

Roller skates The record for a performer on roller skates is $4^7/_{10}$ inches, achieved by Syamala Gowri at Hyderabad, Andhra Pradesh, India on May 10, 1993.

Square dance calling Alan Covacic called for 26 hr. 2 min. for the Wheelers and Dealers Square Dance Club at Halton Royal Air Force Base, Aylesbury, England, November 18–19, 1988.

Tap dancing Fastest tap dancer The fastest rate measured for tap dancing is 32 taps per second, by Stephen Gare (Great Britain) in Birmingham, England on March 28, 1990.

Most taps Roy Castle achieved one million taps in 23 hr. 44 min. at the Guinness World of Records Exhibition, London, England, October 31–November 1, 1985.

Most tap dancers in a routine On August 20, 1995, 6,553 tap dancers tapped through a single routine outside Macy's department store at 34th Street and Sixth Avenue, New York City.

CIRCUS

Oldest circus The oldest circus building is Cirque d'Hiver (originally Cirque Napoléon), which opened in Paris, France on December 11, 1852.

Largest circus The most performers in a circus act was 263 people plus 175 animals, in the 1890 Barnum & Bailey Circus tour of the United States.

The record for an animal-free circus is 61, for Cirque du Soleil's tour of Japan in 1992.

Largest circus tent The traveling circus tent of Ringling Bros. and Barnum & Bailey, used on tours in the United States from 1921 to 1924, covered 91,415 square feet. It consisted of a round top 200 feet in diameter with five middle sections, each 60 feet wide.

A parade of elephants from the Ringling Bros. and Barnum & Bailey
Circus.

Largest circus audience An audience of 52,385 attended the Ringling Bros. and Barnum & Bailey circus at the Superdome, New Orleans, LA on September 14, 1975. The largest audience in a tent was 16,702, also for Ringling Bros. and Barnum & Bailey, in Concordia, KS on September 13, 1924.

Aerial acts The highest trapeze act was performed by Mike Howard (Great Britain) at heights of 19,600 to 20,300 feet, suspended from a hot-air balloon between Glastonbury and Street, England on August 10, 1995.

Janet May Klemke (U.S.) performed 305 1-arm planges at Medina Shrine Circus, Chicago, IL on January 21, 1938.

Flexible pole The only publicly performed quadruple back somersault on the flexible pole was accomplished by Maksim Dobrovitsky (USSR) of the Yegorov Troupe at the International Circus Festival of Monte Carlo in Monaco on February 4, 1989.

Corina Colonelu Mosoianu (Romania) performed a triple full twisting somersault, at Madison Square Garden, New York City, on April 17, 1984.

Flying return trapeze The back somersault record is a quadruple back, by Miguel Vasquez (Mexico) to Juan Vasquez at Ringling Bros. and Barnum & Bailey Circus, Tucson, AZ on July 10, 1982. The greatest number of consecutive triple back somersaults is 135, by Jamie Ibarra (Mexico) to Alejandro Ibarra, between July 23 and October 12, 1989, at various locations in the United States.

High diving Col. Harry A. Froboess (Switzerland) jumped 394 feet into the Bodensee from the airship *Graf Hindenburg* on June 22, 1936.

The greatest height reported for a dive into an air bag is 326 feet, by stuntman Dan Koko, who jumped from the top of Vegas World Hotel and Casino onto a 20 by 40 by 14-foot target on August 13, 1948.

High wire A 7-person pyramid was achieved by the Great Wallendas (Germany) at Wallenda Circus in 1947. The highest high-wire feat (ground supported) was at a height of 1,350 feet by Philippe Petit (France) between the towers of the World Trade Center, New York on August 7, 1974.

Horseback riding James Robinson (U.S.) perfromed 23 consecutive somersaults on horseback at Spalding & Rogers Circus, Pittsburgh, PA in 1856. Willy, Beby, and Rene Fredianis (Italy) performed a 3-high column at Nouveau Cirque, Paris, France in 1908. "Poodles" Hanneford (Ireland; b. England) holds the record for running leaps on and off, with 26 at Barnum & Bailey Circus, New York in 1915.

Human arrow "Ariana" (Vesta Gueschkova; Bulgaria) was fired 75 feet from a crossbow at Ringling Bros. and Barnum & Bailey Circus, Tampa, FL on December 27, 1995.

Human cannonball Emanuel Zacchini (Italy) was fired a record 175 feet from a cannon in the United States in 1940.

Human pyramid The weight record is 1,700 pounds, when Tahar Douis supported 12 members of the Hassani Troupe in Birmingham, England on December 17, 1979. The height record is 39 feet, when Josep-Joan Martinez Lozano of the Colla Vella dels Xiquets mounted a 9-high pyramid at Valls, Spain on October 25, 1981.

Plate spinning The greatest number of plates spun simultaneously is 108, by Dave Spathaky of London, England for the Tarm Pai Du television program in Thailand on November 23, 1992.

Stilt-walking Speed Roy Luiking covered 328 feet on 1-foot-high stilts in 13.01 seconds in Didam, Netherlands on May 28, 1992.
   In 1892, M. Garisoain (France) walked 4.97 miles from Bayonne to Biarritz on stilts in 42 minutes, at an average speed of 7.10 MPH.

Distance Joe Bowen walked 3,008 miles on stilts from Los Angeles, CA to Bowen, KY, February 20–July 26, 1980.

Tallest and heaviest stilts Eddy Wolf ("Steady Eddy") of Loyal, WI mastered stilts measuring 40 ft. 9$\frac{1}{2}$ in. from ground to ankle and weighing 57 pounds each when he walked 25 steps without touching his safety handrail wires on August 3, 1988.

Teeter board The Shanghai Acrobats achieved a 6-person-high unaided column in Shanghai, China in 1993.

Trampoline Marco Canestrelli (U.S.) performed a septuple twisting back somersault to bed at Ringling Bros. and Barnum & Bailey Circus, St. Petersburg, FL on January 5, 1979. He also managed a quintuple twisting back somersault to a 2-high column at Ringling Bros. and Barnum & Bailey Circus, New York City on March 28, 1979.

THEATER

Oldest indoor theater The Teatro Olimpico in Vicenza, Italy was designed in the Roman style by Andrea di Pietro, alias Palladio (1508–80). It was begun three months before his death and finished in 1583. The theater is preserved today in its original form.

Largest theater The Perth Entertainment Center, Western Australia is the largest theater measured by capacity. It was completed in November 1976 and has 8,003 seats. The stage area is 12,000 square feet.

United States The highest-capacity theater in use on Broadway is the Gershwin Theater, with 1,933 seats. Designed by Ralph Alswang, the theater opened in November 1972.

Laurence Olivier in *Hamlet*, the longest of Shakespeare's plays.

Amphitheater   The Colosseum in Rome, Italy, completed in A.D. 80, covers five acres and has a capacity of 87,000. It has a maximum length of 612 feet and a maximum width of 515 feet.

Smallest theater   The smallest regularly operated professional theater in the world is the Piccolo in Juliusstrasse, Hamburg, Germany. It was founded in 1970 and has a maximum capacity of 30 seats.

Largest stage   The Hilton Theater at the Reno Hilton, Reno, NV measures 175 by 241 feet. The stage has three main elevators each capable of raising 40 tons, two 62½-foot-circumference turntables and 800 spotlights.

Longest runs   *The Mousetrap* by Agatha Christie opened on November 25, 1952 at the Ambassadors Theatre, London, England and later moved to the St. Martin's Theatre. The 18,110th performance was on May 28, 1996, and the show has grossed more than £20 million ($36 million).

The Vicksburg Theater Guild, Vicksburg, MS has been playing the melodrama *Gold in the Hills* by J. Frank Davis discontinuously but every season since 1936.

Revue   The greatest number of performances of any theatrical presentation is 47,250, by *The Golden Horseshoe Revue*, a show staged at Disneyland, Anaheim, CA. It started on July 16, 1955 and closed on October 12, 1986.

Musicals   The off-Broadway musical show *The Fantasticks* by Tom Jones and Harvey Schmidt opened on May 3, 1960. As of July 30, 1996, the show had been performed a record 15,007 times at the Sullivan Street Playhouse, Greenwich Village, New York City.

Cats is the longest-running musical in the history of the West End and Broadway. It opened on May 12, 1981 at the New London Theatre, Drury Lane, where the 6,278th show was performed on May 28, 1996.

Most ardent theatergoer   Dr. H. Howard Hughes, Prof. Emeritus of Texas Wesleyan College, Fort Worth, TX attended 6,136 shows in the period 1957–87.

Greatest loss   The greatest loss sustained by a theatrical show was by the American producers of the Royal Shakespeare Company's musical *Carrie*, which closed after five performances on Broadway on May 17, 1988 at a cost of $7 million.

Tony Awards   Hal Prince has won 17 Tonys—the awards of the American Theater Wing—the most for any individual. Prince has won a total of 9 awards as a producer and 8 as a director.

Three plays have won five Tonys: *A Man for All Seasons* (1962), *Who's Afraid of Virginia Woolf?* (1963) and *Amadeus* (1981).

The only person to win five Tonys in starring roles is Julie Harris, in *I am a Camera* (1952), *The Lark* (1956), *Forty Carats* (1969), *The Last of Mrs. Lincoln* (1973) and *The Belle of Amherst* (1977).

One-man shows   The longest run of one-man shows is 849, by Victor Borge (Denmark) in his *Comedy in Music* from October 2, 1953 through January 21, 1956 at the Golden Theater, Broadway, New York City.

The aggregate record for one-man shows is 1,700 performances of *Brief Lives* by Roy Dotrice (Great Britain), including 400 straight at the Mayfair Theatre, London, England ending on July 20, 1974. He was on stage for more than 2½ hours per performance of this 17th-century monologue and required three hours for makeup and an hour for removal of makeup, thus totaling 40 weeks in the chair.

Most durable performer   Kanmi Fujiyama played the lead role in 10,288 performances by comedy company Sochiku Shikigeki from November 1966 to June 1983.

Most durable understudy   In 1994, Nancy Seabrooke, age 79, retired from the company of *The Mousetrap* in London, England, having understudied the part of "Mrs. Boyle" for 15 years or 6,240 performances.

Greatest advance sales   *Miss Saigon*, produced by Cameron Mackintosh, opened on Broadway in April 1991 after generating record advance sales of $36 million.

Most roles   The greatest recorded number of theatrical, film and television roles portrayed is 3,395 since 1951 by Jan Leighton (U.S.).

Theatrical roles   Kanzaburo Nakamura performed in 806 Kabuki titles from November 1926 to January 1987. Since each title in this classical Japanese theatrical form lasts 25 days, he gave 20,150 performances.

Longest Shakespeare play   *Hamlet* is the longest of Shakespeare's 37 plays. Written in 1604, it has 4,042 lines or 29,551 words. The longest of Shakespeare's 1,277 speaking parts is the role of Hamlet, with 11,610 words.

Longest chorus lines   The longest chorus line numbered up to 120 in some of the early *Ziegfeld Follies*. In the finale of *A Chorus Line* on the night of September 29, 1983, when it broke the record as the longest-running Broadway show ever, 332 top-hatted "strutters" performed on stage.

On March 28, 1992 in Eastleigh, England, 543 members of the cast of *Showtime News*, a production by Hampshire West Guides, performed a routine choreographed by professional dancer Sally Horsley.

Hal Prince

Excellence, ticket sales, and controversy: the three leading players of the Tony Awards. The Tonys recognize the best on Broadway, and they also stimulate ticket sales for the winning shows. As a result, few awards have such an impact on their industry. And few spark so much debate. "They don't make any more sense than any other award." The comments of a sore loser? Hardly! These are the words of producer and director Hal Prince, who has won 17 Tony Awards.

"I'm delighted to have received so many Tonys and I think they're good for the industry, but I don't think any awards are artistically significant," says Prince. The Broadway legend received his first Tony in 1954 as co-producer of *The Pajama Game*. Other Tonys have poured in for his work as producer or director (sometimes both), of such hits as *Damn Yankees* (1955), *Fiddler On The Roof* (1964), *Company* (1970), *Evita* (1978), *Phantom of the Opera* (1986) and *Showboat* (1994). But Prince is modest about his success. "I can't take credit for shows like *West Side Story*, which turned out to be a gigantic success. I produced it, that's all." He adds, "By the way, *West Side Story* never won a Tony Award for anyone except the choreographer [Jerome Robbins]."

Although he pooh-poohs awards, Prince thinks his Tony record will be tough to beat. "There's a terrible reason for that. It's harder for someone to have a 40- or 50-year career doing plays on Broadway now. The other reason—I'm blowing the whistle on all of those awards, you understand—is because some are for producing and some directing. There was a period when I got two at a time (for producing and directing the same show). I've had the advantage on guys who just direct or just produce."

Prince is currently planning another collaboration with Andrew Lloyd-Webber (*Whistle Down the Wind*), but he claims he never sets out to win a Tony, even for a Lloyd-Webber musical. His inspiration? "I love subjects that seem unlikely. I can surprise the audience."

But there's no doubt that he would readily accept another Tony. "I think they're lovely. They create a little glamor once a year. They sound the theater hunting horn, if you will, outside New York."

Largest arts festival The largest arts festival is the annual Edinburgh Fringe Festival, held in Edinburgh, Scotland (instituted in 1947). In 1993, its record year, 582 groups gave 14,108 performances of 1,643 shows between August 15 and September 4.

Nigel Tantrum (Great Britain) attended 169 separate performances at the 1994 Edinburgh Festival.

Fashion shows The greatest distance covered by a model on a catwalk is 83.1 miles, by Eddie Warke at Parke's Hotel, Dublin, Republic of Ireland, September 19–21, 1983. The women's record is 71.1 miles, by Roberta Brown and Lorraine McCourt on the same occasion.

Fastest magician Eldon D. Wigton, alias Dr. Eldoonie, performed 225 different tricks in two minutes in Kilbourne, OH on April 21, 1991.

CINEMA

MOVIES

Largest output India's production of feature-length movies was a record 948 in 1990, and its annual output has exceeded 700 every year since 1979.

United States In the United States, 479 movies were produced in 1988, the most in a year since 1968.

Most expensive movie The most expensive movie was Universal's *Waterworld* (U.S., 1995), directed by Kevin Reynolds and starring Kevin Costner and Dennis Hopper, which cost $175 million. Extraordinary special effects and schedule overruns contributed to the huge costs.

In terms of real costs adjusted for inflation, the most expensive movie ever made was *Cleopatra* (U.S., 1963), with a budget of $44 million.

Most expensive movie rights The highest price ever paid for movie rights was $9.5 million, announced on January 20, 1978 by Columbia, for *Annie*, the Broadway musical by Charles Strouse.

Longest movie The longest movie commercially released in its entirety was Edgar Reitz's 25-hr.-32-min. *Die Zweite Heimat* (Germany, 1992), premiered in Munich, September 5–9, 1992.

Highest box office gross The box office champion is Universal's *Jurassic Park*, which earned $912.8 million ($356.8 million in North America) through April 21, 1995.

In July 1996, *Independence Day* (20th Century Fox) passed the $100 million mark in 6.5 days, faster than any other movie.

Batman Forever (Warner Brothers) broke records for both highest opening-day box office gross and highest single-day gross by bringing in $20 million on June 16, 1995.

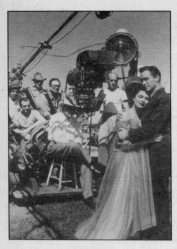

King Vidor directed movies for 67 years.

Foreign language   The highest-grossing foreign language movie in the United States is Alfonso Arau's *Like Water for Chocolate*, which had earned a final domestic gross of $21.7 million as of April 1995.

Largest movie premiere   *A Few Good Men*, starring Tom Cruise, Demi Moore and Jack Nicholson, was simultaneously released in over 50 countries by Columbia Pictures in 1992.

Largest loss   It cost a total $124,053,994 to produce, promote, and distribute *Last Action Hero* (Columbia; U.S., 1993). The movie, starring Arnold Schwarzenegger, is estimated to have earned $44 million worldwide, creating a resounding loss of some $80 million.

Highest earnings   Jack Nicholson stood to receive up to $60 million for playing "The Joker" in Warner Brothers' $50 million *Batman*, through a percentage of the movie's receipts in lieu of salary.

Most profitable series   The most successful movie series is the 18 James Bond movies, from *Dr. No* (1962) starring Sean Connery to *License to Kill* (1989) with Timothy Dalton. The series grossed over $1 billion worldwide.

Largest studios   The largest complex of movie studios in the world is the one at Universal City, Los Angeles, CA. The back lot contains 479 buildings and there are 31 sound stages on the 420-acre site.

Largest studio stage   The 007 stage at Pinewood Studios, Buckinghamshire, England was built in 1976 for the James Bond movie *The Spy Who Loved Me*. It measures 336 by 139 by 41 feet and can accommodate 1.2 million gallons of water, a full-scale 672,000-ton oil tanker and three scaled-down nuclear submarines.

Largest movie set Veniero Colosanti and John Moore designed a Roman Forum measuring 1,312 by 754 feet for Samuel Bronston's production of *The Fall of the Roman Empire* (1964). It was built on a 55-acre site outside Madrid, Spain. It took 1,100 workmen seven months to lay 170,000 cement blocks, erect 22,000 feet of stairways, 601 columns and 350 statues, and construct 27 buildings.

Largest number of extras It is believed that over 300,000 extras appeared in the funeral scene of Sir Richard Attenborough's *Gandhi* (1982).

Most expensive prop In January 1995, the 45-pound statue known as the Maltese Falcon was sold to a secret buyer for a price that cannot be revealed. The Maltese Falcon is described in the 1941 Humphrey Bogart movie of the same name and was sold by Ronald Winston, president of Harry Winston jewelers, for much more than the $398,500 he paid for it at auction in 1994.

Longest directorial career The directorial career of King Vidor lasted for 67 years, beginning with the 2-reel comedy *Hurricane in Galveston* (1913) and culminating in another short, a documentary called *The Metaphor* (1980).

Oldest director The Dutch director Joris Ivens (1898–1989) made the Franco-Italian co-production *Une Histoire de Vent* in 1988 at age 89. He made his directorial debut with the Dutch movie *De Brug* in 1928.

Hollywood George Cukor (1899–1983) made his 50th and final movie, MGM's *Rich and Famous*, in 1981 at age 81.

Youngest director The movie *Lex the Wonderdog* was written, produced, and directed by Sydney Ling (b. 1959) when he was 13 years old. Ling was therefore the youngest director of a professionally made feature-length movie.

Most successful director Steven Spielberg is the most successful filmmaker ever, with seven movies in the all-time top 10. Collectively, his movies have grossed more than $2.17 billion. *Schindler's List*, Spielberg's portrayal of the Holocaust, won him his first "Best Director" Oscar.

Oldest performer The oldest screen performer in a speaking role was Jeanne Louise Calment (b. 1875–*fl.* July 1996), who portrayed herself in the 1990 Canadian movie *Vincent and Me*. (See OLDEST PERSON.)

Most durable performers The record for the longest screen career is 83 years, held by German actor Curt Bois (1900–91), who made his debut in *Der Fidele Bauer* at age eight; one of his most recent movies is *Wings of Desire* (1988).

American actress Helen Hayes (1900–93) first appeared on screen at age 10 in *Jean and the Calico Doll*, with much of her later work being for television. Her last screen role was in *Divine Mercy, No Escape* (1988) in a career lasting 78 years.

The most enduring star of the big screen was Lillian Gish (1893–1993). She made her debut in *An Unseen Enemy* (1912), and her last movie in a career spanning 75 years was *The Whales of August* (1987).

DEAN DEVLIN

Talk about death and destruction: on its preview night, *Independence Day* united citizens of cities across the United States, penetrated the countryside with violent force, and absorbed the mind-sets of officials and civilians alike. Yet not a drop of blood was shed (unlike the plot of the film)—unless you count the moviegoers' wallets, which bled green to the tune of $11.124 million. The previous record, $3.7 million by *Die Hard*, died, well, with a vengeance.

In this movie, an enormous force of technologically advanced aliens arrives in Earth's atmosphere and disperses disc-shaped spaceships to hover over every major city, quietly taking aim. Producer Dean Devlin de-

scribed the goals he and co-writer Roland Emmerich used to come up with this blockbuster: "All we wanted to do was to make the movie we'd like to go see on Friday night." That movie, they realized, would owe a lot to B-movies of the 70s—movies like *Airport* and *The Towering Inferno*, which included guts, gore, and a cast of famous people playing unusual

(for them) roles. *Independence Day* finds Will E. Smith in the role of a fighter pilot, Harry Connick, Jr. as his flaky sidekick, Bill Pullman as the President of the United States, Jeff Goldblum as a cyber-genius, plus appearances by Mary McDonnell, Harvey Fierstein, Judd Hirsch, and more.

"Our plot gave us the liberty to do wide-ranging things in the course of a disaster. People have compared *Independence Day* to *War of the Worlds* (the H. G. Wells story about an alien invasion), but *War of the Worlds* was not fulfilling on an emotional level: it didn't appeal to audiences viscerally." To Devlin and Emmerich, extraterrestrials make ideal villains. "Aliens don't have a political action committee. We have the liberty to portray them as a force of nature. They don't like us or hate us, they just want us gone—kind of the way people feel when they move into an apartment full of cockroaches. So when the President asks the aliens, 'What do you want us to do?' they say what we'd say to cockroaches: 'Die.' "

These aliens, having overrun their own planet, use their technological prowess to try to put Earthlings out of commission. Their bodies, which include an outer shell, are symbolic. "Our theme is the triumph of the human spirit over technology. They come to a planet, consume until the planet is destroyed, then move on. We have such aliens inside ourselves, as people, and we have to fight against ourselves to save our planet."

What starts as an American holiday weekend wrecked by aliens ends as the entire Earth declares its independence together. What happens, in Devlin's mind, after the movie ends? "I'd like to think everyone in the world would get along, but given what's in human nature, I don't know." He and Emmerich will be exploring the possibility of a sequel, while working on their next potential record-breakers, remakes of *Godzilla* and *Fantastic Voyage*, as well as *Supertanker*, a spectacular with a cargo ship at its heart. "We have 11 projects in development. One reason we can be so prolific is the way we write. I write dialogue on my laptop while Roland sits next to me with a drawing board. We question each other relentlessly and are incredibly combative, in a healthy way. By the end of the process, we have a script, we know what special effects and cast we will need, and we've already answered each question that any studio can come up with."

Such speed enabled the crew of thousands to make *Independence Day* in 15 months, and to keep the budget at a relatively low $70 million. "We have a director [Emmerich] who won't do it at just any price. Our hero is Steven-Spielberg, and he never spends that much money." Devlin has a long history of learning from other filmmakers. He's the son of producer Don Devlin (*My Bodyguard*) and took his first role at age 12½, as a pageboy in *Harry and Walter Go to New York*. "I took the money I made in that and

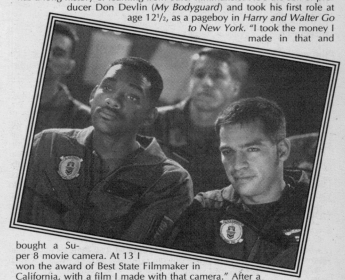

bought a Super 8 movie camera. At 13 I won the award of Best State Filmmaker in California, with a film I made with that camera." After a stint as an actor, Devlin joined with Emmerich and created *Universal Soldier* and the ground-breaking *Stargate*. Experience as an amateur magician helped him form his own philosophy about how a movie should look. And *The Guinness Book of Records* fed his ambition. "I never wanted to try something like pogo stick jumping," he says, then adds laughingly, "but I did always hope I'd have that box office record."

Most generations of screen actors There are four generations of screen actors in the Redgrave family. Roy Redgrave made his screen debut in 1911 and continued to appear in Australian movies until 1920. His son, Sir Michael Redgrave, married actress Rachel Kempson, and their two daughters Vanessa and Lynn and son Corin are all actors. Vanessa's two daughters, Joely and Natasha, and Corin's daughter Jemma, are also actresses.

Most portrayed character The character most frequently recurring on the screen is Sherlock Holmes, created by Sir Arthur Conan Doyle (1859–1930). The Baker Street sleuth has been portrayed by 75 actors in 211 movies since 1900.

In horror movies, the character most often portrayed is Count Dracula, created by the Irish writer Bram Stoker (1847–1912). Representations of the Count or his immediate descendants outnumber those of his closest rival, Frankenstein's monster, by 161 to 117.

Most movies seen Gwilym Hughes of Dolgellau, Wales had seen 22,447 movies as of January 12, 1996. He saw his first movie in 1953 while in the hospital.

Most costumes The largest number of costumes used for any one movie was 32,000 for the 1951 movie *Quo Vadis*.

Most costume changes Elizabeth Taylor changed costume 65 times in *Cleopatra* (1963). The costumes were designed by Irene Sharaff and cost $130,000.

Most expensive costume Constance Bennett's sable coat in *Madame X* was valued at $50,000. The most expensive costume made for a movie was Edith Head's mink-and-sequin dance costume worn by Ginger Rogers in *Lady in the Dark*. It cost Paramount $35,000.

The ruby slippers worn by Judy Garland in *The Wizard of Oz* were sold on June 2, 1988 to a mystery buyer at Christie's, New York City for $165,000.

Oscar winners Walt Disney (1901–66) won more Oscars than any other person. The physical count comprises 20 statuettes and 12 other plaques and certificates, including posthumous awards.

Katharine Hepburn won four Oscars in starring roles, for *Morning Glory* (1932/33), *Guess Who's Coming to Dinner* (1967), *The Lion in Winter* (1968) and *On Golden Pond* (1981).

The movie with the most awards is *Ben Hur* (1959) with 11. The most nominations, 14, went to *All About Eve* (1950), which won 6 awards.

Youngest winners The youngest winner in competition was Tatum O'Neal, who was 10 when she received the award in 1974 for Best Supporting Actress in *Paper Moon* (1973). Shirley Temple was awarded an honorary Oscar at age five in 1934.

Oldest winner The oldest recipient of an Oscar was Jessica Tandy, who won Best Actress for *Driving Miss Daisy* in 1990 at the age of 80.

MOVIE THEATERS

Largest movie theater   Radio City Music Hall, New York City, opened on December 27, 1932, with 5,945 (now 5,910) seats.

Kinepolis, in Brussels, Belgium, has 26 theaters with seating for 160–70 people. It also has an IMAX theater, with a screen measuring 65 ft. 7 in. by 98 ft. 5 in., that can seat 450 people. The total seating capacity of the complex is around 6,000.

Largest movie theater attendance   China had a peak mainland movie theater attendance figure of 21.8 billion in 1988.

Biggest screen   The largest permanent screen has an area of 81 by 109.3 feet. It is located at the Expo '93 Taejon Earthscape Pavilion Sangyong Group Imax Theatre, Taejon, South Korea.

The Six Flags Great America Pictorium, Gurnee, IL has a 3D screen of 96 by 70½ feet.

ADVERTISING

TELEVISION

Highest TV advertising rate   The highest TV advertising rate was $2.3 million per minute for ABC network prime time during the transmission of Super Bowl XXIX on January 29, 1995, watched by 120 million viewers.

Shortest TV commercial   An advertisement lasting only four frames (there are 30 frames in a second) was aired on KING-TV's *Evening Magazine* on November 29, 1993. The ad was for Bon Marche's Frango candies, and cost $3,780 to make.

Fastest production   A 30-second TV advertisement for Reebok Insta-PUMP shoes, starring Emmitt Smith of the Dallas Cowboys, was created, filmed and aired during Super Bowl XXVII on January 31, 1993. Filming continued until the beginning of the fourth quarter, editing began in the middle of the third quarter, and the finished product was aired during the commercial break at the 2-minute warning of the fourth quarter.

Longest-running commercial characters   Jan Miner appeared in U.S. TV commercials as "Madge the Manicurist" from 1965 to 1991, and Dick Wilson, alias "Mr. Whipple," from 1964 to 1989.

SIGNS

Highest advertising sign   The highest advertising sign is the logo "I" at the top of the 73-story, 1,017-foot-tall First Interstate World Center building, Los Angeles, CA.

Most visible advertising sign   The electric Citroën sign on the Eiffel Tower, Paris, France was switched on on July 4, 1925, and could be seen 24 miles

The Citroën sign on the Eiffel Tower was switched on in 1925.

away. It was in six colors with 250,000 bulbs and 56 miles of electric cables. The letter "N" in "Citroën" measured 68 ft. 5 in. high. The whole apparatus was dismantled in 1936.

Largest freestanding advertising sign   The sign at the Hilton Hotel and Casino in Las Vegas, NV was completed in December 1993. Its two faces had a total area of 2,328 square feet and it was 362 feet high when it was completed, but it was damaged in a storm on July 18, 1994, and part of it fell down. Even after this, it is still both the largest and the tallest sign.

Largest advertising signs   The largest advertisement on a building measured 47,385 square feet and was erected to promote the international airline Gulf Air. It was displayed at the side of the M4 motorway near Chiswick, England during May and June 1995.

Airborne   Reebok International Ltd. of Massachusetts flew a banner from a single-seater plane that read "Reebok Totally Beachin." The banner measured 50 feet high and 100 feet long, and was flown for four hours each day between March 13–16 and 20–23, 1990, at Daytona Beach, FL.

Animated   Topsy the Clown, outside the Circus Circus Hotel, Reno, NV, is 127 feet tall and weighs over 45 tons, with 1.4 miles of neon tubing. Topsy's smile measures 14 feet across.

Billboard   The billboard for the Bassat Ogilvy Promotional Campaign for Ford España is 475 ft. 9 in. long and 49 ft. 3 in. high. It is sited at Plaza de Toros Monumental de Barcelona, Barcelona, Spain, and was installed on April 27, 1989.

Largest illuminated advertising signs   A sign measuring 210 feet by 55 feet was built for Marlboro cigarettes in Hung Hom, Kowloon, Hong Kong in May 1986. It contains 35,000 feet of neon tubing and weighs approximately 126 tons.

Longest   The longest illuminated sign measures 197 by 66 feet. It is lit by 62 400-W metal-halide projectors and was erected by Abudi Signs Industry Ltd. in Ramat Gan, Israel.

A larger such sign, measuring 171 by 138 feet, was displayed throughout 1988 on the Australian Mutual Provident Building in Sydney, New South Wales, Australia. The sign, reading "1788–1988," consisted of 4.26 miles of LUMENYTE fiber optics.

Neon   The longest neon sign is the letter "M" installed on the Great Mississippi River Bridge, Old Man River at Memphis, TN. It is 1,800 feet long and is made up of 200 high-intensity lamps.

An interior-lit fascia advertising sign in Clearwater, FL completed by the Adco Sign Corp. in April 1983 measured 1,168 ft. 6½ in. long.

BUSINESS &

LAW

40

COMMERCE

Oldest industry   Flint knapping, involving the production of chopping tools and hand axes, dates from 2.5 million years ago in Ethiopia. Evidence of trading in exotic stone and amber dates from *c.* 28,000 B.C. in Europe.

Oldest company   The oldest existing documented company is Stora Kopparbergs Bergslags of Falun, Sweden, which has been in continuous operation since the 11th century. It is first mentioned in historical records in the year 1288, when a bishop bartered an eighth share in the enterprise, and it was granted a charter in 1347.

Family business   The Hoshi Ryokan, a hotel in Japan, dates back to A.D. 717 and has been run as a family business for 46 generations.

Largest manufacturing company   In terms of revenues and employees, General Motors Corporation of Detroit, MI is the world's largest manufacturing company. It has a workforce of 709,000, and revenues for the company in 1995 totaled $168.8 billion, with assets of $217.1 billion; a profit of $6.88 billion was announced for 1995.

Longest company name   The longest company name on the Index registered under the British Companies Acts is "The Only Ordinary People Trying to Impress the Big Guys with Extra Ordinary Ideas, Sales, Management, Creative Thinking and Problem Solving Consultancy Company Ltd.," Company Number 2660603.

Largest employer   On March 31, 1992, Indian Railways had 1,654,066 employees.

Greatest sales   The *Fortune 500* list of leading industrial corporations in April 1996 was headed by General Motors Corporation of Detroit, MI, with sales of $168.8 billion for 1995.

Greatest corporate profit   The American Telephone and Telegraph Co. (AT&T) made a net profit of $7.6 billion in 12 months from October 1, 1981 to September 30, 1982.

Greatest loss   In 1992, General Motors reported an annual net trading loss of $23.5 billion. The bulk of this figure was, however, due to a single charge of some $21 billion for employees' health costs and pensions and was disclosed because of new U.S. accounting regulations.

Largest corporate takeover bid   On October 24, 1988, the Wall Street leveraged buyout firm Kohlberg Kravis Roberts (KKR) bid $21 billion, or $90 a share, for RJR Nabisco Inc., the tobacco, food and beverage company. By December 1, 1988, the bid, led by Henry Kravis, had reached $109 per share, to total $25 billion.

Biggest bankrupt On September 3, 1992, newspaper heir Kevin Maxwell became the world's biggest bankrupt following the death of his father, Robert Maxwell, with debts of £406.8 million ($813.6 million).

Corporate The biggest corporate bankruptcy in terms of assets was $35.9 billion, filed by Texaco in 1987.

Largest public auction In 1995, the Federal Communications Commission (FCC) raised $7.7 billion for the U.S Treasury by auctioning off 99 licenses to provide advanced digital communication services. The auction was conducted by Kennedy-Wilson International.

Greatest barter deal In July 1984, 30 million barrels of oil, valued at $1.71 billion, were exchanged for 10 Boeing 747s for the Royal Saudi Airline.

Oldest bank The oldest bank in continuous operation in the United States is The Bank of New York, founded in 1834.

Savings and loan association The world's biggest lender is the Japanese government-controlled House Loan Corporation.

United States The largest savings and loan association (S&L) in the United States is Home Savings of America FSB in Irwindale, CA. As of June 1996, the company had total assets of $49.1 billion and total deposits of $33.3 billion.

Largest banks The largest commercial bank is the Bank of Tokyo-Mitsubishi, Ltd. of Tokyo, Japan, with assets of $737 billion as of April 1, 1996.
  The largest commercial bank in the United States is Chase Manhattan of New York City, with total assets of $304.1 billion.
  The International Bank of Reconstruction and Development, also known as the World Bank, is the largest multilateral development bank. Based in Washington, D.C., the bank had total assets of $168.7 billion for the 1995 fiscal year.

Most branches The State Bank of India had 12,704 outlets on April 1, 1994 and assets of $36 billion.

Most cash machines The United States had 109,080 ATM (automated teller machine) cash machines as of September 1, 1994. Bank America in San Francisco, CA had 5,700 cash machines, the most of any city in the U.S.

Largest piggy bank A giant piggy bank called Maximillion, measuring 15 ft. 5 in. long and 8 ft. 8 in. tall, was constructed by The Canadian Imperial Bank of Commerce in Canada in November 1995.

Largest charity food bank The South Plains Food Bank's Breedlove Dehydration Plant in Lubbock, TX can dehydrate 28 million pounds of surplus fruit and vegetables per year, enough to produce 30,000 meals per day.

Charity fund-raising The greatest recorded amount raised by a charity walk or run is $Cdn24.7 million by Terry Fox of Canada, who, with an artificial leg, ran from St. John's, Newfoundland to Thunder Bay, Ontario in 143 days, April 12–September 2, 1980. He covered 3,339 miles.

Largest rummage sale The Cleveland Convention Center, Cleveland, OH White Elephant Sale (instituted 1933) held October 18–19, 1983, raised $427,935.21.

The greatest amount of money raised at a one-day sale was $214,085.99 at the 62nd one-day rummage sale organized by the Winnetka Congregational Church, Winnetka, IL on May 12, 1994.

Largest food company The world's largest food company is the Swiss-based Nestlé, with sales in 1994 totaling SFr56.9 billion ($43.5 billion).

LARGEST SPIRITS COMPANY

The world's most profitable spirits company, and the largest blender and bottler of Scotch whiskey, is United Distillers, the liquor company of Guinness plc. United Distillers made a profit of £673 million ($1.07 billion) in 1995.

See feature (next page)

Most popular soft drink The world's most popular soft drink is Coca-Cola, with sales in 1995 of over 573 million drinks per day. Total Coca-Cola Company sales for 1995 were over $18 billion, representing 47 percent of the world market share.

Largest insurance companies The company with the highest volume of insurance in force in the world is the Metropolitan Life Insurance Co. of New York City, with $1.27 trillion at year end 1994.

The Prudential Insurance Company of America of Newark, NJ has the greatest volume of consolidated assets, totaling $212 billion in 1994.

The largest single insurance association in the world is Blue Cross and Blue Shield of Chicago, IL. As of December 31, 1994, it had a membership of 65.2 million and paid out benefits totaling $71.4 billion.

Largest insurance policies The largest life insurance policy was for $100 million, bought by a major American entertainment corporation on the life of a leading American entertainment industry figure. The policy was sold in July 1990 by Peter Rosengard of London, England and was placed by Albert G. Ruben & Co. Inc. of Beverly Hills, CA and the Feldman Agency, East Liverpool, OH with nine insurance companies to spread the risk.

The highest payout on a single life was reported on November 14, 1970 to be some $18 million to Linda Mullendore, widow of an Oklahoma rancher. Her murdered husband had paid $300,000 in premiums in 1969.

Marine insurance The largest-ever marine insurance loss was approximately $836 million for the Piper Alpha Oil Field in the North Sea. On

A SPIRITED COMPANY

The world's most profitable spirits company is United Distillers. The British-based company is owned by Guinness PLC, which is also the parent company of *The Guinness Book of Records*. United Distillers operates five distilleries in North America: two in Louisville, KY, and others in Plainfield, IL, Valleyfield, Quebec and Tullahoma, TN. These plants produce a variety of spirits products, including gin, vodka, American whiskey and bourbon.

Seen here is the George Dickel Distillery in Tullahoma, which is a record-holder in its own right. George Dickel Whisky has the longest distilling process of any American whiskey: two weeks. The main ingredients of George Dickel are corn, rye and barley. The grains are cooked in a mashing process that naturally creates a sugar-based liquid. Fermentation is the second stage. Yeast is added to convert the sugar into carbon dioxide and ethanol (alcohol). The fermentation process takes up to five days. The next stage is distillation, whereby the grain, yeast and water are separated from the alcohol. George Dickel is distilled twice in a two-step process that takes 24 hours to complete. Finally, the crystal-clear whisky undergoes "chill maple mellowing." The whisky runs through a 10-foot deep, 8-foot-diameter vat filled with hard sugar maple charcoal. Mellowing takes up to 10 days. Once this stage is finished the record-breaking production process is complete.

Once mellowed, however, George Dickel still has a long way to go before it is ready for consumption. The whisky is poured into new barrels made of charred American white oak and is aged and warehoused for 4–12 years. Only when this maturing (or aging) process is completed will the whisky be bottled and sold.

The Tullahoma distillery claims two other features of note, although they're not exactly records. It is the only distillery in the United States that houses a United States Post Office. And its liquor store is the smallest in the state of Tennessee. It has room for exactly 16 cases of whisky. No doubt there is a line outside the door.

July 6, 1988, a leak from a gas compression chamber underneath the living quarters ignited and triggered a series of explosions that blew Piper Alpha apart, killing 169 people.

The largest sum claimed for consequential losses was approximately $1.7 trillion against owning, operating and building corporations and Claude Phillips, resulting from the 55-million-gallon oil spill from MT *Amoco Cadiz* off the coast of France in March 1978.

Largest landowner The United States government has a holding of 728.8 million acres.

Most expensive land The land around the central Tokyo retail food store Mediya Building was quoted in October 1988 by the Japanese National Land Agency at 358.5 million yen ($248,000) per square foot.

Most expensive offices The highest rentals for offices, according to *World Rental Levels* by Richard Ellis (Great Britain), were in Tokyo, Japan at $143.38 per square foot per annum (December 1994) compared with a peak of $206.68 in June 1991. With service charges and rates this increased to $163.13 per square foot (December 1994) and $225.34 in June 1991.

RETAILERS

Largest restaurant chain McDonald's Corporation is the world's largest food service retailer. At the end of 1995, McDonald's operated 18,380 restaurants in 89 countries. Worldwide sales in 1995 were nearly $30 billion.

Largest department store Woolworth Corporation operated 8,178 stores worldwide as of January 1996. Frank Winfield Woolworth opened his first store, "The Great Five Cent Store," in Utica, NY on February 22, 1879.

Largest retailer The largest retailer in the United States is Wal-Mart, Inc. of Bentonville, AR, with sales of $93.6 billion and a net income of $2.74 billion reported on January 31, 1996, when Wal-Mart had over 3,000 retail locations and employed 675,000 people.

Wal-Mart, Inc. is the largest retailer in the United States.

Largest grocery chain   The single largest operator of supermarkets and food stores in the United States is Kroger Co. of Cincinnati, OH, with sales of $23.9 billion as of December 31, 1995. The company also has the most stores in the United States, with 2,144.

Largest drug store chains   The largest chain of drug stores is Rite Aid Corporation of Camp Hill, PA, which had 2,759 stores throughout the United States as of March 2, 1996. The Walgreen Co. of Deerfield, IL has fewer stores, but a larger volume of sales, totaling $10.4 billion in 1995.

STOCK EXCHANGES

Oldest stock exchange   The stock exchange in Amsterdam, Netherlands was founded in 1602 with dealings in printed shares of the United East India Company of the Netherlands in the Oude Zijds Kapel.

Largest stock exchange   The largest in trading volume in 1995 was the New York Stock Exchange, with $3.1 trillion.

New York Stock Exchange   The market value of stocks listed on the New York Stock Exchange reached an all-time high of $6.65 trillion on June 28, 1996.

The record day's trading was 652,829,000 shares on December 15, 1995.

The largest stock trade in the history of the New York Stock Exchange was a 48,788,800-share block of Navistar International Corporation stock at $10 per share on April 10, 1986.

The highest price paid for a seat on the New York Stock Exchange was $1.45 million in 1996. The lowest 20th-century price was $17,000, in 1942.

Closing prices   As of May 22, 1996, the highest index figure on the Dow Jones Industrial average of selected stocks at the close of a day's trading was 5,778.

The Dow Jones Industrial average, which reached 381.71 on September 3, 1929, plunged 30.57 points on October 29, 1929, on its way to the Depression's lowest point of 41.22 on July 2, 1932. The largest decline in a day, 508 points (22.6 percent), occurred on October 19, 1987.

The total lost in security values from September 1, 1929 to June 30, 1932 was $74 billion. The greatest paper loss in a year was $210 billion in 1974.

The record daily increase, on October 21, 1987, was 186.84 points, to 2,027.85.

Largest flotation   The £5.2 billion ($9.9 billion) sale of the 12 British regional electricity companies to 5.7 million stockholders at the end of 1990 was the largest in stock market history.

The earlier flotation of British Gas plc in 1986 had an equity offer that produced the higher sum of £7.75 billion ($10.85 billion), but to only 4.5 million stockholders.

Longest-listed company   Consolidated Edison Company of New York (ConEd) is reported to be the longest continually listed company on the New York Stock Exchange. First traded under the name New York Gas Light Company in 1824, it formed a merger to create the Consolidated Gas Company of New York in 1884. ConEd took its current name in 1936.

The longest-listed company traded under the same name is the Brooklyn Union Gas Company. Originally listed as the Brooklyn Gas Light Company in the late 1830s, it has been traded under its current name since the mid-1860s.

Most valuable company   The greatest market value of any corporation as of year end 1995 was $126.5 billion for General Electric Co., of Fairfield, CT.

Greatest stockholder attendance   In April 1961, a total of 20,109 stockholders attended the annual general meeting of the American Telephone and Telegraph Co. (AT&T), thereby setting a world record.

Longest-serving current member   As of June 1995, the longest-serving current member of the New York Stock Exchange was David Granger. He became a member on February 4, 1926.

Largest rights issue   The largest recorded rights issue was one of £921 million ($1.57 billion) by Barclays Bank, Great Britain, announced on April 7, 1988.

Highest gold price   The highest closing spot price for gold on the Commodities Exchange (COMEX) in New York City was $875 per fine ounce on January 21, 1980.

Highest silver price   The highest closing spot price for silver on the Commodities Exchange (COMEX) in New York City was $50.35 per fine ounce on January 18, 1980.

Highest par value   The highest denomination of any share quoted in the world is a single share in Moeara Enim Petroleum Corporation, worth 165,000 Dutch florins ($75,500) on April 22, 1992.

PERSONAL WEALTH

Richest man   Much of the wealth of the world's monarchs represents national rather than personal assets. The least fettered and most monarchical is HM Sir Muda Hassanal Bolkiah Mu'izzaddin Waddaulah of Brunei. *Fortune* magazine reported in June 1993 that his fortune was $37 billion.

The richest private individual is Microsoft founder Bill Gates. *Forbes* magazine reported in July 1996 that Gates was worth $18 billion. His net worth increased by $5.1 billion in 1995, on top of a $4.7 billion increase from the year before.

Richest woman   Her Majesty Queen Elizabeth II is asserted by some to be the wealthiest woman in the world, and *The Sunday Times* of London, England estimated in April 1993 that she had assets worth £6.75 billion ($11.7 billion). However, few of her assets under the perpetual succession of the Crown are either personal or disposable, and her personal wealth was estimated at £500 million ($900 million). An alternative estimate published by the British magazine *The Economist* in January 1992 placed her personal wealth at much closer to £150 million ($270 million).

Richest families   It has been estimated that the combined value of the assets nominally controlled by the Du Pont family, which has about 1,600 members, may be $150 billion. The family arrived in the United States from France on January 1, 1800. A more conclusive claim is for the Walton retailing family, worth an estimated $23.5 billion.

Youngest millionaire   The youngest self-made millionaire was the American child film actor Jackie Coogan (1914–84), who co-starred with Charlie Chaplin in *The Kid*, made in 1921.

Youngest billionaire   The youngest of the 101 billionaires reported in the United States in 1992 was Bill Gates, cofounder of Microsoft of Seattle, WA, whose *MS/DOS* operating system runs on an estimated 72 million of the United States' 90 million personal computers. Gates was 20 when he set up his company in 1976 and was a billionaire by 31.

40 years ago the first edition of The Guinness Book of Records listed Andrew Carnegie as the "greatest benefactor," noting that his "major bequests totaled $309,940,000." **Today** Walter Annenberg has arranged to donate his entire art collection to the Metropolitan Museum of Art in New York City upon his death. The collection is valued at $1 billion.

"This country has been very good to me and, therefore, I believe it is obligatory that I be good to my country." —Walter Annenberg, June 10, 1996

Highest incomes   The largest incomes derive from the collection of royalties per barrel by rulers of oil-rich sheikhdoms who have not formally revoked personal entitlement. Sheikh Zayid ibn Sultan an-Nuhayan, head of state of the United Arab Emirates, arguably has title to some $9 billion of the country's annual gross national product.

Highest personal tax levy   The highest recorded personal tax levy is one for $336 million on 70 percent of the estate of Howard Hughes.

Largest golden handshake   *Business Week* magazine reported in May 1989 that the largest "golden handshake" ever given was one of $53.8 million, to F. Ross Johnson, who left RJR Nabisco as chairman in February 1989.

Largest dowry In 1929, Don Simón Iturbi Patiño (1861–1947), the Bolivian tin millionaire, bestowed $39 million on his daughter, Elena Patiño. His total fortune was at one time estimated to be worth $607.5 million.

Longest pension Millicent Barclay was born on July 10, 1872, three months after the death of her father, Col. William Barclay, and became eligible for a Madras Military Fund pension to continue until her marriage. She died unmarried on October 26, 1969, having drawn the pension every day of her life of 97 yr. 3 mo.

Largest return of cash In May 1994, Howard Jenkins of Tampa, FL, a 31-year-old roofing company employee, discovered that $88 million had been mistakenly transferred into his account. Although he initially withdrew $4 million, his conscience got the better of him shortly afterward and he returned the $88 million in full.

Largest single bequests American publisher Walter Annenberg announced on March 12, 1991 that he would be leaving his art collection, worth $1 billion, to the Metropolitan Museum of Art in New York City.

The largest single cash bequest was the $500 million gift, announced on December 12, 1955, to 4,157 educational and other institutions from the Ford Foundation (established 1936) of New York.

Highest lottery sales In the 1994 fiscal year (July 1–June 30), the United States Lottery netted record total sales of $33,882,158,000 in North America.

The state with the highest lottery sales is Texas, with $2,681,260,000 in the 1994 fiscal year.

Largest lottery jackpot The largest U.S. lottery jackpot was $118,800,000, in California, on April 17, 1991. Holders of ten tickets shared the prize money.

The highest payout for one ticket was shared by Leslie Robbins and Colleen DeVries of Fond du Lac, WI. The two won $111,200,000 in the Powerball lottery on July 7, 1993; each will receive an annual net sum of $1,500,000 for twenty years.

PAPER MONEY

Oldest paper money The world's earliest bank notes (*banco-sedler*) were issued in Stockholm, Sweden in July 1661. The oldest survivor is a 5-daler note dated December 6, 1662.

Largest paper money The 1-guan note of the Chinese Ming Dynasty issue of 1368–99 measured 9 by 13 inches.

Smallest paper money The smallest national note ever issued was the 10-bani note of the Ministry of Finance of Romania, in 1917. Its printed area measured $1\frac{1}{16}$ by $1\frac{1}{2}$ inches.

Highest values The highest value ever issued by the U.S. Federal Reserve System is a note for $100,000, bearing the head of Woodrow Wilson

(1856–1924), which is only used for transactions between the Federal Reserve and the Treasury Department.

The highest-value notes in circulation are U.S. Federal Reserve $10,000 bank notes, bearing the head of Salmon P. Chase (1808–73). It was announced in 1969 that no further notes higher than $100 would be issued, and only 200 $10,000 bills remain in circulation or unretired.

Most expensive paper money   On February 14, 1991, Richard Lobel paid £240,350 ($478,900) including buyer's premium, on behalf of a consortium, at Phillips, London, England, for a single lot of bank notes. The lot consisted of a cache of British military notes that were found in a vault in Berlin, Germany, and contained more than 17 million notes.

Largest paper money collection   Israel Gerber of Ashdod, Israel has accumulated banknotes from 215 different countries since he started collecting in 1962.

CHECKS AND COINS

Largest check   An internal U.S. Treasury check for $4,176,969,623.57 was drawn on June 30, 1954.

The largest check in terms of physical dimensions measured 70 by 31 feet. It was presented by InterMortgage of Leeds, England to Yorkshire Television's 1992 Telephone Appeal on September 4, 1992, and had a value of £10,000 ($19,000).

Mints Largest   The U.S. Treasury mint was built 1965–1969 on Independence Mall, Philadelphia and covers 11½ acres. The mint has an annual production capacity of 12 billion coins.

Fastest   The Graebner Press high-speed stamping machine can produce coins at a rate of 42,000 per hour. The record production for coins was in 1982, when 19.5 billion were produced between the Philadelphia and Denver mints.

Smallest issuing   The single-press mint belonging to the Sovereign Military Order of Malta, the City of Rome, is housed in one small room and has issued proof coins since 1961.

Most expensive coin collection   The highest price ever paid for a coin collection was $25,235,360 for the Garrett family collection of U.S. and colonial coins, which had been donated to Johns Hopkins University, Baltimore, MD. The sales were made at a series of four auctions held November 28–29, 1979 and March 25–26, 1981 at the Bowers & Ruddy Galleries in Wolfeboro, NH. The collection was put together by members of the Garrett family between 1860 and 1942.

Column of coins   The most valuable column of coins was worth 39,458 Irish pounds ($55,063) and was 6 ft. 2 in. high. It was built by St. Brigid's Family and Community Centre in Waterford, Ireland on November 20, 1993.

COINS

Oldest
Electrum staters of King Gyges of Lydia, Turkey, *c.* 670 B.C. Chinese uninscribed "spade" money of the Zhou dynasty has been dated to *c.* 770 B.C.

Oldest dated
Samian silver tetradrachm struck in Zankle (now Messina), Sicily, dated year 1, viz. 494 B.C.

Heaviest
Swedish 10-daler copper plate, 1644, 43 lb. 7^{1}/$_{4}$ oz.
Gold: Islamic 1,000-muhur, 32 lb., minted in Agra, 1613.

Lightest
Nepalese silver ^{1}/$_{4}$ jawa *c.* 1740, 14,000 to the oz.

Most valuable
Set: $3,190,000 for the King of Siam Proof Set, a set of 1804 and 1834 U.S. coins that had once been given to the King of Siam, purchased by Iraj Sayah and Terry Brand at Superior Galleries, Beverly Hills, CA on May 28, 1990. Included in the set of nine coins was the 1804 silver dollar, which had an estimated value of about $2,000,000.

Individual: $1,500,000 for the U.S. 1907 Double Eagle Ultra High Relief $20 gold coin, sold by MTB Banking Corporation of New York to a private investor on July 9, 1990.

Pile of coins The most valuable pile of coins had a total value of $126,463.61 and consisted of 1,000,298 coins of various denominations. It was constructed by the YWCA of Seattle, King County, WA in Redmond, WA on May 28, 1992.

Line of coins The most valuable line of coins was made up of 1,724,000 quarters with a value of $431,000. It was 25.9 miles long, and was laid at the Atlanta Marriott Marquis Hotel, GA by members of the National Exchange Club on July 25, 1992.

Longest The longest line of coins had a total length of 34.57 miles and comprised 2,367,234 20-sen coins. It was made in Kuala Lumpur, Malaysia and was laid by representatives of WWF (World Wide Fund for Nature) Malaysia and Dumex Sdn Bhd on August 6, 1995.

Coin snatching The greatest number of modern British 10-pence pieces clean-caught from being flipped from the back of a forearm into the same downward palm is 328, by Dean Gould of Felixstowe, England on April 6, 1993.

POSTAGE STAMPS

Oldest
Put on sale May 6, 1840. 1d Penny Black of Great Britain, Queen Victoria, 68,158,080 printed.

U.S.
Put on sale in New York City July 1, 1847. 5-cent red-brown Benjamin Franklin, 3,712,200 issued, and 10-cent black George Washington, 891,000 issued.

Highest price (auction)
SFr 3,400,000 ($2,400,000), including buyer's premium. Penny Black, May 2, 1840 cover, bought at Harmers, Lugano, Switzerland, on behalf of a Japanese buyer on May 23, 1991.

£203,500 ($350,000), including buyer's premium, for a philatelic item. Bermuda 1854 Perot Postmasters' Stamp affixed to a letter, 1d red on bluish wove paper, sold by Christie's Robson Lowe, London, England on June 13, 1991.

U.S.
$1.1 million (including buyer's premium). "Curtiss Jenny" plate block of four 24-cent stamps from 1918 with inverted image of an airplane, bought by an unnamed American executive at Christie's, New York on October 12, 1989.

Largest purchase
$11 million. Marc Haas collection of 3,000 U.S. postal and pre-postal covers to 1869 by Stanley Gibbons International Ltd. of London, England in August 1979.

Largest (special)
$9^3/4$ by $2^3/4$ in. Express Delivery of China, 1913. U.S. $3^3/4$ by 2 in. 1865 newspaper stamps.

Largest (standard)
6.3 by 4.33 in. Marshall Islands 75-cent issued October 30, 1979.

U.S.
$1^1/11$ by $1^5/11$ in. 5-cent blue and carmine Air Beacon issued July 25, 1928, and 2-cent black and carmine George Rogers Clark issued February 25, 1929.

Smallest
0.31 by 0.37 in. 10-cent and 1-peso Colombian State of Bolivar, 1863–66.

Highest denomination
$10,000. Documentary and Stock Transfer stamps, 1952–58.

Coin balancing On March 16, 1993, Mohammad Irshadullah Hamidi of Muzaffarpur, India stacked a pyramid of 870 coins on the edge of a coin freestanding vertically on the base of another coin that was on a table.

The tallest single column of coins ever stacked on the edge of a coin was made up of 253 Indian 1-rupee pieces on top of a vertical 5-rupee coin, by Dipak Syal of Yamuna Nagar, India on May 3, 1991. He also balanced 10 1-rupee coins and 10 10-paise coins alternately horizontally and vertically in a single column on May 1, 1991.

Most valuable hoard The most valuable hoard of coins was one of about 80,000 aurei found in Brescello near Modena, Italy in 1714, and believed to have been deposited *c*. 37 B.C.

POSTAL SERVICES

Largest mail service The country with the largest mail service is the United States.

Its population mailed 177.1 billion letters and packages during the 1994 fiscal year. The average number of letters and packages per capita was 675. The U.S. Postal Service employs 728,944 people, and there are 39,372 post offices in the U.S.

Most post offices The country with the greatest number of post offices is India, with 144,829 in 1988.

Stamp licking Dean Gould of Felixstowe, England licked and affixed 450 stamps in four minutes outside Tower Ramparts Post Office, Ipswich, England on November 24, 1995.

AGRICULTURE

BREWERIES AND VINEYARDS

Oldest brewer Weihenstephan Brewery, Freising, near Munich, Germany, was founded in A.D. 1040.

Oldest vat The oldest vat still in use is at Hugel et Fils (founded 1639), Riqueweihr, Haut-Rhin, France. Twelve generations of the family have used it since 1715.

Oldest vintners The world's oldest champagne firm is Ruinart Père et Fils, founded in 1729. The oldest cognac firm is Augier Frères & Cie, established in 1643.

Largest brewer The largest brewing organization in the world is Anheuser-Busch Inc. of St. Louis, MO, with 12 breweries in the United States. In 1995, the company sold 87.5 million barrels, or 2.713 billion gallons, of beer. One of its brands, Budweiser, is the top-selling beer in the world,

The world's largest vineyard covers 2,075,685 acres.

with 1.163 billion gallons sold in 1995. The company's St. Louis plant covers 100 acres. The completion of modernization projects in 1994 gave the plant an annual capacity of 412 million gallons.

The largest brewery on a single site is Coors Brewing Co. of Golden, CO, where 587 million gallons were produced in 1995. At the same location is the world's largest aluminum can manufacturing plant, with a capacity of more than 4 billion cans annually.

Largest vineyard The vineyard that extends over the Mediterranean slopes between the Pyrenees and the Rhône in the *départements* Gard, Hérault, Aude and Pyrénées-Orientales, France covers an area of 2,075,685 acres.

Largest wine cellars The cellars of the Ko-operatieve Wijnbouwers Vereniging (KWV), Paarl, Cape Province, in the center of the wine-growing district of South Africa, cover an area of 54 acres and have a capacity of 32 million gallons.

Largest vat "Strongbow," used by H. P. Bulmer Ltd., the English cidermakers, measures 64½ feet in height and 75½ feet in diameter, with a capacity of 1.95 million gallons.

The largest wooden winecask in the world is the Heidelberg Tun, completed in 1751, in the cellar of the Friedrichsbau, Heidelberg, Germany. It has a capacity of 58,570 gallons.

Largest vine A grapevine planted in 1842 at Carpinteria, CA yielded more than 9.9 tons of grapes in some years, and averaged 7.7 tons per year until it died in 1920.

FISHERIES

Leading fishing nation United Nations Food and Agricultural Organization figures for 1990 (the last year for which comparable data is available) showed the world's leading fishing nation to be China, with a total catch of 13.44 million tons. The United States was in fifth place with 6.57 million tons out of a worldwide total of 108.86 million tons.

Most valuable catch The record value for a catch by a single trawler is $473,957, from a 41,776-ton catch by the Icelandic vessel *Videy* at Hull, England on August 11, 1987.

The greatest catch ever recorded from a single throw is 2,724 tons, by the purse seine-net boat M/S *Flømann* from Hareide, Norway in the Barents Sea on August 28, 1986. It was estimated that more than 120 million fish were caught in this shoal.

FARMS

Largest cattle ranch The Anna Creek cattle ranch in South Australia, owned by the Kidman family, comprises 11,600 square miles. The biggest component is Strangway, at 5,500 square miles.

Largest egg farm The Agrigeneral Company L.P. in Croton, OH has 4.8 million hens laying 3.7 million eggs daily.

Largest community garden The project operated by the City Beautiful Council and the Benjamin Wegerzyn Garden Center in Dayton, OH comprises 1,173 plots, each measuring 812 square feet.

Largest hop farm The world's leading hop growers are John I. Haas Inc., with farms in Oregon, Washington, Tasmania and Australia, covering a total net area of 5,940 acres. The largest field covers 1,385 acres near Toppenish, WA.

Largest mushroom farm Moonlight Mushrooms Inc. employs over 1,106 people who work in a maze of underground galleries in a disused mine. The farm produces over 54 million pounds of mushrooms per year.

Largest sheep ranch Commonwealth Hill, South Australia grazes between 50,000 and 70,000 sheep, along with 24,000 uninvited kangaroos, in an area of 4,080 square miles enclosed by 138 miles of dog-proof fencing.

The head count on Sir William Stevenson's 40,970-acre Lochinver station in New Zealand was 127,406 on January 1, 1993.

Largest turkey farm The farms of Bernard Matthews plc of Norfolk, England produce 10 million turkeys per year and employ a staff of 2,500. The largest farm, in North Pickenham, England, produces 1 million turkeys.

Combine harvesting Philip Baker of West End Farm, Merton, Bicester, England harvested 182.5 tons of wheat in eight hours using a Massey Ferguson MF 38 combine on August 8, 1989.

On August 9, 1990, an international team from CWS Agriculture, led by estate manager Ian Hanglin, harvested 394.73 tons of wheat in eight hours from 108.72 acres at Cockayne Hatley Estate, Sandy, England.

Bale rolling Michael Priestley and Marcus Stanley of Heckington Young Farmers Club rolled a 3-ft.-11-in.-wide cylindrical bale over a 164-foot course in 18.06 seconds in Sleaford, England on June 25, 1989.

Baling A rick of 40,400 bales of straw was built between July 22 and September 3, 1982 by Nick and Tom Parsons with a gang of eight at Cuckoo Pen Barn Farm, Birdlip, England. It measured 150 by 30 by 60 feet high and weighed some 784 tons. The team baled, hauled and ricked 24,200 bales in seven consecutive days, July 22–29.

Svend Erik Klemmensen of Trustrup, Djursland, Denmark baled 220 tons of straw in 9 hr. 54 min. using a Hesston 4800 baling machine on August 30, 1989.

Plowing The fastest time for plowing an acre by the United Kingdom Society of Ploughmen rules is 9 min. 49.88 sec., by Joe Langcake at Hornby Hall Farm, Brougham, England on October 21, 1989. He used a case IH 7140 Magnum tractor and a Kverneland 4-furrow plow.

The greatest area plowed with a 6-furrow plow to a depth of nine inches in 24 hours is 173 acres, by Richard Gaisford and Peter Gooding of Wiltshire Young Farmers, using a Case IH tractor and a Lemken plow, at Manor Farm, Pewsey, England, September 25–26, 1990.

Field to loaf The fastest time for producing 13 loaves of bread (a baker's dozen) from growing wheat is 8 min. 13.6 sec., by Wheat Montana Farms

& Bakery, Three Forks, MT on September 19, 1995. They used 13 microwave ovens to bake the loaves.

Using a traditional baker's oven to bake the bread, the record time is 19 min. 45 sec., by a team organized by John Haynes of millers Read Woodrow in Alpheton, England on September 19, 1992.

Largest grain elevator The single-unit elevator operated by the C-G-F Grain Co. in Wichita, KS is 2,717 feet long and 100 feet wide. The total storage capacity is 20 million bushels of wheat.

CATTLE

Leading cattle producer India was the world's leading cattle farming nation in 1995, with an estimated 274.2 million head.

United States As of January 1, 1996, there were 103.8 million head of cattle farmed in the United States. The leading cattle producer was Texas, with 15 million head.

Largest cattle breed The heaviest breed of cattle is the Val di Chianini. Bulls average 5 ft. 8 in. at the forequarters and weigh 2,865 pounds, but Chianini oxen have been known to attain heights of 6 ft. 2¾ in.

Heaviest bovine A Holstein–Durham cross named Mount Katahdin, exhibited by A.S. Rand of Maine from 1906 to 1910, frequently weighed in at an even 5,000 pounds. He was 6 ft. 2 in. at the shoulder with a 13-foot girth, and died in a barn fire *c.* 1923.

Smallest cattle breed The smallest breed of domestic cattle is the Ovambo of Namibia. Bulls and cows average 496 pounds and 353 pounds respectively.

Oldest bovine Big Bertha, a Dremon owned by Jerome O'Leary of Blackwatersbridge, County Kerry, Republic of Ireland, died less than three months short of her 49th birthday, on December 31, 1993.

Most reproductive cow On April 25, 1964, it was reported that a cow named Lyubik had given birth to seven calves in Mogilev, Byelarus. A case of five live calves at one birth was reported in 1928 by T.G. Yarwood of Manchester, England. The lifetime breeding record is 39 in the case of Big Bertha.

Heaviest calf The heaviest recorded live birth weight for a calf is 225 pounds for a British Friesian cow at Rockhouse Farm, Bishopston, Wales in 1961.

Lightest calf The lowest live birthweight for a calf is nine pounds, for a Holstein heifer called Christmas, born on December 25, 1993 on the farm of Mark and Wendy Theuringer in Hutchinson, MN.

Highest milk yields In 1995, the United States produced 155.8 billion pounds of cow's milk. As of June 1996, the state producing the most milk was California, with a monthly total of 2.2 billion pounds.

MOST EXPENSIVE LIVESTOCK

Cattle
Joe's Pride (Beefalo); bought by Beefalo Cattle Co., Calgary, Canada, Sept. 9, 1974; $2,500,000

Sheep
Collinsville stud JC&S 43; bought by Willogoleche Pty. Ltd., 1989 Adelaide Ram Sales, South Australia; $358,750

Goat
Angora buck; bought by Elliott Brown Ltd., Waipu, New Zealand, Jan. 25, 1985; $79,000

Pig
Bud (cross-bred barrow); bought by E.A. Bud Olson and Phil Bonzio, Mar. 5, 1983; $56,000

Horse
Farceur (Belgian stallion); bought by C.G. Good, Ogden, IA, Oct. 16, 1917; $47,000

The highest lifetime yield of milk for a single cow is 465,224 pounds, by the unglamorously named cow No. 289 owned by M. G. Maciel & Son of Hanford, CA, to May 1, 1984.

The greatest recorded yield for one lactation (maximum 365 days) is 59,443 pounds in 1995 by the Friesian cow Acme Goldy 2, owned by Bryce Miller of Woodford Grange Farm, Islip, England.

Hand-milking of cows Joseph Love of Kilifi Plantations Ltd., Kenya milked 117 gallons from 30 cows on August 25, 1992.

Highest butterfat yields The world record lifetime yield is 16,370 pounds, by the Holstein Breezewood Patsy Bar Pontiac in 3,979 days.

Largest cheese producer The United States produces the most cheese, with a total of 6.94 billion pounds in 1995.

Highest cheese consumption The most avid cheese-eaters are the French, with an annual average of 43.6 pounds per person.

GOATS

Largest goat A British Saanen named Mostyn Moorcock, owned by Pat Robinson of Ewyas Harold, England, reached a weight of 400 pounds (shoulder height 44 inches and overall length 66 inches).

Oldest goat A Golden Guernsey–Anglo Nubian cross named Naturemade Aphrodite (1975–93), belonging to Katherine Whitwell of Moulton, Newmarket, England, died on August 23, 1993 aged 18 yr. 1 mo.

Most reproductive goat According to the British Goat Society, one or two cases of quintuplets are recorded annually out of the 10,000 goats registered, but some breeders only record the females born.

On January 14, 1980, a nanny goat named Julie, owned by Galen Cowper of Nampah, ID, gave birth to septuplets, but all seven died, along with the mother.

Highest milk yield In 1977, Osory Snow-Goose, owned by Mr. and Mrs. G. Jameson of Leppington, New South Wales, Australia produced 7,714 pounds in 365 days.

Cynthia-Jean (Baba), owned by Carolyn Freund-Nelson of Northport, NY, has lactated continuously since June 1980. Baba celebrated her 16th birthday on April 14, 1995.

PIGS

Largest pig producer The world's leading producer of hogs in 1995 was China, with 414.6 million head from a world total of 759.9 million. As of June 1, 1996, there were 58 million head of pigs and hogs farmed in the United States. The leading state was Iowa with 13.3 million head.

Largest pig A Poland–China hog named Big Bill weighed an astonishing 2,552 pounds just before he was put to sleep after suffering a broken leg en route to the Chicago World's Fair for exhibition in 1933. Other statistics included a shoulder height of five feet and a length of nine feet.

Smallest pig After 10 years of experimentation with Vietnamese potbellied pigs, Stefano Morini of St. Polo d'Enza, Italy developed the Mini Maialino. The pig weigh 20 pounds at maturity.

Largest litter The highest recorded number of piglets in one litter is 37, farrowed on September 21, 1993 by Sow 570, a Meishan cross Large White–Duroc at Mr. and Mrs. M. P. Ford's Eastfield House Farm, Melbourne, England. Of the 36 piglets that were born alive, 33 survived.

Highest birth weight A Hampshire–Yorkshire sow belonging to Rev. John Schroeder of Mountain Grove, MO farrowed a litter of 18 on August 26, 1979. Five were stillborn, including one male that weighed 5 lb. 4 oz.

POULTRY

Largest poultry producer In 1995, the United States was the largest producer of chicken meat, or broiler, with a total of 34.2 billion pounds. The most produced by a state was 5.1 billion pounds, by Georgia. The leading egg producer is China, where an estimated 284.4 billion were laid in 1994. United States egg production in 1995 was 74.3 billion eggs. The state with the highest production was California, with 6.4 billion eggs.

Largest chicken The largest recorded chicken was Big Snow, a rooster weighing 23 lb. 3 oz. on June 12, 1992, with a chest girth of 2 ft. 9 in. and standing 1 ft. 5 in. at the shoulder. Owned and bred by Ronald Alldridge of Deuchar, Queensland, Australia, Big Snow died of natural causes on September 6, 1992.

TIPS

from the
RECORD BREAKERS

EGG-DROPPING

*Imagine having a party trick so popular you got paid to do it.
That's how David Donoghue got started in his lifetime pursuit
of egg dropping. Here are his tips on helping Humpty
Dumpty have a great fall—with a soft landing.*

◆

Get a feel for flinging projectiles around.

When he was in the army in Singapore, Donoghue's friends
paid him $50 to throw eggs over army-issue bungalows—
without breaking them. Donoghue, a helicopter pilot, was
studying the throwing of missiles at targets. "We worked with
the Dam-Buster bomb, and discovered that if it's revolved at
the point that it's thrown, you can dissipate its energy and
create a bounce. I merged what I learned with my egg
findings and discovered that if I increased the forward speed
of the egg, I could drop it from higher and higher."

◆

Choose the right spot.

"Golf courses are brilliant, because they're kept groomed,
soft, and humid." What's more, they often have the kind of
slope that makes the best landing spot. "You have to get the
forward velocity equal to the downward velocity, then get the
egg to land nearly perpendicular on a steep slope."

◆

Find good eggs.

"Organic-farmed eggs from chickens that have eaten a lot of
phosphate, sulfate, and calcium, are strongest."

Most reproductive chicken   A White Leghorn, No. 2988, laid 371 eggs in 364 days in an official test conducted by Prof. Harold V. Biellier ending on August 29, 1979 at the College of Agriculture, University of Missouri.

Most reproductive duck   An Aylesbury duck belonging to Annette and Angela Butler of Princes Risborough, England laid 457 eggs in 463 days, including an uninterrupted run of 375 in as many days. The duck died on February 7, 1986. Another duck of the same breed, owned by Edmond Walsh of Gormanstown, Republic of Ireland, laid eggs every year right up to her 25th birthday. She died on December 3, 1978 at age 28 yr. 6 mo.

Largest chicken egg   A Black Minorca laid a 5-yolked egg of nearly 12 ounces measuring 12¼ inches around the long axis and nine inches around the short, at Mr. Stafford's Damsteads Farm, Mellor, Lancashire, England in 1896.

Heaviest chicken egg   A White Leghorn in Vineland, NJ laid an egg weighing 16 ounces, with double yolk and double shell, on February 25, 1956.

Heaviest goose egg   An egg weighing 24 ounces and measuring 13½ inches around the long axis with a maximum circumference of 9½ inches around the short axis was laid on May 3, 1977 by a white goose named Speckle, owned by Donny Brandenberg of Goshen, OH.

Most-yolked chicken egg   In July 1971, a hen's egg was reported by Diane Hainsworth of Hainsworth Poultry Farms, Mount Morris, NY to have nine yolks. A hen in Kyrgyzstan was also reported to have nine yolks in August 1977.

Egg shelling   Two kitchen hands, Harold Witcomb and Gerald Harding, shelled 1,050 dozen eggs in a 7¼-hour shift at Bowyers, Trowbridge, England on April 23, 1971.

Egg dropping   The greatest height from which fresh eggs have been dropped (to the ground) and remained intact is 700 feet, by David Donoghue from a helicopter on August 22, 1994 on a golf course in Blackpool, England.

Longest chicken flight   Sheena, a barnyard bantam owned by Bill and Bob Knox, flew 630 ft. 2 in. at Parkesburg, PA on May 31, 1985.

Chicken plucking   Ernest Hausen (1877–1955) of Fort Atkinson, WI died undefeated after 33 years as champion chicken plucker. On January 19, 1939 he was timed at 4.4 seconds.

Turkey plucking   Vincent Pilkington of Cootehill, County Cavan, Republic of Ireland killed and plucked 100 turkeys in 7 hr. 32 min. on December 15, 1978. His record for a single turkey is 1 min. 30 sec. in Dublin on November 17, 1980.

SHEEP

Largest sheep producer   The world's leading producer of sheep is China, with a total of 240.5 million head in 1995. As of January 1, 1996, there were

8.5 million head of sheep farmed in the United States, and the leading state was Texas, with 1.7 million head.

Largest sheep   A Suffolk ram named Stratford Whisper 23H weighed 545 pounds and stood 43 inches tall in March 1991. It is owned by Joseph and Susan Schallberger of Boring, OR.

Smallest sheep   The Ouessant, from the Ile d'Ouessant, Brittany, France, weighs 29–35 pounds and stands 18–20 inches at the withers.

Oldest sheep   A crossbred sheep owned by Griffiths & Davies of Dolclettwr Hall, Taliesin, Wales died on January 24, 1989 just one week before her 29th birthday.

Largest litter   A Finnish Landrace ewe owned by the D.M.C. Partnership of Feilding, Manawatu, New Zealand gave birth to eight lambs (five rams and three ewes) at a single birth on September 4, 1991. On December 2, 1992, a Charolais ewe owned by Graham and Jo Partt of Wem, England also gave birth to eight lambs, seven of which survived.

The largest litter of lambs in the United States.

United States   Ewe 2312, belonging to the University of Wisconsin–Madison and part of the flock of the Spooner Agricultural Research Station, Spooner, WI, gave birth to seven live lambs on April 24, 1996.

Heaviest lamb A lamb weighing 38 pounds was born at Clearwater, Sedgwick County, KS in 1975, but neither lamb nor ewe survived. Another lamb of the same weight was born on April 7, 1975 on the Gerald Neises Farm, Howard, SD but died soon afterwards.

Lightest lamb The lowest live birthweight recorded for a lamb is 1 lb. 4 oz. for a female named Princess Pippin, born on March 16, 1995 at Howarton Farm, Speldhurst, England. She is owned by Ann and Adam Massingham of Fordcombe, England.

Sheep to shoulder At the International Wool Secretariat Development Center, Ilkley, England, a team of eight using commercial machinery produced a sweater—from shearing sheep to the finished article—in 2 hr. 28 min. 32 sec. on September 3, 1986.

Sheep shearing The fastest speed for sheep shearing in a working day was by Alan MacDonald, who machine-sheared 805 lambs in nine hours (an average of 40.2 seconds per lamb) at Waitnaguru, New Zealand on December 20, 1990. The hand-shearing record is 353 lambs in nine hours, by Peter Casserly of Christchurch, New Zealand on February 13, 1976.

Longest fleece A Merino wether found on K.P. & B.A. Reynolds Company's Willow Springs Station, South Australia in November 1990 produced 65 pounds of wool from a fleece 25 inches long, representing a 7-year growth.

LAW

LEGISLATION AND LITIGATION

Oldest statute The oldest surviving judicial code is the code of King Ur-Nammu, from the third dynasty of Ur, Iraq, *c.* 2250 B.C.

Most protracted litigation A controversy over the claim of the Prior and Convent (now the Dean and Chapter) of Durham Cathedral in England to administer the diocese during a vacancy in the See grew fierce in 1283. The dispute, with the Archbishop of York, flared up again in 1672 and 1890; an attempt in November 1975 to settle the issue, then 692 years old, was unsuccessful. Neither side admits the legitimacy of writs of appointment issued by the other, even though identical persons are named.

Longest trial Civil The longest civil case heard before a jury is *Kemner* vs. *Monsanto Co.,* which concerned an alleged toxic chemical spill in Sturgeon, MO in 1979. The trial started on February 6, 1984, at St. Clair County Court House, Belleville, IL before Circuit Judge Richard P. Goldenhersh, and ended on October 22, 1987. The testimony lasted 657 days, following which the jury deliberated for two months. The residents of Sturgeon were awarded $1 million nominal compensatory damages and $16,280,000 punitive damages, but these awards were overturned by the Illinois Appellate

Court on June 11, 1991 because the jury in the original trial had not found that any damage had resulted from the spill.

Criminal The longest criminal trial took place in Hong Kong from November 30, 1992 to November 29, 1994. The High Court sat for 398 days to hear murder charges against 14 South Vietnamese boat people accused of murdering 24 North Vietnamese adults and children, who died in a blazing hut during a riot at a refugee camp in Hong Kong, in February 1992. All the defendants were acquitted of murder, but some were convicted of lesser charges.

Greatest damages Civil damages The largest damages awarded in legal history were $11.12 billion to Pennzoil Company against Texaco Inc., as a result of Texaco's allegedly unethical tactics in January 1984 in attempting to break up a merger between Pennzoil and Getty Oil Company. The verdict was handed down in Houston, TX on December 10, 1985. An out-of-court settlement of $5.5 billion was reached after a 48-hour negotiation on December 19, 1987.

The largest damages awarded against an individual were $2.1 billion. On July 10, 1992, Charles H. Keating, Jr., the former owner of Lincoln Savings and Loan of Los Angeles, CA, was ordered by a federal jury to pay this sum to 23,000 small investors who were defrauded by his company. On July 8, 1993, Keating was sentenced to 12½ years in prison.

Personal injury Shiyamala Thirunayagam was awarded $163,882,660 by a jury in the Supreme Court of the State of New York on July 27, 1993. She was almost completely paralyzed after the car in which she was traveling hit a broken-down truck in the fast lane of the New Jersey Turnpike on October 4, 1987. Because the defendants would have challenged the jury's verdict in a higher court, Thirunayagam agreed to accept a lump sum of $8,230,000 for her pain and suffering and a guarantee that the defendants would pay up to $55,000,000 for her future medical expenses.

The compensation for the disaster on December 2–3, 1984 at the Union Carbide Corporation plant in Bhopal, India was agreed at $470 million. The Supreme Court of India passed the order for payment on February 14, 1989 after a settlement between the corporation and the Indian government, which represented the interests of more than 500,000 claimants, including the families of 3,350 people who died.

Sexual harassment The record award in a sexual harassment case was $50 million to Peggy Kimzey, a former employee of the Warsaw, MO Wal-Mart. The award of punitive damages was made by a jury in Jefferson City, MO on June 28, 1995. The jury also awarded Kimzey $35,000 for humiliation and mental anguish and $1 in lost wages. Wal-Mart said it would appeal.

Best-attended trial The greatest attendance at any trial was at that of Major Jesús Sosa Blanco, age 51, for an alleged 108 murders. At one point in the 12½-hour trial (5:30 P.M. to 6 A.M., January 22–23, 1959), 17,000 people were present in the Havana Sports Palace, Cuba. The defendant was found guilty and was executed on February 18, 1959.

Most viewed trial Between January 24 and October 3, 1995, a daily average of 5.5 million Americans watched live coverage of the O. J. Simpson

Sandra Day O'Connor

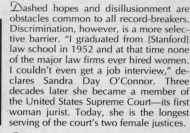

Dashed hopes and disillusionment are obstacles common to all record-breakers. Discrimination, however, is a more selective barrier. "I graduated from [Stanford] law school in 1952 and at that time none of the major law firms ever hired women. I couldn't even get a job interview," declares Sandra Day O'Connor. Three decades later she became a member of the United States Supreme Court—its first woman jurist. Today, she is the longest serving of the court's two female justices.

Justice O'Connor's first job out of law school was as a deputy county attorney in San Mateo, California. "That was in the public sector, of course. I wanted a job as a lawyer and was thrilled to get it." When her husband was drafted, O'Connor joined him in West Germany and worked as a civilian lawyer for the U.S. military. When the couple returned home, O'Connor faced the same barriers as before, only this time in Arizona. "We returned in 1957 and lived in Phoenix. The law firms there weren't hiring women either," says O'Connor. She passed the Arizona bar exam and opened a private legal practice.

O'Connor's ascent to the nation's highest court sets an example for any aspiring jurist. In Arizona she served terms as an Assistant Attorney General, State Senator, Superior Court Judge and Intermediate Court of Appeals member. "Happily, circumstances have changed dramatically during my lifetime. All states, as well as the federal government, have passed laws prohibiting discrimination in hiring, firing and promotions. This has made an enormous difference."

On July 7, 1981, President Ronald Reagan appointed O'Connor to the United States Supreme Court. She was sworn in on September 25. To O'Connor, the Supreme Court's role is "to develop a reasonably uniform and consistent body of federal laws, to accept for review cases in which lower courts have reached conflicting holdings on particular issues." She is confident that the barriers that faced her have been toppled: "I wouldn't expect young women today to experience discrimination. There are some lingering effects from the past, but so much has improved over the last 40 years that I think young women should expect to have opportunities in any field they choose to enter."

trial on three major cable networks. Simpson, a pro football Hall of Famer and actor, was on trial for the murder of his ex-wife, Nicole Brown Simpson, and waiter Ronald Goldman on June 12, 1994. He was acquitted when the jury reached a verdict of not guilty on October 3, 1995.

Greatest compensation for wrongful imprisonment   Robert McLaughlin, 29, was awarded $1,935,000 in October 1989 for wrongful imprisonment for a murder in New York City in 1979 which he did not commit. He had been sentenced to 15 years in prison and had actually served six years, from 1980 to 1986, when he was released after his foster father succeeded in showing the authorities that he had had nothing to do with the crime.

Largest divorce settlement   The largest publicly declared settlement, achieved in 1982 by lawyers for Soraya Khashóggi, was £500 million ($950 million) plus property from her husband Adnan.

Largest alimony suit   Belgian-born Sheika Dena Al-Fassi filed an alimony claim of $3 billion against her former husband, Sheik Mohammed Al-Fassi of the Saudi Arabian royal family, in Los Angeles, CA in February 1982. Attorney Marvin Mitchelson, explaining the size of the settlement claim, alluded to the Sheik's wealth, which included 14 homes in Florida alone and numerous private aircraft. On June 14, 1983, the claimant was awarded $81 million and declared she would be "very very happy" if she were able to collect.

Largest patent violation case   Litton Industries Inc. was awarded $1.2 billion in damages from Honeywell Inc. on August 31, 1993. A jury in Los Angeles, CA decided that Honeywell had violated a Litton patent covering airline navigation systems.

Highest costs   The Blue Arrow trial, involving the illegal support of the company's shares during a rights issue in 1987, is estimated to have cost approximately £35 million (*c.* $60 million). The trial in, London, England lasted a year and ended on February 14, 1992 with four of the defendants being convicted. Although they received suspended prison sentences, they were later cleared on appeal.

United States   The McMartin Preschool case in Los Angeles, CA is estimated to have cost $15 million. The trial, concerning the alleged abuse of children at the school in Manhattan Beach, CA, had begun with jury selection on April 20, 1987 and resulted in the acquittal on January 18, 1990 of the two defendants on 52 counts of child molestation and conspiracy.

Longest lease   A lease on a plot for a sewage tank adjoining Columb Barracks, Mullingar, Ireland was signed on December 3, 1868 for 10 million years.

Oldest will   The oldest written will dates from 2061 B.C. It was carved on the walls of the tomb of Nek'ure, the son of the Egyptian pharaoh Khafre, and indicated that Nek'ure would bequeath 14 towns, two estates and other property to his wife, another woman and three children.

Shortest will   The shortest valid will consists of four characters in Hindi meaning "All to son." It was written by Bimla Rishi of Delhi, India and is dated February 9, 1995.

Longest will   The will of Frederica Evelyn Stilwell Cook (U.S.) was proved in London, England on November 2, 1925. It consisted of four bound volumes containing 95,940 words, primarily concerning some $100,000 worth of property.

Most codicils   The largest number of codicils (supplements modifying the details) to a will admitted to probate is 21, in the case of the will of J. Paul Getty. The will was dated September 22, 1958 and had 21 codicils dating from June 18, 1960 through March 11, 1976. Getty died on June 6, 1976.

Most durable judge   The oldest recorded active judge was Judge Albert R. Alexander of Plattsburg, MO. He was enrolled as a member of the Clinton County Bar in 1926, and was later the magistrate and probate judge of Clinton County until his retirement at age 105 yr. 8 mo. on July 9, 1965.

Narrowest margin   Judge Clarence Thomas was elected to the Supreme Court in 1991 by the narrowest margin ever recorded, 52 votes to 48.

Youngest judge   No collated records on the ages of judicial appointments exist. However, David Elmer Ward had to wait until he reached the legal age of 21 before taking office after nomination in 1932 as judge of the County Court in Fort Myers, FL.
   Muhammad Ilyas passed the examination enabling him to become a civil judge in July 1952 at the age of 20 yr. 9 mo., although formalities such as medicals meant that it was not until eight months later that he started work as a civil judge in Lahore, Pakistan.

Most lawyers   In the United States there were an estimated 946,499 resident and active lawyers as of June 1996, or one lawyer for every 276 people.

Oldest lawyer   The oldest lawyer was Cornelius Van de Steeg (1889–1994) of Perry, IA. He was a practicing lawyer until April 1991, when he was 101 yr. 11 mo. old.

Most acquittals   Sir Lionel Luckhoo, senior partner of Luckhoo and Luckhoo of Georgetown, Guyana, succeeded in getting 245 successive murder charge acquittals between 1940 and 1985.

CRIME

Largest criminal organizations   There are believed to be more than 250,000 members of Chinese triad societies worldwide, but they are fragmented into many groups that often fight each other and compete in disputed areas. Hong Kong alone has some 100,000 members.

In terms of profit, the largest syndicate in organized crime is the Mafia or La Cosa Nostra. The Mafia consists of some 3,000 to 5,000 individuals in 25 "families" federated under "The Commission," with an annual turnover in illegal activities that was estimated by *U.S. News & World Report* in December 1982 to be $200 billion, and a profit estimated in March 1986 by Rudolph Giuliani, United States Attorney for the Southern District of New York, to be $75 billion.

In terms of numbers, the Yamaguchi-gumi gang of the *yakuza* in Japan is the largest, with 30,000 members. There are some 90,000 *yakuza* or gangsters altogether, in more than 3,000 groups. On March 1, 1992, Japan instituted laws to combat their activities, which include drug trafficking, smuggling, prostitution and gambling.

Most assassination attempts   The target of the highest number of *failed* assassination attempts on an individual head of state in modern times was Charles de Gaulle, president of France from 1958 to 1969. He was reputed to have survived 31 plots against his life between 1944 and 1966, although some plots were foiled and did not culminate in actual attacks.

Most murders committed   It was established at the trial of Behram, the Indian Thug, that he had strangled at least 931 victims in the Oudh district between 1790 and 1840. An estimated 2 million Indians were strangled by Thugs during the reign of the Thuggee cult from 1550 until its final suppression by the British raj in 1853.

Twentieth century   A total of 592 deaths was attributed to one Colombian bandit leader, Teófilo ("Sparks") Rojas, between 1948 and his death in an ambush near Armenia, Colombia on January 22, 1963. Some sources attribute 3,500 slayings to him during La Violencia of 1945–62.

United States   The greatest mass murder committed in the United States was the Happy Land fire, which resulted in the deaths of 87 individuals. The fire was set by 36-year-old Julio Gonzalez, on March 25, 1990 at an illegal New York City social club, The Happy Land, in revenge for being thrown out of the club after an argument with a former girlfriend, Lydia Feliciano, who worked at the club. Feliciano was one of six survivors.

Greatest mass arrest   The greatest mass arrest reported in a democratic country was of 15,617 demonstrators on July 11, 1988, rounded up by South Korean police to ensure security in advance of the 1988 Olympic Games in Seoul.

Most lynchings   The worst year in the 20th century for lynchings in the United States was 1901, with 130 lynchings, of which 125 were of blacks and five were of whites. The date on which lynchings were last reported was June 21, 1964, in Philadelphia, MS. Three men—two white and one black—were lynched in the Neshoba County town.

Greatest mass poisoning   On May 1, 1981, an 8-year-old boy became the first of more than 600 victims of the Spanish cooking oil scandal. On June 12, it was discovered that the cause of his death was the use of "denatured" industrial oil from rape-seed. The trial of 38 defendants, including the manufacturers, lasted from March 30, 1987 to June 28, 1988. The 586

Contaminated cooking oil from the worst mass poisoning is tested
in a laboratory (top): above, an angry scene at the start of the trial.

counts on which the prosecution demanded jail sentences totaled 60,000 years.

Biggest robbery The robbery of the Reischbank following Germany's collapse in April–May 1945 was described by the Pentagon in Washington as "an unverified allegation." However, the book *Nazi Gold* by Ian Sayer and Douglas Botting, published in 1984, finally revealed full details and estimated the total haul at what were then current values as £2.5 billion ($3.75 billion).

The government of the Philippines announced on April 23, 1986 that it had succeeded in identifying $860.8 million salted away since 1965 by former President Ferdinand Marcos and his wife Imelda. The total wealth taken by the couple was believed to be $5–$10 billion.

Art It is arguable that the Mona Lisa, though never appraised, is the most valuable object ever stolen. The painting disappeared from the Louvre, Paris, France on August 21, 1911. It was recovered in Italy in 1913, when Vincenzo Perugia was charged with its theft.

Bank During the civil disorder prior to January 22, 1976 in Beirut, Lebanon, a guerrilla force blasted the vaults of the British Bank of the Middle East in Bab Idriss and cleared out safe deposit boxes with contents valued by former Finance Minister Lucien Dahdah at $50 million and by another source at an "absolute minimum" of $20 million.

Jewels The greatest recorded theft of jewels was from the Carlton Hotel, Cannes, France on August 11, 1994. Gems with an estimated value of Fr250 million ($48 million) were stolen from the jewelry store by a 3-man gang. A security guard was seriously injured during the raid.

Train The greatest recorded train robbery occurred on August 8, 1963, when a General Post Office mail train was ambushed at Sears Crossing and robbed at Bridego Bridge, near Mentmore, England. The robbers escaped with £2,631,784 in banknotes; only $343,448 was recovered.

Greatest hijacking ransom The Japanese government paid $6 million to aircraft hijackers for a JAL DC-8 and 38 hostages at Dacca Airport, Bangladesh on October 2, 1977. Six convicted criminals were also exchanged. The Bangladesh government had refused to sanction any retaliatory action.

Greatest kidnapping ransom Historically, the greatest ransom paid was that for Atahualpa by the Incas to Francisco Pizarro in 1532–33 at Cajamarca, Peru. It constituted a hall full of gold and silver, worth some $1.5 billion on today's market. Pizarro did not keep his side of the bargain; he murdered Atahualpa instead of returning him.

The greatest ransom ever reported in modern times was 1,500 million pesos ($60 million) for the release of the brothers Jorge and Juan Born of the firm Bunge and Born, paid to the left-wing urban guerrilla group Montoneros in Buenos Aires, Argentina on June 20, 1975.

Largest narcotics haul In terms of value, the greatest haul in a drug seizure was on September 28, 1989, when cocaine with an estimated street value of $6–7 billion was seized in a raid on a warehouse in Los Angeles, CA.

Largest narcotics operation The bulkiest haul was 3,200 tons of Colombian marijuana in the 14-month-long "Operation Tiburon," carried out by the U.S. Drug Enforcement Administration and Colombian authorities. The arrest of 495 people and the seizure of 95 vessels was announced on February 5, 1982.

The London *Evening Standard* reports the greatest-ever train robbery.

Greatest bank note forgery The German Third Reich's forging operation, code name "Operation Bernhard," was engineered by Major Bernhard Krüger during World War II. It involved more than £130 million worth of British notes, which were produced by 140 Jewish prisoners at Sachsenhausen concentration camp.

Biggest bank fraud The Banca Nazionale del Lavoro of Italy admitted on September 6, 1989 that it had been defrauded of a huge sum, later estimated to be in the region of $5 billion, with the disclosure that its Atlanta, GA branch had made unauthorized loan commitments to Iraq.

Biggest computer fraud Between 1964 and 1973, 64,000 fake insurance policies were created on the computer of the Equity Funding Corporation in the United States, involving $2 billion.

Stanley Mark Rifkin was arrested in Carlsbad, CA by the FBI on November 6, 1978 and charged with defrauding a Los Angeles bank of $10.2 million by manipulation of a computer system. He was sentenced to eight years' imprisonment in June 1980.

Biggest maritime fraud A cargo of 198,414 tons of Kuwaiti crude oil on the supertanker *Salem* at Durban was sold without title to the South African government in December 1979. The ship mysteriously sank off Senegal in 1980, leaving the government to pay £148 million ($318.2 million) to Shell International, which owned the shipment.

FINES

Heaviest fine A fine of $650 million was imposed on the U.S. securities firm of Drexel Burnham Lambert in December 1988 for insider trading. This figure represented $300 million in direct fines, with the balance to be put into an account to satisfy claims of parties who could prove they were defrauded by Drexel's actions.

The record for an individual is $200 million, which Michael Milken agreed to pay on April 24, 1990. In addition, he agreed to settle civil charges filed by the Securities and Exchange Commission. The payments were in settlement of a racketeering and securities fraud suit brought by the U.S. government. On appeal, Milken's sentence was reduced to 33 mo. 26 days. He was released from prison on March 2, 1993, but was required to give 1,800 hours of community service.

CAPITAL PUNISHMENT

Largest hanging The Nazi Feldkommandant simultaneously hanged 50 Greek resistance fighters as a reprisal measure in Athens, Greece on July 22, 1944.

The greatest number of people hanged from one gallows was 38 Sioux Indians, by William J. Duly outside Mankato, MN on December 26, 1862 for the murder of unarmed citizens.

Last public hanging The last public hanging in the United States occurred at Owensboro, KY on August 14, 1936, when Rainey Bethea was hung in a field by the banks of the Ohio River. He was executed in the presence of a crowd of 10–15,000.

Most experienced executioners The Sanson family of France supplied executioners through several generations, from 1688 to 1847. Charles-Henri Sanson, known as Monsieur de Paris, dispatched more than 3,000 victims, most of them in two years, 1793–94, including the king, Louis XVI, on January 21, 1793.

Longest stay on death row Sadamichi Hirasawa (1893–1987) spent 39 years on death row in Sendai Jail, Japan. He was convicted in 1948 of poisoning 12 bank employees with potassium cyanide to effect a theft of $403, and died in prison at age 94.

United States Howard Virgil Lee Douglas spent 17½ years on death row, longer than any other person in American penal history. On May 15, 1991, he was resentenced to life in prison.

PRISON SENTENCES

Longest sentences Chamoy Thipyaso, a Thai woman known as the queen of underground investing, and seven of her associates were each sentenced to serve 141,078 years in jail by the Bangkok Criminal Court, Thailand on

Sadamichi Hirasawa spent a record 39 years on death row.

July 27, 1989 for swindling the public through a multimillion-dollar deposit-taking business.

The longest sentence imposed on a mass murderer was 21 consecutive life sentences and 12 death sentences in the case of John Wayne Gacy, Jr., who killed 33 boys and young men between 1972 and 1978 in Illinois. He was sentenced by a jury in Chicago, IL on March 13, 1980, and executed on May 10, 1994.

Longest time served   Paul Geidel was convicted of second-degree murder on September 5, 1911 when he was a 17-year-old porter in a hotel in New York. He was released from the Fishkill Correctional Facility, Beacon, NY at age 85 on May 7, 1980, having served 68 yr. 8 mo. 2 days—the longest recorded term in U.S. history.

Oldest prisoner   Bill Wallace spent the last 63 years of his life in Aradale Psychiatric Hospital, Ararat, Victoria, Australia. He had shot and killed a man at a restaurant in Melbourne, Victoria in December 1925, and having been found unfit to plead, was transferred to the responsibility of the Mental Health Department in February 1926. He remained at Aradale until his death on July 17, 1989, shortly before his 108th birthday.

PRISONS

Most expensive imprisonment   Spandau Prison, Berlin, Germany, originally built in 1887 for 600 prisoners, was used solely for the Nazi war criminal Rudolf Hess (April 26, 1894–August 17, 1987) for the last 20 years of his life. The cost of maintenance of the staff of 105 was estimated in 1976 to be $415,000 per year.

Longest escape   On December 15, 1923, Leonard T. Fristoe escaped from Nevada State Prison, Carson City, NV, where he was serving time for killing two sheriff's deputies. Fristoe was turned in by his son on November 15, 1969, in Compton, CA, having had nearly 46 years of freedom under the name of Claude R. Willis.

Largest jailbreaks   On February 11, 1979, an Iranian employee of the Electronic Data Systems Corporation led a mob into Gasr prison, Tehran, Iran in an effort to rescue two Americans. Some 11,000 other prisoners took advantage of the situation and became part of history's largest-ever jailbreak. Although it was the Iranian employee's actions that allowed the actual jail break to happen, the plan to get the Americans out was masterminded by their employer, H. Ross Perot.

In September 1971, Raúl Sendic and 105 other Tupamaro guerrillas, plus five nonpolitical prisoners, escaped from a Uruguayan prison through a tunnel 298 feet long.

Highest prison population   Some human rights organizations have estimated that there are 20 million prisoners in China, or 1,658 per 100,000 population, although this figure is not officially acknowledged. Among countries for which statistics are available, the country with the highest per capita prison population is the United States, with 565 prisoners per 100,000 population.

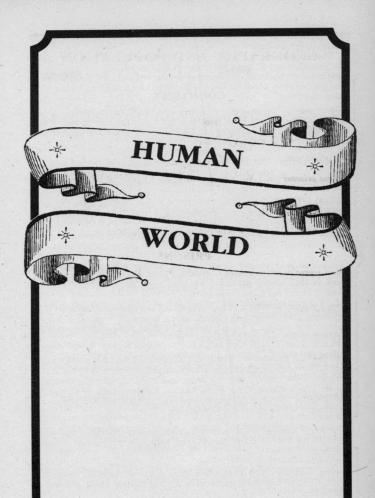

HUMAN

WORLD

40

GEOGRAPHY AND POPULATION

COUNTRIES

Largest country   Russia has a total area of 6,592,800 square miles, or 11.5 percent of the world's land area. It is 1.8 times the size of the United States, but had a population of 147,168,000 people in 1995, around 60 percent the size of the U.S. population.

Smallest country   The smallest independent country in the world is the State of Vatican City or Holy See (Stato della Città del Vaticano), an enclave within the city of Rome, Italy. The enclave has an area of 108.7 acres.

Republic   The world's smallest republic is Nauru, in the Pacific Ocean. It has an area of 5,263 acres and a population of 10,400 (1995 estimate).

Colony   Gibraltar has an area of 1,440 acres. However, Pitcairn Island in the South Pacific (population 55 in late 1993) has an area of 960 acres.

Flattest and most elevated countries   The country with the lowest "high point" is Maldives, at eight feet above sea level. The country with the highest "low point" is Lesotho, at 4,530 feet above sea level.

Largest political division   The Commonwealth, a free association of 52 independent states and their dependencies, covers an area of 12,294,421 square miles and has a population of 1.5 billion. Almost all members belonged to the former British Empire.

Most national boundaries   There are 319 national land boundaries in the world. The continent with the greatest number is Africa, with 109.

China is the country with the most land frontiers, with 16—Mongolia, Russia, North Korea, Hong Kong, Macau, Vietnam, Laos, Myanmar, India, Bhutan, Nepal, Pakistan, Afghanistan, Tajikistan, Kyrgyzstan and Kazakhstan. These extend for 14,900 miles.

Most border crossings   The most frequently crossed frontier is the border between the United States and Mexico, with over 475 million crossings each year.

Longest boundary   The longest boundary in the world is the border between Canada and the conterminous United States, which extends for 3,987 miles.

Maritime   The Greenland–Canada boundary is 1,676 miles long.

Shortest boundary   The land frontier between Gibraltar and Spain at La Linea measures one mile in length.

Longest coastline   Canada has the longest coastline of any country in the world, with 152,100 miles including islands.

Maldives has the lowest "high point" of any country.

Shortest coastline   Monaco has 3½ miles of coastline, excluding piers and breakwaters.

Nearest and farthest capital cities   The nearest capitals of two neighboring countries are the Vatican City and Rome (Italy)—the Vatican is surrounded by Rome. The greatest distance between capitals of countries that share a border is 2,600 miles, for Moscow (Russia) and Pyongyang (Democratic People's Republic of Korea).

STATES

Largest state   The largest state in land area is Alaska, with 591,004 square miles. The largest of the 48 conterminous states is Texas, with 267,017 square miles of land.

Smallest state   The smallest state is Rhode Island, with 1,212 square miles.

Most populous state   The most populous state in the United States as of July 1, 1995 was California, with an estimated 31,589,000 people.

Least populous state   As of July 1, 1995, Wyoming had an estimated 480,000 people.

Longest coastline   Alaska is the state with the longest coastline; it measures 5,580 miles.

COUNTIES

Largest county   The largest in the lower 48 states is San Bernardino County, CA, with an area of 20,062 square miles. The biggest legally established county is the North Slope Borough of Alaska, at 87,860 acres.

Most and fewest counties The state with the most counties is Texas, with 254, and the state with the fewest is Delaware, with three (Kent, New Castle and Sussex).

CITIES AND TOWNS

Oldest town The oldest walled town in the world is Ariha (Jericho), which was inhabited by perhaps 2,700 people as early as 7800 B.C. The settlement of Dolní Věstonice, Czech Republic has been dated to the Gravettian culture *c.* 27,000 B.C.

The oldest town of European origin in the United States is St. Augustine, St. John's County, FL. The town was founded on September 8, 1565, on the site of Seloy, by Pedro Menendez de Aviles. Its present population is 11,933.

Oldest city The oldest capital city in the world is Dimishq (Damascus), Syria. It has been continuously inhabited since *c.* 2500 B.C.

United States The oldest incorporated city is York, ME (present population 14,000), which received an English charter in March 1642, and was incorporated under the name Georgiana.

Most populous city The 1994 Revision of the United Nations publication *World Urbanization Prospects* lists Tokyo, Japan as the most populous agglomeration, with a population of 26,500,000 in 1994.

United States New York City has 18,107,235 residents.

Largest city The world's largest city (defined as a densely populated settlement) is Mount Isa, Queensland, Australia. The City Council administers 15,822 square miles.

Highest town The town of Wenzhuan, founded in 1955 on the Qinghai–Tibet road north of the Tangla range, is the highest in the world, at 16,730 feet above sea level.

United States The highest incorporated city in the United States is Leadville, CO, at 10,152 feet. Leadville has a population of 2,629.

Highest capital city The highest capital in the world, before the domination of Tibet by China, was Lhasa, at an elevation of 12,087 feet above sea level. La Paz, administrative and *de facto* capital of Bolivia, stands at an altitude of 11,913 feet above sea level.

Farthest town from the sea The major town most remote from the sea is Urumqi (Wulumuqi) in Xinjiang, the capital of China's Xinjiang Uygur Autonomous Region, at a distance of about 1,500 miles from the nearest coastline.

Highest settlement The settlement on the T'e-li-mo trail in southern Tibet is sited at an altitude of 19,800 feet.

Lowest settlement The Israeli settlement of Ein Bokek on the shores of the Dead Sea is 1,291 feet below sea level.

Lowest city The lowest incorporated city in the United States is Calipatria, CA, at 184 feet below sea level.

Northernmost settlement Ny Ålesund (78° 55′ N) is a coalmining settlement on King's Bay, Vest-Spitsbergen in the Norwegian territory of Svalbard. Its population varies seasonally from 25 to 100.

The northernmost town is Dikson, Russia (73° 32′ N), with a population of 1,400.

United States The northernmost city in the United States is Barrow, AK (71° 17′ N).

Northernmost capital city The northernmost capital is Reykjavik, Iceland (64° 08′ N). Its population was 103,036 in 1994.

Southernmost settlement The world's southernmost village is Puerto Williams (population 1,550) on the north coast of Isla Navarino, Tierra del Fuego, Chile, 680 miles north of Antarctica.

United States The southernmost city in the United States is Hilo, HI (19° 43′ N).

Southernmost capital city Wellington, the capital of New Zealand (41° 17′ S), has a population of 331,100.

Longest mayoralty Edmond Mathis was the mayor of Ehuns, Haute-Saône, France for 75 years, 1878–1953.

The longest-serving mayor in the United States is Robert P. Linn, who took office as mayor of Beaver, PA in January 1946 and was still serving as of September 1995.

Youngest mayor The youngest-ever mayor was Shane Mack (b. November 15, 1969), who became mayor of Castlewood, SD at the age of 18 yr. 169 days on May 3, 1988. He held office until May 6, 1996.

POPULATION

Most populous country China had an estimated population of 1,206,600,000 in mid-1995 and a rate of natural increase of over 14.3 million per year or more than 39,000 per day. Its population is larger than that of the whole world 150 years ago.

Least populous country The independent state with the smallest population is Vatican City, with 1,000 inhabitants in 1995.

Most densely populated territory The Portuguese province of Macau, with an estimated population of 428,000 (1995) in an area of 6.9 square miles, has a density of 62,029 people per square mile.

Most sparsely populated territory   Antarctica became permanently occupied by relays of scientists from 1943 on. The population now reaches 2,000 at times.

Most houses   For comparison purposes, a dwelling unit is defined as a structurally separated room or rooms occupied by a private household of one or more people and having separate access or a common passageway to the street. The country with the greatest number of dwelling units is China, with 276,947,962 in 1990.

Most emigrants   More people emigrate from Mexico than from any other country, mainly to the United States.

Most immigrants   The country that receives the most legal immigrants is the United States. During fiscal year 1993 (October 1992–September 1993), an estimated 1,024,908 people legally entered the United States.

In fiscal year 1995, a total of 1,394,554 people were apprehended for immigration violations. The largest group by nationality were 1,340,458 from Mexico.

Most tourists   The World Tourism Organization reports that the most popular destination is France, which in 1995 received 60,584,000 foreign tourists. The country with the greatest receipts from tourism is the United States, with $58.6 billion in 1995. The biggest spenders on foreign tourism are Germans, who in the same year spent $47.3 billion abroad.

Most and fewest hospitals   The country with the greatest number of hospitals is China, with 60,784 in 1993. Monaco has the most hospital beds per person (168 for every 10,000 people); Afghanistan, Bangladesh, Ethiopia and Nepal have the fewest (3 per 10,000).

Baragwanath Hospital, in Soweto, South Africa, has more beds than any other hospital, with 3,294.

Highest and lowest death rates   The crude death rate—the number of deaths per 1,000 population of all ages—for the whole world was an estimated 9.3 per 1,000 in the period 1990–95. The highest estimated rate in the period 1990–95 was 25.2 per 1,000 for Sierra Leone. The lowest estimated rate for 1990–95 was 2.7 deaths per 1,000 for the United Arab Emirates.

Highest and lowest suicide rates   The country with the highest suicide rate is Sri Lanka, with a rate of 47 per 100,000 population in 1991. The country with the lowest recorded rate is Jordan, with just a single case in 1970 and hence a rate of 0.04 per 100,000.

Most marriages   The marriage rate for Vanuatu is 34.0 per 1,000 population.

Most divorces   The country with the most divorces is the United States, with 1,191,000 in 1994—a rate of 4.6 per 1,000 population. The all-time high rate was 5.3 per 1,000 people, in 1979 and 1981. The lowest rate on record was 0.7 per 1,000 people, in 1900.

Greatest gender ratio imbalance The country with the largest recorded shortage of women is the United Arab Emirates, with an estimated 566 women for every 1,000 men. The country with the largest recorded shortage of men is Latvia, with an estimated 1,167 women for every 1,000 men.

Japan has the highest life expectancy of any country.

Highest and lowest infant mortality rates   The world infant mortality rate—the number of deaths at ages under one year per 1,000 live births—in 1990–95 was 64 per 1,000 live births. The lowest of the latest recorded rates is 4 per 1,000 in Japan for the period 1990–95. The highest rate recently estimated is 166 per 1,000 in Sierra Leone (1990–95).

United States   Washington, D.C. had the highest infant mortality rate in 1994, with 20.1 percent, while Washington had the lowest, with 5.4 percent.

Life expectancy   World life expectancy has risen from 46.4 years (1950–55) to 64.4 years (1990–95).
   The highest average life expectancy at birth is in Japan, with 82.1 years for women and 76.1 years for men in 1991. The lowest life expectancy at birth for the period 1985–90 is 39.4 years for males in Ethiopia and Sierra Leone, and 42.0 years for females in Afghanistan.

Highest and lowest birthrates   The crude birthrate—the number of births per 1,000 population—for the whole world was estimated to be 25 per 1,000 in the period 1990–95. The highest rate estimated by the United Nations for the period 1990–95 was 52.5 per 1,000 for Niger. Excluding Vatican City, where the rate is negligible, the lowest recorded rate for the period 1990–95 was 9.7 per 1,000 for Spain.

United States   The National Center for Health Statistics (NCHS) estimates that the United States' crude birthrate (the number of babies for every 1,000 people) is 15.7. Official statistics for 1994 show that California led with 581,763 births, while Wyoming had the fewest, with 6,385. The most live births registered in the United States in any year were 4,300,000 in 1957. The highest birthrate recorded after 1909, the first year official records were recognized, was 30.1 in 1910.

Highest and lowest natural increase   The rate of natural increase (crude birthrate minus crude death rate) for the whole world was estimated to be 15.7 (25.0 minus 9.3) per 1,000 in the period 1990–95, compared with a peak of 20.4 per 1,000 in 1965–70. The highest of the latest available recorded rates was 38.8 (43.6 minus 4.8) for Oman in 1990–95. The lowest rate of natural increase in any major independent country in recent times was in Hungary, which experienced a decline in the same period, with a figure of –2.9 per 1,000 (11.7 births and 14.6 deaths).

Most and fewest physicians   The country with the greatest number of physicians is China, which had 1,832,000 physicians in 1993, including those practicing dentistry and those practicing traditional Chinese medicine. The United States had 629,815 physicians as of January 1, 1994.
   Niger has the highest number of people per physician, with 54,472, while at the other extreme, in Italy there is one physician for every 225 people.

Largest religion   Christianity is the world's largest religion, with some 1.90 billion adherents in 1994, or 33.7 percent of the world's population. Of these, 1.06 billion were Roman Catholics. The largest non-Christian religion is Islam, with some 1.03 billion followers in 1994.

40 years ago *The first edition of* The Guinness Book of Records *reported: "Christianity is the world's prevailing religion, with at least 750 million and probably an additional 250 million Protestants who are not in membership with the Church of their baptism. It would appear that the total of 200 million practicing and 250 million non-practicing Protestants is slightly outnumbered by the 460 million who have received baptism into the Roman Catholic Church."* **Today** *Christianity is calculated to be the world's largest religion, with some 1.90 billion adherents as of 1994. Of these, 1.06 billion were Roman Catholics.*

"I'd like to be the guy in Times Square with the Bible in his hand and preach the longest."—George Foreman, boxing champion, May 23, 1996

GENOCIDES AND MASSACRES

Most lives saved The greatest number of people saved from death by one person is estimated to be nearly 100,000 Jews in Budapest, Hungary from July 1944 to January 1945, by Swedish diplomat Raoul Wallenberg. After escaping an assassination attempt by the Nazis, he was imprisoned without trial in the Soviet Union. Although officials claimed that Wallenberg died in Lubyanka Jail, Moscow on July 16, 1947, sighting reports within the gulag system persisted for years after his disappearance.

Worst mass killings Cambodia As a percentage of a nation's total population the worst genocide appears to have taken place in Cambodia during the Khmer Rouge regime of Saloth Sar, alias Pol Pot. According to the foreign minister, Ieng Sary, more than a third of the 8 million Khmers were killed between April 17, 1975, when the Khmer Rouge captured Phnom Penh, and January 1979, when they were overthrown.

China The greatest massacre ever imputed by the government of one sovereign nation to the government of another is that of 26.3 million Chinese during the regime of Mao Zedong (Tse-tung) between 1949 and May 1965. This accusation was made by an agency of the Soviet government in a radio broadcast on April 7, 1969.

The Walker Report, published by the U.S. Senate Committee of the Judiciary in July 1971, placed the death toll within China since 1949 between 32.25 and 61.7 million. An estimate of 63.7 million was published by *Le Figaro Magazine*, November 19–25, 1978.

Nazi Germany   The most extreme extermination campaign against a people was the Holocaust, the genocidal "Final Solution" (End-lösung) ordered by Adolf Hitler, starting by the fall of 1941 and continuing into May 1945. Reliable estimates of the number of victims range from 5.1 million to 6 million Jews. At the SS death camp at Auschwitz-Birkenau in southern Poland, it is estimated that 1,350,000 Jews and 115,000 others were murdered from June 1940 through January 1945. The greatest number killed in a day was 6,000.

Worst terrorist bombing   The largest terrorist attack in the United States was the car bombing of the Alfred P. Murrah Federal Building in Oklahoma City, OK on April 19, 1995. The death toll was 169, including one rescue worker.

DISASTERS

Atomic bomb   On the morning of August 6, 1945, a U.S. B-29 dropped an atomic bomb on Hiroshima, Japan, killing over 130,000. Within a year, another 25,200 died from radiation.

Conventional bombing   A bomb killed 140,000 people on March 10, 1945 in Tokyo, Japan.

Marine disaster   On January 30, 1945, 7,700 people died when the *Wilhelm Gustloff* sank into the Gulf of Danzig. The 25,484-ton German liner was torpedoed by a Russian submarine, leaving only 903 survivors.

Dam burst   The Machhu River dam collapsed due to flooding on August 11, 1979, claiming 5,000 lives in Morvi, India.

Panic   On June 6, 1941, 700 people suffocated in a Chungking underground tunnel where they sheltered during a Japanese air raid.

Smog   In London, England in December 1952, 3,500–4,000 people, mainly elderly and children, died from acute bronchitis caused by smog carrying dirt from industrial cities.

Industrial accident   The December 3, 1984 methyl-isocyanate gas leak at a Union Carbide pesticide plant in Bhopal, India killed 3,350 and left 20,000 to suffer from blindness, cancer, and ulcers.

Fire   The fire in the Hotel Daeyungak, Seoul, South Korea, December 25, 1971, killed 162 people.

Explosion   On December 7, 1917 the French freighter *Mont Blanc*, packed with 5,000 tons of explosives and combustibles, collided with another ship in Halifax Harbour, Nova Scotia, creating a blast felt over 60 miles away and killing 1,635.

Hurricane Andrew was the costliest hurricane in the United States (see also EARTH AND SPACE).

Mining accident A coal dust explosion killed 1,549 miners at Honkeiko Colliery, China, April 26, 1942.

Riots On February 28, 1947, Nationalist police in Taiwan beat and arrested an elderly woman selling black market cigarettes, then shot at the crowd that formed in protest. A riot ensued, and approximately 1,400 people were killed.

The Los Angeles earthquake of 1994 was the most destructive to hit the United States.

Tornado After hundreds united in prayer for rain to end a 4-month drought in Shaturia, Bangladesh, water came on April 26, 1989. Unfortunately, it was brought by a tornado that created winds up to 120 MPH, leaving around 1,300 dead and at least 30,000 homeless.

Mass suicide Rather than submit to the Romans, 960 Jewish zealots committed suicide after a prolonged seige of Massada, their fortress stronghold, during the Roman–Jewish war of A.D. 66–73. In modern times, the greatest mass suicide was on November 18, 1978, when 913 members of the People's Temple cult died of cyanide poisoning near Port Kaituma, Guyana.

Railroad disaster On June 6,1981 an overcrowded passenger train travelling in Bihar, India fell off the Bagmati bridge into the river, leaving at least 800 dead.

Fireworks accident The celebration of the Dauphin's wedding on May 16, 1770 in Paris, France ended in disaster when at least 800 people were trampled to death or drowned in the Seine after the fireworks display went wrong.

Aircraft disaster The worst air crash occurred on March 27, 1977, when two Boeing 747s (Pan-Am and KLM) collided on the runway at Tenerife in the Canary Islands, killing 583 people.

The crash of JAL's Boeing 747, flight 123, near Tokyo on August 12, 1985, in which 520 passengers and crew perished, was the worst crash involving a single plane in aviation history.

Man-eating animal Between 1902 and 1907, 436 people were killed by a man-eating tiger in the Champawat district of India. The tiger was eventually shot by famed hunter Col. Jim Corbett.

Terrorism A bomb exploded on an Air-India Boeing 747, which crashed into the Atlantic southwest of Ireland, killing 329, on June 23, 1985.

Road accident At least 176 Soviet soldiers and Afghani citizens died of carbon monoxide asphyxiation when both ends of the Salang Tunnel in Afghanistan were sealed after a tanker full of petrol collided with the leading Soviet vehicle on November 3, 1982. Western estimates gave the number of deaths at around 1,100.

Latvia has the highest fatality rate in road accidents, with 34.7 deaths per 100,000 population, and Malta the lowest, with 1.6 per 100,000. The worst year for road deaths in the United States was 1972 (56,278).

Offshore oil platform accident A breakdown in production platform communications caused the Piper Alpha oil rig blast, which claimed 167 lives on July 6, 1988 in the North Sea.

Submarine accident The American freighter SS *Thompson Lykes* rammed and sank the Free French submarine *Surcouf*, which was carrying 130 officers and men, in the Caribbean on February 18, 1942. There were no survivors.

Helicopter crash A Russian military helicopter transporting 58 refugees from Abkhaziya on December 14, 1992 was shot down near the Georgian village of Lata. All the refugees and the three crew members died.

Mountaineering accident On July 13, 1990, 43 climbers died when an avalanche triggered by a small earthquake buried their camp on Lenin Peak on the Tajikistan/Kyrgyzstan border.

Ski lift accident On March 9, 1976, 42 skiers fell to their death when their trolley was knocked off its cable, snapping it and causing the car to plummet 250 feet at a resort in northern Italy.

Nuclear reactor disaster Although 31 was the official Soviet total of immediate deaths in the April 26, 1986 Chernobyl disaster, it is not known how many of the c. 200,000 people involved in the cleanup died in the 5-year period following the disaster due to radiation exposure, since no systematic records were kept.

Yacht racing accident High seas claimed 19 lives during the 28th Fastnet Race, held August 13–15, 1979, and left 23 boats sunk or abandoned.

Space disaster On January 23, 1986, the U.S. space shuttle *Challenger* exploded just 73 seconds after take-off at Cape Canaveral, Florida, killing the crew of seven.

In the worst accident on the ground, 91 people died when an R-16 rocket exploded during fueling at the Baikonur Space Center, Kazakhstan, on October 24, 1960.

Nuclear waste accident Overheating of a nuclear waste container caused the 1957 explosion at complex i-Kyshtym, Russia, dipersing radioactive compounds over 23,000 square kilometers. More than 30 small communities in a 460-square-mile area were eliminated from maps of the USSR in the years after the accident, with 17,000 people evacuated. A 1992 report indicated that 8,015 people had died over a 32-year period as a direct result of discharges from the complex.

ECONOMICS

Largest budget The greatest governmental expenditure ever made was $1.519 trillion by the United States government for the fiscal year 1995. The highest revenue figure was $1.355 trillion in the same year.

The greatest fiscal surplus was $8,419,469,844 in the United States in 1947/48. The worst deficit was $290 billion in U.S. fiscal year 1992.

Foreign aid The greatest donor of foreign aid is the United States, which gave a net total of $436.9 billion from July 1, 1945 through May 1, 1995.

The country receiving most U.S. aid in 1994 was Israel, with $4.57 billion for economic and military aid and loan guarantees.

Lowest taxation rates   The sovereign countries with the lowest income tax in the world are Bahrain and Qatar, where the rate is zero, regardless of income. No tax is levied on the inhabitants of Sark in the Channel Islands, Great Britain.

United States   The lowest income tax rate in United States history was 1 percent between 1913 and 1915.

Highest taxation rates   In Denmark, the highest rate of income tax is 68 percent, but a net wealth tax of 1 percent can result in tax of over 100 percent on income in extreme situations.

United States   The highest income tax rate in United States history was implemented in 1944 by the Individual Tax Act with a 91 percent bracket. The current highest income tax bracket is 31 percent.

Balance of payments   The record balance of payments deficit for any country for a calendar year is $173.4 billion in 1995 by the United States. The record surplus was Japan's $117.64 billion (the equivalent of 149 trillion yen) in 1992.

Largest national debt   The United States has the world's largest national debt. By March 31, 1996, it reached $5.153 trillion, with net interest payments on the debt of $163.92 billion and gross interest payments of $263.217 billion.

Most foreign debt   The country most heavily in overseas debt at the end of fiscal year 1994 was the United States, with over $654 billion.

Largest gross national product   The gross national product of the United States was running at $7.2 trillion at the end of 1995.

Richest country   The richest country in the world, according to the United Nations Statistical Division, is Liechtenstein, which in 1992 had an average gross national product per capita of $54,607.

According to the Department of Commerce, in 1995, Connecticut enjoyed the highest per capita income level of any state ($30,303), while Mississippi continued to have the lowest ($16,531). Personal income in the United States averaged $23,192 per person for 1995 and set a record high of $6.1 trillion in the same year.

The median household income in the United States in 1994 was $31,241. Alaska enjoyed the highest level, at $42,931, while Mississippi had the lowest, at $22,191.

Poorest country   Mozambique had the lowest gross national product per capita in 1991, with $70, although there are several countries for which the *World Bank Atlas* is not able to include data.

Largest gold reserves   The country with the greatest monetary gold reserves is the United States, whose Treasury held 261.7 million fine troy ounces as of December 31, 1994. At $383.10 per fine ounce (December 30, 1994, New York Mercantile Exchange, COMEX division price), their value was $100.26 billion.

Worst inflation   In Hungary in June 1946, the 1931 gold pengö was valued at 130 million trillion (1.3×10^{20}) paper pengös. Notes were issued for "Egymillard billion" (one sextillion or 1×10^{21}) pengös on June 3 and withdrawn on July 11, 1946. Vouchers for 1 billion trillion (1×10^{27}) pengös were issued for taxation payment only.

The country with the worst inflation in 1993 was Moldova, where consumer prices rose by 2,707 percent.

The best-known hyperinflationary episode occurred in Germany in 1923. The circulation of the Reichsbank mark reached 400,338,326,350,700,000,000 on November 6 and inflation was 755.7 billion times 1913 levels.

United States   The United States Department of Labor measures changes in the Consumer Price Index (CPI) in 12-month periods ending in December. The Bureau of Labor Statistics first began keeping the CPI in 1913. Since that time, the change of the greatest magnitude was a 20.4 percent increase for the 12-month period ending December 1918, and the largest decline was –10.8 percent in December 1921. The largest peacetime increase, recorded in December 1979, was 13.3 percent.

EMPLOYMENT

Largest labor union   The Professionalniy Soyuz Rabotnikov Agro-Promyshlennogo Kompleksa (Agro-Industrial Complex Workers' Union) in the former Soviet Union had 15.2 million members in 1993.

United States   As of January 1994, the largest labor union in the United States was the National Education Association (NEA), with 2.1 million members.

Smallest labor union   The ultimate in small unions was the Jewelcase and Jewelry Display Makers Union (JJDMU), founded in 1894. It was dissolved on December 31, 1986 by its general secretary, Charles Evans. The motion was seconded by Fergus McCormack, its only other surviving member.

Longest union name   The union with the longest name is the International Association of Marble, Slate and Stone Polishers, Rubbers and Sawyers, Tile and Marble Setters' Helpers and Marble, Mosaic and Terrazzo Workers' Helpers, or the IAMSSPRSTMSHMMTWH, of Washington, D.C.

Longest strike   The longest recorded strike ended on January 4, 1961, after 33 years. It concerned the employment of barbers' assistants in Copenhagen, Denmark.

Industrial   The longest industrial strike was at the plumbing fixtures factory of the Kohler Co. in Sheboygan, WI, between April 1954 and October 1962. The strike is alleged to have cost the United Automobile Workers' Union about $12 million to sustain.

Lowest unemployment   In Switzerland (population 6.6 million), the total number of unemployed in 1973 was reported to be 81.

United States The lowest unemployment average in the United States was 1.2 percent, or 670,000 people, in 1944 during World War II, based on a labor force aged 14 and older.

Highest unemployment The highest annual unemployment average in United States history was 24.9 percent, or 12,830,000 people, in 1933 during the Great Depression.

Longest working career Shigechiyo Izumi began work goading draft animals at a sugar mill at Isen, Tokunoshima, Japan in 1872. He retired as a sugar cane farmer in 1970 at the age of 105, after a working career that lasted for 98 years.

EDUCATION

Oldest university The oldest existing educational institution in the world is the University of Karueein, founded in A.D. 859 in Fez, Morocco.

United States The oldest college in the United States is Harvard College in Cambridge, MA, founded in 1636 as Newtowne College and renamed in 1638 after its first benefactor, John Harvard.

Largest university The largest existing university building in the world is the M. V. Lomonosov State University on the Lenin Hills, south of Moscow, Russia. It stands 787 ft. 5 in. tall, and has 32 stories and 40,000 rooms. It was constructed from 1949 to 1953.

Greatest enrollment The university with the greatest enrollment in the world is the State University of New York, which had 381,568 students at 64 campuses throughout the state in late 1995.

The greatest enrollment at a university centered in one city is at the City University of New York, which had 206,500 students in late 1995. It has 21 campuses throughout the city.

Most graduates in family Mr. and Mrs. Harold Erickson of Naples, FL saw all 14 of their children (11 sons and 3 daughters) obtain university or college degrees between 1962 and 1978. All 14 children (10 sons and 4 daughters) of Mr. and Mrs. Robert Johnson of Edwards, MI also obtained degrees, between 1959 and 1983.

Youngest university student Michael Kearney started studying for an Associate of Science degree at Santa Rosa Junior College, Santa Rosa, CA in September 1990 at the age of 6 yr. 7 mo.

Youngest graduate Michael Kearney became the youngest graduate in June 1994, at age 10 yr. 4 mo., when he obtained his BA in anthropology from the University of South Alabama.

The Oxford Academy is the most expensive school in the United States.

Youngest doctorate   On April 13, 1814, mathematician Carl Witte of Lochau was made a Doctor of Philosophy of the University of Giessen, Germany at age 12.

Youngest college president   The youngest president of a major college was Ellen Futter, who was appointed to head Barnard College, New York City in May 1981 at age 31.

Most schools   The country with the greatest number of primary schools is China, with 861,878 in 1993. San Marino has the lowest pupil-to-teacher ratio, with 5.2 children per teacher.

At general secondary level, India has the most schools, with 241,129 in 1994, while San Marino has the best pupil-to-teacher ratio, with 5.8 pupils per teacher.

Most expensive school   The annual cost of keeping a pupil at the most expensive school in the United States for the academic year 1995/96 was $34,700 at the Oxford Academy in Westbrook, CT.

Largest school   In 1995/96, Rizal High School, Pasig, Manila, Philippines had 19,738 regular students.

Michael Kearney was the youngest-ever university graduate.

Most schools attended   Wilma Williams attended 265 schools from 1933 to 1943 when her parents were in show business traveling around the United States.

Most durable teacher   Medarda de Jesús León de Uzcátegui, alias La Maestra Chucha, has been teaching in Venezuela for 85 years. In 1911, when she was 12, she and her sisters set up a school. Since 1942, La Maestra Chucha has run her own school, which she calls the *Escuela Uzcátegui*, from her home in Caracas.

Highest endowment   The greatest single gift in the history of education was $500 million, to the U.S. public education system by Walter Annenburg in December 1993. The gift was intended to help fight violence in schools.

Highest lecture fee   Dr. Ronald Dante was paid $3,080,000 for lecturing students on hypnotherapy at a 2-day course held in Chicago in June 1986. He taught for eight hours each day and thus earned $192,500 per hour.

HEADS OF STATE AND ROYALTY

Oldest ruling house   The Emperor of Japan, Akihito, is the 125th in line from the first Emperor, Jimmu Tenno, whose reign was traditionally from 660 to 581 B.C., but more probably dates from *c.* 40 B.C. to *c.* 10 B.C.

Longest reign   The reign of Phiops II, or Neferkare, a Sixth Dynasty pharaoh of Egypt, began *c.* 2281 B.C., when he was six years old, and is believed to have lasted for 94 years.

Current   The King of Thailand, Bhumibol Adulyadej (Rama IX), is currently the world's longest-reigning monarch, having succeeded to the throne on June 9, 1946.

Shortest reign   Crown Prince Luis Filipe of Portugal was technically king of Portugal (Dom Luis III) for about 20 minutes. He was fatally wounded when his father was assassinated in Lisbon on February 1, 1908.

Youngest monarch   King Mswati III of Swaziland was crowned on April 25, 1986 at age 18 yr. 6 days.

Most prolific royalty   The most prolific monogamous "royal" was Prince Hartmann of Liechtenstein (1613–86), who had 24 children, of whom 21 were born alive, by Countess Elisabeth zu Salm-Reifferscheidt (1623–88). HRH Duke Roberto I of Parma (1848–1907) also had 24 children, but by two wives.

Highest post-nominal number   The highest post-nominal number ever used to designate a member of a royal house was 75, briefly enjoyed by Count Heinrich LXXV Reuss zu Schleiz (1800–1801).

Heaviest monarch   In September 1976, 6-ft.-3-in.-tall King Taufa'ahau of Tonga recorded a weight of 462 pounds. In early 1993, he weighed 280 pounds.

Oldest head of state   The oldest head of state is Joaquín Balaguer (b. September 1, 1907), president of the Dominican Republic. The oldest monarch is King Taufa'ahau of Tonga (b. July 4, 1918).

Largest gathering of world leaders   In honor of the fiftieth anniversary of the United Nations, a Special Commemorative Meeting of the General Assembly was held at United Nations Headquarters, New York City, October 22–24, 1995. The meeting was addressed by 128 heads of state and heads of government.

UNITED STATES GOVERNMENT

PRESIDENTS

Oldest president   Ronald Reagan was 69 yr. 349 days old when he took the oath of office. He was reelected at age 73.

Youngest president   Vice-President Theodore Roosevelt became president at age 42 yr. 10 mo. when President William McKinley was assassinated in 1901. The youngest president ever elected was John Fitzgerald Kennedy, who took the oath of office at age 43 yr. 236 days in 1961.

Longest and shortest terms of office   Franklin D. Roosevelt served in office for 12 yr. 39 days (1933–45). The shortest term in office was 32 days (March 4–April 4, 1841) by William Henry Harrison.

Longest and shortest inaugural speeches William Henry Harrison's inaugural speech of 1841 lasted for two hours. George Washington's second inaugural speech of March 4, 1793 lasted only 90 seconds.

Largest presidential gathering On December 30, 1834, eight men who had been or would become president gathered together in the old House Chamber of the Capitol: ex-president John Quincy Adams; ex-president Andrew Jackson; Vice-President Martin Van Buren; Senator John Tyler; Senator James Buchanan; and Representatives James K. Polk, Millard Fillmore and Franklin Pierce.

Most handshakes The most hands shaken by a public figure at an official function was 8,513, by President Theodore Roosevelt at a New Year's Day White House presentation in Washington, D.C. in 1907.

ELECTIONS

Largest popular majority The greatest majority won was 17,994,460 votes in 1972, when President Richard M. Nixon (Republican) defeated George S. McGovern (Democrat) with 47,165,234 votes to 29,170,774.

Smallest popular majority The smallest popular majority was 7,023 votes in 1880, when President James A. Garfield (Republican) defeated Winfield Scott Hancock (Democrat) with 4,449,053 votes to 4,442,030.

Largest electoral college majority Since 1872, the greatest electoral college majority was 515 votes in 1936 when President Franklin D. Roosevelt (Democrat) defeated Alfred M. Landon (Republican) with 523 votes to 8.

VICE-PRESIDENTS

Youngest vice-president The youngest man to become vice-president was John Cabell Breckinridge (Democrat), who took office on March 4, 1857 at age 36 yr. 1 mo.

Oldest vice-president Alben William Barkley (Democrat) took office on January 20, 1949 at age 71 yr. 40 days. He served a full 4-year term.

Longest-lived vice-president John Nance Garner served under Franklin D. Roosevelt from 1933 to 1941. He was born in 1868 and died on November 7, 1967 at age 98.

GOVERNORS

Oldest governor Walter S. Goodland became governor of Wisconsin in 1943, at age 84.

Youngest governor Stevens T. Mason was 24 years old when he was elected governor of Michigan in 1835.

CONGRESS

Most expensive election The Federal Election Commission reported on April 28, 1995 that the 1994 congressional campaign was the most expensive in history. Candidates spent a total of $724 million.

Longest congressional service Carl Hayden (1877–1972; D-Arizona) holds the record for the longest congressional service, a total of 57 consecutive years (1912–1969), of which 42 years were spent as a senator and the remainder as a representative.

Longest-serving speaker The longest time served by any speaker was 17 years, by Sam Rayburn (D-Texas). Rayburn served three terms: 1940–47, 1949–53, and 1955–61.

Shortest term The shortest term of any speaker was one day, March 3, 1869, served by Theodore Medad Pomeroy (R-New York).

Oldest speaker Sam Rayburn (D-Texas) was reelected speaker on January 3, 1961 at age 78 yr. 11 mo.

Youngest speaker Robert Mercer Taliaferro Hunter (D-Virginia) was chosen speaker for the 26th Congress on December 2, 1839 at age 30 yr. 7 mo.

Longest-serving representative Rep. Jamie L. Whitten (D-Mississippi) began his career on November 4, 1941 and retired on January 3, 1995, after 53 yr. 2 mo.

Youngest representative The youngest person to serve in the House was William Charles Cole Claiborne (1775–1817; Jeffersonian Democrat-Tennessee), who, in contravention of the 25-year age requirement of the Constitution, was elected in August 1797 at age 22.

Oldest representative The oldest person ever elected representative was Claude Pepper (D-Florida), who was reelected on November 8, 1988 at age 88 yr. 2 mo.

Oldest senator The greatest age at which anyone has been returned as a senator is 87 yr. 11 mo., the age at which Strom Thurmond (R-South Carolina) was reelected in 1990.

OLDEST SENATOR

The greatest age at which anyone has been returned as a senator is 87 yr. 11 mo., the age at which Strom Thurmond (R-South Carolina) was reelected in 1990.

See feature (next page)

See feature (next page)

STROM THURMOND

"My motto is helping people. Pass good laws and help people, and stop bad laws," says Sen. Strom Thurmond (R-South Carolina). This motto has guided him since 1933, when he first won election to the South Carolina Senate. Now 93 years young, he is a 40-year veteran (and counting) of the United States Senate and the oldest person ever to serve as a United States Senator.

The ultimate elder statesman was an educator before he entered politics. "I was first a teacher and then a coach," says Thurmond. Stints as a school superintendent, attorney and judge followed. On his return from duty in World War II, Thurmond quickly reentered politics. "I went back on the bench for a few months, resigned in 1946, then ran for governor and won," summarizes the senator. In 1948 Thurmond ran for the presidency as a "States' Rights Democrat" (Dixiecrat), winning four states and 39 electoral votes.

But Thurmond's mark on American history has been made on Capitol Hill. He was first elected to the Senate in 1954. The circumstances were unique: "The Democratic leaders didn't hold a primary and selected

Edgar A. Brown. People were so upset, they came to me to run. I defeated him nearly 2 to 1 on a write-in basis," remembers Thurmond. Keeping his campaign promise, Thurmond resigned in April 1956 to run in the full senatorial election in the fall. He won that election, and every one since. "When I came to the Senate, the law of every state in the south provided for the separation of races." Although an opponent of civil rights legislation, Thurmond now says, "I believe in equal opportunity for everybody, regardless of race and religion. Looking back, I think it's better now."

Thurmond brands the budget deficit as a change for the worse. "As time passed, the federal government went into almost every conceivable field of activity. That's why we have a big deficit. It was a great mistake," declares the senator. "I have voted against big spending all the time." Thurmond is seeking reelection in 1996. "The experience I've had in the Senate is helpful to people in my state. You can do more because of your seniority," he says.

The senator offers this advice to politicians eyeing his record: "Be willing to work hard, be honest and get pleasure out of helping people. You'll be fine." Assessing his own career, he says, "I'm proud of everything I've done. I don't regret any stances."

Longest-serving senator The longest any senator has ever served is 42 years, by Carl Trumbull Hayden (D-Arizona), who served in the Senate from 1927 to 1969. The current longest-serving member of the Senate is Strom Thurmond (R-South Carolina). As of June 1996, Thurmond had served for 40 yr. 11 mo. He was elected as a Democrat in 1954, but became a Republican in 1964.

Youngest senator The youngest person elected senator was Brig. Gen. Armistead Thomson Mason (D-Virginia), who was sworn in on January 22 at age 28 yr. 5 mo. 18 days. The youngest senator was John Henry Eaton (D-Tennessee), who was sworn in on November 16, at age 28 yr. 4 mo. 29 days.

Most expensive senate race In 1994, Democratic incumbent Dianne Feinstein and Republican Michael Huffington spent a combined $44,590,675. Despite Huffington's record expenditure of $29,992,884, he lost the race to Feinstein, who spent $14,597,791.

Most roll calls Senator William Proxmire (D-Wisconsin) did not miss a single one of the 9,695 roll calls from April 1966 to August 27, 1987. Rep. William H. Natcher (D-Kentucky) cast 18,401 consecutive roll call votes, January 6, 1954–March 3, 1994.

Longest filibuster The longest continuous speech in Senate history was by Senator Wayne Morse (D-Oregon) on April 24–25, 1953, when he spoke on the Tidelands oil bill for 22 hr. 26 min without resuming his seat.

Interrupted only briefly by the swearing-in of a new senator, Senator Strom Thurmond (R-South Carolina) spoke against a civil rights bill for 24 hr. 19 min., August 28–29, 1957.

WORLD LEGISLATURES

PARLIAMENTS

Oldest legislative body The Althing of Iceland was founded in A.D. 930. This body was abolished in 1800, but restored by Denmark to a consultative status in 1843 and a legislative status in 1874.

The legislative assembly with the oldest *continuous* history is the Tynwald of the Isle of Man, Great Britain, which may have its origins in the late ninth century and possibly predates the Althing.

Largest legislative body The National People's Congress of the People's Republic of China has 2,978 single-party members who are indirectly elected for a 5-year term.

Highest-paid legislators The most highly paid of all the world's legislators are the Japanese. The prime minister has an annual salary of 38,463,360 yen ($343,000) including monthly allowances and bonuses. Members of the

House of Representatives and the House of Councilors have annual salaries of 23,633,565 yen ($211,000) including bonuses.

Smallest quorum The House of Lords in Great Britain has the smallest quorum, expressed as a percentage of members eligible to vote, of any legislative body in the world—less than one-third of 1 percent of 1,205 members. To transact business, there need be only three peers present, including the lord chancellor or his deputy.

Largest petition The largest petition on record was signed by 21,202,192 people, mainly from South Korea, between June 1, 1993 and October 31, 1994. They were protesting against the forced separation of families since the Korean war, and the division of the country into North and South Korea.

Longest membership The longest span as a legislator was 83 years, by József Madarász (1814–1915). He attended the Hungarian Parliament 1832–38 as *absentium oblegatus* (i.e., on behalf of an absent deputy), and was a full member from 1848 to 1850 and from 1861 until his death on January 31, 1915.

Longest speech Chief Mangosuthu Buthelezi, the Zulu leader, gave an address to the KwaZulu legislative assembly, March 12–29, 1993. He spoke on 11 of the 18 days, averaging nearly 2½ hours on each of those days.

The longest continuous speech made in the United Nations was one of 4 hr. 29 min. on September 26, 1960 by President Fidel Castro of Cuba.

Oldest treaty The oldest treaty still in force is the Anglo-Portuguese Treaty, which was signed in London, England on June 16, 1373.

Oldest constitution The world's oldest national constitution still in uninterrupted use is that of the United States of America, ratified by the necessary ninth state (New Hampshire) on June 21, 1788 and declared to be in effect on March 4, 1789.

ELECTIONS

Largest election The largest election began on May 20, 1991 for the Indian Lower House, which has 543 elective seats. A total of 315,439,908 people cast their votes out of an eligible electorate of 488,678,993. The election was contested by 359 parties, and there were nearly 565,000 polling stations manned by 3 million people. As a result of the election, a new government was formed under the leadership of P. V. Narasimha Rao of the Congress (I) Party.

Closest election On January 18, 1961 in Zanzibar (now part of Tanzania), the Afro-Shirazi Party won the general elections by a single seat, after the seat of Chake-Chake on Pemba Island was won by a single vote.

The narrowest recorded percentage win in an election was for the office of Southern District Highway Commissioner in Mississippi on August 7, 1979. Robert E. Joiner was declared the winner over W. H. Pyron, with 133,587 votes to 133,582. The loser thus obtained more than 49.999 percent of the votes.

Most decisive election North Korea recorded a 100 percent turnout and a 100 percent vote for the Workers' Party of Korea in the general election of October 8, 1962.

An almost unanimous vote occurred in Albania on November 14, 1982, when a single voter spoiled national unanimity for the official (and only) candidates, who consequently obtained 99.99993 percent of the vote in a reported 100 percent turnout of 1,627,968.

Most crooked election In the 1927 Liberian presidential election, President Charles D. B. King (1875–1961) was returned with an officially announced majority of 234,000 over his opponent, Thomas J. R. Faulkner of the People's Party. King thus claimed a "majority" more than 15½ times greater than the entire electorate.

Most elections contested John C. 'The Engineer' Turmel, of Nepean, Ontario, Canada has contested a record 40 elections as an Independent candidate at a municipal, provincial and federal level since 1979. He founded the federal Abolitionist Party of Canada in 1993.

Longest in power In Mongolia, the Communists (Mongolian People's Revolutionary Party) have been in power since 1924, although only since July 1990 within a multiparty system. In February 1992, the term "People's Republic" was dropped from the official name of Mongolia.

Highest personal majority The highest-ever personal majority for any politician was 4,726,112 by Boris Yeltsin, the people's deputy candidate for Moscow, in the parliamentary elections held in the Soviet Union on March 26, 1989. Yeltsin received 5,118,745 votes out of the 5,722,937 that were cast in the Moscow constituency. His closest rival received 392,633 votes.

Benazir Bhutto achieved 98.48 percent of the vote in the Larkana-III constituency in the 1990 general election in Pakistan, with 94,462 votes. The next-highest candidate obtained just 718 votes.

Largest political party The Chinese Communist Party, formed in 1920, had a membership of 55 million in 1995.

Largest field of candidates There were 301 candidates running to represent one seat, that of Belgaum City, in the State Assembly (Vidhan Sabha) elections in Karnataka, India on March 5, 1985.

Most coups Statisticians contend that Bolivia, since it became a sovereign country in 1825, has had 191 coups. The latest was on June 30, 1984, when President Hernan Siles Zuazo was temporarily kidnapped from his official residence by a group of more than 60 armed men who were masquerading as police officers.

PRIME MINISTERS AND HEADS OF STATE

Oldest prime minister El Hadji Muhammad el Mokri, Grand Vizier of Morocco, died on September 16, 1957 at a reputed age of 116 Muslim (*Hijri*) years, equivalent to 112½ years.

The oldest age at first appointment was 81, in the case of Morarji Ranchhodji Desai of India (1896–1995) in March 1977.

Philippe Pétain (1856–1951), although not prime minister, became "chief of state" of the French state on July 10, 1940 at age 84.

YOUNGEST HEAD OF GOVERNMENT

Dr. Mario Frick (b. May 8, 1965) became prime minister of Liechtenstein at age 28 on December 15, 1993.

See feature (next page)

Longest-serving prime minister   The longest-serving prime minister of a sovereign state is Khalifa bin Sulman al-Khalifa (b. July 3, 1933) of Bahrain, who took office 1½ years before Bahrain became independent in August 1971.

Marshall Kim Il Sung was head of government or head of state of the Democratic People's Republic of Korea from August 25, 1948 until his death on July 8, 1994.

Woman   Indira Ghandhi (1917–84) of India was prime minister for 15 years—in two spans, 1966–77 and 1980–84.

Eugenia Charles (b. May 15, 1919) of Dominica is the current record holder; she took office when her Dominica Freedom Party won the elections in July 1980.

Most women in a cabinet   In Sweden, following a general election in March 1996, a new cabinet was formed containing 11 women out of a total 22 ministers.

MILITARY AND DEFENSE

WAR

Oldest weapon   The oldest weapon is a broken wooden spear found in April 1911 in Clacton-on-Sea, England. It is beyond the limit of radiocarbon dating but is estimated to have been made before 200,000 B.C.

Longest continuous war   The Thirty Years' War, between various European countries, was fought continuously from 1618 to 1648. The *Reconquista*—the campaigns in the Iberian Peninsula to recover the region from the Moors—began in 718 and continued intermittently until 1492, when Granada, the last Moorish stronghold, was conquered.

Bloodiest war.   The most costly war in terms of human life was World War II (1939–45). The total number of fatalities, including battle deaths and

Mario Frick

Two parts mountains, one part valleys, Liechtenstein nestles between Austria and Switzerland. Difficult to find on a map, this tiny landlocked nation holds a unique spot in political affairs—its prime minister, the Hon. Dr. Mario Frick, is the world's youngest head of government.

"My party [the Patriotic Union Party] decided we should have some young people in the government. I was appointed deputy prime minister in May 1993," explains Frick. Later that year the coalition government collapsed. Frick's party won the subsequent election and at 28 years old, he became Prime Minister. Age was an issue, concedes Frick: "Most people said, 'He's 28, we need people who know life and know people.' I succeeded in telling them it's not only a question of youth, but personality, character, knowledge and the way you treat people."

The Prime Minister's day usually starts at 6 A.M.: "I must give my son his bottle. He's 18 months old," says Frick. He drives himself to work. "My first meeting is at 8:30 A.M. with other members of the government or other officials." He adds, "Being prime minister means a lot of talking with people, reading reports and taking positions."

The Liechtenstein constitution sets the minimum age requirement for any elective office, including prime minister, at 20 years old. A doctor of international law, Frick sees no reason for change: "Liechtenstein has 30,000 people, so it's easier to get an overview of the country. If you want to be president of the United States or chancellor of Germany, it's more complicated. You need to know more people."

Now 31, the Prime Minister has great ambitions for his country: "Liechtenstein is a small, beautiful country, but it's very competitive. Our communities are small with no noise or crime. That's what makes our country so attractive." Frick adds, "I want Liechtenstein to become a center for investment banking, insurance, and telecommunications."

And his own ambitions? "I could be the prime minister until I die, if the people wanted me to. Personally, I hope to serve three terms, until 2005."

civilians, is estimated to have been 56.4 million. The country that suffered most was Poland, with 6,028,000 or 17.2 percent of its population of 35.1 million killed.

Civil   The bloodiest civil war in history was the Taiping rebellion, a revolt against the Chinese Qing Dynasty between 1851 and 1864. According to the best estimates, the loss of life was some 20 million.

Most costly war   The material cost of World War II far transcended that of all the rest of history's wars put together and has been estimated at $1.5 trillion.

Bloodiest battles   The Battle of the Somme, France (July 1–November 19, 1916) produced 1.22 million casualties (dead and wounded); of these, 623,907 were Allied. The greatest death toll in a battle has been estimated at 1,109,000 in the Battle of Stalingrad, USSR, ending with the German surrender on January 31, 1943. The Germans suffered 200,000 losses. About 650,800 soldiers from the Soviet army were injured but survived. Only 1,515 civilians from a pre-war population of more than 500,000 were found alive after the battle.

The final drive on Berlin, Germany by the Soviet army, and the battle that followed, April 16–May 2, 1945, involved 3.5 million men, 52,000 guns and mortars, 7,750 tanks and 11,000 aircraft.

United States   The American Civil War (1861–65) claimed 200,000 lives and left 469,000 wounded. The bloodiest battle was at Gettysburg, PA, July 1–3, 1863, when the Union reported 23,000 killed, wounded and missing, and the Confederacy approximately 28,000 killed, wounded and missing.

Greatest naval battles   The greatest number of ships and aircraft ever involved in a sea–air action was 282 ships and 1,996 aircraft in the Battle of Leyte Gulf, in the Philippines, during World War II. It raged from October 22 through October 27, 1944, with 218 Allied and 64 Japanese warships engaged, of which 26 Japanese and 6 U.S. ships were sunk. In addition, 1,280 U.S. and 716 Japanese aircraft were engaged.

GREATEST INVASION

The greatest invasion in military history was the Allied operation against the Normandy coast of France starting on June 6, 1944. Thirty-eight convoys of 745 ships moved in during the first three days, supported by 4,066 landing craft, carrying 185,000 men, 20,000 vehicles and 347 minesweepers. The air assault comprised 18,000 paratroopers from 1,087 aircraft. The 42 divisions had air support from 13,175 aircraft.

See feature (next page)

THE
MOST
IMPORTANT
DAY

*1*85,000 men, 745 ships, 4,066 landing craft, 20,000 vehicles, 347 minesweepers, 18,000 paratroopers, 13,175 aircraft and thousands of casualties. These are the chilling statistics of the first three days of the largest invasion in military history, the Normandy Landings begun on June 6, 1944, D-Day. The outcome, however, not the statistics, is the true significance of D-Day.

"*D*-Day was the most important day of the 20th Century," says Stephen E. Ambrose, the preeminent expert on the life of Gen. Dwight D. Eisenhower, leader of the Allied invasion. Ambrose explains: "World War II was a struggle between three ideologies: fascism, democracy and communism. The Normandy invasion had the decisive effect on Nazi Germany. It turned a three-way struggle into a two-way struggle between the democracies and communism. If D-Day had failed, the Germans would have faced the Soviet Union and whoever won was going to control Europe."

*F*ailure was a distinct possibility. Weather and the nature of democracy were the deciding factors in the Allied victory, according to Ambrose. "The weather was a determining factor because the German defenses were strong enough that with the help of the weather, they could have turned back the invasion." He adds, "The ultimate winning factor for the Allies was that they were democracies. Junior officers in the Allied armies took the initiative, made decisions and moved against their foes. The Germans were hamstrung by the 'Fuhrer Principle,' which made it impossible for their commanders to act on their own initiative."

*U*niversally hailed for his leadership of the invasion, Eisenhower became an American folk hero and later President. Ambrose joins the cheers for Eisenhower: "He was the one in charge of training, planning and operations. And he was the one who made the decision to go in a time of great uncertainty about the weather. He is first among equals without any question." He adds, "In the end it came down to one guy and he had to decide."

Airborne The largest airborne invasion was the British–American assault by three divisions (34,000 men), with 2,800 aircraft and 1,600 gliders, near Arnhem, Netherlands, on September 17, 1944.

Longest-range attacks The longest-range attacks were undertaken by seven B-52G bombers that took off from Barksdale Air Force Base, LA on January 16, 1991 to deliver air-launched cruise missiles against targets in Iraq. Each bomber flew 14,000 miles, with the round-trip mission lasting some 35 hours.

Greatest evacuation The greatest evacuation in military history was carried out by 1,200 Allied naval and civilian craft from the beachhead at Dunkerque (Dunkirk), France, May 26–June 4, 1940. A total of 338,226 British and French troops were evacuated.

Largest civilian evacuation Following the Iraqi invasion of Kuwait in August 1990, Air India evacuated 111,711 Indian nationals who were working in Kuwait. Beginning on August 13, 488 flights took the expatriates back to India over a 2-month period.

Longest march The longest march in military history was the Long March by the Chinese Communists, 1934–35. In 368 days, of which 268 were days of movement, their force of some 100,000 covered 6,000 miles from Ruijin, in Jiangxi, to Yan'an, in Shaanxi. They reached Yan'an with about 8,000 survivors, following continual rearguard actions against Kuomintang (KMT) forces.

Worst sieges The worst siege in history was the 880-day siege of Leningrad, USSR (now St. Petersburg, Russia) by the German army, from August 30, 1941 through January 27, 1944. The best estimate is that 1.3–1.5 million defenders and citizens died. This included 641,000 people who died of hunger in the city and 17,000 civilians killed by shelling. More than 150,000 shells and 100,000 bombs were dropped on the city.

The longest recorded siege was in Azotus (now Ashdod), Israel, which according to Herodotus was besieged by Psamtik I of Egypt for 29 years, during the period 664–610 B.C.

Chemical warfare The greatest number of people killed in a single chemical warfare attack were the 4,000 Kurds who died at Halabja, Iraq in March 1988 when President Saddam Hussein used chemical weapons against Iraq's Kurds in revenge for the support they had given to Iran in the Iran–Iraq war.

Biggest demonstration A figure of 2.7 million was reported from China for a demonstration against the USSR in Shanghai, March 3–4, 1969 following border clashes.

ARMED FORCES

Largest armed force The strength of China's People's Liberation Army in 1994 was estimated to be 2,930,000 troops. Its reserves number 1.2 million.

Largest navy The largest navy in terms of personnel is the United States Navy, with a total of 420,149 active-duty servicemen and servicewomen, plus 174,000 active-duty Marines in mid-1996. As of March 1996, the navy's active strength included 8 nuclear-powered aircraft carriers, 4 conventionally powered aircraft carriers, 16 ballistic missile submarines, 78 nuclear attack submarines, 31 cruisers, 51 destroyers, 34 frigates, and 40 amphibious warfare ships.

Oldest army The 80–90-strong Pontifical Swiss Guard in Vatican City was founded January 21, 1506. Its origins, however, predate 1400.

Largest army The army of the People's Republic of China had a total strength of some 2.2 million in mid-1994.

Oldest soldier John B. Salling of the Army of the Confederate States of America was the last accepted survivor of the Civil War (1861–65). He died in Kingsport, TN on March 16, 1959, aged 112 yr. 305 days.

Tallest soldier Väinö Myllyrinne was conscripted into the Finnish army when he was 7 ft. 3 in.; he later grew to 8 ft. 3 in.

Oldest air force The oldest autonomous air force is the Royal Air Force, which can be traced back to 1878, when the British War Office commissioned the building of a military balloon. The Royal Air Force itself came into existence on April 1, 1918. Balloons had also been used for military observation by the French in June 1794 during the French Revolutionary Wars.

Largest air force The United States Army Air Corps had 79,908 aircraft in July 1944 and 2,411,294 personnel in March 1944. In mid-1996, the U.S. Air Force, including strategic missile forces, had 387,275 personnel and 6,633 aircraft (plus more in storage).

BOMBS

Heaviest bomb The heaviest conventional bomb ever used operationally was the Royal Air Force's Grand Slam, weighing 22,000 pounds and measuring 25 ft. 5 in. long, dropped on Bielefeld railroad viaduct, Germany on March 14, 1945.

In 1949, the United States Air Force tested a bomb weighing 42,000 pounds at Muroc Dry Lake, CA.

Nuclear The heaviest known nuclear bomb was the MK 17, carried by U.S. B-36 bombers in the mid-1950s. It weighed 42,000 pounds and was 24 ft. 6 in. long.

Most powerful thermonuclear device The most powerful thermonuclear device so far tested has a power equivalent to that of approximately 57 megatons of TNT, and was detonated by the former USSR in the Novaya Zemlya area on October 30, 1961. The largest U.S. H-bomb tested was the 18–22 megaton *Bravo* at Bikini Atoll, Marshall Islands on March 1, 1954.

Largest nuclear weapons   The most powerful ICBM (intercontinental ballistic missile) is the former USSR's SS–18 (Model 5), believed to be armed with ten 750-kiloton MIRVs (multiple independently targetable reentry vehicles). SS–18 ICBMs are located on both Russian and Kazakhstan territory, although the dismantling of those in Kazakhstan has begun.

GUNS

Largest gun   A gun with a caliber of 31½ inches and a barrel 94 ft. 8½ in. long was used by German forces in the siege of Sevastopol, USSR (now Ukraine) in July 1942. The gun was 141 feet long and weighed 1,481.5 tons, with a crew of 1,500. The range for a 5.3-ton projectile was 29 miles.

Heaviest gun   The heaviest gun in the U.S. Army is the MK19-3 40mm automatic grenade launcher, which weighs 72.5 pounds and has the greatest range of any U.S. Army weapon: about 1,650 yards at point targets, over 2,400 yards at area targets. The bullets can penetrate two inches into armor at 2,400 yards.

Largest cannon   The *Tsar Pushka*, now housed in the Kremlin, Moscow, Russia, was built in the 16th century with a bore of 35 inches and a barrel 17 ft. 6 in. long. It weighs 44 tons.

HONORS, DECORATIONS AND AWARDS

Oldest order   The oldest honor known is the "Gold of Honor" for extraordinary valor, which was awarded in the 18th Dynasty *c.* 1440–1400 B.C. A representative statuette was found at Qan-el-Kebri, Egypt. The oldest true order is the Order of St. John of Jerusalem (the direct descendant of which is the Sovereign Military Order of Malta), legitimized in 1113.

Youngest awardees   Kristina Stragauskaite of Skirmantiskes, Lithuania was awarded a medal "For Courage in Fire" when she was just 4 yr. 252 days old. She had saved the lives of her younger brother and sister in April 1989 when a fire broke out in the family's home while her parents were out. The award was decreed by the Presidium of the then Lithuanian Soviet Socialist Republic.

   The youngest person to receive an official gallantry award is Julius Rosenberg of Winnipeg, Canada, who was given the Medal of Bravery on March 30, 1994 for stopping a black bear that attacked his 3-year-old sister on September 20, 1992. Aged five at the time of the incident, he saved his sister's life by growling at the bear.

Most titles   The 18th Duchess of Alba, Doña María del Rosario Cayetana Fitz-James Stuart y Silva, is 14 times a Spanish grandee, 5 times a duchess, once a countess-duchess, 18 times a marchioness, 18 times a countess and once a viscountess.

Most valuable annual prize The most valuable annual prize is the Louis Jeantet Prize for Medicine, which in 1996 was worth SFr2.1 million (equivalent to approximately $1,840,000). It was first awarded in 1986 and is intended to "provide substantial funds for the support of biomedical research projects."

Most statues The world record for raising statues to oneself was set by Joseph Stalin (1879–1953), leader of the Soviet Union, 1924–53. It is estimated that during the Stalin era there were *c.* 6,000 statues to him throughout the USSR and in many cities in Eastern Europe.

The man to whom the most statues have been raised is Buddha. The 20th-century champion is Vladimir Ilyich Ulyanov, alias Lenin (1870–1924), busts of whom have been mass-produced.

Most honorary degrees The greatest number of honorary degrees awarded is 131, given to Rev. Father Theodore M. Hesburgh, president of the University of Notre Dame, South Bend, IN. These have been accumulated since 1954.

More statues have been raised to Buddha than to anyone else.

HUMAN

ACHIEVEMENTS

40

ADVENTURE

Most-traveled person   John D. Clouse of Evansville, IN had visited all 192 sovereign countries and all but six of the nonsovereign or other territories that existed in early 1996.

Couple   Dr. Robert and Carmen Becker of East Northport, NY have visited all of the sovereign countries and all but seven of the nonsovereign or other territories.

Most counties visited   Allen F. Zondlak of St. Clair Shores, MI visited all 3,142 counties and county equivalents in the United States, completing his travels in 1991.

Most miles walked   Arthur Blessitt of North Fort Myers, FL has walked 31,416 miles in more than 27 years since December 25, 1969. He has been to all seven continents, including Antarctica, carrying a 12-foot cross and preaching throughout his walk.

The longest distance walked by a woman was 19,586 miles, by Ffyona Campbell (Great Britain), who walked around the world in five phases, covering four continents and 20 countries. She left John o' Groat's, Scotland on August 16, 1983 and returned there on October 14, 1994.

Rick Hansen (Canada), who was paralyzed from the waist down in 1973 as a result of a car accident, wheeled his wheelchair 24,901.55 miles through four continents and 34 countries. He started his journey from Vancouver, British Columbia on March 21, 1985 and arrived back there on May 22, 1987.

Trans-Americas   George Meegan (Great Britain) walked 19,019 miles from Ushuaia, in the southern tip of South America, to Prudhoe Bay in northern Alaska, taking 2,426 days from January 26, 1977 to September 18, 1983.

Trans-America   Sean Eugene McGuire (U.S.) walked 7,327 miles from the Yukon River, north of Livengood, AK to Key West, FL in 307 days, from June 6, 1978 to April 9, 1979.

John Lees (Great Britain) walked 2,876 miles across the United States from City Hall, Los Angeles to City Hall, New York City in 53 days 12 hr. 15 min. (averaging 53.75 miles a day) between April 11 and June 3, 1972.

Trans-Canada   Clyde McRae walked 3,764 miles from Halifax to Vancouver in 96 days, from May 1 to August 4, 1973.

MOUNTAINEERING

Climbing Mount Everest Most conquests   Ang Rita Sherpa has scaled Mount Everest (29,029 feet) eight times, with ascents in 1983, 1984, 1985, 1987, 1988, 1990, 1992, and 1993, all without the use of bottled oxygen.

Most climbers   The Mount Everest International Peace Climb, a team of American, Russian and Chinese climbers, led by James W. Whittaker (U.S.), succeeded in putting the greatest number of people on the summit, 20, on May 7–10, 1990.

Most in a day   Nine separate expeditions (32 men and 8 women from the United States, Canada, Australia, Great Britain, Russia, New Zealand, Finland, Lithuania, India and Nepal) reached the summit on May 12, 1992.

Sea level to summit   Timothy John Macartney-Snape (Australia) traversed Mt. Everest's entire altitude from sea level to summit. He set off on foot from the Bay of Bengal near Calcutta, India on February 5, 1990 and reached the summit on May 11, having walked approximately 745 miles.

Oldest   Ramon Blanco (Spain) was 60 years old when he reached the summit on October 7, 1993.

Most summits   Reinhold Messner scaled all 14 of the world's mountains of over 26,250 feet, all without oxygen.

Oldest mountain climber   Ichijirou Araya (Japan) climbed Mt. Fuji (12,388 feet) at the age of 100 yr. 258 days on August 5, 1994.

Greatest walls   The highest final stage in any wall climb is the one on the south face of Annapurna I (26,545 feet). It was climbed by the British expedition led by Christian John Storey Bonington, when, from April 2 to May 27, 1970, using 18,000 feet of rope, Donald Whillans and Dougal Haston scaled to the summit.

The longest wall climb is on the Rupal-Flank from the base camp, at 11,680 feet, to the South Point, at 26,384 feet, of Nanga Parbat—a vertical ascent of 14,704 feet. This was scaled by the Austro-German-Italian expedition led by Dr. Karl Maria Herrligkoffer in April 1970.

Highest bivouac   Four Nepalese summiters bivouacked at more than 28,870 feet in their descent from the summit of Everest on the night of April 23, 1990. They were Ang Rita Sherpa, on his record-breaking sixth ascent of Everest; Ang Kami Sherpa; Pasang Norbu Sherpa; and Top Bahadur Khatri.

Highest unclimbed mountain   The highest unclimbed mountain is Kankar Punsum (24,741 feet), on the Bhutan–Tibet border. It is the 67th highest mountain in the world.

The highest unclimbed summit is Lhotse Middle (27,605 feet), one of the peaks of Lhotse, in the Khumbu district of the Nepal Himalaya. It is the tenth highest individually recognized peak in the world, Lhotse being the fourth highest mountain.

Human fly   The longest climb on the vertical face of a building occurred on May 25, 1981, when Daniel Goodwin climbed a record 1,454 feet up the outside of the Sears Tower in Chicago, using suction cups and metal clips for support.

Ffoyna Campbell has walked more miles than any other woman.

OCEAN EXPLORATION

Greatest ocean descent The record ocean descent was achieved in the Challenger Deep of the Mariana Trench, where the U.S. Navy bathyscaphe *Trieste*, manned by Dr. Jacques Piccard (Switzerland) and Lt. Donald Walsh (U.S.N.), reached a depth of 35,797 feet on January 23, 1960. The descent took 4 hr. 48 min. and the ascent 3 hr. 17 min.

Deepest dive The record depth for the dangerous (and ill-advised) activity of breath-held diving is 428 feet, by Francisco "Pipín" Ferreras (Cuba) off Cabo San Lucas, Mexico on March 10, 1996. He was underwater for 2 min. 11 sec.

The record dive with scuba gear is 437 feet, by John J. Gruener and R. Neal Watson (U.S.) off Freeport, Grand Bahama on October 14, 1968.

The record dive utilizing gas mixtures was a simulated dive to a depth of 2,300 feet of sea-water by Théo Mavrostomos as part of the HYDRA 10 operation at the Hyperbaric Center of Comex in Marseilles, France on November 20, 1992, during a 43-day dive. He was breathing "hydreliox" (hydrogen, oxygen and helium).

Arnaud de Nechaud de Feral performed a saturation dive of 73 days, October 9–December 21, 1989, in a hyperbaric chamber simulating a depth of 985 feet, as part of the Comex HYDRA 9 operation. He was breathing "hydrox," a mixture of hydrogen and oxygen.

Richard Presley spent 69 days 19 min. in an underwater module in a lagoon in Key Largo, FL, May 6–July 14, 1992. The test was carried out as part of a mission called Project Atlantis that explored the human factors of living in an undersea environment.

High altitude diving The record for high altitude diving is 19,357 feet, in a lagoon in the crater of Licancabur, a volcano on the border between Chile and Bolivia. Johann Reinhard of Sea World Research Institute in San Diego, together with a team of scuba divers, made a series of dives there between November 14 and November 17, 1994. Henri García of the Chilean *Expedición America* team spent 1 hr. 8 min. exploring the lake at depths of 16–23 feet on January 16, 1995.

Deepest underwater escapes The deepest underwater rescue ever achieved was of the *Pisces III*, in which Roger R. Chapman and Roger Mallinson were trapped for 76 hours when their vessel sank to 1,575 feet, 150 miles southeast of Cork, Ireland on August 29, 1973. It was hauled to the surface on September 1 by the cable ship *John Cabot* after work by *Pisces V*, *Pisces II* and the remote-control recovery vessel *Curv* (Controlled Underwater Recovery Vehicle).

The greatest depth from which an unaided escape without equipment has been made is 225 feet, by Richard A. Slater from the rammed submersible *Nekton Beta* off Catalina Island, CA on September 28, 1970.

The record for an escape with equipment was by Norman Cooke and Hamish Jones on July 22, 1987. During a naval exercise they escaped from a depth of 601 feet from the submarine HMS *Otus* off Bergen, Norway. They were wearing standard suits with a built-in life jacket.

Deepest salvage The greatest depth at which salvage has been successfully carried out is 17,251 feet, in the case of a helicopter that crashed into the Pacific Ocean in August 1991 with the loss of four lives. The crew of the U.S.S. *Salvor* and personnel from East Port International raised the wreckage to the surface on February 27, 1992 so that the authorities could try to determine the cause of the accident.

The deepest salvage operation ever achieved with divers was on the wreck of HM cruiser *Edinburgh*, sunk on May 2, 1942 in the Barents Sea off northern Norway, inside the Arctic Circle, in 803 feet of water. Over 32 days (September 7–October 7, 1981), 12 divers worked on the wreck in pairs, using a bell from the *Stephaniturm* (1,594 tons).

Longest survival at sea Tabwai Mikaie and Arenta Tebeitabu, two fishermen from the island of Nikunau in Kiribati, were found alive on May 12,

1992 after surviving for a record 177 days adrift at sea in their 13-foot open dinghy.

Longest on a raft   The longest survival alone on a raft is 133 days (4½ months) by Second Steward Poon Lim of Great Britain's Merchant Navy, whose ship, the SS *Ben Lomond*, was torpedoed in the Atlantic 565 miles west of St. Paul's Rocks at Lat. 00° 30′ N, Long. 38° 45′ W at 11:45 A.M. on November 23, 1942. He was picked up by a Brazilian fishing boat off Salinópolis, Brazil on April 5, 1943.

POLAR EXPLORATION

Longest sled journey   The longest polar sled journey was undertaken by the International Trans-Antarctica Expedition (six members), who traveled about 3,750 miles by sled in 220 days, from July 27, 1989 (Seal Nunataks) to March 3, 1990 (Mirnyy). The expedition was supported by aircraft throughout its duration.

The longest *self-supporting* polar sled journey was one of 1,350 miles from Gould Bay to the Ross Ice Shelf by Sir Ranulph Fiennes and Dr. Michael Stroud, November 9, 1992–February 11, 1993.

Oldest to reach both poles   Major Will Lacy (Great Britain) went to the North Pole on April 9, 1990 at age 82 and the South Pole on December 20, 1991 at age 84. He traveled by aircraft on both trips.

Youngest to reach both poles   Robert Schumann (Great Britain) went to the North Pole on April 6, 1992 at age 10 and the South Pole on December 29, 1993 at age 11. He reached the North Pole by air and the South Pole by mountain bike (having flown to within a short distance of the pole).

Fastest Antarctic crossing   The 2,600-mile trans-Antarctic leg from Sanae to Scott Base of the 1980–82 British Trans-Globe Expedition was achieved in 67 days and eight rest days, from October 28, 1980 to January 11, 1981, the expedition having reached the South Pole on December 15, 1980. The 3-man snowmobile team comprised Sir Ranulph Fiennes, Oliver Shepard and Charles Burton.

BIG DEALS

Because of the infinite number of objects it is possible to collect, we can include only a small number of claims—those that in our experience reflect proven widespread interest.

We are more likely to consider claims for items accumulated on a personal basis over a significant period of time, made through recognized organizations, as these organizations are often in a better position to comment authoritatively in record terms.

Ax   A steel ax 60 feet long, 23 feet wide and weighing 7.7 tons was designed and built by BID Ltd. of Woodstock, New Brunswick, Canada. The ax was presented to the town of Nackawic, also in New Brunswick, on May 11, 1991 to commemorate the town's selection as Forestry Capital of Canada for 1991.

Balloon sculpture The largest balloon sculpture was a reproduction of Van Gogh's *Fishing Boats on the Beach of Les Saintes Maries*, made out of 25,344 colored balloons on June 28, 1992. Students from Haarlem Business School created the picture at a harbor in Ouddorp, Netherlands.

Basket A hand-woven maple basket measuring 48 by 23 by 19 feet was made by the Longaberger Company of Dresden, OH in 1990.

Beer cans William B. Christiensen of Madison, NJ collected over 75,000 different cans from 125 different countries, colonies and territories.

Most expensive A Rosalie Pilsner can sold for $6,000 in the United States in April 1981.

Beer labels Jan Solberg of Oslo, Norway had collected 424,868 different labels from around the world as of June 1995.

Blanket A hand-knitted, machine-knitted and crocheted blanket measuring a record 186,107.8 square feet was made by members of the Knitting and Crochet Guild worldwide, coordinated by Gloria Buckley of Bradford, England, and assembled at Dishforth Airfield, Thirsk, England on May 30, 1993.

Bottle A soda bottle 10 ft. 2 in. tall and 11 ft. 6 in. in circumference was filled with Schweppes Lemonade in Melbourne, Australia on March 17, 1994 to celebrate 200 years of Schweppes.

Bottle caps Starting in 1956, Paul Høegh Poulsen of Rødovre, Denmark amassed 82,169 different bottle caps from 179 countries.

Pyramid A pyramid consisting of 362,194 bottle caps was constructed by a team of 11 led by Yevgeniy Lepechov at Chernigov, Kiev, Ukraine, November 17–22, 1990.

Bottle collections George E. Terren of Southboro, MA had a collection of 31,804 miniature liquor bottles on May 31, 1993.

The record for beer is 8,131 unduplicated full bottles from 110 countries, collected by Peter Broeker of Geesthacht, Germany.

David L. Maund (Great Britain) had a collection of 11,476 miniature Scotch whiskey bottles as of May 1995.

Edoardo Giaccone of Gardone Riviera, Brescia, Italy has a total of 5,502 unduplicated full-size whisky bottles in his collection, which is housed in his specially-built "whiskyteca."

Christopher Weide of Jacksonville, FL had collected 6,510 different soda bottles as of August 1993.

Bouquet A team of students and community helpers led by Susan Williams of Victoria, British Columbia constructed a giant bouquet of 10,011 roses measuring 41.9 feet long in August 1994.

Can construction A 1:4 scale model of the Basilica di Sant'Antonio di Padova was built from 3,245,000 empty beverage cans in Padova (Padua), Italy by the charities AMNIUP, AIDO, AVIS and GPDS. The model, measuring 96 by 75 by 56 feet, was completed on December 20, 1992 after 20,000 hours of work.

Can pyramid Ten science students at University College Dublin, Belfield, Ireland built a pyramid of 5,525 empty cans in 30 minutes on February 14, 1995 in Belfield, Ireland. Ten students from Nakamura Elementary School, Yokohama, Japan equaled the record on August 16, 1995.

Schweppes created a soda bottle over 10 feet tall.

Carpets and rugs Largest The largest ancient carpet was a gold-enriched silk one of Hashim (dated A.D. 743) of the Abbasid caliphate in Baghdad, Iraq. It is reputed to have measured 180 by 300 feet (54,000 square feet).

A 52,225-square-foot, 31.4-ton red carpet was laid on February 13, 1982, by the Allied Corporation, from Radio City Music Hall to the New York Hilton along the Avenue of the Americas, in New York City.

Most finely woven The most finely woven carpet known is a silk hand-knotted example with 4,224 knots per square inch, measuring 14 by 22 inches. It was made over a period of 22 months by the Kapoor Rug Corporation of Jaipur, India and completed in May 1993.

Chair The largest is the Washington Chair, a 53-ft.-4-in.-high replica of the chair George Washington sat in when he presided over the Constitutional Convention in Philadelphia in 1787. Built by NSA and first displayed in Los Angeles, CA on December 9, 1988, the chair was designed to withstand earthquakes and 70-MPH winds.

Chandelier The world's largest chandelier was created by the Kookje Lighting Co. Ltd. of Seoul, South Korea. It is 39 feet high, weighs 11.8 tons and has 700 bulbs. Completed in November 1988, the chandelier now occupies three floors of the Lotte Chamshil Department Store in Seoul.

Christmas cracker The largest functional Christmas cracker ever constructed was 150 feet long and 10 feet in diameter. It was made by Ray Price for Markson Sparks! of New South Wales, Australia and pulled at Westfield Shopping Town, Chatswood, Sydney, Australia on November 9, 1991.

Christmas tree A 221-foot Douglas fir (*Pseudotsuga menziesii*) was erected at Northgate Shopping Center, Seattle, WA in December 1950.

Coasters The world's largest collection of coasters is owned by Leo Pisker of Langenzersdorf, Austria, who has collected 148,230 different coasters from 163 countries to date.

Credit cards The largest collection of valid credit cards to date is one of 1,397 (all different) by Walter Cavanagh of Santa Clara, CA. The cost of acquisition for "Mr. Plastic Fantastic" was zero, and he keeps the cards in the world's longest wallet—250 feet long, weighing 38 lb. 8 oz. and containing cards worth more than $1.65 million in credit.

Crossword puzzle In July 1982, Robert Turcot of Québec, Canada compiled the largest crossword puzzle ever published, comprising 82,951 squares. It contained 12,489 clues across, 13,125 down, and covered 38.28 square feet.

Daisy chain The longest daisy chain measured 6,980 ft. 7 in. and was made in seven hours by villagers of Good Easter, England on May 27, 1985. The team in this competition is limited to 16.

Doll The largest rag doll in the United States is 41 ft. 11 in. in total length, and was created by Apryl Scott at Autoworld in Flint, MI on November 20, 1990.

Dress A wedding outfit created by Hélène Gainville with jewels by Alexander Reza is believed to be worth $7,301,587.20 precisely. The dress is embroidered with diamonds mounted on platinum and was unveiled in Paris, France on March 23, 1989.

Dress train The world's longest wedding dress train measured 515 feet and was made by the Hansel and Gretel bridal outfitters of Guriskirchen, Germany in 1992.

Earrings Carol McFadden of Oil City, PA had collected 22,623 different pairs of earrings as of April 1996.

Egg The largest and most elaborate jeweled egg stands two feet tall and was fashioned from 37 pounds of gold, studded with 20,000 pink diamonds. Designed by British jeweler Paul Kutchinsky, the Argyle Library Egg took six British craftsmen 7,000 hours to create and has a price tag of £7 million ($12 million). It was unveiled on April 30, 1990 before going on display at the Victoria and Albert Museum, London, England.

Fabrics Oldest The oldest surviving fabric, radiocarbon dated to 7000 B.C., was reported in July 1993 to have been discovered in southeastern Turkey. The semi-fossilized cloth, measuring roughly 3 by 1½ inches, was believed to be linen.

Most expensive The most expensive wool fabric is one manufactured by Fujii Keori Ltd. of Osaka, Japan that retailed at 3 million yen ($30,000) per meter in January 1989.

Fan A handpainted fan made of chintz and wood, measuring 26 ft. 3 in. when unfolded and 14 ft. 8 in. high, was made by Victor Troyas Oses of Peralta, Spain in October 1994.

Fireworks Largest The largest firework ever produced was *Universe I Part II*, exploded for the Lake Toya Festival, Hokkaido, Japan on July 15, 1988. The 1,543-pound shell was 54.7 inches in diameter and burst to a diameter of 3,937 feet.

Catherine wheel A self-propelled horizontal firework wheel measuring 47 ft. 4 in. in diameter, built by Florida Pyrotechnic Arts Guild, was displayed at the Pyrotechnics Guild International Convention in Idaho Falls, ID on August 14, 1992. It functioned for 3 min. 45 sec.

Flags Oldest The oldest Stars and Stripes in existence is preserved in the Bennington Historical Museum in Old Bennington, VT, and dates from the 18th century.

Largest The largest flag in the world, measuring 505 by 255 feet and weighing 1.36 tons, is the American "Superflag," owned by Ski Demski of Long Beach, CA. On May 1, 1996, "Superflag" was unfurled and suspended from cables strung across Hoover Dam.

Float The world's largest float was 184 ft. 8 in. long. It was produced by the World of Dreams Foundation for the St. Patrick's Day parade, Montreal, Quebec, Canada in 1993.

"Superflag" is the world's largest flag, at 505 feet long.

Four-leaf clover collection   Norman W. Bright of Heber Springs, AR had collected 7,116 4-leaf clovers as of May 20, 1995.

Garbage can   The world's largest garbage can was made by Natsales of Durban, South Africa for "Keep Durban Beautiful Association Week," September 16–22, 1991. The 19-ft.-9-in.-tall fiberglass can is a replica of Natsales' standard model and has a capacity of 11,493 gallons.

Globe   The revolving "Globe of Peace," built between 1982 and 1987 by Orfeo Bartolucci of Apecchi, Pesaro, Italy, is 33 feet in diameter and weighs 33 tons.

Greeting cards   Craig Shergold of Carshalton, England was reported to have collected a record 33 million get-well cards by May 1991, when his mother pleaded for no more.

Gum wrapper chain   The longest gum wrapper chain on record measured 18,721 feet long, and was made by Gary Duschl of Waterdown, Ontario, Canada between 1965 and 1996.

Jack-o'-lanterns   The record for most jack-o'-lanterns in one place at one time is 10,540, on October 29, 1994. The pumpkins were carved for the Harvest Festival in Keene, NH, a Center Stage Cheshire County event sponsored by Paragon Cable.

   The largest jack-o'-lantern in the world was carved from a 827-pound pumpkin by Michael Green, Regina Johnson and Daniel Salcedo at Nut Tree, CA on October 30, 1992.

Jigsaw puzzles Largest   The world's largest jigsaw puzzle measures 51,484 square feet and consists of 43,924 pieces. Assembled on July 8, 1992, it was devised by Centre Socio-Culturel d'Endoume in Marseilles, France and was designed on the theme of the environment.

TIPS

from the
RECORD BREAKERS
LARGEST FLAG

Ski Demski resides in Long Beach, CA with his 3,000-pound co-star, the world's largest flag. In order to make it into The Guinness Book of Records *as a flag, the item in question has to be hoisted—and that's where advice from Demski comes in.*

◆

Find a *big* display area.
Superflag—a 505-by-255-foot version of "Old Glory"—was hung on cables across the Hoover Dam to mark the 1996 Olympic torch relay. "It wasn't easy," is Demski's comment. Superflag, which weighs in at 3,000 pounds, has its own motor home trailer to travel in. No special equipment is required to move it, says Demski. "You just need a bunch of people to manhandle it."

◆

Reinforce your flag.
Demski's flag was made of cloth and sewn together in Pennsylvania, and delivered to him on Flag Day (June 14), 1992. It was made to his specifications, with steel grommets every 30 inches.

◆

Use strong cables.
Superflag's grommets were attached to heavy steel cables attached to the Hoover Dam by officials of the U.S. Bureau of Reclamation, which operates the Dam. The grommets weren't strong enough to hold the flag in heavy wind, and soon after the Guinness-required time period had passed, one cable snapped.

A puzzle consisting of 204,484 pieces was made by BCF Holland b.v. of Almelo, Netherlands and assembled by students of the local Gravenvoorde School, from May 25 to June 1, 1991. The completed puzzle measured 1,036 square feet.

Knife The penknife with the greatest number of blades is the Year Knife, made by cutlers Joseph Rodgers & Sons, of Sheffield, England, whose trademark was granted in 1682. The knife was made in 1822 with 1,822 blades, and a blade was added every year until 1973, when there was no more space. It was acquired by British hand tool manufacturers Stanley Works (Great Britain) Ltd. in 1970.

Matchbook covers Ed Brassard of Seattle, WA had a collection of 3,159,119 matchbook covers as of March 1995.

Matchstick model Joseph Sciberras (Malta) constructed an exact replica, including the interior, of St. Publius Parish Church, Floriana, Malta, consisting of over 3 million matchsticks. The model, made to scale, is 6½ by 6½ by 5 ft.

Origami It took residents of the district of Gunma, Maebashi, Japan six hours to fold a paper crane measuring 52 ft. 6 in. tall, with a wingspan of 117 ft. 2 in., on October 28, 1995.

Pencil A pencil measuring 8.9 feet long and weighing 53 pounds was constructed by students at Huddersfield Technical College, Huddersfield, England in 1995.

The world's most expensive pen costs $121,000.

Pens Vilma Valma Turpeinen of Tampere, Finland had collected 14,492 different pens as of April 29, 1992.

The Meisterstück Solitaire Royal fountain pen, made by Montblanc, is made of solid gold and is encased with 4,810 diamonds—the height in meters of Mont Blanc mountain. The pen can be made to order for £75,000 ($121,000), and takes six months to make.

A Japanese collector paid Fr1.3 million ($2,340,000) in February 1988 for the "Anémone" fountain pen made by Réden, France. It was encrusted with 600 precious stones, including emeralds, amethysts, rubies, sapphires and onyx, and took craftsmen over a year to complete.

Piggy bank Ove Nordström of Spånga, Sweden has collected 3,075 pig-shaped money boxes over the past 39 years.

Piñata The world's biggest piñata measured 27 feet high with a diameter of 30 feet, a circumference of 100 feet and a weight of 10,000 pounds. It was built in March 1990 during the celebrations for Carnaval Miami in Miami, FL.

Pottery The largest thrown vase on record is one measuring 18 ft. 7 in. high. It was completed on February 10, 1996 by Ray Sparks of The Creative Clay Company, Queensland, Australia.

Quilt The world's largest quilt was made by the Saskatchewan Seniors' Association of Saskatchewan, Canada. It measured 155 ft. 4½ in. by 82 ft. 8 in., and was completed on June 13, 1994.

Refrigerator magnets Louise J. Greenfarb of Spanaway, WA had collected 15,500 refrigerator magnets as of January 1996.

Rope A giant tug of war rope measuring 564 ft. 4 in. feet long, with a diameter of 5 ft. ½ in., was made from rice straw for the annual festival in Naha City, Japan in October 1995. It is the largest rope made from natural materials and weighs 58,929 pounds.

The largest rope in the world was made from rice straw.

Scarf The longest scarf ever knitted measured 20 miles long. It was knitted by residents of Abbeyfield Houses for the Abbeyfield Society in Potters Bar, England and was completed on May 29, 1988.

Shoes Emperor Field Marshal Jean Fedor Bokassa of the Central African Empire (now Republic) commissioned pearl-studded shoes at a cost of

$85,000 from the House of Berluti, Paris, France for his self-coronation on December 4, 1977.

The most expensive manufactured shoes are mink-lined golf shoes with 18-carat gold embellishments and ruby-tipped spikes, made by Stylo Matchmakers International of Northampton, England, which retail for $23,000 per pair.

Silver   The largest single pieces of silver are a pair of water jugs of 10,408 troy ounces (4.77 cwt) made in 1902 for the Maharaja of Jaipur (1861–1922). They are 5 ft. 3 in. tall, with a circumference of 8 ft. 1½ in., and have a capacity of 2,160 gallons. They are now in the City Palace, Jaipur, India.

Snowman   The tallest snowman was built by a team of local residents at Ohkura Village, Yamagata, Japan. They spent 10 days and nights building the 96-ft.-7-in.-tall snowman, which was completed on March 10, 1995.

Sofa   In May 1995, a red leather sofa 24 feet long was made by Art Forma (Furniture) Ltd. of Castle Donington, England for the Swiss company Spühl AG.

String ball   The largest ball of string on record is one 13 ft. 2½ in. in diameter, 41 ft. 6 in. in circumference, amassed by J. C. Payne of Valley View, TX between 1989 and 1991.

Table   The longest table was set up in Pesaro, Italy on June 20, 1988 by the U.S. Libertas Scavolini basketball team. It was 10,072 feet long and seated 12,000 people.

Tablecloth   The world's largest tablecloth is 1,502 feet long and 4½ feet wide, and was made by the Sportex division of Artex International in Highland, IL on October 17, 1990.

Tapestry and embroidery   The largest tapestry ever woven is the *History of Iraq*, with an area of 13,370.7 square feet. It was designed by the Yugoslavian artist Frane Delale and produced by the Zivtex Regeneracija Workshop in Zabok, Yugoslavia. The tapestry was completed in 1986, and it now adorns the wall of an amphitheater in Baghdad, Iraq.

Embroidery   An 8-inch-deep, 1,338-foot-long embroidery of scenes from C. S. Lewis's *Narnia* children's stories was worked by Margaret S. Pollard (Great Britain) to the order of Michael Maine. Its total area is about 937 square feet.

Ties   A collection of 10,453 ties accumulated by Bill McDaniel of Santa Maria, CA was sold to a museum in St. Augustine, FL in 1992.

Wallet   The most expensive wallet ever made is a platinum-cornered, diamond-studded crocodile creation made by Louis Quatorze of Paris, France and Mikimoto of Tokyo, selling in September 1984 for $84,000.

Yo-yo   A yo-yo measuring 10 ft. 4 in. in diameter and weighing 897 pounds was devised by J. N. Nichols (Vimto) Ltd. and made by engineering students at Stockport College, Stockport, England. It was suspended from a

The largest yo-yo was suspended from a crane and yo-yoed four times.

187-foot crane in Wythenshawe, England on August 1, 1993, and "yo-yoed" about four times.

Zipper   The world's longest zipper was laid around the center of Sneek, Netherlands on September 5, 1989. The brass zipper, made by Yoshida (Netherlands) Ltd., is 9,353.56 feet long and consists of 2,565,900 teeth.

FANTASTIC FEATS

Apple peeling   The longest single unbroken apple peel on record measures 172 ft. 4 in. It was peeled by Kathy Wafler of Wolcott, NY in 11 hr. 30 min. at Long Ridge Mall, Rochester, NY on October 16, 1976. The apple weighed 20 ounces.

Apple picking   The greatest recorded performance is 15,830 pounds picked in eight hours by George Adrian of Indianapolis, IN on September 23, 1980.

Balloon release   A mass release of 1,592,744 balloons was staged by Disney Home Video at Longleat House, England on August 27, 1994.

Barrel rolling   The record for rolling a full 36-gallon metal beer barrel over a measured mile is 8 min. 7.2 sec., by Phillip Randle, Steve Hewitt, John Round, Trevor Bradley, Colin Barnes and Ray Glover of Haunchwood Collieries Institute and Social Club, Nuneaton, England on August 15, 1982.

Barrow pushing   A 1-wheeled barrow loaded with bricks weighing a gross 8,275 pounds was pushed a distance of 243 feet by John Sarich in London, Ontario, Canada on February 19, 1987.

Barrow racing   The fastest time attained in a one-mile wheelbarrow race is 4 min. 48.51 sec., by Piet Pitzer and Jaco Erasmus at Transvalia High School, Vanderbijlpark, South Africa on October 3, 1987.

Bathtub racing   The record for a 36-mile bathtub race is 1 hr. 22 min. 27 sec., by Greg Mutton at the Grafton Jacaranda Festival, New South Wales, Australia on November 8, 1987. Tubs are limited to 75 inches and 6-hp motors.

   The greatest distance for paddling a hand-propelled bathtub in still water in 24 hours is 90½ miles, by 13 members of Aldington Prison Officers Social Club, near Ashford, Kent, England, May 28–29, 1983.

Bed making   The pair record for making a bed with one blanket, two sheets, an undersheet, an uncased pillow, one bedspread and "hospital" corners is 14.0 seconds, by Sister Sharon Stringer and Nurse Michelle Benkel of the Royal Masonic Hospital, London, England on November 26, 1993.

The record time for one person to make a bed is 28.2 seconds, by Wendy Wall, 34, of Sydney, Australia on November 30, 1978.

Bed pushing A wheeled hospital bed was pushed 3,233 miles by a team of nine employees of Bruntsfield Bedding Center, Edinburgh, Scotland, June 21–July 26, 1979.

Bed race The course record for a 10-mile bed race is 50 minutes, as established by the Westbury Harriers' 3-man bed team at Chew Valley, Avon, England.

Beer coaster flipping Dean Gould of Felixstowe, England flipped a pile of 111 coasters (0.047-inch wood pulp board) through 180 degrees and caught them all on January 13, 1993.

Beer keg lifting George Olesen raised a keg of beer weighing 138 lb. 11 oz. above his head 737 times in six hours in Horsens, Denmark on May 1, 1994.

Beer stein carrying Duane Osborn covered a distance of 49 ft. 2½ in. in 3.65 seconds with five full steins in each hand in Cadillac, MI on July 10, 1992.

Brick balancing Terry Cole of Walthamstow, England balanced 75 bricks (weighing a total of 328 lb. 2 oz.) on his head for 19 seconds on May 4, 1996.

Brick carrying The greatest distance achieved for carrying a 9-pound brick in one ungloved hand using an uncradled downward pincer grip is 71.03 miles, by Ashrita Furman of Jamaica, NY on June 3–4, 1995. The women's record for carrying a 9-lb.-12-oz. brick is 22.5 miles, by Wendy Morris of Walsall, England on April 28, 1986.

Brick lifting Russell Bradley of Worcester, England lifted 31 bricks laid side by side off a table, raising them to chest height and holding them there for two seconds, on June 14, 1992.

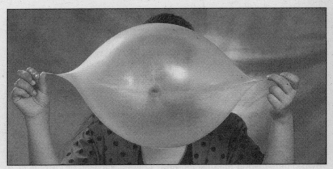

Susan Montgomery Williams is the bubble-gum blowing champ.

The greatest weight of bricks lifted was by Fred Burton of Cheadle, Staffordshire, England, who lifted 20 far heavier bricks weighing 202 lb. 5 oz. on May 4, 1996, holding them for two seconds.

Bubble blowing   Alan McKay of Wellington, New Zealand created a bubble 63 ft. 10 in. long on July 30, 1995. He made it using a bubble wand, dishwashing liquid, glycerine and water.

Bubble-gum blowing   The greatest reported diameter for a bubble-gum bubble under the strict rules of this highly competitive activity is 23 inches, by Susan Montgomery Williams of Fresno, CA on July 19, 1994.

Carriage pushing   The greatest distance covered in 24 hours while pushing a baby carriage is 350.22 miles, by 60 members of the Oost-Vlanderen branch of Amnesty International in Lede, Belgium on October 15, 1988.

A 10-man team from the Royal Marines School of Music, Deal, England, with an adult "baby," covered 271.7 miles in 24 hours, November 22–23, 1990.

Car washing   Students from Carroll High School, Yakima, WA washed 3,844 cars in eight hours on May 7, 1983.

Cherry stem tying   Al Gliniecki (U.S.) tied 833 cherry stems into knots with his tongue in one hour on April 21, 1995.

Cigar box balancing   Terry Cole of London, England balanced 220 unmodified cigar boxes on his chin for nine seconds on April 24, 1992.

Clapping   The duration record for continuous clapping (sustaining an average of 160 claps per minute, audible at 120 yards) is 58 hr. 9 min. by V. Jeyaraman of Tamil Nadu, India, February 12–15, 1988.

Coal shoveling   The record for filling a 1,120-pound hopper with coal is 26.59 seconds, by Wayne Miller in Wonthaggi, Victoria, Australia on April 17, 1995. The record by a team of two is 15.01 seconds, by Brian McArdle and Rodney Spark at the Fingal Valley Festival in Fingal, Tasmania, Australia on March 5, 1994.

Crawling   The longest continuous voluntary crawl (progression with one knee or the other in unbroken contact with the ground) on record is 31.5 miles, by Peter McKinlay and John Murrie, who covered 115 laps of an athletic track at Falkirk, Scotland, March 28–29, 1992.

Over a 15-month period ending on March 9, 1985, Jagdish Chander crawled 870 miles from Aligarh to Jamma, India to propitiate his revered Hindu goddess, Mata.

Crossword puzzle solving *Fastest*   The fastest time for completing *The Times* (London) crossword puzzle under test conditions is 3 min. 45 sec., by Roy Dean (Great Britain) on December 19, 1970.

Slowest   In May 1966, *The Times* of London received an announcement from a Fijian woman that she had just completed their crossword puzzle No. 673, published in the issue of April 4, 1932. The problem wasn't that the puzzle was fiendishly difficult—it was just that it was in an edition that

TIPS

from the
RECORD BREAKERS
GRAPE CATCHING

Paul Tavilla is part of a big family that owns a wholesale fruit business. He knows his fruit and has gone to great lengths to prove it: he can use his mouth to catch a grape thrown from 327 feet away. We got these tips straight from the grape-catcher's mouth.

◆

Choose your grape carefully.

"I use only black grapes—because they're big and heavy, and easy to see." Tavilla's recommendation: "California Ribier grapes grown in July or August, when they come really big. If I have to, I'll go to Chilean Red Globe grapes."

◆

Catch with your eyes.

"You're not catching it with your mouth," Tavilla reveals. "I've been catching things in my mouth since I was a kid, and now I teach other kids how to do it. I say, 'I'll aim at your head. Watch my hand.' They'll get it in the head, or in the nose, until they really learn to follow the grape with their eyes."

◆

Choose your students carefully.

Tavilla is a favorite of TV talk shows. But some of his hosts have gotten in trouble by trying to emulate the master. "The writer George Plimpton had people throwing grapes from the Trump Tower in New York City. I caught one, but Plimpton slipped on the sidewalk and went over backward." Johnny Carson hardly had better luck. "I told him to catch with his eyes, and that's just what he did. He got a grape right in the eye!"

had been used to wrap a package, and had subsequently lain uncompleted for 34 years.

Cucumber slicing   Norman Johnson (Great Britain) set a record of 13.4 seconds for slicing a 12-inch cucumber, 1½ inches in diameter, at 22 slices to the inch (total 264 slices) at Westdeutsche Rundfunk in Cologne, Germany on April 3, 1983.

Egg and spoon racing   Dale Lyons of Meriden, England ran 26 mi. 385 yd. (the classic marathon distance) while carrying a dessert spoon with a fresh egg on it in 3 hr. 47 min. on April 23, 1990.

Egg hunt   The greatest egg hunt in the United States involved 120,000 plastic and candy eggs at a community Easter egg hunt at Coquina Beach in Manatee, FL on March 23, 1991. The event, hosted by Meals on Wheels PLUS of Manatee, Inc., entertained 1,870 children.

Longest incarceration in an elevator   Graham Coates of Brighton, England was trapped in an elevator in Brighton for 62 hours, May 24–27, 1986.

Escalator riding   The record distance traveled on a pair of up and down escalators is 133.18 miles, by David Beattie and Adrian Simons at Top Shop in London, England, July 17–21, 1989. They each completed 7,032 circuits.

Fire bucket brigade   The longest fire company bucket brigade stretched over 11,471 feet, with 2,271 people passing 50 buckets along the complete course, at the Centennial Parade and Muster, Hudson, NY on July 11, 1992.

Garbage collecting   The greatest number of volunteers involved in collecting garbage in one location in one day is 50,405, along the coastline of California on October 2, 1993, in conjunction with the International Coast Cleanup.

Glass balancing   Ashrita Furman of Jamaica, NY balanced 57 pint glasses on his chin for 11.9 seconds on May 18, 1996.

Gold panning   The fastest time for "panning" eight planted gold nuggets in a 10-inch-diameter pan is 7.55 seconds, by Don Roberts of Diamond Bar, CA in the 27th World Gold Panning Championship on April 16, 1989 in Dahlonega, GA. The women's record is 10.03 seconds, by Susan Bryeans of Fullerton, CA at the 23rd World Gold Panning Championship on March 6, 1983 at Knott's Berry Farm, Buena Park, CA.

Grape catching   The greatest distance at which a grape thrown from level ground has been caught in the mouth is 327 ft. 6 in., by Paul J. Tavilla in East Boston, MA on May 27, 1991. The grape was thrown by James Deady.

Hair splitting   Alfred West (Great Britain) split a human hair 17 times into 18 parts on eight occasions.

Handshaking   Yogesh Sharma shook hands with 31,118 different people in eight hours at the Gwalior Trade Fair, Gwalior, Madhya Pradesh, India on January 14, 1996.

Hopscotch   The greatest number of games of hopscotch successfully completed in 24 hours is 390, by Ashrita Furman of Jamaica, NY, April 2–3, 1995.

Human centipede   The largest "human centipede" to move 98 ft. 5 in. (30 meters), with ankles firmly tied together, consisted of 1,601 students from Nanyang Technological University, Singapore on July 29, 1995. Nobody fell over in the course of the walk.

Human logo   The largest human logo ever made was the Human U.S. Shield consisting of 30,000 officers and men at Camp Custer, Battle Creek, MI on November 10, 1918.

Joke telling   Working on the premise that a joke must have a beginning, a middle and an end, Felipe Carbonell of Lima, Peru told 345 jokes in one hour on July 29, 1993.

Mike Hessman of Columbus, OH told 12,682 jokes in 24 hours on November 16–17, 1992.

Juggling   *"Juggled" means that the number of catches made equals twice the number of objects multiplied by the number of hands. "Flashed" means the number of catches made equals at least the number of objects, but less than a "juggle."*

* These records are reported to have been achieved, but indisputable evidence is not available.

Most objects aloft   826 jugglers kept 2,478 objects in the air simultaneously, each person juggling at least three objects, in Glastonbury, England on June 26, 1994.

11 rings (juggled)   Albert Petrovski* (USSR), 1963; Eugene Belaur* (USSR), 1968; Sergei Ignatov* (USSR), 1973.

12 rings (flashed)   Albert Lucas (U.S.), 1995 (1984*); Anthony Gatto (U.S.), 1993.

7 clubs (juggled)   Albert Petrovski* (USSR), 1963; Sorin Munteanu* (Romania), 1975; Jack Bremlov* (Czechoslovakia), 1985; Albert Lucas (U.S.), 1996 (1985*); Anthony Gatto (U.S.), 1988; Bruce Tiemann (U.S.), 1995.

8 clubs (flashed)   Anthony Gatto (U.S.), 1989; Scott Sorensen (U.S.), 1995.

10 balls (juggled)   Enrico Rastelli* (Italy), 1920s; Bruce Sarafian (U.S.), 1996.

10 balls (bounce juggled)   Tim Nolan* (U.S.), 1988.

12 balls (flashed)   Bruce Sarafian (U.S.), 1995.

8 plates (juggled)   Enrico Rastelli* (Italy), 1920s.

8 plates (flashed)   Albert Lucas (U.S.), 1993.

7 flaming torches (juggled)   Anthony Gatto (U.S.), 1989.

Passing 11 clubs (juggled)   Owen Morse and John Wee (U.S.), 1995.

Passing 15 balls (flashed)   Peter Kaseman and Rob Vancko (U.S.), 1995.

5 balls inverted   Bobby May (U.S.), 1953.

Ball spinning (on one hand)   François Chotard (France), 9 balls, 1990.

Basketball spinning   Bruce Crevier (U.S.), 18 basketballs (whole body), 1994.

Duration: 5 clubs without a drop   45 min. 2 sec., Anthony Gatto (U.S.), 1989.

Duration: 3 objects without a drop   Terry Cole (Great Britain), 11 hr. 4 min. 22 sec., 1995.

Kissing   Alfred A. E. Wolfram of New Brighton, MN kissed 10,504 people in eight hours at the Minnesota Renaissance Festival on August 19, 1995.
   The most couples kissing simultaneously in one place was 1,420, at the University of Maine, Orono, ME on February 14, 1996.

Kite flying   The following records are all recognized by *Kite Lines* Magazine:

Highest   A record height of 31,955 feet was reached by a train of eight kites over Lindenberg, Germany on August 1, 1919.
   The altitude record for a single kite is 12,471 feet, in the case of a kite flown by Henry Helm Clayton and A. E. Sweetland at the Blue Hill Weather Station, Milton, MA on February 28, 1898.

Longest   The longest kite flown was 3,394 feet long. It was made and flown by Michel Trouillet and a team of helpers in Nîmes, France on November 18, 1990.

Largest   The largest kite flown was 5,952 square feet. It was first flown by a Dutch team on the beach at Scheveningen, Netherlands on August 8, 1991.

Fastest   The fastest speed attained by a kite was 120 MPH for a kite flown by Pete DiGiacomo in Ocean City, MD on September 22, 1989.

Most figure eights   The greatest number of figure eights achieved with a kite in an hour is 2,911, by Stu Cohen in Ocean City, MD on September 25, 1988.

ALBERT LUCAS

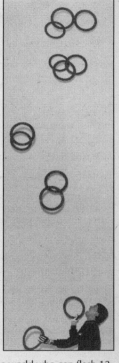

*A*lbert Lucas is one of the best jugglers in the world. If he had his way, though, many more people would become jugglers and make their bids to surpass him. Lucas took some time out from competing at the International Jugglers' Association World Championship in Rapid City, SD, where he received a lifetime achievement award (at age 36), to talk to *The Guinness Book of Records.*

*J*uggling, says Lucas, is an art form, and an athletic one at that. He comes from a family tradition of athletic artists: his father, Albert Moreira, was a world-famous acrobat (with the troupe Los Gatos) who started in the circus, went on to vaudeville, and worked with the likes of Sammy Davis, Jr., Donald O'Connor and Milton Berle. "My father worked with the best jugglers of his era, and I got my start learning from them," says Lucas. His brother, a neurosurgeon, is an expert juggler who attributes his surgical prowess to his juggling background.

*"E*veryone—especially every youngster—has the potential to juggle. The Soviet Union used to teach many of its athletes to juggle, no matter what sport was their forte. If you want to improve your hand–eye coordination, or your judgment of distances, learn to juggle." Lucas has taught many others, from movement-impaired children who learn to juggle silk scarves to Julius "Dr. J." Erving, who honed his hand–eye coordination by juggling socks in the locker room.

*N*owadays Lucas is one of only two people in the world who can flash 12 rings at once. His next attempt, with 14 rings, will be made at MIT, where physicists think it can't be done. "They've studied the problem of juggling to determine how many rings can be kept in the air at once, based on the gravitational pull of the earth." Lucas has also worked on the problem, and thinks he'll succeed. "Every time you add a ring, you must increase the height and speed of your toss by one-third," he states. "There's a limit to your hand capacity and your hand speed. The first rings you throw have to be the fastest—and it's tough because your hands carry the weight of the other rings. It's like getting the Saturn rocket off the ground: the first few seconds are the hardest."

Most on a single line   The greatest number of kites flown on a single line is 11,284, by Sadao Harada and a team of helpers in Sakurajima, Kagoshima, Japan on October 18, 1990.

Longest duration   The longest recorded flight is one of 180 hr. 17 min. by the Edmonds Community College team at Long Beach, WA, August 21–29, 1982. Managing the flight of this J-25 parafoil was Harry N. Osborne.

Knitting   The world's fastest hand-knitter was Gwen Matthewman of Featherstone, England. She attained a speed of 111 stitches per minute in a test at Phildar's Wool Shop, Leeds, England on September 29, 1980.

The Exeter Spinners—Audrey Felton, Christine Heap, Eileen Lancaster, Marjorie Mellis, Ann Sandercock and Maria Scott—produced a sweater by hand from raw fleece in 1 hr. 55 min. 50.2 sec. on September 25, 1983 at British Broadcasting Corporation Television Centre, London, England.

Knot tying   The fastest recorded time for tying the six Boy Scout Handbook knots (square knot, sheet bend, sheepshank, clove hitch, round turn and two half hitches, and bowline) on individual ropes is 8.1 seconds, by Clinton R. Bailey, Sr. of Pacific City, OR on April 13, 1977.

Ladder climbing   A team of 10 firefighters from Royal Berkshire Fire and Rescue Service climbed a vertical height of 47.58 miles up a standard fire-service ladder in 24 hours in Reading, England, April 28–29, 1995.

Leapfrogging   The greatest distance covered is 996.2 miles, by 14 students from Trancos dormitory at Stanford University, Stanford, CA. They started leapfrogging on May 16, 1991 and stopped 244 hr. 43 min. later on May 26.

Log rolling   The record number of International Championships won is 10, by Jubiel Wickheim of Shawnigan Lake, British Columbia, Canada, between 1956 and 1969.

Mantle of bees   Jed Shaner was covered by a mantle of an estimated 343,000 bees weighing an aggregate of 80 pounds in Staunton, VA on June 29, 1991.

Milk bottle balancing   The greatest distance walked by a person continuously balancing a milk bottle on the head is 70.16 miles, by Ashrita Furman in Jamaica, NY, August 1–2, 1993. It took him 18 hr. 46 min. to complete the walk.

Milk crate balancing   Terry Cole of Walthamstow, England balanced 29 crates on his chin for the minimum specified 10 seconds on May 16, 1994.

John Evans of Marlpool, England balanced 92 crates (each weighing three pounds) on his head for 10 seconds for the British television show *Good Morning with Anne and Nick,* filmed in Birmingham, England, on March 27, 1996.

Oyster opening   The record for opening oysters is 100 in 2 min. 20.07 sec., by Mike Racz in Invercargill, New Zealand on July 16, 1990.

Paper chain A paper chain 36.69 miles long was made by 60 students from University College Dublin, Republic of Ireland, as part of UCD Science Day in Dublin, February 11–12, 1993. The chain consisted of nearly 400,000 links and was made over a period of 24 hours.

Paper clip chain A 9.31-mile-long chain of paper clips was made by 40 members of Boon Lay Community Centre Youth Group, Singapore, July 13–14, 1996.

Pass the parcel The largest game of pass the parcel involved 3,464 people who removed 2,000 wrappers in two hours from a parcel measuring 5 by 3 by 3 feet at Alton Towers, Alton, England on November 8, 1992. The event was organized by Parcelforce International.

Pedal-boating Kenichi Horie of Kobe, Japan set a pedal-boating distance record of 4,660 miles, leaving Honolulu, HI on October 30, 1992 and arriving in Naha, Okinawa, Japan on February 17, 1993.

40 years ago *the first edition of* The Guinness Book of Records *noted that in 1892, French stilt-walker M. Garisoain walked 4.97 miles in 42 minutes.* **Today** *M. Garisoain's record still stands. It is, however, under threat. Ashrita Furman, who has set more Guinness records than anyone else, has set his sights on the stilt-walking speed record.*

"The attraction [of the stilt-walking record] is that it has stood for over a hundred years. Humanity must have made enough progress that this record is ripe for breaking. I feel that it is my responsibility to do so." —Ashrita Furman, July 30, 1996

Pogo stick jumping The greatest number of jumps achieved is 177,737, by Gary Stewart at Huntington Beach, Los Angeles, CA, May 25–26, 1990. Ashrita Furman of Jamaica, NY set a distance record of 16 miles in 6 hr. 40 min. on October 8, 1993 in Gotemba, Japan.

Potato peeling On September 19, 1992, Marj Killian, Terry Anderson, Barbara Pearson, Marilyn Small and Janene Utkin peeled 1,064 lb. 6 oz. (net) of potatoes to an institutional cookery standard with standard kitchen knives in 45 minutes at the 64th Annual Idaho Spud Day celebration, held in Shelley, ID.

Rope slide   The greatest distance recorded in a rope slide is 5,730 feet, by Lance Corporal Peter Baldwin of the British Royal Marines and Stu Leggett of the Canadian School of Rescue Training, from the top of Mt. Gibraltar, near Calgary, Canada down to level ground on August 31, 1994. Some of the descent was done at speeds in excess of 100 MPH.

Spitting   The greatest recorded distance for spitting a cherry stone is 95 ft. 1 in., by Horst Ortmann in Langenthal, Germany on August 27, 1994. The record for projecting a watermelon seed is 75 ft. 2 in., by Jason Schayot in De Leon, TX on August 12, 1995.

United States   David O'Dell of Apple Valley, CA spat a tobacco wad 49 ft. 5½ in. at the 19th World Tobacco Spitting Championships, Calico Ghost Town, CA on March 26, 1994.

Standing   The longest period on record that anyone has continuously stood is more than 17 years in the case of Swami Maujgiri Maharaj when performing the *Tapasya* or penance from 1955 to November 1973 in Shahjahanpur, Uttar Pradesh, India. When sleeping he would lean against a plank. He died at age 85 in September 1980.

Step-ups   Terry Cole of Walthamstow, England completed 2,970 step-ups in one hour on May 24, 1996, using a 15-inch-high exercise bench.

Stone skipping   The video-verified stone skipping record is 38 skips, achieved by Jerdone in Wimberley, TX on October 20, 1991.

Stretcher bearing   The record for carrying a stretcher case with a 140-pound "body" is 167.86 miles in 49 hr. 2 min., April 29–May 1, 1993. This was achieved by two 4-man teams from the 85th CFB (Canadian Forces Base) Trenton in and around Trenton, Ontario, Canada.

Tailoring   The shortest time for production of a 3-piece suit from sheep to finished article was 1 hr. 34 min. 33.42 sec., by 65 members of the Melbourne College of Textiles, Pascoe Vale, Victoria, Australia on June 24, 1982. Catching and fleecing took 2 min. 21 sec., and carding, spinning, weaving and tailoring occupied the remaining time.

Tiddlywinks   Larry Kahn has won the Tiddlywinks World Championships singles title 14 times, 1983–95. Geoff Meyers and Andy Purvis have won a record seven pairs titles, 1991–95.

Tightrope walking   The oldest tightrope walker was "Professor" William Ivy Baldwin, who crossed the South Boulder Canyon in Colorado on a 320-foot wire with a 125-foot drop on his 82nd birthday on July 31, 1948.

The tightrope endurance record is 205 days, by Jorge Ojeda-Guzman of Orlando, FL, on a wire 36 feet long and 35 feet above the ground. He was there from January 1 to July 25, 1993 and entertained onlookers by walking, balancing on a chair and dancing. His main luxury was a wooden cabin measuring 3 by 3 feet at one end of the tightrope.

Ashley Brophy of Neilborough, Victoria, Australia walked 7.19 miles on a wire 147.64 feet long and 32.81 feet above the ground in Adelaide, Australia on November 1, 1985 in 3½ hours.

The greatest drop over which anyone has walked on a tightrope is 10,335 feet above the French countryside, by Michel Menin (France) on August 4, 1989.

 **40 years ago** *no tiddlywinks records had yet gained entry to the Guinness pages; it was in 1966 that various tiddlywinks feats were listed for the first time. Among them was the fastest time for potting 10,000 winks: 3 hr. 51 min. 46 sec., by Allen Astles in February 1966.* **Today** *Astles' record still stands.*

"We knew Guinness as kids. Like all the other kids we would sit around the pub thinking up categories . . . like being the tiddlywinks champion."
—Paul McCartney, May 8, 1996

Top spinning   A team of 25 from the Mizushima Plant of Kawasaki Steel Works in Okayama, Japan spun a giant top 6 ft. 6¾ in. tall and 8 ft. 6¼ in. in diameter, weighing 793.6 pounds, for 1 hr. 21 min. 35 sec. on November 3, 1986.

Train pulling   Grant Edwards single-handedly pulled a train weighing 223 tons a distance of 120 ft. 9 in. along a train track in Thirlmere, New South Wales, Australia on April 4, 1996.

Tree climbing   On July 3, 1988, Guy German of Sitka, AK climbed up a 100-foot tree trunk and back down to the ground in 24.82 seconds at the World Championship Timber Carnival in Albany, OR.

Tree planting   The most trees planted in one day by an unlimited number of volunteers is 10,136. The trees were planted as part of a project called Pinte Bauru de Verde ("Paint Bauru Green") in Bauru, São Paulo, Brazil on June 15, 1993.

The most trees planted by no more than 300 volunteers is 2,589, by 218 students of Peel Hall Primary School and Joseph Eastham High, New Madamswood, England on March 14, 1995.

Tree sitting   The duration record for staying in a tree is more than 25 years, by Bungkas, who went up a palm tree in the Indonesian village of Bengkes in 1970 and has been there ever since. He lives in a nest made from branches and leaves. Repeated efforts have been made to persuade him to come down, but without success.

Typewriting   The highest recorded speeds attained with a 10-word penalty per error on a manual machine are as follows: Five minutes: 176 WPM by Carole Forristall Waldschlager Bechen in Dixon, IL on April 2, 1959; one hour: 147 WPM by Albert Tangora (U.S.) on an Underwood Standard, October 21, 1923.

The official 1-hour record on an electric typewriter is 9,316 words (40 errors) on an IBM machine, giving a net rate of 149 WPM, by Margaret Hamma (later Dilmore) in Brooklyn, NY on June 20, 1941.

In an official test in 1946, Stella Pajunas (later Garnand) typed 216 words in one minute on an IBM machine in Chicago, IL.

Gregory Arakelian of Herndon, VA set a speed record of 158 WPM, with two errors, on a personal computer in the Key Tronic World Invitational Type-off, which attracted some 10,000 entrants worldwide. He recorded this speed in a 3-minute test in the semifinal on September 24, 1991.

Mikhail Shestov of Fredriksberg, Denmark set a numerical record for a PC on April 2, 1996, by typing spaced numbers from 1 to 801 in five minutes at Baruch College, New York City. He did not make any errors and was not aided by a correction device.

Les Stewart of Mudjimba Beach, Queensland, Australia had typed the numbers 1 to 894,000 in *words* on 17,770 quarto sheets as of April 11, 1996. His target is to become a "millionaire."

Unsupported circle   An unsupported circle of 10,323 employees of the Nissan Motor Co. was formed at Komazawa Stadium, Tokyo, Japan on October 23, 1982.

Whip cracking   The longest whip ever cracked (i.e., the end made to travel faster than the speed of sound) is one of 184 ft. 6 in., excluding the handle, wielded by Krist King of Pettisville, OH on September 17, 1991.

Wine glass stacking   Alain Fournier (Canada) put in position and held 45 wine glasses in one hand on "Live! With Regis and Kathie Lee" on July 20, 1994.

Writing   During the mid 1950s, Horace Dall of Luton, England built a pantograph—which reduces movement—fitted with a diamond stylus, with which he engraved writing small enough to fit 140 Bibles to one square inch. In the 1990s, the movement of small atoms under an electron microscope now allows engraving of letters five atoms tall. At this size, several Bibles could be printed on a single bacterium.

Yo-yo   Fast Eddy McDonald of Toronto, Canada completed 21,663 loops in three hours on October 14, 1990 in Boston, MA. McDonald also set a 1-hour speed record of 8,437 loops in Cavendish, Prince Edward Island, Canada on July 14, 1990.

FOOD AND DRINK

Alcohol consumption   Russia has the highest consumption of hard liquor per person, with an average of 9.3 pints of pure alcohol according to 1994 figures. In the same year, the Czech Republic was the leading beer consumer, with 338.1 pints per person, and France headed the list for wine, with 132 pints per person.

Most alcoholic drink   When Estonia was independent, between the two World Wars, the Estonian Liquor Monopoly marketed 98 percent alcohol (196 proof) distilled from potatoes. In 31 states, Everclear, 190 proof or 95 percent alcohol by volume, is marketed by the American Distilling Co. "primarily as a base for home-made cordials."

Banana split   The longest banana split ever created measured 4.55 miles long, and was made by residents of Selinsgrove, PA on April 30, 1988.

Strongest beer   Baz's Super Brew, brewed by Barrie Parish and on sale at The Parish Brewery, Somerby, England, has an alcohol volume of 23.0 percent.

United States   Samuel Adams Triple Bock, brewed by the Boston Beer Company, is 17.7 percent alcohol by volume.

Burrito   A burrito weighing 4,217 pounds and measuring 3,112.99 feet long was created by El Pollo Loco in Anaheim, CA on July 31, 1995.

Cake Largest   The largest cake ever created weighed 128,238 lb. 8 oz., including 16,209 pounds of icing. It was made to celebrate the 100th birthday of Fort Payne, AL, and was in the shape of Alabama. The cake was prepared by a local bakery, EarthGrains, and the first cut was made by 100-year-old resident Ed Henderson on October 18, 1989.

Tallest   The tallest cake was 101 ft. 2½ in. high. It was created by Beth Cornell Trevorrow and her team of helpers at the Shiawassee County Fairgrounds, MI. The cake consisted of 100 tiers, and work was completed on August 5, 1990.

Oldest   The Alimentarium Food Museum in Vevey, Switzerland has on display the world's oldest cake, which was sealed and "vacuum-packed" in the grave of Pepionkh, who lived in ancient Egypt around 2200 B.C. The 4.3-inch-wide cake has sesame on it and honey inside, and was possibly made with milk.

Candy   The largest candy was a marzipan chocolate weighing 4,078 lb. 8 oz., made at the Ven International Fresh Market, Diemen, Netherlands, May 11–13, 1990.

Champagne cork flight   The longest flight of a cork from an untreated and unheated bottle four feet from level ground is 177 ft. 9 in., reached by Prof.

MAX CLOUGH

What do you do when you're just a small soda company, competing with the really, really big guys? According to Max Clough, a director of the Thomas Kemper Soda Company, you do something really, really big. "It was our ambition to create a little splash of our own," says Clough. Since root beer is the company's best seller, a giant root beer float seemed like the natural thing.

The event was staged in a park in downtown Seattle, a few blocks from the Kemper brewery. A local construction company lent the crane that moved a 4,000-ton carbonating tank to the park, and a dairy donated a hundred 3-gallon containers of ice cream. "We dumped the ice cream in first," Clough recalls. "Then we brewed up a batch of root beer back at our plant. A pumper truck came and pumped the soda out of the brewery tank and trucked it over to the park.

We pumped it into the carbonation tank, and started passing out root beer floats!" The outcome: a 2,166.5-gallon root beer float.

Thomas Kemper root beer was born at an Oktoberfest in 1990. Clough's wife, Laura, had invested in a micro-brewery that produced beer for the Oktoberfest. To help make the event a family affair, Laura Clough and her sister, Carol Clemency, brewed up a batch of root beer. "It was an instant success," recalls Max Clough. "The demand was higher for the root beer than for the beer."

Root beer is a quintessentially American quaff. "It was created in the late 1800s. As brewers, we try to capture the traditional flavors and quality of

old time soda pop. People tell us they haven't tried root beer in 20 years, and tasting ours reminds them of reaching into their grandmother's refrigerator." Root beer floats be-came popular in the 1950s, thanks to the ice cream soda culture of drive-ins.

Clough hopes the world's largest root beer float will win a new gener-ation of root beer drinkers. The float was created as an event to support new construction of parks in downtown Seattle, and combination of parks and pop attracted a large group of children. "They even made up a root beer song and sang it to us," laughs Clough. "We had a good time, even though we had standard Seattle weather conditions: a cold downpour."

Emeritus Heinrich Medicus, Rensselaer Polytechnic Institute, at the Woodbury Vineyards Winery, NY on June 5, 1988.

Champagne fountain The greatest number of stories achieved in a champagne fountain, successfully filled from the top and using traditional long-stem glasses, is 47 (height 25 ft. 9 in.), achieved by Moet et Chandon Champagne with 23,642 glasses at Caesars Palace, Las Vegas, NV, July 19–23, 1993.

Cheese The largest cheese ever created was a cheddar weighing 57,508 lb. 8 oz., made on September 7, 1995 by Loblaws Supermarkets Limited and Agropur Dairies in Granby, Quebec, Canada. It was subsequently taken on tour in a refrigerated truck that had been specially designed for the purpose.

Chocolate model The largest chocolate model weighed 4.4 tons, and was in the shape of a traditional Spanish sailing ship. It was made by Gremi Provincial de Pastisseria, Confiteria i Bolleria school, Barcelona in February 1991 and measured 42 ft. 8 in. by 27 ft. 10½ in. by 8 ft. 2½ in.

Cocktail The largest cocktail on record was a Finlandia Sea Breeze of 2,933 gallons, made at Maui Entertainment Center, Philadelphia, PA on August 5, 1994. It consisted of Finlandia vodka, cranberry juice, grapefruit juice and ice.

Cookie On April 2, 1996, a chocolate chip cookie with an area of 5,241.5 square feet and a diameter of 81 ft. 8 in. was made by Cookie Time, in Christchurch, New Zealand. It contained approximately 2.8 tons of chocolate.

Crepe The largest crepe was 49 ft. 3 in. in diameter and one inch deep, and weighed 6,614 pounds. It was made and flipped in Rochdale, England on August 13, 1994.

Crepe tossing The greatest number of times a crepe has been tossed in two minutes is 349, by Dean Gould in Felixstowe, England on January 14, 1995.

Dish The largest item on any menu in the world is roasted camel, prepared occasionally for Bedouin wedding feasts. Cooked eggs are stuffed into fish, the fish stuffed into cooked chickens, the chickens stuffed into a roasted sheep's carcass and the sheep stuffed into a whole camel.

Doughnut The largest doughnut ever made weighed 3,739 pounds. It was 16 feet in diameter and 16 inches high in the center. The jelly doughnut was made by representatives from Hemstrought's Bakeries, Donato's Bakery and radio station WKLL-FM in Utica, NY on January 21, 1993.

Easter egg The heaviest chocolate Easter egg on record, and also the tallest, weighed 10,482 lb. 14 oz., and was 23 ft. 3 in. high. It was made by the staff of Cadbury Red Tulip at their factory at Ringwood, Victoria, Australia, and completed on April 9, 1992.

Float On May 18, 1996, the Thomas Kemper Soda Company of Seattle, WA concocted a 2,166.5-gallon root beer float. Some 500 people enjoyed the finished product.

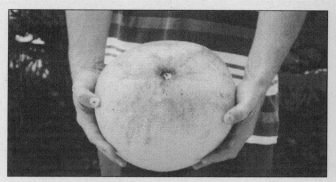

The world's largest grapefruit was grown in Australia in 1995.

Hamburger The largest hamburger on record weighed 5,520 pounds and was 21 feet in diameter. The burger was made at the Outagamie County Fairgrounds, Seymour, WI on August 5, 1989.

Ice-cream bar The world's largest ice-cream bar was a vanilla, chocolate and nut one of 19,357 pounds, made by the staff of Augusto Ltd. in Kalisz, Poland, September 18–29, 1994.

Ice-cream sandwich Interbake Dairy Ingredients made an 830-pound ice-cream sandwich, measuring 3 feet by 8 feet by 1 foot, on June 22, 1995.

Ice-cream sundae The largest ice-cream sundae weighed 54,914 lb. 13 oz., and was made by Palm Dairies Ltd. under the supervision of Mike Rogiani in Edmonton, Alberta, Canada on July 24, 1988. It consisted of 44,689 lb. 8 oz. of ice cream, 9,688 lb. 2 oz. of syrup and 537 lb. 3 oz. of topping.

Jell-O A 9,246-gallon watermelon-flavored pink Jell-O was made by Paul Squires and Geoff Ross at Roma Street Forum, Brisbane, Australia on February 5, 1981, in a tank supplied by Pool Fab.

Jelly bean jar The largest jar of jelly beans was 96 inches high and contained 378,000 jelly beans weighing a total of 2,910 pounds. The Disney Channel sponsored the jar, which was unveiled in October 1992 at Westside Pavilion, Los Angeles, CA.

Lasagne The largest lasagne weighed 8,188 lb. 8 oz. and measured 70 feet by 7 feet. It was made by the Food Bank for Monterey County in Salinas, CA on October 14, 1993.

FLOWERS, FRUITS AND VEGETABLES

World Records

In the interest of fairness and to minimize the risk of mistakes being made, all plants should, where possible, be entered in official international, national or local garden contests. Only produce grown primarily for human consumption will be considered for publication.

Type	Size	Grower/Location	Year
Apple	3 lb. 2 oz.	Miklovic family, Caro, MI	1992
Beetroot	40 lb. 8 oz.	I. Neale, Newport, Wales	1994
Cabbage	124 lb.	B. Lavery, Llanharry, Wales	1989
Cantaloupe	62 lb.	G. Draughtridge, Rocky Mount, NC	1991
Carrot	15 lb. 11½ oz.	B. Lavery, Llanharry, Wales	1996
Celery	46 lb. 1 oz.	B. Lavery, Llanharry, Wales	1990
Chrysanthemum	8 ft. 10 in.	M. Comer, Desford, England	1992
Cucumber	20 lb. 1 oz.	B. Lavery, Llanharry, Wales	1991
Dahlia	25 ft. 7 in.	R. Blythe, Nannup, Western Australia	1990
Garlic	2 lb. 10 oz.	R. Kirkpatrick, Eureka, CA	1985
Grapefruit	6 lb. 12 oz.	D. Hazelton, Queensland, Australia	1995
Grapes	20 lb. 11½ oz.	Bozzolo y Perut Ltda, Santiago, Chile	1984
Green bean	48 in.	Bill Rogerson, Robersonville, NC	1994
Leek (pot)	12 lb. 2 oz.	P. Harrigan, Linton, England	1987
Lemon	8 lb. 8 oz.	C. and D. Knutzen, Whittier, CA	1983
Long gourd	110⅝ in.	Peter Waterman, NY	1994
Okra	19 ft. 9⅞ in.	David Mikulka, FL	1994
Onion	12 lb. 4 oz.	M. Ednie, Anstruther, Scotland	1994

Parsnip	171¾ in.	B. Lavery, Llanharry, Wales ...1990
Petunia	13 ft. 8 in.	B. Lawrence, Windham, NY ...1985
Philodendron	1,114 ft.	F. Francis, University of Massachusetts ...1984
Pineapple	17 lb. 12 oz.	E. Kamuk, Ais Village, WBNP, Papua New Guinea ...1994
Potato	7 lb. 13 oz.	K. Sloane, Patrick, Isle of Man ...1994
Pumpkin	990 lb.	H. Bax, Lyon, Ontario, Canada ...1994
Radish	37 lb. 15 oz.	Litterini family, Tanunda, South Australia ...1992
Rhubarb	5 lb. 14 oz.	E. Stone, East Woodyates, England ...1985
Runner bean	39½ in.	J. Taylor, Shifnal, England ...1986
Rutabaga	62 lb. 3 oz.	N. Craven, Stouffville, Ontario, Canada ...1993
Squash	900 lb. 12 oz.	J. & C. Lyons, Baltimore, Canada ...1994
Strawberry	8.17 oz.	G. Anderson, Folkestone, England ...1983
Sunflower	25 ft. 5½ in.	M. Heijms, Oirschot, Netherlands ...1986
Tomato	7 lb. 12 oz.	G. Graham, Edmond, OK ...1986
Tomato plant	53 ft. 6 in.	G. Graham, Edmond, OK ...1985
Watermelon	262 lb.	B. Carson, Arrington, TN ...1990
Zucchini	64·lb. 8 oz.	B. Lavery, Llanharry, Wales ...1990

FLOWERS, FRUITS AND VEGETABLES

U.S. National Records

Collard	41¼ in. tall	B. Rackley, Rocky Mount, NC	1989
Corn	31 ft. tall	D. Radda, Washington, IA	1946
Dahlia	16 ft. 5 in.	S. & P. Barnes, Chattahoochee, FL	1982
Eggplant	5 lb. 5¼ oz.	J. & I. Charles, Summerville, SC	1984
Bushel gourd	231.5 lb.	Richard Wright, NJ	1992
Kohlrabi	36 lb.	E. Krejci, Mt. Clemens, MI	1979
Lima bean	14 in.	N. McCoy, Hubert, NC	1979
Onion	7½ lb.	N. W. Hope, Tempe, AZ	1984
Peanut	4 in.	E. Adkins, Enfield, NC	1990
Pepper	13½ in.	J. Rutherford, Hatch, NM	1975
Pepper plant	12 ft. 3 in.	F. Melton, Jacksonville, FL	1992
Rutabaga	53.35 lb.	J. & M. Evans, Palmer, AK	1994
Squash	821 lb	L. Stellpflug, Rush, NY	1990
Sweet potato	40¾ lb.	O. Harrison, Kite, GA	1982
Tomato (cherry)	28 ft. 7 in.	C. H. Wilber, Crane Hill, AL	1985
Zucchini	35.6 lb.	D. Schroer, Homer, AK	1992

Liquor *Most expensive* A bottle of 50-year-old Glenfiddich Scotch was sold for a record price of 99,999,999 lire (approximately $71,200) to an anonymous Italian businessman at a charity auction in Milan, Italy.

Loaf The longest loaf on record was a Rosca de Reyes measuring 3,491 ft. 9 in. long, baked at the Hyatt Regency Hotel in Guadalajara, Mexico on January 6, 1991.

The largest pan loaf weighed 3,163 lb. 10 oz. and measured 9 ft. 10 in. by 4 ft. 1 in. by 3 ft. 7 in. It was made by the staff of Sasko in Johannesburg, South Africa on March 18, 1988.

Lollipop A peppermint-flavored lollipop weighing 3,011 pounds was made by the staff of BonBon in Holme Olstrup, Denmark, April 22, 1994.

Meat pie A chicken pie weighing 22,178 pounds and measuring 12 feet in diameter was made by KFC in New York City on October 18, 1995.

Milk shake A chocolate milk shake of 1,955.1 gallons was made by the Nelspruit and District Welfare Society and the Fundraising Five in Nelspruit, South Africa on March 5, 1994.

Noodle making Simon Sang Koon Sung (Singapore) made 8,192 noodle strings from one piece of dough in 59.29 seconds during the Singapore Food Festival on July 31, 1994.

Omelet The largest omelet had an area of 1,383 square feet and contained 160,000 eggs. It was cooked by representatives of Swatch in Yokohama, Japan, March 19, 1994.

Omelet making The greatest number of 2-egg omelets made in 30 minutes is 427, by Howard Helmer in Atlanta, GA on February 2, 1990.

Pastry The longest pastry was a cream puff 3,403 feet long, made by employees of Pidy, in Ypres, Belgium, September 4–5, 1992.

Pie A pecan pie weighing 40,266 pounds and measuring 40 feet in diameter was baked on June 16, 1989 for the Pecan Festival in Okmulgee, OK.

Pizza The largest pizza was 122 ft. 8 in. in diameter with an area of 11,816 square feet. It was made at Norwood Hypermarket, Norwood, South Africa on December 8, 1990.

Popcorn A container measuring 40 feet long, 28 feet wide and 6 ft. 8 in. high was filled with 7,466 cubic feet of popped corn by students from Pittsville Elementary School, Pittsville, WI, with help from local residents, March 22–26, 1996.

Popcorn ball The Boy Scouts of America Gateway Area Council created a 2,377-pound popcorn ball in La Crosse, WI, September 23–27, 1995. The finished ball was 7 ft. 7 in. tall and 23 ft. 5 in. in circumference.

Popsicle A 17,450-pound orange popsicle was made in Millinocket, ME on July 30, 1995 on behalf of the Katahdin Nursing Home.

Rice Krispies treat   The Wood Company created a 1,064-pound Kellogg's Rice Krispies treat in Fort Meade, MD on September 17, 1995.

The largest Rice Krispies treat weighed 1,064 pounds.

Salami   The longest salami was 68 ft. 9 in. long with a circumference of 25 inches, and weighed 1,492 lb. 5 oz. It was made by A/S Svindlands Pølsefabrikk, Flekkefjord, Norway, July 6–16, 1992.

Sausage   The longest continuous sausage was one of 28.77 miles, made by M & M Meat Shops in partnership with J. M. Schneider Inc. in Kitchener, Ontario, Canada on April 28–29, 1995.

Shortcake   A blueberry shortcake measuring 49 ft. 4 in. by 9 ft. was made at the Salem & Hillsborough Railroad, Hillsborough, New Brunswick, Canada on September 19, 1995. The 1,640.85-pound shortcake included 800 pounds of blueberries.

Spice Hottest   The hottest spice is believed to be Red "Savina" Habanero (1994 special), developed by GNS Spices of Walnut, CA. A single dried gram will produce detectable "heat" in 1,272 pounds of bland sauce.

Most expensive   Prices for wild ginseng from the Chan Pak Mountain area of China were reported in 1979 to be as high as $23,000 per ounce in Hong Kong.

Strawberry bowl   The largest bowl of strawberries had a net weight of 5,266 pounds. The strawberries were picked at Joe Moss Farms near Embro, Ontario, Canada and the bowl was filled at the Kitchener-Waterloo Hospital, also in Ontario, on June 29, 1993.

Wine Most expensive   £105,000 ($131,250) was paid for a bottle of 1787 Château Lafite claret engraved with Thomas Jefferson's initials, sold to Christopher Forbes (U.S.) at Christie's, London, England on December 5, 1985.

The first glass of Beaujolais Nouveau 1993 (from Maison Jaffelin) was bought for Fr8,600 ($1,447) by Robert Denby at Pickwick's, a British pub in Beaune, France, on November 18, 1993.

Wine tasting   At a wine tasting staged by WQED on November 22, 1986 in San Francisco, CA, 4,000 tasters consumed 9,360 bottles of wine.

FEASTS AND CELEBRATIONS

Largest banquet   There were 150,000 guests at the renunciation ceremony of Atul Dalpatlal Shah, when he became a monk, in Ahmedabad, India on June 2, 1991.

Indoor   The greatest number of people served indoors at a single sitting was 18,000 municipal leaders at the Palais de l'Industrie, Paris, France, August 18, 1889.

Largest barbecue   The record attendance at a one-day barbecue was 44,158 at Warwick Farm Racecourse, Sydney, Australia on October 10, 1993. The greatest meat consumption at a barbecue was at the Lancaster Sertoma Club's Chicken Bar-B-Que in Lancaster, PA, on May 21, 1994, when 44,010 pounds or 31,500 chicken halves were consumed in eight hours.

Most restaurants visited   Fred E. Magel of Chicago, IL dined out 46,000 times in 60 countries over 50 years as a restaurant grader. He claimed that the restaurant that served the largest helpings was Zehnder's Hotel, Frankenmuth, MI. Magel's favorite dishes were South African rock lobster and mousse of fresh English strawberries.

Largest party   The International Year of the Child children's party in Hyde Park, London, England, May 30–31, 1979 was attended by 160,000 children.

Birthday   The world's biggest birthday party was attended by an estimated 100,000 people in Aberdeen, Scotland on July 24, 1994. It was held to celebrate the 200th birthday of Union Street, the main street in the city.
   The largest birthday party held for someone who actually went to the party was attended by an estimated 35,000 people in Louisville, KY on September 8, 1979, to celebrate the 89th birthday of Col. Harland Sanders, the founder of Kentucky Fried Chicken.

Christmas   The largest Christmas party was thrown by the Boeing Co. in the 65,000-seat Kingdome, Seattle, WA. The party was held in two parts on December 15, 1979, and a total of 103,152 people attended.

Teddy bear picnic   The largest teddy bear picnic ever staged was attended by 33,573 bears and their owners at Dublin Zoo, Republic of Ireland on June 24, 1995.

MARRIAGES

Longest engagement   The longest engagement was between Octavio Guillén and Adriana Martínez. They took the plunge after 67 years in Mexico City in June 1969, when they were 82 years old.

Most marriages   The greatest number of marriages contracted by one person in the monogamous world is 28, by former Baptist minister Glynn "Scotty" Wolfe of Blythe, CA, who first married in 1927.

The greatest number of monogamous marriages by a woman is 22, by Linda Lou Essex of Anderson, IN, who has been married to 15 different men since 1957. Her most recent marriage was in October 1991, but that ended in divorce, like the others.

The record for bigamous marriages is 104, by a man using the name Giovanni Vigliotto, from 1949 to 1981 in 27 states and 14 countries. On March 28, 1983 in Phoenix, AZ, Vigliotto received a sentence of 28 years for fraud and six for bigamy, and was fined $336,000.

Oldest bride and bridegroom   The oldest recorded bridegroom was Harry Stevens, age 103, who married Thelma Lucas, 84, in Beloit, WI on December 3, 1984.

The oldest bride was Minnie Munro, age 102, who married Dudley Reid, 83, in Point Clare, New South Wales, Australia on May 31, 1991.

Youngest married couple   In 1986 an 11-month-old boy was married to a 3-month-old girl in Bangladesh to end a 20-year feud over a disputed farm.

The Olympic Stadium in Seoul was the site of the largest mass wedding.

Longest marriages The longest marriages were both of 86 years. Sir Temulji Bhicaji Nariman and Lady Nariman were married from 1853 until 1940, when Sir Temulji died in Bombay, India. Lazarus Rowe of Greenland, NH and Molly Webber married in 1743. She died in 1829, also after 86 years of marriage.

Golden weddings The most golden weddings in a family is 10. The six sons and four daughters of Joseph and Sophia Gresl of Manitowoc, WI celebrated golden weddings between 1962 and 1988; the six sons and four daughters of George and Eleonora Hopkins of Patrick County, VA celebrated golden weddings between 1961 and 1988; and the five sons and five daughters of Alonzo and Willie Alpharetta Cagle of McLennan County, TX celebrated golden weddings between 1971 and 1993.

Wedding ceremonies The largest mass wedding was one of 35,000 couples officiated over by Sun Myung Moon of the Holy Spirit Association for the Unification of World Christianity in Seoul, South Korea on August 25, 1995. Another 325,000 couples around the world took part through a satellite link.

Most ceremonies Richard and Carole Roble of South Hempstead, NY have married each other 56 times, starting in 1969.

Most expensive The wedding of Mohammed, son of Shaik Rashid Bin Saeed Al Maktoum, to Princess Salama in Dubai in May 1981 lasted seven days and cost $44 million.

Best man In March 1996, Ting Ming Siong (Malaysia) was best man at a wedding for the 1,035th time since September 1975.

SPORTS & GAMES

For a full roundup of records set at the 1996 Summer Olympics, see Extra! Extra! (page 636).

GENERAL RECORDS

Fastest sport The fastest projectile speed in any moving ball game is *c.* 188 MPH, in jai alai. This compares with 170 MPH (electronically timed) for a golf ball driven off a tee.

Youngest record breaker The youngest age at which anybody has broken a nonmechanical world record is 12 yr. 298 days for Gertrude Ederle (U.S.), with 13 min. 19.0 sec. for women's 880-yard freestyle swimming, in Indianapolis, IN on August 17, 1919.

Oldest record breaker Gerhard Weidner (Germany) set a 20-mile walk record on May 25, 1974, at age 41 yr. 71 days, thus becoming the oldest to set an official world record recognized by an international governing body.

Most records broken Between January 24, 1970 and November 1, 1977, Vasiliy Alekseyev (USSR) broke 80 official world records in weightlifting.

Youngest champions Olympic The youngest Olympic champion was a French boy, whose name is not recorded, who coxed the Netherlands' Olympic pair in the rowing competition at Paris, France on August 26, 1900. He was not more than 10 and may have been as young as seven.

The youngest individual Olympic winner was Marjorie Gestring (U.S.), who took the springboard diving title at the age of 13 yr. 268 days at the Olympic Games in Berlin, Germany on August 12, 1936.

Fu Mingxia (China, b. August 16, 1978) won the women's world title for platform diving in Perth, Australia on January 4, 1991, at age 12 yr. 141 days.

Oldest champion Fred Davis (Great Britain; b. February 14, 1913) won the world professional billiards title in 1980, at age 67.

Heaviest sportsman Professional wrestler William J. Cobb of Macon, GA, who in 1962 was billed as "Happy Humphrey," weighed 802 pounds. The heaviest player of any ball game was Bob Pointer, the 487-pound football tackle on the 1967 Santa Barbara, CA High School team.

Longest-reigning champion Jacques Barre (France) was a world champion for 33 years (1829–62) at court tennis.

Largest crowds It is estimated that more than 10 million people see the annual Tour de France cycling race, which is spread over three weeks. The greatest number of live spectators for any 1-day sporting spectacle is the estimated 2.5 million who have lined the route of the New York City Marathon.

Stadium   A crowd of 199,854 attended the Brazil vs. Uruguay World Cup Finals deciding soccer game, in the Maracanã Municipal Stadium, Rio de Janeiro, Brazil on July 16, 1950.

Most participants   On May 15, 1988, an estimated 110,000 (including unregistered athletes) ran in the *Examiner* Bay-to-Breakers 7.6-mile race in San Francisco, CA.

Worst sports disaster   The stands at the Hong Kong Jockey Club racetrack collapsed and caught fire on February 26, 1918, killing an estimated 604 people.

AEROBATICS

World Championships   The former USSR has won the men's team competition a record six times. The most victories in the men's individual championship is two, by Petr Jirmus (Czechoslovakia), 1984 and 1986. In the women's event the record is also two titles, by Betty Stewart (U.S.), 1980 and 1982.

Longest inverted flight   The duration record is 4 hr. 38 min. 10 sec. by Joann Osterud (U.S.) from Vancouver to Vanderhoof, Canada on July 24, 1991.

Most loops   Joann Osterud achieved 208 outside loops in a "Supernova" Hyperbipe over North Bend, OR on July 13, 1989. On August 9, 1986, David Childs performed 2,368 inside loops in a Bellanca Decathlon over North Pole, AK.

AIR RACING

NATIONAL CHAMPIONSHIP AIR RACES

Unlimited class   In this class the aircraft must use piston engines, be propeller-driven and be capable of pulling six g's. The planes race over a 9.128-mile course marked with pylons.

Most titles   Darryl Greenmyer has won seven NCAR titles in the unlimited class, the top level of the sport: 1965–69, 1971 and 1977.

Fastest average speed (race)   Lyle Shelton won the 1991 NCAR title recording the fastest average speed at 481.618 MPH, in his "Rare Bear."

Fastest qualifying speed   The 1-lap NCAR qualifying record is 482.892 MPH, by Lyle Shelton in 1992.

The Tour de France attracts over 10 million spectators each year.

ARCHERY

Olympic Games   Hubert van Innis (Belgium) won six gold and three silver medals at the 1900 and 1920 Olympic Games. The most successful U.S. archer at the Olympic Games is Darrell Pace, gold medalist in 1976 and 1984.

ARCHERY RECORDS

Events	Points	Possible	Name and Country	Year
MEN (SINGLE FITA ROUNDS)				
FITA	1,368	1,440	Kyo-moon Oh (South Korea)	1995
90 m	330	360	Vladimir Yesheyev (USSR)	1990
70 m	344	360	Hiroshi Yamamoto (Japan)	1990
50 m	348	360	Seung-hun Han (South Korea)	1994
30 m	360	360	Seung-hun Han	1994
Team	4,035	4,320	South Korea (Kim Kyeng-ho, Seung-hun Han, Park Kyeng-moo)	1993
WOMEN (SINGLE FITA ROUNDS)				
FITA	1,375	1,440	Cho Youn-jeong (South Korea)	1992
70 m	341*	360	Kim Soo-nyung (South Korea)	1990
	338	360	Cho Youn-jeong	1992
60 m	349	360	He Ying (China)	1995
50 m	340	360	Lim Jung (South Korea)	1994
30 m	357	360	Joanne Edens (Great Britain)	1990
Team	4,094	4,320	South Korea (Kim Soo-nyung, Lee Eun-kyung, Cho Yuon-jeng)	1992

unofficial

INDOOR DOUBLE FITA ROUNDS AT 25 METERS

Men	577	600	Tom Henrikson (Denmark)	1994
Women	556	600	Annette Frederiksen (Sweden)	1994

INDOOR FITA ROUNDS AT 18 METERS

Men	596	600	Magnus Pattersson (Sweden)	1995
Women	590	600	Nalalya Valeyeva (Moldova)	1995

World Championships   The most titles won is seven, by Janina Spychajowa-Kurkowska (Poland) in 1931–34, 1936, 1939 and 1947. The most titles won by a man is four, by Hans Deutgen (Sweden), 1947–50. The U.S. has won a record 14 men's and eight women's team titles.

United States   The most individual world titles by a U.S. archer is three, by Rick McKinney: 1977, 1983 and 1985. Jean Lee is the only U.S. woman to have won two individual world titles (1950, 1952).

U.S. Championships   The U.S. National Championships were first held in Chicago, IL, August 12–14, 1879, and are staged annually. The most U.S. archery titles won is 17, by Lida Howell (née Scott), from 20 contested between 1883 and 1907. The most men's titles is nine, by Rick McKinney, 1977, 1979–83, 1985–87.

The greatest span of title winning is 29 years, by William Henry Thompson, who was the first U.S. champion in 1879, and won his fifth and last men's title in 1908.

Highest score in 24 hours   The highest recorded score over 24 hours by a pair of archers is 76,158, during 70 Portsmouth Rounds (60 arrows per round at 20 yards at 2-foot FITA targets) by Simon Tarplee and David Hathaway in Evesham, England on April 1, 1991. During this attempt Tarplee set an individual record of 38,500.

Greatest draw on a longbow   Gary Sentman of Roseberg, OR drew a longbow weighing a record 176 pounds to the maximum draw on the arrow of 28¼ inches at Forksville, PA on September 20, 1975.

Longest arrow flight   The furthest an arrow has been shot is 2,047 yd. 2 in. by Harry Drake (U.S.), using a crossbow at the Smith Creek Flight Range near Austin, NV on July 30, 1988.

AUTO RACING

Oldest race   The oldest auto race still regularly run is the Royal Automobile Club (RAC) Tourist Trophy, first staged on September 14, 1905 on the Isle of Man, Great Britain.

Oldest winner   The oldest winner of a professionally sanctioned race is Charles F. Grabiak, M.D. (U.S.; b. March 9, 1920), who was 72 years old when he finished first in a nationally sanctioned auto race in 1992 at Watkins Glen, NY.

Fastest circuits   The highest average lap speed attained on any closed circuit is 250.958 MPH, in a trial by Dr. Hans Liebold (Germany), who lapped the 7.85-mile high-speed track at Nardo, Italy in 1 min. 52.67 sec. in a Mercedes-Benz C111-IV on May 5, 1979. It was powered by a V8 engine with two KKK turbochargers, with an output of 500 hp at 6,200 rpm.

Fastest race   The fastest race is the Busch Clash at Daytona, FL over 50 miles on a 31-degree banked track 2½ miles long. In 1987, Bill Elliott (U.S.) averaged 197.802 MPH in a Ford Thunderbird.

500 miles   Al Unser, Jr. (U.S.) set the world record for a 500-mile race when he won the Michigan 500 on August 9, 1990 at an average speed of 189.727 MPH.

NASCAR

Most titles   The NASCAR (National Association for Stock Car Auto Racing, Inc.) championship, now called the Winston Cup Championship, has been won a record seven times by two drivers: Richard Petty (U.S.), in 1964, 1967, 1971–72, 1974–75 and 1979; and Dale Earnhardt (U.S.), in 1980, 1986–87, 1990–91, and 1993–94. Petty won 200 NASCAR Winston Cup races in 1,185 starts from 1958 to 1992, and his best season was 1967, with 27 wins.

Most consecutive titles   Cale Yarborough is the only driver to be a NASCAR champion three times, winning in 1976–78.

Highest earnings   The NASCAR career money record is $27,115,271 to July 24, 1996, by Dale Earnhardt (U.S.). The single-season earnings record is $4,347,343, by Jeff Gordon in 1995.

Dale Earnhardt has earned more money than any other NASCAR driver.

DAYTONA 500

Most titles   The Daytona 500 has been held at the 2½-mile oval Daytona International Speedway in Daytona, FL since 1959. Richard Petty has a record seven wins—1964, 1966, 1971, 1973–74, 1979 and 1981.

Fastest speed   The record average speed for the race is 177.602 MPH, by Buddy Baker in an Oldsmobile in 1980. The qualifying speed record is 210.364 MPH, by Bill Elliott in a Ford Thunderbird in 1987.

INDY CAR

Most wins National Championships   The most successful driver is A. J. Foyt, Jr., who has won 67 races and seven championships (1960–61, 1963–64, 1967, 1975 and 1979). The record for the most victories in a season is 10, shared by two drivers: A. J. Foyt, Jr. (1964) and Al Unser (1970).

Most laps led   Mario Andretti (U.S.) has the most laps led (7,587), 1964–94. He also holds the record for most pole positions, at 67.

Highest career earnings   As of July 1996, Al Unser, Jr. had earned $17,184,656. The single-season earnings record is $2,999,269, by Jacques Villeneuve (Canada) in 1995.

INDIANAPOLIS 500

Most titles   The Indianapolis 500-mile race (200 laps) was inaugurated in the United States on May 30, 1911. Three drivers have four wins: A. J. Foyt, Jr. (U.S.) in 1961, 1964, 1967 and 1977; Al Unser (U.S.) in 1970–71, 1978 and 1987; and Rick Mears (U.S.) in 1979, 1984, 1988 and 1991.

Fastest speed   The record time is 2 hr. 41 min. 18.404 sec. (185.981 MPH) by Arie Luyendyk (Netherlands) driving a Lola-Chevrolet on May 27, 1990. The record average speed for four laps qualifying is 236.986 MPH by Arie Luyendyk in a Reynard-Ford-Cosworth (including a one-lap record of 237.498 MPH) on May 12, 1996.

Most starts   A. J. Foyt, Jr. has started a record 35 races, 1958–92, and Rick Mears has started from pole position a record six times, 1979, 1982, 1986, 1988–89, and 1991.

Highest earnings   The record prize fund is $8,114,600 awarded in 1996. The individual prize record is $1,373,813 by Al Unser, Jr., in 1994. Rick Mears leads in career earnings, with $4,299,392 from 15 starts, 1978–92.

Closest finish   Al Unser, Jr. edged Scott Goodyear by 0.043 seconds in 1992.

FORMULA ONE GRAND PRIX

Most successful drivers   The World Drivers' Championship, inaugurated in 1950, was won five times by Juan-Manuel Fangio (Argentina), in 1951 and 1954–57. He won 24 Grand Prix races (two shared) from 51 starts.

The following records stand for Formula One Grand Prix auto racing: Alain Prost (France) holds the records for both the most points in a career, 798.5, and the most victories, 51 from 199 races, 1980–93. The most victories in a year is nine, by two drivers: Nigel Mansell (Great Britain) in 1992, and Michael Schumacher (Germany) in 1995. The most starts is 256, by Ricardo Patrese (Italy), 1977–93. The greatest number of pole positions is 65, by Ayrton Senna (Brazil) from 161 races (41 wins), 1984–94.

Two U.S. drivers have won the World Drivers' Championship—Phil Hill in 1961, and Mario Andretti in 1978. Andretti has the most Grand Prix wins by a U.S. driver: 12 in 128 races, 1968–82.

Fastest race   The fastest overall average speed for a Grand Prix race on a circuit in current use is 150.759 MPH, by Peter Gethin (Great Britain) in a BRM in Monza in the Italian Grand Prix on September 5, 1971. The qualifying lap record was set by Keke Rosberg (Finland) at 1 min. 05.59 sec., an average speed of 160.817 MPH, in a Williams-Honda at Silverstone in the British Grand Prix on July 20, 1985.

Closest finish   The closest finish to a World Championship race was when Peter Gethin (Great Britain) beat Ronnie Peterson (Sweden) by 0.01 seconds in the Italian Grand Prix in Monza on September 5, 1971. Since 1982, timing has been to thousandths of a second; the closest finish since then was when Ayrton Senna (Brazil) beat Nigel Mansell (Great Britain) by 0.014 seconds in the Spanish Grand Prix in Jerez de la Frontera on April 13, 1986.

LE MANS

Most wins   The most wins by a driver is six, by Jacky Ickx (Belgium), 1969, 1975–77 and 1981–82.

Greatest distance   The greatest distance covered in the 24-hour *Grand Prix d'Endurance* (first held May 26–27, 1923) on the old Sarthe circuit at Le Mans, France is 3,315.203 miles, by Dr. Helmut Marko (Austria) and Gijs van Lennep (Netherlands) in a 4,907-cc flat-12 Porsche 917K Group 5 sports car, June 12–13, 1971.

The record for the greatest distance covered for the current circuit is 3,313.150 miles (average speed 137.047 MPH) by Jan Lammers (Netherlands), Johnny Dumfries and Andy Wallace (both Great Britain) in a Jaguar XJR9 on June 11–12, 1988.

Fastest lap   The race lap record (now 8.411-mile lap) is 3 min. 21.27 sec. (average speed 150.429 MPH) by Alain Ferté (France) in a Jaguar XRJ-9 on June 10, 1989. Hans Stück (West Germany) set the practice lap speed record of 156.377 MPH.

RALLYING

Longest rally   The Singapore Airlines London–Sydney Rally was held over 19,329 miles from Covent Garden, London, England on August 14, 1977 to Sydney Opera House, Australia. It was won on September 28, 1977 by Andrew Cowan, Colin Malkin and Michael Broad in a Mercedes 280E.

Monte Carlo   The Monte Carlo Rally (first run in 1911) has been won four times by Sandro Munari (Italy), in 1972, 1975, 1976 and 1977; and by Walter Röhrl (West Germany) (with co-driver Christian Geistdorfer) in 1980 and 1982–84.

World Championship   The World Drivers' Championships (instituted 1979) have been won four times by Juha Kankkunen (Finland), 1986–87, 1991, 1993. The most wins in a season is six, by Didier Auriol (France) in 1992. The most wins in World Championship races is 21, by Juha Kankkunen. The youngest winner is Colin McRae (Great Britain), who was 27 yr. 89 days old when he won in 1995.

DRAG RACING

Piston-engined The lowest elapsed time recorded by a piston-engined dragster from a standing start for 440 yards is 4.592 seconds, by Blaine Johnson (U.S.) in Topeca, KS on July 7, 1996. The highest terminal velocity at the end of a 440-yard run is 315.67 MPH, by Scott Kalitta (U.S.), in Topeka, KS on July 7, 1996.

In the Funny Car category, John Force (U.S.) had the quickest run at 4.889 seconds on July 7, 1996, in Topeka, KS. A top speed of 311.20 MPH was achieved by Cruz Pedregon (U.S.) in Topeka, KS on July 7, 1996.

For a gasoline-driven piston-engined car, the lowest elapsed time is 6.948 seconds, by Warren Johnson (U.S.) in Baytown, TX on March 10, 1995. On that day, Johnson also set the highest terminal velocity mark of 199.15 MPH.

The lowest elapsed time for a gasoline-driven piston-engined motorcycle is 7.386 seconds, by David Schultz in Gainesville, FL in March 1996. John Myers (U.S.) set the highest terminal velocity mark, at 185.18 MPH in March 1996 in Gainesville, FL.

NHRA titles The National Hot Rod Association (NHRA) World Championship Series was inaugurated in 1951. Since 1975, the series has been called the NHRA Winston Drag Racing Series.

Top Fuel Joe Amato has won a record five national titles: 1984, 1988 and 1990–92.

Funny Car Two drivers have won four national titles: Don Prudhomme, 1975–78, and Kenny Bernstein, 1985–88.

Pro Stock Bob Glidden has won a record 10 national titles, in 1974–75, 1978–80 and 1985–89.

Pro Stock Motorcycle David Schultz has won a record five national titles, 1987–88, 1991 and 1993–94.

BADMINTON

World Championships Individual In this competition, instituted in 1977 and staged biennially, a record five titles have been won by Park Joo-bong (South Korea)—men's doubles, 1985 and 1991, and mixed doubles, 1985, 1989 and 1991.

Three Chinese players have won two individual world titles: (men's) Yang Yang, 1987 and 1989; (women's) Li Ling Wei in 1983 and 1989; Han Aiping in 1985 and 1987.

Team The most wins in the men's World Team Badminton Championship for the Thomas Cup (instituted 1948) is ten, by Indonesia (1958, 1961, 1964, 1970, 1973, 1976, 1979, 1984, 1994 and 1996).

The most wins in the women's World Team Badminton Championship for the Uber Cup (instituted 1956) is five, by Japan (1966, 1969, 1972, 1978 and 1981) and China (1984, 1986, 1988, 1990 and 1992).

United States Championships The annual competition was first held in 1937.

Most titles Judy Hashman won a record 31 U.S. titles: 12 women's singles, 1954, 1956–63, 1965–67; 12 women's doubles, 1953–55, 1957–63, 1966–67 (11 with her sister Susan); and seven mixed doubles, 1956–59, 1961–62, 1967. David Freeman won seven singles titles: 1939–42, 1947–48, 1953.

Longest badminton rally In the men's singles final of the 1987 All-England Championships between Morten Frost (Denmark) and Icuk Sugiarto (Indonesia), there were two successive rallies of over 90 strokes.

Shortest badminton game Ra Kyung-min (South Korea) beat Julia Mann (England) 11–2, 11–1 in six minutes during the 1996 Uber Cup in Hong Kong on May 19, 1996.

BASEBALL

MAJOR LEAGUE

Longest sports strike The longest strike in the history of professional sports was in major league baseball, August 12, 1994–April 4, 1995—a total of 234 days. For the first time in 90 years, the World Series was not held.

Most games played Pete Rose played in a record 3,562 games with a record 14,053 at-bats, for the Cincinnati Reds (NL), 1963–78 and 1984–86, the Philadelphia Phillies (NL), 1979–83, and the Montreal Expos (NL), 1984.

Cal Ripken Jr., of the Baltimore Orioles (AL), had played in 2,243 successive games as of July 15, 1996.

Most home runs Career Hank Aaron holds the major league career record with 755 home runs—733 for the Milwaukee (1954–65) and Atlanta (1966–74) Braves (NL) and 22 for the Milwaukee Brewers (AL) 1975–76. On April 8, 1974 he bettered the previous record of 714 by Babe Ruth (1895–1948). Ruth hit his home runs in 8,399 times at bat, achieving the highest home run percentage of 8.5 percent.

Season The major league record for home runs in a season is 61, by Roger Maris (1934–85) for the New York Yankees (AL) in 162 games in 1961.

The most official home runs in a minor league season is 72, by Joe Bauman of the Roswell Rockets of the Longhorn League in 1954.

Game The most home runs in a major league game is four. The feat has been achieved 12 times.

Consecutive games   The most home runs hit in consecutive games is eight, set by Dale Long for the Pittsburgh Pirates (NL), May 19–28, 1956, and tied by Don Mattingly for the New York Yankees (AL), on July 18, 1987, and by Ken Griffey Jr., Seattle Mariners (AL) on July 28, 1993.

Grand slams   Seven players have hit two grand slams in a single game. They are: Tony Lazzeri (1903–46) for the New York Yankees (AL) on May 24, 1936; Jim Tabor (1916–53) for the Boston Red Sox (AL) on July 4, 1939; Rudy York (1913–70) for the Boston Red Sox (AL) on July 27, 1946; Diamond Jim Gentile for the Baltimore Orioles (AL) on May 9, 1961; Tony Cloninger for the Atlanta Braves (NL) on July 3, 1966; Jim Northrup for the Detroit Tigers (AL) on June 24, 1968; and Frank Robinson for the Baltimore Orioles (AL) on June 26, 1970.

Don Mattingly of the New York Yankees (AL) hit six grand slams in 1987, the most in one season. Lou Gehrig hit 23 grand slams during his 16 seasons with the New York Yankees (AL), 1923–39, the most in one lifetime.

Fastest base runner   The fastest time for circling bases is 13.3 seconds, by Ernest Swanson in Columbus, OH in 1931, at an average speed of 18.45 MPH.

Most career hits   The career record for most hits is 4,256, by Pete Rose. Rose's record hits total came from a record 14,053 at-bats, which gave him a career batting average of .303.

Most consecutive hits   Pinky Higgins had 12 consecutive hits for the Boston Red Sox (AL) in a 4-game span, June 19–21, 1938. This was equaled by Moose Dropo for the Detroit Tigers (AL), July 14–15, 1952.

Joe DiMaggio hit in a record 56 consecutive games for the New York Yankees (AL) in 1941; he went to bat 223 times, with 91 hits, totaling 56 singles, 16 doubles, 4 triples and 15 home runs.

Largest baseball bat   The Baseball Hall of Fame in Cooperstown, NY possesses a baseball bat over 11 feet long. It was turned from a telephone pole by Ernst Anderson of Gardner, MA, and the citizens of Gardner presented the it to Ted Williams of the Boston Red Sox (AL) in 1946.

Home runs and stolen bases   The only player to have hit 40 or more home runs and have 40 stolen bases in a season was Jose Canseco for the Oakland Athletics (AL) in 1988. His totals were 42 and 40 respectively.

Longest home run   The longest measured home run in a major league game was 643 feet, by Mickey Mantle for the New York Yankees vs. Detroit Tigers on September 10, 1960 at Briggs Stadium in Detroit.

Most stolen bases   As of July 17, 1996, Rickey Henderson of the San Diego Padres (NL) had stolen a record 1,173 bases. Henderson also holds the mark for most stolen bases in a season, with 130 in 1982.

Most walks   Babe Ruth holds the record for career walks, 2,056, and the single-season record, 170 in 1923.

Three players share a record six walks for a single game. Walt Wilmot of the Chicago White Stockings (NL; later known as the Chicago Cubs) set

THE CY YOUNG AWARD

At the turn of the 20th century, baseball's dominant player was pitcher Denton True Young, dubbed "The Cyclone." Today, he's known simply as Cy Young. The Hall of Famer still holds baseball's records for most wins (511), most complete games (749), most innings pitched (7,356.2) and most games played (815). In 1956, the Baseball Writers' Association of America established the Cy Young Award to be presented to the season's best pitcher. Here, four winners discuss the award.

Greg Maddux (1992, 1993, 1994, 1995)

In 1995 Maddux won his fourth award, tying Steve Carlton's all-time tally. Maddux is the only pitcher to win four in a row.

GBR: What does winning four straight Cy Young Awards mean to you?

GM: The Cy Young just snuck up on me. It really hasn't sunk in yet. When I'm done playing I think I'll look back on my career and appreciate it.

GBR: As a young pitcher, did you dream of winning the Cy Young?

GM: You don't think about winning it. You just try to pitch and be as good as you can. It's too easy to go out and give up seven runs in one game. That knocks your chances of winning something like the Cy Young.

GBR: What are your remaining goals in baseball?

GM: My goal is to win the World Series again. It's like going to Disneyland and getting on the best ride. As soon as you get off, you want to get on again.

Dwight Gooden (1985)

Gooden is the youngest player ever to win the award, winning in 1985 when he was 20 years old.

GBR: How do you account for winning the award in only your second season?

DG: I didn't really think about the Cy Young until after the All-Star break in 1985. There were a couple of other guys in the race. Fernando Valenzuela was there, John Tudor, too. Those guys had great years. It's definitely an honor I'll never live down.

GBR: Was it your goal to win the Cy Young as such a young pitcher?

DG: No. When you're in the minor leagues, your dream is to get to the majors, and then do what you can to stay in the major leagues.

GBR: Would you rather have a solid 20-win season or win the Cy Young Award?

DG: I would definitely rather have a Cy Young. Because if you get the Cy Young that means you've won at least 20-plus games. It's like getting both ends of the stick with that.

Orel Hershiser (1988)

During his Cy Young year, Hershiser broke Don Drysdale's "unbeatable" consecutive scoreless innings streak record. In addition, he gained World Series MVP honors in leading the Los Angeles Dodgers to the world title.

GBR: How do you compare the Cy Young Award to the innings streak?

OH: They're completely different. The streak happened over a short burst. The Cy Young is a whole season. That's more of a career feat.

GBR: What was the biggest challenge during the record streak?

OH: It was fighting the negative of everybody saying, "It's not going to be done," and just focusing on one batter at a time.

GBR: What did winning the Cy Young mean to you?

OH: It was fun and important, but the best thing about it was that it happened with a championship season with my team. It's fun to win your own award because everybody pats you on the back. But it's another thing to win it as a team when everybody is patting each other on the back.

Jim Palmer (1973, 1975, 1976)

Palmer was the first American League pitcher to win three Cy Young Awards. Roger Clemens is the only other AL pitcher to win three awards.

GBR: What did it mean to you to be the first three-time Cy Young winner in the American League?

JP: It was an affirmation that I had done my work. It was very satisfying. It meant I had committed myself intellectually, spiritually, emotionally and physically to having as good a year as I could.

GBR: Do you agree that pitching is a lost art in baseball?

JP: It has never been more difficult to pitch than it is now, especially in the American League. The new ball parks are smaller, the strike zone has been reduced and the hitters are bigger and more aggressive.

GBR: Does winning the Cy Young make you famous?

JP: It's an interesting phenomenon. When I won the Cy Young I became better known. But once I started doing underwear ads on TV, everyone knew me.

the mark on August 22, 1891, and the record was tied by Jimmie Foxx of the Boston Red Sox (AL) on June 16, 1938 and by Andre Thornton of the Cleveland Indians (AL) on May 2, 1984 in a game that went 18 innings.

Most strikeouts   The batter with the career strikeout record is Reggie Jackson, who struck out 2,597 times in 21 seasons with four teams. The season record is 189, by Bobby Bonds, right fielder for the San Francisco Giants in 1970. The longest run of games without striking out is 115, by Joe Sewell while playing third base for the Cleveland Indians (AL) in 1929.

Most games won by a pitcher   Cy Young had a record 511 wins and a record 749 complete games from a total of 906 games and 815 starts in his career for the Cleveland Spiders (NL) 1890–98, the St. Louis Cardinals (NL) 1899–1900, the Boston Red Sox (AL) 1901–08, the Cleveland Indians (AL) 1909–11 and the Boston Braves (NL) 1911. He pitched a total of 7,356 innings.

The career record for most pitching appearances is 1,070, by Hoyt Wilhelm for a total of nine teams between 1952 and 1972. The season's record is 106 appearances, by Mike Marshall for the Los Angeles Dodgers (NL) in 1974.

Most consecutive games won by a pitcher   New York Giants (NL) pitcher Carl Hubbell won a record 24 consecutive games—16 in 1936 and eight in 1937.

Longest baseball throw   Glen Gorbous (Canada) threw a baseball 445 ft. 10 in. on August 1, 1957.

Most shutouts   Walter Johnson pitched 110 shutouts in his 21-season career with the Washington Senators (AL), 1907–27. Don Drysdale pitched six consecutive shutouts for the Los Angeles Dodgers (NL) between May 14 and June 4, 1968. Orel Hershiser pitched a record 59 consecutive shutout innings for the Los Angeles Dodgers (NL), August 30–September 28, 1988.

Most no-hitters   Nolan Ryan, playing for the Texas Rangers (AL) against the Toronto Blue Jays (AL), pitched his record seventh no-hitter on May 1, 1991. Johnny Vander Meer of the Cincinnati Reds (NL) is the only player to have pitched consecutive no-hitters, June 11–15, 1938.

Most walks   Nolan Ryan holds the record for the greatest number of walks, giving up 2,795, 1966–93.

Perfect game   In a perfect game, the pitcher allows the opposition no hits, no runs and does not allow a man to reach first base. There have been 14 perfect 9-inning games, but no pitcher has achieved this feat more than once.

On May 26, 1959 Harvey Haddix, Jr. for Pittsburgh pitched a perfect 12 innings against Milwaukee in the National League, but lost in the 13th.

Most saves   Bobby Thigpen saved 57 games for the Chicago White Sox (AL) in 1990. The career record is 473 as of July 22, 1996, by Lee Smith in

WORLD SERIES RECORDS

American League (AL), National League (NL)

Most wins	23 .....New York Yankees–AL 1923–96
Most series played	14 ......Yogi Berra (New York Yankees–AL) 1947–63
Most series played by pitcher	11 ......Whitey Ford (New York Yankees–AL) 1950–64

World Series Career Records

Batting average (min. 75 at-bats)	.391 .....Lou Brock (St. Louis Cardinals–NL; 34 hits in 87 at-bats, 3 series) 1964–68
Runs scored	42 ......Mickey Mantle (New York Yankees–AL) 1951–64
Runs batted in (RBIs)	40 ......Mickey Mantle (New York Yankees–AL) 1951–64
Base hits	71 ......Yogi Berra (New York Yankees–AL) 1947–63
Home runs	18 ......Mickey Mantle (New York Yankees–AL) 1951–64
Victories pitching	10 ......Whitey Ford (New York Yankees–AL) 1950–64
Strikeouts	94 ......Whitey Ford (New York Yankees–AL) 1950–64

World Series Single Series Records

Batting average (4 or more games)	.750 .....Billy Hatcher (Cincinnati Reds–NL; 9 hits in 12 at-bats in four-game series) 1990
Runs scored	10 ......Reggie Jackson (New York Yankees–AL) 1977
Runs batted in (RBI's)	12 ......Bobby Richardson (New York Yankees–AL) 1960

Base hits (7-game series)	13 .....Bobby Richardson (New York Yankees–AL)	1960
	13 .....Lou Brock (St. Louis Cardinals–NL)	1968
	13 .....Marty Barrett (Boston Red Sox–AL)	1986
Home runs	5 .....Reggie Jackson (New York Yankees–AL; in 20 at-bats)	1977
Victories pitching	3 .....Christy Mathewson (New York Yankees–AL; in 5-game series)	1905
	3 .....Jack Coombs (Philadelphia A's–AL; in 5-game series)	1910
	Ten other pitchers have won three games in more than five games.	
Strikeouts	35 .....Bob Gibson (St. Louis Cardinals–NL; in 7 games)	1968
	23 .....Sandy Koufax (Los Angeles Dodgers–NL; in 4 games)	1963

World Series Game Records

Home runs	3 .....Babe Ruth (New York Yankees–AL) vs. St. Louis Cardinals	......Oct. 6, 1926
	3 .....Babe Ruth (New York Yankees–AL) vs. St. Louis Cardinals	......Oct. 9, 1928
	3 .....Reggie Jackson (New York Yankees–AL) vs. Los Angeles Dodgers	......Oct. 18, 1977
Runs batted in (RBIs) in a game	6 .....Bobby Richardson (New York Yankees–AL) vs. Pittsburgh Pirates	......Oct. 8, 1960
Strikeouts by pitcher in a game	17 .....Bob Gibson (St. Louis Cardinals–NL) vs. Detroit Tigers	......Oct. 2, 1968
Perfect game (9 innings)	.....Don Larsen (New York Yankees–AL) vs. Brooklyn Dodgers	......Oct. 8, 1956

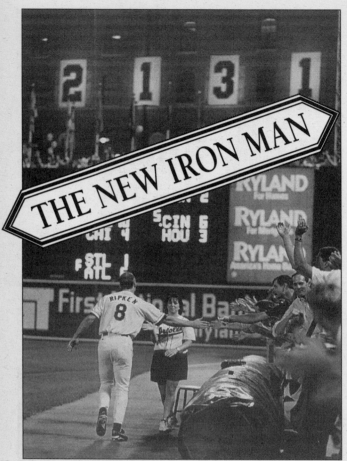

THE NEW IRON MAN

On September 6, 1995, Baltimore Orioles shortstop Cal Ripken, Jr. surpassed one of baseball's legendary records. In playing his 2,131st consecutive game, Ripken bested the total of 2,130 set by the New York Yankees great Lou Gehrig between 1925 and 1939. Ripken's feat was celebrated throughout the baseball world. But, in fact, Ripken still had one more streak to beat. From October 19, 1970 through October 22, 1987, Sachio Kinugasa played 2,215 consecutive games for the Hiroshima Carp of the Japanese Central League. With Kinugasa in attendance, Ripken eclipsed the world record tally on June 14, 1996, in a game against the Kansas

Royals. And the streak goes on. Here Ripken discusses his feelings about the record and the men he bypassed to reach it.

GBR: How did it feel to beat Gehrig's "unbeatable" record?

CR: Last year was a great celebration all the way around. There was no way that we could have expected, or even planned how that whole thing was going to come down. It really came out nice.

GBR: Did you set out to beat Gehrig's record?

CR: I didn't set out to do this. I didn't set out to break Gehrig's record.

GBR: Was beating Kinugasa's record a different experience?

CR: It was almost exactly the same. Afterward, I got the chance to sit and meet with Mr. Kinugasa. We talked and shared philosophies and approaches to baseball. I kind of wish I'd had the opportunity to sit down and talk with Lou Gehrig.

The Most Admired Record

Ripken's streak may hold the record for most-admired record. Here are comments of other record-breakers on the new Iron Man:

"I think Cal Ripken's streak is unbelievable. It's absolutely unbelievable."—*Orel Hershiser, Cleveland Indians pitcher*

"Cal Ripken is the baseball record-holder I most admire."—*Jim Palmer, retired Baltimore Orioles pitcher*

"When I think of what Cal Ripken has done to break Lou Gehrig's record, I just stand back and applaud."—*Don Shula, retired Miami Dolphins head coach*

his 17th season, playing for the Chicago Cubs (NL) 1980–87; the Boston Red Sox (NL) 1988–90; the St. Louis Cardinals (NL) 1990–93; the New York Yankees (AL) 1993; the Baltimore Orioles (AL) 1994; and the California Angels (AL) 1995–96; and the Cincinnati Reds (NL) 1996.

Highest career fielding percentage   Three people share the record for highest career fielding percentage, at .996: Wes Parker, Los Angeles Dodgers (NL), 1964–72; Steve Garvey, Los Angeles Dodgers (NL), 1969–87; and Don Mattingly, New York Yankees (AL), 1982–95.

Youngest player   The youngest major league player was the Cincinnati Reds (NL) pitcher Joe Nuxhall, who played one game on June 10, 1944, at age 15 yr. 314 days. He did not play again in the National League until 1952.

Oldest player   Satchel Paige pitched for the Kansas City A's (AL) at 59 yr. 78 days on September 25, 1965.

Shortest player   The shortest major league player was Eddie Gaedel, who measured 3 ft. 7 in. and weighed 65 pounds. Gaedel pinch-hit for the St. Louis Browns (AL) vs. the Detroit Tigers (AL) on August 19, 1951; wearing number ⅛, the batter with the smallest-ever major league strike zone walked on four pitches.

Tallest player   The tallest major leaguers of all time are two pitchers measuring 6 ft. 10 in.: Randy Johnson, who played in his first game for the Montreal Expos (NL) on September 15, 1988, and Eric Hillman, who debuted for the New York Mets (NL) on May 18, 1992.

Most Valuable Player Award   The most selections in the annual vote (instituted in 1931) of the Baseball Writers' Association for Most Valuable Player of the Year (MVP) in the major leagues is three, won by: *National League*: Stan Musial (St. Louis), 1943, 1946, 1948; Roy Campanella (Brooklyn), 1951, 1953, 1955; Mike Schmidt (Philadelphia), 1980–81, 1986; Barry Bonds (Pittsburgh, San Francisco), 1990, 1992–93; *American League*:

Lee Smith holds the career record for most saves.

TIPS

from the
RECORD BREAKERS

HITTING

Wade Boggs is one of baseball's all-time great hitters. Among his many feats, the New York Yankees third baseman holds the modern era consecutive seasons records for leading the league in intentional walks (6, 1987–92) and 200+ hits (7, 1983–89). Here he offers hitting tips to aspiring ballplayers.

◆

Practice, practice, practice.

"Practice is how you get better." Advises Boggs, "Quality is better than quantity. Take 30 to 45 minutes of good quality batting practice and get a lot out of it. That is better than hitting for three hours until your hands bleed."

◆

Stay with your own style.

"Work on various methods to try and get a good swing. Find your own style and then stick with it," says Boggs. "Don't keep having a new stance every year. You need to form muscle memory. That will help you get better." A "good eye" can be developed: "Learn the strike zone. Know where the ball is when it's released from the hand of the pitcher. And recognize what the ball's going to do."

◆

Eat chicken before every game.

Boggs' pregame rituals are almost as famous as his hitting. He eats chicken before every game: "That's one of the superstitions that's really never changed." He thinks rituals can help any athlete, but he cautions, "If they're consuming your life, then they're a hindrance."

Jimmie Foxx (Philadelphia), 1932–33, 1938; Joe DiMaggio (New York), 1939, 1941, 1947; Yogi Berra (New York), 1951, 1954–55; Mickey Mantle (New York), 1956–57, 1962.

Cy Young Award   The Cy Young Award has been given annually since 1956 to the outstanding pitcher in the major leagues. The most wins is four, by Steve Carlton (Philadelphia Phillies), 1972, 1977, 1980 and 1982, and Greg Maddux (Chicago Cubs, Atlanta Braves, NL), 1992–95. Maddux is the only pitcher to win four times in a row.

Dwight Gooden (b. November 16, 1964) of the New York Mets became the youngest pitcher to win the Cy Young Award in 1985.

Longest game   The longest game was a minor league game in 1981 that lasted 33 innings. At the end of nine innings the score was tied 1–1, with the Rochester (NY) Red Wings battling the home team Pawtucket (RI) Red Sox. After 21 innings it was tied 2–2, and at the end of 32 innings, the score was still 2–2, at which point the game was suspended. Two months later, play was resumed, and 18 minutes later, Pawtucket scored one run and won. The winning pitcher was the Red Sox's Bob Ojeda.

The Chicago White Sox (AL) played the longest major league ballgame in elapsed time, 8 hr. 6 min., beating the Milwaukee Brewers, 7–6, in the 25th inning on May 9, 1984 in Chicago. The game started on Tuesday night and was still tied at 3–3 when the 1 A.M. curfew caused suspension until Wednesday night. The most innings in a major league game were 26, when the Brooklyn Dodgers (NL) and the Boston Braves (NL) played to a 1–1 tie on May 1, 1920.

The New York Yankees (AL) played the longest 9-inning game, 4 hr. 21 min., beating the Baltimore Orioles 13–10 on April 30, 1996.

Shortest game   In the shortest major league game on record, the New York Giants (NL) beat the Philadelphia Phillies (NL), 6–1, in nine innings in 51 minutes on September 28, 1919.

Largest crowd   The all-time season record for attendance for both leagues is 70,257,938 in 1993. The record for an individual league is 36,924,573, for the National League in 1993. The record for an individual team is 4,483,350 for the home games of the Colorado Rockies (NL) at Mile High Stadium, Denver, CO in 1993.

Around the majors   Wayne Zumwalt of Colorado Springs, CO attended a major league baseball game at all 28 major league stadiums in 28 consecutive days, from June 10 to July 7, 1993.

Most successful managers   Connie Mack managed in the major leagues for 53 seasons and achieved 3,731 regular-season victories (and 3,948 losses)—149 wins and 134 losses for the Pittsburgh Pirates (NL) 1894–96, and 3,582 wins and 3,814 losses for the Philadelphia Athletics (AL), 1901–50.

The most successful in the World Series was Casey Stengel, who managed the New York Yankees (AL) to seven wins in 10 World Series, winning in 1949–53, 1956 and 1958, and losing in 1955, 1957 and 1960. Joe McCarthy also led the New York Yankees to seven wins, 1932, 1936–39, 1941, 1943, and his teams lost in 1929 (Chicago) and 1942 (New York). He had the highest win percentage of managers who achieved at least 1,500 regular-season wins, with .615—2,125 wins and 1,333 losses in his 24-year career with the Chicago Cubs (NL) 1926–30, the New York Yankees (AL) 1931–46, and the Boston Red Sox (AL) 1948–50, during which he never had an overall losing season.

WORLD SERIES

Most wins   The most wins in the World Series is 23, by the New York Yankees between 1923 and 1996, during a record 34 Series appearances.

The most wins by a National League team is nine, by the St. Louis Cardinals, 1926, 1931, 1934, 1942, 1944, 1946, 1964, 1967 and 1982.

Most Valuable Player   Sandy Koufax (Los Angeles, NL, 1963, 1965), Bob Gibson (St. Louis, NL, 1964, 1967) and Reggie Jackson (Oakland, AL, 1973; New York, AL, 1977) have won twice.

LEAGUE CHAMPIONSHIP SERIES

Most series played   Reggie Jackson has played in 11 series, with the Oakland Athletics (AL), 1971–75; New York Yankees (AL), 1977–78 and 1980–81; California Angels (AL), 1982, 1986.

Most games played   The record for most games played is 45, by Reggie Jackson. Jackson played for the Oakland Athletics (AL) from 1971–75; the New York Yankees (AL) from 1977–78 and 1980–81; and the California Angels (AL) during the 1982 and 1986 seasons.

Batting average (minimum 50 at-bats)   Playing for the California Angels (AL, 1986) and the Toronto Blue Jays (AL, 1991–93), Devon White had a batting average of .392 during 74 at-bats in 20 games.

Most series pitched   Bob Welch has pitched in eight, with the Los Angeles Dodgers (NL), 1978, 1981, 1983, 1985; and the Oakland Athletics (AL), 1988–90 and 1992.

Most games pitched   The record for most games pitched is 15, shared by Tug McGraw, New York Mets (NL), 1969, 1973, Philadelphia Phillies (NL), 1976–78, 1980; and Dennis Eckersley, Chicago Cubs (NL), 1984, Oakland Athletics (AL), 1988–90, 1992.

COLLEGE BASEBALL

NCAA Division I regular season Hitting records   The most career home runs was 100, by Pete Incaviglia for Oklahoma State in three seasons, 1983–85. The most career hits was 418, by Phil Stephenson for Wichita State in four seasons, 1979–82.

Pitching records   Don Heinkel won 51 games for Wichita State in four seasons, 1979–82. John Powell struck out 602 batters for Auburn University in five seasons, 1990–94.

College World Series   The first College World Series was played in 1947 in Kalamazoo, MI. Since 1950, the College World Series has been played annually at Rosenblatt Stadium in Omaha, NE.

MAJOR LEAGUE RECORDS

American League (AL)
National League (NL)

Career Batting Records

Batting average	.367	Ty Cobb (Detroit–AL, Philadelphia–AL) 1905–28
Runs scored	2,245	Ty Cobb 1905–28
Runs batted in (RBIs)	2,297	Hank Aaron (Milwaukee, Atlanta–NL, Milwaukee–AL) 1954–76
Base hits	4,256	Pete Rose (Cincinnati–NL, Philadelphia–NL, Montreal–NL) 1963–86
Total bases	6,856	Hank Aaron (Milwaukee, Atlanta–NL, Milwaukee–AL) 1954–76

Season Batting Records

Batting average	.438	Hugh Duffy (Boston–NL; 236 hits in 539 at-bats) 1894
1900–present	.424	Rogers Hornsby (St. Louis–NL; 227 hits in 536 at-bats) 1924
Runs scored	196	Billy Hamilton (Philadelphia–NL; in 131 games) 1894
1900–present	177	Babe Ruth (New York–AL; in 152 games) 1921
Runs batted in (RBIs)	190	Hack Wilson (Chicago–NL; in 155 games) 1930
Base hits	257	George Sisler (St. Louis–AL; 631 times at bat, 143 games) 1920
Singles	202	"Willie" Keeler (Baltimore–NL; in 128 games) 1898
1900–present	198	Lloyd Waner (Pittsburgh–NL; in 150 games) 1927
Doubles	67	Earl Webb (Boston–AL; in 151 games) 1931
Triples	36	Owen Wilson (Pittsburgh–NL; in 152 games) 1912
Total bases	457	Babe Ruth (New York–AL); 85 singles, 44 doubles, 16 triples, 59 home runs 1921

Single-Game Batting Records

Runs batted in (RBIs) 12   Jim Bottomley (St Louis–NL) vs. Brooklyn ......Sep. 16, 1924

                     12   Mark Whiten (St Louis–NL) vs. Cincinnati ......Sep. 7, 1993

Base hits 9   Johnny Burnett (Cleveland–AL; in 18 innings) ......Jul. 10, 1932

Total bases 18   Joe Adcock (Milwaukee–AL); 1 double, 4 home runs ......Jul. 31, 1954

Career Pitching Records

Games won 511   Cy Young (in 906 games; Cleveland,
St Louis, Boston–NL and Cleveland, Boston–AL) 1890–1911

Shutouts 110   Walter Johnson (Washington–AL; in 802 games) 1907–27

Strikeouts 5,714   Nolan Ryan (New York–NL, California–AL, Houston–NL, Texas–AL) 1968–93

Season Pitching Records

Games won 60   "Old Hoss" Radbourn (Providence–NL; and 12 losses) 1884

   1900–present 41   Jack Chesbro (New York–AL) 1904

Shutouts 16   George Bradley (St Louis–NL; in 64 games) 1876

   1900–present 16   Grover Alexander (Philadelphia–NL; 48 games) 1916

Strikeouts 513   Matt Kilroy (Baltimore–AL) 1886

   1900–present 383   Nolan Ryan (California–AL) 1973

Single-Game Pitching Records

Strikeouts (9 innings) 20   Roger Clemens (Boston–AL) vs. Seattle ......Apr. 29, 1986

Strikeouts in extra innings 21   Tom Cheney (Washington–AL) vs. Baltimore (16 innings) ......Sep. 12, 1962

Most championships The most wins in Division I is 11, by the University of Southern California (USC) in 1948, 1958, 1961, 1963, 1968, 1970–74 and 1978.

Most home runs The most career home runs in the College World Series is five, by J.D. Drew (Florida State University) in 1995–96.

Most hits Keith Moreland of the University of Texas holds the record for most career hits in the College World Series, with 23 in three series, 1973–75.

Most wins The record for most career wins in the College World Series is four, shared by nine pitchers: Bruce Gardner (University of Southern California), 1958, 1960; Steve Arlin (Ohio State), 1965–66; Bert Hooten (University of Texas at Austin), 1969–70; Steve Rogers (University of Tulsa), 1969, 1971; Russ McQueen (University of Southern California), 1972–73; Mark Bull (University of Southern California), 1973–74; Greg Swindell (University of Texas), 1984–85; Kevin Sheary (University of Miami of Florida), 1984–85; Greg Brummett (Wichita State), 1988–89.

Most strikeouts Carl Thomas of the University of Arizona struck out 64 batters in three College World Series, 1954–56.

BASKETBALL

Highest score In a senior international match, Iraq scored 251 points against Yemen (33) in New Delhi, India, in November 1982 at the Asian Games.

Most points Mats Wermelin, 13 years old, scored all 272 points in a 272–0 win in a regional boys' basketball tournament in Stockholm, Sweden, February 5, 1974.

The record score by a woman is 156 points by Marie Boyd (later Eichler) of Central High School, Lonaconing, MD in a 163–3 defeat of Ursaline Academy, Cumbria on February 25, 1924.

Largest attendance A crowd of 80,000 attended the final of the European Cup Winners' Cup between AEK Athens (89) and Slavia Prague (82) at the Olympic stadium, Athens, Greece on April 4, 1968.

Dribbling Jamie Borges (U.S.) dribbled a basketball without "traveling" a distance of 85.25 miles in 24 hours at Middletown High School, Middletown, RI on September 7–8, 1995.

Longest goal Christopher Eddy scored a field goal measured at 90 ft. 2¼ in. for Fairview High School vs. Iroquois High School in Erie, PA on February 25, 1989. The shot was made as time expired in overtime and it won the game for Fairview, 51–50.

Nikki Fierstos scored a field goal of approximately 79 feet, the longest by a woman, on January 2, 1993 at Huntington North High School, Huntington, IN.

Shooting skills The greatest goal-shooting demonstration was by Thomas Amberry (U.S.), who scored 2,750 consecutive free throws in Seal Beach, CA in November 1993. On June 11, 1992, Jeff Liles scored 231 out of 240 attempts in 10 minutes at Southern Nazarene University, Bethany, OK. He repeated this total of 231 (241 attempts) on June 16. This speed record is achieved using one ball and one rebounder.

In one minute, from seven scoring positions, Jeff Liles scored 25 out of 29 attempts in Bethany, OK on September 18, 1994.

In 24 hours, Fred Newman scored 20,371 free throws from a total of 22,049 taken (92.39 percent) at Caltech, Pasadena, CA, September 29–30, 1990.

Steve Bontrager (U.S.) of the British team Polycell Kingston scored 21 points in one minute from seven positions in a demonstration on October 29, 1986.

Highest vertical dunk Joey Johnson of San Pedro, CA successfully dunked a basketball at a rim height of 11 ft. 7 in. at the One-on-One Collegiate Challenge on June 25, 1990 at Trump Plaza Hotel and Casino in Atlantic City, NJ.

Most valuable basket Don Calhoun, a spectator at a Chicago Bulls home game on April 14, 1993, sank a basket from the opposite foul line—a distance of 75 feet—and won $1 million. He was randomly picked from the crowd to try his luck as part of a promotional stunt.

NATIONAL BASKETBALL ASSOCIATION

Most championships The Boston Celtics have won a record 16 NBA titles—1957, 1959–66, 1968–69, 1974, 1976, 1981, 1984 and 1986.

Highest attendance In the 1995–96 season, the NBA had a record regular-season attendance of 20,513,218.

Most games played Robert Parish played in a record 1,568 NBA regular-season games over 20 seasons, totaling 45,298 minutes played, for the Golden State Warriors, 1976–80; Boston Celtics, 1981–94; and Charlotte Hornets, 1994–96.

The most successive games played is 906, by Randy Smith for the Buffalo Braves, the San Diego Clippers, the Cleveland Cavaliers and the New York Knicks, from February 18, 1972 to March 13, 1983.

The record for most complete games played in one season is 79, by Wilt Chamberlain for Philadelphia in 1962, when he was on court for a record 3,882 minutes. Chamberlain went through his entire career of 1,045 games without fouling out. Moses Malone played his 1,212th consecutive game without fouling out to the end of the 1994/95 season. In his career, Malone has played 1,329 games, fouling out on only five occasions.

Most minutes played The career record for minutes played in the NBA is 57,446 by Kareem Abdul-Jabbar, Milwaukee Bucks, 1969–75, and Los Angeles Lakers, 1975–89. The season record is 3,882 minutes, by Wilt Cham-

NBA RECORDS

Career Records

Points	38,387	Kareem Abdul-Jabbar: Milwaukee Bucks, Los Angeles Lakers 1970–89
Field-goal percentage	599	Artis Gilmore: Chicago Bulls, San Antonio Spurs, Boston Celtics; min. 2,000 field goals. 1977–88
Free throws made	8,531	Moses Malone: Buffalo Braves, Houston Rockets, Philadelphia 76ers, Washington Bullets, Atlanta Hawks, Milwaukee Bucks, San Antonio Spurs 1976–95
Free-throw percentage	906	Mark Price: Cleveland Cavaliers, Washington Bullets. 1986–96
Field goals	15,837	Kareem Abdul-Jabbar 1970–89
3-point field goals	1,269	Dale Ellis: Dallas Mavericks, Seattle SuperSonics, Milwaukee Bucks, San Antonio Spurs, Denver Nuggets 1983–96
Rebounds	23,924	Wilt Chamberlain: Philadelphia / San Francisco Warriors, Philadelphia 76ers, Los Angeles Lakers 1960–73
Steals	2,310	Maurice Cheeks: Philadelphia 76ers, San Antonio Spurs, New York Knicks, Atlanta Hawks, New Jersey Nets 1979–93
Assists	11,310	John Stockton: Utah Jazz 1984–96

Season Records

Points	4,029	Wilt Chamberlain: Philadelphia Warriors 1962
Field-goal percentage	727	Wilt Chamberlain: Los Angeles Lakers; 426 of 586 attempts 1972
Free throws made	840	Jerry West: Los Angeles Lakers; from 977 attempts 1966
Free-throw percentage	958	Calvin Murphy: Houston Rockets; 206 of 215 attempts 1981
Field goals	1,597	Wilt Chamberlain: Philadelphia Warriors 1962
3-point field goals	267	Dennis Scott: Orlando Magic. 1995–96
Rebounds	2,149	Wilt Chamberlain: Philadelphia Warriors 1961
Assists	1,164	John Stockton: Utah Jazz 1991
Steals	301	Alvin Robertson: San Antonio Spurs 1986

Single-Game Records

Points	100	Wilt Chamberlain: Philadelphia Warriors vs. New York Knicks ....Mar. 2, 1962
Field goals	36	Wilt Chamberlain ....Mar. 2, 1962
3-point field goals	11	Dennis Scott: Orlando Magic vs. Atlanta Hawks. ....Apr. 18, 1996
Free throws made	28	Wilt Chamberlain ....Mar. 2, 1962
	28	Adrian Dantley: Utah Jazz vs. Houston Rockets ....Jan. 5, 1984

Rebounds 55   Wilt Chamberlain: Philadelphia Warriors vs. Boston Celtics ....Nov. 24, 1960
Assists 30   Scott Skiles: Orlando Magic vs. Denver Nuggets ....Dec. 30, 1990
Steals 11   Larry Kenon: San Antonio Spurs vs. Kansas City Kings ....Dec. 26, 1976

NBA PLAYOFF RECORDS

Career Records

Most games played 237   Kareem Abdul-Jabbar: Milwaukee Bucks, Los Angeles Lakers 1970–89
Points 5,762   Kareem Abdul-Jabbar (in 237 playoff games) 1970–89
Field goals 2,356   Kareem Abdul-Jabbar 1970–89
Free throws made 1,213   Jerry West: Los Angeles Lakers; from 1,507 attempts 1961–74
Assists 2,168   Magic Johnson: Los Angeles Lakers 1980–91, 1996
Rebounds 4,104   Bill Russell: Boston Celtics 1957–69

Series Records

Points 284   Elgin Baylor: Los Angeles Lakers (vs. Boston Celtics); in 7 games 1962
Field goals 113   Wilt Chamberlain: San Francisco (vs. St. Louis); in 6 games 1964
Free throws made 86   Jerry West: Los Angeles Lakers (vs. Baltimore); in 6 games 1965
Rebounds 220   Wilt Chamberlain: Philadelphia 76ers (vs. Boston Celtics); in 7 games 1965
Assists 115   John Stockton: Utah Jazz (vs. Los Angeles Lakers); in 7 games 1988

Single-Game Records

Points 63   Michael Jordan: Chicago Bulls (vs. Boston Celtics); includes two overtime periods ....Apr. 20, 1986
Field goals 61   Elgin Baylor: Los Angeles Lakers (vs. Boston Celtics) ....Apr. 14, 1962
....24   Wilt Chamberlain: Philadelphia 76ers vs. Syracuse Nationals; in 42 attempts ....Mar. 14, 1960
....24   John Havlicek: Boston Celtics vs. Atlanta Hawks; in 36 attempts ....Apr. 1, 1973
....24   Michael Jordan: Chicago Bulls (vs. Cleveland Cavaliers); in 45 attempts ....May 1, 1988
Free throws made 30   Bob Cousy: Boston Celtics (vs. Syracuse Nationals); includes four overtime periods and 32 attempts ....Mar. 21, 1953
....23   Michael Jordan: Chicago Bulls (vs. New York Knicks); in 28 attempts ....May 14, 1989
Rebounds 41   Wilt Chamberlain: Philadelphia 76ers (vs. Boston Celtics) ....Apr. 5, 1967
Assists 24   Magic Johnson: Los Angeles Lakers (vs. Phoenix Suns) ....May 15, 1984
....24   John Stockton: Utah Jazz (vs. Los Angeles Lakers) ....May 17, 1988

Bullish on NBA Wins

*I*t wasn't a piece of cake, but the 1995–96 NBA season did feature many happy returns for the Chicago Bulls. The campaign started with Michael Jordan's return for his first full NBA season since his retirement in 1993. The season ended with the return of the NBA championship after a two-year hiatus. In between, the Bulls netted several NBA records, including the most wins in a season, 72.

*T*he record-breaking trend was set early in the season. The Bulls won their first four home games to set a franchise mark for most consecutive home wins to start the season. In January the Bulls won all 14 games they played, the first time the franchise went unbeaten for a month. In February the NBA records began to tumble. On February 1, a defeat of the Sacramento Kings raised the Bulls' win–loss tally to 40 and 3, setting a new NBA record for most wins with only three losses. The record was extended to 41–3, before a defeat in Denver foiled the Bulls. At the end of February the Bulls had raised their record to 50 and 6, a new league mark for fewest losses in compiling 50 victories.

A defeat of the New York Knicks on March 21 saw another NBA record. It was the Bulls' 41st consecutive home victory, besting the Orlando

Magic mark of 40. This record was extended to 44 games before the Charlotte Hornets snapped the streak on April 8.

*T*he Bulls' great season became a historic one on April 14 when they beat the Cleveland Cavaliers. It was the team's 69th win and it tied the all-time NBA record for most wins in a season, set by the 1971–72 Los Angeles Lakers.

*T*he Bulls took possession of the single-season wins record on April 16 when they defeated the Milwaukee Bucks. At season's end the Bulls' win–loss record was 72-10, the best finish ever in the NBA.

*I*n the playoffs the Bulls continued their dominance of the league, winning 15 games against three losses. Two of those losses were to the Seattle Supersonics in the NBA Finals. The Bulls won the NBA championship 4 games to 2. Michael Jordan was named MVP of both the regular season and the playoffs—a very happy return indeed.

berlain for the Philadelphia Warriors, 1961–62. The single-game record is 69 minutes, by Dale Ellis for the Seattle SuperSonics vs. Milwaukee Bucks on November 9, 1989 in a 5-overtime game.

Highest scoring average   The highest scoring average during the regular season for players exceeding 10,000 points is 32.0 points per game, by Michael Jordan, who scored 24,489 points in 766 games for the Chicago Bulls, 1984–93, 1994–96. The season record is 50.4 per game, set by Wilt Chamberlain, Philadelphia Warriors, 1961–62.

Playoffs   The highest scoring average record for the playoffs is held by Michael Jordan, at 33.9 points per game. He scored 4,717 points in 139 games, 1984–93, 1994–96.

Most assists   John Stockton (Utah Jazz) made 11,310 assists, 1984–96.

Most blocked shots   The record for most blocked shots in an NBA game is 17, by Elmore Smith for Los Angeles vs. Portland in Los Angeles on October 28, 1973. The season record is 456, by Mark Eaton, Utah Jazz during the 1984–85 season. The career mark is held by Hakeem Olajuwon, at 3,190 with the Houston Rockets, 1984–96.

Most ejections   The career record for ejections (for a player) is 127, by Vern Mikkelsen, Minneapolis Lakers, 1950–59. The season mark is 26, by Don Meineke, Fort Wayne Pistons, 1952–53.

Most personal fouls   Kareem Abdul-Jabbar had 4,657 personal fouls called on him in his career. The single-season record is 386, by Darryl Dawkins, New Jersey Nets, 1983–84. The NBA record for most fouls in a game is eight, committed by Don Otten, Tri-Cities vs. Sheboygan on November 24, 1949.

Most Valuable Player   Kareem Abdul-Jabbar was elected the NBA's Most Valuable Player a record six times, 1971–72, 1974, 1976–77 and 1980.

Youngest and oldest players   The youngest NBA player was Bill Willoughby, who made his debut for the Atlanta Hawks on October 23, 1975 at 18 yr. 156 days. The oldest NBA regular player was Kareem Abdul-Jabbar, who made his last appearance for the Los Angeles Lakers at age 42 yr. 59 days in 1989.

Tallest player   The tallest player in NBA history is Gheorghe Muresan (Romania) of the Washington Bullets, at 7 ft. 7 in. He made his pro debut in 1994.

Highest score   The highest aggregate score in an NBA game is 370, when the Detroit Pistons (186) beat the Denver Nuggets (184) in Denver, CO on December 13, 1983. Overtime was played after a 145–145 tie in regulation time. The record in regulation time is 320, when the Golden State Warriors beat Denver 162–158 in Denver on November 2, 1990. The most points in a half is 107, by the Phoenix Suns in the first half vs. the Denver Nuggets on November 11, 1990. The most points in a quarter is 58, in the fourth quarter, by Buffalo vs. Boston on October 20, 1972.

Greatest winning margin The greatest winning margin in an NBA game is 68 points, by which the Cleveland Cavaliers, 148, beat the Miami Heat, 80, on December 17, 1991.

Longest winning streak The Los Angeles Lakers won a record 33 NBA games in succession from November 5, 1971 to January 7, 1972, as during the 1971/72 season they won a record 69 games with 13 losses. The most wins in a season is 72, by the Chicago Bulls in 1995/96.

Most successful coaches The most successful coach in NBA history is Lenny Wilkens, with a career coaching record of 1,014–850 through the 1995/96 season. Wilkens coached for the Seattle SuperSonics (1969–72, 1977–85), the Portland Trail Blazers (1974–76), the Cleveland Cavaliers (1986–93), and the Atlanta Hawks (1994–96).

Pat Riley has the highest winning percentage, with a .702 average (798 wins, 339 losses) coaching the Los Angeles Lakers (1981–90), the New York Knicks (1991–95), and the Miami Heat (1996).

The most games coached is 1,886, by Bill Fitch: Cleveland Cavaliers, 1970–79; Boston Celtics, 1979–83; Houston Rockets, 1983–88; New Jersey Nets, 1989–92; and Los Angeles Clippers, 1994–96. Fitch's career totals are 891 wins and 995 losses.

Playoffs Pat Riley has won a record 137 playoff games, 102 with the Los Angeles Lakers (1981–90) and 35 with the New York Knicks (1992–95), to set the NBA all-time mark.

NCAA RECORDS

Most wins In this competition, first held in 1939, the most Division I titles is 11, by the University of California at Los Angeles (UCLA), 1964–65, 1967–73, 1975, and 1995.

The UCLA Bruins have won a record 11 NCAA titles.

Most Valuable Player   The only player to have been voted the Most Valuable Player in the NCAA final three times has been Lew Alcindor of UCLA in 1967–69. He subsequently changed his name to Kareem Abdul-Jabbar.

Highest score   The NCAA aggregate record is 399, when Troy State (258) beat De Vry Institute, Atlanta (141) in Troy, AL on January 12, 1992. Troy's total was also the highest individual team score in a game.

Most points scored   The most points scored in an NCAA game is 113, by Clarence "Bevo" Francis, Rio Grande (Div. II), vs. Hillsdale on February 2, 1954. Pete Maravich, Louisiana State (Div. I) holds the season record. He scored 1,381 points in 1970 (522 field goals and 337 free throws). The career scoring record is 4,045 points, held by Travis Grant, Kentucky State (Div. II), 1969–72.

Most goals   The single-game field goal record is 41, by Frank Selvy, Furman (Div. I) vs. Newberry on February 13, 1954. The season record is 539, by Travis Grant, Kentucky State in 1972. Grant also holds the career mark, 1,760.

Most assists   The most assists in a game is 26, by Robert James, Kean (Div. III) vs. New Jersey Tech on March 11, 1989. The season mark is 406, by Mark Wade, UNLV (Div. I) in 1987. The career record is 1,076, by Bobby Hurley, Duke (Div. I), 1990–93.

Consecutive records (Division I) Individual   The record for scoring 10 or more points in consecutive games is 115, by Lionel Simmons for La Salle, 1987–90. The consecutive 50-plus points tally is three games, by Pete Maravich, Louisiana State, February 10–15, 1969. The longest field goal streak is 25, by Ray Voelkel, American, over nine games, November 24–December 16, 1978. The single-game mark is 16 field goals, by Doug Grayson, Kent vs. North Carolina on December 6, 1967. The most consecutive 3-point shots made is 15, by Todd Leslie, Northwestern, over four games, December 15–28, 1990.

Team   UCLA set the NCAA mark for consecutive victories (including the playoffs) at 88 games. The streak started on January 30, 1971 and ended on January 19, 1974, when the Bruins were defeated by Notre Dame, 71–70.

Most successful coaches   The coach with the most victories in NCAA Division I competition is Adolph Rupp at Kentucky, with 876 wins (and 190 losses), 1931–72. The highest winning percentage for a Division I coach is .837, by Jerry Tarkanian, Long Beach State, 1969–73; UNLV, 1974–92, with 625 wins, 122 losses. John Wooden coached UCLA to 10 NCAA titles.

Longest coaching career   In his 48-year career Phog Allen coached four teams: Baker, 1906–08; Kansas, 1908–09, 1920–56; Haskell, 1909; and Central Missouri State, 1913–19.

NCAA MEN'S DIVISION I RECORDS

Career Records

Points	3,667	Pete Maravich: Louisiana State	1968–70
Field goals	1,387	Pete Maravich: Louisiana State	1968–70
Best percentage	.690	Ricky Need: Appalachian State	1991–94
3-point field goals	.401	Doug Day: Radford	1990–93
Free throws	.905	Dickie Hemric: Wake Forest	1952–55
Rebounds	2,201	Tom Gola: La Salle	1952–55
Assists	1,076	Bobby Hurley: Duke	1990–93
Blocked shots	.453	Alonzo Mourning: Georgetown	1989–92
Steals	.376	Eric Murdock: Providence	1988–91

Season Records

Points	1,381	Pete Maravich: Louisiana State	1970
Field goals	.522	Pete Maravich: Louisiana State (from 1,168 attempts)	1970
Best percentage	.746	Steve Johnson: Oregon State	1981
3-point field goals	.158	Darrin Fitzgerald: Butler (in 362 attempts)	1987
Free throws	.355	Frank Selvy: Furman (in 444 attempts)	1954
Best percentage	.959	Craig Collins: Penn State	1985
Rebounds	.734	Walt Dukes: Seton Hall (in 33 games)	1953
Assists	.406	Mark Wade: Nevada–Las Vegas	1987
Blocked shots	.207	David Robinson: Navy (in 35 games)	1986
Steals	.150	Mookie Blaylock: Oklahoma	1988

Game Records

Points	100	Frank Selvy: Furman (vs. Newberry)	Feb. 13, 1954
Field goals	41	Frank Selvy: Furman	Feb. 13, 1954
3-point field goals	14	Dave Jamerson: Ohio (vs. Charleston)	Dec. 21, 1989
	14	Askia Jones: Kansas State (vs. Fresno State)	Mar. 24, 1994
Free throws	30	Pete Maravich: Louisiana State (vs. Oregon State)	Dec. 22, 1969
Rebounds	51	Bill Chambers: William and Mary (vs. Virginia)	Feb. 14, 1953
Assists	22	Tony Fairly: Baptist (vs. Armstrong State)	Feb. 9, 1987
	22	Avery Johnson: Southern–B.R. (vs. Texas Southern)	Jan. 25, 1988
	22	Sherman Douglas: Syracuse (vs. Providence)	Jan. 28, 1989
Blocked shots	14	David Robinson: Navy (vs. North Carolina–Wilmington)	Jan. 4, 1986
	14	Shawn Bradley: BYU (vs. Eastern Kentucky)	Dec. 7, 1990
Steals	13	Mookie Blaylock: Oklahoma (vs. Centenary)	Dec. 12, 1987
	13	Mookie Blaylock: Oklahoma (vs. Loyola Marymount)	Dec. 17, 1988

WOMEN'S BASKETBALL

Women's championships   In this competition, first held in 1982, the record for most Division I titles is four, by Tennessee, 1987, 1989, 1991 and 1996. The regular-season game aggregate record is 261, when St. Joseph's (Indiana) beat North Kentucky 131–130 on February 27, 1988.

Sheryl Swoopes has scored 16 field goals in championship games.

Most successful coaches   Jody Conradt of the University of Texas has won the most games in Women's NCAA Division I competition, with 675 victories through the 1995/96 season.

The coach was the highest winning percentage is Leon Barmore of

Louisiana Tech, who compiled a .863 average (397 wins, 63 losses), 1985–96.

Most points Pearl Moore scored 4,061 points in her college career: 177 points in eight games for Anderson Junior College, Anderson, SC, and 3,884 points for Francis Marion College, Florence, SC, 1975–79. Francis Marion was a member of the Association of Intercollegiate Athletics for Women (AIWA) during Moore's career.

Perfect season Two teams have completed Division I seasons without losing: the University of Texas in 1986 (34–0) and the University of Connecticut in 1995 (35–0).

UCONN'S DREAM SEASON: 35–0

During the University of Connecticut women's 1994–95 undefeated season, not only did they claim the record for the most victories of any Division I team, men or women, in an undefeated season (35–0), but they shattered many women's team records in Division I as well. The following are records UCONN set as a team in 1995.

Assists

786

Blocked shots

250

Scoring margin

33.2 average points (between Connecticut and opponent): their average number of points scored was 89.5 and the average number of points scored against them as 56.3

Field goals made

1,184 field goals made out of 2,334 attempts

Field-goal percentage defense

.315 (of all the field goals attempted, only 31.5 percent made it past the UCONN defense and into the basket)

Won–lost percentage

Tied with Texas at 1,000 (Texas had 34 victories in their undefeated season)

Most victories in a season

35, tied with Texas, 1982, Louisiana Tech, 1962, Tennessee, 1989

Rebecca Lobo of UCONN.

NCAA WOMEN'S DIVISION I RECORDS

Most points   The career points leader in NCAA Division I competition is Patricia Hoskins of Mississippi Valley State, with 3,122 points (1985–89). The season record is 974 points, by Cindy Brown, Long Beach State in 1987. Brown also holds the single-game mark; she scored 60 points vs. San Jose State on February 16, 1987.

Most assists   The most helpful player in NCAA history is Suzie Mc-Connell, Penn State. She holds the career mark, at 1,307, 1984–88, and the single-season mark, with 355 assists in 1987. Michelle Burden, Kent, has the most assists in a game, 23, vs. Ball State on February 6, 1991.

Most rebounds   Drake's Wanda Ford holds career and season bests, at 1,887 and 534 rebounds respectively. Her career spanned 1983–86, and she set the season mark in 1985. The outstanding single-game record is 40 re-

NCAA WOMEN'S DIVISION I CHAMPIONSHIP GAME RECORDS

Team Records

Most championships	4	Tennessee 1987, 1989, 1991, 1996
Points	97	Texas (vs. USC) 1986
Field goals	40	Texas (vs. USC) 1986
Best percentage	.588	Texas (vs. USC; 40–68) 1986
3-point field goals	11	Stanford (vs. Auburn) 1990
Rebounds	57	Old Dominion (vs. Georgia) ... 1985
Assists (since 1985)	22	Texas (vs. USC) 1986
Blocked shots (since 1988)	7	Tennessee (vs. Auburn) 1989
Steals (since 1988)	12	Louisiana Tech (vs. Auburn) ... 1988
	12	Louisiana Tech (vs. North Carolina) ... 1994

Individual Records

Points	47	Sheryl Swoopes: Texas Tech (vs. Ohio State) ... 1993
Field goals	16	Sheryl Swoopes: Texas Tech (vs. Ohio State) ... 1993
Best percentage	.889	Jennifer White: Louisiana Tech (vs. USC; 8–9) ... 1983
3-point field goals (since 1988)	6	Katy Steding: Stanford (vs. Auburn) ... 1990
Rebounds	23	Charlotte Smith: North Carolina (vs. Louisiana Tech) ... 1994
Assists (since 1985)	10	Kamie Ethridge: Texas (vs. USC) ... 1986
	10	Melissa McCray: Tennessee (vs. Auburn) ... 1989
Blocked shots (since 1988)	5	Sheila Frost: Tennessee (vs. Auburn) ... 1989
Steals (since 1988)	6	Erica Westbrooks: Louisiana Tech (vs. Auburn) ... 1988

bounds, by Deborah Temple, Delta State vs. Alabama-Birmingham, February 14, 1983.

Most field goals   The all-time leader for field goals is Joyce Walker, Louisiana State, with 1,259, 1981–84. The season mark was set by Clemson's Barbara Kennedy in 1982, when she hit 392 goals. The single-game record is 27, by Lorri Bauman, Drake vs. Southwest Missouri State, January 6, 1984.

Highest scores   The highest-scoring game was Virginia's defeat of North Carolina State, 123–120, for an aggregate of 243 points. Played on January 12, 1991, the game went to three overtimes.

The most points scored by a team in one game is 149, by Long Beach State, in their defeat of San Jose State (69 points) on February 16, 1987.

OTHER RECORDS

Olympic Games   Six men and two women have won two Olympic gold medals: Bob Kurland in 1948 and 1952; Bill Houghland in 1952 and 1956; Michael Jordan, Patrick Ewing, and Chris Mullin, all in 1984 and 1992; Burdette Eliele Haldorson in 1956 and 1960; Anne Theresa Donovan and Theresa Edwards, both in 1984 and 1988.

Most titles Olympic   The United States has won 10 men's Olympic titles. From the time the sport was introduced to the Games in 1936 until 1972, the U.S. won 63 consecutive matches in the Olympic Games, until it lost 51–50 to the USSR in the disputed final match in Munich, Germany.

The women's title has been won a record three times by the USSR, in 1976, 1980 and 1992 (by the Unified team from the republics of the former USSR). The U.S. team won the title in 1984 and 1988.

World   The USSR has won the most titles in both the men's World Championships (instituted 1950) with three (1967, 1974 and 1982) and women's (instituted 1953), with six (1959, 1964, 1967, 1971, 1975 and 1983). Both Yugoslavia and the U.S. have also won three men's world titles: Yugoslavia in 1970, 1978 and 1990, and the U.S. in 1954, 1986, and 1994.

BIATHLON

Most titles Olympic   The most individual titles is two, by Magnar Solberg (Norway), in 1968 and 1972; and Franz-Peter Rötsch (East Germany) in both 10 km and 20 km in 1988. The USSR won six 4 × 7.5-km relays, 1968–88. Aleksandr Tikhonov, who was a member of the first four teams, also won a silver in the 1968 20 km.

World   Frank Ullrich (East Germany) has won a record six individual world titles—four in 10 km, 1978–81, including the 1980 Olympics, and two in 20 km, 1982–83. Aleksandr Tikhonov was on 10 winning Soviet relay teams, 1968–80, and won four individual titles. The Biathlon World Cup was won four times by Frank Ullrich, 1978 and 1980–82; and by Franz-Peter Rötsch (East Germany), 1984–85 and 1987–88.

Women The most individual titles is three, by Anne-Elinor Elvebakk (Norway), 10 km 1988, 7.5 km 1989–90. Kaya Parve (USSR) has won six titles, two individual and four relay, 1984–86, 1988. A women's biathlon was included in the 1992 Olympics. Myriam Bédard (Canada) is the only double Olympic champion. She won the 7.5 km and 15 km events in 1994.

United States National Championships In this competition, first held in 1965 in Rosendale, NY, men's events have been staged annually. Women's events were first included in 1982.

Most titles Lyle Nelson has won seven titles: five in the 10 km, 1976, 1979, 1981, 1985, 1987; and two in the 20 km, 1977, 1985. Anna Sonnerup holds the women's record with five titles: three in the 7.5 km, 1986–87, 1989; and two in the 15 km, 1989, 1991.

Myriam Bédard is the only double Olympic biathlon winner.

BOBSLED AND LUGE

BOBSLEDDING

Oldest sled run   The oldest sled run is the Cresta Run, which was constructed in St. Moritz, Switzerland in 1902.

Oldest sledder   The oldest person to travel the whole length of the Cresta Run is Robin Todhunter (Great Britain), who completed the course at age 83 yr. 239 days in February 1987.

Most titles   The Olympic 4-man bob title (instituted 1924) has been won five times by Switzerland (1924, 1936, 1956, 1972 and 1988).

The Olympic 2-man bob title (instituted 1932) has been won four times by Switzerland (1948, 1980, 1992 and 1994).

The most gold medals won by an individual is three, by Meinhard Nehmer (East Germany) and by Bernhard Germeshausen (East Germany) in the 1976 2-man, 1976 and 1980 4-man events.

The most medals won is seven (one gold, five silver, one bronze) by Bogdan Musiol (East Germany), 1980–92.

World and Olympic   The world 4-man bob title (instituted 1924) has been won 20 times by Switzerland (1924, 1936, 1939, 1947, 1954–57, 1971–73, 1975, 1982–83, 1986–90, 1993), including its five Olympic victories. Switzerland won the 2-man title 17 times (1935, 1947–50, 1953, 1955, 1977–80 and 1982–83, 1987, 1990, 1992 and 1994), including four Olympic successes.

Eugenio Monti was on 11 world championship crews, eight 2-man and three 4-man, in 1957–68.

United States   Two American bobsledders have won two gold medals: Billy Fiske and Clifford Grey in 1928 and 1932.

Oldest gold medalist   The oldest age at which a gold medal has been won in any Winter Olympic sport is 49 yr. 7 days, for James Jay O'Brien (U.S.) in 4-man bob in 1932.

LUGEING

Most titles   The most successful rider in the World Championships was Thomas Köhler (East Germany), who won the single-seater title in 1962, 1964 (Olympic), 1967, and shared the 2-seater title in 1965, 1967, 1968 (Olympic). Georg Hackl (GDR/Germany) has won four single-seater titles, 1989, 1990, 1992 (Olympic), 1994 (Olympic). Margit Schumann (East Germany) won five women's titles, 1973–75, 1976 (Olympic), 1977.

United States National Championships Most titles   Frank Masley has won a record six men's championships, 1979, 1981–83 and 1987–88. Bonny Warner, 1983–84, 1987–88 and 1990, and Cammy Miller, 1985, 1989, and 1991–93, have each won a record five women's titles.

Fastest lugeing speed The fastest recorded photo-timed speed is 85.38 MPH, by Asle Strand (Norway) in Tandådalens Linbana, Sälen, Sweden on May 1, 1982.

BOWLING

Highest bowling score—24 hours A team of six scored 242,665 at Dover Bowl, Dover, DE, March 18–19, 1995. During this attempt, a member of the team, Richard Ranshaw, set an individual record of 51,064.

Largest bowling center The Fukuyama Bowl, Osaka, Japan has 144 lanes. The Tokyo World Lanes Center, Japan, now closed, had 252 lanes.

Consecutive strikes, spares and splits The record for most consecutive strikes is 40, by Jeanne Maiden. Mabel Henry had 30 consecutive spares in the 1986/87 season. Shirley Tophigh rolled 14 consecutive splits in 1968/69.

World Championships The World *(Fédération Internationale des Quilleurs)* Championships were instituted for men in 1954 and for women in 1963.

The highest pinfall in the individual men's event is 5,963 (in 28 games) by Ed Luther (U.S.) in Milwaukee, WI on August 28, 1971.

For the current schedule of 24 games the men's record is 5,261, by Rick Steelsmith (U.S.), and the women's record is 4,894, by Sandra Jo Shiery (U.S.), both in Helsinki, Finland in June 1987.

The World Cup (instituted 1965) is contested annually by the national champions of each member of FIQ. The most wins is three, by Paeng Nepomuceno (Philippines), 1976, 1980 and 1992.

Highest scores The highest individual score for three sanctioned games (out of a possible 900) is 899, by Thomas Jordan (U.S.) in Union, NJ on March 7, 1989 and Ron Prettyman in Newark DE on February 10, 1996. Jordan followed his 3-game mark with a 299, setting a 4-game series record of 1,198 pins.

The record by a woman is 865, by Anne Marie Duggan (U.S.) in Edmond, OK on July 18, 1993.

Youngest 300 bowler Scott Owsley of Fontana, CA scored 300 at age 10 yr. 9 mo. 6 days on March 26, 1994. The youngest girl to roll a 300 game is Nicole Long of Columbia, MO, at age 12 yr. 5 mo. on May 27, 1995.

Oldest 300 bowler Jerry Whelman of Port St. Lucie, FL scored 300 in April 1992 at age 81. The oldest woman to score 300 is Evelyn Culbert at Echo Lanes, Austin, MN in April 1993, at age 66.

PROFESSIONAL BOWLERS ASSOCIATION (PBA)

Most titles Earl Anthony (U.S.) has won a lifetime total of 41 PBA titles. The record number of titles won in one PBA season is eight, by Mark Roth of Lake Heights, NJ, in 1978.

Consecutive titles   Only three bowlers have ever won three consecutive professional tournaments—Dick Weber (three times), in 1959, 1960 and 1961; Johnny Petraglia in 1971; and Mark Roth in 1977.

Perfect games   A total of 210 perfect (300-pin) games were bowled in PBA tournaments in 1993, the most ever for one year.

Walter Ray Williams Jr. bowled four perfect games in one tournament, in Mechanicsburg, PA in 1993. Kelly Coffman rolled eight perfect games on the 1994 tour.

U.S. Open   The most wins in this tournament is four, by two bowlers: Don Carter in 1953–54 and 1957–58, and Dick Weber in 1962–63 and 1965–66.

PBA National Championship   The most wins in this tournament is six, by Earl Anthony in 1973–75 and 1981–83.

Firestone Tournament of Champions   The most wins is three, by Mike Durbin in 1972, 1982 and 1984.

Highest earners   Pete Weber had won a record $1,746,040 in PBA competitions through June 25, 1996.

Mike Aulby of Indianapolis, IN holds the single-season earnings mark of $298,237, reached in 1989.

LADIES PROFESSIONAL BOWLERS TOUR (LPBT)

Most titles   Lisa Wagner has won 30 tournaments, 1980–96. Patty Costello won a season high seven tournaments in 1976.

Highest earnings   Aleta Sill has won a career record $764,512 in prize money through July 23, 1996. She also had the season high record in 1994, with $126,325 in earnings.

AMERICAN BOWLING CONGRESS (ABC)

Highest scores   The highest individual score for three games is 899, by Thomas Jordan in Union, NJ on March 7, 1989 and Ron Prettyman in Newark DE on February 10, 1996 (see BOWLING: HIGHEST SCORES). The highest 3-game team score is 3,868, by Hurst Bowling Supplies of Luzerne, PA on February 23, 1994.

The highest season average attained in sanctioned competition is 247.9, by Jeff Phipps of Salem, OR in the 1992/93 season. The all-time ABC-sanctioned 2-man single-game record is 600, held jointly by the teams of John Cotta (300) and Steve Larson (300) on May 1, 1981, at the Manteca, CA Bowling Association Tournament; Jeff Mraz and Dave Roney of Canton, OH on November 8, 1987 in the Ann Doubles Classic in Canton, OH; William Gruner and Dave Conway of Oceanside, CA on February 27, 1990; Scott Williams and Willie Hammar of Utica, MI on January 7, 1990; and Darrell Guertin and George Tignor of Rutland, VT on February 20, 1993; Ken Mayo and Mike Mayo of Peoria, IL on January 22, 1995; Keith Nusbaum and Dale Ellis of Toledo, OH on February 5, 1995; Ryan Boyd and Clayton Hicks of Miami, FL on July 27, 1995; Duke Matties and Dave Frascatore of Albany, NY on November 27, 1995.

Perfect scores   Mike Whalin of Cincinnati, OH has bowled 52 sanctioned 300 games.

Two perfect games were rolled back-to-back twice by three bowlers: Al Spotts of West Reading, PA, on March 14, 1982 and again on February 1, 1985; Gerry Wright of Idaho Falls, ID, on January 9, 1992 and again on February 26, 1992; and Steve Gehringer of Reading, PA on October 3, 1991 and again on February 7, 1992.

WOMEN'S INTERNATIONAL BOWLING CONGRESS (WIBC)

Highest scores   Elizabeth Johnson of Niagara Falls, NY had a record 234 single-season average in the 1993/94 season. Patty Ann of Appleton, WI had a record 5-year composite average of 227 through the 1985/86 season. The highest 5-woman team score for a 3-game series is 3,536, by Contour Power Grips on August 29, 1994.

Perfect games   Jeanne Nacarrato (née Maiden) of Tacoma, WA has rolled 21 perfect games to set the WIBC career record. She also set a record of 40 consecutive strikes in 1986 and rolled an 864 on games of 300–300–264.

BOXING

Most knockdowns in a title fight   Vic Toweel (South Africa) knocked down Danny O'Sullivan of London, England 14 times in 10 rounds in their world bantamweight fight in Johannesburg, South Africa on December 2, 1950, before the latter retired.

Longest fight   The longest recorded world title fight with gloves was between Andy Bowen of New Orleans and Jack Burke in New Orleans, LA, April 6–7, 1893. It lasted 110 rounds, 7 hr. 19 min. (9:15 P.M.–4:34 A.M.), and was declared a no-contest (later changed to a draw).

Most fights without loss   Pedro Carrasco (Spain) won 83 consecutive fights from April 22, 1964 to September 3, 1970, drew once and had a further nine wins, for an undefeated streak of 93 fights (1 draw).

Most knockouts   The greatest number of finishes classed as "knockouts" in a career (1936–63) is 145 (129 in professional bouts), by Archie Moore (born Archibald Lee Wright; U.S.).

Highest attendance   The greatest paid attendance at any boxing match is 132,274 for four world title fights at the Aztec Stadium, Mexico City on February 20, 1993, headed by the successful WBC light-welterweight defense by Julio César Chávez (Mexico) over Greg Haugen (U.S.).

The indoor record is 63,350, at the Muhammad Ali vs. Leon Spinks fight in the Superdome, New Orleans, LA on September 15, 1978.

The highest nonpaying attendance is 135,132, at the Tony Zale vs. Billy Pryor fight at Juneau Park, Milwaukee, WI on August 16, 1941.

George Foreman

"I was 37 years old. I was scared," says George Foreman. The heavyweight boxer wasn't concerned for his health, but for the youth center he had founded in Houston, Texas. Financial resources were dwindling but Foreman was reluctant to ask for money to help save the center: "It sounded like I was begging," he recalls.

Foreman decided to take matters into his own hands, literally. "I'm going to be heavyweight champion again," he announced in 1987. Critics were amused, but seven years later he made good on his word. On November 5, 1994 he knocked out Michael Moorer to regain the title. At 45 years 287 days, Foreman was the oldest man ever to win the heavyweight crown.

Foreman returned to the ring with a plan. "The second time around I made certain that I wouldn't start out on top. I wanted to start at the bottom and go to the top." Explains Foreman: "I saw Joe Louis and Joe Frazier. They didn't want to restart at the bottom and work their way up. They said 'Been there, done that,' but if you restart at the top you only go down."

The "top" in boxing is the world heavyweight championship. Foreman had first won the title in 1973, when he defeated Joe Frazier in Jamaica. He had also reached the boxing summit of the amateur ranks, winning the 1968 Olympic title. An explosive puncher, Foreman was pegged for a long reign as champion. But that didn't happen. He defended his title only twice. In 1974 he fought Muhammed Ali in their famous "Rumble in the Jungle" bout in Kinshasa, Zaire. In a stunning upset, Ali knocked out Foreman.

Ironically, Ali had been Foreman's inspiration: "The first knowledge I had of boxing was Ali fighting Sonny Liston [in 1964]. Ali didn't smoke or drink. All my friends were leaning towards smoking and drinking, but I said no because of Ali." "The Greatest" was also part of Foreman's historic comeback victory over Moorer: Foreman wore the same boxing trunks in both fights.

Despite two unsuccessful attempts to win back the title in 1991 and 1993, and despite being ridiculed by sports writers and late-night comedians, Foreman stayed with his plan. "It doesn't matter what people say about you. Look in the mirror and never put yourself down." And above all, he says, "Give yourself time and anything can be accomplished."

Lowest attendance The smallest attendance at a world heavyweight title fight was 2,434, at the Cassius Clay vs. Sonny Liston fight in Lewiston, ME on May 25, 1965. Clay changed his name to Muhammad Ali after the bout.

WORLD HEAVYWEIGHT

Longest-reigning heavyweight champion Joe Louis (U.S.) was champion for 11 yr. 252 days, from June 22, 1937, when he knocked out James Joseph Braddock in the eighth round in Chicago, IL, until announcing his retirement on March 1, 1949. During his reign Louis made a record 25 defenses of his title.

Shortest-reigning heavyweight champion Tony Tucker (U.S.) was IBF champion for 64 days, May 30–August 2, 1987, the shortest duration of a title won and lost in the ring.

Most recaptures Muhammad Ali (b. Cassius Clay) is the only man to have regained the heavyweight championship twice. Ali first won the title on February 25, 1964, defeating Sonny Liston. He defeated George Foreman on October 30, 1974, after having been stripped of the title by the world boxing authorities on April 28, 1967. He won the WBA title from Leon Spinks on September 15, 1978, having previously lost to him on February 15, 1978.

Undefeated Rocky Marciano (U.S.) is the only world champion in any weight to have won every fight of his entire professional career from March 17, 1947 to September 21, 1955 (he announced his retirement on April 27, 1956); 43 of his 49 fights were by knockouts or stoppages.

Lightest heavyweight champion Robert James "Bob" Fitzsimmons of Great Britain weighed 165 pounds when he won the title by knocking out James J. Corbett in Carson City, NV on March 17, 1897.

Heaviest heavyweight champion Primo Carnera (Italy), the "Ambling Alp," who won the title from Jack Sharkey in New York City on June 29, 1933, scaled 260½ pounds for this fight, but he reached his peak weight, 270 pounds, on March 1, 1934. He had an expanded chest measurement of 54 inches and the longest reach at 85½ inches (fingertip to fingertip).

Oldest heavyweight champion George Foreman (U.S.; b. January 22, 1949) was 45 yr. 287 days old when he knocked out Michael Moorer (U.S.) in Las Vegas, NV on November 5, 1994 for the WBA/IBF heavyweight title.

Youngest heavyweight champion Mike Tyson (U.S.) was 20 yr. 144 days when he beat Trevor Berbick (U.S.) to win the WBC version in Las Vegas, NV on November 22, 1986. He added the WBA title when he beat James "Bone-crusher" Smith on March 7, 1987 at 20 yr. 249 days. He became undisputed champion on August 2, 1987 when he beat Tony Tucker (U.S.) for the IBF title.

Greatest weight difference When Primo Carnera (Italy), 270 pounds, fought Tommy Loughran (U.S.), 184 pounds, for the world heavyweight title in Miami, FL on March 1, 1934, there was a weight difference of 86 pounds between the two fighters. Carnera won the fight on points.

WORLD CHAMPIONS ANY WEIGHT

Longest reign   Joe Louis' heavyweight duration record of 11 yr. 252 days stands for all divisions.

Shortest reign   Tony Canzoneri (U.S.) was world light-welterweight champion for 33 days, May 21 to June 23, 1933, the shortest period for a boxer to have won and lost the world title in the ring.

Youngest world champion   Wilfred Benitez of Puerto Rico was 17 yr. 176 days old when he won the WBA light-welterweight title in San Juan, Puerto Rico on March 6, 1976.

Oldest world champion   Archie Moore, who was recognized as a light-heavyweight champion up to February 10, 1962 when his title was removed, was then believed to be between 45 and 48 years old.

Longest fight   The longest world title fight (under Queensberry Rules) was that between the lightweights Joe Gans (U.S.) and "Battling" Nelson, the "Durable Dane," in Goldfield, NV on September 3, 1906. It was terminated in the 42nd round when Gans was declared the winner on a foul.

Most recaptures   The only boxer to win a world title five times at one weight is Sugar Ray Robinson (U.S.; b. Walker Smith, Jr.), who beat Carmen Basilio (U.S.) in Chicago, IL on March 25, 1958 to regain the world middleweight title for the fourth time.

Most title bouts   The record number of title bouts in a career is 37, of which 18 ended in "no decision," by 3-time world welterweight champion Jack Britton (U.S.) in 1915–22. The record for most contests without a "no decision" is 29, including a record 28 wins by Julio César Chávez (Mexico), 1984–94.

Greatest "tonnage"   The highest aggregate weight recorded in any fight is 699 pounds, when Claude "Humphrey" McBride (Oklahoma), 339½ pounds, knocked out Jimmy Black (Houston, TX), 359½ pounds, in the third round in Oklahoma City, OK on June 1, 1971.

AMATEUR

Olympic titles   Only two boxers have won three Olympic gold medals: southpaw László Papp (Hungary), middleweight winner 1948, light-middleweight winner 1952 and 1956; and Teófilo Stevenson (Cuba), heavyweight winner 1972, 1976 and 1980.

The only man to win two titles in one Olympic celebration was Oliver L. Kirk (U.S.), who won both bantam and featherweight titles in St. Louis, MO in 1904, but he needed only one bout in each class.

Youngest   The youngest Olympic boxing champion was Jackie Fields (born Finkelstein; U.S.), who won the 1924 featherweight title at age 16 yr. 162 days. The minimum age for Olympic boxing competitors is now 17.

Oldest gold medalist   Richard Gunn (Great Britain) won the Olympic featherweight gold medal on October 27, 1908 in London, England at age 37 yr. 254 days.

World Championships   A record of five world titles (instituted 1974) have been won by Félix Savon (Cuba), heavyweight winner 1986, 1989, 1991, and 91 kg 1993 and 1995.

BUNGEE JUMPING

Longest bungee cord   Gregory Riffi used an 820-foot-long bungee cord when he jumped from a helicopter above the Loire Valley, France in February 1992. The cord stretched to 2,000 feet during the jump.

CANOEING

Most titles Olympics   Gert Fredriksson (Sweden) won a record six Olympic gold medals, 1948–60. He added a silver and a bronze, for a record eight medals.

The most by a woman is four, by Birgit Schmidt (née Fischer; Germany, formerly GDR), 1980–92. The most gold medals won at one Games is three, by Vladimir Parfenovich (USSR), 1980, and Ian Ferguson (New Zealand), 1984.

World   Including the Olympic Games, a record 24 titles have been won by Birgit Schmidt, 1979–93. The men's record is 13, by Gert Fredriksson, 1948–60; Rüdiger Helm (East Germany), 1976–83; and Ivan Patzaichin (Romania), 1968–84.

United States   The only American canoeist to have won two Olympic gold medals is Greg Barton, who won in K1 and K2 1,000 m events in 1988. He also has a U.S. record three medals, as he took bronze in K1 1,000 m in 1984.

Most U.S. titles   Marcia Smoke won 35 U.S. national titles between 1962 and 1981. The men's record is 33 U.S. titles, by Ernest Riedel between 1930 and 1948, mostly in kayak events.

Fastest speed   The German 4-man kayak Olympic champions in 1992 in Barcelona, Spain covered 1,000 m in 2 min. 52.17 sec. in a heat on August 4. This represents an average speed of 12.98 MPH. At the 1988 Olympics in Seoul, South Korea, the Norwegian four achieved a 250 m split of 42.08 seconds between 500 m and 750 m for a speed of 13.29 MPH.

Longest journey Father and son Dana and Donald Starkell paddled from Winnipeg, Manitoba, Canada by ocean and river to Belem, Brazil, a distance of 12,181 miles, from June 1, 1980 to May 1, 1982. All portages were human-powered. Without portages or aid of any kind, the longest journey is one of 6,102 miles, by Richard H. Grant and Ernest "Moose" Lassy, circumnavigating the eastern United States via Chicago, New Orleans, Miami, New York City and the Great Lakes, September 22, 1930 to August 15, 1931.

24 hours Zdzislaw Szubski paddled 157.1 miles in a Jaguar K1 canoe on the Vistula River, Wockawek to Gdansk, Poland, September 11–12, 1987.

Flat water Marinda Hartzenberg (South Africa) paddled, without benefit of current, 137.13 miles on Loch Logan, Bloemfontein, South Africa, December 31, 1990–January 1, 1991.

Open sea Randy Fine (U.S.) paddled 120.6 miles along the Florida coast, June 26–27, 1986.

Greatest lifetime distance Fritz Lindner of Berlin, Germany totaled 64,278 miles of canoeing from 1928 to 1987.

Eskimo rolls Ray Hudspith achieved 1,000 rolls in 34 min. 43 sec. at the Elswick Pool, Newcastle-upon-Tyne, England on March 20, 1987. He completed 100 rolls in 3 min. 7.25 sec. at Killingworth Leisure Centre, Tyne & Wear, England on March 3, 1991.
  Randy Fine (U.S.) completed 1,796 continuous rolls at Biscayne Bay, Miami, FL on June 8, 1991.

Hand rolls Colin Brian Hill achieved 1,000 rolls in 31 min. 55.62 sec. in Consett, England on March 12, 1987. He also achieved 100 rolls in 2 min. 39.2 sec. in London, England on February 22, 1987. He completed 3,700 continuous rolls at Durham City Swimming Baths, Durham, England on May 1, 1989.

Canoe raft A raft of 582 kayaks and canoes, organized by Cleveland Metroparks, was held together by hands only for 30 seconds while free floating on Hinckley Lake, Cleveland, OH on May 21, 1995.

Longest race The Canadian Government Centennial Voyageur Canoe Pageant and Race from Rocky Mountain House, Alberta to the Expo 67 site in Montreal, Quebec was 3,283 miles. Ten canoes represented Canadian provinces and territories. The winner of the race, which lasted from May 24 to September 4, 1967, was the Province of Manitoba canoe Radisson.

Fastest Rhine crossing The fastest time to paddle the length of the River Rhine is 10 days 12 hr. 9 min. by Frank Palmer (Great Britain), May 15–25, 1988. The supported team record is 7 days 23 hr. 31 sec. by the RAF Laarbruch Canoe Club, led by Andy Goodsell (Great Britain), May 17–24, 1989.

CRICKET

TEST CRICKET

Career records   The most runs scored by an individual is 11,174, by Allan Border (Australia) in 156 Tests, 1978–94. The most wickets taken by a bowler is 434, by Kapil Dev (India) in 131 Tests, 1978–94. The most dismissals by a wicket-keeper is 355, by Rodney Marsh (Australia), in 96 Tests, 1970–84. The most catches by a fielder is 156, by Allan Border in 156 Tests, 1978–94.

The best all-around Test career record is that of Kapil Dev, with 5,248 runs, 434 wickets and 64 catches in 131 matches, 1978–94.

ONE-DAY CRICKET

World Cup   The West Indies are the only double winners, in 1975 and 1979.

International Team   The highest innings scored by a team is 398–5 by Sri Lanka vs. Kenya in a World Cup match in Kandy, Sri Lanka on March 6, 1996. The lowest completed innings total is 43 by Pakistan vs. the West Indies in Cape Town, South Africa on February 25, 1993. The largest victory margin is 232 runs by Australia vs. Sri Lanka (323–2 to 91), in Adelaide, Australia on January 28, 1985.

Individual   The highest individual score is 189 not out by Viv Richards for the West Indies vs. England in Manchester, England on May 31, 1984. The best bowling analysis is 7–37 by Aqib Javed for Pakistan vs. India in Sharjah, UAE on October 25, 1991. The best partnership is 263 by Aamir Sohail (134) and Inzamam-ul-Haq (137 not out) for Pakistan vs. New Zealand in Sharjah on April 20, 1994.

Career   The most matches played is 273 by Allan Border (Australia), 1979–94. The most runs scored is 8,648 (av. 41.37) by Desmond Haynes (West Indies) in 238 matches, 1977–94; . The most wickets taken is 285 (av. 22.51) by Wasim Akram (Pakistan) in 198 matches, 1985–96. The most dismissals is 209 (177 catches, 32 stumpings) by Ian Healy (Australia) in 146 matches, 1988–96. The most catches by a fielder is 127 by Border.

WOMEN'S CRICKET

World Cup   Australia has won three times, in 1978, 1982 and 1988. The highest individual score is 143 not out by Lindsay Reeler for Australia vs. Netherlands in Perth, Australia on November 29, 1988. The most wickets taken is 39, by Lyn Fullston (Australia).

Most appearances   The greatest number of international appearances is 83 (15 Tests, 68 1-day internationals), by Deborah Hockley (New Zealand).

CROQUET

International trophy   The MacRobertson Shield (instituted 1925 and held every three years) has been won a record nine times by Great Britain, in 1925, 1937, 1956, 1963, 1969, 1974, 1982, 1990 and 1993.

A record seven appearances have been made by John G. Prince (New Zealand), in 1963, 1969, 1975, 1979, 1982, 1986 and 1990; on his debut he was the youngest-ever international, at 17 yr. 190 days.

World Championships   The first World Championships were held at the Hurlingham Club, London, England in 1989. The most wins is three, by Robert Fulford (Great Britain), 1990, 1992 and 1994.

USCA National Championships   The first United States Championships were played in 1977. J. Archie Peck has won the singles title a record four times, 1977, 1979–80 and 1982. Ted Prentis has won the doubles title four times, 1978, 1980–81 and 1988. The teams of Ted Prentis and Ned Prentis (1980–81), Dana Dribben and Ray Bell (1985–86), and Reid Fleming and Debbie Cornelius (1990–91) have each won the doubles title twice. The New York Croquet Club has won a record six National Club Championships, 1980–83, 1986 and 1988.

CROSS-COUNTRY RUNNING

World Championships   The greatest margin of victory is 56 seconds or 390 yards by Jack Holden (England) at Ayr Racecourse, Strathclyde, Scotland on March 24, 1934.

Since 1973, the events have been official World Championships under the auspices of the International Amateur Athletic Federation.

United States   Lynn Jennings has won the women's individual title three times, 1990–92, and Craig Virgin won the men's individual race twice, in 1980–81.

Most wins   England has the most team victories, with 45 for the men's team. The U.S. and the USSR each have a record eight women's team victories.

The greatest team domination was by Kenya in Auckland, New Zealand on March 26, 1988. Kenya's senior men's team finished eight men in the first nine, with a low score of 23 (six to score), and its junior men's team set a record low score, 11 (four to score) with six in the first seven.

Kenya won the men's senior team title for a record 10th time in succession at the 1995 World Cross-Country Championships.

The greatest number of individual victories is five, by John Ngugi

(Kenya), 1986–89 and 1992; by Doris Brown-Heritage (U.S.), 1967–71; and by Grete Waitz (née Andersen; Norway), 1978–81 and 1983.

Most appearances Marcel van de Wattyne (Belgium) ran in a record 20 races, 1946–65. The women's record is 16, by Jean Lochhead (Wales), 1967–79, 1981, 1983–84.

U.S. National Championships In this competition, first staged in 1890, the most wins in the men's race is eight, by Pat Porter, 1982–89. The most wins in the women's championships is eight, by Lynn A. Jennings, 1985 and 1987–93.

Largest cross-country field The largest recorded field in any cross-country race was 11,763 starters (10,810 finished), in the 18.6-mile Lidingöloppet, near Stockholm, Sweden on October 3, 1982.

Lynn Jennings has won the U.S. National Championships twice.

CURLING

Most titles   Canada has won the men's World Championships 24 times, 1959–64, 1966, 1968–72, 1980, 1982–83, 1985–87, 1989–90, and 1993–96.

The most women's World Championships (instituted 1979) is nine, by Canada (1980, 1984–87, 1989, 1993–94 and 1996).

United States   The U.S. has won the men's world title four times, with Bud Somerville skip on the first two winning teams, 1965 and 1974.

United States National Championship Men   Two curlers have been skips on five championship teams: Bud Somerville (Superior, WI Curling Club in 1965, 1968–69, 1974, 1981), and Bruce Roberts (Hibbing, MN Curling Club in 1966–67, 1976–77, 1984). Bill Strum of the Superior Curling Club has been on five title teams, 1965, 1967, 1969, 1974, and 1978.

Women   Nancy Langley (Seattle, WA) has been the skip of a record four championship teams, 1979, 1981, 1983 and 1988.

Fastest game   Eight curlers from the Burlington Golf and Country Club curled an 8-end game in 47 min. 24 sec., with time penalties of 5 min. 30 sec., in Burlington, Ontario, Canada on April 4, 1986, following rules agreed upon with the Ontario Curling Association. The time is taken from when the first rock crosses the near hogline until the game's last rock comes to a complete stop.

Largest bonspiel   The largest bonspiel is the annual Manitoba Curling Association Bonspiel, held in Winnipeg, Canada. In 1988, 1,424 4-man teams used 187 sheets of ice.

Longest curling throw   The longest throw of a curling stone was 576 ft. 4 in., by Eddie Kulbacki (Canada) at Park Lake, Neepawa, Manitoba, Canada on January 29, 1989. The attempt took place on a specially prepared sheet of curling ice on frozen Park Lake.

CYCLING

Fastest speed   The fastest speed achieved on a bicycle is 166.944 MPH, by Fred Rompelberg (Netherlands) behind a windshield at Bonneville Salt Flats, UT on October 3, 1995.

The 24-hour record behind pace is 1,216.8 miles, by Michael Secrest at Phoenix International Raceway, AZ, April 26–27, 1990.

Fastest rollercycling speed   James Baker (U.S.) achieved a record speed of 153.2 MPH at El Con Mall, Tucson, AZ on January 28, 1989.

Catherine Marsal cycled a women's record 47.112 km in an hour.

Most titles Olympic The most gold medals won is three, by Paul Masson (France) in 1896; Francisco Verri (Italy) in 1906; Robert Charpentier (France) in 1936; and Daniel Morelon (France) in 1968 and 1972.

Burton Cecil Down (U.S.) won a record six medals at the 1904 Games—two gold, three silver and one bronze. The only American woman to win a cycling gold medal is Connie Carpenter-Phinney, who won the individual road race in 1984.

World World Championships are contested annually. They were first staged for amateurs in 1893 and for professionals in 1895.

The most wins in a particular event is 10, by Koichi Nakano (Japan), professional sprint 1977–86.

The most world titles won by a U.S. cyclist is five, in women's 3 km pursuit, by Rebecca Twigg, 1982, 1984–85, 1987 and 1993. The most successful man is Greg LeMond, winner of the individual road race in 1983 and 1989.

United States National cycling championships have been held annually since 1899. Women's events were first included in 1937.

Leonard Nitz has won the most titles, 16: five pursuit (1976 and 1980–83); eight team pursuit (1980–84, 1986 and 1988–89); two 1-km timetrial (1982 and 1984); and one criterium (1986). Rebecca Twigg has won 14 titles in women's events: five time trials (1982, 1984, 1986, 1993–94); one points race (1984); one match sprint (1984); five pursuits (1981–82, 1984, 1986, 1992); one criterium (1993); and one road race (1983).

Tour de France The greatest number of wins in the Tour de France is five, by Jacques Anquetil (France), 1957, 1961–64; Eddy Merckx (Belgium),

Miguel Induráin set the fastest average speed record in the Tour de France.

CYCLING RECORDS

These records are those recognized by the Union Cycliste Internationale (UCI). From January 1, 1993, its severely reduced list no longer distinguished between those set by professionals and amateurs, indoor and outdoor, at altitude and at sea level.

	min : sec	Name and Country	Place	Date
MEN				
Unpaced Standing Start				
1 km	1:02.091	Maic Malchow (East Germany)	Colorado Springs,CO	Aug. 28, 1986
4 km	4:20.894	Graeme Obree (Great Britain)	Hamar, Norway	Aug. 19, 1993
4 km team	4:03.840	Australia	Hamar, Norway	Aug. 20, 1993
Unpaced Flying Start				
200 meters	0:10.099	Vladimir Adamashvili (Russia)	Moscow, Russia	Aug. 6, 1990
500 meters	0:26.649	Aleksandr Kirichenko (Russia)	Moscow, Russia	Oct. 29, 1988
Unpaced—One Hour	55.291 km	Tony Rominger (Switzerland)	Bordeaux, France	Nov. 6, 1994
WOMEN				
Unpaced Standing Start				
500 m	0:33.438	Galina Yenyukhina (Russia)	Moscow, Russia	Apr. 29, 1993
3 km	3:31.924	Antonella Bellutti (Italy)	Cali, Colombia	Apr. 6, 1996
Unpaced Flying Start				
200 meters	0:10.831	Olga Slyusareva (Russia)	Moscow, Russia	Aug. 6, 1990
500 meters	0:29.655	Erika Salumäe (Russia)	Moscow, Russia	Aug. 6, 1987
Unpaced—One Hour	47.112 km	Catherine Marsal (France)	Bordeaux, France	Apr. 29, 1995

1969–72 and 1974; Bernard Hinault (France), 1978–79, 1981–82 and 1985; and Miguel Induráin (Spain), 1991–95. Greg LeMond (U.S.) won in 1986, 1989 and 1990.

The closest race ever was in 1989, when after 2,030 miles over 23 days (July 1–23) Greg LeMond, who completed the Tour in 87 hr. 38 min. 35 sec., beat Laurent Fignon (France) in Paris, France by only eight seconds.

The fastest average speed was 24.547 MPH, by Miguel Induráin (Spain) in 1992.

Women   The inaugural women's Tour de France was staged in 1984. Jeannie Longo (France) has won the event a record four times, 1987–90.

Longest one-day race   The longest single-day "massed start" road race is the Bordeaux–Paris, France event of 342–385 miles. The highest average speed was 29.32 MPH, by Herman van Springel (Belgium) for 363.1 miles in 13 hr. 35 min. 18 sec., in 1981.

Cross-America   The trans-America solo record recognized by the Ultra-Marathon Cycling Association is 8 days 3 hr. 11 min., by Rob Kish from Costa, CA to New York, in the 1992 Race Across AMerica.

The women's record is 9 days 8 hr. 54 min., by Seana Hogan, also in the Race Across AMerica.

Most wins   Five cyclists have won two titles: Bob Fourney, 1990–91; Lon Haldeman, 1982–83; Rob Kish, 1992, 1994; Susan Notorangelo, 1985, 1989; and Pete Penseyres, 1984, 1986. Seana Hogan has won the Women's Division three times: 1992–93 and 1994.

Circumnavigation   Tal Burt (Israel) circumnavigated the world (13,523 road miles) from Place du Trocadero, Paris, France in 77 days 14 hr., from June 1 to August 17, 1992.

Cycling the length of the Americas   Daniel Buettner, Bret Anderson, Martin Engel and Anne Knabe cycled the length of the Americas, from Prudhoe Bay, AK to the Beagle Channel, Ushuaia, Argentina from August 8, 1986 to June 13, 1987. They cycled 15,266 miles.

Cross-Canada   The trans-Canada record is 13 days 9 hr. 6 min., by Bill Narasnek (Canada), cycling 3,751 miles from Vancouver to Halifax, Nova Scotia, July 5–18, 1991.

Greatest distance   Thomas Godwin (Great Britain), cycling every day during the 365 days of 1939, covered 75,065 miles, or an average of 205.65 miles per day. Continuing his effort, he went on to complete 100,000 miles in 500 days to May 14, 1940.

Greatest distance in one hour   The greatest distance covered in one hour is 122.28 km, by Leon Vanderstuyft (Belgium) on the Montlhéry Motor Circuit, France, on September 30, 1928, from a standing start paced by a motorcycle.

Cycle touring   The greatest mileage amassed in a cycle tour was more than 402,000 miles, by Walter Stolle from January 24, 1959 to December 12, 1976. Starting from Romford, England, he visited 159 countries.

From 1922 to December 25, 1973, Tommy Chambers of Glasgow, Scotland rode a verified total of 799,405 miles.

Visiting every continent, John W. Hathaway (Great Britain) of Vancouver, British Columbia, Canada covered 50,600 miles from November 10, 1974 to October 6, 1976.

Ronald and Sandra Slaughter hold the U.S. record for tandem bicycling, having traveled 18,077.5 miles around the world from December 30, 1989 to July 28, 1991.

The most participants in a bicycle tour were 31,678, in the 56-mile London-to-Brighton Bike Ride (England) on June 19, 1988.

High altitude cycling Canadians Bruce Bell, Philip Whelan and Suzanne MacFadyen cycled at an altitude of 22,834 feet on the peak of Mt. Aconcagua, Argentina in January 1991. This feat was matched by Mozart Hastenreiter Catão (Brazil) in March 1993 and by Tim Sumner (Great Britain) and Jonathan Greene (Great Britain) in January 1994.

CYCLO-CROSS

The greatest number of World Championships (instituted 1950) has been won by Eric de Vlaeminck (Belgium), with the Amateur and Open in 1966 and six Professional titles in 1968–73.

DARTS

PROFESSIONAL DARTS

Most titles Eric Bristow (Great Britain) has the most wins in the World Masters Championship (instituted 1974) with five, 1977, 1979, 1981, 1983–84; the most in the World Professional Championship (instituted 1978) with five, 1980–81, 1984–86; and the most in the World Cup Singles (instituted 1977) with four, 1983, 1985, 1987, 1989.

SCORING RECORDS

Fewest darts The lowest number of darts thrown for a score of 1,001 is 19, by Cliff Inglis (Great Britain) (160, 180, 140, 180, 121, 180, 40) at the Bromfield Men's Club, Devon, England on November 11, 1975; and by Jocky Wilson (Great Britain) (140, 140, 180, 180, 180, 131, Bull) at The London Pride, Bletchley, England on March 23, 1989.

A score of 2,001 in 52 darts was achieved by Alan Evans in Ferndale, Wales on September 3, 1976.

A score of 3,001 in 73 darts was thrown by Tony Benson at the Plough Inn, Gorton, England on July 12, 1986. Linda Batten set a women's 3,001 record of 117 darts at the Old Wheatsheaf, London, England on April 2, 1986.

A score of 100,001 was achieved in 3,579 darts by Chris Gray at the Dolphin, Cromer, England on April 27, 1993.

Roy Blowes (Canada) achieved a 501 in nine darts, "double-on, double-off," at the Widgeons Pub, Calgary, Canada on March 9, 1987. His scores were: bull, treble 20, treble 17, five treble 20s and a double 20 to finish. This was equaled by Steve Draper (Great Britain) at the Ex-Servicemen's Club in Wellingborough, England on November 10, 1994. His scores were: double 20, six treble 20s, treble 17 and bull.

Highest score Team   The highest 24-hour score is 1,722,249, by the Broken Hill Darts Club (eight players) in Broken Hill, New South Wales, Australia, September 28–29, 1985.

The women's record is 744,439 by a team of eight players from the Lord Clyde, London, England, October 13–14, 1990.

Doubles   The highest score by a 2-man team retrieving their own darts, in 10 hours, is 465,919 by Jon Archer and Neil Rankin on November 17, 1990 at the Royal Oak, Cossington, Leicester, England.

Individual   The highest 24-hour score by an individual is 566,175, by Russell Locke in Hugglescote, England, September 17–18, 1993.

Bulls and 25s   An 8-member team scored 526,750 points at the George Inn, Morden, England, July 1–2, 1994.

Million and One Up Men (8 players)   36,583 darts by a team at Buzzy's Pub and Grub, Lynn, MA, October 19–20, 1991.

Women (8 players)   70,019 darts by The Delinquents darts team at the Top George Pub, Combe Martin, England, September 11–13, 1987.

10-hour bulls (individual)   1,320, by John Lowe (U.S.) at The Unicorn Tavern, Chesterfield, England on October 27, 1994.

10-hour trebles   3,056, by Paul Taylor (Great Britain) at the Woodhouse Tavern, Leytonstone, England on October 19, 1985.

10-hour doubles   3,265, by Paul Taylor at the Lord Brooke, Walthamstow, England on September 5, 1987.

SPEED RECORDS

The fastest time taken to complete three games of 301, finishing on doubles, is 1 min. 38 sec., by Ritchie Gardner on the British TV show *Record Breakers*, on September 12, 1989.

The record time for going around the board clockwise in "doubles" at arm's length is 9.2 seconds, by Dennis Gower at the Millers Arms, Hastings, England, October 12, 1975.

The record for around-the-board in numerical order is 14.5 seconds by Jim Pike at the Craven Club, Newmarket, England, March 1944.

The record for this feat at the 9-foot throwing distance, retrieving own darts, is 2 min. 13 sec. by Bill Duddy at The Plough, London, England on October 29, 1972.

EQUESTRIAN SPORTS

CARRIAGE DRIVING

World Championships were first held in 1972. Three titles have been won by Great Britain, 1972, 1974, 1980; Hungary, 1976, 1978, 1984; and Netherlands, 1982, 1986, 1988.

Most titles   Two individual titles have been won by György Bárdos (Hungary), 1978 and 1980; by Tjeerd Velstra (Netherlands), 1982 and 1986; and by Ijsbrand Chardon (Netherlands), 1988 and 1992.

Most animals in a hitch   Willard McWilliams of Navan, Ontario, Canada drove 50 horses in a single hitch at the 50th Navan Fair on August 13, 1995. The lead horses were on reins 168 feet long.

Willard McWilliams drove 50 horses in a single hitch.

Floyd Zopfi of Stratford, WI has driven 52 llamas in a hitch on several occasions since 1990, with the lead llamas on 150-foot reins.

Coaching   The longest horse-drawn procession was a cavalcade of 68 carriages that measured 3,018 feet "nose to tail," organized by the Spies Traveling Company of Denmark on May 7, 1986. It carried 810 people through the woods around Copenhagen to celebrate the coming of spring.

DRESSAGE

Olympic Games and World Championships   Germany (West Germany 1968–90) has won a record eight team Olympic gold medals, 1928, 1936, 1964, 1968, 1976, 1984, 1988, and 1992, and has the most team wins, seven, at the World Championships (instituted 1966). Reiner Klimke (West Germany) has won six Olympic golds (team 1964–88, individual, 1984). He won individual bronze in 1976, for a record seven medals overall, and is the only rider to have won two world titles, on Mehmed in 1974 and on Ahlerich in 1982. Henri St. Cyr (Sweden) won two individual Olympic gold medals, in 1952 and 1956. This was equaled by Nicole Uphoff (Germany) in 1992; she had previously won in 1988.

World Cup   Instituted in 1986, this competition has had three double winners: Christine Stückelberger (Switzerland) on Gauguin de Lully in 1987–88; Monica Theodorescu (Greece) on Ganimedes Tecrent in 1993–94; and Anky van Grunsven (Netherlands) on Camelion Bonfire, 1995–96.

SHOW JUMPING

Olympic Games   The most Olympic gold medals won by a rider is five, by Hans-Günter Winkler (West Germany)—four team wins in 1956, 1960, 1964 and 1972 and the individual Grand Prix in 1956. He also won team silver in 1976 and team bronze in 1968, for a record seven medals overall.

The most team wins in the Prix des Nations is six, by Germany in 1936, 1956, 1960, 1964 and as West Germany in 1972 and 1988.

The lowest score obtained by a winner is no faults, by Frantisek Ventura (Czechoslovakia) on Eliot, 1928; Alwin Schockemöhle (West Germany) on Warwick Rex, 1976; and Ludger Beerbaum (Germany) on Classic Touch, 1992.

Pierre Jonquères d'Oriola (France) uniquely won the individual gold medal twice, in 1952 and 1964.

United States   Two U.S. riders have won individual gold medals: Bill Steinkraus won in 1968 and also won two silvers and a bronze, 1952–68; and Joe Fargis won both individual and team gold medals in 1984 as well as team silver in 1988.

World Championships   The men's World Championships (instituted 1953) have been won twice by Hans-Günter Winkler (West Germany) (1954–55) and Raimondo d'Inzeo (Italy) (1956 and 1960).

The women's title (1965–74) was won twice by Janou Tissot (née Lefebvre; France) on Rocket (1970 and 1974). A team competition was introduced in 1978, and the most wins is two, by France, 1982 and 1990.

President's Cup   Instituted in 1965 for Nations Cup teams, it has been won a record 14 times by Great Britain, in 1965, 1967, 1970, 1972–74, 1977–79, 1983, 1985–86, 1989 and 1991.

World Cup   In this competition, instituted in 1979, double winners have been Conrad Homfeld (U.S.), 1980 and 1985; Ian Millar (Canada), 1988 and 1989; and John Whitaker (Great Britain), 1990–91.

John Whitaker (on Henderson Milton) is one of three double World Cup winners.

Jumping   The official *Fédération Equestre Internationale* records are: high jump, 8 ft. 1¼ in., by Huasó, ridden by Capt. Alberto Larraguibel Morales (Chile) at Viña del Mar, Santiago, Chile on February 5, 1949; long jump over water, 27 ft. 6¾ in., by Something, ridden by André Ferreira (South Africa) in Johannesburg, South Africa on April, 25 1975.

THREE-DAY EVENT

Olympic Games and World Championships   Charles Pahud de Mortanges (Netherlands) won four Olympic gold medals—team 1924 and 1928, individual 1928 and 1932; he also won a team silver in 1932. Bruce Davidson (U.S.) is the only rider to have won two world titles (instituted 1966), in 1974 and in 1978.

Badminton Horse Trials   The Badminton Three-Day Event, instituted in 1949, is the premier annual competition in the sport. Lucinda Green (née Prior-Palmer; Great Britain) has won the event a record six times, 1973, 1976, 1977, 1979 , 1983, and 1984.

FENCING

Most titles Olympic   The most individual Olympic gold medals won is three, by Ramón Fonst (Cuba) in 1900 and 1904 (two); and by Nedo Nadi

(Italy) in 1912 and 1920 (two). Nadi also won three team gold medals in 1920, making five gold medals at one celebration, the record for fencing. Aladár Gerevich (Hungary) won seven golds—one individual and six team.

Edoardo Mangiarotti (Italy), with six gold, five silver and two bronze, holds the record of 13 Olympic medals in fencing. He won them for foil and épée from 1936 to 1960.

The most gold medals won by a woman is four (one individual, three team) by Yelena Novikova (née Belova; USSR) from 1968 to 1976, and the women's record for all medals is seven (two gold, three silver, two bronze) by Ildikó Sági (formerly Ujlaki, née Retjö; Hungary), 1960–76.

United States   The only U.S. Olympic champion was Albertson Van Zo Post, who won the men's single sticks and team foil (with two Cubans) at the 1904 Games.

World   The greatest number of individual world titles won is five, by Aleksandr Romankov (USSR), in foil 1974, 1977, 1979, 1982 and 1983. Christian d'Oriola (France) won four world foil titles, 1947, 1949, 1953–54, as well as two individual Olympic titles (1952 and 1956).

Four women foilists have won three world titles: Helene Mayer (Germany), 1929, 1931, 1937; Ilona Schacherer-Elek (Hungary), 1934–35, 1951; Ellen Müller-Preis (Austria), 1947, 1949–50; and Cornelia Hanisch (West Germany), 1979, 1981, 1985.

The longest time span for winning an individual world or Olympic title is 20 years, by Aladár Gerevich (Hungary) in saber, 1935–55.

Cornelia Hanisch (right) has won three world titles.

United States National Championships   The most U.S. titles won in one weapon is 13 in saber, by Peter J. Westbrook, in 1974, 1975, 1979–86, 1988, 1989 and 1995. The women's record is 10 in foil, by Janice Romary in 1950–51, 1956–57, 1960–61, 1964–66 and 1968.

The most men's individual foil championships won is eight, by Michael Marx in 1977, 1979, 1982, 1985–87, 1990 and 1993. L. G. Nunes won the most épée championships, with six—1917, 1922, 1924, 1926, 1928 and 1932. Vincent Bradford won a record number of women's épée championships, with four in 1982–84 and 1986.

NCAA Championship Division I Men   Inaugurated in 1941, this event was won a record 12 times by New York University (1947, 1954, 1957, 1960–61, 1966–67, 1970–71, 1973–74, 1976). In 1989 the event was combined with the team title.

Michael Lofton (New York University) has won the most titles in a career, with four victories in saber, 1984–87. Abraham Balk (New York University) is the only man to win two individual titles in one year, 1947 (foil and épée).

Women   In this event, inaugurated in 1982, Wayne State (MI) has won the most titles: three (1982, 1988–89).

Caitlin Bilodeaux (Columbia-Barnard) and Molly Sullivan (Notre Dame) have both won the individual title twice—Bilodeaux in 1985 and 1987; Sullivan in 1986 and 1988.

Team   In 1990, the NCAA team competition was combined for the first time. Penn State has won the team title four times, in 1990–91 and 1995–96.

FIELD HOCKEY

Most Olympic medals   India was Olympic champion from the reintroduction of Olympic hockey in 1928 until 1960, when Pakistan beat India 1–0 in Rome. India had its eighth win in 1980.

United States   U.S. men won the bronze medal in 1932, but only three teams played that year; U.S. women won the bronze in 1984.

World Cup   The World Cup for men was first held in 1971, and for women in 1974. The most wins are: (men) four by Pakistan, 1971, 1978, 1982 and 1994; (women) five by Netherlands, 1974, 1978, 1983, 1986 and 1990.

MEN

Highest international score   The highest score was achieved when India defeated the U.S. 24–1 in Los Angeles, CA in the 1932 Olympic Games.

Most international appearances   Heiner Dopp represented West Germany 286 times between 1975 and 1990, indoors and out.

Most goals   The most goals scored in international hockey is 267, by Paul Litjens (Netherlands) in 177 games.

Best goalkeeping   Richard Allen (India) did not concede a goal during the 1928 Olympic tournament and gave up a total of only three in 1936.

Fastest goal in an international game John French scored seven seconds after the bully-off for England vs. West Germany in Nottingham, England on April 25, 1971.

WOMEN

Most international appearances Alison Ramsay has made a record 257 international appearances, 150 for Scotland and 107 for Great Britain, 1982–95.

United States As of April 3, 1996, Barbara Marois had made a record 140 appearances for the U.S.

Highest scores The highest score in an international game was when England beat France 23–0 in Merton, London, England on February 3, 1923.

NCAA Division I In this competition, inaugurated in 1981, Old Dominion University, Norfolk, VA has won the most championships with seven titles: 1982–84, 1988 and 1990–92.

FISHING

Largest single catch The largest officially ratified fish ever caught on a rod was a great white shark (*Carcharodon carcharias*) weighing 2,664 pounds and measuring 16 ft. 10 in. long, caught on a 130-pound test line by Alf Dean in Denial Bay, near Ceduna, South Australia on April 21, 1959. A great white shark weighing 3,388 pounds was caught by Clive Green off Albany, Western Australia on April 26, 1976 but will remain unratified because whale meat was used as bait.

The largest fish ever taken underwater was an 804-pound giant black grouper by Don Pinder of the Miami Triton Club, FL in 1955.

Longest fight The longest recorded individual fight with a fish is 37 hours, by Bob Ploeger (U.S.) with a King salmon on July 12–13, 1989.

World Freshwater Championship France won the European title in 1956 and 13 world titles between 1959 and 1995.

The individual title has been won a record three times by Robert Tesse (France), 1959–60 and 1965; and by Bob Nudd (England), 1990–91, 1994.

The record weight (team) is 76.52 pounds in three hours by West Germany on the Neckar in Mannheim, Germany on September 21, 1980.

The individual record is 37.45 pounds, by Wolf-Rüdiger Kremkus (West Germany) in Mannheim on September 20, 1980. The most fish caught is 652, by Jacques Isenbaert (Belgium) in Danaújváros, Hungary on August 27, 1967.

International Game Fish Association (IGFA) The heaviest freshwater category recognized by the International Game Fish Association is for the stur-

40 years ago the largest blue marlin ever caught was a 756-pounder caught off San Juan, Puerto Rico by A. Sherman. He landed the big catch on April 24, 1956. **Today** the record for the largest blue marlin, as recognized by the International Game Fish Association, stands at 1,402 lb. 2 oz. Roberto Amorim hooked this massive marlin on February 29, 1992 off the coast of Brazil.

"I'd like to break the record on the blue marlin. Eventually, when I get more time, I'll focus on chasing such things."—Greg Norman, highest-earning golfer, June 4, 1996

geon; the record weight in this category is 468 pounds, caught by Joey Pallotta III on July 9, 1983 off Benicia, CA.

Fly fishing World fly fishing championships were inaugurated by the CIPS (Confédération Internationale de la Pêche Sportive) in 1981. The most team titles is five, by Italy, 1982–84, 1986, 1992. The most individual titles is two, by Brian Leadbetter (Great Britain), 1987 and 1991.

Casting The longest freshwater cast ratified under ICF (International Casting Federation) rules is 574 ft. 2 in., by Walter Kummerow (Germany), for the Bait Distance Double-Handed 30 g event held in Lenzerheide, Switzerland in the 1968 Championships.

At the currently contested weight of 17.7 g, known as 18 g Bait Distance, the longest Double-Handed cast is 457 ft. ½ in., by Kevin Carriero (U.S.) in Toronto, Ontario, Canada on July 24, 1984.

The longest Fly Distance Double-Handed cast is 319 ft. 1 in., by Wolfgang Feige (Germany) in Toronto, Ontario, Canada on July 23, 1984.

FOOTBAG

Open singles The record for keeping a footbag airborne is 51,155 consecutive kicks or hacks in 7 hr. 1 min. 37 sec., by Ted Martin (U.S.) at the Green/White Soccer Center, Chicago, IL on May 29, 1993.

Women's singles   The women's record is held by Constance Constable (U.S.), with 18,936 kicks in 3 hr. 14 min. 42 sec. on August 1, 1995 in Menlo Park, CA.

Open doubles   The record is 123,456 hacks, by Tricia George and Gary Lautt (both U.S.) on November 12, 1995 at Lia Way Rec Center, Chico, CA. The pair kept the footbag aloft for 19 hr. 38 min. 20 sec.

Women's doubles   The record is 34,543 kicks, by Constance Constable and Tricia George (both U.S.) on February 18, 1995. The pair kept the footbag aloft for 5 hr. 38 min. 22 sec.

Most kicks in five minutes   Andy Linder (U.S.) achieved 1,017 kicks in five minutes on March 29, 1996 in Carol Stream, IL. The women's record is 769 by Ida Bettis-Fogle (U.S.) on April 13, 1996 in Columbia, MO.

Largest footbag circle   The largest continuous circle of people playing footbag was 932. This gathering was staged at St. Patrick High School Campus, Chicago, IL on May 3, 1996.

FOOTBALL

NATIONAL FOOTBALL LEAGUE (NFL) RECORDS

Most championships   The Green Bay Packers have won a record 11 NFL titles, 1929–31, 1936, 1939, 1944, 1961–62, 1965–67.

Most consecutive wins (regular season and playoffs)   The Chicago Bears have won 18 consecutive games twice, in 1933–34 and 1941–42. This was matched by the Miami Dolphins in 1972–73 and by the San Francisco 49ers in 1989–90. The most consecutive games without defeat is 25, by the Canton Bulldogs (22 wins and 3 ties) in 1921–23.

Most games played   George Blanda played in a record 340 games in a record 26 seasons in the NFL, for the Chicago Bears (1948–58), the Baltimore Colts (1950), the Houston Oilers (1960–66), and the Oakland Raiders (1967–75).

   The most consecutive games played is 282, by Jim Marshall for the Cleveland Browns (1960) and the Minnesota Vikings (1961–79).

Longest run from scrimmage   Tony Dorsett completed a touchdown after a run of 99 yards for the Dallas Cowboys vs. the Minnesota Vikings on January 3, 1983.

Longest field goal   The longest field goal was 63 yards by Tom Dempsey for the New Orleans Saints vs. the Detroit Lions, November 8, 1970.

Longest pass completion   A pass completion of 99 yards has been achieved eight times and has always resulted in a touchdown. The most recent was a pass from Brett Favre to Robert Brooks of the Green Bay Packers against the Chicago Bears on September 11, 1995.

Longest punt   The longest was 98 yards by Steve O'Neal for the New York Jets vs. the Denver Broncos, September 21, 1969.

Longest interception return   The longest interception return is 103 yards, by two players: Vencie Glenn, San Diego Chargers vs. Denver Broncos, No-

Dan Marino holds records for most passes completed and most yards gained passing.

Emmitt Smith holds the season record of 25 touchdowns.

vember 29, 1987; and Louis Oliver, Miami Dolphins vs. Buffalo Bills, October 4, 1992, both for touchdowns.

Longest kickoff return   Three players share the record for a kickoff return at 106 yards: Al Carmichael, Green Bay Packers vs. Chicago Bears, October 7, 1956; Noland Smith, Kansas City Chiefs vs. Denver Broncos, December 17, 1967; and Roy Green, St. Louis Cardinals vs. Dallas Cowboys, October 21, 1979. All three players scored touchdowns.

Longest punt return   Robert Bailey of the Los Angeles Rams set the record for the longest punt return, at 103 yards, while playing against the New Orleans Saints on October 23, 1994.

Largest deficit overcome   On January 3, 1993, the Buffalo Bills, playing at home in the AFC Wild Card game, trailed the Houston Oilers 35–3 with 28 minutes remaining. The Bills won the game in overtime, overcoming a 32-point deficit—the largest in NFL history.

Most successful coaches   The most successful coach in NFL history is Don Shula, with 347 victories: 73 with the Baltimore Colts (1963–69) and 274 with the Miami Dolphins (1970–present). The highest winning percentage was .740, achieved by Vince Lombardi (1913–70): 105 wins, 35 losses and 6 ties with the Green Bay Packers, 1959–67, and the Washington Redskins, 1969.

Highest attendance   The largest crowd for a regular season game was 102,368, for the Los Angeles Rams against the San Francisco 49ers at the Los Angeles Coliseum, Los Angeles, CA on November 10, 1957.

NFL RECORDS

Most points

Career 2,002, George Blanda (Chicago Bears, Baltimore Colts, Houston Oilers, Oakland Raiders), 1949–75. *Season* 176, Paul Hornung (Green Bay Packers), 1960. *Game* 40, Ernie Nevers (Chicago Cardinals), November 28, 1929.

Most touchdowns

Career 156, Jerry Rice (San Francisco 49ers), 1985–95. *Season* 25, Emmitt Smith (Dallas Cowboys), 1995. *Game* 6, Ernie Nevers (Chicago Cardinals), November 28, 1929; William "Dub" Jones (Cleveland Browns) November 25, 1951; Gale Sayers (Chicago Bears), December 12, 1965.

Most yards gained rushing

Career 16,726, Walter Payton (Chicago Bears), 1975–87. *Season* 2,105, Eric Dickerson (Los Angeles Rams), 1984. *Game* 275, Walter Payton (Chicago Bears), November 20, 1977. Highest career average 5.22 yd. per game (12,352 yd. from 2,359 attempts), Jim Brown (Cleveland Browns), 1957–65.

Most yards gained receiving

Career 15,123 Jerry Rice (San Francisco 49ers) 1985–95. *Season* 1,848, Jerry Rice (San Francisco 49ers), 1995. *Game* 336, Willie Anderson (Los Angeles Rams), November 26, 1989.

Most yards gained passing

Career 48,841, Dan Marino (Miami Dolphins), 1983–95. *Season* 5,084, Dan Marino (Miami Dolphins), 1984. *Game* 554, Norm Van Brocklin (Los Angeles Rams), September 28, 1951.

Most combined net yards gained

Career 21,803 Walter Payton (Chicago Bears), 1975–87. *Season* 2,535, Lionel James (San Diego Chargers), 1985. Game 404, Glyn Milburn (Denver Broncos vs. Seattle Seahawks), December 10, 1995.

Passing attempts

Career 6,531 Dan Marino (Miami Dolphins), 1983–95. *Season* 691 Drew Bledsoe (New England Patriots), 1994. *Game* 70 Drew Bledsoe (New England Patriots), November 13, 1994.

Most passes completed

Career 3,913, Dan Marino (Miami Dolphins), 1983–95. *Season* 404, Warren Moon (Houston Oilers), 1991. *Game* 45 (from 70 attempts), Drew Bledsoe (New England Patriots), November 13, 1994. Consecutive 22, Joe Montana (San Francisco 49ers), Nov. 29, 1987 vs. Cleveland Browns (5); December 6, 1987 vs. Green Bay Packers (17).

Pass receptions

Career 942, Jerry Rice (San Francisco 49ers), 1985–96. *Season* 123, Herman Moore (Detroit Lions), 1995. *Game* 18, Tom Fears (Los Angeles Rams), December 3, 1950.

Field goals

Career 373, Jan Stenerud (Kansas City Chiefs, Green Bay Packers, Minnesota Vikings), 1967–85. *Season* 35, Ali Haji-Sheikh (New York Giants), 1983; Jeff Jaeger (Los Angeles Raiders), 1993. *Game* 7, Jim Bakken (St. Louis Cardinals), Sepember 24, 1967; Rich Karlis (Minnesota Vikings), November 5, 1989.

Punting

Career 1,154, Dave Jennings (New York Giants, New York Jets), 1974–87. *Season* 114, Bob Parsons (Chicago Bears), 1981. *Game* 15, John Teltschik (Philadelphia Eagles vs. New York Giants), December 6, 1987.

Sacks

Career 157, Reggie White (Philadelphia Eagles, Green Bay Packers), 1985–95. *Season* 22, Mark Gastineau (New York Jets), 1984. *Game* 7, Derrick Thomas (Kansas City Chiefs vs. Seattle Seahawks), November 11, 1990.

Most Interceptions

Career 81, Paul Krause (Washington Redskins, Minnesota Vikings), 1964–79. *Season* 14, Dick Lane (Los Angeles Rams), 1952. *Game* 4, by 16 players.

NCAA DIVISION I-A INDIVIDUAL RECORDS

Points
Game ....48........Howard Griffith (Illinois vs. Southern Illinois; 8 touchdowns) ....Sep. 22, 1990
Season ....234........Barry Sanders (Oklahoma State; 39 touchdowns in 11 games) 1988
Career ....423........Roman Anderson (Houston; 70 field goals, 213 point-after-touchdowns) 1988–91

Total yardage
Game ....732........David Klingler (Houston vs. Arizona State; 716 passing, 16 rushing) ....Dec. 1, 1990
Season ....5,221........David Klingler (Houston; 5,140 passing, 81 rushing) 1995
Career ....14,665........Ty Detmer (Brigham Young; 15,031 passing, 366 rushing) 1988–91

Yards gained rushing
Game ....396........Tony Sands (Kansas vs. Missouri) ....Nov. 23, 1991
Season ....2,628........Barry Sanders (Oklahoma State; 344 rushes in 11 games, record av. 238.9) 1988
Career ....6,082........Tony Dorsett (Pittsburgh) 1973–76

Yards gained passing
Game ....716........David Klingler (Houston vs. Arizona State) ....Dec. 1, 1990
Season ....5,188........Ty Detmer (Brigham Young) 1990
Career ....15,031........Ty Detmer (Brigham Young; completed 958 of 1,530) 1988–91

Pass completions
Game ....55........Rusty LaRue (Wake Forest vs. Duke) ....Oct. 28, 1995
Season ....374........David Klingler (Houston) 1990
Career ....958........Ty Detmer (Brigham Young; 1,530 attempts) 1988–91

Touchdown passes
Game ....11........David Klingler (Houston vs. Eastern Washington) ....Nov. 17, 1990
Season ....54........David Klingler (Houston) 1990
Career ....121........Ty Detmer (Brigham Young) 1988–91

Pass receptions

Game	23	Randy Gatewood (UNLV vs. Idaho)	Sep. 17, 1994
Season	142	Emmanuel Hazard (Houston)	1989
Career	266	Aaron Turner (Pacific)	1989–92

Yards gained receiving

Game	363	Randy Gatewood (UNLV vs. Idaho)	Sep. 17, 1994
Season	1,854	Alex Van Dyke (Nevada)	1995
Career	4,357	Ryan Yarborough (Wyoming)	1990–93

Pass interceptions

Game	5	Dan Rebsch (Miami [Ohio] vs. Western Michigan; 88 yards; three others with less yards)	Nov. 4, 1972
Season	14	Al Worley (Washington; 130 yards, in 10 games)	1968
Career	29	Al Brosky (Illinois; 356 yards, 27 games)	1950–52

Touchdowns (receiving)

Game	6	Tim Delaney (San Diego State vs. New Mexico State)	Nov. 15, 1969
Season	22	Emmanuel Hazard (Houston)	1989
Career	43	Aaron Turner (Pacific)	1989–92

Field goals

Game	7	Mike Prindle (West Michigan vs. Marshall)	Sep. 29, 1984
	7	Dale Klein (Nebraska vs. Missouri)	Oct. 19, 1985
Season	29	John Lee (UCLA)	1984
Career	80	Jeff Jaeger (Washington)	1983–86
Consecutive	30	Chuck Nelson (Washington)	1981–82

Touchdowns

Game	8	Howard Griffith (Illinois vs. Southern Illinois)	Sep. 22, 1990
Season	39	Barry Sanders (Oklahoma State)	1988
Career	65	Anthony Thompson (Indiana)	1986–89

DON SHULA

"Have a clear vision of what you would like to accomplish and then be willing to do the things that are necessary day in and day out to put yourself in a position to accomplish those goals," advises Don Shula. As a head football coach for 33 seasons, including 26 with the Miami Dolphins, Coach Shula did just that. His 347 victories, six Super Bowl appearances, and one perfect season are all National Football League (NFL) records.

Shula was appointed head coach of the Baltimore Colts in 1963 and joined the Dolphins in 1970. "When you start out, you want to do the best job you can every day, every week, every year and try to be a winner," he says. Although he lost his first game, a 37–28 defeat to the New York Giants, Shula rapidly piled up the Ws. He won his 100th game during his 10th season in the league and his 200th in his 19th, the earliest any coach has reached those landmarks. In 1991 he gained his 300th win and on November 14, 1993 surpassed the Chicago Bears' George Halas's all-time mark of 324 wins, when the Dolphins defeated the Eagles 19–14 in Philadelphia. "When you break a record held by a man like George Halas it makes you all the more proud of the accomplishment. The career win record is important to me because it is measured over a period of time." The coach adds, "I'm just three games shy of averaging 10 wins per year for 33 years."

The coach attributes his consistent success to a balanced perspective. "I didn't get consumed by losses and I didn't get overwhelmed by successes." Shula's 1972 Dolphin team posted the only perfect season, 17–0, in NFL history. "Every week, especially when we got to 12 and 0, and 13 and 0, and 14 and 0, I made a specific emphasis on where we were and concentrated on the upcoming opponents," recalls Shula. The biggest challenge of the undefeated season was the Super Bowl game. "The Redskins were favored in the Super Bowl. It made me want to win all the more. Sixteen and 1 would have been successful by other standards, but for me it would have been utter failure."

Despite his record six Super Bowl appearances, Shula doesn't have fond memories of the NFL's championship game. "I'm 2 and 4 in Super Bowls. I'm not very proud of that. I'd like to be 6 and 0 instead," admits Shula. "When you get there, they're talking about both teams, but when you leave they're only talking about one team—the winner."

At the end of the 1995 season Shula retired from coaching. He continues his legendary association with the Dolphins as a part-owner of the team. During his 43 years in the NFL, (he was drafted as a defensive back by the Cleveland Browns), Shula has seen tremendous changes in football, but the formula for winning in the NFL remains the same. "You have to be willing to do the little things. The nonglamorous, hard-work necessities to prepare yourself for competition: listen in the meetings, pay attention to detail, take pride in your practice approach." Above all, "Try to eliminate errors in practice. If you don't, there is not going to be a magic turnaround on game day."

THE SUPER BOWL

The Super Bowl was first held in 1967 between the winners of the NFL and AFL championships. Since 1970, it has been contested by the winners of the National and American Conferences of the NFL. The most wins is five, by the San Francisco 49ers in 1982, 1985, 1989–90 and 1995 and by the Dallas Cowboys, 1972, 1978, 1993–94 and 1996.

Most appearances   The Dallas Cowboys have played in eight Super Bowls: V, VI, X, XII, XIII, XXVII, XXVIII and XXX. The Cowboys have won five and lost three.

Don Shula has coached six Super Bowls: Baltimore Colts, 1968; Miami Dolphins, 1971–73, 1982, 1984. He won two games and lost four.

Highest scores   The highest aggregate score was 75 points, set when the San Francisco 49ers beat the San Diego Chargers 49–26 in Superbowl XXIX on January 29, 1995.

Smallest margin of victory   The narrowest margin of victory was one point, when the New York Giants defeated the Buffalo Bills 20–19 on January 27, 1991.

Individual game records *Points*   The most points scored is 18, by three players: Roger Craig, San Francisco 49ers (vs. Denver Broncos, 1989); Jerry Rice, San Francisco 49ers (vs. Denver Broncos, 1989 and vs. San Diego Chargers, 1995); and Ricky Watters, San Francisco 49ers (vs. San Diego Chargers, 1995).

Touchdowns   The most touchdowns thrown is 6, by Steve Young, San Francisco 49ers (vs. San Diego Chargers, 1995).

The most touchdowns scored is 3, by three players: Roger Craig, San Francisco 49ers (vs. Miami Dolphins, 1984); Jerry Rice, San Francisco 49ers (vs. Denver Broncos, 1989 and vs. San Diego Chargers, 1995); and Ricky Watters, San Francisco 49ers (vs. San Diego Chargers, 1995).

Yards gained   The most yards gained rushing is 204, by Timmy Smith, Washington Redskins (vs. Denver Broncos, 1987). The most yards gained passing is 357, by Joe Montana, San Francisco 49ers (vs. Cincinnati Bengals, 1988). The most yards gained receiving is 215, by Jerry Rice, San Francisco 49ers (vs. Cincinnati Bengals, 1988).

Completions   The most completions thrown is 31, by Jim Kelly, Buffalo Bills (vs. Dallas Cowboys, 1994). The highest pass completion mark is 88 percent (22–25) by Phil Simms, New York Giants (vs. Denver Broncos, 1986).

Receptions   The most receptions is 11, by two players: Dan Ross, Cincinnati Bengals (vs. San Francisco 49ers, 1981) and Jerry Rice, San Francisco 49ers (vs. Cincinnati Bengals, 1988).

COLLEGE FOOTBALL (NCAA)

Team records *Most wins*   Michigan has won 756 games out of 1,042 played, 1879–1996.

Highest winning percentage The highest winning percentage in college football history is .760, by Notre Dame. The Fighting Irish have won 738, lost 219 and tied 42 out of 999 games played, 1887–1996.

Career records (Divisions I-A, I-AA, II and III) Points scored 528, Carey Bender, Coe College (Div. III), 1991–94.

Rushing (yards) 6,320, Johnny Bailey, Texas A&I (Div. II), 1986–89.

Passing (yards) 15,031, Ty Detmer, Brigham Young (Div. I-A), 1988–91.

Receptions (yards) 4,693, Jerry Rice, Mississippi Valley (Div. I-AA), 1981–84.

Receptions (most) 301, Jerry Rice, Mississippi Valley (Div. I-AA), 1981–84.

Field goals (game) 8, Goran Lingmerth, Northern Arizona (Div. I-AA). Booting 8 out of 8 kicks, Lingmerth set the record on October 25, 1986 vs. Idaho.

Longest streak The University of Oklahoma won 47 successive games 1953–57, until they were beaten 7–0 by Notre Dame. The longest unbeaten streak is 63 (59 won, 4 tied) by Washington, 1907–17, ended by a 27–0 loss to California.

Most successful coaches In Division I-A competition, Paul "Bear" Bryant won more games than any other coach, with 323 wins over 38 years: Maryland 1945, Kentucky 1946–53, Texas A&M 1954–57 and Alabama 1958–82. He led Alabama to five national titles and 15 bowl wins, including seven Sugar Bowls. The best win percentage in Division I-A was .881, by Knute Rockne (1888–1931), with 105 wins, 12 losses and 5 ties, 12,847 points for and 667 against, at Notre Dame 1918–30. In overall NCAA competition, Eddie Robinson, Grambling (Division 1-AA) holds the mark for most victories, with 402 through 1995.

Largest crowds The highest attendances at college football games were estimated crowds of 120,000 at Soldier Field, Chicago, IL on November 26, 1927 when Notre Dame beat Southern California 7–6, and on October 13, 1928 when Notre Dame beat Navy 7–0. The highest average attendance for home games was 106,217 by Michigan in 1994.

Most games attended Roger and Doris Goodridge of Baldwinsville, NY have attended every Colgate University football game since 1940, both at home and away. During this streak, they have cheered for the Red Raiders through 529 games.

National College Football Champions The most wins in the national journalists' poll, established in 1936 to determine the college team of the year, is eight, by Notre Dame, 1943, 1946–47, 1949, 1966, 1973, 1977 and 1988.

Bowl games The oldest college bowl game is the Rose Bowl. It was first played on January 1, 1902 at Tournament Park, Pasadena, CA, when Michigan beat Stanford 49–0. The University of Southern California

(USC) has a record 19 wins in the Rose Bowl. The University of Alabama has made a record 47 bowl appearances and has had 27 wins (including 18 wins in 31 "big four" appearances). Most wins in the other "big four" bowl games: Orange Bowl: 11, Oklahoma; Sugar Bowl: 8, Alabama; Cotton Bowl: 9, Texas. Alabama, Georgia, Georgia Tech and Notre Dame are the only four teams to have won each of the "big four" bowl games.

Heisman Memorial Trophy   The only double winner was Archie Griffin of Ohio State, 1974–75. The University of Notre Dame has had more Heisman Trophy winners than any other school, with seven selections.

GAMES

Shortest backgammon game   Alan Malcolm Beckerson devised a game of 16 throws in 1982.

Biggest board game   The world's biggest commercially available board game is Galaxion, created by Cerebe Design International of Hong Kong. The board measures 33 by 33 inches.

Most expensive board game   The deluxe version of Outrage!, produced by Imperial Games of Southport, England, retails for £3,995 ($6,392). The object of the game is to steal the Crown Jewels from the Tower of London.

Card holding   Ralf Laue held 326 standard playing cards in a fan in one hand, so that the value and color of each one was visible, in Leipzig, Germany, on March 18, 1994.

Card throwing   Jim Karol of Catasauqua, PA threw a standard playing card 201 feet at Mount Ida College, Newton Centre, MA on October 18, 1992.

Shortest solitaire game   The shortest time to complete the game of solitaire is 10.0 seconds, by Stephen Twigge in Scissett Baths, England on August 2, 1991.

BINGO

Largest house   The largest "house" in bingo sessions was 15,756, at the Canadian National Exhibition, Toronto on August 19, 1983, staged by the Variety Club of Ontario Tent Number 28. There was total prize money of $Cdn250,000 with a record 1-game payout of $Cdn100,000.

Earliest and latest full house   A "full house" call occurred on the 15th number by Norman A. Wilson at Guide Post Working Men's Club, Bedlington, England on June 22, 1978; by Anne Wintle of Brynrethin, Wales, on a bus trip to Bath, England on August 17, 1982; and by Shirley Lord at Kahibah Bowling Club, New South Wales, Australia on October 24, 1983.

"House" was not called until the 86th number at the Hillsborough

Working Men's Club, Sheffield, England on January 11, 1982. There were 32 winners.

CHECKERS

World champion Walter Hellman (U.S.) won a record eight world titles during his tenure as world champion, 1948–75.

Youngest and oldest national champion Asa A. Long became the youngest U.S. national champion, at age 18 yr. 64 days, when he won in Boston, MA on October 23, 1922. He became the oldest, age 79 yr. 334 days, when he won his sixth title in Tupelo, MS on July 21, 1984.

Most opponents Charles Walker played a record 306 games simultaneously, winning 300, drawing 5 and losing 1, at Dollywood, Pigeon Force, TN on October 22, 1994.

The largest number of opponents played without a defeat or draw is 172, by Nate Cohen of Portland, ME in Portland on July 26, 1981. This was not a simultaneous attempt, but consecutive play over four hours.

Newell W. Banks played 140 games simultaneously, winning 133 and drawing seven, in Chicago, IL in 1933. His total playing time was 145 minutes, thus averaging about one move per second. In 1947, he played blindfolded for four hours per day for 45 consecutive days, winning 1,331 games, drawing 54 and losing only two, while playing six games at a time.

Longest game In competition, the prescribed rate of play is not less than 30 moves per hour, with the average game lasting about 90 minutes. In 1958, a game between Dr. Marion Tinsley (U.S.) and Derek Oldbury (Great Britain) lasted 7 hr. 30 min. (played under the 5-minutes-a-move rule).

CHESS

World Championships World champions have been officially recognized since 1886. The longest undisputed tenure was 26 yr. 337 days, by Dr. Emanuel Lasker of Germany, 1894–1921.

The women's world championship title was held by Vera Francevna Stevenson-Menchik (USSR, later Great Britain) from 1927 until her death in 1944, and was successfully defended a record seven times.

Team The USSR won the biennial men's team title (Olympiad) a record 18 times between 1952 and 1990, with Russia winning twice, in 1992 and 1994. The women's title has been won 11 times by the USSR from its introduction in 1957 to 1986, with Georgia winning in 1992 and 1995.

The U.S. has won the men's title five times: 1931, 1933, 1935, 1937 and 1976.

Youngest world champion Maya Chiburdanidze (USSR; b. January 17, 1961) won the women's title in 1978 when she was only 17. Gary Kasparov (USSR) won the title on November 9, 1985 at age 22 yr. 210 days.

Oldest world champion Wilhelm Steinitz (Austria, later U.S.) was 58 yr. 10 days when he lost his title to Lasker on May 26, 1894.

Most active world champion Anatoliy Karpov (USSR) in his tenure as champion, 1975–85, averaged 45.2 competitive games per year, played in 32 tournaments and finished first in 26.

Gary Kasparov was the youngest male world champion in chess.

Youngest Grand Master The youngest individual to qualify as an International Grand Master is Peter Leko (Hungary), at age 14 yr. 145 days on January 30, 1994. The youngest female Grand Master is Judit Polgar (Hungary), at age 15 yr. 150 days on December 20, 1991.

United States The youngest U.S. Grand Master was Bobby Fischer (b. March 9, 1943) in 1958.

Youngest Master In January 1995, Vinay Bhat of San Jose, CA became the youngest person in the history of the United States Chess Foundation to attain a master rating, at 10 yr. 176 days.

Highest rating The highest rating ever attained on the officially adopted Elo System (devised by Arpad E. Elo) is 2,805, by Gary Kasparov (USSR) at the end of 1992.

The women's record is held by Judit Polgar, who achieved a peak rating of 2,630 at the end of 1993.

Fewest games lost by a world champion José Raúl Capablanca (Cuba) lost only 34 games (out of 571) in his adult career, 1909–39. He was unbeaten from February 10, 1916 to March 21, 1924 (63 games) and was world champion 1921–27.

U.S. Championships The most wins since the U.S. Championships became determined by match play competition in 1888 is eight, by Bobby Fischer, 1957–66.

Most opponents The record for most consecutive games played is 663, by Vlastimil Hort (Czechoslovakia, later Germany) over 32½ hours in Porz, Germany, October 5–6, 1984. He played 60–120 opponents at a time, scoring over 80 percent wins and averaging 30 moves per game. He also holds the record for most games played simultaneously, 201 during 550 consecutive games of which he lost only 10, in Seltjarnes, Iceland, April 23–24, 1977.

Eric G. J. Knoppert (Netherlands) played 500 games of 10-minute chess against opponents, averaging 2,002 on the Elo scale, September 13–16, 1985. He scored 413 points (1 for win, ½ for draw), a success rate of 82.6 percent.

Most moves The Master chess game with the most moves on record was one of 269 moves, when Ivan Nikolić drew with Goran Arsović in Belgrade, Yugoslavia on February 17, 1989. The game took 20 hr. 15 min.

Slowest moves In a 15-hour chess game between Louis Paulsen (Germany) and Paul Charles Morphy (U.S.) at the first American Chess Congress, NY on October 29, 1857 (before time clocks were used), a total of 56 moves were made. The game ended in a draw, Paulsen having used about 11 hours of play.

Grand Master Friedrich Sämisch (Germany) ran out of the allotted time (2 hr. 30 min. for 45 moves) after only 12 moves, in Prague, Czechoslovakia, in 1938.

The slowest move played since time clocks were introduced was in Vigo, Spain in 1980 when Francisco R. Torres Trois took 2 hr. 20 min. for his seventh move vs. Luis M. C. P. Santos.

Oldest chess pieces The oldest chess pieces were found in Nashipur, and were dated to c. A.D. 900.

CONTRACT BRIDGE

Biggest tournament The Epson World Bridge Championship, held June 20–21, 1992, was contested by 102,000 players playing the same hands, at 2,000 centers worldwide.

Most world titles The World Championship (Bermuda Bowl) has been won a record 14 times by the U.S., 1950–51, 1953–54, 1970–71, 1976–77, 1979, 1981, 1983, 1985, 1987 and 1995. Italy's Blue Team (*Squadra Azzura*) won 13 world titles and an additional three team Olympiads between 1957 and 1975. Giorgio Belladonna was on all the Italian winning teams.

The U.S. has six wins in the women's world championship for the Venice Trophy, 1974, 1976, 1978, 1987, 1989 and 1991, and three women's wins in the World Team Olympiad, 1976, 1980 and 1984.

Most world championship hands In the 1989 Bermuda Bowl in Perth, Australia, Marcel Branco and Gabriel Chagas, both of Brazil, played a record 752 out of a possible 784 boards.

Possible bridge auctions The number of possible auctions with North as dealer is 128,745,650,347,030,683,120,231,926,111,609,371,363,122,697,557.

CRIBBAGE

Rare hands Five maximum 29-point hands have been achieved by Sean Daniels of Astoria, OR, 1989–92. Paul Nault of Athol, MA had two such hands within eight games in a tournament on March 19, 1977.

Most points in 24 hours The most points scored by a team of four, playing singles in two pairs, is 139,454, by Colin Cooper, John Dunk, Peter Hyham and John Wilson at Her Majesty's Prison, Doncaster, England, September 16–17, 1995.

DOMINOES

Domino toppling The greatest number set up single-handedly and toppled is 281,581 out of 320,236, by Klaus Friedrich, 22, in Fürth, Germany on January 27, 1984. The dominoes fell within 12 min. 57.3 sec., having taken 31 days (10 hours daily) to set up.

Thirty students at Delft, Eindhoven and Twente Technical Universities in the Netherlands set up 1,500,000 dominoes representing all the European Community countries. Of these, 1,382,101 were toppled by one push on January 2, 1988.

Domino stacking Aleksandr Bendikov of Mogilev, Belarus stacked 522 dominoes on a single supporting domino on September 21, 1994.

HORSESHOE PITCHING

World Championships Most titles (men) Ted Allen (U.S.) has won 10 world titles: 1933–35, 1940, 1946, 1953, 1955–57 and 1959.

Most titles (women) Vicki Winston (née Chapelle) has won a record 10 women's titles: 1956, 1958–59, 1961, 1963, 1966–67, 1969, 1975 and 1981.

Longest perfect game At the 1968 World Championship, Elmer Hohl (Canada) threw 56 consecutive ringers.

Most perfect games In World Championship play, only three pitchers have thrown perfect games: Guy Zimmerman (U.S.), 1948; Elmer Hohl (Canada) in 1968; and Jim Walters (U.S.) in 1993.

JUMP ROPE

10-mile skip–run Vadivelu Karunakaren (India) jumped rope 10 miles in 58 minutes in Madras, India, February 1, 1990.

Most turns of the rope One hour 14,628, by Park Bong Tae (South Korea) in Pusan, South Korea, July 2, 1989.

On a single rope, team of 90 206, by students from the Minamikayabe-Chyoritu-Makou Elementary School, Hokkaido, Japan on August 19, 1995.

On a tightrope 521 (consecutive), by Walfer Guerrero (Colombia) in Haarlem, Netherlands on June 1, 1995.

Most on a 50-meter (164-foot) rope (minimum 12 turns obligatory)   220, by a team at the International Rope Skipping Competition, Greeley, CO on June 28, 1990.

SCRABBLE

Highest scores   The highest competitive game score is 1,049 by Phil Appleby in June 1989. His opponent scored 253, and the margin of victory, 796 points, is also a record. His score included a single turn of 374 for the word "OXIDIZERS."

The highest competitive single-turn score recorded, however, is 392, by Dr. Saladin Karl Khoshnaw (of Kurdish origin) in Manchester, England in April 1982. He laid down "CAZIQUES," which means "native chiefs of West Indian aborigines."

The highest score achieved on a single opening move is 124, by Sam Kantimathi in Portland, OR in July 1993. He laid down "BEZIQUE."

United States   The highest score in a tournament game (American-style competitive) is 770 points by game inventor Mark Lansberg (Los Angeles) at the Scrabble tournament in Eagle Rock, CA on June 13, 1993. His opponent, Alan Stern, scored 338 points; their combined total of 1,108 points is also a record for American-style competitive tournament play.

Most tournaments   Chuck Armstrong of Saline, MI, won the most tournaments—65 to the end of 1989.

TWISTER

Most participants   The greatest number of participants in a game of Twister is 4,160 people, at the University of Massachusetts at Amherst on May 2, 1987. Allison Culler won the game.

GOLF

Oldest club   The oldest club of which there is written evidence is the Gentlemen Golfers (now the Honourable Company of Edinburgh Golfers) formed in March 1744. The Royal Burgess Golfing Society of Edinburgh, Scotland claims to have been founded in 1735.

United States   Two golf clubs claim to be the first established in the United States: the Foxburg Golf Club, Clarion Co., PA (1887) and St. Andrews Golf Club of Yonkers, NY (1888).

Largest tournament   The Volkswagen Grand Prix Open Amateur Championship in Great Britain attracted a record 321,778 (206,820 men and 114,958 women) competitors in 1984.

Longest course   The world's longest course is the par-77 8,325-yard International Golf Club in Bolton, MA from the "Tiger" tees, remodeled in 1969 by Robert Trent Jones.

Floyd Satterlee Rood used the entire United States as a course, when he played from the Pacific surf to the Atlantic surf from September 14, 1963 to October 3, 1964 in 114,737 strokes. He lost 3,511 balls on the 3,397.7-mile trail.

Largest green   Probably the largest green in the world is that of the par-6 695-yard fifth hole at International Golf Club, Bolton, MA with an area greater than 28,000 square feet.

Biggest bunker   The biggest bunker is Hell's Half Acre on the 585-yard seventh hole of the Pine Valley course, Clementon, NJ, built in 1912 and generally regarded as the world's most trying course.

Longest hole   The seventh hole (par-7) of the Satsuki Golf Club, Sano, Japan measures 964 yards.

United States   The longest hole in the United States is the 12th hole at Meadows Farm Golf Course in Locust Grove, VA, at a distance of 841 yards.

Longest drive   The greatest recorded drive on a standard course is one of 515 yards, by Michael Hoke Austin of Los Angeles, CA, in the U.S. National Seniors Open Championship at Las Vegas, NV on September 25, 1974.

Kelly Robbins struck the longest recorded drive by a woman, 429.7 yards, at the Elmira Corning Regional Airport in Corning, NY on May 22, 1995.

Most balls hit in one hour   The most balls driven in one hour, over 100 yards and into a target area, is 2,146, by Sean Murphy (Canada) at Swifts Practice Range, Carlisle, England on June 30, 1995.

Longest putt   The longest recorded holed putt in a professional tournament is 110 feet, by Jack Nicklaus in the 1964 Tournament of Champions; and by Nick Price in the 1992 United States PGA Championship.

Bob Cook (U.S.) sank a putt measured at 140 ft. 2³/₄ in. on the 18th at St. Andrews, Scotland in the International Fourball Pro Am Tournament on October 1, 1976.

SCORES

Lowest 18 holes Men   At least four players have played a long course (over 6,561 yards) in a score of 58—most recently Monte Carlo Money (U.S.), at the par-72, 6,607-yard Las Vegas Municipal Golf Club, NV on March 11, 1981.

The PGA tournament record for 18 holes is 59 (30 + 29), by Àl Geiberger in the second round of the Danny Thomas Classic, on the 72-par 7,249-yard Colonial Golf Club course, Memphis, TN on June 10, 1977; and by Chip Beck in the third round of the Las Vegas Invitational, on the

PGA TOUR ALL-TIME SCORING RECORDS

All records are for 72-hole tournaments.

Lowest score (9 holes)	27	Mike Souchak, Texas Open (back nine)	1955
	27	Andy North, B.C. Open (back nine)	1975
Lowest score (18 holes)	59	Al Geiberger, Danny Thomas Memphis Classic (2nd round)	1977
	59	Chip Beck, Las Vegas Invitational (3rd round)	1991
Lowest score (36 holes)	125	Gay Brewer, Pensacola Open (2nd and 3rd rounds)	1967
	125	Ron Streck, Texas Open (3rd and 4th rounds)	1978
	125	Blaine McCallister, Hardee's Golf Classic (2nd and 3rd rounds)	1988
Lowest score (54 holes)	189	Chandler Harper, Texas Open (2nd, 3rd and 4th rounds)	1954
	189	John Cook, Federal Express St. Jude Classic (1st, 2nd and 3rd rounds)	1996
Lowest score (72 holes)	257	Mike Souchak, Texas Open	1955
Most shots under par	27	Ben Hogan, Portland Invitational	1945
	27	Mike Souchak, Texas Open	1955
Fewest putts (18 holes)	18	Sam Trahan, IVB-Philadelphia Golf Classic (4th round)	1979
	18	Mike McGee, Federal Express St. Jude Classic (1st round)	1987
	18	Kenny Knox, MCI Heritage Classic (1st round)	1989
	18	Andy North, Anheuser Busch Golf Classic (2nd round)	1990
	18	Jim McGovern, Federal Express St. Jude Classic (2nd round)	1992
Fewest putts (72 holes)	93	Kenny Knox, MCI Heritage Classic	1989

PGA Tour

72-par 6,979-yard Sunrise Golf Club course, Las Vegas, NV on October 11, 1991.

Women   The lowest score on an 18-hole course over 5,000 yards is 60 (31 + 29) by Wanda Morgan, on the Westgate and Birchington Golf Club course, Kent, England, on July 11, 1929.

The lowest recorded score in an LPGA tour event on an 18-hole course (over 5,600 yards) is 62 (30 + 32) by Mickey Wright (U.S.) on the Hogan Park Course (par-71, 6,286 yards) in Midland, TX, in November 1964; Vicki Fergon at the 1984 San Jose Classic, San Jose, CA; Laura Davies (Great Britain) (32 + 30) at the Rail Golf Club, Springfield, IL on August 31, 1991; and Hollis Stacy (U.S.) (30 + 32) at the Meridian Valley CC, Seattle, WA on September 18, 1992.

Lowest 72 holes Men   Horton Smith scored 245 (63, 58, 61 and 63) for 72 holes on the 4,700-yard course (par-64) at Catalina Country Club, CA to win the Catalina Open, December 21–23, 1928.

The lowest 72 holes in a PGA tour event is 257 (60, 68, 64, 65), by Mike Souchak in the 1955 Texas Open in San Antonio.

Women   Trish Johnson (Great Britain) scored 242 (64, 60, 60, 58; 21 under par) in the Bloor Homes Eastleigh Classic at the Fleming Park Course (4,402 yards) in Eastleigh, England, July 22–25, 1987.

The lowest score in an LPGA tour event is 267 (68, 66, 67, 66), by Betsy King in the 1992 Mazda LPGA championship.

Most consecutive birdies   The official PGA tour record is eight, recorded by three players: Bob Goalby, during the fourth round of the 1961 St. Petersburg Open; Fuzzy Zoeller, during the opening round of the 1976 Quad Cities Open; and Dewey Arnette, during the opening round of the 1987 Buick Open. Goalby was the only golfer to win his event.

Most shots under par   35, by Tom Kite at the 90-hole 1993 Bob Hope Chrysler Classic, February 11–14, 1993.

Fastest rounds Individual   With wide variations in the lengths of courses, speed records, even for rounds under par, are of little comparative value. The fastest round played with the golf ball coming to rest before each new stroke is 27 min. 9 sec., by James Carvill at Warrenpoint Golf Course, County Down, Northern Ireland (18 holes, 6,154 yards) on June 18, 1987.

Team   The 35 members of the Team Balls Out Diving completed the 18-hole 5,516-meter John E. Clark course in Point Micu, CA in 9 min. 39 sec. on November 16, 1992. They scored 71.

Most holes in 24 hours   *On foot*   Ian Colston, 35, played 22 rounds plus five holes (401 holes in all) at Bendigo Golf Club, Victoria, Australia (par-73, 6,061 yards), November 27–28, 1971.

Using golf carts   David Cavalier played 846 holes at Arrowhead Country Club, North Canton, OH (9 holes, 3,013 yards), August 6–7, 1990. The women's record is held by Cyndy Lent (U.S.), who played 509 holes at Twin Lakes Country Club, Twin Lakes, WI on August 7–8, 1994.

Most holes in 12 hours   Doug Wert played 440 holes in 12 hours on the 6,044-yard course at Tournament Players Club, Coral Springs, FL on June 7, 1993.

Most holes played in a week   Steve Hylton played 1,128 holes at the Mason Rudolph Golf Club (6,060 yards), Clarksville, TN, August 25–31, 1980. Using a golf cart, Leroy Kilpatrick (U.S.) completed 1,363 holes at Jack Gaither Golf Course, Tallahassee, FL, October 23–29, 1995.

World One-Club Championship   Thad Daber (U.S.), with a 6-iron, played the 6,037-yard Lochmore Golf Club course, Cary, NC in 70 to win the 1987 World One-Club Championship.

MEN'S CHAMPIONSHIP RECORDS

Grand Slam   The four grand slam events are the Masters, the U.S. Open, the British Open and the PGA Championship. No player has won all four events in one calendar year. Ben Hogan came closest to succeeding in 1951, when he won the first three legs, but he could not return to the United States from Britain in time for the PGA Championship. Jack Nicklaus has won the most major championships, with 18 professional titles (6 Masters, 4 U.S. Opens, 3 British Opens and 5 PGA Championships). Additionally, Nicklaus has won two U.S. Amateur titles, which are often included in calculating major championship victories.

Masters   *(played on the 6,925-yard Augusta National Golf Course, GA, first in 1934)*

Most wins   Jack Nicklaus has won six green jackets (1963, 1965–66, 1972, 1975, 1986). Two players have won consecutive Masters: Jack Nicklaus (1965–66) and Nick Faldo (Great Britain; 1989–90).

Lowest total aggregate   271, by Jack Nicklaus (67, 71, 64, 69) in 1965, and by Raymond Loran Floyd (65, 66, 70, 70) in 1976.

U.S. Open (inaugurated 1895)

Most wins   Four players have won the title four times: Willie Anderson (1901, 1903–05), Bobby Jones (1923, 1926, 1929–30), Ben Hogan (1948, 1950–51, 1953) and Jack Nicklaus (1962, 1967, 1972, 1980). Willie Anderson gained three successive titles, 1903–05.

Lowest total aggregate   The lowest 72-hole score is 272, achieved by two players: Jack Nicklaus, 272 (63, 71, 70, 68) on the lower course (7,015 yards) at Baltusrol Country Club, NJ, June 12–15, 1980; and Lee Janzen (67, 67, 69, 69), also at Baltusrol, June 17–20, 1993.

British Open (inaugurated 1860)

Most wins   Harry Vardon won six titles, in 1896, 1898–99, 1903, 1911 and 1914. Tom Morris, Jr. won four successive British Opens, from 1868 to 1872 (the event was not held in 1871).

Lowest total aggregate   267 (66, 68, 69, 64) by Greg Norman (Australia) at Royal St. George's, in July 1993.

Professional Golfers Association (PGA) Championship *(inaugurated 1916)*

Most wins   Two players have won the title five times: Walter Hagen (1921, 1924–27) and Jack Nicklaus (1963, 1971, 1973, 1975, 1980). Walter Hagen won four consecutive titles from 1924 to 1927.

Lowest total aggregate   267, by Steve Elkington (Australia) (68, 67, 68, 64) and Colin Montgomerie (Great Britain) (68, 67, 67, 65) at the Riviera Country Club, Pacific Palisades, CA in 1995. Elkington defeated Montgomerie in a playoff.

WOMEN'S CHAMPIONSHIP RECORDS

Grand Slam   The Grand Slam of women's golf has consisted of four tournaments since 1955. Since 1983, the U.S. Open, LPGA Championship, du Maurier Classic and Nabisco Dinah Shore have been the major events. Patty Berg has won 15 professional Grand Slam events: U.S. Open (1), Titleholders (7), Western Open (7); the latter two are now defunct. She also won one U.S. Amateur title.

U.S. Open (inaugurated 1946)

Most wins   The most wins is four, by Betsy Rawls, 1951, 1953, 1957 and 1960, and by Mickey Wright, in 1958–59, 1961 and 1964.

40 years ago *the lowest score for 18 holes by a professional woman golfer was 64, by Patty Berg. Her historic round occurred on April 29, 1952. Berg went out in 30 and came home in 34.* **Today** *the 18-hole record for the LPGA Tour is 62, shared by four players: Mickey Wright (1964), Vicki Fergon (1984), Laura Davies (1991) and Hollis Stacy (1992). Playing a par-73 course, Fergon knocked in 11 birdies during her round, the all-time LPGA record.*

"Her mother and I were there that day. It was glorious."—Ed Fergon, Vicki's father, February 20, 1996

Annika Sorenstam (Sweden) won the U.S. Open in 1995 and 1996.

Lowest total aggregate The lowest 72-hole aggregate is 277, by Liselotte Newman (Sweden), 1988, and by Patty Sheehan (U.S.), 1994.

Ladies Professional Golfers Association (LPGA) Championship *(inaugurated 1955)*

Most wins Mickey Wright won four times, in 1958, 1960–61 and 1963.

Lowest total aggregate The lowest score for 72 holes is 267, by Betsy King at the Bethesda Country Club, MD in 1992.

Du Maurier Classic *(inaugurated 1973)*

Most wins Pat Bradley holds the record for most wins, with three titles won in 1980, 1985–86.

Lowest total aggregate The lowest score for 72 holes is 272, by Jody Rosenthal in 1987.

Nabisco Dinah Shore *(inaugurated 1972)*

Most wins Amy Alcott won three times, in 1983, 1988 and 1991.

Lowest total aggregate The lowest score for 72 holes is 273, by Amy Alcott in 1991.

INDIVIDUAL RECORDS

Biggest prizes The greatest first-place prize money ever won is $1 million, awarded in the Sun City Challenge, 1987–91. Bophuthatswana, South Africa. The greatest total prize money is $2.7 million (including a $550,000 first prize) for the Johnnie Walker World Championship at Tryall Golf Course, Montego Bay, Jamaica in 1992, 1993, and 1994.

GREG NORMAN

"The earnings record doesn't mean a whole lot, to tell you the truth. I go out there to play because I love to play the game," says Greg Norman. The PGA Tour's all-time leading money winner, "the Great White Shark" is proudest of his British Open triumph at Royal St. George's in 1993. His winning score of 267 was the lowest in the history of the event.

"**I**t was one of the greatest championships ever played. All the great play-ers—Faldo, Price, Pavin, Langer and myself—peaked at the same time. That is very unusual in a major," recalls Norman. "Everybody raised their level to a different standard that week. That's the thing that stands out in my mind."

The 1993 win was Norman's second British Open title. The first came in 1986 at Turnberry. There he tied the all-time low 18-hole score, post-ing a 63 in the second round. "I still can't believe I finished the last two holes, three-putt, three-putt," laments the Shark. Norman also shares the low-18 score for the Masters at Augusta National. He tied Nick Price's mark in the first round of the 1996 event. "I would say the 63 at Turn-berry was superior to the one at Augusta. The conditions at Turnberry were extremely demanding, a lot of rough, very high fairways, and the weather wasn't good." Norman doesn't think about shooting record scores on the course: "You just play one shot at a time. Even when you're playing poorly, you don't want to think what you are shooting because that's not the way you play the game mentally. When I tied both of those records, I had no idea when I made the putt on 18."

Norman's record at this year's Masters was overshadowed by the cir-cumstances of his subsequent defeat when he held a six-shot lead after the third round, but finished second to Nick Faldo. The Shark is philo-sophical: "If I had started with a 78 and finished with a 63, everybody would have thought I had come back with a phenomenal score."

Norman has experienced more than his fair share of tough losses. His graciousness in defeat, particularly in the wake of his Masters collapse, has been a model of sportsmanship. "It's frustrating when you know you've put in a 101 percent and you come up short. But deep down in-side you know that the game of golf is bigger than anybody." Norman adds, "There's a great old saying: 'The journey is the reward.' If you make your journey in life enjoyable, then your reward is how you've taken that journey. For me, the journey is the reward, win lose or draw."

Highest earnings   Greg Norman (Australia) has won a record $14,618,816 worldwide, 1976–95.

PGA and LPGA circuits   Greg Norman won a season's record $1,654,959 in 1995. Norman also holds the PGA career earnings record. As of July 28, 1996, his career total stood at $10,363,740.

The record career earnings for a woman is $5,443,144 to July 23, 1996, by Betsy King. The season record for a woman is $863,578, by Beth Daniel in 1990.

Most times leading money winner   Jack Nicklaus has been the PGA tour leading money winner eight times—1964–65, 1967, 1971–73, 1975–76. Kathy Whitworth headed the LPGA list eight times—1965–68, 1970–73.

Most tournament wins   Byron Nelson (U.S.) won a record 18 tournaments (plus one unofficial) in one year, including a record 11 consecutively from March 8 to August 4, 1945.

The LPGA record for one year is 13, by Mickey Wright (1963). She also holds the record for most wins in scheduled events, with four between August and September 1962 and between May and June 1963, a record matched by Kathy Whitworth between March and April 1969.

Successive wins   Between May and June 1978, Nancy Lopez won all five tournaments that she entered; however, these events did not follow each other and are therefore not considered consecutive tournament victories.

Career wins   Sam Snead won 84 official PGA tour events, 1936–65. The LPGA record is 88, by Kathy Whitworth, 1959–91.

Oldest winner   Sam Snead won a PGA tournament at age 52 yr. 312 days at the 1965 Greater Greensboro Open.

Greatest winning margin   The greatest margin of victory in a professional tournament is 21 strokes, by Jerry Pate (U.S.), who won the Colombian Open with 262, December 10–13, 1981.

The greatest margin of victory in a PGA tour event is 16 strokes, by Joe Kirkwood, Sr. (U.S.) in the 1924 Corpus Christi Open, and by Bobby Locke (South Africa) in 1948 at the Chicago Victory National Championship.

NCAA Championships   Two golfers have won three NCAA titles: Ben Daniel Crenshaw of the University of Texas in 1971–73, tying with Tom Kite in 1972; and Phil Mickelson of Arizona State University in 1989–90, 1992.

Oldest player to score his age   The oldest player to achieve a score equal to his age is C. Arthur Thompson (1869–1975) of Victoria, British Columbia, Canada, who scored 103, on the Uplands course of 6,215 yards in 1973.

Golf ball balancing   Lang Martin balanced seven golf balls vertically on a flat surface without adhesive in Charlotte, NC on February 9, 1980.

Throwing a golf ball   The lowest recorded score for throwing a golf ball around 18 holes (over 6,000 yards) is 82, by Joe Flynn (U.S.), 21, at the 6,228-yard Port Royal course, Bermuda on March 27, 1975.

HOLES IN ONE

Longest hole in one   The longest hole ever sunk in one shot was the "dog-leg" 496-yard 17th at Teign Valley Golf Course, Exeter, England, by Shaun Lynch on July 24, 1995. The women's record is 393 yards, by Marie Robie on the first hole of the Furnace Brook Golf Club, Wollaston, MA on September 4, 1949.

Consecutive holes in one   There are at least 20 cases of "aces" being achieved in consecutive holes, of which the greatest was Norman L. Manley's unique "double albatross" on the par-4 330-yard seventh and par-4 290-yard eighth holes on the Del Valle Country Club course, Saugus, CA on September 2, 1964.

Youngest and oldest   The youngest golfer recorded to have shot a hole in one is Coby Orr (5 years) of Littleton, CO on the 103-yard fifth at the Riverside Golf Course, San Antonio, TX in 1975. The youngest girl is Nicola Mylonas (10 yr. 64 days) on the 133-yard 1st at South Course, Nudgee, Australia on September 18, 1993. The youngest American girl to score an ace was Tara Wilkens, at Square Butte Creek Golf Course, Center, ND, June 11, 1995, at age 10 yr. 92 days.

The oldest golfers to have performed this feat are: (men) 99 yr. 244 days, Otto Bucher (Switzerland) on the 130-yard 12th at La Manga Golf Club, Spain on January 13, 1985; (women) 95 yr. 257 days, Erna Ross on the 112-yard 17th at The Everglades Club, Palm Beach, FL on April 23, 1986.

Most rewarding hole in one   On November 1, 1992, Jason Bohn (U.S.) won $1 million when he made a hole in one in a charity contest. He aced the 136-yard second hole at the Harry S. Pritchett Gold Course, Tuscaloosa, AL using a 9-iron.

TEAM COMPETITIONS

World Cup (formerly Canada Cup)   The World Cup (formerly Canada Cup) has been won most often by the U.S., with 21 victories between 1955 and 1995.

The only men to have been on six winning teams are Arnold Palmer (1960, 1962–64, 1966–67) and Jack Nicklaus (1963–64, 1966–67, 1971 and 1973). Only Nicklaus has taken the individual title three times (1963–64, 1971).

The lowest aggregate score for 144 holes is 536, by the U.S., Fredrick Stephen Couples and Davis Love III, in Dorado, Puerto Rico, November 10–13, 1994.

The lowest individual score is 269, by Roberto de Vicenzo (Argentina) in 1970.

Ryder Cup   The U.S. has won 23 to 6 (with 2 ties) to 1995.

Arnold Palmer has won the most Ryder Cup matches, with 22 out of 32 played, with 2 halved and 8 lost, in six contests from 1963 to 1973. Christy O'Connor, Sr. (Ireland) played in 10 contests, 1955–73; this was equaled by Nick Faldo, 1977–95. Three players have played in eight U.S. Ryder Cup teams: Billy Casper (1965–75), Raymond Floyd (1969–93) and Lanny Wadkins (1977–93).

Walker Cup   The series was instituted in 1921 (for the Walker Cup since 1922 and now held biennially). The U.S. has won 30 matches, Great Britain and Ireland 4 (1938, 1971, 1989, 1995), and the 1965 match was tied.

Jay Sigel (U.S.) has won a record 18 matches, with 5 halved and 10 lost, 1977–93. Joseph Boynton Carr (Great Britain & Ireland) played in 10 contests, 1947–67.

Curtis Cup   The biennial ladies' Curtis Cup match between the U.S. and Great Britain & Ireland was first held in 1932. The U.S. has won 20 to 1994, Great Britain & Ireland six (1952, 1956, 1986, 1988, 1992 and 1994), and three matches have been tied.

GREYHOUND RACING

Derby   Two greyhounds have won the American Derby twice, in Taunton, MA: Real Huntsman in 1950–51, and Dutch Bahama in 1984–85.

Fastest greyhound   The fastest speed at which any greyhound has been timed is 41.83 MPH (400 yards in 19.57 seconds) by Star Title on the straightaway track in Wyong, New South Wales, Australia on March 5, 1994.

United States   My Bold Girl ran $5/16$ mile in 29.58 seconds at Bluffs Run, Council Bluffs, IA in 1994. The fastest $3/8$-mile time was 36.43 seconds by P's Rambling in Hollywood, FL in 1987. Runaround Sue ran a $7/16$-mile track in 42.57 seconds in Hollywood, FL in 1991.

Most wins   The most career wins is 143, by JR's Ripper of Multnomah, Fairview, OR and Tucson, AZ, 1982–86. The most wins in a year is 61, by Indy Ann in Mexico and the United States in 1956.

The most consecutive victories is 37, by J. J. Doc Richard, owned by Jack Boyd.

Highest earnings   The career earnings record is held by Mo Kick, with $314,067, 1990–94. The most money won in a single race is $130,000, by Design Time, at the 1994 Great Greyhound Futurity, in the Woodlands, Kansas City, KS.

Most stakes victories   Real Huntsman achieved 10 wins from 1949 to 1951, including the American Derby twice.

Longest odds   Apollo Prince won at odds of 250–1 at Sandown Greyhound Race Course, Springvale, Victoria, Australia on November 14, 1968.

GYMNASTICS

Largest gymnastics/aerobics display   The largest number of participants was 30,517 for the Great Singapore Workout at The Padang, Singapore on August 27, 1995.

World Championships Women   The greatest number of titles won in the World Championships (including Olympic Games) is 12 individual wins and six team, by Larisa Latynina (USSR), 1954–64.

The USSR won 21 team titles (11 world and 10 Olympic).

Men   Vitaliy Scherbo (Belarus) won 13 individual titles and one team title, 1992–95.

Vitaliy Scherbo won a record six gold medals at the 1992 Olympics.

The USSR won the team title a record 13 times (eight World Championships, five Olympics) between 1952 and 1992.

United States   Shannon Miller has won five gold medals, in all-around, floor exercise and uneven bars in 1993 and all-around and beam in 1994. The men's record is three gold medals, by Kurt Thomas, in floor exercise in 1978–79 and horizontal bar in 1979.

Youngest champions   Aurelia Dobre (Romania) won the women's overall world title at age 14 yr. 352 days on October 23, 1987. Daniela Silivas (Romania) revealed in 1990 that she was born in 1971, a year later than previously claimed, so that she was age 14 yr. 185 days when she won the gold medal for balance beam on November 10, 1985.

The youngest male world champion was Dmitriy Bilozerchev (USSR), at 16 yr. 315 days in Budapest, Hungary on October 28, 1983.

Olympics   The USSR won the women's title 10 times (1952–80, 1988 and 1992). The successes in 1992 were by the Unified Team from the republics of the former USSR. The men's title has been won a record five times, by Japan (in 1960, 1964, 1968, 1972 and 1976) and the USSR (1952, 1956, 1980, 1988 and 1992).

Vera Cáslavská-Odlozil (Czechoslovakia) has won the most individual gold medals, with seven, three in 1964 and four (one shared) in 1968.

The most men's individual gold medals is six, by Boris Shakhlin, one in 1956, four (two shared) in 1960 and one in 1964; and by Nikolay Yefimovich (USSR), one in 1972, four in 1976 and one in 1980.

Larisa Latynina won six individual gold medals and was on three winning teams, 1956–64, earning nine gold medals. She also won five silver and four bronze, 18 in all—an Olympic record.

The most medals for a male gymnast is 15, by Nikolay Andrianov (USSR)—seven gold, five silver and three bronze, 1972–80.

Aleksandr Dityatin (USSR) is the only man to win a medal in all eight categories in the same Games, with three gold, four silver and one bronze in Moscow in 1980.

Vitaliy Scherbo (Belarus) won a record six golds at one Games in 1992: four individual titles, the all-around and the team gold that he won with the Unified Team.

United States   The best U.S. performances were in the 1904 Games, when there was limited international participation. Anton Heida won five gold medals and a silver, and George Eyser, who had a wooden leg, won three gold, two silver and a bronze medal. Mary Lou Retton won a women's record five medals in 1984—gold in all-around, two silver and two bronze.

Highest score   Hans Eugster (Switzerland) scored a perfect 10.00 in the compulsory parallel bars at the 1950 World Championships. Nadia Comaneci (Romania) achieved seven perfect scores at the Olympics in Montreal, Canada in July 1976.

U.S. Championships   Alfred A. Jochim (1902–81) won seven men's all-around U.S. titles, 1925–30 and 1933, and a total of 34 in all events, 1923–34. The women's record is six all-around, 1945–46 and 1949–52, and 39 in all exercises, including 11 in succession on balance beam, 1941–51, by Clara Marie Lomady.

EXERCISES

Speed and Stamina

Records are for the most repetitions of the following activities within the given time span.

Chins—consecutive 370, Lee Chin-yong (South Korea) at Backyon Gymnasium, Seoul, South Korea on May 14, 1988.

Chins—consecutive, one arm, from a ring 22, Robert Chisnall at Queen's University, Kingston, Ontario, Canada on December 3, 1982. (Also 18 2-finger chins, 12 1-finger chins).

Parallel bar dips—1 hour 3,726, Kim Yang-ki (South Korea) at the Rivera Hotel, Seoul, South Korea on November 28, 1991.

Push-ups—24 hours 46,001, Charles Servizio (U.S.) at Fontana City Hall, Fontana, CA on April 24–25, 1993.

Push-ups—one arm, 5 hours 8,794, Paddy Doyle (Great Britain) at Stamina's Kickboxing Self Defence Gym, Birmingham, England on February 12, 1996.

Push-ups—fingertip, 5 hours 7,011, Kim Yang-ki (South Korea) at the Swiss Guard Hotel, Seoul, South Korea on August 30, 1990.

Push-ups—consecutive, one finger 124, Paul Lynch (Great Britain) at the Hippodrome, London, England on April 21, 1992.

Push-ups in a year Paddy Doyle (Great Britain) achieved a documented 1,500,230 push-ups, October 1988–October 1989.

Leg lifts—12 hours 41,788, Lou Scripa, Jr. at Jack La Lanne's American Health & Fitness Spa, Sacramento, CA on December 2, 1988.

Somersaults Ashrita Furman performed 8,341 forward rolls in 10 hr. 30 min. over 12 miles 390 yd., Lexington to Charleston, MA on April 30, 1986.

Backwards somersaults—Shigeru Iwasaki somersaulted backwards 54.68 yd. in 10.8 sec. in Tokyo, Japan on March 30, 1980.

Squats—1 hour 4,289, Paul Wai Man Chung at the Yee Gin Kung Fu of Chung Sze Health (HK) Association, Kowloon, Hong Kong on April 5, 1993.

Squat thrusts—1 hour 3,552, Paul Wai Man Chung at the Yee Gin Kung Fu of Chung Sze Kung Fu (HK) Association, Kowloon, Hong Kong on April 21, 1992.

Burpees—1 hour 1,840, Paddy Doyle at the Bull's Head, Polesworth, England on February 6, 1994.

Pummel horse double circles—consecutive 97, Tyler Farstad (Canada) at Surrey Gymnastic Society, Surrey, British Columbia on November 27, 1993.

Static wall sit (Samson's chair) 11 hr. 5 min., Rajikumar Chakraborty (India) at Panposh Sports Hostel, Rourkel, India on April 22, 1994.

NCAA Championships Men The men's competition was first held in 1932. The most team championships won is nine, by two colleges: University of Illinois, 1939–42, 1950, 1955–56, 1958, 1989; and Pennsylvania State University, 1948, 1953–54, 1957, 1959–61, 1965, 1976.

The most individual titles in a career is seven, by Joe Giallombardo, University of Illinois, tumbling, 1938–40, all-around title, 1938–40, and floor exercise, 1938; and by Jim Hartung, University c. Nebraska, all-around title, 1980–81, rings, 1980–82, and parallel bar, 1981–82.

Women The women's competition was first held in 1982. The most team championships is eight, by the University of Utah, 1982–86, 1990, 1992 and 1994.

The most individual titles in a career is five, by Missy Marlowe, University of Utah—all-around title, 1992, balance beam, 1991–92, uneven bars, 1992, floor exercise, 1992.

Modern rhythmic gymnastics The most overall individual world titles is three, by Maria Gigova (Bulgaria) in 1969, 1971 and 1973 (shared), and by Maria Petrova (Bulgaria), 1993, 1994, and 1995 (shared). Bulgaria won nine team titles, 1969, 1971, 1981, 1983, 1985, 1987, 1989 (shared), 1993, 1995.

Bianka Panova (Bulgaria) won four apparatus gold medals with maximum scores, and won a team gold in 1987. Lilia Ignatova (Bulgaria) has won two individual World Cup titles, in 1983 and 1986. Marina Lobach (USSR) won the 1988 Olympic title with perfect scores for all six disciplines.

HOCKEY

NATIONAL HOCKEY LEAGUE (NHL)

Most wins The Detroit Red Wings won a record 62 games in the 1995/96 season. The Montreal Canadiens won a record 132 points (60 wins and 12 ties) in 80 games played in 1976/77; their eight losses were also a record, the least ever in a season of 70 or more games. The highest percentage of wins in a season was .875, achieved by the Boston Bruins, with 30 wins in 44 games in 1929/30.

The longest undefeated run during a season, 35 games (25 wins and 10 ties), was established by the Philadelphia Flyers from October 14, 1979 to January 6, 1980.

The most goals scored in a season is 446, by the Edmonton Oilers in 1983/84, when they also achieved a record 1,182 points.

The most assists in a season was the 737 by the Edmonton Oilers during the 1985–86 season.

The most power-play goals scored in a season is 119, by the Pittsburgh Penguins during the 1988–89 season. The most shorthanded goals scored in a season is 36, by the Edmonton Oilers during the 1983/84 season.

The most shutouts in a season is 22, in 1928/29 by the Montreal Canadiens, in just 44 games, all by George Hainsworth, who also achieved a record low goals-against average of .98 that season.

The Detroit Red Wings won 62 games in the 1995/96 season.

Most goals in a game   The NHL record is 21 goals, when the Montreal Canadiens beat Toronto St. Patrick's, 14–7, in Montreal on January 10, 1920, and the Edmonton Oilers beat the Chicago Blackhawks, 12–9, in Chicago on December 11, 1985. The NHL single-team record is 16, by the Montreal Canadiens vs. the Québec Bulldogs (3), in Québec City on November 3, 1920.

Longest hockey game   The longest game, and the longest single shutout, was 2 hr. 56 min. 30 sec. (playing time) when the Detroit Red Wings beat the Montreal Maroons 1–0 in the sixth period of overtime at the Forum, Montreal, at 2:25 A.M. on March 25, 1936.

Fastest goals   Toronto scored eight goals in 4 min. 52 sec. vs. the New York Americans on March 19, 1938.

INDIVIDUAL RECORDS

Most games played   Gordie Howe played in a record 1,767 NHL regular-season games (and 157 playoff games) over a record 26 seasons, from 1946 to 1971, for the Detroit Red Wings, and in 1979/80 for the Hartford Whalers.

Fastest goals   Joseph A. C. Provost (Montreal Canadiens) scored after four seconds vs. Boston Bruins in the second period in Montreal on November 9, 1957. Denis J. Savard (Chicago Blackhawks) equaled this feat on January 12, 1986 vs. Hartford Whalers in the third period in Chicago. From the opening whistle, the fastest is five seconds, by Doug Smail (Winnipeg Jets) vs. St. Louis Blues in Winnipeg on December 20, 1981, and by Bryan John Trottier (New York Islanders) vs. Boston Bruins in Boston on March 22, 1984. Bill Mosienko (Chicago Blackhawks) scored three goals in 21 seconds vs. New York Rangers on March 23, 1952.

Most goals, assists and points Career   Wayne Gretzky holds the NHL's three most coveted records, all-time leader in goals, assists and points. During his career (Edmonton Oilers 1979–88, Los Angeles Kings 1988–96, St. Louis Blues 1996) he has scored 837 goals, 1,771 assists and 2,608 points from 1,253 games.

Season   The most goals scored in a season in the NHL is 92, in the 1981/82 season by Wayne Gretzky for the Edmonton Oilers. He scored a record 215 points, including a record 163 assists, in 1985/86.

Game   The most goals in an NHL game is seven, by Michael Joe Malone in Québec's 10–6 win over Toronto St. Patricks in Québec City on January 31, 1920.

The most assists in an NHL game is seven, once by Billy Taylor for Detroit, 10–6 vs. Chicago on March 16, 1947, and three times by Wayne Gretzky for Edmonton, 8–2 vs. Washington on February 15, 1980, 12–9 vs. Chicago on December 11, 1985, and 8–2 vs. Québec on February 14, 1986.

The record number of assists in one period is five, by Dale Hawerchuk, for the Winnipeg Jets vs. the Los Angeles Kings on March 6, 1984.

Consecutive games   Harry Broadbent scored in 16 consecutive games for Ottawa in the 1921/22 season.

Most hat tricks   The most hat tricks (three or more goals in a game) in a career is 49, by Wayne Gretzky through the 1995/96 season for the Edmonton Oilers, the Los Angeles Kings and the St. Louis Blues. Gretzky also holds the record for most hat tricks in a season, 10, in both the 1982 and 1984 seasons for the Oilers.

Most points in one game   The NHL record for most points scored in one game is 10, by Darryl Sittler—six goals, four assists for the Toronto Maple Leafs vs. the Boston Bruins in an NHL game in Toronto on February 7, 1976.

Period   The most points in one period is six, by Bryan Trottier—three goals and three assists in the second period, for the New York Islanders vs. the New York Rangers (9–4) on December 23, 1978. Nine players have a record four goals in one period.

Most consecutive games played   A record of 964 consecutive games played was achieved by Doug Jarvis for the Montreal Canadiens, the Washington Capitals and the Hartford Whalers from October 8,1975 to October 10, 1987.

Most consecutive 50-or-more-goal seasons   Mike Bossy (New York Islanders) scored at least 50 goals in nine consecutive seasons from 1977/78 through 1985/86. Wayne Gretzky (Edmonton Oilers, Los Angeles Kings) has also scored at least 50 goals in one season nine times, but his longest streak is eight seasons.

Most consecutive points   The most consecutive games scoring points was 51, by Wayne Gretzky from October 5, 1983 to January 27, 1984 for the Edmonton Oilers.

Goaltending   Terry Sawchuk played a record 971 games as a goaltender, for the Detroit Red Wings, the Boston Bruins, the Toronto Maple Leafs, the Los Angeles Kings and the New York Rangers, from 1949 to 1970. He achieved a record 435 wins (to 337 losses, and 188 ties). Jacques Plante, with 434 NHL wins, surpassed Sawchuk's figure by adding 15 wins in his one season in the WHA, for a total of 449 in 868 games.

Bernie Parent achieved a record 47 wins in a season, with 13 losses and 12 ties, for Philadelphia in 1973/74.

Most successful goaltending   The most shutouts played by a goaltender in an NHL career is 103, by Terry Sawchuck of Detroit, Boston, Toronto, Los Angeles and New York Rangers, between 1949 and 1970. Gerry Cheevers (Boston Bruins) went a record 32 successive games without a defeat in 1971/72.

George Hainsworth completed 22 shutouts for the Montreal Canadiens in 1928/29. Alex Connell played 461 min. 29 sec. without conceding a goal for Ottawa in the 1928/29 season. Roy Worters saved 70 shots for the Pittsburgh Pirates vs. the New York Americans on December 24, 1925.

Defensemen   Paul Coffey (Edmonton Oilers 1980–87, Pittsburgh Penguins 1988–92, Los Angeles Kings 1992–93, Detroit Red Wings 1996) holds the record for most goals (372), assists (1,038) and points (1,410) by a defenseman. He scored a record 48 goals in 1985/86. Bobby Orr (Boston Bruins) holds the single-season marks for assists (102) and points (139), both of which were set in 1970/71.

Brian Leetch shares the record for most goals in a game by a defenseman.

Player awards   The Hart Trophy, awarded annually starting with the 1923/24 season by the Professional Hockey Writers Association as the Most Valuable Player award of the NHL, has been won a record nine times by Wayne Gretzky, 1980–87, 1989. Gretzky has also won the Art Ross Trophy a record 10 times, 1981–87, 1990–91 and 1994; this trophy has been awarded annually since 1947/48 to the NHL season's leading scorer.

Bobby Orr of Boston won the James Norris Memorial Trophy, awarded annually starting with the 1953/54 season to the league's leading defenseman, a record eight times, 1968–75.

Most successful coach   Scotty Bowman holds the records for most victories, highest winning percentage and most games coached by an NHL coach. He won 975 games (110, St. Louis Blues 1967–71; 419, Montreal Canadiens

1971–79; 210, Buffalo Sabres 1979–87; 95, Pittsburgh Penguins, 1991–93; 141, Detroit Red Wings, 1993–96). His career record is 975 wins, 434 losses, 245 ties for a record .664 winning percentage from a record 1,654 games.

Scotty Bowman is the most successful coach in the NHL.

STANLEY CUP

The Stanley Cup has been won 24 times by the Montreal Canadiens, 1916, 1924, 1930–31, 1944, 1946, 1953, 1956–60, 1965–66, 1968–69, 1971, 1973, 1976–79, 1986, 1993 from a record 33 finals. The longest Stanley Cup final game was settled after 115 min. 13 sec., in the third period of overtime, when the Edmonton Oilers beat the Boston Bruins 3–2 on May 15, 1990. Henri Richard played on a record 11 winning teams for the Montreal Canadiens between 1956 and 1973.

Most games played Larry Robinson played in 227 Stanley Cup playoff games, for the Montreal Canadiens (1973–89) and the Los Angeles Kings (1990–92).

Highest scores Wayne Gretzky (Edmonton Oilers, Los Angeles Kings, St. Louis Blues) has scored 378 points in Stanley Cup games, 114 goals and 264 assists. Gretzky scored a playoff record 47 points (17 goals, a record 30 assists) in 1985.

Five goals in a Stanley Cup game were scored by Newsy LaLonde in Montreal's 6–3 victory over Ottawa on March 1, 1919; by Maurice Richard in Montreal's 5–1 win over the Toronto Maple Leafs on March 23, 1944; by Darryl Glen Sittler for Toronto's 8–5 victory over Philadelphia on April 22, 1976; by Reggie Leach for Philadelphia's 6–3 victory over the Boston Bruins on May 6, 1976; and by Mario Lemieux for the Pittsburgh Penguins' 10–7 win over Philadelphia on April 25, 1989.

A record six assists in a game were achieved by Mikko Leinonen (Finland) for the New York Rangers in their 7–3 victory over Philadelphia on

April 8, 1982, and by Wayne Gretzky for Edmonton's 13–3 victory over Los Angeles on April 9, 1987, when his team set a Stanley Cup game record of 13 goals. The most points in a game is eight, by Patrik Sundström (Sweden), three goals and five assists, for the New Jersey Devils (10) vs. the Washington Capitals (4) on April 22, 1988, and by Mario Lemieux, five goals and three assists, for the Pittsburgh Penguins (10) vs. the Philadelphia Flyers (7) on April 25, 1989.

Point-scoring streak Bryan Trottier (New York Islanders) scored a point in 27 playoff games over three seasons (1980–82), scoring 16 goals and 26 assists for 42 points.

Goal-scoring streak Reggie Leach (Philadelphia Flyers) scored at least one goal in nine consecutive playoff games, April 17–May 9, 1976. Overall, he scored 14 goals.

Goaltending Two players share the record of 15 shutouts in a playoff career: Jacques Plante of the Montreal Canadiens (1953–63) and the St. Louis Blues (1969–70), and Clint Benedict of the Montreal Maroons (1917–30). The most victories in a playoff career is 88, by Billy Smith for the New York Islanders (1975–88).

Defensemen During his career with the Edmonton Oilers, 1980–87, Paul Coffey set marks for the most points in a playoff game (6) and in a season (37)—both set in 1985. Also in 1985, Coffey set the record for most goals by a defenseman in a playoff season, with 12 in 18 games. The record for most goals in a game by a defenseman is three, shared by eight players: Bobby Orr (Boston Bruins vs. Montreal Canadiens, April 11, 1971); Dick Redmond (Chicago Blackhawks vs. St. Louis Blues, April 4, 1973); Denis Potvin (New York Islanders vs. Edmonton Oilers, April 17, 1981); Paul Reinhart twice (Calgary Flames vs. Edmonton Oilers, April 14, 1983; vs. Vancouver Canucks, April 8, 1984); Doug Halward (Vancouver Canucks vs. Calgary Flames, April 7, 1984); Al Iafrate (Washington Capitals vs. New York Islanders, April 26, 1993); Eric Desjardins (Montreal Canadiens vs. Los Angeles Kings, June 3, 1993); Gary Suter (Chicago Blackhawks vs. Toronto Maple Leafs, April 24, 1994); and Brian Leetch (Ottawa Senators vs. New York Rangers, May 22, 1995).

Most valuable player The Conn Smythe Trophy for the most valuable player has been awarded annually since 1965. It has been won twice by Bobby Orr (Boston), 1970, 1972; Bernie Parent (Philadelphia), 1974–75; Wayne Gretzky (Edmonton), 1985, 1988; Mario Lemieux (Pittsburgh), 1991–92; and Patrick Roy (Montreal), 1986, 1993.

Most successful coaches Toe Blake coached the Montreal Canadiens to eight championships (1956–60, 1965–66, 1968), the most of any coach. Scotty Bowman holds the record for most playoff wins at 162: 26, St. Louis Blues, 1967–71; 70, Montreal Canadiens, 1971–79; 18, Buffalo Sabres, 1979–87; 23, Pittsburgh Penguins, 1991–93; 25, Detroit Red Wings, 1993–96.

WORLD CHAMPIONSHIPS AND OLYMPIC GAMES

World Championships were first held for amateurs in 1920 in conjunction with the Olympic Games, which were also considered world championships up to 1968. Since 1976, the World Championships have been open to professionals. The USSR won 22 world titles between 1954 and 1990 (with Russia winning a further title in 1993), including the Olympic titles of 1956, 1964 and 1968. It has a record eight Olympic titles with a further five in 1972, 1976, 1984, 1988 and 1992 (as the Unified Team). The most gold medals won by any player is three, achieved by Soviet players Vitaliy Davydov, Anatoliy Firsov, Viktor Kuzkin and Aleksandr Ragulin in 1964, 1968 and 1972, and by Vladislav Tretyak in 1972, 1976 and 1984.

Women's World Championships Three world championships have been won by Canada, 1990, 1992, and 1994.

HORSE RACING

Highest prizes The highest prize money won for a day's racing is $10 million, for the Breeders' Cup series of seven races staged annually since 1984.

The largest single race purse is $4 million, awarded at two races: the Dubai World Cup and the Breeders' Cup Classic.

A record first prize of $2.4 million was won by Cigar at the Dubai World Cup on March 27, 1996.

Breeders' Cup Pat Day has a record eight wins in Breeders' Cup races: Classic (1984, 1990); Distaff (1986, 1991); Turf (1987); Juvenile Fillies (1987, 1994); and Juvenile (1994).

Highest earnings Pat Day has won a record $12,447,000 in Breeders' Cup racing, 1984–95.

Biggest payout Anthony A. Speelman and Nicholas John Cowan (both Great Britain) won $1,627,084.40, after federal income tax of $406,768.00 was withheld, on a $64 9-horse accumulator at Santa Anita Racetrack, Arcadia, CA on April 19, 1987. Their first seven selections won, and the payout was for a jackpot accumulated over 24 days. .

Most successful owners The most lifetime wins by an owner is 4,775, by Marion H. Van Berg (1895–1971), in North America, in 35 years.

The most wins in a year is 494, by Dan R. Lasater (U.S.) in 1974.

The greatest amount won in a year is $6,881,902, by Sam-Son Farm in North America in 1991.

Most successful trainers Jack Charles Van Berg (U.S.) has the greatest number of wins in a year, 496 in 1976.

The career record is 6,362, by Dale Baird (U.S.) from 1962 to the end of 1993.

The greatest amount won in a year is $17,842,358, by D. Wayne Lukas (U.S.) in 1988; he has won a record $140,024,750 in his career.

TRIPLE CROWN

Race (instituted)	Record time	Most Wins by a jockey	Most Wins by a trainer	Most Wins by an owner	Largest field
Kentucky Derby (1875) 1¼ miles Churchill Downs, Louisville, KY	1 min. 59.4 sec. Secretariat, 1973	5—Eddie Arcaro 1938, '41, '45, '48, '52 5—Bill Hartack 1957, '60, '62, '64, '69	6—Ben Jones 1938, '41, '44, '48, '49, '52	8—Calumet Farm 1941, '44, '48, '49, '52, '57, '58, '68	23 (1974)
Preakness Stakes (1873) 1 mile 1½ furlongs, Pimlico, Baltimore, MD	1 min. 53.2 sec. Tank's Prospect, 1985	6—Eddie Arcaro 1941, '48, '50, '51, '55, '57	7—Robert Wyndham Walden 1875, '78, '79, '80, '81, '82, '88	5—George Lorillard 1878, '79, '80, '81, '82	18 (1928)
Belmont Stakes (1867) 1½ miles Belmont Park, NY	2 min. 24.0 sec. Secretariat, 1973 (by a record 31 lengths)	6—Jimmy McLaughlin 1882, '83, '84, '86, '87, '88 6—Eddie Arcaro 1941, '42, '45, '48, '52, '55	8—James Rowe Sr. 1883, '84, 1901, '04, '07, '08, '10, '13	5—Dwyer Bros. 1883, '84, '86, '87, '88 5—James R. Keene 1901, '04, '07, '08, '10 5—William Woodward Sr. (Belair Stud) 1930, '32, '35, '36, '39	15 (1983)

HORSES

Most valuable horse   The most valuable animals are racehorses. The most ever paid for a yearling was $13.1 million on July 23, 1985 in Keeneland, KY by Robert Sangster and partners for Seattle Dancer.

Oldest thoroughbred   The greatest age recorded for a thoroughbred race-horse is 42 years, in the case of the chestnut gelding Tango Duke (foaled 1935), owned by Carmen J. Koper of Barongarook, Victoria, Australia. The horse died on January 25, 1978.

Most successful horse   The horse with the best win–loss record was Kinc-sem, a Hungarian mare foaled in 1874, who was unbeaten in 54 races (1876–79) throughout Europe, including the Goodwood Cup (Great Britain) of 1878.

Longest winning sequence   Camarero, foaled in 1951, was undefeated in 56 races in Puerto Rico from April 19, 1953 to his first defeat on August 17, 1955 (in his career to 1956, he won 73 of 77 races).

Career   Chorisbar (foaled 1935) won 197 of his 325 races in Puerto Rico, 1937–47. Lenoxbar (foaled 1935) won 46 races in one year, 1940, in Puerto Rico from 56 starts.

United States   The most career wins in the United States is 89, by Kingston in 138 starts, 1886–94. This included 33 in stakes races, but the horse with the most wins in stakes races in the U.S. is Exterminator (foaled 1915), with 34 between 1918 and 1923.

John Henry (foaled 1975) won a record 25 graded stakes races, including 16 at Grade 1, 1978–84. On his retirement in 1984, his career prize money was $6,597,947, nearly twice as much as the next best. Of 83 races, he won 39, was second 15 times and third 9 times.

Same race   Doctor Syntax (foaled 1811) won the Preston Gold Cup on seven successive occasions, 1815–21.

Triple Crown winners   The Triple Crown (Kentucky Derby, Preakness Stakes, Belmont Stakes) has been achieved 11 times, most recently by Affirmed in 1978.

Eddie Arcaro is the only jockey to have ridden two Triple Crown winners, Whirlaway in 1941 and Citation in 1948.

Two trainers have schooled two Triple Crown winners: James Fitzsimmons, Gallant Fox in 1930 and Omaha in 1935; Ben A. Jones, Whirlaway in 1941 and Citation in 1948.

Greatest winnings   The career earnings record is $9,663,593, by the 1994 Japanese Triple Crown winner Narita Brian (foaled 1991) to June 1996.

United States   The career earnings record for the United States is $7,669,015, by Cigar (1993–96).

The most prize money earned in a year is $4,578,454, by Sunday Silence (foaled 1986) in 1989. The record was set in nine races, Sunday Silence winning seven times and finishing second twice.

Cigar has won more money than any other U.S. racehorse.

The leading money-winning mare is Hishi Amazon (foaled 1991), with $6,089,196, in Japan, to June 1996.

The one-race record is $2.6 million, by Spend a Buck (foaled 1982), for the Jersey Derby, Garden State Park, NJ on May 27, 1985, of which $2 million was a bonus for having previously won the Kentucky Derby and two preparatory races at Garden State Park.

Fastest horses The fastest race speed recorded is 43.26 MPH, by Big Racket, 20.8 seconds for ¾ mile, in Mexico City, Mexico on February 5, 1945. The 4-year-old carried 114 pounds.

The record for 1½ miles is 37.82 MPH, by 3-year-old Hawkster (carrying 121 pounds) at Santa Anita Park, Arcadia, CA on October 14, 1989, with 2 min. 22.8 sec.

JOCKEYS

Most successful jockeys Willie Shoemaker (U.S.), whose racing weight was 97 pounds at 4 ft. 11 in., rode 8,833 winners out of 40,350 mounts from March 19, 1949 to his retirement on February 3, 1990.

Chris McCarron (U.S.) has earned a career record $192 million from 1974 to May 1996.

The most races won by a jockey in a year is 598, in 2,312 rides, by Kent Jason Desormeaux (U.S.) in 1989.

The greatest amount won in a year is 3,133,742,006 yen ($28.4 million) by Yutaka Take (Japan) in Japan in 1993.

The greatest amount won in the United States in a year is $14,877,298, by José Adeon Santos (U.S.) in 1988.

Mike Smith (U.S.) rode a season record 62 stakes race winners in 1993.

Most wins One day The most winners ridden in one day is nine, by Chris Antley (U.S.) on October 31, 1987. They consisted of four in the afternoon at Aqueduct, NY and five in the evening at The Meadowlands, East–Rutherford, NJ.

One card   The most winners ridden on one card is eight, by six riders, most recently by Pat Day, in only nine rides in Arlington, IL on September 13, 1989.

Consecutive   The longest winning streak is 12, by Sir Gordon Richards (Great Britain)—one race in Nottingham, England on October 3, six out of six at Chepstow on October 4, and the first five races next day at Chepstow, in 1933; and by Pieter Stroebel in Bulawayo, Southern Rhodesia (now Zimbabwe), June 7 to July 7, 1958.

United States   The longest winning streak for an American jockey is nine races, by Albert Adams (U.S.) at Marlboro Racetrack, MD over three days, September 10–12, 1930. He won two races on September 10, six races on September 11 and one race on September 12.

HARNESS RACING

Most successful horses   The trotter Goldsmith Maid won an all-time record 350 races (including dashes and heats) from 1864 to 1877. The career record tally for a pacer is 262 wins (including dashes and heats) by Single G, 1918–26. The season record is 65 races, by the pacer Victory Hy in 1950. The record for a trotter is 53 victories, by Make Believe in 1949.

HARNESS RACING MILE RECORDS

Trotting	Time	Horse (driver)	Place	Date
World	1:51	*Pine Chip* (John Campbell)	Lexington, KY	Oct. 1, 1994
Race	1:51 4/5	*Beat the Wheel* (Cat Manzi)	East Rutherford, NJ	Jul. 7, 1994
Pacing				
World	1:46 1/5	*Cambest* (Bill O'Donnell)	Springfield, IL	Aug. 16, 1993
Race	1:47 3/5	*Jenna's Beach Boy* (William R. Fahy)	East Rutherford, NJ	Jun. 22, 1996

Most successful driver   The most successful sulky driver in North American harness racing history is Herve Filion of Québec, Canada, who had achieved 14,783 wins and prize earnings of $85,044,328 through July 6, 1996. The most wins in a year is 843, by Walter Case (U.S.) in 1992. The most wins in a day is 12, by Mike Lechance at Yonkers Raceway, NY on June 23, 1987.

John D. Campbell (U.S.) has the highest career earnings, $141,905,446, with a total of 7,202 wins through July 6, 1996. This includes a season record of $11,620,878 in 1990, when he won 543 races.

Triple Crown Trotters   The Triple Crown consists of three races: Hambletonian, Kentucky Futurity, and Yonkers Trot. Six trotters have won the Triple Crown. Stanley Dancer is the only driver to win two Triple Crowns, 1968 and 1972.

Hambletonian: The record time is 1 min. 53$^1/_5$ sec., by American Winner, driven by Ron Pierce in 1993.

Kentucky Futurity: The race record time is 1 min. 52$^3/_5$ sec., by Pine Chip, driven by John Campbell in 1993.

Yonkers Trot: The race record time is 1 min. 56 sec., by CR Kay Suzie, driven by Rod Allen, in 1996.

Pacers   The Triple Crown consists of three races: Cane Pace, Little Brown Jug, and Messenger Stakes. Seven horses have won the Triple Crown, each with different drivers.

Cane Pace: The race record time is 1 min. 51$^2/_5$ sec., by Riyadh, driven by Jim Morrill Jr., in 1993.

Little Brown Jug: The race record time is 1 min. 51$^2/_5$ sec., by Nick's Fantasy, driven by John D. Campbell, in 1996.

Messenger Stakes: The race record time is 1 min. 51 sec., by Cam's Card Shark, driven by John Campbell, in 1994.

Highest price   The highest price paid was $19.2 million for Nihilator (a pacer), who was syndicated by Wall Street Stable and Almahurst Stud Farm in 1984.

Greatest winnings   For any harness horse the record amount is $4,907,307, by the trotter Peace Corps, 1988–93.

The single-season record is $2,264,714 by the pacer Cam's Card Shark in 1994.

The largest-ever purse was $2,161,000, for the Woodrow Wilson 2-year-old race over one mile at The Meadowlands, East Rutherford, NJ on August 16, 1984. Of this sum a record $1,080,500 went to the winner, Nihilator, driven by William O'Donnell.

HURLING

Most titles All-Ireland   The greatest number of All-Ireland Championships won by one team is 27, by Cork, between 1890 and 1990. The greatest number of successive wins is four, by Cork (1941–44).

Most appearances   The most appearances in All-Ireland finals is 10, shared by Christy Ring (Cork and Munster) and John Doyle (Tipperary). They also share the record of All-Ireland medals, won with eight each. Ring's appearances on the winning side were in 1941–44, 1946 and 1952–54, while Doyle's were in 1949–51, 1958, 1961–62 and 1964–65. Ring also played in a record 22 interprovincial finals (1942–63), and was on the winning side 18 times.

Highest and lowest scores   The highest score in an All-Ireland final (60 minutes) was in 1989, when Tipperary, 41 (4 goals, 29 points) beat Antrim, 18 (3 goals, 9 points). The record aggregate score was when Cork, 39 (6 goals, 21 points) defeated Wexford, 25 (5 goals, 10 points), in the 80-minute final of 1970. A goal equals three points.

The highest recorded individual score was by Nick Rackard (Wexford), who scored 7 goals and 7 points against Antrim in the 1954 All-Ireland semifinal.

The lowest score in an All-Ireland final was when Tipperary (1 goal, 1 point) beat Galway (zero) in the first championship at Birr in 1887.

Largest crowd The largest crowd was 84,865 for the All-Ireland Final between Cork and Wexford at Croke Park, Dublin in 1954.

ICE AND SAND YACHTING

Fastest speeds Ice The fastest speed officially recorded is 143 MPH, by John D. Buckstaff in a Class A stern-steerer on Lake Winnebago, WI in 1938.

Sand The official world record for a sand yacht is 66.48 MPH, set by Christian-Yves Nau (France) in *Mobil* in Le Touquet, France on March 22, 1981, when the wind speed reached 75 MPH. A speed of 88.4 MPH was attained by Nord Embroden (U.S.) in *Midnight at the Oasis* on Superior Dry Lake, CA on April 15, 1976.

Largest ice yacht The largest ice yacht was *Icicle*, built for Commodore John E. Roosevelt for racing on the Hudson River, NY in 1869. It was 68 ft. 11 in. long.

ICE SKATING

Largest rink The world's largest indoor ice rink is in the Moscow Olympic Arena, which has an ice area of 86,800 square feet. The five rinks at Fujikyu Highland Skating Center in Japan total 285,243 square feet.

Barrel jumping on ice skates The official distance record is 29 ft. 5 in. over 18 barrels, by Yvon Jolin in Terrebonne, Québec, Canada on January 25, 1981. The women's record is 22 ft. 5¼ in. over 11 barrels, by Marie Josée Houle in Lasalle, Québec, Canada on March 1, 1987.

FIGURE SKATING

Most titles Olympic The most Olympic gold medals won by a figure skater is three: by Gillis Grafström (Sweden) in 1920, 1924 and 1928 (also silver medal in 1932); by Sonja Henie (Norway) in 1928, 1932 and 1936; and by Irina Rodnina (USSR) with two different partners in the pairs in 1972, 1976 and 1980.

Triple Crown Karl Schäfer (Austria) and Sonja Henie achieved double "Triple Crowns" (world, Olympic and European or U.S. titles won in the same year), both in the years 1932 and 1936. This feat was repeated by Katarina Witt (East Germany) in 1984 and 1988.

World The greatest number of men's individual world figure skating titles (instituted 1896) is 10, by Ulrich Salchow (Sweden) in 1901–05 and 1907–11. The women's record (instituted 1906) is also 10 individual titles, by Sonja Henie between 1927 and 1936. Irina Rodnina won 10 pairs titles (instituted 1908), four with Aleksey Ulanov, 1969–72, and six with her former husband Aleksandr Zaitsev, 1973–78. The most ice dance titles (instituted 1952) won is six, by Lyudmila Pakhomova and her husband Aleksandr Gorshkov (USSR), 1970–74 and 1976. They also won the first-ever Olympic ice dance title in 1976.

Dick Button set U.S. records with two Olympic gold medals, 1948 and 1952, and five world titles, 1948–52. Five women's world titles were won by Carol Heise, 1956–60, as well as the 1960 Olympic gold.

United States The U.S. Championships were first held in 1914. The most titles won by an individual is nine, by Maribel Y. Vinson, 1928–33 and 1935–37.

She also won six pairs titles, and her total of 15 titles is equaled by Therese Blanchard, who won six individual and nine pairs titles, 1914–27. The men's individual record is seven, by Roger Turner, 1928–34, and Dick Button, 1946–52.

Highest marks The highest tally of maximum six marks awarded in an international championship was 29, to Jayne Torvill and Christopher Dean (both Great Britain) in the World Ice Dance Championships in Ottawa, Canada, March 22–24, 1984. This comprised seven in the compulsory dances, a perfect set of nine for presentation in the set pattern dance, and 13 in the free dance, including another perfect set from all nine judges for artistic presentation.

The most by a soloist is seven: by Donald Jackson (Canada) in the World Men's Championship in Prague, Czechoslovakia in 1962; and by Midori Ito (Japan) in the World Women's Championships in Paris, France in 1989.

Greatest jump Robin Cousins (Great Britain) achieved 19 ft. 1 in. in an axel jump and 18 feet with a back flip in Richmond, England in 1983.

SPEED SKATING

Most medals Olympic The most Olympic gold medals ever won in speed skating is six, by Lidiya Skoblikova (USSR) in 1960 (two) and 1964 (four).

The men's record is five, by Clas Thunberg (Finland), in 1924 and 1928 (including one tied); and by Eric Heiden (U.S.), uniquely at one Games on Lake Placid, NY in 1980.

The most medals won is seven, by Clas Thunberg, who won a silver and a bronze in addition to his five gold medals, and by Ivar Ballangrud (Norway), four gold, two silver and a bronze, 1928–36.

World The greatest number of world overall titles (instituted 1893) won by any skater is five—by Oscar Mathisen (Norway) in 1908–09 and 1912–14; by Clas Thunberg in 1923, 1925, 1928–29 and 1931; and by Karin Kania (née Enke; East Germany) in 1982, 1984, 1986–88. Kania also won a

In 1996, 15-year-old Michelle Kwan became the youngest American
to win the World Figure Skating Championships.

record six overall titles at the World Sprint Championships, 1980–81, 1983–84, 1986–87. A record six men's sprint overall titles have been won by Igor Zhelezovskiy (USSR/Belarus), 1985–86, 1989 and 1991–93.

United States Eric Heiden won a U.S. record three overall world titles, 1977–79. He also won four overall titles at the World Sprint Championships, 1977–80. Beth Heiden became the only U.S. women's all-around champion in 1979. Bonnie Blair has won a U.S. women's record three overall World Sprint Championships, 1989, 1994–95. Sheila Young has also won three, 1973, 1975–76.

Bonnie Blair has won more Olympic medals—five gold and one bronze—than any other U.S. citizen.

World Short-Track Championships The most successful skater in these championships (instituted 1978) is Sylvie Daigle (Canada), women's overall champion in 1979, 1983 and 1989–90.

Longest race The "Elfstedentocht," which originated in the 17th century, was held in the Netherlands, 1909–63, and again in 1985 and 1986, covering 200 km (124 miles 483 yards). As the weather does not permit an annual race in the Netherlands, alternative "Elfstedentocht" have taken place on Lake Vesijärvi, near Lahti, Finland; Ottawa River, Canada; and Lake Weissensee, Austria. The record time for 200 km is: *(men)* 5 hr. 40 min. 37 sec., by Dries van Wijhe (Netherlands); and *(women)* 5 hr. 48 min. 8 sec., by Alida Pasveer (Netherlands), both on Lake Weissensee (altitude 3,609 feet), Austria on February 11, 1989. Jan-Roelof Kruithof (Netherlands) won the race nine times—1974, 1976–77, 1979–84. An estimated 16,000 skaters took part in 1986.

Bonnie Blair has won five Olympic gold medals.

SPEED SKATING RECORDS

Event	Time	Name and Country	Place	Date
MEN				
500	0:35.39	Hiroyasu Shimizu (Japan)	Calgary, Canada	Mar. 1, 1996
1,000	1:11.67	Manabu Horii (Japan)	Calgary, Canada	Mar. 1, 1996
1,500	1:51.29	Johann-Olav Koss (Norway)	Hamar, Norway	Feb. 16, 1994
3,000	3:56.16	Thomas Bos (Netherlands)	Calgary, Canada	Mar. 3, 1992
5,000	6:34.96	Johann-Olav Koss	Hamar, Norway	Feb. 13, 1994
10,000	13:30.55	Johann-Olav Koss	Hamar, Norway	Feb. 20, 1994
WOMEN				
500	0:38.69	Bonnie Blair (U.S.)	Calgary, Canada	Feb. 12, 1995
1,000	1:17.65	Christa Rothenburger (now Luding; East Germany)	Calgary, Canada	Feb. 26, 1988
1,500	1:59.30†	Karin Kania (East Germany)	Medeo, USSR	Mar. 22, 1986
3,000	4:09.32	Gunda Niemann (née Kleeman; Germany)	Calgary, Canada	Mar. 25, 1994
5,000	7:03.26	Gunda Niemann	Calgary, Canada	Mar. 26, 1994

† Set at high altitude.

SHORT TRACK

MEN

500	0:42.68	Mirko Vuillermin (Italy)	Lake Placid, U.S. ....Mar. 29, 1996
1,000	1:28.47	Mike McMillen (New Zealand)	Denver, CO ....Apr. 4, 1992
1,500	2:18.16	Mark Gagnon (Canada)	The Hague, Netherlands........Mar. 1, 1996
3,000	4:56.29	Chae Ji-hoon (South Korea)	Gyovik, Norway ....Mar. 19, 1995
5,000 relay	7:04.92	Italy	The Hauge, Netherlands........Mar. 3, 1996

WOMEN

500	0:45.25	Isabelle Charest (Canada)	The Hague, Netherlands........Mar 2, 1996
1,000	1:34.07	Nathalie Lambert (Canada)	Hamar, Norway........Nov. 7, 1993
1,500	2:27.27	Marianella Canclini (Italy)	Guildford, England ....Feb. 6, 1996
3,000	5:02.18	Chun Lee-kyung (South Korea)	Gyovik, Norway ....Mar. 19, 1995
3,000 relay	4:21.50	China	The Hague, Netherlands........Mar. 3, 1996

Greatest 24-hour distance Martinus Kuiper (Netherlands) skated 339.67 miles in 24 hours in Alkmaar, Netherlands, December 12–13, 1988.

JAI ALAI (PELOTA VASCA)

World Championships The *Federacion Internacional de Pelota Vasca* stages World Championships every four years (the first in 1952). The most successful pair has been Roberto Elias and Juan Labat (Argentina), who won the *Trinquete Share* four times, 1952, 1958, 1962 and 1966. Labat won a record seven world titles in all between 1952 and 1966. Riccardo Bizzozero (Argentina) also won seven world titles in various *Trinquete* and *Frontón corto* events, 1970–82. The most wins in the long court game Cesta Punta is three, by José Hamuy (Mexico; 1934–83), with two different partners, 1958, 1962 and 1966.

Fastest speed An electronically measured ball velocity of 188 MPH was recorded by José Ramon Areitio (Spain) at the Newport Jai Alai, RI on August 3, 1979.

Longest domination The longest domination as the world's No. 1 player was enjoyed by Chiquito de Cambo (France; born Joseph Apesteguy) from the beginning of the century until 1938.

Largest frontón The world's largest frontón (enclosed stadium) is the Palm Beach Jai Alai, West Palm Beach, which has a seating capacity of 6,000 and covers three acres.

Largest crowd The record attendance for a jai alai contest was 15,052 people at the World Jai Alai in Miami, FL on December 27, 1975. The frontón has seating capacity for only 3,884.

JUDO

Most titles World and Olympic World Championships for men were inaugurated in Tokyo, Japan in 1956. Judo was made an Olympic medal event at the 1972 games. Women's championships were first held in 1980 in New York. Yashiro Yamashita won nine consecutive Japanese titles from 1977 to 1985; four world titles (Over 95 kg in 1979, 1981 and 1983; Open in 1981); and the Olympic Open category in 1984. He retired undefeated after 203 successive wins between 1977 and 1985. Two other men have won four world titles—Shozo Fujii (Japan), Under 80 kg 1971, 1973 and 1975, Under 78 kg 1979; and Naoya Ogawa (Japan), Open 1987, 1989, 1991 and Over 95 kg 1989.

The only men to have won two Olympic gold medals are Wilhelm Ruska

(Netherlands), Over 93 kg and Open in 1972; Peter Seisenbacher (Austria), 86 kg 1984 and 1988; Hitoshi Saito (Japan), Over 95 kg 1984 and 1988; and Waldemar Legien (Poland), 78 kg 1988 and 86 kg 1992. Ingrid Berghmans (Belgium) has won a record six women's world titles (first held 1980): Open 1980, 1982, 1984 and 1986 and Under 72 kg in 1984 and 1989. She has also won four silver medals and a bronze. She won the Olympic 72 kg title in 1988, when women's judo was introduced as a demonstration sport.

The only U.S. judo players to win world titles were Michael Swain, in the men's 71 kg class in 1987, and Ann-Maria Bernadette Burns in the women's 56 kg in 1984.

Most throws Brian Woodward and David Norman completed 33,681 judo throws in 10 hours in Rainham, England on April 10, 1994.

KARATE

World Championships Great Britain has won a record six world titles (instituted 1970) in the kumite team event, in 1975, 1982, 1984, 1986, 1988 and 1990. Two men's individual kumite titles have been won by Pat McKay (Great Britain) in Under 80 kg, 1982 and 1984; Emmanuel Pinda (France) in Open, 1984, and Over 80 kg, 1988; Theirry Masci (France) in Under 70 kg, in 1986 and 1988; and José Manuel Egea (Spain) in Under 80 kg, 1990 and 1992. Four women's kumite titles have been won by Guus van Mourik (Netherlands) in Over 60 kg, in 1982, 1984, 1986 and 1988. Three individual kata titles have been won by: *(men)* Tsuguo Sakumoto (Japan) in 1984, 1986 and 1988; *(women)* Mie Nakayama (Japan) in 1982, 1984 and 1986, and Yuki Mimura (Japan) in 1988, 1990, and 1992.

"Tokey" Hill is the only American ever to win a gold medal at the Karate World Championships in Madrid, Spain. He won the 80 kg division on November 27, 1980.

LACROSSE

MEN

Most titles World   The U.S. has won six of the seven World Champi-onships, in 1967, 1974, 1982, 1986, 1990 and 1994. Canada won the other world title in 1978, beating the U.S. 17–16 in overtime; this was the first tied international match.

NCAA   National champions have been decided by NCAA playoffs since 1971. Johns Hopkins University has the most wins overall: seven NCAA ti-tles between 1974 and 1987, and six wins and five ties between 1941 and 1970.

Most points   The record for most points in the NCAA lacrosse tournament is 25, by Eamon McEneaney (Cornell) in 1977 and Tim Goldstein (Cor-nell) in 1987. Both players played in three games. Two players are tied with 12 points in one championship game: Ed Mullen scored 12, for Maryland vs. Navy in the 1976 championship game; and Gary Gait scored 12 on May 22, 1988, for Syracuse vs. Navy.

Highest score   The highest score in an international lacrosse match is Scot-land's 34–3 win over Germany in Manchester, England on July 25, 1994.

WOMEN

The first reported playing of lacrosse by women was in 1886. The women's game has evolved separately from the men's game, so the rules differ consider-ably.

World Championships/World Cup   The first World Cup was held in 1982, replacing the world championships that had been held three times since 1969. The U.S. has won four times, in 1974, 1982, 1989 and 1993.

NCAA   The NCAA first staged a women's national championship in 1982.

Most titles   Maryland has won the most titles, with three: 1986, 1992, and 1995.

MODERN PENTATHLON

Most titles World   András Balczó (Hungary) won the record number of world titles (instituted 1949), six individual and seven team. He won the world individual title in 1963, 1965–67 and 1969 and the Olympic title in

1972. His seven team titles (1960–70) comprised five world and two Olympic.

The USSR has won a record 15 world and four Olympic team titles. Hungary has also won a record four Olympic team titles and 10 world titles.

Women's World Championships were first held in 1981, replacing the World Cup, which began in 1978. Poland has won a record seven women's

Cathy Nelson of the University of Maryland, which has won three NCAA titles.

world team titles: 1985, 1988–92 and 1995. Eva Fjellerup (Denmark) has won the individual title four times, 1990–91, 1993–94.

The only U.S. modern pentathletes to win world titles have been Robert Nieman, 1979, when the men's team also won, and Lori Norwood (women's) in 1989.

Olympic   The greatest number of Olympic gold medals won in pentathlon is three, by András Balczó, a member of the winning team in 1960 and 1968 and the 1972 individual champion.

Lars Hall (Sweden) has uniquely won two individual championships (1952 and 1956). Pavel Serafimovich Lednyev (USSR) won a record seven medals (two team gold, one team silver, one individual silver, three individual bronze), 1968–80.

U.S. National Championships   The women's championship was first held in 1977; Kim Dunlop (née Arata) has won nine titles (1979–80, 1984–89 and 1991). The men's championship was inaugurated in 1955. Mike Burley has won four titles (1977, 1979, 1981, 1985).

MOTORCYCLE RACING

Oldest race   The oldest continuous motorcycle races in the world are the Auto-Cycle Union Tourist Trophy (TT) series, first held on the 15.81-mile "Peel" (St. John's) course in the Isle of Man, Great Britain in 1907, and still run on the "Mountain" circuit.

Fastest circuits   The highest average lap speed attained on any closed circuit 541 is 160.288 MPH, by Yvon du Hamel (Canada) on a modified 903 cc 4-cylinder Kawasaki Z1 at the 31-degree banked 2.5-mile Daytona International Speedway, FL in March 1973. His lap time was 56.149 seconds.

The fastest road circuit used to be Francorchamps circuit near Spa, Belgium, then 8.77 miles long. It was lapped in 3 min. 50.3 sec. (average speed 137.150 MPH) by Barry Sheene (Great Britain) on a 495 cc 4-cylinder Suzuki during the Belgian Grand Prix on July 3, 1977. On that occasion he set a record time for this 10-lap (87.74-mile) race of 38 min. 58.5 sec. (average speed 135.068 MPH).

Longest circuit   The 37.73-mile "Mountain" circuit on the Isle of Man, over which the Tourist Trophy (TT) races have been run since 1911, has 264 curves and corners and is the longest used for any motorcycle race.

Most successful riders   Giacomo Agostini (Italy) won 122 races (68 in 500 cc, 54 in 350 cc) in the World Championship series between April 24, 1965 and September 25, 1977, including a record 19 in 1970, a season's total also achieved by Mike Hailwood (Great Britain) in 1966.

The record number of career wins for any one class is 78, by Rolf Biland in sidecar.

Angel Roldan Nieto (Spain) won a record seven 125 cc titles, 1971–72, 1979, 1981–84, and he also won a record six titles in 50 cc, 1969–70, 1972,

1975–77. Phil Read (Great Britain) won a record four 250 cc titles, 1964–65, 1968, 1971.

Sidecar Rolf Biland (Switzerland), won seven world sidecar titles, 1978–79, 1981, 1983 and 1992–94.

World Championships The most World Championship titles (instituted by the *Fédération Internationale Motocycliste* in 1949) won is 15, by Giacomo Agostini—seven in 350 cc, 1968–74, and eight in 500 cc in 1966–72, 1975.

The most world titles won by an American motorcyclist is four, by Edie Lawson, in 500 cc in 1984, 1986, 1988–89.

Trials A record six World Trials Championships have been won by Jordi Tarrès (Spain), 1987, 1989–91, 1993–94.

Youngest and oldest world champions Loris Capirossi (Italy) is the youngest to win a World Championship. He was 17 yr. 165 days old when he won the 125 cc title on September 16, 1990. The oldest was Hermann-Peter Müller of West Germany, who won the 250 cc title in 1955 at age 46.

MOTO-CROSS

World Championships Joël Robert (Belgium) won six 250-cc Moto-cross World Championships (1964, 1968–72). Between April 25, 1964 and June 18, 1972 he won a record 50 250-cc Grand Prix. Eric Geboers (Belgium) has uniquely won all three categories of the Moto-cross World Championships, in 125 cc in 1982 and 1983, 250 cc in 1987 and 500 cc in 1988 and 1990.

Youngest champion The youngest moto-cross world champion was Dave Strijbos (Netherlands), who won the 125 cc title at the age of 18 yr. 296 days on August 31, 1986.

United States The youngest female moto-cross champion in the United States is Kristy Shealy (born December 12, 1978), who, at age 14, won the women's division in the 1993 AMA Amateur/Youth National Moto-cross at Loretta Lynn's. In the same year, at the GNC Motocross 21st Annual Texas Series, she became the youngest racer to win the 125 Novice Class. In 1994, at age 15, Shealy became the youngest to win in the Ladies class at the GNC International Moto-cross Final.

OLYMPICS

For a full roundup of records set at the 1996 Atlanta games, see Extra! Extra! (page 636).

Most participants The greatest number of competitors at a Summer Games celebration was 9,369 (6,659 men, 2,710 women), who represented a record 169 nations, in Barcelona, Spain in 1992. The greatest number at a Winter Games was 1,737 (1,216 men, 521 women) representing 64 countries, in Lillehammer, Norway in 1994.

Largest crowd   The largest crowd at any Olympic site was 104,102 in the 1952 ski-jumping competition at the Holmenkøllen, outside Oslo, Norway. Estimates of the number of spectators of the marathon race through Tokyo, Japan on October 21, 1964 ranged from 500,000 to 1.5 million. The total spectator attendance in Los Angeles in 1984 was given as 5,797,923.

Olympic torch relay   The longest journey of the torch within one country was for the XV Olympic Winter Games in Canada in 1988. The torch arrived from Greece in St. John's, Newfoundland on November 17, 1987 and was transported 11,222 miles (5,088 miles on foot, 4,419 miles by aircraft/ferry, 1,712 miles by snowmobile and 3 miles by dogsled) until its arrival in Calgary on February 13, 1988.

Most medals   In the ancient Olympic Games, Leonidas of Rhodos won 12 running titles, 164–152 B.C.

The most individual gold medals won by a male competitor in the modern Games is 10, by Ray Ewry (U.S.) (see TRACK AND FIELD). The women's record is seven, by Vera Cáslavská-Odlozil (Czechoslovakia) (see GYMNASTICS).

The most gold medals won by an American woman is five, by speedskater Bonnie Blair. She won the 500 meter event in 1988, 1992 and 1994 and the 1,000 meter in 1992 and 1994. The most medals won by an American woman is eight, by swimmer Shirley Babashoff—gold in 4 × 100 meters freestyle relay 1972 and 1976, and six silver medals 1972–76, a record for any competitor in Olympic history.

Gymnast Larisa Latynina (USSR) won a record 18 medals, and the men's record is 15, by Nikolay Andrianov (see GYMNASTICS). The record at one celebration is eight, by gymnast Aleksandr Dityatin (USSR) in 1980.

The most medals won by an American Olympian is 11, in shooting, by Carl Townsend Osburn from 1912 to 1924—five gold, four silver, two bronze; by Mark Spitz, in swimming, 1968–72—nine gold, one silver, one bronze; and by Matt Biondi, in swimming, 1984–92—eight gold, two silver, one bronze.

The only Olympian to win four consecutive individual titles in the same event was Alfred Adolph Oerter (U.S.), who won the discus in 1956–68. However, Raymond Ewry (U.S.) won both the standing long jump and the standing high jump at four games in succession, 1900, 1904, 1906 (the Intercalated Games) and 1908. Also, Paul B. Elvstrøm won four successive gold medals in monotype yachting events, 1948–60, but there was a class change (1948 Firefly class, 1952–60 Finn class).

Swimmer Mark Spitz (U.S.) won seven golds at one celebration, in Munich in 1972, including three in relays. The most won in individual events at one celebration is five, by speed skater Eric Heiden (U.S.) at Lake Placid, NY in 1980.

The only man to win a gold medal in both the Summer and Winter Games is Edward Patrick Francis Eagan (U.S.), who won the 1920 light-heavyweight boxing title and was a member of the winning 4-man bob in 1932.

Christa Luding (née Rothenburger; East Germany) became the only woman to win a medal at both the Summer and Winter Games when she won a silver in the cycling sprint in 1988. She had previously won medals

Evelyn Ashford (above) and Janet Evans (top) have both won four gold medals in Summer Games.

for speed skating (500 meter gold in 1984, and 1,000 meter gold and 500 meter silver in 1988.

Youngest medal winners The youngest winner was a French boy (whose name is not recorded) who coxed the Netherlands pair in rowing in 1900. He was 7–10 years old and he substituted for Dr. Hermanus Brockmann, who coxed in the heats but proved too heavy. The youngest female was Kim Yoon-mi (South Korea), age 13 yr. 83 days, in the 1994 3,000 m short-track speed skating relay event.

United States The youngest American medalist and participant was Dorothy Poynton, who won the springboard diving bronze medal at 13 yr. 23 days in 1928. The youngest American male medalist was Donald Wills Douglas, Jr. with silver in 6-meter yachting in 1932, at 15 yr. 40 days. The youngest American gold medalist was Jackie Fields, who won the 1924 featherweight boxing title at 16 yr. 161 days.

The 1994 Winter Games had 1,737 competitors; shown here is Bjorn Daehlie (Norway).

Oldest medal winners Oscar Swahn (Sweden) won a silver medal in running deer shooting at 72 yr. 280 days in 1920.

United States The oldest American Olympic champion was retired minister Galen Spencer, who won a gold medal in the Team Round archery event two days after his 64th birthday in 1904.

The oldest American medalist and Olympic participant was Samuel Harding Duvall, who was 68 yr. 194 days when he was a member of the 1904 silver medal team.

Longest span The longest span of an Olympic competitor is 40 years, by Dr. Ivan Osiier (Denmark) in fencing, 1908–32 and 1948; Magnus Konow (Norway; 1887–1972) in yachting, 1908–20, 1928 and 1936–48; Paul

Elvstrøm (Denmark) in yachting, 1948–1960, 1968–72 and 1984–88; and Durward Knowles (Great Britain 1948, then Bahamas) in yachting, 1948–72 and 1988. Raimondo d'Inzeo competed for Italy in equestrian events at a record eight celebrations from 1948–76, gaining one gold, two silver and three bronze medals. D'Inzeo's record was equaled by Paul Elvstrøm and Durward Knowles in 1988. The longest span by a woman is 28 years, by Anne Ransehousen (née Newberry; U.S.) in dressage, 1960, 1964 and 1988. Fencer Kerstin Palm (Sweden) competed in a women's record seven competitions, 1964–88.

United States   The longest span of Olympic competition by a U.S. man is 32 years, by equestrian Michael J. Plumb, who competed in seven Olympics. Janice Lee York Romary competed in fencing in six Games.

ORIENTEERING

Most titles   Sweden has won the women's relay ten times—1966, 1970, 1974, 1976, 1981, 1983, 1985, 1989, 1991 and 1993. The men's relay has been won a record seven times by Norway—1970, 1978, 1981, 1983, 1985, 1987 and 1989. Three women's individual titles have been won by Annichen Kringstad (Sweden), in 1981, 1983 and 1985. The men's title has been won twice by Åge Hadler (Norway), in 1966 and 1972; Egil Johansen (Norway), in 1976 and 1978; Øyvin Thon (Norway), in 1979 and 1981; and Jorgen Martensson (Sweden), in 1991 and 1995.

Most competitors   The most competitors in a one-day orienteering event was 38,000, in the Ruf des Herbstes held in Sibiu, Romania in 1982. The largest event is the 5-day Swedish O-Ringen in Småland, which attracted 120,000 competitors in July 1983.

U.S. National Championships   Sharon Crawford, of the New England Orienteering Club, has won a record 11 overall women's titles, 1977–82, 1984–87, 1989. Mikell Platt, of the Rocky Mountain Orienteering Club, has won a record seven overall men's titles, 1985 and 1988–93.

Ski orienteering   Sweden has won the men's relay six times (1977, 1980, 1982, 1984, 1990 and 1996) and Finland has won the women's relay five times (1975, 1977, 1980, 1988 and 1990). The most individual titles is four, by Ragnhild Bratberg (Norway), Classic 1986, 1990, Sprint 1988, 1990. The men's record is three, shared by Anssi Juutilainen (Finland), Classic 1984, 1988, Sprint 1992 and Nicolo Corradini (Italy), Classic 1994, 1996 and Sprint 1994.

PARACHUTING

World championships *Team*   The USSR won the men's team title in 1954, 1958, 1960, 1966, 1972, 1976 and 1980, and the women's team title in 1956, 1958, 1966, 1968, 1972 and 1976.

Individual   Nikolay Ushamyev (USSR) has won the individual title twice, in 1974 and 1980.

Greatest accuracy   Dwight Reynolds scored a record 105 daytime dead centers, and Bill Wenger and Phil Munden tied with 43 night-time dead centers, competing as members of the U.S. Army Golden Knights in Yuma, AZ, in March 1978.

With electronic measuring, the official *Fédération Aeronautique Internationale* (FAI) record is 50 dead centers, by Linger Abdurakhmanov (USSR) in Fergana in 1988, when the women's record was set at 41, by Natalya Filinkova (USSR).

The Men's Night Accuracy Landing record on an electronic score pad is 31 consecutive dead centers, by Vladimir Buchenev (USSR) on October 30, 1986. The women's record is 21, by Inessa Stepanova (USSR) in Fergana on October 18, 1988.

Paragliding   The greatest distance flown is 176.4 miles by Alex François Louw (South Africa) from Kuruman, South Africa on December 31, 1992. The women's record is 113.2 miles, by Kat Thurston (Great Britain) from Cabo Paquica, Chile on November 19, 1994. The men's height gain record is 14,849 feet by Robby Whittal (Great Britain), in Brandvlei, South Africa on January 6, 1993, and the women's record is 9,747 feet by Verena Mühr

Parachute Records

Longest-Duration Fall • Lt. Col. Wm H. Rankin (USMC) 40 min. due to thermals, North Carolina, Jul. 26, 1956.

Longest-Delayed Drop • Capt. Joseph W. Kittinger, 84,700 ft. (16.04 miles), from balloon at 102,800 ft., Tularosa, NM, Aug. 16, 1960.

Women's Record • Elvira Fomitcheva (USSR), 48,556 ft. over Odessa, USSR (now Ukraine), Oct. 26, 1977.

Highest Base Jump • Nicholas Feteris and Dr. Glenn Singleman from the "Great Trango Tower" at 19,300 ft. in Karakoram, Pakistan, Aug. 26, 1992. Jumps from buildings and claims for lowest base jumps will not be accepted.

Lowest Mid-Air Rescue • Eddie Turner saved Frank Farnan (unconscious), who had been injured in a collision after jumping out of an aircraft at 13,000 ft. He pulled his ripcord at 1,800 ft.—less than 10 seconds from impact—over Clewiston, FL on Oct. 16, 1988.

Highest Escape • Flt. Lt. J. de Salis (RAF) and Fg. Off. P. Lowe (RAF), 56,000 ft., Monyash, Derby, England, Apr. 9, 1958.

Lowest Escape • S/Ldr. Terence Spencer (DFC, RAF), 30–40 ft., Wismar Bay, Baltic, Apr. 19, 1945.

Highest Landing • Ten USSR parachutists (of whom four were killed), 23,405 ft., Lenina Peak, USSR (now Tajikistan/Kyrgyzstan border), May 1969.

Cross-Channel (lateral fall) • Sgt. Bob Walters with three soldiers and two British Royal Marines, 22 miles from 25,000 ft., Dover, Great Britain to Sangatte, France, Aug. 31, 1980.

Total Sport Parachuting Descents • Don Kellner (U.S.), 21,000, various locations, up to Oct. 2, 1994.

Women's Record • Cheryl Stearns (U.S.), 10,100, various locations, up to Aug. 2, 1995.

24-Hour Total • Jay Stokes (U.S.), 331 (in accordance with United States Parachute Association rules). Raeford, NC, May 30–31, 1995.

Women's Record • Cheryl Stearns (U.S.), 352 at Lodi, CA, Nov. 8–9, 1995.

Most Traveled • Kevin Seaman from a Cessna Skylane (pilot Charles E. Merritt), 12,186 miles, jumps in all 50 states, Jul. 26–Oct. 15, 1972.

Heaviest Load • Space shuttle *Columbia*, booster rocket retrieval, 80-ton capacity, triple array, each 120 ft. in diameter, Atlantic, off Cape Canaveral, FL, Apr. 12, 1981.

Highest Canopy Formation • 37, a team of French parachutists at Brienne le Chateau, Troyes, France, held for 13 sec. on Aug. 16, 1992.

Largest Free-fall Formation • 216, from 23 countries, held for 8.21 seconds from 21,000 ft. over Bratislava, Slovakia, Aug. 19, 1994 (unofficial). 200, from 10 countries, held for

6.47 sec. from 16,500 ft., Myrtle Beach, SC, Oct. 23, 1992 (record recognized by FAI).

Women's Record • 100, from 20 countries, held for 5.97 sec., from 17,000 ft., Aéreodrome du Cannet des Maures, France, Aug. 14, 1992.

Oldest • Edwin C. Townsend (d. Nov. 7, 1987), 89 years, Vermillion Bay, LA, Feb. 5, 1986.

Women's Record • Sylvia Brett (Great Britain), 80 yr. 166 days, Cranfield, England, Aug. 23, 1986.

Oldest Tandem • Hildegarde Ferrera (U.S.), 99 years, Mokuleia, HI, Feb. 17, 1996.

Men's Record • Edward Royds-Jones, 95 yr, 170 days, Dunkeswell, England, Jul. 2, 1994.

Survival from Longest Fall without Parachute • Vesna Vulovic (Yugoslavia), flight attendant on DC–9 that blew up at 33,330 ft. over Srbská Kamenice, Czechoslovakia (now Czech Republic), Jan. 26, 1972.

(Germany) in Bitterwasser, Namibia on December 13, 1991. All these records were tow launched.

Nigel Horder scored four successive dead centers at the 1983 Dutch Open, Flevhof, Netherlands.

POLO

World Championships   The first F.I.P. World Championships were held in Berlin, Germany in 1989. The U.S. won the title, defeating Great Britain 7–6 in the final.

The United States Open Championship has been won 28 times by the Meadow Brook Polo Club, in 1916, 1920, 1923–41, 1946–51 and 1953.

Highest score   The highest aggregate number of goals scored in an international polo match is 30, when Argentina beat the U.S. 21–9 in Meadowbrook, Long Island, NY in September 1936.

Highest handicap   The highest handicap based on six 7½-minute "chukkas" is 10 goals, introduced in the United States in 1891. A total of 41 players have received 10-goal U.S.A. handicaps.

A match of two 40-goal teams has been staged on three occasions—in Argentina in 1975, in the United States in 1990, and in Australia in 1991.

Most chukkas   The greatest number of chukkas played on one ground in a day is 43. This was achieved by the Pony Club in Kirtlington Park, England on July 31, 1991.

POOL

14.1 CONTINUOUS POOL
(AMERICAN STRAIGHT POOL)

World Championship The two most dominant 14.1 players were Ralph Greenleaf (U.S.), who won the "world" professional title six times and defended it 13 times (1919–37), and Willie Mosconi (U.S.), who dominated the game from 1941 to 1956, winning the title six times and defending it 13 times.

Most balls pocketed The greatest number of balls pocketed in 24 hours is 16,497, by Paul Sullivan in Selby, England, April 16–17, 1993.

Pool pocketing speed The record times for pocketing all 15 balls are: *(men)* 32.72 seconds, by Paul Sullivan at the Excelsior Pool and Snooker Club, Leeds, England on September 26, 1995; *(women)* 42.28 seconds, by Susan Thompson at the Ferry Inn, Holmsgarth, Shetland Isles on January 28, 1995.

POWERBOAT RACING

APBA Gold Cup The American Powerboat Association (APBA) Gold Cup race has been won 10 times by Chip Hanauer (U.S.), 1982–88, 1992–93 and 1995.

The highest average speed for the race is 149.160 MPH by Chip Hanauer, piloting *Miss Budweiser* in Detroit, MI on June 4, 1995.

Chip Hanauer, in *Miss Budweiser*, set the average speed mark in the APBA Gold Cup.

Longest races The longest offshore race was the Port Richborough, London, England to Monte Carlo Marathon Offshore international event. The race extended over 2,947 miles in 14 stages, June 10–25, 1972. It was won by *H.T.S.* (Great Britain), driven by Mike Bellamy, Eddie Chater and Jim Brooker, in 71 hr. 35 min. 56 sec., for an average of 41.15 MPH.

The longest circuit race is the 24-hour race held annually since 1962 on the River Seine in Rouen, France.

Fastest water speed Kenneth Peter Warby achieved 300 knots (345.48 MPH) on Blowering Dam Lake, New South Wales, Australia on November 20, 1977 in his unlimited hydroplane *Spirit of Australia*.

The official world water speed record is 275.8 knots (511.11 kilometers per hour) set on October 8, 1978 by Warby on Blowering Dam Lake.

Mary Rife of Flint, TX set a women's unofficial record of 206.72 MPH in her blown fuel hydro *Proud Mary* in Tulsa, OK on July 23, 1977. Her official record is 197 MPH.

David Mischke set the APBA electric powerboat speed record of 70.597 MPH in a 14-foot outboard hydroplane with a 48-volt motor at Kilometer Speed Trials, Devil's Lake, Lincoln City, OR on October 14, 1995.

David Mischke set the electric powerboat record of 70.597 MPH.

PROJECTILE THROWING

Longest throw The longest independently authenticated throw of any inert object heavier than air is 1,265 ft. 9 in., for a lead weight with a long string tail attached, thrown by David Engvall in El Mirage, CA on October 17,

1993. The record for an object without any velocity-aiding feature is 1,257 feet by Scott Zimmerman, with a flying ring on July 8, 1986 in Fort Funston, CA.

Records achieved with other miscellaneous objects:

Boomerang juggling   The greatest number of consecutive catches with two boomerangs, keeping at least one boomerang aloft at all times, is 555, by Yannick Charles (France) in Strasbourg, France on September 4, 1995.

Boomerang throwing   The greatest number of consecutive 2-handed catches is 817, by Michael Girvin (U.S.) on July 17, 1994 in Oakland, CA.

Longest out-and-return distance   489 ft. 3 in., by Michel Dufayard (France) on July 5, 1992 in Shrewsbury, England.

Longest flight duration (with self-catch), 2 min. 59.94 sec. by Dennis Joyce (U.S.) in Bethlehem, PA, June 25, 1987.

Brick   146 ft. 1 in. (standard 5-pound building brick), Geoff Capes (Great Britain) at Braybrook School, Orton Goldhay, England on July 19, 1978.

Cow chip tossing   The greatest distance under the "non-sphericalization and 100 percent organic" rule is 266 feet, by Steve Urner at the Mountain Festival, Tehachapi, CA on August 14, 1981.

Egg (fresh hen's)   323 ft. 2½ in. (without breaking it), Johnny Dell Foley to Keith Thomas in Jewett, TX on November 12, 1978.

Rolling pin   175 ft. 5 in. (two pounds), Lori La Deane Adams at Iowa State Fair, IA on August 21, 1979.

Slingshot   1,565 ft. 4 in. (50-inch-long sling and a 2¼-ounce dart), David P. Engvall in Baldwin Lake, CA on September 13, 1992.

Spear throwing   848 ft. 6½ in. (using an atlatl or hand-held device that fits onto a short spear), David Engvall in Aurora, CO on July 15, 1995.

Flying disc throwing (formerly Frisbee)   The World Flying Disc Federation distance records are: *(men)* 656 ft. 2 in., by Scott Stokely (U.S.) on May 14, 1995 in Fort Collins, CO; *(women)* 447 ft. 3 in., by Anni Kreml (U.S.) on August 21, 1994, also in Fort Collins, CO.

The throw, run and catch records are: *(men)* 303 ft. 11 in., by Hiroshi Oshima (Japan) on July 20, 1988 in San Francisco, CA; *(women)* 196 ft. 11 in., by Judy Horowitz (U.S.) on June 29, 1985 in La Mirada, CA.

The 24-hour distance records for a pair are: *(men)* 367.94 miles, by Conrad Damon and Pete Fust (U.S.) on April 24–25, 1993 in San Marino, CA; *(women)* 115.65 miles, by Jo Cahow and Amy Berard (U.S.), December 30–31, 1979 in Pasadena, CA.

The records for maximum time aloft are: *(men)* 16.72 seconds, by Don Cain (U.S.) on May 26, 1984 in Philadelphia, PA; *(women)* 11.81 seconds, by Amy Bekken (U.S.) on August 1, 1991.

RACQUETBALL

World Championships First held in 1982, the International Racquetball Federation (IRF) World Championships have been held biennially since 1984. The United States has won all seven team titles, in 1981, 1984, 1986 (tie with Canada), 1988, 1990, 1992, and 1994. Egan Inoue (U.S.) has won the most men's singles titles with two, in 1986 and 1990. Three women have won the world singles championships twice: Cindy Baxter (U.S.) in 1981 and 1986; Heather Stupp (Canada) in 1988 and 1990; and Michelle Gould (née Gilman; U.S.), in 1992 and 1994.

U.S. titles In 1968, championships were initiated by the American Amateur Racquetball Association (AARA). A record seven women's open titles have been won by Michelle Gilman-Gould, 1989–93 and 1995–96. Four men's open titles have been won by Ed Andrews of California, 1980–81 and 1985–86.

RAPPELING

Distance A team of four Royal Marines set an overall distance record of 3,627 feet, by each rappeling down the Boulby Potash Mine, Cleveland, England from 25 feet below ground level to the shaft bottom on November 2, 1993.

The longest descent down the side of a building is one of 1,465 feet by two teams of twelve people representing the British Royal Marines and the Canadian School of Rescue Training. All 24 people rappeled to the ground from the Space Deck of the CN Tower in Toronto, Ontario, Canada on July 1, 1992. Two ropes were used, the first member of each team reaching the ground at exactly the same time. The greatest distance rappeled by 10 people in an 8-hour period is 67.68 miles, by a team from the British 10th (Volunteer) Battalion, Parachute Regiment. They rappeled 1,427 times down the side of Barclays Bank on Fenchurch Street, London, England on May 6, 1995.

RODEO

Largest rodeo The National Finals Rodeo is organized by the Professional Rodeo Cowboys Association (PRCA) and the Women's Professional Rodeo Association (WPRA). The 1991 Finals had a paid attendance of

171,414 for 10 performances. In 1995, a record $3,047,455 in prize money was offered for the event.

Most world titles   The record number of all-around titles (awarded to the leading money winner in a single season in two or more events) in the PRCA World Championships is six, by Larry Mahan (U.S.) in 1966–70 and 1973; Tom Ferguson, 1974–79; and Ty Murray, 1989–94. Jim Shoulders of Henrietta, TX won a record 16 World Championships in four events between 1949 and 1959.

Earnings records   Roy Cooper holds the career rodeo earnings mark at $1,584,297 through June 1996. The record figure for prize money in a single season is $297,896 by Ty Murray in 1993.

Fastest times   The fastest time recorded for calf-roping under the current PRCA rules is 6.7 seconds, by Joe Beaver in West Jordan, UT in 1986, and the fastest time for steer wrestling is 2.4 seconds, by James Bynum in Marietta, OK in 1955; Carl Deaton in Tulsa, OK in 1976; and Gene Melton in Pecatonica, IL in 1976. The fastest team roping time is 3.7 seconds, by Bob Harris and Tee Woolman in Spanish Fork, UT in 1986. The fastest in the steer roping event is 8.4 seconds, by Guy Allen in Garden City, KS in 1991. Allen later matched the time at rodeos in Roswell, NM and El Campo, TX.

Women's barrel racing   The greatest number of titles won in women's barrel racing is 10, by Charmayne Rodman, 1984–93.

Youngest rodeo champions   The youngest winner of a world title in rodeo is Anne Lewis (b. September 1, 1958), who won the WPRA barrel racing title in 1968, at 10 years of age. Ty Murray (b. October 11, 1969) is the youngest cowboy to win the PRCA All-Around Champion title, at age 20, in 1989.

Bull riding   The highest score in bull riding was 100 points out of a possible 100, by Wade Leslie on Wolfman Skoal in Central Point, OR in 1991.

Top bull   The top bucking bull Red Rock dislodged 312 riders, 1980–88, and was finally ridden to the 8-second bell by Lane Frost (1963–89; world champion bull rider, 1987) on May 20, 1988.

Saddle bronc riding   The highest scored saddle bronc ride is 95 out of a possible 100, by Doug Vold on Transport in Meadow Lake, Saskatchewan, Canada in 1979. Descent, a saddle bronc owned by Beutler Brothers and Cervi Rodeo Company, received a record six PRCA Saddle Bronc of the Year awards, 1966–69, 1971–72.

Bareback riding   Joe Alexander of Cora, WY scored 93 out of a possible 100 on Marlboro in Cheyenne, WY in 1974.

Sippin' Velvet, owned by Bernis Johnson, has been awarded five PRCA Bareback Horse of the Year titles: 1978, 1983–84 and 1986–87.

Texas skips   Vince Bruce (U.S.) performed 4,001 Texas skips on July 22, 1991 in New York City.

Largest loop Using 100 feet of rope, Kalvin Cook spun a loop of 95 feet at the Hacienda Hotel, Las Vegas, NV on March 27, 1994.

ROLLER SPORTS

INLINE SKATING

World Championships The first world championships took place in 1992. Derek Parra of Dover, DE has won two overall world titles: overall track champion, 1993 and overall road champion, 1994. No woman in-line skater has won more than one overall title.

Solo records The Inline Skating Records Association recognizes the following world records:

One hour (track) Haico Bauma (Netherlands) skated 22.11 miles in one hour on August 16, 1994 in Gronigen, Netherlands. The women's record is held by Karin Verhoef (Netherlands), who accomplished 18.98 miles on August 14, 1990 in Vriezenveen, Netherlands.

One hour (road) Eddy Matzger (U.S.) holds the men's 1-hour record of 21.64 miles, set on February 2, 1991 in Long Beach, CA.

Six hours (road) Jonathan Seutter (U.S.) holds the men's 6-hour record of 91.35 miles, set on February 2, 1991 in Long Beach, CA. Kimberly Pavek (U.S.) holds the women's record of 90.54 miles, set on October 30, 1993 in Minneapolis, MN.

12 hours (road) Jonathan Seutter (U.S.) bladed 177.63 miles in 12 hours on February 2, 1991 in Long Beach, CA. Kimberley Ames (U.S.) is the women's record holder, with 162.26 miles on October 2, 1994 in Portland, OR.

24 hours (road) The 24-hour world record is held by Kimberly Ames (U.S.), who skated 283.07 miles on October 2, 1994 in Portland, OR. The men's record is held by Jonathan Seutter (U.S.), who bladed 271.25 miles on October 31, 1993 in Minneapolis, MN.

Paced records 1,500 m (road) Derek Parra (U.S.) in 2:04.26 on August 26, 1994 in Gujan Maestras, France.

20 km (road) Arnaud Gicquel (France) in 31:23.320 on August 27, 1994 in Gujan Maestras, France.

42 km (marathon) Derek Parra (U.S.) in 1:04:27.986 on August 28, 1994 in Gujan Maestras, France.

ROLLER SKATING

Most titles Speed   The most world speed titles won is 18, by two women: Alberta Vianello (Italy), eight track and 10 road, 1953–65; and Annie Lambrechts (Belgium), one track and 17 road, 1964–81, at distances from 500 meters to 10,000 meters.

Figure   The records for combined figure and free skating titles are five, by two men, Karl Heinz Losch (West Germany) in 1958–59, 1961–62 and 1966, and Sandro Guerra (Italy), 1987–89 and 1991–92, and one woman, Rafaella del Vinaccio (Italy), 1988–92. The most world pair titles is six, by Tammy Jeru (U.S.) in 1983–86 (with John Arishita), and in 1990–91 (with Larry McGrew).

Speed skating   The fastest speed posted in an official world record is 27.46 MPH, when Luca Antoniel (Italy) recorded 24.678 seconds for 300 meters on a road in Bello, Colombia on November 15, 1990. The women's record is 25.04 MPH, by Marisa Canofoglia (Italy) for 300 meters on the road in Grenoble, France on August 27, 1987.

The world records for 10,000 meters on a road or track are: *(men)* 14 min. 55.64 sec., Giuseppe de Persio (Italy), Gujan Maestras, France, August 1, 1988; *(women)* 15 min. 58.022 sec., Marisa Canofoglia (Italy), Grenoble, France, August 30, 1987.

Roller limbo   On May 10, 1993, Syamala Gowri roller-skated under a limbo bar set at 4.7 inches in Hyderabad, India.

ROLLER HOCKEY

Most titles   Portugal has won most titles, with 14: 1947–50, 1952, 1956, 1958, 1960, 1962, 1968, 1974, 1982, 1991, and 1993.

ROWING

Most Olympic medals   Seven oarsmen have won three gold medals: John Brenden Kelly (U.S.), who won in single sculls (1920) and double sculls (1920, 1924); Paul Vincent Costello (U.S.), double sculls (1920, 1924, 1928); Jack Beresford, Jr. (Great Britain), single sculls (1924), coxless fours (1932) and double sculls (1936); Vyacheslav Nikolayevich Ivanov (USSR), single sculls (1956, 1960, 1964); Siegfried Brietzke (East Germany), coxless pairs (1972) and coxless fours (1976, 1980); Pertti Karppinen (Finland), single sculls (1976, 1980, 1984); and Steven Redgrave (Great Britain), coxed fours (1984) and coxless pairs (1988, 1992).

World Championships   World rowing championships distinct from the Olympic Games were first held in 1962, and were held every four years at first, but from 1974 were held annually, except in Olympic years.

The most gold medals won at World Championships and Olympic Games is nine, by the Abbagnale brothers, Guiseppe and Carmine (Italy) and their cox, Guiseppe di Capua: World in 1981–82, 1985, 1987, 1989–91, and Olympics in 1984 and 1988; and by Steven Redgrave: World in coxed pairs, 1986 and coxless pairs, 1987, 1991, 1993–95, and Olympics in coxed fours, 1984 and coxless pairs, 1988 and 1992. Francesco Esposito (Italy) has won nine titles in lightweight events; coxless pairs, 1980–84, 1988, and 1994, and coxless fours in 1990 and 1992. At women's events, Yelena Tereshina (USSR) has won a record seven golds, all in eights, in 1978–79, 1981–83, and 1985–86.

The most wins in single sculls is five, by Peter-Michael Kolbe (West Germany), 1975, 1978, 1981, 1983 and 1986; Pertti Karppinen, 1979 and 1985, and with his three Olympic wins (above); Thomas Lange (Germany), 1987, 1989 and 1991 and two Olympics 1988 and 1992; and in the women's events by Christine Hahn (née Scheiblich; East Germany), 1974–75, 1977–78 (and the 1976 Olympic title).

Three-time Olympic gold medalist Steve Redgrave (left) trains with teammate Matthew Pinsent.

Collegiate Championships   The first intercollegiate boat race in the United States was between Harvard and Yale in 1852. The Intercollegiate Rowing Association (IRA) was formed in 1895, and in 1898 inaugurated the Varsity Challenge Cup, which was recognized as the national championship. In 1982, the United States Rowing Assocation introduced the National Collegiate Championships, and this race now decides the national champion. Overall, Cornell University has won the most national championships, with 25 titles (all Varsity Cup wins). Since 1982, Harvard University has won six titles (1983, 1985, 1987–89, 1992).

The women's national championship (inaugurated 1979) has been won seven times by the University of Washington (1981–85, 1987–88).

Longest race   The longest annual rowing race is the annual Tour du Lac Leman, Geneva, Switzerland for coxed fours (the 5-man crew taking turns as cox) over 99 miles. The record winning time is 12 hr. 22 min. 29 sec., by RG Red Bull, Bonn, Germany on October 2, 1994.

Fastest speed   The record time for 2,187 yards on non-tidal water is 5 min. 24.28 sec. (13.79 MPH) by an eight from Hansa Dortmund (Germany), in Essen, Germany on May 17, 1992. The women's record is 5 min. 58.50 sec., by Romania in Duisburg, Germany, on May 18, 1996.

The single sculls record is 6 min. 37.03 sec. (11.26 MPH), by Juri Jaanson (Estonia) in Lucerne, Switzerland, on July 9, 1995. On July 17, 1994, Silken Laumann (Canada) set a women's record of 7 min. 17.09 sec. in Lucerne.

Greatest 24-hour distance   The greatest distance rowed in 24 hours (upstream and downstream) is 141.26 miles, by six members of Dittons Skiff & Punting Club on the River Thames between Hampton Court and Teddington, England on June 3–4, 1994.

International Dragon Boat Race   In this race, held annually in Hong Kong, the fastest time achieved for the 700-yard course is 2 min. 27.45 sec., by the Chinese Shun De team on January 30, 1985.

RUGBY

Records are based on the scoring system that was in use at the time.

Rugby all-arounder   Canadian international Barrie Burnham scored all possible ways—try, conversion, penalty goal, drop goal, goal from mark—for Meralomas vs. Georgians (20–11) in Vancouver, British Columbia, Canada on February 26, 1966.

Gavin Hastings (Scotland) is the leading scorer in the Rugby World Cup.

Highest rugby posts   The world's highest rubgy union goal posts are 110 ft. $\frac{1}{2}$ in. high, at the Roan Antelope Rugby Union Club, Luanshya, Zambia.

OLYMPIC GAMES

In competitions held 1900–24, the only double gold medalist was the United States, which won in 1920 and 1924, defeating France in the final on both occasions.

WORLD CUP

The World Cup has been held on three occasions, 1987, 1991 and 1995, with the winners being New Zealand, Australia and South Africa respectively. The highest team score was New Zealand's 145–17 victory over Japan in Bloemfontein, South Africa on June 4, 1995. The individual match record was 45 (20 conversions, 1 try), by Simon Culhane (New Zealand) vs. Japan in Bloemfontein, South Africa on June 4, 1995. The leading scorer in the tournament was Gavin Hastings (Scotland), with 227 points.

HIGHEST SCORES

Teams   The highest score in any full international was when Hong Kong beat Singapore 164–13 in a World Cup qualifying match in Kuala Lumpur, Malaysia, on October 27, 1994.

Individuals Most points   Ashley Billington (Hong Kong) scored 50 points (10 tries) in the World Cup qualifying match in Kuala Lumpur, Malaysia, on October 27, 1994, when Hong Kong won 164–13.

Most penalty goals   The most penalty goals kicked in a match is eight, by Mark Andrew Wyatt (Canada) vs. Scotland in St. John, New Brunswick, Canada on May 25, 1991; Neil Roger Jenkins (Wales) vs. Canada in Cardiff, Wales on November 10, 1993; Santiago Meson (Argentina) vs. Canada in Buenos Aires, Argentina on March 12, 1995; Gavin Hastings (Scotland) vs. Tonga in Pretoria, South Africa on May 30, 1995; and Thierry Lacroix (France) vs. Ireland at Durban, South Africa on June 10, 1995.

Career   In all internationals, Michael Lynagh scored a record 911 points in 72 matches for Australia, 1984–95. The most tries is 63, by David Campese in 95 internationals for Australia, 1982–96.

SEVEN-A-SIDES

Hong Kong Sevens   The record of seven wins is held by Fiji, 1977–78, 1980, 1984, 1990–92.

SHOOTING

Most Olympic medals Carl Townsend Osburn (U.S.) won 11 medals, in 1912, 1920 and 1924—five gold, four silver and two bronze. Gudbrand Gudbrandsönn Skatteboe (Norway) is the only marksman to have won three individual gold medals, in 1906.

Highest shooting score in 24 hours The Easingwold Rifle and Pistol Club (Yorkshire, England) team of John Smith, Edward Kendall, Phillip Kendall and Paul Duffield scored 120,242 points (averaging 95.66 per card), August 6–7, 1983.

Bench rest shooting The smallest group on record at 1,000 yards is 3.960 inches, by Frank Weber (U.S.) with a .308 Baer Magnum in Williamsport, PA on November 14, 1993.

The smallest at 500 meters (546 yards) is 1.5 inches, by Ross Hicks (Australia) using a .30–06 rifle of his own design in Canberra, Australia on March 12, 1994.

Clay pigeon The most world titles have been won by Susan Nattrass (Canada) with six, 1974–75, 1977–79, 1981. The record number of clay birds shot in an hour is 4,551, by John Cloherty (U.S.) in Seattle, WA on August 31, 1992.

The maximum 200/200 was achieved by Ricardo Ruiz Rumoroso at the Spanish Clay Pigeon Championships in Zaragossa on June 12, 1983.

Noel D. Townend achieved the maximum 200 consecutive down-the-line targets in Nottingham, England on August 21, 1983.

SKATEBOARDING

Distance Eleftherios Argiropoulos covered 271.3 miles in 36 hr. 33 min. 17 sec. in Ekali, Greece, November 4–5, 1993.

Fastest speed The fastest speed recorded on a skateboard is 78.37 MPH in a prone position by Roger Hickey, on a course near Los Angeles, CA on March 15, 1990.

The stand-up record is 55.43 MPH, achieved by Roger Hickey, in San Demas, CA on July 3, 1990.

Highest jump The high-jump record is 5 ft. 5³/₄ in., by Trevor Baxter of Burgess Hill, England in Grenoble, France on September 14, 1982.

Longest jump At the World Professional Championships in Long Beach, CA, on September 25, 1977, Tony Alva jumped 17 barrels (17 feet).

SHOOTING—INDIVIDUAL RECORDS

In 1986, the International Shooting Union (UIT) introduced new regulations for determining major championships and world records. Now the leading competitors undertake an additional round with a target subdivided to tenths of a point for rifle and pistol shooting, and an extra 25 shots for trap and skeet. Harder targets have since been introduced, and the table below shows the world records, as recognized by the UIT, for the 13 Olympic shooting disciplines, giving in parentheses the score for the number of shots specified plus the score in the additional round.

Event	Score	Name and Country	Place	Date
MEN				
Free Rifle 50 m 3 × 40 shots	1,287.9	(1,186 + 101.9) ...Rajmond Debevec (Slovenia)	Munich, Germany	Aug. 29, 1992
Free Rifle 50 m 60 shots prone	703.5	(599 + 104.5) ...Jens Harskov (Denmark)	Zürich, Switzerland	Jun. 6, 1991
Air Rifle 10 m 60 shots	699.4	(596 + 103.4) ...Rajmond Debevec (Yugoslavia)	Zürich, Switzerland	Jun. 8, 1990
Free Pistol 50 m 60 shots	675.3	(580 + 95.3) ...Taniu Kirlakov (Bulgaria)	Hiroshima, Japan	Apr. 21, 1995
Rapid-Free Pistol 25 m 60 shots	699.7	(596 + 107.5) ...Ralf Schumann (Germany)	Barcelona, Spain	Jun. 8, 1994
Air Pistol 10 m 60 shots	695.1	(593 + 102.1) ...Sergey Pyzhyanov (USSR)	Munich, Germany	Oct. 13, 1989
Running Target 50 m 30 + 30 shots	679	(582 + 97) ...Lubos Racansky (Czechoslovakia)	Munich, Germany	May 30, 1991
WOMEN				
Standard Rifle 50 m 3 × 20 shots	689.7	(592 + 97.7) ...Vessela Letcheva (Bulgaria)	Munich, Germany	Jun. 15, 1995
Air Rifle 10 m 40 shots	501.1	(396 + 105.1) ...Bettina Knells (Germany)	Hiroshima, Japan	Apr. 23, 1995
Sport Pistol 25 m 60 shots	696.2	(594 + 102.2) ...Diana Jorgova (Bulgaria)	Milan, Italy	May 31, 1994
Air Pistol 10 m 40 shots	492.4	(392 + 100.4) ...Lieslotte Breker (West Germany)	Zagreb, Yugoslavia	May 18, 1989
OPEN				
Trap 200 targets	148	(124 + 24) ...Giovanni Pellielo (Italy)	Fagnano, Italy	Jun. 5, 1993
	148	(124 + 24) ...Marco Venturini (Netherlands)	Barcelona, Spain	Jun. 15, 1993
Skeet 200 targets	149	(124 + 25) ...Dean Clark (U.S.)	Barcelona, Spain	Jun. 20, 1993

SKIING

Most titles *World/Olympic Championships—Alpine* The greatest number of titles were won by Christl Cranz of Germany, with seven individual— four slalom (1934, 1937–39) and three downhill (1935, 1937, 1939), and five combined (1934–35, 1937–39). The most won by a man is seven, by Toni Sailer (Austria), who won all four in 1956 (giant slalom, slalom, downhill and the non-Olympic Alpine combination) and the downhill, giant slalom and combined in 1958.

The only U.S. skier to win two Olympic gold medals is Andrea Mead-Lawrence, in slalom and giant slalom in 1952.

World/Olympic Championships—Nordic The first World Nordic Championships were those of the 1924 Winter Olympics in Chamonix, France. The greatest number of titles won is 11, by Gunde Svan (Sweden), seven individual—15 km 1989, 30 km 1985 and 1991, 50 km 1985 and 1989, and Olympics, 15 km 1984, 50 km 1988; and four relays—4 × 10 km, 1987 and 1989, and Olympics, 1984 and 1988. The most titles won by a woman is 11, by Yelena Välbe (née Trubizinina; Russia), with six individual and five relay, 1989–95. The most medals is 23, by Raisa Smetanina (USSR), including seven gold, 1974–92. The record for a ski-jumper is five, by Birger Ruud (Norway), in 1931–32 and 1935–37.

Vreni Schneider won 13 World Cup events in 1988/89.

World Cup The World Cup was introduced for Alpine events in 1967, and Nordic events were officially integrated into the World Cup in the 1983/84 season. The most individual event wins is 86 (46 giant slalom, 40 slalom from a total of 287 races) by Ingemar Stenmark (Sweden) in 1974–89, including a men's record 13 in one season in 1978/79, of which 10 were part of a record 14 successive giant slalom wins from March 18, 1978 to January 21, 1980. Franz Klammer (Austria) won 25 downhill races, 1974–84. Annemarie Moser (née Pröll; Austria) won a women's record 62 individual event wins, 1970–79. She had 11 consecutive downhill wins from December 1972 to January 1974.

Vreni Schneider (Switzerland) won a record 13 events and a combined, including all seven slalom events in 1988/89.

United States   The most successful U.S. skier was Phil Mahre, winner of the overall title three times, 1981–83, with two wins in giant slalom and one in slalom. The most successful U.S. woman was Tamara McKinney, overall winner 1983, giant slalom 1981 and 1983, and slalom 1984.

The only American to win a Nordic skiing World Cup title was William Koch, in cross-country in 1982.

Longest ski-jump   The longest ski-jump ever recorded is 686 feet, by Espen Bredesen (Norway) in Planica, Slovenia on March 18, 1994. The women's record is 367 feet, by Eva Ganster (Austria), in Bischofshofen, Austria on January 7, 1994.

Fastest speed   The official world record, as recognized by the International Ski Federation, is 150.028 MPH, by Jeffrey Hamilton (U.S.) on April 14, 1995 in Vars, France.

The fastest speed by a woman is 140.864 MPH, by Karine Dubouchet (France) on April 20, 1996 in Les Arcs, France.

On April 16, 1988 Patrick Knaff (France) set a one-legged record of 115.306 MPH.

The fastest average speed in the Olympic downhill race is 64.95 MPH, by Bill Johnson (U.S.), in Sarajevo, Yugoslavia on February 16, 1984. The fastest in a World Cup downhill is 69.8 MPH, by Armin Assinger (Austria) in Sierra Nevada, Spain on March 15, 1993.

Fastest speed—cross-country   The record time for a 50-km race in a major championship is 1 hr. 54 min. 46 sec., at an average speed of 16.24 MPH, by Aleksey Prokurorov (Russia), at Thunder Bay, Canada on March 19, 1994.

40 years ago the fastest speed attained on a pair of skis was 109.11 MPH by Ralph Miller (U.S.). He set the record in Portillos, Chile in July 1955. **Today** the official world record is 150.028 MPH. Jeffrey Hamilton (U.S.) set the mark on April 14, 1995 in Vars, France.

"I started skiing last year on my 67th birthday. I would love to be a world-class skier."—Hal Prince, Broadway legend, April 16, 1996

Longest run The longest all-downhill ski run in the world is the Weissfluhjoch-Küblis Parsenn course, near Davos, Switzerland, which measures 7.6 miles.

The run from the Aiguille du Midi top of the Chamonix lift across the Vallée Blanche is 13 miles.

Long-distance *Nordic* In 24 hours, Seppo-Juhani Savolainen covered 258.2 miles in Saariselkä, Finland, April 8–9, 1988.

The women's 24-hour record is 205.05 miles, by Sisko Kainulaisen in Jyväskylä, Finland, March 23–24, 1985.

In 48 hours, Bjørn Løkken (Norway) covered 319 mi. 205 yd., March 11–13, 1982.

Alpine During calendar year 1994, Lucy Dicker and Arnie Wilson (both Great Britain) skied every day in an around-the-world expedition. They skied a total of 3,678 miles and 472,050 feet at 237 resorts in 13 countries on five continents.

Longest races The longest Nordic ski race is the Vasaloppet, at 55.3 miles. There were a record 10,934 starters on March 6, 1977 and a record 10,650 finishers on March 4, 1979. The fastest time is 3 hr. 48 min. 55 sec., by Bengt Hassis (Sweden) in 1986.

The 1984 Finlandia Ski Race, 46.6 miles from Hämeenlinna to Lahti, had 13,226 starters and 12,909 finishers.

The longest downhill race is the Inferno in Switzerland, 9.8 miles from the top of the Schilthorn to Lauterbrunnen. The record number of entries was 1,401 in 1981, and the record time was 13 min. 53.40 sec. by Urs von Allmen (Switzerland) in 1991.

Freestyle skiing The first World Championships were held in Tignes, France in 1986. Edgar Grospiron (France) has won a record three titles: moguls, 1989, 1991 and 1995. Grospiron has also won an Olympic title, in 1992. The most Overall titles in the World Cup (instituted 1980) is 10, by

MOST WORLD CUP TITLES

ALPINE SKIING (instituted 1967)

Men

Overall ....5......Marc Girardelli (Luxembourg) 1985–86, 1989, 1991, 1993

Downhill ....5......Franz Klammer (Austria) 1975–76; 1983

Slalom ....8......Ingemar Stenmark (Sweden) 1975–81, 1983

Giant Slalom 7......Ingemar Stenmark (Sweden) 1975–76, 1978–81, 1984

Super Giant
   Slalom ......4......Pirmin Zurbriggen (Switzerland) 1987–90

Two men have won four titles in one year: Jean-Claude Killy (France) won all four possible disciplines (downhill, slalom, giant slalom and overall) in 1967; and Pirmin Zurbriggen (Switzerland) won four of the five possible disciplines (downhill, giant slalom, super giant slalom [added 1986] and overall) in 1987.

Women

Overall ....6......Annemarie Moser-Pröll (Austria) 1971–75, 1979

Downhill ....7......Annemarie Moser-Pröll 1971–75, 1978–79

Slalom ....6......Vreni Schneider (Switzerland) 1989–90, 1992–95

Giant Slalom 5......Vreni Schneider (Switzerland) 1986–87, 1989, 1991, 1995

Super Giant
   Slalom ......4......Carole Merle (France) 1989–92

           4......Katja Seizinger (Germany) 1993–96

NORDIC SKIING (instituted 1981)

Men

Jumping ....4......Matti Nykänen (Finland) 1983, 1985–86, 1988

Cross-
   Country ...5......Gunde Svan (Sweden) 1984–86, 1988–89

Women

Cross-
   Country ....4......Yelena Välbe (USSR/Russia) 1989, 1991–92, 1995

Connie Kissling (Switzerland), 1983–92. The men's record is four, by Eric Laboureix (France), 1986–87, 1990–91.

Longest ski lift The longest gondola ski lift is 3.88 miles long, in Grindelwald-Männlichen, Switzerland (in two sections, but one gondola).

Ski-bob Fastest speed The fastest speed attained is 103.1 MPH, by Erich Brenter (Austria), in Cervinia, Italy in 1964.

World Championships The only ski-bobbers to retain a world championship are: *(men)* Alois Fischbauer (Austria), 1973 and 1975; Robert Mühlberger (West Germany), 1979 and 1981; *(women)* Gerhilde Schiffkorn (Austria), 1967 and 1969; Gertrude Geberth (Austria), 1971 and 1973.

GRASS SKIING

Most titles The biennial World Championships (now awarded for Super G, giant slalom, slalom and combined) were first held in 1979. The most titles won is 14, by Ingrid Hirschhofer (Austria), 1979–93. The most by a man is seven, by Erwin Gansner (Switzerland), 1981–87, and Rainer Grossman, 1985–93.

The feat of winning all four titles in one year has been achieved by *(men)* Erwin Gansner, 1987, and Rainer Grossman, 1991, and by *(women)* Katja Krey (West Germany), 1989, and Ingrid Hirschhofer, 1993.

Fastest speed Klaus Spinka (Austria) set a record of 57.21 MPH in Waldassen, Germany on September 24, 1989.

SLED DOG RACING

Iditarod trail Now recognized as the world's most prestigious sled dog race, the Iditarod trail is also the oldest established trail. It has existed since 1910 and has been raced annually since 1967, 1,049 miles from Anchorage to Nome, AK.

The fastest time was set by Doug Swingley (U.S.) in 1995, with 9 days 2 hr. 42 min. 19 sec. Rick Swenson (U.S.) has won the race five times (1977, 1979, 1981–82 and 1991).

Longest trail The longest race is the 1,243-mile Benergia Trail from Esso to Markovo, Russia. The 1991 race was won by Pavel Lazarev in 10 days 18 hr. 17 min. 56 sec.

SOARING

Most titles The most World Individual Championships won is four, by Ingo Renner (Australia) in 1976 (Standard class), 1983, 1985 and 1987 (Open). The most titles won by a U.S. pilot is two, by George Moffat, in the Open category, 1970 and 1974.

HANG GLIDING

World Championships The World Team Championships have been won most often by Great Britain (1981, 1985, 1989 and 1991).

World records The *Fédération Aéronautique Internationale* recognizes world records for rigid-wing, flex-wing and multiplace flex-wing. The following records are for the greatest distance by flex-wing gliders.

Men Greatest distance in straight line and declared goal distance: 303.3 miles, Larry Tudor (U.S.), Hobbs Airpark, NM to Elkhart, KS, July 3, 1990.

Height gain: 14,250 feet, Larry Tudor, Owens Valley, CA, August 4, 1985.

Out and return distance: 192.8 miles, Larry Tudor and Geoffrey Loyns (Great Britain), Owens Valley, June 26, 1988.

Triangular course distance: 121.79 miles, James Lee (U.S.), Wild Horse Mesa, CO, July 4, 1991.

Women Greatest distance: 208.6 miles, Kari Castle (U.S.), Owens Valley, July 22, 1991.

Height gain: 13,025 feet, Judy Leden (Great Britain), Kuruman, South Africa, December 1, 1992.

Out and return distance in a single turn: 181.5 miles, Kari Castle, Hobbs Airpark, July 1, 1990.

Declared goal distance: 132.04 miles, Liavan Mallin (Ireland), Owens Valley, July 13, 1989.

Triangular course distance: Judy Leden, 70.9 miles, Kössen, Austria, June 22, 1991.

SOCCER

Ball control Ricardinho Neves (Brazil) juggled a regulation soccer ball for 19 hr. 5 min. 31 sec. nonstop with feet, legs and head, without the ball ever touching the ground, at the Los Angeles Convention Center, CA, on July 15–16, 1994. The heading record is 7 hr. 17 min. 5 sec. by Tomas Lundman (Sweden) in Chertsey, England on June 27, 1995.

Most dismissive referee It was reported on June 1, 1993 that in a league soccer match between Sportivo Ameliano and General Caballero in Paraguay, referee William Weiler ejected 20 players. Trouble flared after two Sportivo players were thrown out, a 10-minute fight ensued, and Weiler then dismissed a further 18 players, including the rest of the Sportivo team. Not surprisingly, the game was abandoned.

THE FIFA WORLD CUP

Three wins have been achieved by Brazil, in 1958, 1962 and 1970; Italy, in 1934, 1938 and 1982; and West Germany, in 1954, 1974 and 1990.

Team records Most appearances Brazil is the only country to qualify for all 15 World Cup tournaments.

Marcello Balbao has played the most games for the U.S.

Most goals The most goals scored in one game occurred when New Zealand beat Fiji 13–0 in a qualifying game in Auckland on August 15, 1981. The highest score during the final stages is 10, scored by Hungary in a 10–1 defeat of El Salvador in Elche, Spain on June 15, 1982. The highest game aggregate in the finals tournament is 12, when Austria defeated Switzerland 7–5 in Lausanne, Switzerland on June 26, 1954.

Tournament The most goals in a single finals tournament is 27 (five games) by Hungary in 1954. Brazil has scored the most overall, with 159 in 73 games.

Individual records *Most wins* Pelé (Brazil) is the only player to have played on three winning teams, 1958, 1962 and 1970. He played during the 1962 Finals, but was injured before the final match and was therefore unable to play in it.

Most goals The most goals scored in a final is three, by Geoff Hurst for England vs. West Germany on July 30, 1966.

Most games played   Four players have appeared in 21 games in the finals tournament: Uwe Seeler (West Germany) 1958–70; and Wladyslaw Zmuda (Poland) 1974–86; Diego Maradona (Argentina), 1982–94; and Lothar Matthaüs (Germany), 1982–94.

Most goals scored   The most goals scored in one tournament is 13, by Just Fontaine (France) in 1958, in six games. The most goals scored in a career is 14, by Gerd Muller (West Germany), 10 goals in 1970 and four in 1974.

Women's World Cup   The U.S. won the inaugural World Cup in 1991, beating Norway 2–1 in the final. The second competition, in 1995, was won by Norway, which beat Germany 2–0 in the final.

Olympic Games   The leading gold medal winner is Hungary, with three wins (1952, 1964, 1968). The highest Olympic score is 17, by Denmark vs. France in 1908. A record 126 nations took part in qualifying for the 1992 tournament.

NCAA DIVISION I CHAMPIONSHIPS

Men   In this competition, first held in 1959, the University of St. Louis has won the most Division I titles with 10 victories, including one tie: 1959–60, 1962–63, 1965, 1967, 1969–70, 1972–73.

Women   In this competition, first held in 1982, the University of North Carolina has won 10 Division I titles, in 1982–84 and 1986–92.

Largest soccer crowds   The top attendance for a soccer match in the United States was 101,799, for France's 2–0 Olympic final win over Brazil at the Rose Bowl, Pasadena, CA on August 11, 1984.

SOFTBALL

Most titles   The U.S. has won the men's World Championship (instituted 1966) five times, 1966, 1968, 1976 (shared), 1980 and 1988, and the women's title (instituted 1965) five times, in 1974, 1978, 1986, 1990, and 1994.

U.S. National Championships   The most wins in the fast pitch championships (first held in 1933) for men is 10, by the Clearwater (Florida) Bombers between 1950 and 1973, and for women is 23, by the Raybestos Brakettes of Stratford, CT, between 1958 and 1992.

Slow pitch championships have been staged annually since 1953 for men and since 1962 for women. Three wins for men have been achieved by Skip Hogan A.C. of Pittsburgh, 1962, 1964–65, and by Joe Gatliff Auto Sales of Newport, KY, 1956–57, 1963.

At super slow pitch, four wins have been achieved by Steele's Silver Bullets, Grafton, OH, 1985–87 and 1990. The Dots of Miami, FL have a record five women's titles, playing as the Converse Dots, 1969; Marks

Brothers, 1974–75; North Miami Dots, 1974–75; and Bob Hoffman Dots, 1978–79.

Perfect game Carol Christ Hampton, pitcher for Les's Legacy, Seattle, WA, pitched an entire game with all strikes except for three balls called at the ASA Class C Women's National Softball Championship, St. Augustine, FL on September 25, 1994.

SQUASH

World Championships Jansher Khan (Pakistan) has won seven World Open titles, in 1987, 1989–90, and 1992–95. Geoffrey B. Hunt (Australia) won four World Open titles, 1976–77 and 1979–80, and three World Amateur, 1967, 1969 and 1971. The most women's World Open titles is four, by Susan Devoy (New Zealand), 1985, 1987, 1990, and 1992.

Australia (1967, 1969, 1971, 1973, 1989 and 1991) and Pakistan (1977, 1981, 1983, 1985, 1987 and 1993) have each won six men's world team titles. The women's world team title has been won four times, by England (1985, 1987, 1989 and 1990) and by Australia (1981, 1983, 1992 and 1994).

Most titles Open Championship The most wins in the Open Championship, held annually in Britain, is 10, by Jahangir Khan, 1982–91. Hashim Khan (Pakistan) won seven times, 1950–55 and 1957, and also won the Vintage title six times, 1978–83.

The most British Open women's titles is 16, by Heather McKay (née Blundell; Australia), 1961–77.

United States The U.S. amateur squash championships were first held for men in 1907 and for women in 1928; the most singles wins is six, by Stanley W. Pearson, 1915–17 and 1921–23. G. Diehl Mateer won a record 11 men's doubles titles between 1949 and 1966 with five different partners. Sharif Khan (Pakistan) won a record 13 North American Open Championships (instituted 1953), 1969–74 and 1976–82. Alicia McConnell has won seven women's national championships (1982–88).

Unbeaten sequences Heather McKay was unbeaten from 1962 to 1980. Jahangir Khan was unbeaten from his loss to Geoff Hunt at the British Open on April 10, 1981 until his loss to Ross Norman (New Zealand) in the World Open final on November 11, 1986.

Longest and shortest championship matches The longest recorded competitive match was one of 2 hr. 45 min. when Jahangir Khan beat Gamal Awad (Egypt) 9–10, 9–5, 9–7, 9–2, the first game lasting a record 1 hr. 11 min., in the final of the Patrick International Festival in Chichester, England on March 30, 1983. Philip Kenyon (England) beat Salah Nadi (Egypt) in just 6 min. 37 sec. (9–0, 9–0, 9–0) in the British Open at Lamb's Squash Club, London, England on April 9, 1992.

Most international appearances The men's record is 122 by David Gotto for Ireland. The women's record is 108 by Marjorie Croke (née Burke) for Ireland, 1981–93.

SURFING

Most titles World Amateur Championships were inaugurated in May 1964. The most titles is three, by Michael Novakov (Australia), who won the Kneeboard event in 1982, 1984 and 1986. A World Professional series was started in 1975. The men's title has been won five times, by Mark Richards (Australia), 1975 and from 1979 to 1982, and the women's title (instituted 1979) four times, by Frieda Zamba (U.S.), 1984–86, 1988; and by Wendy Botha (Australia, formerly South Africa), 1987, 1989, 1991–92.

Youngest surfing champion Frieda Zamba was 19 years old when she won the 1984 title. The youngest men's champion was Kelly Slater (U.S.), who won the 1992 crown at age 20.

Highest career earnings The career earnings leader through January 1, 1996 is Barton Lynch (Australia) with $550,187. The women's leader is Pam Burridge (Australia), with $220,540.

SWIMMING

Fastest swimmer In a 25-yard pool, Tom Jager (U.S.) achieved an average speed of 5.37 MPH for 50 yards in 19.05 seconds in Nashville, TN on March 23, 1990.

Most world records *Men:* 32, Arne Borg (Sweden), 1921–29. *Women*: 42, Ragnhild Hveger (Denmark), 1936–42. For currently recognized events (only metric distances in 50-meter pools) the most is (men) 26, by Mark Spitz (U.S.), 1967–72, and (women) 23, by Kornelia Ender (East Germany), 1973–76. The most by a U.S. woman is 15, by Debbie Meyer, 1967–70.

Most world titles In the World Championships (instituted 1973) the most medals won is 13, by Michael Gross (West Germany)—5 gold, 5 silver and 3 bronze, 1982–90. The most medals won by a woman is 10, by Kornelia Ender, with eight gold and two silver in 1973 and 1975. The most gold medals won is six (two individual and four relay) by Jim Montgomery (U.S.) in 1973 and 1975.

The most medals won in a single championship is seven, by Matt Biondi (U.S.)—3 gold, 1 silver, 3 bronze, in 1986.

The most gold medals won by an American woman is five, by Tracy

Caulkins, all in 1978; she also won a silver. The most medals overall is nine, by Mary Terstegge Meagher—2 gold, 5 silver, 2 bronze, 1978–82.

U.S. Championships Tracy Caulkins won a record 48 U.S. swimming titles and set 60 U.S. records in her career, 1977–84. The men's record is 36 titles, by Johnny Weissmuller, 1921–28.

Sponsored swim The greatest amount of money collected in a charity swim was £122,983.19 (*c.* $350,000) in "Splash '92," organized by the Royal Bank of Scotland Swimming Club and held at the Royal Commonwealth Pool, Edinburgh, Scotland on January 25–26, 1992 with 3,218 participants.

Most Golden Gate crossings Joseph Bruno has crossed the Golden Gate strait 61 times. He first performed the feat on September 17, 1933. His latest crossing was on September 11, 1993, two months shy of his 81st birthday.

Youngest to cross the Golden Gate Andrew Pinetti swam the strait on August 11, 1993, when he was 10 years old.

OLYMPIC RECORDS

Most medals Men The greatest number of Olympic gold medals won is nine, by Mark Spitz (U.S.): 100 m and 200 m freestyle, 1972; 100 m and 200 m butterfly, 1972; 4 × 100 m freestyle, 1968 and 1972; 4 × 200 m freestyle, 1968 and 1972; 4 × 100 m medley, 1972. All but one of these performances (the 4 × 200 m freestyle of 1968) were also new world records. He also won a silver (100 m butterfly) and a bronze (100 m freestyle) in 1968, for a record 11 medals. His record seven medals at one Games in 1972 was equaled by Matt Biondi (U.S.), who took five gold, a silver and a bronze in 1988. Biondi has also won a record 11 medals in total, winning a gold in 1984, and two golds and a silver in 1992.

Women The record number of gold medals won by a woman is six, by Kristin Otto (East Germany) in Seoul in 1988: 100 m freestyle, backstroke

Kieren Perkins set the 400 meter freestyle record in Rome in 1994.

Jeff Rouse set the 100 meter backstroke mark in Barcelona in 1992.

and butterfly, 50 m freestyle, 4 × 100 m freestyle and 4 × 100 m medley. Dawn Fraser (Australia) is the only swimmer to win the same event, the 100 m freestyle, on three successive occasions (1956, 1960 and 1964). The most gold medals won by a U.S. woman is three, by 14 swimmers.

The most medals won by a woman is eight, by three swimmers: Dawn Fraser—four golds (100 m freestyle, 1956, 1960 and 1964, 4 × 100 m freestyle, 1956) and four silvers (400 m freestyle, 1956, 4 × 100 m freestyle, 1960 and 1964, 4 × 100 m medley, 1960); Kornelia Ender—four golds (100 m and 200 m freestyle, 100 m butterfly, and 4 × 100 m medley in 1976) and four silvers (200 m individual medley, 1972, 4 × 100 m medley, 1972, 4 × 100 m freestyle, 1972 and 1976); and Shirley Babashoff (U.S.), who won two golds (4 × 100 m freestyle, 1972 and 1976) and six silvers (100 m freestyle, 1972, 200 m freestyle, 1972 and 1976, 400 m and 800 m freestyle, 1976, 4 × 100 m medley, 1976).

Most individual gold medals   The record number of individual gold medals won is four, by Charles Meldrum Daniels (U.S.): 100 m freestyle, 1906 and 1908, 220 yd freestyle, 1904, 440 yd freestyle, 1904); by Roland Matthes (East Germany) with 100 m and 200 m backstroke in 1968 and 1972; by Mark Spitz and Kristin Otto (see MOST MEDALS); and by the divers Pat McCormick and Greg Louganis (see DIVING).

DIVING

Most Olympic medals   The most medals won by a diver is five, by Klaus Dibiasi (Austria), three gold, two silver, 1964–76; and by Greg Louganis (U.S.), four golds, one silver, 1976, 1984–88. Dibiasi is the only diver to win the same event (highboard) at three successive Games (1968, 1972 and 1976). Two divers have won the highboard and springboard doubles at two Games: Pat McCormick (née Keller), 1952 and 1956, and Greg Louganis, 1984 and 1988.

Most world titles   Greg Louganis (U.S.) won five world titles—highboard in 1978, highboard and springboard in 1982 and 1986, and four Olympic

SHORT-COURSE SWIMMING RECORDS

(set in 25-meter pools)

Event	Time	Name & Country	Place	Date
MEN				
Freestyle				
50 meters	0:21.50	Aleksandr Popov (Russia)	Desenzano, Italy	Mar. 13, 1994
100 meters*	0:46.74	Aleksandr Popov (Russia)	Gelsenkirchen, Germany	Mar. 19, 1994
200 meters	1:43.64	Giorgio Lamberti (Italy)	Bonn, Germany	Feb. 11, 1990
400 meters	3:40.46	Danyon Loader (New Zealand)	Sheffield, England	Feb. 11, 1995
800 meters	7:34.90	Kieren Perkins (Australia)	Sydney, Australia	Jul. 25, 1993
1,500 meters	14:26.52	Kieren Perkins (Australia)	Auckland, New Zealand	Jul. 15, 1993
4 × 50 meters	1:27.62	Sweden	Stavanger, Norway	Dec. 2, 1994
4 × 100 meters	3:12.11	Brazil	Palma de Mallorca, Spain	Dec. 5, 1993
4 × 200 meters	7:05.17	West Germany	Bonn, Germany	Feb. 9, 1986
Backstroke				
50 meters	0:24.37	Jeff Rouse (U.S.)	Sheffield, England	Feb. 12, 1995
100 meters	0:51.43	Jeff Rouse (U.S.)	Sheffield, England	Apr. 11, 1993
200 meters	1:52.51	Martin Lopez-Zubero (Spain)	Gainesville, FL	Apr. 10, 1991
Breaststroke				
50 meters	0:27.00	Mark Warnecke (Germany)	Gelsenkirchen, Germany	Feb. 18, 1995
100 meters	0:59.02	Frédéric Deburghgraeve (Belgium)	Bastogne, Belgium	Feb. 17, 1996
200 meters	2:07.80	Philip John Rogers (Australia)	Melbourne, Australia	Aug. 28, 1993
Butterfly				
50 meters	0:23.55	Mark Foster (Great Britain)	Sheffield, England	Feb. 11, 1995
100 meters	0:51.94	Denis Pankratov (Russia)	Paris, France	Feb. 4, 1996
200 meters	1:52.34	Denis Pankratov (Russia)	Paris, France	Feb. 3, 1996
Medley				
100 meters	0:53.10	Jani Sievinen (Finland)	Malmö, Sweden	Jan. 30, 1996
200 meters	1:54.65	Jani Sievinen (Finland)	Kuopio, Finland	Jan. 19, 1996
400 meters	4:06.03	Jani Sievinen (Finland)	Lappeenranta, Finland	Feb. 9, 1992
4 × 50 meters	1:38.01	Germany	Stavanger, Norway	Dec. 3, 1994
4 × 100 meters	3:32.57	U.S.	Palma de Mallorca, Spain	Dec. 2, 1993

WOMEN

Freestyle

50 meters	0:24.23	Le Jingyi (China)	Palma de Mallorca, Spain	Dec. 3, 1993
100 meters	0:53.01	Le Jingyi (China)	Palma de Mallorca, Spain	Dec. 2, 1993
200 meters	1:55.84	Franziska van Almsick (Germany)	Beijing, China	Jan. 9, 1993
400 meters	4:02.05	Astrid Strauss (East Germany)	Bonn, Germany	Feb. 8, 1987
800 meters	8:15.34	Astrid Strauss (East Germany)	Bonn, Germany	Feb. 6, 1987
1,500 meters	15:43.31	Petra Schneider (East Germany)	Gainesville, FL	Jan. 10, 1982
4 × 50 meters	1:40.63	Germany	Espoo, Finland	Nov. 22, 1992
4 × 100 meters	3:35.97	China	Palma de Mallorca, Spain	Dec. 4, 1993
4 × 200 meters	7:52.45	China	Palma de Mallorca, Spain	Dec. 2, 1993

Backstroke

50 meters	0:27.64	Bai Xiuyu (China)	Desenzano, Italy	Mar. 12, 1994
100 meters	0:58.50	Angel Martino (U.S.)	Palma de Mallorca, Spain	Dec. 3, 1993
200 meters	2:06.09	He Cihong (China)	Palma de Mallorca, Spain	Dec. 5, 1993

Breaststroke

50 meters	0:31.19	Louise Karlsson (Sweden)	Espoo, Finland	Nov. 21, 1992
100 meters	1:06.58	Dai Guohong (China)	Palma de Mallorca, Spain	Dec. 4, 1993
200 meters	2:21.99	Dai Guohong (China)	Palma de Mallorca, Spain	Dec. 3, 1993

Butterfly

50 meters	0:26.56	Angela Kennedy (Australia)	Sheffield, England	Feb. 12, 1995
100 meters**	0:58.77	Angela Kennedy (Australia)	Gelsenkirchen, Germany	Feb. 18, 1995
200 meters	2:05.65	Mary Meagher (U.S.)	Gainesville, FL	Jan. 2, 1981

Medley

100 meters	1:01.03	Louise Karlsson (Sweden)	Espoo, Finland	Nov. 22, 1992
200 meters	2:07.79	Allison Wagner (U.S.)	Palma de Mallorca, Spain	Dec. 5, 1993
400 meters	4:29.00	Dai Guohong (China)	Palma de Mallorca, Spain	Dec. 2, 1993
4 × 50 meters	1:52.44	Germany	Espoo, Finland	Nov. 21, 1992
4 × 100 meters	3:57.73	China	Palma de Mallorca, Spain	Dec. 5, 1993

* Hand timed for first leg.
**Slower than long-course bests.

SWIMMING RECORDS (set in 50-meter pools)

Event	Time	Name and Country	Place	Date
MEN				
Freestyle				
50 meters	0:21.81	Tom Jager (U.S.)	Nashville, TN	Mar. 24, 1990
100 meters	0:48.21	Aleksandr Popov (Russia)	Monte Carlo, Monaco	Jun. 18, 1994
200 meters	1:46.69	Giorgis Lamberti (Italy)	Bonn, Germany	Aug. 15, 1989
400 meters	3:43.80	Kieren Perkins (Australia)	Rome, Italy	Sep. 9, 1994
800 meters	7:46.00	Kieren Perkins (Australia)	Victoria, Canada	Aug. 24, 1994
1,500 meters	14:41.66	Kieren Perkins (Australia)	Victoria, Canada	Aug. 24, 1994
4 × 100 meter relay	3:16.53	United States (David Fox, Joe Hudjpohi, Jon Olsen, Gary Hall)	Atlanta, GA	Aug. 12, 1995
4 × 200 meter relay	7:11.95	EUN (Dmitriy Lepikov, Vladimir Pychenko, Venyamin Tayanovich, Yevgeniy Sadoviy)	Barcelona, Spain	Jul. 27, 1992
Breaststroke				
100 meters	1:00.95	Karoly Guttler (Hungary)	Sheffield, England	Aug. 3, 1993
200 meters	2:10.16	Michael Barrowman (U.S.)	Barcelona, Spain	Jul. 29, 1992
Butterfly				
100 meters	0:52.32	Denis Pankratov (Russia)	Vienna, Austria	Mar. 23, 1995
200 meters	1:55.22	Denis Pankratov (Russia)	Canet-en-Roussillon, France	Jun. 14, 1995
Backstroke				
100 meters	0:53.86	Jeff Rouse (U.S.—relay leg)	Barcelona, Spain	Jul. 31, 1992
200 meters	1:56.57	Martin Lopez-Zubero (Spain)	Tuscaloosa, AL	Nov. 23, 1991
Medley				
200 meters	1:58.16	Jani Nikanor Sievenen (Finland)	Rome, Italy	Sep. 11, 1994
400 meters	4:12.30	Tom Dolan (U.S.)	Rome, Italy	Sep. 6, 1994
4 × 100 meter relay	3:36.93	United States (David Berkoff, Richard Schroeder, Matt Biondi, Christopher Jacobs)	Seoul, South Korea	Sep. 25, 1988
	3:36.93	United States (Jeff Rouse, Nelson Diebel, Pablo Morales, Jon Olsen)	Barcelona Spain	Jul. 13, 1992

WOMEN

Freestyle

50 meters	0:24.51	Le Jingyi (China)	Rome, Italy	Sep. 11, 1994
100 meters	0:54.01	Le Jingyi (China)	Rome, Italy	Sep. 5, 1994
200 meters	1:56.78	Franziska van Almsick (Germany)	Rome, Italy	Sep. 6, 1994
400 meters	4:03.85	Janet B. Evans (U.S.)	Seoul, South Korea	Sep. 22, 1988
800 meters	8:16.22	Janet B. Evans (U.S.)	Tokyo, Japan	Aug. 20, 1989
1,500 meters	15:52.10	Janet B. Evans (U.S.)	Orlando, FL	Mar. 26, 1988
4 × 100 meter relay	3:37.91	China (Le Jingyi, Shan Ying, Le Ying, Lu Bin)	Rome, Italy	Sep. 7, 1994
4 × 200 meter relay	7:55.47	East Germany (Manuela Stellmach, Astrid Strauss, Anke Möhring, Heike Friedrich)	Strasbourg, France	Aug. 18, 1987

Breaststroke

100 meters	1:07.46	Samantha Riley (Australia)	Durban, South Africa	Mar. 4, 1996
200 meters	2:24.76	Rebecca Brown (Australia)	Brisbane, Australia	Mar. 16, 1994

Butterfly

100 meters	0:57.93	Mary Terstegge Meagher (U.S.)	Milwaukee, WI	Aug. 16, 1981
200 meters	2:05.96	Mary Terstegge Meagher (U.S.)	Milwaukee, WI	Aug. 13, 1981

Backstroke

100 meters	1:00.16	He Cihong (China)	Rome, Italy	Sep. 11, 1994
200 meters	2:06.62	Krisztina Egerszegi (Hungary)	Athens, Greece	Aug. 25, 1991

Medley

200 meters	2:11.65	Li Lin (China)	Barcelona, Spain	Jul. 30, 1992
400 meters	4:36.10	Petra Schneider (East Germany)	Guayaquil, Ecuador	Aug. 1, 1982
4 × 100 meter relay	4:01.67	China (He Cihong, Dai Guohong, Liu Limin, Le Jingyi)	Rome, Italy	Sep. 11, 1994

U.S. NATIONAL SWIMMING RECORDS (set in 50-meter pools)

Event	Time	Name	Place	Date
MEN				
Freestyle				
50 meters	0:21.81	Tom Jager	Nashville, TN	Mar. 24, 1990
100 meters	0:48.42	Matt Biondi	Austin, TX	Aug. 10, 1988
200 meters	1:47.72	Matt Biondi	Austin, TX	Aug. 8, 1988
400 meters	3:48.06	Matt Cetlinski	Austin, TX	Aug. 11, 1988
800 meters	7:52.45	Sean Killion	Clovis, CA	Jul. 27, 1987
1,500 meters	15:01.51	George DiCarlo	Indianapolis, IN	Jun. 30, 1984
4 × 100 meter relay	3:15.11	United States (David Fox, Joe Hudipohi, Jon Olsen, Gary Hall)	Atlanta, GA	Aug. 12, 1995
4 × 200 meter relay	7:12.51	United States (Troy Dalbey, Matthew Cetinski, Douglas Gjertsen, Matt Biondi)	Seoul, South Korea	Sep. 21, 1988
Breaststroke				
100 meters	1:01.40	Nelson Diebel	Indianapolis, IN	Mar. 1, 1992
		Seth Van Neerdan	Indianapolis, IN	Aug. 14, 1994
200 meters	2:10.16	Michael Barrowman	Barcelona, Spain	Jul. 29, 1992
Butterfly				
100 meters	0:52.84	Pablo Morales	Orlando, FL	Jun. 23, 1986
200 meters	1:55.69	Melvin Stewart	Perth, Australia	Jan. 12, 1991
Backstroke				
100 meters	0:53.86	Jeff Rouse	Barcelona, Spain	Jul. 31, 1992
200 meters	1:58.33	Tripp Schwank	Pasadena, CA	Aug. 1, 1995
Medley				
200 meters	2:00.11	David Wharton	Tokyo, Japan	Aug. 20, 1989
400 meters	4:12.30	Tom Dolan	Rome, Italy	Sep. 6, 1994
4 × 100 meter relay	3:36.93	United States (David Berkoff, Richard Schroeder, Matt Biondi, Christopher Jacobs)	Seoul, South Korea	Sep. 25, 1988

WOMEN

Freestyle

50 meters	0:25.08	Amy Van Dyken	Atlanta, GA	Aug. 13, 1995
100 meters	0:54.48	Jenny Thompson	Indianapolis, IN	Mar. 1, 1992
200 meters	1:57.90	Nicole Haislett	Barcelona, Spain	Jul. 27, 1992
400 meters	4:03.85	Janet B. Evans	Seoul, South Korea	Sep. 22, 1988
800 meters	8:16.22	Janet B. Evans	Tokyo, Japan	Aug. 20, 1989
1,500 meters	15:52.10	Janet B. Evans	Orlando, FL	Mar. 26, 1988
4 × 100 meter relay	3:39.46	United States (Nicole Haislett, Dara Torres, Angel Martino, Jenny Thompson)	Barcelona, Spain	Jul. 28, 1992
4 × 200 meter relay	8:02.12	United States (Betsy Mitchell, Mary Terstege Meagher, Kim Brown, Mary Alice Wayte)	Madrid, Spain	Aug. 22, 1986

Breaststroke

100 meters	1:08.17	Anita Nall	Barcelona, Spain	Jul. 29, 1992
200 meters	2:25.35	Anita Nall	Indianapolis, IN	Mar. 2, 1992

Butterfly

100 meters	0:57.93	Mary T. Meagher	Brown Deer, WI	Aug. 16, 1981
200 meters	2:05.96	Mary T. Meagher	Brown Deer, WI	Aug. 13, 1981

Backstroke

100 meters	1:00.82	Lea Loveless	Barcelona, Spain	Jul. 30, 1992
200 meters	2:08.60	Betsy Mitchell	Orlando, FL	Jun. 27, 1986

Medley

200 meters	2:11.91	Summer Sanders	Barcelona, Spain	Jul. 28, 1992
400 meters	4:37.58	Summer Sanders	Barcelona, Spain	Jul. 26, 1992
4 × 100 meter relay	4:02.54	United States (Lea Loveless, Anita Nall, Crissy Ahmann-Leighton, Jenny Thompson)	Barcelona, Spain	Jul. 30, 1992

gold medals in 1984 and 1988. Three gold medals in one event have also been won by Philip Boggs (U.S.)—springboard, 1973, 1975 and 1978.

United States Championships *Most titles* Greg Louganis has won 47 national titles: 17 in 1 m springboard; 17 in 3 m springboard; 13 in platform. In women's competition, Cynthia Potter has won 28 titles.

Highest scores *Men* Greg Louganis achieved record scores at the 1984 Olympic Games in Los Angeles, CA, with 754.41 points for the 11-dive springboard event and 710.91 for the highboard.

In non-Olympic competitions, Mark Lenzi set the record for the springboard, with 764.52 points at the 1996 U.S. Olympic team trials in Atlanta, GA. The record for the highboard is 723.45 points, awarded to Dmitry Sautin at the 1996 Southern Cross Invitational.

Women In 1988, Gao Min (China) won 614.07 points in a 10-dive springboard event at Dive Canada, in Québec, Canada. Since 1995, the women's highboard event has required nine dives instead of eight. Chi Bin (China) holds the women's highboard record for her nine dives at the 1995 China Open, which earned 549.81 points.

High diving The highest regularly performed head-first dives are those of professional divers from La Quebrada in Acapulco, Mexico, a height of 87½ feet. The base rocks necessitate a leap of 27 feet out. The water is 12 feet deep.

The highest dive from a diving board is 176 ft. 10 in., by Olivier Favre (Switzerland) in Villers-le-Lac, France on August 30, 1987. The women's record is 120 ft. 9 in., by Lucy Wardle (U.S.) in Ocean Park, Hong Kong on April 6, 1985.

CHANNEL SWIMMING

As of May 1996, there had been 6,381 attempts to swim the English Channel, by 4,387 people. Of these, 485 individuals (324 men and 161 women) from 42 countries have made 761 successful crossings: 708 solo, 22 double and 3 triple.

Fastest crossing The official Channel Swimming Association (founded 1927) record is 7 hr. 17 min., by Chad Hundeby (U.S.), from Shakespeare Beach, Dover, to Cap Gris-Nez, France, on September 27, 1994.

The official women's record is 7 hr. 40 min., by Penny Dean (U.S.) from Shakespeare Beach, Dover to Cap Gris-Nez, France, on July 29, 1978.

The fastest France–England time is 8 hr. 5 min., by Richard Davey (Great Britain) in 1988.

The fastest crossing by a relay team is 6 hr. 52 min. (England to France), by the U.S. National Swim Team on August 1, 1990. They went on to complete the fastest two-way relay in 14 hr. 18 min.

Fastest double crossing Philip Rush (New Zealand) completed the fastest double crossing in 16 hr. 10 min. on August 17, 1987. He also completed the fastest triple crossing in 28 hr. 21 min., August 17–18, 1987.

The women's record is 17 hr. 14 min., by Susie Maroney (Australia) on July 23, 1991.

Most Channel conquests   The greatest number of Channel conquests is 32, by Alison Streeter (Great Britain), from 1982 to September 1995 (including a record seven in one year in 1992). The most by a man is 31, by Michael Read (Great Britain), between August 24, 1969–August 19, 1984.

Oldest Channel swimmer   Bertram Clifford Batt (Australia) was 67 yr. 241 days old when he swam from Cap Gris-Nez, France to Dover, England in 18 hr. 37 min. on August 19–20, 1987.

Susan Fraenkel (South Africa) was 46 yr. 93 days old when she swam the Channel in 12 hr. 5 min. on July 24, 1994.

LONG-DISTANCE SWIMMING

Longest swims   The greatest recorded distance ever swum is 1,826 miles down the Mississippi River between Ford Dam near Minneapolis, MN and Carrollton Ave., New Orleans, LA, by Fred P. Newton of Clinton, OK from July 6 to December 29, 1930. He was in the water for 742 hours.

Greatest 24-hour distance   Anders Forvass (Sweden) swam 63.3 miles at the 25-meter Linköping public swimming pool, Sweden, October 28–29, 1989.

In a 50-meter pool, Evan Barry (Australia) swam 60.08 miles, at the Valley Pool, Brisbane, Australia, December 19–20, 1987.

The women's record is 58.17 miles, by Susie Maroney (Australia) at Carss Park, Sydney, Australia, April 21–22, 1995.

Manhattan swim   The fastest swim around Manhattan Island in New York City was in 5 hr. 53 min. 57 sec., by Kris Rutford (U.S.) on August 29, 1992. Shelley Taylor set the women's record, 6 hr. 12 min. 29 sec., on October 15, 1985.

Kris Rutford also holds the record for swimming clockwise around Manhattan, at 17 hr. 48 min. 30 sec.

Long-distance relays   The New Zealand national relay team of 20 swimmers swam a record 113.59 miles in Lower Hutt, New Zealand in 24 hours, passing 100 miles in 20 hr. 47 min. 13 sec., December 9–10, 1983.

The 24-hour club record by a team of five is 100.99 miles, by the Portsmouth Northsea SC at the Victoria Swimming Centre, Portsmouth, England, March 4–5, 1993.

The women's record is 88.93 miles by the City of Newcastle ASC, December 16–17, 1986.

The most participants in a one-day swim relay is 2,375, each swimming a length, at Liverpool High School, Liverpool, New York, NY, May 20–21, 1994.

Underwater swimming   Paul Cryne (Great Britain) and Samir Sawan al Awami (Qatar) swam 49.04 miles in 24 hours from Doha, Qatar to Umm Said and back, February 21–22, 1985, using sub-aqua equipment. They were underwater 95.5 percent of the time.

A relay team of six swam 94.44 miles in a swimming pool in Olomouc, Czechoslovakia, October 17–18, 1987.

TABLE TENNIS

Most titles World (instituted 1926) G. Viktor Barna (b. Gyözö Braun; Hungary) won a record five singles, 1930, 1932–35, and eight men's doubles, 1929–35, 1939, in the World Championships (first held in 1926). Angelica Rozeanu (Romania) won a record six women's singles, 1950–55, and Maria Mednyanszky (Hungary) won seven women's doubles, 1928, 1930–35. With two more at mixed doubles and seven team, Barna won 22 world titles in all, while Mednyanszky won 18.

The most men's team titles (Swaythling Cup) is 12, by Hungary, 1927–31, 1933–35, 1938, 1949, 1952 and 1979.

The women's record (Marcel Corbillon Cup) is 11, by China, 1965, 1975–89 (biennially), 1993 and 1995.

United States The U.S. won the Swaythling Cup in 1937 and the Corbillon Cup in 1937 and 1949. Ruth Aarons was the women's world champion in 1936 and 1937, sharing the title in the latter year.

James McClure won three men's doubles titles, with Robert Blattner, 1936–37, and with Sol Schiff, 1938.

U.S. Championships U.S. national championships were first held in 1931. Leah Neuberger (née Thall) won a record 21 titles between 1941 and 1961: nine women's singles, 12 women's doubles. Richard Miles won a record 10 men's singles titles between 1945 and 1962.

The longest span for winning a national championship is 61 years, by Keith Gledhill. He won the U.S. National Boys' Doubles Championship (with Sidney Wood) in 1926. In 1987, he won the U.S. National 75 and Over Doubles Championship (with Elbert Lewis).

Counter hitting The record number of hits in 60 seconds is 173, by Jackie Bellinger and Lisa Lomas, at the Northgate Sports Centre, Ipswich, England, on February 7, 1993.

With a paddle in each hand, S. Ramesh Babu (India) completed 5,000 consecutive volleys over the net in 41 min. 27 sec. in Swargate, India on April 14, 1995.

TAEKWONDO

Most titles Chung Kook-hyun (South Korea) won four world titles as a light-middleweight in 1982 and 1983 and as a welterweight in 1985 and 1987. Lynette Love (U.S.) also took four world titles, all as a heavyweight, in 1985, 1987–88 and 1991.

Most consecutive U.S. titles Lynette Love (heavyweight) and Dae Sung Lee (finweight) held national titles from 1979 to 1987.

TEAM HANDBALL

Most championships Olympic The USSR won five titles—(men) 1976, 1988 and 1992 (by the Unified Team from the republics of the former USSR), (women) 1976 and 1980. South Korea has also won two women's titles, in 1988 and 1992.

World Championships (instituted 1938) For indoor handball (now the predominant version of the game), the most men's titles won is four, by Ro-

South Korea has won two Olympic women's handball titles.

mania, 1961, 1964, 1970 and 1974; and by Sweden, 1954, 1958 and 1990. However, Germany/West Germany won the outdoor title five times, 1938–66, and has won the indoor title twice, 1938 and 1978. Three women's titles have been won by three teams: Romania, 1956, 1960 (both outdoor) and 1962 (indoor); the GDR, 1971, 1975 and 1978 (all indoor); and the USSR, 1982, 1986 and 1990 (all indoor).

Highest score   The highest score in an international match was recorded when the USSR beat Afghanistan 86–2 in the "Friendly Army Tournament" in Miskolc, Hungary in August 1981.

TENNIS

Longest match   The longest match in a grand slam tournament is 5 hr. 26 min. between Stefan Edberg (Sweden) and Michael Chang (U.S.) for the semifinal of the U.S. Championships, September 12, 1992. Edberg won 6–7, 7–5, 7–6, 5–7, 6–4.

Fastest service   The fastest service timed with modern equipment is 138 MPH, by Steve Denton (U.S.) in Beaver Creek, CO on July 29, 1984. The women's best is 121.8 MPH. by Brenda Shultz-McCarthy, at the 1996 Australian Open.

Grand slam   The grand slam for a tennis player is winning the Australian Open, French Open, Wimbledon and U.S. Open in the same calendar year. Rod Laver (Australia) achieved the grand slam twice, as an amateur in 1962 and again in 1969, when the titles were open to professionals.

Four women have achieved the grand slam: Maureen Connolly (U.S.) in 1953; Margaret Court (Australia) in 1970; Martina Navratilova in 1983–84; and Steffi Graf (Germany) in 1988.

The most singles championships won in grand slam tournaments is 24, by Margaret Court (11 Australian, 5 U.S., 5 French, 3 Wimbledon), 1960–73. She also won the U.S. Amateur in 1969 and 1970 when this was held, as well as the U.S. Open. The men's record is 12, by Roy Stanley Emerson (Australia), 6 Australian, 2 each French, U.S., Wimbledon, 1961–67.

Pam Shriver (U.S.) with Martina Navratilova won a record eight successive grand slam tournament women's doubles titles, and 109 successive matches in all events, from April 1983 to July 1985.

The most grand slam tournament wins by a doubles partnership is 20, by Althea Louise Brough (U.S.) and Margaret Evelyn du Pont (née Osborne; U.S.)—12 U.S., 5 Wimbledon, 3 French, 1942–57; and by Martina Navratilova and Pam Shriver—7 Australian, 5 Wimbledon, 4 French, 4 U.S., 1981–89.

United States   The most singles wins in grand slam tournaments by a U.S. player is 19, by Helen Moody—8 Wimbledon, 7 U.S. and 4 French.

Martina Navratilova (formerly of Czechoslovakia) has won 56 grand slam titles—18 singles, a record 31 women's doubles and 7 mixed doubles.

Billie Jean King has the most of U.S.-born players, with 39 titles—12 singles, 16 women's doubles and 11 mixed doubles.

"Golden set" The only known example of a "golden set" (winning a set 6–0 without dropping a single point, i.e., winning 24 consecutive points) in professional tennis was achieved by Bill Scanlon (U.S.) against Marcos Hocevar (Brazil) in the first round of the WCT Gold Coast Classic in Del Ray, FL on February 22, 1983. Scanlon won the match, 6–2, 6–0.

WIMBLEDON CHAMPIONSHIPS

Most wins Women Billie Jean King won 20 titles between 1961 and 1979—6 singles, 10 women's doubles and 4 mixed doubles. Elizabeth Montague Ryan (U.S.) won 19 doubles (12 women's, seven mixed) titles from 1914 to 1934.

Men The most titles by a man was 13, by Hugh Doherty (Great Britain) with 5 singles titles (1902–06) and a record 8 men's doubles (1897–1901, 1903–05).

United States The most titles won by a U.S. man is eight, by John McEnroe—singles 1981, 1983 and 1984; men's doubles 1979, 1981, 1983–84 (all with Peter Fleming), and 1992 (with Michael Stich).

Singles Martina Navratilova won a record nine titles, 1978–79, 1982–87 and 1990. The most men's singles wins since the Challenge Round was abolished in 1922 is five consecutively, by Björn Borg (Sweden) in 1976–80. William Charles Renshaw (Great Britain) won seven singles, in 1881–86 and 1889.

Youngest champions The youngest champion was Lottie Dod (Great Britain), who was 15 yr. 285 days when she won in 1887. The youngest male champion was Boris Becker (West Germany), who won the men's singles title in 1985 at 17 yr. 227 days.

U.S. OPEN

Most wins Margaret Evelyn du Pont won a record 25 titles between 1941 and 1960. She won 13 women's doubles, 9 mixed doubles and 3 singles. The men's record is 16, by Bill Tilden, including seven men's singles, 1920–25, 1929—a record for singles shared with: Richard Dudley Sears, 1881–87; William A. Larned, 1901–02, 1907–11; and in women's singles by Molla Mallory (née Bjurstedt), 1915–16, 1918, 1920–22, 1926; and Helen Wills Moody, 1923–25, 1927–29, 1931.

Youngest champions The youngest champion was Vincent Richards, who was 15 yr. 139 days when he won the men's doubles with Bill Tilden in 1918. The youngest singles champion was Tracy Ann Austin, who was 16 yr. 271 days when she won the women's singles in 1979.

Steffi Graf

On August 17, 1987, Steffi Graf ascended above Martina Navratilova to the top of the WTA rankings for the first time. Graf held the top spot for a record 186 consecutive weeks until March 10, 1991. During the next five years, Graf, Monica Seles and Arantxa Sánchez Vicario traded the number one spot several times. Graf regained the top spot outright on

June 12, 1995, a status she currently shares with Seles. On May 13, 1996, Graf topped Navratilova's career mark of 331 weeks as the world's number one player. By July 15, 1996 she had extended her record to 341 weeks and counting.

"The most important thing for me is knowing I've achieved something no one else in tennis history has done. The record has never been the main goal," says Graf. The Wimbledon champion does not set her sights on records: "I'm not playing to continue to be number one but because I love the game." Graf and Seles have shared the number one ranking since August 15, 1995. Seles, stabbed during a tennis match in Hamburg, Germany, had taken a sabbatical to recover. The WTA established the joint ranking upon Seles' return. "It was a condition to help her get back on tour. It was the right decision," says Graf.

In 1988, Graf won the Olympic gold medal, creating the Golden Slam: winning the four Grand Slam events (Australian Open, French Open, Wimbledon and U.S. Open), and the Olympic title in the same year. She is the only player to achieve this feat. "I realize now what an achievement it was, but at the time there was a lot of pressure. People kept asking, 'Can she make it? Can she make it?' I was under so much stress that it was difficult to enjoy," recalls Graf.

Graf's 1996 Wimbledon victory was her 20th Grand Slam singles title, four shy of Margaret Court's all-time mark. "My main focus is to win the Grand Slam tournaments," says Graf. Winning, however, is not everything for the German legend. "My main goal has always been to play the best tennis I can. I never set any goals in terms of Grand Slam victories or being number one, but to be the best on the court—that has always given me the most pleasure."

This year's Wimbledon win was also Graf's 100th tournament victory. In recent years, many of those titles have come while playing through injuries or illness, but Graf doesn't consider herself "tough." "I'm more surprised than anyone else. I've been in these situations quite a few times. I tell myself I have nothing to lose. If I don't succeed, I've tried everything I could." Graf adds, "I love to play and when I get on the court I block out the injuries."

Injury did force Graf to withdraw from the 1996 Olympics, but she's not ready to hang up her tennis shoes. "I haven't put a time on my career. I'll play for as long as I am motivated and enjoy it. When the time comes to retire, hopefully I'll realize it," she says. And are there any other tennis records she'd like to break? "If I can dream, it would be the Wimbledon record," she admits.

FRENCH OPEN

Most wins (from international status 1925)   Margaret Court won a record 13 titles—5 singles, 4 women's doubles and 4 mixed doubles, 1962–73. The men's record is 9, by Henri Cochet (France)—4 singles, 3 men's doubles and 2 mixed doubles, 1926–30. The singles record is seven, by Chris Evert (U.S.), 1974–75, 1979–80, 1983, 1985–86. Björn Borg won six men's singles, 1974–75, 1978–81.

Youngest champions   The youngest doubles champions were the 1981 mixed doubles winners Andrea Jaeger, at 15 yr. 339 days, and Jimmy Arias, at 16 yr. 296 days. The youngest singles winners were Monica Seles (Yugoslavia), who won the 1990 women's title at 16 yr. 169 days in 1990, and Michael Chang (U.S.), who won the men's title at 17 yr. 109 days in 1989.

AUSTRALIAN OPEN

Most wins   Margaret Court won the women's singles 11 times (1960–66, 1969–71 and 1973) as well as eight women's doubles and two mixed doubles, for a record total of 21 titles. Six men's singles were won by Roy Emerson, 1961 and 1963–67. Thelma Long (née Coyne) won a record 12 women's doubles and four mixed doubles for a record total of 16 doubles titles. Adrian Quist won 10 consecutive men's doubles from 1936 to 1950 and three men's singles.

Youngest champions   The youngest champions were Rodney W. Heath, age 17 when he won the men's singles in 1905, and Monica Seles (Yugoslavia), who won the women's singles at 17 yr. 55 days in 1991.

OLYMPIC GAMES

Most medals   Four gold medals, as well as a silver and a bronze, were won by Max Decugis (France), 1900–20. A women's record five medals (one gold, two silver, two bronze) were won by Kitty McKane (Great Britain) in 1920 and 1924.

INTERNATIONAL TEAM

Davis Cup (instituted 1900)   The most wins in the Davis Cup is 30, by the U.S. between 1900 and 1995. The most appearances for Cup winners is eight, by Roy Emerson (Australia), 1959–62, 1964–67. Bill Tilden (U.S.) played in a record 28 matches in the final, winning a record 21—17 out of 22 singles and four out of six doubles.

Nicola Pietrangeli (Italy) played a record 163 rubbers (66 ties), 1954 to 1972, winning 120. He played 109 singles (winning 78) and 54 doubles (winning 42).

John McEnroe has played for the U.S. on 31 occasions, 1978–92. He also has the most wins—60 matches in Davis Cup competition (41 singles and 19 doubles).

Federation Cup (instituted 1963 and known as the Fed Cup from 1995)   The most wins in the Federation Cup is 14, by the U.S., 1963–90. Virginia Wade (Great Britain) played each year, 1967–83, in a record 57 ties, playing 100 rubbers, including 56 singles (winning 36) and 44 doubles (winning

30). Chris Evert won her first 29 singles matches, 1977–86. Her overall record, 1977–89, is 40 wins in 42 singles and 16 wins in 18 doubles matches.

Highest earnings Pete Sampras (U.S.) won a men's season's record of $5,415,066 in 1995. Arantxa Sánchez Vicario (Spain) won a women's record of $2,943,665 in 1994. As of July 1996, the career records are $22,680,850 by Pete Sampras, and $20,344,061 by Martina Navratilova.

The greatest first-place prize money ever won is $2 million, by Pete Sampras when he won the Grand Slam Cup in Munich, Germany on December 16, 1990. The highest total prize money was $10,893,890 for the U.S. Open Championships in 1996.

Number one ranking The greatest number of weeks any player has held the number one ranking is 341, by Steffi Graf (Germany). The longest streak at number one is 186 weeks, by Graf, August 17, 1987 to March 10, 1991.

Longest game The longest singles game was one of 37 deuces (80 points) between Anthony Fawcett (Rhodesia) and Keith Glass (Great Britain) in the first round of the Surrey Championships in Surbiton, England on May 26, 1975. It lasted 31 minutes. Noëlle van Lottum and Sandra Begijn played a 52-minute game in the semifinals of the 1984 Dutch Indoor Championships.

The longest tiebreak was 26–24 for the first round men's doubles at the Wimbledon Championships on July 1, 1985. Jan Gunnarsson (Sweden) and Michael Mortensen (Denmark) defeated John Frawley (Australia) and Victor Pecci (Paraguay) 6–3, 6–4, 3–6, 7–6.

The 1995 U.S. Davis Cup team celebrates a 3–2 victory over Russia.

TRACK AND FIELD

Fastest speed   An analysis of split times in each 10 meters in the 1988 Olympic Games 100 m final in Seoul, South Korea on September 24, 1988, won by Ben Johnson (Canada) in 9.79 seconds (average speed 22.85 MPH), with Carl Lewis (U.S.) finishing in 9.92 seconds, showed that both men reached a peak speed of 0.83 seconds for 10 m, i.e., 26.95 MPH. Johnson's record was disallowed as a result of his positive drug test for steroids. In the women's final, Florence Griffith Joyner was timed at 0.91 seconds for each 10 m from 60 m to 90 m, i.e., 24.58 MPH.

Most track records in a day   Jesse Owens (U.S.) set six world records in 45 minutes in Ann Arbor, MI on May 25, 1935, with a 9.4-second 100 yards, a 26 ft. 8¼ in. long jump, a 20.3-second 220 yards (and 200 m), and a 22.6-second 220 yards (and 200 m) low hurdles.

Highest jump   The greatest height cleared above an athlete's own head is 23¼ inches, by Franklin Jacobs (U.S.), 5 ft. 8 in. tall, who jumped 7 ft. 7¼ in. in New York City, on January 27, 1978. The women's record is 12¾ inches, by Yolanda Henry (U.S.), 5 ft. 6 in. tall, who jumped 6 ft. 6¾ in. in Seville, Spain on May 30, 1990.

Highest standing jump   The best high jump from a standing position is 6 ft. 2¾ in., by Rune Almen (Sweden) in Karlstad, Sweden on May 3, 1980. The women's best is 4 ft. 11¾ in., by Grete Bjørdalsbakka (Norway) in Flisa, Norway in 1984.

Longest standing jump   The best long jump from a standing position is 12 ft. 2 in., by Arne Tvervaag (Norway) in 1968. The women's record is 9 ft. 7 in., by Annelin Mannes (Norway) in Flisa, Norway on March 7, 1981.

Most Olympic titles   The most Olympic gold medals won is 10 (an absolute Olympic record), by Raymond Ewry (U.S.) in the standing high, long and triple jumps in 1900, 1904, 1906 and 1908.

Women   The most gold medals won by a woman is four, shared by Fanny E. Blankers-Koen (Netherlands), with 100 m, 200 m, 80 m hurdles and 4 × 100 m relay, 1948; Betty Cuthbert (Australia), with 100 m, 200 m, 4 × 100 m relay, 1956 and 400 m, 1964; Bärbel Wöckel (née Eckert; East Germany), with 200 m and 4 × 100 m relay in 1976 and 1980; and Evelyn Ashford (U.S.), 100 m and 4 × 100 m relay in 1984, 4 × 100 m relay in 1988 and 1992.

Most wins at one Games   The most gold medals at one celebration is five, by Paavo Nurmi (Finland) in 1924: 1,500 m, 5,000 m, 10,000 m cross-country, 3,000 m team and cross-country team. The most in individual events is four, by Alvin Kraenzlein (U.S.) in 1900: 60 m, 110 m hurdles, 200 m hurdles and long jump.

Most Olympic medals   The most medals won is 12 (nine gold and three silver), by Paavo Nurmi (Finland) in the Games of 1920, 1924 and 1928. The most medals won by a woman athlete is seven, by Shirley Barbara de la Hunty (née Strickland; Australia) with 3 gold, 1 silver and 3 bronze in the 1948, 1952 and 1956 Games. Irena Szewinska (née Kirszenstein; Poland) won 3 gold, 2 silver and 2 bronze in 1964, 1968, 1972 and 1976, and is the only woman athlete to win a medal in four successive Games.

United States   The most Olympic medals won is 10, by Ray Ewry (see MOST OLYMPIC TITLES). The most by a woman is five, by Florence Griffith Joyner: silver in 200 m in 1984, gold in 100 m, 200 m and 4 × 100 m relay, silver in 4 × 400 m relay in 1988, and by Evelyn Ashford: gold in 100 m and 4 × 100 m relay in 1984, gold in 4 × 100 m relay and silver in 100 m in 1988, and gold in 4 × 100 m relay in 1992.

Four gold medals at one Game were won by Alvin Kraenzlein (see above). Jesse Owens in 1936 and Carl Lewis in 1984 both won four gold medals at one Games, both in 100 m, 200 m, long jump and the 4 × 100 m relay.

Olympic champions Oldest and youngest   The oldest athlete to win an Olympic title was Irish-born Babe McDonald (b. McDonnell; U.S.), who was age 42 yr. 26 days when he won the 56 lb. weight throw in Antwerp, Belgium on August 21, 1920. The oldest female champion was Lia Manoliu (Romania), age 36 yr. 176 days when she won the discus in Mexico City on October 18, 1968. The youngest gold medalist was Barbara Pearl Jones (U.S.), who at 15 yr. 123 days was a member of the winning 4 × 100 m relay team, in Helsinki, Finland on July 27, 1952. The youngest male champion was Bob Mathias (U.S.), age 17 yr. 263 days when he won the decathlon at the London Games, August 5–6, 1948.

The oldest Olympic medalist was Tebbs Lloyd Johnson (Great Britain), age 48 yr. 115 days when he was third in the 1948 50,000 m walk. The oldest woman medalist was Dana Zátopková (Czechoslovakia), age 37 yr. 348 days when she was second in the javelin in 1960.

Sonia O'Sullivan (Ireland).

TRACK AND FIELD RECORDS—Men

World records for the men's events scheduled by the International Amateur Athletic Federation.
Fully automatic electric timing is mandatory for events up to 400 meters.

Running	Time	Name & Country	Place	Date
100 meters	0:9.85*	Leroy Burrell (U.S.)	Lausanne, Switzerland	Jul. 6, 1994
200 meters	0:19.66	Michael Johnson (U.S.)	Atlanta, GA	Jun. 23, 1996
400 meters	0:43.29	Butch Reynolds, Jr. (U.S.)	Zürich, Switzerland	Aug. 17, 1988
800 meters	1:41.73	Sebastian Coe (Great Britain)	Florence, Italy	Jun. 10, 1981
1,000 meters	2:12.18	Sebastian Coe	Oslo, Norway	Jul. 11, 1981
1,500 meters	3:27.37	Noureddine Morceli (Algeria)	Nice, France	Jul. 12, 1995
1 mile	3:44.39	Noureddine Morceli	Rieti, Italy	Sep. 5, 1993
2,000 meters	4:47.88	Noureddine Morceli	Paris, France	Jul. 3, 1995
3,000 meters	7:25.11	Noureddine Morceli	Monte Carlo, Monaco	Aug. 2, 1994
5,000 meters	12:55.30	Moses Kiptanui (Kenya)	Rome, Italy	Jun. 8, 1995
10,000 meters	26:43.53	Haile Gebrselassie (Ethiopia)	Hengelo, Netherlands	Jun. 5, 1995
20,000 meters	56:55.6	Arturo Barrios (Mexico)	La Flèche, France	Mar. 30, 1991
25,000 meters	1 hr. 13:55.8	Toshihiko Seko (Japan)	Christchurch, New Zealand	Mar. 22, 1981
30,000 meters	1 hr. 29:18.8	Toshihiko Seko	Christchurch, New Zealand	Mar. 22, 1981
1 hour	13.111 miles	Arturo Barrios (Mexico)	La Flèche, France	May 30, 1991

Ben Johnson (Canada) ran 100 m in 9.79 seconds in Seoul, South Korea on Sep. 24, 1988, but was subsequently disqualified when he tested positive for steroids. He later admitted to having taken drugs over many years, and this also invalidated his 9.83 sec. in Rome, Italy on Aug. 30, 1987.

Hurdling				
110 meters (3' 6")	0:12.91	Colin Jackson (Great Britain)	Stuttgart, Germany	Aug. 20, 1993
400 meters (3' 0")	0:46.78	Kevin Young (U.S.)	Barcelona, Spain	Aug. 6, 1992
3,000 meter steeplechase	7:59.18	Moses Kiptanui (Kenya)	Zürich, Switzerland	Aug. 16, 1995

Relays

4 × 100 meters	0:37.40	United States	Barcelona, Spain	Aug. 8, 1992
		(Mike Marsh, Leroy Burrell, Dennis Mitchell, Carl Lewis)		
	0:37.40	United States	Stuttgart, Germany	Aug. 21, 1993
		(John A. Drummond Jr., Andre Cason, Dennis A. Mitchell, Leroy Burrell)		
4 × 200 meters	1:18.68	Santa Monica Track Club	Walnut, CA	Apr. 17, 1994
		(Mike Marsh, Leroy Burrell, Floyd Heard, Carl Lewis)		
4 × 400 meters	2:54.29	United States	Stuttgart, Germany	Aug. 21, 1993
		(Andrew Valmon, Quincy Watts, Butch Reynolds, Michael Johnson)		
4 × 800 meters	7:03.89	Great Britain	London, England	Aug. 30, 1982
		(Peter Elliott, Garry Peter Cook, Steven Cram, Sebastian Coe)		
4 × 1,500 meters	14:38.8	Germany	Cologne, Germany	Aug. 17, 1977
		(Thomas Wessinghage, Harald Hudak, Michael Lederer, Karl Fleschen)		

Field Events

	m	ft.	in.			
High jump	2.45	8	0½	Javier Sotomayor (Cuba)	Salamanca, Spain	Jul. 27, 1993
Pole vault	6.14*	20	1¾	Sergey Bubka (Ukraine)	Sestriere, Italy	Jul. 31, 1994
Long jump	8.96	29	4¾	Iván Pedroso (Cuba)	Sestriere, Italy	Jul. 29, 1995
Triple jump	18.29	60	¼	Jonathan Edwards (Great Britain)	Gothenburg, Sweden	Aug. 7, 1995
Shot 16 lb.	23.12	75	10¼	Randy Barnes (U.S.)	Los Angeles, CA	May 20, 1990
Discus 4 lb. 8 oz.	74.08	243	.0	Jürgen Schult (East Germany)	Neubrandenburg, Germany	Jun. 6, 1986
Hammer 16 lb.	86.74	284	.7	Yuriy Sedykh (USSR)	Stuttgart, Germany	Aug. 30, 1986
Javelin	98.48	323	.1	Jan Zelezny (Czech Republic)	Jena, Germany	May 25, 1996
Decathlon	8,891 points			Dan O'Brien (U.S.)	Talence, France	Sep. 4–5, 1992

*This record was set at high altitude. Best mark at low altitude: 20 ft. 1¼ in. by Sergey Bubka, Tokyo, Japan, Sep. 19, 1992.

Sergey Bubka (Ukraine).

Michael Johnson holds the U.S. and world records for 200 meters.

TRACK AND FIELD RECORDS—*Women*

World records for the women's events scheduled by the International Amateur Athletic Federation.

Running	Time	Name & Country	Place	Date
100 meters	0:10.49	Florence Griffith Joyner (U.S.)	Indianapolis, IN	Jul. 16, 1988
200 meters	0:21.34	Florence Griffith Joyner (U.S.)	Seoul, South Korea	Sep. 29, 1988
400 meters	0:47.60	Marita Koch (East Germany)	Canberra, Australia	Oct. 6, 1985
800 meters	1:53.28	Jarmila Kratochvílová (Czechoslovakia)	Munich, Germany	Jul. 26, 1983
1,000 meters	2:29.34	Maria Mutola (Mozambique)	Brussels, Belgium	Aug. 25, 1995
1,500 meters	3:50.46	Qu Yunxia (China)	Beijing, China	Sep. 11, 1993
1 mile	4:15.61	Paula Ivan (Romania)	Nice, France	Jul. 10, 1989
2,000 meters	5:25.36	Sonia O'Sullivan (Ireland)	Edinburgh, Scotland	Jul. 8, 1994
3,000 meters	8:06.11	Wang Junxia (China)	Beijing, China	Sep. 13, 1993
5,000 meters	14:36.45	Fernanda Ribeiro (Portugal)	Hechtel, Belgium	Jul. 22, 1995
10,000 meters	29:31.78	Wang Junxia (China)	Beijing, China	Sep. 8, 1993

Hurdling				
100 meters (2' 9")	0:12.21	Yordanka Donkova (Bulgaria)	Stara Zagora, Bulgaria	Aug. 20, 1988
400 meters (2' 6")	0:52.61	Kim Batten (U.S.)	Gothenburg, Sweden	Aug. 11, 1995

Relays

4 × 100 meters	0:41.37	East Germany	Canberra, Australia	Oct. 6, 1985
		(Silke Gladisch [now Möller], Sabine Rieger [now Günther], Ingrid Auerswald, Marlies Göhr)		
4 × 200 meters	1:28.15	East Germany	Jena, Germany	Aug. 9, 1980
		(Marlies Göhr, Romy Müller, Bärbel Wöckel, Marita Koch)		
4 × 400 meters	3:15.17	USSR	Seoul, South Korea	Oct. 1, 1988
		(Tatyana Ledovskaya, Olga Nazarova, Maria Pinigina, Olga Bryzgina)		
4 × 800 meters	7:50.17	USSR	Moscow, USSR	Aug. 5, 1984
		(Nadezhda Olizarenko, Lyubov Gurina, Lyudmila Borisova, Irina Podyalovskaya)		

Field Events

	m	ft.	in.			
High jump	2.09	6	10¼	Stefka Kostadinova (Bulgaria)	Rome, Italy	Aug. 30, 1987
Pole vault	4.42	14	6	Emma George (Australia)	Reims, France	Jul. 1, 1996
Long jump	7.52	24	8¼	Galina Chistyakova (USSR)	Leningrad, USSR	Jun. 11, 1988
Triple jump	15.50	50	8	Inessa Kravets (Ukraine)	Gothenburg, Sweden	Aug. 10, 1995
Shot 8 lb. 13 oz.	22.63	74	3	Natalya Lisovskaya (USSR)	Moscow, USSR	Jun. 7, 1987
Discus 2 lb. 3 oz.	76.80	25	20	Gabriele Reinsch (East Germany)	Neubrandenburg, Germany	Jul. 9, 1988
Javelin 24 lb. 7 oz.	80.00	26	25	Petra Felke (East Germany)	Potsdam, Germany	Sep. 9, 1988
Heptathlon	7,291 points			Jacqueline Joyner-Kersee (U.S.)	Seoul, South Korea	Sep. 23–24, 1988

TRACK AND FIELD RECORDS

U.S. National Records—*Women*

Running

	Time	Name	Place	Date
100 meters	0:10.49	Florence Griffith Joyner	Indianapolis, IN	Jul. 16, 1988
200 meters	0:21.34	Florence Griffith Joyner	Seoul, South Korea	Sep. 29, 1988
400 meters	0:48.83	Valerie Ann Brisco	Los Angeles, CA	Aug. 6, 1984
800 meters	1:56.90	Mary Slaney (née Decker)	Berne, Switzerland	Aug. 16, 1985
1,000 meters	2:34.04	Julie Jenkins	Berlin, Germany	Aug. 17, 1990
1,500 meters	3:57.12	Mary Slaney	Stockholm, Sweden	Jul. 26, 1983
1 mile	4:16.71	Mary Slaney	Zürich, Switzerland	Aug. 21, 1985
2,000 meters	5:32.7	Mary Slaney	Eugene, OR	Aug. 3, 1984
3,000 meters	8:25.83	Mary Slaney	Rome, Italy	Sep. 7, 1985
5,000 meters	14:56.04	Amy Rudolph	Stockholm, Sweden	Jul. 8, 1996
10,000 meters	31:19.89	Lynn Jennings	Barcelona, Spain	Aug. 7, 1992
Marathon	2 hr. 21:21	Joan Samuelson (née Benoit)	Chicago, IL	Oct. 20, 1985

Hurdling

	Time	Name	Place	Date
100 meters	0:12.46	Gail Devers	Stuttgart, Germany	Aug. 20, 1993
400 meters	0:52.61	Kim Batten	Gothenburg, Sweden	Aug. 11, 1995

Relays

4 × 100 meters	0:41.49	National Team .....Stuttgart, Germany ....Aug. 22, 1993
		(Michelle Finn, Gwen Torrance, Wendy Vereen, Gail Devers)
4 × 200 meters	1:32.55	Louisiana State University .....Philadelphia, PA ....Apr. 30, 1994
		(D'Andre Hill, Karen Boone, Eureka Hall, Cheryl Taplin)
4 × 400 meters	3:15.51	National Team .....Seoul, South Korea ....Oct. 1, 1988
		(Denean Howard, Diane Lynn Dixon, Valerie Brisco, Florence Griffith Joyner)
4 × 800 meters	8:17.09	Athletics West .....Walnut, CA ....Apr. 24, 1983
		(Susan Addison, Lee Arbogast, Mary Decker, Chris Mullen)

Field Events

	ft.	in.			
High jump	6	8	Louise Ritter	Austin, TX	Jul. 8, 1988
Pole vault	13	1¾	Louise Ritter	Seoul, South Korea	Sep. 30, 1988
Long jump	24	7	Melissa Price	Walnut, CA	Jun. 24, 1995
Triple jump	47	3½	Jacqueline Joyner-Kersee	New York, NY	May 22, 1994
Shot	66	2½	Sheila Hudson	Stockholm, Sweden	Jul. 8, 1996
Discus	216		Ramona Pagel (née Ebert)	San Diego, CA	Jun. 25, 1988
Javelin	227		Carol Cady	San Jose, CA	May 31, 1986
Heptathlon	7,291 points		Kate Schmidt	Fürth, Germany	Sep. 11, 1977
			Jacqueline Joyner-Kersee	Seoul, South Korea	Sep. 23–24, 1988

TRACK AND FIELD RECORDS

U.S. National Records—*Men*

Running	Time	Name	Place	Date
100 meters	0:09.85	Leroy Burrell	Lausanne, Switzerland	Jul. 6, 1994
200 meters	0:19.66	Michael Johnson	Atlanta, GA	Jun. 23, 1996
400 meters	0:43.29	Harry "Butch" Reynolds, Jr.	Zürich, Switzerland	Aug. 17, 1988
800 meters	1:42.60	Johnny Gray	Koblenz, Germany	Aug. 28, 1985
1,000 meters	2:13.9	Rick Wohlhuter	Oslo, Norway	Jul. 30, 1974
1,500 meters	3:29.77	Sydney Maree	Cologne, Germany	Aug. 25, 1985
1 mile	3:47.69	Steve Scott	Oslo, Norway	Jul. 7, 1982
2,000 meters	4:52.44	Jim Spivey	Lausanne, Switzerland	Sep. 15, 1987
3,000 meters	7:33.37	Sydney Maree*	London, England	Jul. 17, 1982
	7:35.33	Bob Kennedy	Nice, France	Jul. 18, 1994
5,000 meters	12:58.75	Bob Kennedy	Stockholm, Sweden	Jul. 8, 1996
10,000 meters	27:20.56	Marcus Nenow	Brussels, Belgium	Sep. 5, 1986
15,000 meters	43:39.8	Bill Rodgers	Boston, MA	Aug. 9, 1977
20,000 meters	58:25.0	Bill Rodgers	Boston, MA	Aug. 9, 1977
25,000 meters	1 hr 14:11.8	Bill Rodgers	Saratoga, NY	Feb. 21, 1979
30,000 meters	1 hr 31:49	Bill Rodgers	Saratoga, NY	Feb. 21, 1979
1 hour	12 mi. 1,350 yd.	Bill Rodgers	Boston, MA	Aug. 9, 1977
Marathon	2 hr. 08:47	Robert Kempainen**	Boston, MA	Apr. 18, 1994

* *Prior to obtaining U.S. citizenship.*

** *Course overall downhill, and with following wind. Official U.S. record: 2 hr 10:04, by Pat Peterson, London, Apr. 23, 1989.*

Hurdling				
110 meters	0:12.92	Roger Kingdom	Zürich, Switzerland	Aug. 16, 1989
	0:12.92	Allen Johnson	Atlanta, GA	Jun. 23, 1996

400 meters	0:46.78	Kevin Young	Barcelona, Spain	Aug. 6, 1992
3,000 meter steeplechase	8:09.17	Henry Marsh	Koblenz, Germany	Aug. 28, 1985

Relays

4 × 100 meters	0:37.40	National Team	Barcelona, Spain	Aug. 8, 1992
		(Michael Marsh, Leroy Burrell, Dennis Mitchell, Carl Lewis)		
	0:37.40	National Team	Stuttgart, Germany	Aug. 21, 1993
		(Jon Drummond, Andre Cason, Dennis Mitchell, Leroy Burrell)		
4 × 200 meters	1:18.68	Santa Monica Track Club	Walnut, CA	Apr. 17, 1994
		(Michael Marsh, Leroy Burrell, Floyd Heard, Carl Lewis)		
4 × 400 meters	2:54.29	National Team	Stuttgart, Germany	Aug. 21, 1993
		(Andrew Valmon, Quincy Watts, Butch Reynolds, Michael Johnson)		
4 × 800 meters	7:06.5	Santa Monica Track Club	Walnut, CA	Apr. 26, 1986
		(James Robinson, David Mack, Earl Jones, Johnny Gray)		
4 × 1,000 meters	14:46.3	National Team	Bourges, France	Jun. 24, 1969

Field Events

	ft.	in.			
High jump	7	10½	Charles Austin	Zürich, Switzerland	Aug. 7, 1991
Pole vault	19	7	Scott Huffman	Knoxville, TN	Jun. 18, 1994
Long jump	29	4½	Mike Powell	Tokyo, Japan	Aug. 30, 1991
Triple jump	58	11½	Willie Banks	Indianapolis, IN	Jun. 16, 1985
Shot	75	10¼	Randy Barnes	Westwood, LA	May 20, 1990
Discus*	237	4	Ben Plunknett	Stockholm, Sweden	Jul. 7, 1981
Hammer	270	8	Lance Deal	Knoxville, TN	Jun. 17, 1994
Javelin	282	3	Tom Pukstys	Paris, France	Jun. 28, 1996
Decathlon	8,891 points		Dan O'Brien	Talence, France	Sep. 4–5, 1992

Ratified despite the fact that it was achieved after a positive drug test.

TRACK AND FIELD RECORDS—*Indoor*

Track performances around a turn must be made on a track of circumference no longer than 200 meters.

Event	Time	Name & Country	Place	Date
MEN				
Running				
50 meters	0:5.56*	Donovan Bailey (Canada)	Reno, NV	Feb. 9, 1996
60 meters	0:6.41	Andre Cason (U.S.)	Madrid, Spain	Feb. 14, 1992
200 meters	0:19.92	Frank Fredericks (Namibia)	Liévin, France	Feb. 18, 1996
400 meters	0:44.63	Michael Johnson (U.S.)	Atlanta, GA	Mar. 4, 1995
800 meters	1:44.84	Paul Ereng (Kenya)	Budapest, Hungary	Mar. 4, 1989
1,000 meters	2:15.26	Noureddine Morceli (Algeria)	Birmingham, England	Feb. 22, 1992
1,500 meters	3:34.16	Noureddine Morceli (Algeria)	Seville, Spain	Feb. 28, 1991
1 mile	3:49.78	Eamonn Coghlan (Ireland)	East Rutherford, NJ	Feb. 27, 1983
3,000 meters	7:35.15	Moses Kiptanui (Kenya)	Ghent, Belgium	Feb. 12, 1995
5,000 meters	7:30.72	Haile Gebrselassie (Ethiopia)	Stuttgart, Germany	Feb. 4, 1996
50 meter hurdles	0:6.25	Mark McKoy (Canada)	Kobe, Japan	Mar. 5, 1986
60 meter hurdles	0:7.30	Colin Jackson (Great Britain)	Sindelfingen, Germany	Mar. 6, 1994

* Set at high altitude; best at low altitude: 5.61 sec. by Manfred Kokot (GDR) in Berlin, Germany on Feb. 4, 1973 and James Sanford (U.S.) in San Diego, CA on Feb. 20, 1981.

Event	Time	Name & Country	Place	Date
Relays				
4 × 200 meters	1:22.11	United Kingdom	Glasgow, Scotland	Mar. 3, 1991
		(Linford Christie, Darren Braithwaite, Ade Mafe, John Regis)		
4 × 400 meter	3:03.05	Germany	Seville, Spain	Mar. 10, 1991
		(Rico Lieder, Jens Carlowitz, Karsten Just, Thomas Schönlebe)		

Walking

5,000 meters	18:07.08		Mikhail Schennikov (Russia)	Moscow, Russia	Feb. 14, 1995

Field Events

	m	ft.	in.			
High jump	2.43	7	11½	Javier Sotomayor (Cuba)	Budapest, Hungary	Mar. 4, 1989
Pole vault	6.15	20	2¼	Sergey Nazarovich Bubka (Ukraine)	Donetsk, Ukraine	Feb. 21, 1993
Long jump	8.79	28	10¼	Carl Lewis (U.S.)	New York, NY	Jan. 27, 1984
Triple jump	17.77	58	3½	Leonid Voloshin (Russia)	Grenoble France	Feb. 6, 1994
Shot	22.66	74	4¼	Randy Barnes (U.S.)	Los Angeles, CA	Jan. 20, 1989
Heptathlon	6,476 points			Dan O'Brien (U.S.)	Toronto, Canada	Mar. 13–14, 1993

WOMEN

Running

50 meters	0:5.96	Irina Privalova (Russia)	Madrid, Spain	Feb. 9, 1995
60 meters	0:6.92	Irina Privalova	Madrid, Spain	Feb. 11, 1993
60 meters	0:6.92	Irina Privalova	Madrid, Spain	Feb. 9, 1995
200 meters	0:21.87	Merlene Ottey (Jamaica)	Liévin, France	Feb. 13, 1994
400 meters	0:49.59	Jarmila Kratochvílová (Czechoslovakia)	Milan, Italy	Mar. 7, 1982
800 meters	1:56.40	Christine Wachtel (East Germany)	Vienna, Austria	Feb. 13, 1988
1,000 meters	2:31.23	Maria Mutola (Mozambique)	Stockholm, Sweden	Feb. 25, 1996
1,500 meters	4:00.27	Doina Melinte (Romania)	East Rutherford, NJ	Feb. 9, 1990
1 mile	4:17.14	Doina Melinte	East Rutherford, NJ	Feb. 9, 1990
3,000 meters	8:33.82	Elly van Hulst (Netherlands)	Budapest, Hungary	Mar. 4, 1989
5,000 meters	15:03.17	Elizabeth McColgan (Great Britain)	Birmingham, England	Feb. 22, 1992
50 meter hurdles	0:6.58	Cornelia Oschkenat (East Germany)	Berlin, Germany	Feb. 20, 1988
60 meter hurdles	0:7.69*	Lyudmila Narozhilenko (USSR)	Chelyabinsk, Russia	Feb. 4, 1993

*Narozhilenko recorded a time of 7.63 in Seville, Spain on November 4, 1993, but was disqualified on a positive drugs test.

Relays

4 × 200 meters	1:32.55	S. C. Eintracht Hamm (West Germany)	Dortmund, Germany	Feb. 19, 1988
		(Helga Arendt, Silke-Beate Knoll, Mechthild Kluth, Gisela Kinzel)		
4 × 400 meters	3:27.22	Germany	Seville, Spain	Mar. 10, 1992
		(Sandra Seuser, Katrin Schreiter, Annet Hesselbarth, Grit Breuer)		

Walking

3,000 meters	11:44.00	Alina Ivanova (Ukraine)	Moscow, Russia	Feb. 7, 1992

Field Events

	m	ft.	in.			
High jump	2.07	6	9½	Heike Henkel (Germany)	Karlsruhe, Germany	Feb. 9, 1992
Pole vault	4.28	14	0¼	Sun Caiyun (China)	Tianjin, China	Feb. 27, 1996
Long jump	7.37	24	2¼	Heike Drechsler (East Germany)	Vienna, Austria	Feb. 13, 1988
Triple jump	15.03	49	3½	Yolanda Chen (Russia)	Barcelona, Spain	Mar. 11, 1995
Shot	22.50	73	10	Helena Fibingerová (Czechoslovakia)	Jablonec, Czechoslovakia	Feb. 19, 1977
Pentathlon	4,991 points			Irina Belova (Russia)	Berlin, Germany	Feb.14–15, 1992

Frank Fredericks (Namibia).

ULTRA LONG DISTANCE RECORDS

Event	Time	Name and Country	Place	Date
MEN				
Track				
50 km	2:48:06	Jeff Norman (Great Britain)	Manchester, England	Jun. 7, 1980
50 miles	4:51:49	Don Ritchie (Great Britain)	London, England	Mar. 12, 1983
100 km	6:10:20	Don Ritchie	London, England	Oct. 28, 1978
100 miles	11:30:51	Don Ritchie	London, England	Oct. 15, 1977
200 km	15:11:10*	Yiannis Kouros (Greece)	Montauban, France	Mar. 15–16, 1985
200 miles	27:48:35	Yiannis Kouros	Montauban, France	Mar. 15–16, 1985
500 km	60:23:00	Yiannis Kouros	Colac, Australia	Nov. 26–29, 1984
500 miles	105:42:09	Yiannis Kouros	Colac, Australia	Nov. 26–30, 1984
1,000 km	136:17:00	Yiannis Kouros	Colac, Australia	Nov. 26–Dec. 1, 1984
Kilometers				
24 hours	293.704	Yiannis Kouros (Greece; now Australia)	Coburg, Australia	Apr. 13–14, 1996
48 hours	473.496	Yiannis Kouros (Greece; now Australia)	Surgères, France	May 3–5, 1996
6 days	1,022.068	Yiannis Kouros (Greece)	New York City	Jul. 2–8, 1984
Road	**Time**			
50 km	2:43:38	Thompson Magawana (South Africa)	Claremont–Kirstenbosch, South Africa	Apr. 12, 1988
50 miles	4:50:21	Bruce Fordyce (South Africa)	London–Brighton, England	Sep. 25, 1983
1,000 miles	10 days 10:30:35**	Yiannis Kouros (Greece)	New York City	May 21–30, 1988
Kilometers				
24 hours	286.463	Yiannis Kouros (Greece)	New York City	Sep. 28–29, 1985
6 days	1,028.370	Yiannis Kouros	New York City	May 21–26, 1988

WOMEN

Track

	Time			
50 km	3:18:52	Carolyn Hunter-Rowe	Barry, Wales	Mar. 3, 1996
50 miles	6:07:58	Linda Meadows (Australia)	Burwood, Australia	Jun. 18, 1994
100 km	7:50:09	Ann Trason (U.S.)	Hayward, CA	Aug. 3-4, 1991
100 miles	14:29:44	Ann Trason (U.S.)	Santa Rosa, CA	Mar. 18-19, 1989
200 km	19:28:48 ‡	Eleanor Adams (Great Britain)	Melbourne, Australia	Aug. 19-20, 1989
200 miles	39:09:03	Hilary Walker (Great Britain)	Blackpool, England	Nov. 5-6, 1988
500 km	77:53:46	Eleanor Adams (Great Britain)	Colac, Australia	Nov. 13-15, 1989
500 miles	130:59:58	Sandra Barwick (New Zealand)	Campbelltown, Australia	Nov. 18-23, 1990

Kilometers

1 hour	18.084	Silvana Cruciata (Italy)	Rome, Italy	May 4, 1981
24 hours	240.169	Eleanor Adams (Great Britain)	Melbourne, Australia	Aug. 19-20, 1989
48 hours	366.512	Hilary Walker (Great Britain)	Blackpool, England	Nov. 5-7, 1988
6 days	883.631	Sandra Barwick (New Zealand)	Campbelltown, Australia	Nov. 18-24, 1990

Road

	Time			
30 km	1:38:27	Ingrid Kristiansen (Norway)	London, England	May 10, 1987
50 km	3:08:39	Frith van der Merwe (South Africa)	Claremont-Kirstenbosch, South Africa	Mar. 25, 1989
50 miles	5:40:18	Ann Trason (U.S.)	Houston, TX	Feb. 23, 1991
100 km	7:09:44	Ann Trason	Amiens, France	Sep. 27, 1993
100 miles	13:47:41	Ann Trason	Queens, NY	May 4, 1991
200 km	19:08:21	Sigrid Lomsky (Germany)	Basel, Switzerland	May 1-2, 1993
(indoors)	19:00:31	Eleanor Adams (Great Britain)	Milton Keynes, England	Feb. 3-4, 1990
1,000 km	7 days 1:11:00	Sandra Barwick (New Zealand)	Queens, NY	Sep. 16-23, 1991
1,000 miles	12 days 14:38:40	Sandra Barwick	Queens, NY	Sep. 16-29, 1991

* Where superior to track bests and run on properly measured road courses. Road times must be assessed with care as course conditions can vary considerably. ** Only one stopped time. ‡ No stopped time known.

World Championships Quadrennial World Championships were inaugurated in 1983, when they were held in Helsinki, Finland. In 1991, the event became a biennial championship. The most medals won is 13, by Merlene Ottey (Jamaica)—three gold, four silver and six bronze, 1983–95. The most medals won by a man is 10, by Carl Lewis (U.S.)—a record eight gold, one silver and one bronze, 1983–93. The most gold medals won by a woman is four, by Jackie Joyner-Kersee (U.S.)—long jump 1987, 1991; heptathlon 1987, 1993.

Carl Lewis has won a record 10 World Championship medals.

Indoor The most individual titles is four, shared by Stefka Kostadinova (Bulgaria), high jump 1985, 1987, 1989, 1993; by Mikhail Shchennikov (Russia), 5,000 m walk 1987, 1989, 1991, 1993; and by Sergey Bubka (Ukraine), pole vault 1985, 1987, 1991, 1995.

Oldest record breaker For the greatest age at which anyone has set a world record under IAAF jurisdiction, see GENERAL RECORDS. The women's record, is held by Marina Styepanova (USSR), with 52.94 seconds for the 400 m hurdles in Tashkent, USSR on September 17, 1986.

Youngest record breaker The youngest individual record-breaker is Wang Yan (China), who set a women's 5,000 m walk record at age 14 yr. 334 days with 21 min. 33.8 sec. in Jian, China on March 9, 1986. The youngest male is Thomas Ray (Great Britain) at 17 yr. 198 days when he pole-vaulted 11 ft. 2³/₄ in. on September 19, 1879 (prior to IAAF ratification).

U.S. Championships The most American national titles won in all events, indoors and out, is 65, by Ronald Owen Laird in various walks events between 1958 and 1976. Excluding the walks, the record is 41, by Stella Walsh (née Walasiewicz), who won women's events between 1930 and 1954—33 outdoors and 8 indoors.

The most wins outdoors in one event in AAU/TAC history is 11, by James Sarsfield Mitchel in 56 lb weight in 1888, 1891–97, 1900, 1903, 1905; Stella Walsh, in 220 yd/200 m 1930–31, 1939–40, 1942–48, and in long jump

1930, 1939–46, 1948 and 1951; Maren Seidler in shot 1967–68, 1972–80; and Dorothy Dodson in javelin 1939–49.

Longest winning sequence Iolanda Balas (Romania) won 150 consecutive competitions in high jump, 1956–67. The record in a track event is 122, in 400 m hurdles, by Edwin Moses (U.S.) between his loss to Harald Schmid (West Germany) in Berlin, Germany on August 26, 1977 and his loss to Danny Lee Harris (U.S.) in Madrid, Spain on June 4, 1987.

Longest running races The longest race staged annually is the New York 1,300 Mile race, held in Ward Island Park, NY. The fastest time to complete the race is 16 days 14 hr. 28 min. 19 sec. by Georg Jermolajevs (Latvia), September 11–28, 1995.

Longest runs The longest run by an individual is one of 11,134 miles around the United States, by Sarah Covington-Fulcher (U.S.), starting and finishing in Los Angeles, CA, from July 21, 1987 to October 2, 1988.

Al Howie (Great Britain) ran across Canada, from St. Johns, Newfoundland to Victoria, British Columbia, a distance of 4,533.2 miles, in 72 days 10 hr. 23 min., from June 21 to September 1, 1991.

Robert J. Sweetgall (U.S.) ran 10,608 miles around the perimeter of the United States, starting and finishing in Washington, D.C., from October 9, 1982 to July 15, 1983.

Max Telford (New Zealand) ran 5,110 miles from Anchorage, AK to Halifax, Nova Scotia, in 106 days 18 hr. 45 min. from July 25, to November 9, 1977.

The fastest time for the cross-America run is 46 days 8 hr. 36 min., by Frank Giannino, Jr. (U.S.) for the 3,100 miles from San Francisco to New York, September 1 to October 17, 1980. The women's record is 69 days 2 hr. 40 min., by Mavis Hutchinson (South Africa), March 12 to May 21, 1978.

Mass relays The record for 100 miles by 100 runners from one club is 7 hr. 53 min. 52.1 sec., by the Baltimore Road Runners Club, Towson, MD on May 17, 1981. The women's record is 10 hr. 15 min. 29.5 sec. on July 29, 1995, by the Dolphin South End Runners, Los Altos Hills, CA.

The record for 100 × 100 m is 19 min. 14.19 sec., by a team from Antwerp in Merksem, Belgium on September 23, 1989.

The greatest distance covered in 24 hours by a team of 10 is 302.281 miles, by Puma Tyneside RC at Monkton Stadium, Jarrow, England, September 10–11, 1994.

Joggling 3 objects Owen Morse (U.S.), 100 m in 11.68 seconds, 1989, and 400 m in 57.32 seconds, 1990. Kirk Swenson (U.S.), one mile in 4 min. 43 sec., 1986, and 5,000 m (3.1 miles) in 16 min. 55 sec., 1986. Ashrita Furman (U.S.), marathon—26 mi. 385 yd.—in 3 hr. 22 min. 32.5 sec., 1988, and 50 miles in 8 hr. 52 min. 7 sec., 1989. Michael Hout (U.S.), 110 m hurdles in 18.9 seconds, 1993. Albert Lucas (U.S.), 400 m hurdles in 1 min. 7 sec., 1993. Owen Morse, Albert Lucas, Tuey Wilson and John Wee (all U.S.), one mile relay in 3 min. 57.38 sec., 1990.

5 objects Owen Morse (U.S.), 100 m in 13.8 seconds, 1988. Bill Gillen (U.S.), 1 mile in 7 min. 41.01 sec., 1989, and 3.1 miles in 28 min. 11 sec., 1989.

MARATHON

Fastest marathon There are no official records for the marathon, and courses may vary in severity. The following are the best times recorded on courses whose distances have been verified.

Men 2 hr. 6 min. 50 sec.; Belayneh Dinsamo (Ethiopia), Rotterdam, Netherlands, April 17, 1988.

Women 2 hr. 21 min. 6 sec.; Ingrid Kristiansen (Norway), London, England, April 21, 1985.

Boston Marathon First run by 15 men on April 19, 1897 over a distance of 24 mi. 1,232 yd., the Boston Marathon is the world's oldest annual marathon. The full marathon distance was first run in 1927.

The most wins is seven, by Clarence DeMar, in 1911, 1922–24, 1927–28 and 1930. Rosa Mota (Portugal) has a record three wins, 1987–88 and 1990, in the women's competition.

The course record for men is 2 hr. 7 min. 15 sec. by Cosmas Ndeti (Kenya) in 1994. The women's record is 2 hr. 21 min. 45 sec., by Uta Pippig (Germany) in 1994.

John A. Kelley (U.S.) finished the Boston Marathon 62 times through 1993, winning twice, in 1933 and 1945.

Uta Pippig is the fastest woman finisher in the Boston Marathon.

New York City Marathon In the 1994 New York City Marathon, there were a record 29,735 finishers.

Grete Waitz (née Andersen; Norway) was the women's winner nine times, in 1978–80, 1982–86 and 1988. Bill Rodgers (U.S.) had a record four wins, 1976–79.

The course record is 2 hr. 8 min. 1 sec., by Juma Ikangaa (Tanzania), set in 1989.

Lisa Ondieki (Australia) set the course record for women, 2 hr. 24 min. 40 sec., in 1992.

Highest altitude The highest start for a marathon is the biennially held Everest Marathon, first run on November 27, 1987. It begins at Gorak Shep at 17,100 feet and ends at Namche Bazar, 11,300 feet. The fastest times to complete this race are *(men)* 3 hr. 59 min. 4 sec., by Jack Maitland in 1989; *(women)* 5 hr. 32 min. 43 sec., by Cath Proctor in 1993.

Most competitors The record number of confirmed finishers in a marathon is 38,706 in the centennial Boston race on April 15, 1996.

Most marathons run by an individual As at May 29, 1996, Horst Preisler (Germany) had run 631 races of 26 mi. 385 yd. or longer, starting in 1974. Henri Girault (France) has run 330 races of 100 km (an IAAF-recognized distance) from 1979 to June 1996 and has completed a run on every continent except Antarctica.

Three marathons in three days The fastest combined time 'for three marathons in three days is 8 hr. 22 min. 31 sec., by Raymond Hubbard (Belfast, Northern Ireland: 2 hr. 45 min. 55 sec.; London, England: 2 hr. 48 min. 45 sec.; and Boston: 2 hr. 47 min. 51 sec.), April 16–18, 1988.

Oldest marathon finishers Dimitrion Yordanidis (Greece) was aged 98 when he completed a marathon in Athens, Greece on October 10, 1976 in 7 hr. 33 min. The women's record was set by Thelma Pitt-Turner (New Zealand) in August 1985 when she completed the Hastings, New Zealand Marathon in 7 hr. 58 min. at age 82.

Pancake race Dominic M. Cuzzacrea (U.S.) of Lockport, NY ran the Buffalo, New York Nissan Marathon (26.2 miles) while flipping a pancake in a time of 3 hr. 6 min. 22 sec. on May 6, 1990.

Half marathon The world best time on a properly measured course is 58 min. 31 sec. by Paul Tergat (Kenya) in Milan, Italy on March 30, 1996.

Ingrid Kristiansen (Norway) ran 66 min. 40 sec. in Sandes, Norway on April 5, 1987, but the course measurement has not been confirmed. Liz McColgan ran 67 min. 11 sec. in Tokyo, Japan on January 26, 1992, but the course was 33 m downhill, a little more than the allowable 1 in 1,000 drop.

Baby carriage-pushing Tabby Puzey pushed a baby buggy while running the Abingdon half marathon in Abingdon, England, on April 13, 1986 in 2 hr. 4 min. 9 sec.

Backwards running Bud Badyna (U.S.) ran the fastest backwards marathon in 3 hr. 53 min. 17 sec. in Toledo, OH on April 24, 1994. He also ran 10 km in 45 min. 37 sec. in Toledo on July 13, 1991. Donald Davis (U.S.) ran one mile in 6 min. 7.1 sec. at the University of Hawaii on February 21, 1983. Ferdie Ato Adoboe (Ghana) ran 100 yards in 12.7 seconds at Smith College, Northampton, MA on July 25, 1991.

Arvind Pandya of India ran backwards across the U.S., Los Angeles to New York, in 107 days, August 18–December 3, 1984. He also ran back-

TRACK WALKING RECORDS

The International Amateur Athletic Federation recognizes men's records at 20 km,
30 km, 50 km and 2 hours, and women's at 5 km and 10 km.

Event	Time	Name and Country	Place	Date
MEN				
10 km	38:02.60	Jozef Pribilinec (Czechoslovakia)	Banská Bystrica, Czechoslovakia	Aug. 30, 1985
20 km	1:17:25.6	Bernardo Segura (Mexico)	Fana, Norway	May 7, 1994
30 km	2:01:44.1	Maurizio Damilano (Italy)	Cuneo, Italy	Oct. 4, 1992
50 km	3:41:28.2	René Piller (France)	Fana, Norway	May 7, 1994
1 hour	15,577 m	Bernardo Segura (Mexico)	Fana, Norway	May 7, 1994
2 hours	29,572 m	Maurizio Damilano (Italy)	Cuneo, Italy	Oct. 4, 1992
WOMEN				
3 km	11:48.24	Ileana Salvador (Italy)	Padua, Italy	Aug. 19, 1993
5 km	20:13.26	Kerry Saxby-Juna (Australia)	Hobart, Australia	Feb. 25, 1996
10 km	41:56.23	Nadezhda Ryashkina (USSR)	Seattle, WA	Jul. 24, 1990

wards from John O'Groat's to Land's End in 26 days 7 hr., April 6–May 2, 1990.

Greatest 1,000-hour distance   Ron Grant (Australia) ran 1.86 miles within an hour, every hour, for 1,000 consecutive hours in New Farm Park, Brisbane, Queensland, Australia from February 6 to March 20, 1991.

Roof of the world run   Ultra runner Hilary Walker ran from Lhasa, Tibet to Kathmandu, Nepal, a distance of 590 miles, in 14 days 9 hr. 36 min. from September 18 to October 2, 1991. The run was made at an average altitude of 13,780 feet.

WALKING

Most titles   Four-time Olympian Ronald Owen Laird of the New York Athletic Club won a total of 65 U.S. national titles from 1958 to 1976, plus four Canadian championships.

Andrey Perlov holds the 30 km and 50 km road walking marks.

ROAD WALKING

*The severity of the road race courses and the accuracy of their
measurement may vary, sometimes making comparisons
of times unreliable.*

MEN
30 km: 2 hr. 2 min. 41 sec., Andrey Perlov (USSR) at Sochi, USSR on
Feb. 19, 1989.

50 km: 3 hr. 37 min. 41 sec., Andrey Perlov (USSR) at Leningrad,
USSR on Aug. 5, 1989.

WOMEN
10 km: 41 min. 4 sec., Yelena Nikolayeva (Russia) in Sochi, Russia on
Apr. 20, 1996.

20 km: 1 hr. 27 min. 30 sec., Liu Hongyu (China) in Beijing, China on
May 1, 1995.

50 km: 4 hr. 50 min. 28 sec., Kora Sommerfield (Australia) at Neuilly-
sur-Marne, France on Sep. 13, 1993.

Most Olympic medals   Walking races have been included in the Olympics
since 1906. The only walker to win three gold medals has been Ugo Frige-
rio (Italy) with the 3,000 m in 1920, and 10,000 m in 1920 and 1924. He
also holds the record for most medals, with four (he won the bronze medal
in 50,000 m in 1932), a total shared with Vladimir Stepanovich Golub-
nichiy (USSR), who won gold medals for the 20,000 m in 1960 and 1968,
the silver in 1972 and the bronze in 1964.

Longest race   The race from Paris to Colmar (until 1980 from Strasbourg
to Paris) in France (instituted 1926 in the reverse direction), now about
325 miles, is the world's longest annual race walk.

  The fastest performance is by Robert Pietquin (Belgium), who walked
315 miles in the 1980 race in 60 hr. 1 min. 10 sec. (after deducting 4-hour
compulsory stops). This represents an average speed of 5.25 MPH. Roger
Quémener (France) has won a record seven times, 1979, 1983, 1985–89.

Greatest 24-hour distance   Jesse Castenada (U.S.) walked 142 mi. 440 yd.
in Albuquerque, NM, September 18–19, 1976. The best 24-hour distance
by a woman is 131.27 miles, by Annie van der Meer-Timmerman (Netherlands) in Rouen, France, May 10–11, 1986.

Backwards walking   The greatest-ever distance was 8,000 miles, by Plennie
L. Wingo, who walked backwards from Santa Monica, CA to Istanbul,
Turkey from April 15, 1931 to October 24, 1932. The longest distance
recorded for walking backwards in 24 hours is 95.40 miles, by Anthony
Thornton (U.S.) in Minneapolis, MN, December 31, 1988 to January 1,
1989.

Walking on hands   The distance record is 870 miles, by Johann Hurlinger of Austria, who averaged 1.58 MPH from Vienna, Austria to Paris, France in 1900. The 4-man relay team of David Lutterman, Brendan Price, Philip Savage and Danny Scannell covered one mile in 24 min. 48 sec. on March 15, 1987 in Knoxville, TN.

Shin Don-mok (South Korea) completed a 50-meter inverted sprint in 17.44 seconds in Saitama, Japan on November 14, 1986.

TRAMPOLINING

World Championships   World Championships were instituted in 1964 and have been held biennially since 1968. The most titles won is nine, by Judy Wills (U.S.)—a record 5 individual 1964–68, 2 pairs 1966–67 and 2 tumbling 1965–66. The men's record is 5, by Aleksandr Moskalenko (Russia), 3 individual 1990–94, and 2 pairs 1992–94. Brett Austine (Australia) won three individual titles in double mini, 1982–86.

United States Championships *Most titles*   Stuart Ransom has won a record 12 national titles: six individual (1975–76, 1978–80, 1982); three synchronized (1975, 1979–80); and three double mini-tramp (1979–80, 1982). Karl Heger has also won 12 titles: four individual (1991–94); two synchronized (1982, 1986); and six double mini-tramp (1986, 1991–94). Leigh Hennessy has won a record 10 women's titles: 1 individual (1978); eight synchronized (1972–73, 1976–78, 1980–82); and one double mini-tramp (1978).

Most somersaults   Christopher Gibson performed 3,025 consecutive somersaults in Shipley Park, Derbyshire, England on November 17, 1989.

The most complete somersaults in one minute is 75, by Richard Cobbing of Lightwater, England, in London, England on November 8, 1989. The most baranis in a minute is 78, by Zoe Finn of Chatham, England in London, England on January 25, 1988.

TRIATHLON

The triathlon combines long-distance swimming, cycling and running. Distances for each of the phases can vary, but for the best-established event—the Hawaii Ironman—competitors first swim 2.4 miles, cycle 112 miles, and run a full marathon of 26 mi. 385 yd.

Fastest triathlon   The fastest time recorded over the Ironman distances is 8 hr. 1 min. 32 sec., by Dave Scott (U.S.) at Lake Biwa, Japan on July 30, 1989. The fastest time record for a woman is 8 hr. 55 min., by Paula Newby-Fraser (Zimbabwe), in Roth, Germany on July 12, 1992.

Dave Scott has won the Hawaii Ironman six times.

World Championships *L'Union Internationale de Triathlon* (UIT) staged the first official World Championships in August 1989. The men's race has been won twice by Spencer Smith (Great Britain; 1993–94) and by Simon Lessing (Great Britain; 1992, 1995). The women's race has been won twice by Michelle Jones (Australia), 1992–93 and by Karen Smyers (U.S), 1990 and 1995.

A World Championship race has been held annually in Nice, France from 1982; the distances are 3,200 m, 120 km and 32 km respectively, with the swim increased to 4,000 m from 1988 on. Mark Allen (U.S.) has won 10 times, 1982–86, 1989–93. Paula Newby-Fraser has a record four women's wins, 1989–92. The fastest times are: (men) 5 hr. 46 min. 10 sec. in 1988, by Mark Allen; (women) 6 hr. 27 min. 6 sec. in 1988, by Erin Baker (New Zealand).

Hawaii Ironman   The most wins is seven, by Paula Newby-Fraser, in 1986, 1988–89, and 1991–94. The most wins in the men's race is six, by Dave Scott (U.S.) in 1980, 1982–84, 1986–87, and by Mark Allen in 1989–93 and 1995. Allen holds the record for fastest time, at 8 hr. 7 min. 45 sec. in 1993. Newby-Fraser holds the course record for women at 8 hr. 55 min. 28 sec. on October 10, 1992.

Oldest   The oldest triathlete to finish the Ironman Triathlon was 73-year-old Walt Stack in 1981. Stack completed the course in a time of 26 hr. 20 min., the longest elapsed time ever.

TUG OF WAR

Most titles   In the World Championships, England has won 16 titles in all categories, 1975–93. Sweden has won the 520 kg and the 560 kg three times at the Womens' World Championships (held biennially since 1986), 1986–94.

Longest pulls Duration   The longest recorded pull (prior to the introduction of AAA rules) is one of 2 hr. 41 min. when "H" Company beat "E" Company of the 2nd Battalion of the Sherwood Foresters (Derbyshire Regiment) in Jubbulpore, India on August 12, 1889.
   The longest recorded pull under AAA rules (in which lying on the ground or entrenching the feet is not permitted) is one of 24 min. 45 sec. for the first pull between the Republic of Ireland and England during the world championships (640 kg class) in Malmö, Sweden on September 18, 1988.
   The record time for "The Pull" (instituted 1898), across the Black River, between freshman and sophomore teams at Hope College, Holland, MI, is 3 hr. 51 min. on September 23, 1977, but the method of bracing the feet precludes this replacing the preceding records.

Greatest distance   The record distance for a tug of war contest is 3,962 yards, between Freedom Square and Independence Square, in Lodz, Poland on May 28, 1994.

VOLLEYBALL

Most Olympic titles   The sport was introduced to the Olympic Games for both men and women in 1964. The USSR won a record three men's (1964, 1968 and 1980) and four women's (1968, 1972, 1980 and 1988) titles.
   The only player to win four medals is Inna Valeryevna Ryskal (USSR), who won women's silver medals in 1964 and 1976 and golds in 1968 and 1972. The record for men is held by Yuriy Mikhailovich Poyarkov (USSR),

who won gold medals in 1964 and 1968 and a bronze in 1972; and by Katsutoshi Nekoda (Japan), who won gold in 1972, silver in 1968 and bronze in 1964.

United States The U.S. won the men's championship in 1984 and 1988. Three men played on each of the winning teams and on the only U.S. teams to win the World Cup (1985) and World Championships (1986): Craig Buck, Karch Kiraly, and Stephen Timmons. Karch Kiraly is the only player to win an Olympic gold medal and the beach volleyball World Championship.

Most world titles in volleyball World Championships were instituted in 1949 for men and in 1952 for women. The USSR won six men's titles (1949, 1952, 1960, 1962, 1978 and 1982) and five women's (1952, 1956, 1960, 1970 and 1990).

BEACH VOLLEYBALL

U.S. Championships *Most wins* Four players have won five titles: Sinjin Smith (U.S.), 1979 and 1981 (with K. Kiraly), 1982, 1988 and 1990 (with Randy Stoklos); Karch Kiraly (U.S.), 1979 and 1981 (with S. Smith), and 1992, 1993 and 1994 (with Kent Steffes); and Mike Dodd (U.S.) and Tim Hovland (U.S.), who teamed up to win the 1983, 1985–87, and 1989 titles.

AVP Tour *Most wins* Sinjin Smith (U.S.) has won a record 139 AVP tour events, 1977–95.

Highest earnings Karch Kiraly has the highest career earnings, reaching $2,075,759 at the end of the 1995 season.

Karch Kiraly holds the beach volleyball career earnings record.

WATER POLO

Most Olympic titles   Hungary has won the Olympic tournament six times, in 1932, 1936, 1952, 1956, 1964 and 1976.

Five players share the record of three gold medals: Britons George Wilkinson, in 1900, 1908, 1912; Paul Radmilovic, and Charles Sidney Smith, in 1908, 1912, 1920; and Hungarians Deszö Gyarmati and György Kárpáti, in 1952, 1956, and 1964. Paul Radmilovic also won a gold medal for 4 × 200 m freestyle swimming in 1908.

Italy is one of three teams to win the Water Polo World Championships twice.

United States U.S. teams took all the medals in 1904, but there were no foreign contestants. Since then, their best result has been silver in 1984 and 1988.

World Championships This competition was first held at the World Swimming Championships in 1973. The most wins is two, by the USSR, 1975 and 1982; Yugoslavia, 1986 and 1991; and Italy, 1978 and 1994. A women's competition was introduced in 1986, when it was won by Australia. The Netherlands won the title in 1991, and Hungary won in 1994.

Most goals The greatest number of goals scored by an individual in an international match is 13, by Debbie Handley for Australia (16) vs. Canada (10) at the World Championship in Guayaquil, Ecuador in 1982.

Most international appearances The greatest number of international appearances is 412, by Aleksey Stepanovich Barkalov (USSR), 1965–80.

U.S. National Championships In this competition, inaugurated in 1891, the New York Athletic Club has won a record 25 men's championships: 1892–96, 1903–04, 1906–08, 1922, 1929–31, 1933–35, 1937–39, 1954, 1956, 1960–61, 1971. The women's championship was first held in 1926; the Industry Hills Athletic Club (California) has won a record five titles: 1980–81, 1983–85.

WATERSKIING

Most titles World Overall Championships (instituted 1949) have been won four times by Sammy Duvall (U.S.), in 1981, 1983, 1985 and 1987, and Patrice Martin (France), in 1989, 1991, 1993 and 1995; and three times by two women, Willa Worthington McGuire (U.S.), in 1949–50 and 1955, and Liz Allan-Shetter (U.S.), in 1965, 1969 and 1975. Allan-Shetter has won eight individual championship events and is the only person to win all four titles—slalom, jumping, tricks and overall—in one year, in Copenhagen, Denmark in 1969. Patrice Martin (France) has won a men's record seven titles. The United States has won the team championship on 21 successive occasions, 1949–89.

United States U.S. national championships were first held at Marine Stadium, Jones Beach State Park, Long Island, NY on July 22, 1939. The most overall titles is nine, by Carl Roberge, 1980–83, 1985–88, and 1990. The women's record is eight titles, by Willa Worthington McGuire, 1946–51 and 1954–55, and by Liz Allan-Shetter, 1968–75.

Fastest speed The fastest waterskiing speed recorded is 143.08 MPH, by Christopher Michael Massey (Australia) on the Hawkesbury River, Windsor, New South Wales, Australia on March 6, 1983. Donna Patterson Brice set a women's record of 111.11 MPH in Long Beach, CA on August 21, 1977.

WATERSKIING RECORDS

Slalom

Men: 4 buoys on a 10.25 m line, Andrew Mapple (Great Britain) in Charleston, SC on September 4, 1994.

Women: 2.25 buoys on a 10.75-m line, Susi Graham (Canada) in Santa Rosa, FL on September 25, 1994.

Tricks

Men: 11,590 points, Aymeric Benet (France) in West Palm Beach, FL on October 30, 1994.

Women: 8,580 points, Tawn Larsen (U.S.) in Groveland, FL on July 4, 1992.

Jumping

Men: 220 ft., Sammy Duvall (U.S.) in Santa Rosa Beach, FL on October 10, 1993.

Women: 156 ft., Deena Mapple (née Brush; U.S.) in Charlotte, MI on July 9, 1988.

Most skiers towed by one boat   A record 100 waterskiers were towed on double skis over a nautical mile by the cruiser *Reef Cat* in Cairns, Queensland, Australia on October 18, 1986. This feat, organized by the Cairns and District Powerboat and Ski Club, was then replicated by 100 skiers on single skis.

Barefoot   The barefoot duration record is 2 hr. 42 min. 39 sec., by Billy Nichols (U.S.) on Lake Weir, FL on November 19, 1978. The backwards barefoot record is 1 hr. 27 min. 3.96 sec., by Steve Fontaine in Jupiter, FL, on August 31, 1989.

World Championships (instituted 1978)   The most overall titles is four, by Kim Lampard (Australia), 1980, 1982, 1985, 1986; and the men's record is three, by Brett Wing (Australia), 1978, 1980, 1982. The team title has been won five times by Australia, 1978, 1980, 1982, 1985 and 1986.

The official barefoot speed record is 135.74 MPH, by Scott Michael Pellaton over a ¼-mile course in Chandler, CA, in November 1989. The fastest by a woman is 73.67 MPH, by Karen Toms (Australia) on the Hawkesbury River, Windsor, New South Wales on March 31, 1984.

The fastest official speed backwards barefoot is 62 MPH, by Robert Wing (Australia) on April 3, 1982.

The barefoot jump record is: *(men)* 90 ft. 3 in., by Richard Mainwaring in Thurrock, England on August 20, 1994; and *(women)* 54 ft. 5 in., by Sharon Stekelenberg (Australia) in 1991.

Walking on water   Rémy Bricka of Paris, France "walked" across the lantic Ocean on waterskis 13 ft. 9 in. long in 1988. Leaving Tenerif nary Islands on April 2, 1988, he covered 3,502 miles, arriving in on May 31, 1988.

Bricka also set a speed record of 7 min. 7.41 sec. for 1,094 yards in the Olympic pool in Montreal, Canada on August 2, 1989.

Wearing 11-foot waterski shoes, called Skijaks, and using a twin-bladed paddle, David Kiner walked 155 miles on the Hudson River from Albany, NY to Battery Park, New York City. His walk took him 57 hours, June 22–27, 1987.

Longest jet-ski journey Gary Frick (U.S.) traveled 5,040 miles along the United States coastline on a stand-up Kawasaki 650sx Jet Ski. He left Lubec, ME on May 8, 1993 and arrived in Seattle, WA on September 16, 1993.

WEIGHTLIFTING

Most titles Olympic medals Norbert Schemansky (U.S.) won a record four Olympic medals: gold, middle heavyweight 1952; silver, heavyweight 1948; bronze, heavyweight 1960 and 1964.

World The most world title wins (overall), including Olympic Games, is eight, shared by John Henry Davis (U.S.) in 1938, 1946–52; Tommy Kono (U.S.) in 1952–59; Vasiliy Alekseiev (USSR), 1970–77; and Naim Suleymanoglu (Turkey; previously Neum Shalamanov [Bulgaria]), 1985–86, 1988–89, 1991–94.

Two American women have won world titles. In the 82-kg category, Karyn Marshall won a title in 1987 by lifting a total of 220 kg (a 95-kg snatch and a 125-kg clean and jerk). In 1994, Robin Byrd-Goad won a 50-kg title with a total weight of 175 kg.

United States The most U.S. national titles won is 13, by Anthony Terlazzo, in 137 lb, 1932 and 1936 and in 148 lb., 1933, 1935, 1937–45.

Youngest world record holder Naim Suleimanov set 56-kg world records for clean and jerk (160 kg) and total (285 kg), at 16 yr. 62 days, in Allentown, NJ on March 26, 1983.

Oldest world record holder The oldest is Norbert Schemansky (U.S.), who snatched 164.2 kg in the then unlimited Heavyweight class, aged 37 yr. 333 days, in Detroit, MI on April 28, 1962.

Heaviest lift to body weight Stefan Topurov (Bulgaria) managed to clean and jerk more than three times his body weight when he lifted $396\frac{3}{4}$ pounds in Moscow, USSR on October 24, 1983.

Women's World Championships These are held annually; the first was held in Daytona Beach, FL in October 1987. Women's world records have been ratified for the best marks at these championships. The most gold medals 12, by Peng Li Ping (China) with snatch, jerk and total in the 52-kg class ch year, 1988–89 and 1991–92; and Milena Tendafilova (Bulgaria), 67.5-70-kg classes, 1989–93.

Milena Tendafilova is the second woman to take 12 gold medals in the Women's World Championships.

Peng Li Ping has won 12 Women's World Championships.

WEIGHTLIFTING RECORDS—MEN

From January 1, 1993, the International Weightlifting Federation (IWF) introduced modified weight categories, thereby making the then world records redundant. This is the current list for the new weight categories with, for some events, world standards that have yet to be met.

Bodyweight	Lift.	kg	lb	Name and Country	Place	Date
54 kg *119 lb.*	Snatch	130.5	*287 1/2*	Halil Mutlu (Turkey)	Warsaw, Poland	May 3, 1995
	Jerk	160	*352 3/4*	Halil Mutlu (Turkey)	Istanbul, Turkey	Nov. 18, 1994
	Total	290	*639 1/4*	Halil Mutlu (Turkey)	Istanbul, Turkey	Nov. 18, 1994
59 kg *130 lb.*	Snatch	140	*308 1/2*	Hafiz Suleymanoglu	Warsaw, Poland	May 3, 1995
	Jerk	170	*370 1/4*	Nikolai Pershalov (Bulgaria)	Warsaw, Poland	May 3, 1995
	Total	305	*672 1/4*	Nikolai Pershalov (Bulgaria)	Melbourne, Australia	Nov. 13, 1993
64 kg *141 lb.*	Snatch	148.5	*327 1/4*	Wang Guohua (China)	Yachiyo, Japan	Apr. 5, 1996
	Jerk	183.0	*403 1/2*	Valerios Leonidis (Greece)	Warsaw, Poland	Apr. 5, 1995
	Total	330	*727 1/2*	Naim Suleymanoglu (Turkey)*	Istanbul, Turkey	Nov. 20, 1994
70 kg *154 1/4 lb.*	Snatch	161	*354 3/4*	Kim Myong-nam (North Korea)	Yachiyo, Japan	Apr. 6, 1996
	Jerk	193.5	*426 1/2*	Kim Myong-nam (North Korea)	Yachiyo, Japan	Apr. 6, 1996
	Total	352.5	*777*	Kim Myong-nam (North Korea)	Yachiyo, Japan	Apr. 6, 1996
76 kg *167 1/2 lb.*	Snatch	170	*374 3/4*	Ruslan Savchenko (Ukraine)	Melbourne, Australia	Nov. 16, 1993
	Jerk	208	*458 1/2*	Pablo Lara (Cuba)	Sveksard, Hungary	Apr. 20, 1996
	Total	72.5	*821*	Pablo Lara (Cuba)	Sveksard, Hungary	Apr. 20, 1996
83 kg *183 lb.*	Snatch	177.5	*391 1/2*	Pyrros Dimas (Greece)	Warsaw, Poland	May 5, 1995
	Jerk	212.5	*468 1/4*	Pyrros Dimas (Greece)	Guangzhou, China	Nov. 22, 1995
	Total	387.5	*854 1/2*	Pyrros Dimas (Greece)	Warsaw, Poland	May 5, 1995
91 kg *200 1/2 lb.*	Snatch	186	*410*	Aleksey Petrov (Russia)	Istanbul, Turkey	Nov. 24, 1994
	Jerk	228.5	*503 3/4*	Kakhi Kakhiasvilis (Greece)	Warsaw, Poland	Jun. 5, 1995
	Total	412.5	*909 1/4*	Aleksey Petrov (Russia)	Sokolov, Czech Republic	May 7, 1994
99 kg *218 1/2 lb.*	Snatch	192.5	*424 1/4*	Sergey Syrtsov (Russia)	Istanbul, Turkey	Nov. 25, 1994
	Jerk	228	*502 1/2*	Anatoliy Khrapaty (Kazakhstan)	Yachiyo, Japan	Apr. 8, 1996
	Total	417.5	*920 1/4*	Sergey Syrtsov (Russia)	Istanbul, Turkey	Nov. 25, 1994
108 kg *238 lb.*	Snatch	200	*441*	Timour Taimazov (Ukraine)	Istanbul, Turkey	Nov. 26, 1994
	Jerk	235.5	*519*	Timour Taimazov (Ukraine)	Sokolov, Czech Republic	May 8, 1994
	Total	435	*959*	Timour Taimazov (Ukraine)	Istanbul, Turkey	Nov. 26, 1994
108+ kg	Snatch	205	*452*	Aleksandr Kurlovich (Belarus)	Istanbul, Turkey	Nov. 27, 1994
	Jerk	253.5	559	Andrei Tchemerkin (Kazakhstan)	Warsaw, Poland	Jul. 5, 1995
	Total	457.5	992	Aleksandr Kurlovich (Belarus)	Istanbul, Turkey	Nov. 27, 1994

** Formerly Naim Suleimanov or Neum Shalamanov of Bulgaria.*

WEIGHTLIFTING RECORDS—WOMEN

Class	Lift	kg	lb	Name	Location	Date
46 kg 101¼ lb.	Snatch	81	178½	Guang Hong (China)	Guangzhou, China	Nov. 17, 1995
	Jerk	105	231½	Guang Hong (China)	Yachyp, Japan	Apr. 4, 1996
	Total	185	407¾	Guang Hong (China)	Yachyp, Japan	Apr. 4, 1996
50 kg 110¼ lb.	Snatch	88	194	Baoyu Jiang (China)	Pusan, South Korea	Mar. 7, 1995
	Jerk	110.5	243½	Liu Xiuhia (China)	Hiroshima, Japan	Oct. 3, 1994
	Total	197.5	435¼	Liu Xiuhia (China)	Hiroshima, Japan	Oct. 3, 1994
54 kg 119 lb.	Snatch	92.5	204	Zhang Juhua (China)	Hiroshima, Japan	Oct. 3, 1994
	Jerk	113.5	250	Zhang Xixiang (China)	Yachyp, Japan	Apr. 5, 1996
	Total	202.5	446¼	Zhang Juhua (China)	Hiroshima, Japan	Oct. 3, 1994
59 kg 130 lb.	Snatch	99	218¼	Chen Xiaomin (China)	Warsaw, Poland	May 6, 1996
	Jerk	124	273¼	Xiu Xiongying (China)	Warsaw, Poland	May 6, 1996
	Total	220	485	Chen Xiaomin (China)	Warsaw, Poland	Oct. 4, 1994
64 kg 141 lb.	Snatch	106	233½	Li Hongyun (China)	Hiroshima, Japan	May 7, 1996
	Jerk	130	286½	Li Hongyun (China)	Warsaw, Poland	Nov. 22, 1994
	Total	235	518	Li Hongyun (China)	Istanbul, Turkey	Nov. 22, 1994
70 kg 154¼ lb.	Snatch	102.5	226	Tang Weifang (China)	Hiroshima, Japan	Oct. 4, 1994
	Jerk	129	284¼	Tang Weifang (China)	Guangzhou, China	Nov. 22, 1995
	Total	230	507	Tang Weifang (China)	Hiroshima, Japan	Oct. 4, 1994
76 kg 167¼ lb.	Snatch	106	233½	Dai Yanan (China)	Warsaw, Poland	May 10, 1996
	Jerk	140	308½	Zhang Guimei (China)	Shilong, China	Dec. 18, 1993
	Total	235	518	Zhang Guimei (China)	Shilong, China	Dec. 18, 1993
83 kg 183 lb.	Snatch	110	242½	Wei Xiangying (China)	Warsaw, Poland	May 11, 1996
	Jerk	135	297½	Chen Shu-Chih (Taiwan)	Guangzhou, China	Nov. 24, 1995
	Total	242.5	534½	Wei Xiangying (China)	Warsaw, Poland	May 11, 1996
83+ kg	Snatch	108.5	232½	Wang Yanmei (China)	Warsaw, Poland	May 11, 1996
	Jerk	155	341½	Li Yajuan (China)	Melbourne, Australia	Nov. 20, 1993
	Total	260	573	Li Yajuan (China)	Melbourne, Australia	Nov. 20, 1993

POWERLIFTING RECORDS (All weights in kilograms)

Class	Squat	Bench Press	Deadlift	Total
MEN				
52 kg	270.5.....Andrzej Stanaszek (Pol.) 1995	177.5.....Andrzej Stanashek 1994	256.....E. S. Bhaskaran (India) 1993	590.....Andrzej Stanaszek, 1995
56 kg	277.5...Magnus Karlsson (Swed.) 1995	175.5...Magnus Karlsson 1995	289.5...Lamar Gant (U.S.) 1982	625.....Lamar Gant 1982
60 kg	295.5...Magnus Karlsson 1994	180.5...Magnus Karlsson 1993	310.....Lamar Gant 1988	707.5...Joe Bradley (U.S.) 1982
67.5 kg	300.....Jessie Jackson (U.S.) 1987	200.....Kristoffer Hulecki (Swed.) 1985	316.....Daniel Austin (U.S.) 1991	765.....Aleksey Sivokon (Kaz.) 1994
75 kg	328.....Ausby Alexander (U.S.) 1989	217.5...James Rouse (U.S.) 1980	337.5...Daniel Austin (U.S.) 1994	850.....Rick Gaugler (U.S.) 1982
82.5 kg	379.5..Mike Bridges (U.S.) 1982	240.....Mike Bridges 1981	357.5...Veli Kumpuniemi (Fin.) 1980	952.5...Mike Bridges 1982
90 kg	375.....Fred Hatfield (U.S.) 1980	255.....Mike MacDonald (U.S.) 1980	372.5...Walter Thomas (U.S.) 1982	937.5...Mike Bridges 1980
100 kg	423.....Ed Coan (U.S.) 1994	261.5...Mike MacDonald 1977	390.....Ed Coan 1993	1035...Ed Coan 1994
110 kg	415.....Kirk Karwoski (U.S.) 1994	270.....Jeffrey Magruder (U.S.) 1982	395.....John Kuc (U.S.) 1980	1000...John Kuc 1980
125 kg	455.....Kirk Karwoski 1995	278.5...Tom Hardman (U.S.) 1982	387.5...Lars Norén (Swed.) 1987	1045...Kirk Karwoski (U.S.) 1995
125+ kg	447.5..Shane Hamman (U.S.) 1994	310.....Anthony Clark (U.S.) 1994	406.....Lars Norén 1988	1100...Bill Kazmaier 1981
WOMEN				
44 kg	156.....Raija Koskinen (Fin.) 1995	82.5....Irina Krylova (Rus.) 1993	165.....Nancy Belliveau (U.S.) 1985	372.5...Svetlana Tesleva (Rus.) 1995
48 kg	167.5..Raija Koskinen 1995	96.....Irina Krylova 1995	182.5...Majik Jones (U.S.) 1984	402.5...Yelena Yamkich (Rus.) 1995
52 kg	175.5..Mary Jeffrey (U.S.) 1991	105.....Mary Jeffrey 1991	197.5...Diana Rowell (U.S.) 1984	452.5...Mary Jeffrey 1991
56 kg	191.5..Carrie Boudreau (U.S.) 1995	115.....Mary Jeffrey 1988	222.5...Carrie Boudreau (U.S.) 1995	522.5...Carrie Boudreau 1995
60 kg	210.....Beate Amdahl (Nor.) 1993	115.5...Eriko Himeno (Jap.) 1995	213.....Ruthi Shafer 1983	502.5...Vicki Steenrod 1985
67.5 kg	230.....Ruthi Shafer (U.S.) 1984	120.....Vicki Steenrod (U.S.) 1990	244.....Ruthi Shafer 1984	565.....Ruthi Shafer 1984
75 kg	240.5..Yelena Sukhoruk (Ukr.) 1995	143.....Tammy Diande (U.S.), 1994	252.5...Yelena Sukhoruk 1995	605.....Yelena Sukhoruk 1995
82.5 kg	240.....Cathy Millen (N.Z.) 1991	150.5...Cathy Millen 1993	257.5...Cathy Millen 1993	637.5...Cathy Millen 1993
90 kg	260.....Cathy Millen 1994	160.....Cathy Millen 1994	260.....Cathy Millen 1994	682.5...Cathy Millen 1994
90+ kg	277.5..Juanita Trujillo (U.S.) 1993	157.5...Ulrike Herchenhein (Ger.) 1994	240.....Ulrike Herchenhein 1994	640.....Juanita Trujillo 1994

POWERLIFTING

Most world titles   Hideaki Inaba (Japan) has won 17 world titles, in 52 kg, 1974–83, 1985–91.

Lamar Gant (U.S.) holds the record for an American with 15 titles, in 56 kg, 1975–77, 1979, 1982–84; and in 60 kg, 1978, 1980–81 and 1986–90. The most by a woman is six, shared by Beverley Francis (Australia), in 75 kg 1980, 1982; 82.5 kg 1981, 1983–85; and Sisi Dolman (Netherlands) in 52 kg 1985–86, 1988–91.

Timed lifts 24 hours   A team of 10 deadlifted 6,705,241 pounds in 24 hours at the Forum Health Club, Birmingham, England on March 30–31, 1996.

The 24-hour individual deadlift record is 818,121 pounds, by Anthony Wright at Her Majesty's Prison, Featherstone, England, August 31–September 1, 1990.

12 hours   An individual bench press record of 1,181,312 pounds was set by Chris Lawton at the Waterside Wine Bar, Solihull, England on June 3, 1994.

A bench press record of 8,873,860 pounds was set by a 9-man team from the Forum Health Club, Chelmsleywood, England, March 19–20, 1994.

A squat record of 4,780,994 pounds was set by a 10-man team from St. Albans Weightlifting Club and Ware Boys Club, Hertfordshire, England, July 20–21, 1986.

A record 133,380 arm-curling repetitions using three 48¼-pound weightlifting bars and dumbbells was achieved by a team of nine from Intrim Health and Fitness Club in Gosport, England, August 4–5, 1989.

WINDSURFING

Boardsailing (windsurfing)   World Championships were first held in 1973 and the sport was added to the Olympic Games in 1984, when the winner was Stephan van den Berg (Netherlands), who also won five world titles 1979–83.

Longest sailboard   A sailboard of 165 feet was constructed in Fredrikstad, Norway. It was first sailed on June 28, 1986.

The longest snake of sailboards was made by 70 windsurfers in a row at the Sailboard Show '89 event in Narrabeen Lakes, Manly, Australia on October 21, 1989.

WRESTLING

Most Olympic titles Three Olympic titles have been won by Carl Wester-gren (Sweden), in 1920, 1924 and 1932; Ivar Johansson (Sweden), in 1932 (two) and 1936; and Aleksandr Vasilyevich Medved (USSR), in 1964, 1968 and 1972. Four Olympic medals were won by Eino Leino (Finland) in free style 1920–32; and by Imre Polyák (Hungary) in Greco-Roman in 1952–64.

United States Three U.S. wrestlers have won two Olympic freestyle titles: George Nicholas Mehnert, flyweight in 1904 and bantamweight in 1908; John Smith, featherweight in 1988 and 1992; and Bruce Baumgartner, su-per-heavyweight in 1984 and 1992. The only U.S. men to win a Greco-Roman title are Steven Fraser at 198 pounds and Jeffrey Blatnick in super-heavyweight in 1984.

John Smith is the U.S. wrestler with the most world titles.

Most World titles The freestyler Aleksandr Medved (USSR) won a record 10 World Championships, 1962–64, 1966–72 in three weight categories.

United States The most world titles won by a U.S. wrestler is six (four world, two Olympic), by John Smith, featherweight 1987–92.

Most wins In international competition, Osamu Watanabe (Japan), the 1964 Olympic freestyle 63 kg champion, was unbeaten and did not concede a score in 189 consecutive matches.

Outside of FILA sanctioned competition, Wade Schalles (U.S.) won 821 bouts from 1964 to 1984, with 530 of these victories by pin.

NCAA Division I Championship Including five unofficial titles, Oklahoma State has won a record 30 NCAA titles, in 1928–31, 1933–35, 1937–42, 1946, 1948–49, 1954–56, 1958–59, 1961–62, 1964, 1966, 1968, 1971, 1989–90 and 1994. The University of Iowa has won the most consecutive titles, with nine championships from 1978 to 1986.

Heaviest heavyweight The heaviest wrestler in Olympic history was Chris Taylor (U.S.), bronze medalist in the super-heavyweight class in 1972, who stood 6 ft. 5 in. tall and weighed over 420 pounds.

FILA introduced an upper weight limit of 286 pounds for international competition in 1985.

SUMO

The heaviest-ever *rikishi*, or wrestler, is Samoan-American Salevaa Fuali Atisnoe of Hawaii, alias Konishiki, who weighed in at 580 pounds at Tokyo's Ryogaku Kokugikau on January 4, 1993. He is the only foreign *rikishi* to attain the second highest rank of *ozeki*, or champion. Weight is gained by eating large quantities of a high-protein stew called *chankonabe*.

Most successful sumo wrestlers The most successful wrestlers have been *yokozuna* (grand champion) Sadaji Akiyoshi, alias Futabayama, winner of 69 consecutive bouts in the 1930s; *yokozuna* Koki Naya, alias Taiho, who won the Emperor's Cup 32 times up to his retirement in 1971; and the *ozeki* Tameemon Torokichi, alias Raiden, who in 21 years (1789–1810) won 254 bouts and lost only 10, for the highest-ever winning percentage of 96.2. Taiho and Futabayama share the record of eight perfect tournaments without a single loss.

Yokozuna Mitsugu Akimoto, alias Chiyonofuji, set a record for domination of one of the six annual tournaments by winning the Kyushu Basho for eight years, 1981–88. He also holds the record for most career wins, 1,045, and *Makunoiuchi* (top division) wins, 807.

Hawaiian-born Jesse Kuhaulua, now a Japanese citizen named Daigoro Watanabe, set a record of 1,231 consecutive top-division bouts in September 1981.

Kenji Hatano, alias Oshio, contested a record 1,891 bouts in his 26-year career, 1962–88, the longest in modern sumo history.

Yukio Shoji, alias Aobajo, contested a record 1,631 consecutive bouts in his 22-year career, 1964–86.

Katsumi Yamanaka, alias Akinoshima, set a new *kinboshi* (gold star) record of 13 upsets over *yokozuna* by a *maegashira*.

Hawaiian-born Chad Rowan, alias Akebono, scored a majority of wins for a record 18 consecutive tournaments, March 1988–March 1991. He is the tallest (6 ft. 8 in.) and heaviest (467½ pounds) *yokozuna* in sumo history.

Youngest   The youngest of the 64 men to attain the rank of *yokozuna* was Toshimitsu Ogata, alias Kitanoumi, in July 1974 at age 21 yr. 2 mo. He set a record in 1978, winning 82 of the 90 bouts that top *rikishi* fight annually.

Longest sumo bout   The longest recorded wrestling bout was 11 hr. 40 min., when Martin Klein (Russia) beat Alfred Asikáinen (Finland) for the Greco-Roman 75-kg "A" event silver medal in the 1912 Olympic Games in Stockholm, Sweden.

YACHTING

Oldest race   The oldest race for any type of craft on either fresh or salt water is the Chicago-to-Mackinac race on Lakes Michigan and Huron, first sailed in 1898. It was held again in 1904, and has been held almost every year since then. The record for the course (333 nautical miles) is 1 day 1 hr. 50 min. (average speed 12.89 knots), set in 1987 by the sloop *Pied Piper*, owned by Dick Jennings (U.S.).

Olympic titles   Paul B. Elvstrøm (Denmark) won individual gold medals in four successive Olympic Games, in the Firefly class in 1948 and the Finn class in 1952, 1956 and 1960. He also won eight other world titles in a total of six classes. The lowest number of penalty points by the winner of any class in an Olympic regatta is three points (five wins, one disqualified and one second in seven starts) by *Superdocious* of the Flying Dutchman class (Lt. Rodney Stuart Pattisson and Iain Somerled Macdonald-Smith), in Acapulco Bay, Mexico in October 1968.

United States   The only U.S. yachtsman to have won two gold medals is Herman Frasch Whiton, in 6-meter class, in 1948 and 1952.

America's Cup   The America's Cup was originally won as an outright prize (with no special name) by the schooner *America* on August 22, 1851 in Cowes, Great Britain and was later offered by the New York Yacht Club as a challenge trophy.

There have been 29 challenges since August 8, 1870, with the United States winning on every occasion until 1983, when *Australia II*, skippered by John Bertrand and owned by a Perth syndicate headed by Alan Bond, beat *Liberty* 4–3 in Newport, RI, the narrowest series victory ever. In San Diego in 1995, the United States lost again, 5–0, to New Zealand's *Black Magic I*, skippered by Russell Coutts and owned by an Auckland syndicate headed by Peter Blake.

Dennis Walter Conner (U.S.) has been helms man of American boats five times in succession: in 1980, when he successfully defended; in 1983, when he steered the defender, but lost; in 1987, when the American challenger regained the trophy; in 1988, when he again successfully defended; and in 1995, when he lost. He was also starting helmsman in 1974, with Ted Hood as skipper.

The largest yacht to have competed in the America's Cup was the 1903 defender, the gaff rigged cutter *Reliance*, with an overall length of 144 feet, a record sail area of 16,160 square feet and a rig 175 feet high.

The Whitbread Round the World Race was first held in 1973.

Longest sailing race   The Vendée Globe Challenge, first held in Les Sables d'Olonne, France on November 26, 1989, has a nonstop circumnavigated distance of 22,500 nautical miles and is for boats between 50–60 feet, sailed single-handedly. The record time on the course is 109 days 8 hr. 48 min. 50 sec., by Titouan Lamazou (France) in the sloop *Ecureuil d'Aquitaine*, which finished in Les Sables on March 19, 1990.

The oldest regular transglobal sailing race is the quadrennial Whitbread Round the World Race (instituted August 1973) organized by the British Royal Naval Sailing Association. It starts in England, but the course and the number of legs with stops at specified ports are varied from race to race. The 1993–94 race covered 32,000 nautical miles from Southampton, England and return, with stops and restarts in Punta del Este, Uruguay; Fremantle, Australia; Auckland, New Zealand; Punta del Este, Uruguay; and Fort Lauderdale, FL.

Fastest speeds   The fastest speed reached under sail on water by any craft over a 500-meter timed run is 46.25 knots, by Simon McKeon and Tim Daddo (Australia) in the trifoiler *Yellow Pages Endeavour c.* October 26, 1993 in Shallow Inlet near Melbourne. The women's record is held by boardsailer Babethe Coquelle (France), who achieved 40.38 knots in Ta-rifa, Spain on July 7, 1995.

The fastest speed by a true yacht is 36.22 knots (41.68 MPH), by Jean

Saucet (France) in *Charante Maritime* on the Bassin de Thau, near Sete, on October 5, 1992.

The record for a boat is 43.55 knots (80.65 kilometers per hour) by *Longshot*, steered by Russell Long (U.S.) in Tarifa, Spain in July 1992.

United States   The American with the best time under sail over a 500-meter run is Jimmy Lewis, with 38.68 knots in Saintes Maries-de-la-Mer, France in February 1988.

Most competitors   The most boats ever to start in a single race was 2,072 in the Round Zeeland (Denmark) race on June 21, 1984, over a course of 235 nautical miles.

The largest transoceanic race was the ARC (Atlantic Rally for Cruisers), when 204 boats of the 209 starters completed the race from Las Palmas de Gran Canaria (Canary Islands) to Barbados in 1989.

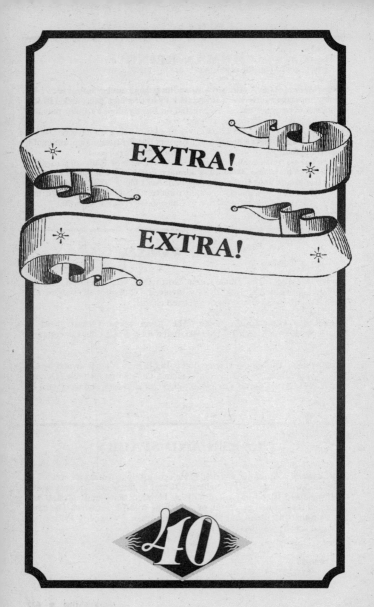

HUMAN BEING

Balancing on one foot   Amresh Kumar Jha balanced on one foot for 71 hr. 40 min. in Bihar, India from September 13 to September 16, 1995. In this activity, the free foot may not be rested on the standing foot, nor may any object be used for support or balance.

Most blood donors   The San Diego Chargers Blood Drive on December 14, 1993 attracted 1,853 donors, the record for a one-day drive.

Lightest triplets United States   On January 27, 1990, Mrs. Vincent of Aurora, IL gave birth to Joel (1 lb. 8.64 oz.), Ariel (1 lb. 2.27 oz.) and Bethel (1 lb. 7.23 oz.). The triplets were approximately $2^1/2$ months premature, and were delivered by cesarean section at Chicago Osteopathic Hospital.

LIVING WORLD

Largest dog walk   The 3-mile Great North Dog Walk, held on May 19, 1996 in South Shields, Great Britain, involved 672 dogs of 103 breeds. The annual event raises money for dog-related charities.

Largest dog show United States   The Kentuckiana Cluster, held in Louisville, KY on March 14–18, 1995, had a record 4,254 dogs in competition.

Smallest dog   The smallest living dog is Big Boss, a Yorkie owned by Dr. Chai Khanchanakom of Bangkok, Thailand. On his first birthday (December 7, 1995) he measured $4^7/10$ inches tall, $5^1/10$ inches long and weighed 1 lb. 1 oz.

EARTH AND SPACE

Newest island   An island in Tonga's Ha'apai group, covering an area of 12 acres and with a maximum height of 131 feet, is the world's newest island. The unnamed island is located halfway between the islands of Kao and Late and was formed as a result of submarine volcanic activities. The earliest date that the island can be said to have existed is June 6, 1995, when volcanic activity was first observed.

Big Boss is the world's smallest living dog.

SCIENCE AND TECHNOLOGY

Largest kaleidoscope   The Kaatskill Kaleidoscope at Catskill Corners, Mt. Tremper, NY measures 56 ft. 3 in. long. Viewers can step inside the kaleidoscope to experience America: The House We Live In, an adventure through 200 years of American history.

Most powerful laser   The "Petawatt" Laser at the Lawrence Livermore National Laboratory, CA produces laser pulses of more than 1.3 quadrillion watts (1.3 petawatts) at peak power. This is more than 1,300 times the entire electrical capacity of the United States, although each pulse lasts less than half a trillionth of a second.

Longest spaceflight *United States*   Shannon Lucid holds the record for the longest single space flight by a U.S. astronaut, with 118 days as of July 18, 1996. She is also the most experienced U.S. astronaut, with 152 days in space as of July 18, 1996.

BUILDINGS AND STRUCTURES

Bricklaying   Travis McGee of Monroe, NC laid 1,494 bricks in 60 minutes on May 17, 1996. The record was set under the normal working conditions of an average bricklayer in a charity event for Habitat for Humanity in Dallas, TX.

Busiest telephone exchange   The busiest telecommunications exchange was the Bellsouth network used at the International Broadcast Center, Atlanta, GA during the 1996 Olympic Games from July 19 to August 4. It could transmit 100 billion bits of information per second.

TRANSPORT

Largest automobile plant *United States*   The largest automobile plant in the United States is Ford Motor Company's Lorain, OH plant. The plant had a capacity of 493,000 vans and cars at the end of 1995.

Longest scheduled flight   The longest scheduled flight, in terms of time taken, is for the United Airlines Chicago to Hong Kong flight, which takes 15 hr. 55 min.

ARTS AND ENTERTAINMENT

Most No. 1 singles   The Beatles have had the most number No. 1 singles, with 22.

Tap dancing   The longest distance ever tap danced by one person was 17.9 miles, by Laurie Churchwell, who tap danced for six hours around the campus of Howard College in Big Spring, TX on March 9, 1996.

Most prolific TV producer   Aaron Spelling has produced more than 3,097 TV episodes totaling more than 3,099 hours of airtime.

Laurie Churchwell tap danced 17.9 miles in 6 hours.

HUMAN WORLD

Most graduates in a family   Dan and Helen Fagan of Bessemer, AL saw 15 of their 16 children—8 daughters and 7 sons—obtain bachelor's degrees from a university or college between 1969 and 1992.

Oldest head of state   The oldest head of state is Nouhak Phoumsavan (b. April 9, 1914), president of Laos.

Most elections contested   John C. "The Engineer" Turmel, of Nepean, Ontario, Canada has contested a record 41 elections as an Independent candidate at a municipal, provincial and federal level since 1979. He founded the federal Abolitionist Party of Canada in 1993.

Worst train disaster Approximately 300 people were killed when the underground train they were travelling in caught fire in Baku, Azerbaijan on October 28, 1995.

HUMAN ACHIEVEMENTS

Bagel On July 24, 1996 Kraft Foods and Lender's Bagels in Mattoon, IL made a bagel weighing 563 pounds and measuring 59³/₁₆ inches in diameter and 12¹/₂ inches in height.

The largest bagel weighed 563 pounds.

Maze The K.I.D.S. maze in Shaw Park, Clayton, MO was made of PVC posts, with fencing and clear plastic stretched between the posts. It covered an area of 175,250 square feet, with a total path length of 2.47 miles. The maze was erected in May 1996 and taken down in June 1996.

Shortcake A strawberry shortcake measuring 81 feet long by 7 feet wide was made in Bellevue Square, Bellevue, WA by Biringer Farm on June 22,

1996. The shortcake was made with 2,610 pounds of strawberries, 1,632 pounds of shortcake and mounds of whipped cream.

The largest strawberry shortcake was made in Bellevue, WA.

Stretcher bearing The record for carrying a stretcher case with a 140-pound "body" is 186.66 miles in 59 hr. 19 min., May 27–30, 1996. This was achieved by two teams of four from 1 Field Ambulance, Canadian Forces Base Calgary, starting from Edmonton, Alberta, Canada and finishing in Calgary, Alberta.

The K.I.D.S. maze was 2.47 miles long.

Paper chain   A paper chain 37.04 miles long was made by 60 members of the Wernersville Service Unit of the Great Valley Girl Scout Council in Robesonia, PA, April 26–27, 1996. The chain consisted of nearly 400,000 links and was made over a period of 24 hours.

SPORTS AND GAMES

BASEBALL

Consecutive Saves   Reliever John Wetteland, New York Yankees (AL) saved 24 consecutive games, May 31–July 14, 1996.

BASKETBALL

Olympic Games   At the '96 Games, Teresa Edwards (U.S.) played on her third gold medal-winning team, the most of any basketball player. She led the U.S. women's team in its 111–87 defeat of Brazil in the gold medal game. Charles Barkley, David Robinson, John Stockton, Karl Malone and Scottie Pippen gained their second gold medals at the Atlanta Games. They joined six other men as 2-time basketball gold medalists.

CANOEING

Most titles Olympics   Birgit Fischer (Germany), the most successful woman kayaker in Olympic history, won her fifth gold medal at the Atlanta Games. She was a member of the K-4 500 meter gold medal winning team.

EQUESTRIAN SPORTS

Dressage Olympic Games   Germany won a record ninth team event at the '96 Games.

Show Jumping Olympic Games   Ulrich Kirchhoff (Germany) became the fourth rider to win the individual show jumping gold medal event with two clear rounds. Kirchhoff's mount was Jus de Pommes.

GYMNASTICS

Olympics (United States)   The United States women's gymnastics team won the Olympic title on July 23, 1996. This was the first time either a men's or women's team from the United States won a team gold medal at the Olympics. At the '96 Games, Shannon Miller became the most successful American gymnast in Olympic history. She starred on the women's gold medal winning team and won another gold medal in the balance beam event, raising her tally of Olympic medals to an American record seven medals: 2 gold, 1 silver and 4 bronze, 1992–96.

Olympic Games   A record 197 nations competed in the 1996 Olympic Games held in Atlanta, GA, July 19–August 4, 1996. An estimated 10,000 athletes competed in the Centennial Games.

Most medals   Swimmer Jenny Thompson won three gold medals at the Atlanta Games, tying Bonnie Blair's record for the most gold medals won by an American woman at the Olympics. All of Thompson's golds have come in relay events. In Atlanta she swam in the 4 × 100 meter and 4 × 200 freestyle finals. She also swam in the preliminary heats of the 4 × 100 meter medley relay. Under the rules of the swimming competition, Thompson received a gold medal for the medley relay even though she didn't swim in the final.

Most medals (consecutive)   On July 27, 1996 rower Steve Redgrave (Great Britain) won the coxless pairs title. He became the fourth person to win a gold medal in four consecutive Olympiads. On July 29, 1996, Carl Lewis (U.S.) became the fifth Olympian to win gold medals in four consecutive Games. His victory in the long jump made him the second athlete to win in four consecutive individual events.

ROWING

Most Olympic medals   Steve Redgrave (Great Britain) won a record fourth gold medal at the Atlanta Games, winning the coxless pairs with Matthew Pinsent on July 27, 1996.

SHOOTING

Olympic medals   Kim Rhodes (U.S.) won the women's double trap gold medal on July 23, 1996. At 17, she was the youngest winner of an Olympic shooting title.

World records—men Free rifle—50 m, 60 shots prone   704.8 points, Christian Klees (Germany) July 25, 1996.

SOCCER

Olympic Games   The United States defeated China 2–1 to win the first women's Olympic soccer tournament on August 1, 1996.

SWIMMING

Olympic Games Most medals   Kristina Egerszegi (Hungary) won the 200 meter backstroke for the third consecutive time at the 1996 Games. This tied Dawn Fraser's mark for consecutive victories in one event.

Olympic Games United States   The most gold medals won by a female swimmer in Olympic competition is five, by Jenny Thompson. She won three golds at the Atlanta Games to go with the two she won in Barcelona in 1992. Amy Van Dyken tied Janet Evans' mark for most gold medals at one Olympics by a woman swimmer. Van Dyken won four events: 50 meter freestyle, 100 meter butterfly, 4 × 100 meter relay and 4 × 100 meter medley relay.

World records—men 100 meter breaststroke   1:00.60, Frederik Deburgh-graeve (Belgium), July 20, 1996.

100 meter butterfly   52.27, Denis Pankratov (Russia), July 24, 1996.

4 × 100 meter medley relay   3:34.84, United States (Gary Hall, Jr., Mark Henderson, Jeremy Linn, Jeff Rouse), July 26, 1996.

World records—women 100 meter breaststroke   1:07.02, Penny Heyns (South Africa), July 21, 1996.

United States records—men 100 meter breaststroke   1:00.77, Jeremy Linn, July 20, 1996.

4 × 100 meter medley relay   3:34.84, United States (Gary Hall, Jr., Mark Henderson, Jeremy Linn, Jeff Rouse), July 26, 1996.

United States records—women 50 meter freestyle   24.70, Amy Van Dyken, July 26, 1996.

100 meter breaststroke   1:08.09, Amanda Beard, July 21, 1996.

4 × 100 meter relay   3:39.29, United States (Angel Martino, Amy Van Dyken, Catherine Fox, Jenny Thompson), July 22, 1996.

TRACK AND FIELD

World Records—men 100 meters   9.84, Donovan Bailey (Canada), July 27, 1996.

200 meters   19.32, Michael Johnson (U.S.), August 1, 1996.

United States records—men Triple jump   59 ft. 1¼ in., Kenny Harrison, July 27, 1996.

VOLLEYBALL

Most Olympic titles   Karch Kiraly and Kent Steffes (U.S.) won the inaugural men's beach volleyball tournament at the '96 Games. Kiraly's third gold medal for volleyball set a new record.

WEIGHTLIFTING

Olympic   Naim Suleymanoglu (Turkey) won his third consecutive Olympic title in the 64 kg class on July 22, 1996.

World records—men 54 kg (119 lb.)—Snatch   132.5 kg, Halil Mutlu (Turkey), July 20, 1996.

59 kg (130 lb.)—Total   307.5 kg, Tang Ningsheng (China), July 21, 1996.

64 kg (141 lb.)—Snatch   147.5 kg, Naim Suleymanoglu (Turkey), July 22, 1996; *Jerk*   187.5 kg, Valerios Leonidis (Greece), July 22, 1996; *Total* 335.0 kg, Naim Suleymanoglu, July 22, 1996.

70 kg (154¹/₄ lb.)—Snatch   162.5 kg, Zhan Xugang (China), July 23, 1996; *Jerk*   195.0 kg, Zhan Xugang, July 23, 1996; *Total*   357.5 kg, Zhan Xugang, July 23, 1996.

83 kg (183 lb.)—Snatch   180.0 kg, Pyrros Dimas (Greece), July 26, 1996; *Jerk*   213.5 kg, Marc Huster (Germany), July 26, 1996; *Total*   392.5 kg, Pyrros Dimas, July 26, 1996.

91 kg (200¹/₂ lb.)—Snatch   187.5 kg, Aleksey Petrov (Russia), July 27, 1996.

99 kg (218 lb.)—Jerk   235.0 kg, Akakide Kakhiashvilis (Greece), July 28, 1996; *Total*   420.0 kg, Akakide Kakhiashvilis, July 28, 1996.

Over 108 kg (238 lb.)—Jerk   260.0 kg, Andrey Chemerkin (Russia), July 30, 1996; *Total*   457.5 kg, Andrey Chemerkin, July 30, 1996.

WRESTLING

Most Olympic titles   Alexander Karelin (Russia) won the 286 lb. class Greco-Roman wrestling gold medal. This was Karelin's third Olympic title, equaling the mark for most wins, shared by three other wrestlers.

THE
CENTENNIAL
OLYMPIC
GAMES:
ATLANTA 1996

The Centennial Olympic Games opened in Atlanta, GA on July 19, 1996. Former Olympian Muhammed Ali ignited the Olympic flame, opening the largest sporting event in history. During 16 days of competition, over 10,000 athletes representing a record 197 nations participated in 31 sports. Atlanta saw the introduction of new sports to the Games, such as beach volleyball, mountain biking and softball. New countries made debuts too, Slovakia, Burundi and many of the former Soviet Republics among them.

Terrorism returned to the Olympics. One person was killed and 111 concert-goers were injured in a pipe-bomb blast in Centennial Olympic Park. The Games continued without delay, although the horror lingered.

Records tumbled throughout the Olympiad. Fastest times became even faster, gold medal collections swelled and age barriers were conquered. Highlighted here are many of the record-breaking feats of the Centennial Games.

The oldest living Olympian, 97-year-old Leon Stukelj of Slovenia, was an inspiring presence at the opening ceremony. American diver Mary Ellen Clark won a bronze medal in the platform event. At 33 years old, she was the oldest diver ever to win an Olympic medal. At the other end of the age spectrum, 17-year-old Kim Rhodes (U.S.) became the youngest-ever shooting champion when she won the double trap shooting title.

Women's soccer made its debut in Atlanta. The United States *(page 650 bottom)* defeated China 2–1 in the final. A crowd of 76,841 people attended the game, the most people ever to watch a women's soccer match.

German kayaker Birgit Fischer extended her Olympic gold medal tally to five with her victory in the K-4 500 meter race. Teresa Edwards *(page 652 bottom)* was a leader of the American women's basketball team that went unbeaten throughout the tournament. It was Edwards' third Olympic victory, making her the most successful basketball Olympian ever.

In the closest marathon ever, eight seconds separated the medal winners in the men's marathon. Josia Thugwane (South Africa) won the race in 2:12.36, three seconds ahead of silver medalist Lee Bong Ju (South Korea) and eight seconds ahead of bronze medalist Eric Wainaina (Kenya).

More countries won medals in Atlanta than at any other Olympiad. For some, the first medal was golden. Ghada Shouaa won the heptathlon to gain Syria's first medal. Jefferson Perez gained Ecuador's first medal by winning the 20 km walk. Hong Kong's first medal was earned by Lee Lai Shan. She won the women's mistral event. Burundi made the medal table when Venuste Niyongabo won the men's 5,000 meters.

Greek gymnast Ioannis Melissanidis won the men's floor exercise in Atlanta. It was the first time that a Greek gymnast had won an Olympic title since Ioannis Mitropoulos won gold in the rings in 1896 at the first Olympic Games of the modern era.

Triple Success

Three athletes in three sports won gold medals for the third Olympics in succession, tying or beating marks in their sports. Turkish weightlifter Naim Suleymanoglu *(page 650 center)* set three world records to win his weight class for the third time. His victory made him the most successful weight lifter in Olympic history. Hungarian swimmer Kristina Egerszegi *(page 654 bottom right)* won her third successive 200 meter backstroke title; her victory tied the all-time mark of Australian Dawn Fraser. Super-heavyweight Greco-Roman wrestler Aleksander Karelin won his third consecutive gold medal. He joined three other wrestlers as a three-time Olympic champion.

Sprint Double

Canada's Donovan Bailey *(page 650 top)* won the 100 meters in a world record 9.84 seconds. "The world's fastest human" was overshadowed by the feats of Michael Johnson *(page 652 top right)*. He became the first man to win both the 400 meters and 200 meters at the same Games.

Johnson set a world record of 19.32 seconds in the 200 meters, besting his own previous mark by an astonishing 0.34 seconds.

Four-In-A-Row

British rower Steven Redgrave *(below left, with partner Matthew Pinsent)* and American track star Carl Lewis *(page 652 top left)* both captured gold at the Atlanta games. For both it was the fourth Olympiad in succession that they had won a gold medal, tying the all-time mark. Lewis became only the second athlete to win the same event in four consecutive Games.

American Success

In gymnastics, the United States women's team won the team title for the first time. Team leader Shannon Miller *(page 654 bottom left)* won two gold medals in Atlanta, increasing her Olympic medal tally to seven, the most of any American gymnast.

Water Marks

Penny Heyns *(page 654 center right)* won South Africa's first gold medals since the country's reentry to the Olympic Games. In the process, she set a new world record in the 100 meter backstroke. Amy Van Dyken *(page 654 top left)* won four gold medals in the pool, the most by an American woman swimmer at one Games, Freestyler Jenny Thompson (page 654

top left) became the most successful American woman Olympian ever. She won three golds in Atlanta to add to the two she earned in Barcelona.

Equestrian Conquest

The German team *(below)* gained its record seventh victory in the team dressage competition at the Atlanta Games. In show jumping, Germany's Ulrich Kirchhoff became the fourth rider to win the event with a double clear round. His mount, Jus de Pommes, shares the record.

Moving Outdoors

Karch Kiraly *(below)* has been a member of two Olympic indoor championship teams. At Atlanta he teamed with Kent Steffes to win the first beach volleyball gold medal. Kiraly's third gold medal made him volleyball's most decorated Olympian.

INDEX

T

U

PHOTO CREDITS